World Religions in America

CONTRIBUTORS

Carlos F. Cardoza-Orlandi, *Columbia Theological Seminary*

George D. Chryssides, *University of Birmingham*

Mark A. Csikszentmihalyi, *University of California at Berkeley*

Dell deChant, *University of South Florida*

Malcolm David Eckel, *Boston University*

Robert S. Ellwood, *University of Southern California*

John L. Esposito, *Georgetown University*

Fred Frohock, *University of Miami*

Sam Gill, *University of Colorado at Boulder*

Justo L. González, *Columbia Theological Seminary*

Andrew M. Greeley, *University of Arizona and University of Chicago*

William Scott Green, *University of Miami*

Danny L. Jorgensen, *University of South Florida*

Gerald James Larson, *University of California at Santa Barbara*

Martin E. Marty, *University of Chicago*

John McGuckin, *Union Theological Seminary*

Mike McMullen, *University of Houston–Clear Lake*

†Paul Murray, *Bard College*

Jacob Neusner, *Bard College*

Peter J. Paris, *Princeton Theological Seminary*

Jaroslav Pelikan, *Yale University*

Eleanor J. Stebner, *Simon Fraser University*

World Religions in America

An Introduction

Fourth edition

JACOB NEUSNER
Editor

WESTMINSTER
JOHN KNOX PRESS
LOUISVILLE · KENTUCKY

Book design by Sharon Adams
Cover design by designpointinc.com

This book is printed on acid-free paper that meets the American National Standards Institute Z39.48 standard. ∞

PRINTED IN THE UNITED STATES OF AMERICA

09 10 11 12 13 14 15 16 17 18 — 10 9 8 7 6 5 4 3 2 1

Library of Congress Cataloging-in-Publication Data

World religions in America : an introduction/Jacob Neusner, editor.—4th ed.
   p. cm.
  Includes bibliographical references and index.
  ISBN 978-0-664-23320-4 (alk. paper)
  1. United States—Religion. I. Neusner, Jacob, 1932–

BL2525.W67 2009
200.973—dc22   2009006573

CONTENTS

PART FIVE: MADE (OR RE-MADE) IN THE U.S.A.

PART SIX: ISSUES IN AMERICAN RELIGION

PREFACE TO THE FOURTH EDITION

The publication of a fourth edition of this textbook responds to the acceptance of the first three editions and also to the passage of time. We realized that the story of what has happened to world religions in the USA has opened a new chapter and requires amplification. We are serving two audiences here, those interested in religion in America and those interested in world religions compared and contrasted.

For this new edition we have commissioned three completely new chapters, which are on the Unification Church (popularly known as the Moonies), New Thought, and Women and Religion in America. In addition, all the existing chapters have been revised and updated to take account of recent developments and trends.

The entire textbook has been reorganized to take account of a more logical sequence of topics. In addition we have added timelines of important events and persons, sidebars on key movements or controversies, sidebars with personal stories from members of various faiths, and lists of suggested websites, books, and topics for further study. The editor thanks the contributors both old and new for their participation in what has become a long-term project, and also the following people at Westminster John Knox Press: editors Gavin Stephens and Jana Riess, who supervised the changes and additions for this edition; production professionals Julie Tonini and Erika Lundbom; and marketing director Jennifer Cox.

JACOB NEUSNER

ACKNOWLEDGMENTS

As organizer and editor of this project, I acknowledge with real thanks the contributions of many people. It is right and proper to name each one.

The literary editor of this book is Naomi Pasachoff. She read each chapter as it came in and corresponded with the various authors, making numerous important suggestions for the improvement of the early drafts. An accomplished textbook writer in her own career, she brought to the study of religion those skills of presentation to students that have made her one of the country's leading writers of science textbooks, and textbooks for the synagogues' schools of Judaism. We were fortunate indeed to have her participation in this volume, and all of the authors join me in expressing our thanks to her.

The study-guide material and the Glossary are the work of Dr. Mark Ledbetter. The weight of his contribution may be simply stated: Without it, the book would be much less effective as an instrument of teaching. All parties to the book concur that he has given us just what we needed, and it is his skill as a teacher that has shaped the study-guide material.

My thinking about the need for a project of just this kind—combining the study of world religions with a close reading of religions in America—was shaped in conversations with Professor William Scott Green, then of the University of Rochester. No detail of the planning of this book, the definition of its purpose, the outline of its chapters, and its execution throughout, was finally defined without discussion with him. He has served not only as a consultant, but as an active partner in the conception and completion of the book.

A word of thanks and admiration goes, also, to the authors of the various chapters. I learned about religion, as well as about the study and teaching of religion, from each chapter in succession as it reached me. First, all authors kept to our timetable, and none caused a day of delay, so we were able to produce the book within that precise schedule projected at the outset. Readers who have organized academic projects will know what high praise that simple sentence accords to every author in this book. Second, each one of them gave thought to the program and problems of the book, responding to my questions and taking up my intellectual challenge for them: Can we talk to young Americans about the things they see and know from day to day, so that out of the known they may learn about what the here and now represents? Can we discover the character of religion throughout the world through the facts of religions in America? Those who use this book will concur that every author answered these questions, and that all of them did so in an imaginative and passionate way.

I wanted the authors to write out of emotion and commitment, as well as objective learning—to tell young people what they cared about and why, not only what they know and how they know it. Every chapter in this book has met that aspiration. If the book engages its intended audience, it is because each of these authors has responded to the challenge, and I am proud to have worked with all of them.

Beyond what I owe to all of them equally, I am personally obligated to three of the authors. Professor Andrew M. Greeley of the University of Chicago was my other conversation partner in the formation of the book; most of what I know about religion in America, how it should be studied, and why it is important, I learned from his writings and from conversation and letters exchanged with him. It is from his imaginative and original thought that I got the idea for the book to begin with. Professor Martin Marty made a contribution to my chapter that he cannot have realized he was offering. When I conceived of this book, I did not know whether or not anyone could carry it off. I wanted major scholars to write for young

Americans. I wanted every American student to find himself or herself in the pages of this book. I wanted the book to express passion and commitment to learning about religion as a critical component of intellectual life. I also did not know whether I personally could write a chapter that would serve. I had no model in my own mind for what I needed to do; I knew only that we, and I, faced a mighty worthwhile challenge in writing. The first of the chapters to come back to me came—predictably—from Professor Marty, who is justly famed in the study of religion both for the quantity and the quality of his writing, and also for the vitality and excellence of his thinking. His chapter assured me that the project was feasible, because he provided precisely the kind of writing that I had hoped to elicit for the book. Once I read his chapter, I knew the work could be done, and I also had a model for my own chapter. I do not claim to write nearly so powerfully as he does, but he at least gave me a standard by which to measure my own work. I had invited the late Professor John Meyendorff to write the chapter on Orthodox Christianity. Shortly after he signed the contract, he died suddenly and unexpectedly. Left with a deadline I wanted to preserve and an unassigned chapter I deemed essential to the book—Orthodox Christianity sometimes being slighted in the study of Christianity in the world today—I turned to Professor Jaroslav Pelikan. Overburdened with a vast range of important scholarly projects, he accepted the assignment and produced a chapter that admirably met the needs of the book. Professor Pelikan's willingness to take up the burden at the last minute represents a gift beyond the measure of the law, and I am thankful to him for his understanding and cooperation. His death in 2006 was a loss to the entire scholarly community.

JACOB NEUSNER

Introduction

JACOB NEUSNER

This book introduces you to the world's religions in the United States today. Such an introduction is important because to understand America,* you have to know about religion. Most, though not all, Americans say they are religious, and the world's religions flourish in today's America. Most Americans would agree that "in God we trust." But each does so in his or her quite special way, and that is what makes religion in America interesting. This book does not advocate religion, or any particular religion. Its purpose is only to describe and explain religion as an important factor in American society.

AMERICANS ARE
A RELIGIOUS PEOPLE

Most Americans are religious. They believe in God. They pray. They practice a religion. They explain what happens in their lives by appeal to God's will and word and work, and they form their ideal for the American nation by reference to the teachings of religion: "one nation, under God." This statement, from the Pledge of Allegiance, describes how most Americans view our country. Americans act on their religious beliefs. A 2008 Pew study found that nearly all Americans (92 percent) profess belief in God. More than half pray

at least once a day. Most Christians go to church every week; nearly all Jews observe the Passover festival and most keep the Days of Awe (New Year, Day of Atonement) and other religious celebrations. Religiosity is a fundamental trait of the American people and has been from the very beginning.

THE RELIGIONS OF THE
WORLD FLOURISH IN
TODAY'S AMERICA

Americans are not only a religious people. We also are a people of many religions. Most of the religions of the world are practiced in America, and the number of people who profess to be Protestant is decreasing. According to a study released in 2004 by the National Opinion Research Center at the University of Chicago, about 52 percent of the American people are Protestants, down from 63 percent in 1993. Another 25 percent are Roman Catholics, a figure that has held steady through the years. Slightly less than two percent are Jews. "Other" religions—which the study defined as including Islam, Buddhism, Eastern Orthodoxy, and Hinduism, among others—clocked in at seven percent, more than triple its 1972 share of 1.9 percent. Another growth area

---

*Although Canadians, Mexicans, and Latin Americans of South America also are Americans, this work concentrates on the United States in particular, and in these pages we use "Americans" to mean residents of the United States.

is nonbelief; nearly fourteen percent of the American people profess no religion at all, double what it was thirty years ago.

One cannot understand America without making some sense of its diverse religious life. The marvel of America is its capacity to give a home to nearly every religion in the world, and the will of the American people to get along with one another, with the rich mixture of religions that flourish here. This book presents not only the better-known religions of America, Christianity and Judaism, but also the religious world of Native Americans, African Americans, and Hispanic or Latin Americans, as well as the old religions newly arrived in this country, such as Islam, Hinduism, and Buddhism.

America Began Because of Religion: Religion played a fundamental role in America's development by Europeans. The eastern part of this country was settled by people from Great Britain as an act of religion. The Southwest was founded by people from Spain and Latin America as an act of religion.

New England was settled by British Puritans from the East Anglia; Virginia and the Chesapeake area, by British Anglicans (Episcopalians); Pennsylvania and New Jersey, by British Quakers; and the Appalachian South, from West Virginia and western Pennsylvania south through Piedmont North and South Carolina, by British Presbyterians from the area around the Irish Sea, the border regions of Scotland and Northern England, and the Irish counties of Ulster, in particular.

The first European settlements in Texas, New Mexico, Arizona, and California were established by Roman Catholic missionaries and soldiers coming north from Mexico, who wanted to bring Christianity to the native peoples. Many of the place-names in the American Southwest were given by Hispanic pioneers, who acted in the name of Jesus Christ and the Roman Catholic faith. The earliest European explorers and settlers from Detroit to New Orleans were Roman Catholic missionaries and traders from Quebec, in French Canada.

From colonial times onward, many groups that joined in the adventure of building the American nation brought with them their religious hopes and founded in this country a particularly American expression of religions from all parts of the world: Africa, Asia, Europe, and Latin America. Entire American states and regions took shape because of religiously motivated groups—for example, Utah and the intermountain West through the Latter-day Saints ("Mormons"). So our country is a fundamentally religious nation, and in our country today, nearly every living religion is now represented in a significant way.

Is America a Christian Country?

Some people think America is basically a Christian country because different forms of Christianity have predominated through its history and have defined much of its culture and society. The vast majority of Americans who are religious—and that means most of us—are Christians. But to be a true American, one can hold another religion or no religion at all. The first religions of America were those of the Native Americans. And although Protestant and Roman Catholic Christianity laid the foundations of American society, America had a Jewish community from nearly the beginning; the first synagogues date back to the mid-seventeenth century. Today this country has become the meeting place for nearly all of the living religions of the world, with the Zoroastrian, Shinto, Muslim, Buddhist, and Hindu religions well represented. Various religious groups from the Caribbean and from Africa and Latin America likewise flourish. What you learn in this book is that nearly every religion in the world is practiced by some Americans.

America Is Different

Other countries have difficulty dealing with more than a single skin color, or with more than a single religion or ethnic group, and nations today break apart because of ethnic and religious difference. But America holds together because of the American ideal that anyone, of any race, creed, color, language, religion, gender, sexual preference, or country of origin, can become a good American under this nation's Constitution and Bill of Rights, its political institutions and social ideals. And while religions separate people from one another, shared religious attitudes, such as a belief in God, unite people as well.

America is different because, except for Native Americans, it has always been a land of immigrants. From the very beginning, but especially before World War I and after World War II, people have come to this country from all parts of the world. Today the great religious traditions of the world are practiced in America, where many of them have become distinctively American. This book presents the world's religions both as they flourish universally and also in their distinctively American forms.

WHY STUDY THE WORLD'S RELIGIONS IN THE AMERICAN SETTING?

America is the right place in which to study the religions of the world because nearly all of them can be found here (and in nearby Canada). But America is religiously more interesting than most countries in another way. Not only do we have Judaism and the various kinds of European Christianity, we also have Christian traditions deriving from places besides Europe, for instance, from Africa, China, Korea, Japan, Southeast Asia, and the Pacific islands. To give one example, the Unification Church, which began in Korea, flourishes in America today. Distinctive forms of Christianity from Latin America, both Pentecostal and Roman Catholic, have also become part of the tapestry woven by world religions into the fabric of American society. All of these important components of religion in America are described in this book.

WHAT YOU WILL LEARN IN THIS BOOK ABOUT RELIGIONS IN PARTICULAR

This book first examines religions one by one, and then religion in America in general. Part 1 starts with the first set of religions to exist in America, the diverse faith of Native Americans. We turn next to the Christian foundations of American religion in Part 2. Protestant Christianity is addressed first, because the founders of the earliest American settlements, in Virginia and Massachusetts, were Protestants. Because Protestants form the most complex and also the largest single component of religious life in America, Protestant Christianity is treated in a chapter twice as long as those devoted to the other American representatives of the religions of the world. African Americans have formulated a distinctive religious expression within Protestant Christianity, and they were among the earliest settlers, so we turn then to African American religious life.

Next we discuss Catholic Christianity, represented in the eastern part of the United States nearly from the beginning, and also the foundation religion of the great Southwest. Because Hispanic Americans today comprise nearly half of all Roman Catholic Christians in the United States, we take up Hispanic religious life in America, both Roman Catholic and Protestant. We round out our section on Christian foundations by addressing Orthodox Christianity, especially as it came to America from Russia and Greece.

Part 3 explores the other major monotheistic traditions in America. We first turn to Judaism, a most ancient religion that has produced a strikingly contemporary and distinctively American statement of its own. We learn much about America from how Judaism has evolved within this country's open society. Next, we encounter Islam, a fast-growing religion in America, and the Bahá'í Faith, an offshoot of Islam that emphasizes unity and harmony of religion.

Part 4 takes up some American religions that have achieved importance on the national scene in our own day—newer religions of this country, but older religions of humanity, including Buddhism, Hinduism, and East Asian faiths like Confucianism and Shinto. We pay particular attention to the religious traditions brought to the United States by Japanese, Korean, and Chinese immigrants, many of whom are Christian but some of whom practice other religious traditions of the eastern shores of Asia.

Part 5 introduces some religions made in the United States such as Mormonism, Christian Science, Jehovah's Witnesses, and Scientology, as well as those that did not begin here but have taken a remarkable foothold, like the Unification Church. This section also explores the growth of Wicca and nature religions in America.

Each chapter in Parts 1 through 5 treats its subject in accord with a single plan: How do we encounter this religion today? What is the definition and history? In what ways does the American expression of this religion teach us about religion in America and what being religious in America means? In answering these questions, the authors tell you about world religions in general and also about world religions in America in particular. Having mastered the contents of these chapters, you should be able to make sense out of the great religions of the world as America knows them, and also the diverse meanings of religious life in America.

What You Will
Learn in This Book
About Religion
in General

To make sense of our country's complex life—its politics, culture, society—we need generalizations, which brings us to the final section of this book. Part 6 promotes an understanding of religion in general, and not just particular faiths, that sheds light on these aspects of American life. We therefore consider three questions that pertain to all religions. The first concerns how religion is shaped in this country by women: What do we learn about religion from the ways in which women are religious? Next, we turn to the immediate question of politics: How does religion affect the political life of this country? Our political system carefully distinguishes state from church, so that no governing body may favor or discriminate against a particular religion or religion in general. But religious people—that is, nearly all Americans—bring to politics important religious beliefs and commitments. How religion comes to expression in American political life teaches us much about religion. Finally, we undertake the relationship between religion and society: How does religion shape American life?

Why This Book Differs
from Other Books
About the World's Religions
in American Life

In general, up to the end of World War II people defined the three religions of the United States as Catholicism, Protestantism, and Judaism. The other great world religions, such as Islam, Buddhism, and Hinduism, were not broadly represented here. In addition, it was not widely recognized that African Americans had formed a powerful and distinctive statement of Protestant Christianity, and that Latin Americans had formed in this country an equally important and distinctive expression of Catholic Christianity. Also, the importance of Pentecostal Christianity in Latin America was just then emerging. So chapters on other world religions, besides Christianity and Judaism, or on how other non-European formulations of great religions flourished in America, would not likely have been written just a few decades ago.

And, if the truth be told, half a century ago chapters on Catholic Christianity and on Judaism might also have been left out, since not a few people saw America as not only Christian, but also—and exclusively—Protestant. According to this school of thought, "others"—not white, not Protestant, not Christian, not European, not English-speaking, or not from the northeastern part of Europe (Britain, excluding Ireland, Germany, or Scandinavia)—really were not authentic Americans at all. That is what made them different and somehow abnormal, just as in that time people thought it was "normal" to be a man and not "normal" to be a woman. But that narrow conception of what it means to be an American—and normal—is no longer taken seriously. We now accept that Americans come in all colors, shapes, and sizes, in both genders, and from every corner of the world. We now know that anyone can become a real American. And America has the power to make its own all the religions of the world. In America, there is no "other." Everyone is one of us. That is the message of this book: we all belong. Therefore, all of us bear the same tasks and responsibilities to make this a better country.

HOW TO STUDY ABOUT OTHER RELIGIONS

The future of America depends on the answer to the question, How are religions going to relate to one another in this country? Shall we refight in our own country the world's religious wars, Protestant against Catholic, Christian against Jew, Muslim against Hindu, and so on?

Religions think about outsiders, that is, other religions, in four ways.

1. *Exclusivist:* "My religion is not only true, but it is the only truth." This view of religious truth is natural to many believers, whether or not their religion officially takes such a position. If I believe something about God, how can I imagine any other belief is valid?

2. *Inclusivist:* "My religion is true for me; your religion is true for you." This position is common in a tolerant society, such as, in general, America. It is sometimes called "relativism," meaning that truth is relative to the person who holds it; if you think up and I think down, for you it's up and for me it's down. Religious beliefs can be true only for those who hold them.

3. *Pluralist:* "Every religion has something true to tell us." God works in ways we do not always understand. We had best try to make sense of each of those ways. One way of doing so is to realize that different religions ask different questions, so you really cannot compare the statements of one religion with those of another.

4. *Empathetic Interest in Other People:* The way taken in the pages of this book concerns not whether religions are true (which in the end is for God to decide) but how all religions are interesting and important. We maintain here that every religion has something to teach us about what it means to be a human being. Here we take a different path from the one that leads us to questions about religious truth. It is a path that carries us to a position of empathy for our fellow Americans, in all their rich diversity.

We are trying to understand others and to explain ourselves in terms others can understand. That is the American way: to learn to live happily with difference, and not only to respect but to value the other. We teach the lesson that religion is a powerful force in shaping society, making history, and defining the life and purpose of individuals and entire groups. That is why we want to understand religion—and, among the many true and valuable things about religion that there are to comprehend, that is what we in particular want in these pages.

HOW WILL YOU KNOW WHETHER THIS BOOK HAS SUCCEEDED?

If, when you meet someone of another religion, you find yourself able to understand what is important to that person about the religion he or she believes in, then the course in which this book has been used is a success for you. The goal of this course is to help you better understand the world you live in, which means understanding the people you meet. America is a huge and diverse country, and the secret of its national unity lies in its power to teach people to respect one another, not despite difference but in full regard for difference. We like one another as we are, or, at least, we try to. And when we do not succeed, we know we have failed our country. A good American is a person who cares for the other with all due regard for the way in which the other is different.

STUDY QUESTIONS

1. Do you believe that most Americans are religious persons? If yes, explain why you think so, and give specific examples of persons "being religious" or "acting out" their religion to support your answer. If no, explain why you think so, and give specific examples.

2. Why do you think that America has such religious diversity? Is this a positive and/or negative feature of American society?

3. Why would Christians tend to describe America as a Christian nation? Why should persons be careful in defining America in this way? Should we/Can we talk about "being religious" in America and include everyone, Christian and non-Christian?

PART ONE

In the Beginning

Native Americans and Their Religions

SAM GILL

When Americans are asked to say what distinguishes our country from all other nations in the world, it isn't long before we begin to talk about Native Americans. When talking about Native Americans it isn't long before we say something about dances, rituals, ceremonies, spirituality, and stories. Today people the world over, but especially Americans, look to Native Americans to find inspiration, a spiritual centeredness, a religious connectedness to the land and to nature. Native American religions frequently play a role in film, television, and literature. Native American religions are important to the way we think about America. Significantly, Native American dancers represented the United States in the festivals that opened the 1984 Summer Olympic Games in Los Angeles, as well as the 2002 Winter Games in Salt Lake City. The Vancouver Olympics in 2010 have designated three mascots based on First Nations culture and heritage.

There are four predominant categories of Native American religions in today's America, categories that native practitioners may or may not recognize. Each category is distinguished not only by its form but also by its history. 1. Today many Native American religions are identified with specific cultures. We will call them *tribal traditions.* These religious cultures have distinctive histories running for hundreds, often thousands, of years. Each tribal tra-

dition has its distinguishing character and history, but we find some common traits and attributes among them. For example, all of these traditions have a strong attachment to the specific landscape they designate as their place of origin and where they continue to flourish.

2. Missionaries were often successful in introducing various forms of Christianity to Native Americans. Today Christianity is their most widely practiced religion. Native American Christianity has taken on characteristics distinctive to specific Native American communities. There are fascinating surprises here.

3. Native Americans have developed new religious forms that extend beyond specific tribes, yet are distinct from European American religions. The most common of these is *peyote religion*, practiced in a variety of traditions and institutionalized as the Native American Church.

4. When Native Americans of different cultures talk to one another they often emphasize how they and their cultures differ. But when Native Americans of different cultures talk about their histories, or find themselves joined together to deal with the U.S. government or with Christian missionaries, they talk about an identity they hold in common, whatever their tribal identities. This "Indian" identity is often expressed as an alternative to the modern, technologically

based, capitalistic, and materialistic character of much of America. Though this identity is political, it is also religious in that it strives to recover ancient sensitivities, particularly those that connect people religiously to the land, to nature, and to all living things. This Native American religiousness, called *Indian spirituality*, is at once old and new. It is the form of Native American religion publicly most observable in today's America.)

The following presentation of Native American religions in today's America will explore each of these four categories more fully. Most Native Americans inhabit more than one of these categories either serially or simultaneously.

TRIBAL TRADITIONS

Since a time thousands of years before Columbus, hundreds of relatively small groups of people have lived on the lands we now know as the Americas. Many of these groups continue to exist today. It is difficult to know in much detail the religions of these peoples before Europeans began to write descriptions of them, and even these records are rather sketchy. There are some clear defining traits, however, that are present today as in the past.

The peoples of these cultures self-consciously distinguish themselves from their neighbors. They speak different languages than other tribes around them. They have distinctive houses and styles of clothes. Every tribe or nation has rules defining marriages. Some tribes are patrilineal—that is, they transmit lineage through the father as we do when we receive our father's family name. Many other tribes are matrilineal—that is, a woman and her daughters and granddaughters are the lineage of the family. All of these many cultures tell their own stories, perform their own rituals, and have ritual leaders or medicine societies. These various factors, and many other things, make each of these cultures distinctive. So we must always think of Native American tribal traditions as many and varied and con-

stantly changing. Today in North America there are still more than one hundred Native American tribal traditions. Most Native Americans now speak English, but many also speak their native languages. Many Native American communities understand that keeping alive their own native language is important to the survival of their culture.

Oral Traditions

While there are many Native American languages, none of them are written. You may have heard about a Cherokee man named Sequoya who developed a way to write the Cherokee language, but this is an exception and is not even much used by Cherokees. Native American tribal religious traditions are shaped by the fact that these languages are not written. Just think about how important scriptures, written histories, and interpretive writings are to Christianity, Judaism, Islam, and other religions in America. Native American tribal traditions are composed of stories told orally by one person to others and of rituals passed from one generation to the next.

Though the lack of a written tradition may involve some shortcomings, it also ensures that the religious lives of Native Americans have a sense of immediacy, urgency, and relevance. Native American traditions are always on the edge of extinction because what is not remembered, kept vital, or seen as important enough to pass on to the next generation is irrevocably lost. The wisdom, experience, knowledge, and achievement of a people gained throughout their history must be borne in the memories of the living members of the culture. Story and narrative are essential vehhicles for exclusively oral culture. Every person bears some responsibility for the history and wisdom of her or his culture.

America is obsessed with the development of literacy, the very emblem of civilization and the measure of superiority in the world. The verbal SAT score is a primary measure of our secondary educational system. Native

Americans are not unaware of literacy. Some have even suggested reasons for resisting it. A member of the Carrier tribe in British Columbia told anthropologist Diamond Jenness, "The white man writes everything down in a book so that it might not be forgotten; but our ancestors married the animals, learned their ways, and passed on the knowledge from one generation to another."[1] An old Inuit (Eskimo) woman told the Danish ethnologist Knud Rasmussen, "Our forefathers talked much of the making of the world. . . . They did not understand how to hide words in strokes, like you do; they only told things by word of mouth, . . . they told many things . . . which we have heard repeated time after time, ever since we were children. Old women do not fling their words about without meaning, and we believe them. There are no lies with age."[2]

The Zuni in New Mexico tell stories of their origins. In the earliest era the ancestors of the Zuni people lived in dark, crowded caves deep within the earth. The Sun Father sent his two warrior sons to lead the people out. When they emerged as "sunlight people" the Sun Father told them to travel in search of their home, "the middle place of the world." During their travels the people found a rain priest. Their own rain priest prayed with him, and together they made it rain. A water strider, an insect that skates on the surface of the water, came along and stretched its legs out to the edges of the earth. Where its heart touched the earth marked the middle. The Zuni had finally found *itiwana*, the middle place of the world.

Today, as in the past, the Zuni see the world as divided into sections corresponding mainly with the four cardinal directions, but they also consider the regions above and below as important. The Zuni are matrilineal. Each person is born into her or his mother's family and receives her clan, a named social designation. Each clan is associated with one of these directions. For example, if your mother's clan is Evergreen-oak, this is your clan. Evergreen-oak, green even in winter, is associated with the north and with winter.

Yellow, the color of morning and evening light in winter, is associated with northern clans. One's clan determines the range of occupations and religious activities one has. Because the north correlates with war and destruction, a person in the Evergreen-oak clan would be encouraged to engage in war-related occupations and religious activities. One must always marry outside of one's own clan.

The Zuni priesthoods stand at the pivot and meeting place of all these divisions. For the Zuni the center represents totality and summation. The Zuni annual calendar is divided at the solstices into two halves, each containing six lunar months. Around the time of the solstices are twenty-day periods of intense religious activities, known as *itiwana*, marking the center or turning places within the yearly cycle.

The Zuni village, known also as *itiwana*, bears the prestige and power of a center place, of being at the conjunction of all places in the universe.

The Seneca, who live in upper New York State, tell stories about a woman who fell from the sky into this world. A flock of birds caught this woman. The world was then covered by water, so the only support they could find for her was on the back of a turtle swimming in the water. One by one, many animals tried to dive to the bottom of the water to get a bit of earth from which to make the world. After many failed, one finally succeeded, and the Earth Maker, a creator, expanded this bit of soil into the present earth, which is supported on the back of the turtle.

The woman who fell from the sky gave birth to a daughter. The daughter was the mother of corn as well as of twin boys who represent the negative and positive forces constantly at struggle in life.

We may think that no one could really believe such a fanciful story, and we might even be a little suspicious of anyone who claimed they believed it. These stories are, however, quite interesting, and they are among the ways Native American people express such important things as what they understand to be good and bad, how the world came to be, what makes life meaningful, and how to relate to one another. These stories tell how members of a particular Native American culture strive to understand the world.

This kind of story, which we call a myth, can be used in very serious ways. For example, for decades the Navajo and Hopi peoples have been in conflict over lands declared for their joint use by a U.S. government treaty. Though there have been many court battles

Mother Earth

Contemporary Indians refer often to the figure "Mother Earth" (sometimes connected with Father Sky). The frequency of this story across native cultures is remarkable. Comparative academic studies of the ideology, symbology, theology, mythology, language, ritual, and history of the hundreds of cultures that comprise native North America show that the differences among the cultures are so vast as to exclude almost anything held in common that is not also common to all human beings (one might think of archetypes). Yet Native Americans have increasingly identified Mother Earth as distinctive to Indian belief and identity, particularly as opposed to Americans with European ancestry. Studies of the historical record of the emergence of these references indicate that the figure known by the English term "Mother Earth" emerged from the discourse of Native Americans attempting to defend their ancestral lands against claims made by those of European heritage. Today, in broad terms, Mother Earth has become a powerful figure that is actively used to demonstrate Native American distinctiveness.

and efforts made by the federal government to resolve the situation, the peoples themselves remain unsatisfied. Several years ago the Hopi and Navajo tribal chairpersons met in public to discuss this conflict. Both appeared dressed in business suits. Both

were well versed in the law and government policy. Each, when it was his time to speak, told the story of the creation of the world. Each showed how the particular landscape in question is essential to the identity of the people in his tribe.

The Hopi tribal chairperson described how the Hopi people were led out of the lower worlds onto this surface of the earth through an emergence hole (*sipapuni*) in the canyon of the Little Colorado River. From there they migrated in clan groupings to their present homes atop the mesas in northeastern Arizona.

The Navajo tribal chairperson told the story of how, before the Navajo world was created, the Navajo ancestors traveled through worlds below this one. Eventually they emerged at a location somewhere in the four corners region, where present-day Arizona, Utah, Colorado, and New Mexico meet. The Navajo world was then created, bound by four mountains, one in each of the four cardinal directions, each identified with a mountain that Navajos can see in their land today.

While expressed in a political and legal setting, these stories are no less religiously significant today, for they continue to perform the cultural work of defining people to themselves and to others around them, including the federal government and the broader public. Both cultures depend for their very lives on the land they occupy. Each culture's identity depends on its creation story and on living in the landscape created for it. These stories are the basis for a meaningful life for individuals and cultures.

Art and Architecture

Native Americans' homes are commonly models of the universe. This makes homes religiously important. Every architectural feature, every way a house is used, reflects something meaningful. The way Native Americans build, divide up, and use parts of their houses correlates with their way of life. Many Native Americans perform ceremonials in the home. Yet there is also specialized religious architecture. *Sweat lodges*, found in many styles throughout North America, are small houses in which people go to purify themselves, to learn religious information, and to talk about serious things. Pueblo people use *kivas*, partly underground rooms, for performing rituals. Large Eskimo ceremonial houses called *qasgiq* are entered through a tunnel and a hole in the floor. These houses contain marionettes; for use in dramatic performances there are screens, behind which the performer can dress or otherwise prepare; even the entry tunnel and the skylight window are used to dramatic effect. Enormous clan houses of the Pacific Northwest have elaborately painted fronts and doorways that represent an orifice of the body of a mythic ancestor. Just imagine that every time you enter your house you step through the mouth or vagina of a mythic ancestor!

The designs on clothing, pottery, baskets, and tools frequently correspond with images from stories, features of the landscape, and clan symbols. By wearing clothing and using pottery and baskets, Native Americans are reminded of their stories; they are surrounded by the patterns that they associate with what makes their life and culture meaningful. For example, Navajos believe that closed circles constrict movement and thereby life. To bring harm to another, one need only draw a closed circle around her or his house. Navajos insist on openings in all encircling designs. The characteristic design woven into Navajo wedding baskets is always open, and the opening corresponds with the beginning and ending coil at the center and perimeter of the basket. The border designs in Navajo weavings always have a thread carried from the interior to the outside signifying the opening for the movement of life. A personified rainbow surrounds sandpaintings (discussed below) on three sides, being open on the east.

It is more appropriate to think of Native American art as a verb, as "arting," to focus attention on the creation process and the use of the objects produced. In Eskimo carving, the carver picks up the raw material, a piece of ivory or stone. Turning it about, the carver tries to see the shape contained within. To assert one's will upon the material is not the goal of carving. Rather the carver serves as an agent to reveal or release a shape already in the material—a seal, a bear, a whale.

Navajo sandpainting, so commonly known in the craft or fine art form, is always a part of a ritual process in traditional Navajo culture. Sandpainting is a ritual act of curing performed as a part of healing ceremonials that often last many days. These pictures are associated with stories about heroes or heroines who are cured of some illness they suffer. Sandpaintings are made on smooth, clean sand bases on the floors of Navajo *hogans* (houses). They are often ten feet or larger in diameter. The elaborate designs must be produced accurately, but none of the hundreds of paintings that can be prepared exists anywhere in permanent form. Their every detail must be remembered by the medicine people who know these ceremonials. When the painting is finished, the person to be treated walks on and sits in the middle of the painting. The medicine person or a masked spirit being known as *ye'ii* begins to treat the person. The medicine person's or the ye'ii's hands are moistened with an herbal medicine lotion and placed on the story figures in the picture. Particles of sand are transferred from the body parts of each figure in the sandpainting to the corresponding body parts of the suffering person. This identifies the person with story. The painting is smeared in this process. After the ritual is performed upon the sandpainting, the medicine person destroys and removes it from the hogan. For Navajos, a sandpainting functions less as a work of art than as a tool to make a healthy human being and world. What a sandpainting helps create is beauty of the highest order.

For Native Americans, art and arting have a religious aspect. By making and using art, Native Americans continue the creation process begun so long ago by gods and ancestors.

Rituals

The rituals of Native American tribal traditions are rarely performed simply to celebrate or commemorate some event or time. Native American rituals are performed to bring something about—a stage of life, a successful hunt, a change in season. In other words, rituals do more than celebrate something already done.

Girls' puberty rites are performed throughout the region west of the Rocky Mountains. The Apache people call their girls' puberty rite the Sunrise Dance. After an Apache girl begins menstruation, her family may sponsor a Sunrise Dance involving not only the extended family but the whole community. After days of preparation accompanied by social dances in the evenings, the formal ceremonial begins. In an elaborate buckskin dress, the initiate dances to songs that tell the stories of creation. The girl is identified with White Shell Woman, and through her dance she reenacts the events that created the world, when White Shell Woman had sexual union with the Sun. During this rite the pubescent girl is identified with the powers that created the whole world. Contact with her, even being present at the ceremony, promotes health and life. Near the end of the ceremonial, baskets of fruit and candies are poured over the girl's head. Everyone present scrambles for the goodies, made powerful by their contact with the girl.

The Apache, and similarly the Navajo, are exceptional in their approach to female coming-of-age. Many cultures, in contrast, consider menstrual blood a pollutant, and menstruating females are isolated from the community.

Among tribes throughout the northern Plains and Northwest, males come of age by fasting for a vision. A Lakota (Sioux) male wishing to complete his passage to manhood seeks a vision through a period of ritual and fasting. Isolated on a hilltop, he fasts and offers prayers using a pipe and pointing its stem in each of the four directions—north, south, east, and west. He humbles himself before the powers of the world; he cries for a vision. Visions are described by visionaries as sequences of images strong in their potential for meaning. After a vision, the visionary consults with medicine men who help him discover the possible meanings of the vision. These images serve as a guide to be consulted throughout life. When a man must make decisions at the crossroads of life, he will look to his vision for help. The vision thus serves as a guardian spirit or a spiritual helper available in times of need.

A fascinating example of the transformative powers of ritual is the Hopi initiation of eight- to ten-year-old children, who thus begin their formal religious lives. Much of Hopi religion involves the frequent appearance of masked dancers, known as *kachinas,* representing spiritual messengers. For more than half of every year dancing and performing kachinas are common in Hopi villages. Before their initiation, children do not see either unmasked kachinas or unoccupied masks. When they undergo their initiation rites, the children hear stories about the kachinas, especially about their origins. They go to a nighttime kiva dance from which they have always been excluded. The kachinas enter the kiva where the children await. What is important is that these kachinas do not wear masks. When the children see that what they thought were spirits are actually their uncles and fathers, they are shocked, angered, and disenchanted. They wonder if they will ever be able to trust adults again.

This seems harsh treatment for children, and it is. But the children learn something very important through this experience. They have until now seen the world naively, believing that the world is exactly as it appears to be. This disenchantment gives them the experience that there is more to the world than meets the eye. As they begin to participate in their religious lives, they listen to the stories with greater care. This initiation by disenchantment opens the children to the world of mystery, beauty, and power that can only be known through devoted participation and can only be experienced with a sensitivity attuned to the reality that surpasses the merely physical.

The Sun Dance was prohibited in the late nineteenth century by U.S. government regulation. It returned in the mid-twentieth century, especially among tribes in the northern Plains. The Sun Dance is an annual ritual involving many in the community. The world is re-created and renewed in this new year's rite. All the people are released from grievances and social strife. Everyone is rededicated to his or her role as woman, man, leader, hunter, warrior, or child. The Sun Dance provides an opportunity to perform vows made in return for favors asked of spirit beings. These vows often take the form of physical suffering. After the ritual construction of a Sun Dance lodge, dances are performed by individuals attached to the center pole of the lodge by leather thongs and skewers, which are inserted through the flesh above the dancer's pectoral muscles. These dances are central to the Sun Dance ceremonial. The dancer's suffering fulfills a vow made in promise for some spiritual favor and serves to humble the dancer before the spiritual powers.

The Sun Dance innovatively combines features from old fertility rites of corn-growing peoples who lived along the rivers in the central and eastern Plains with the hunting rituals of cultures that hunted buffalo and other game on the Plains. For thousands of years physical survival of Native American peoples depended on some combination of successful hunting, gathering, agriculture, and fishing. It is little surprise that animals and plants are central to the religions of tribal traditions. Not only are such animals and plants used as powerful ritual objects, they express central religious concepts. The buffalo, whose head adorns the center pole in the Sun Dance lodge, designates the source and power of life itself.

Corn, corn pollen, and cornmeal are used ritually by agricultural Native American tribes. Corn, in a personified form, plays a major role in ritual and story. The Cherokee tell a story of Selu, a woman who is corn, who provides food for her family by rubbing epidermal waste from her skin or by defecating. When her children discover how she produces food, they consider it witchcraft and decide to kill her. Knowing of their plans, Selu instructs them to plow an area of ground and to drag her bleeding body over the upturned soil after they kill her. They do as she asks, and where her blood touches the soil corn plants grow. Many Native American cultures tell stories of a corn woman who magically provides corn to feed her people. When mistreated she leaves, and her departure marks the beginning of the human cultivation of corn. In some southwestern tribes, at initiation a child is given an ear of corn, known as a corn mother, as a guide and protector. Pollen or cornmeal strewn or sprinkled is a blessing and an act of prayer.

Even though the horse was introduced to North America only with the coming of the Spanish in the sixteenth century, it has become central to many tribal traditions. The most respected of Navajo songs are the horse songs, which depict its cosmic dimensions:

> Its feet are made of mirage
> Its gait is a rainbow
> Its bridle of sun strings
> Its heart is made of red stone
> Its intestines are made of water of all
>   kinds
> Its tail of black rain
> Its mane is a cloud with a little rain.[3]

From the circumpolar region southward throughout much of North America, bears have played a religious role for thousands of years. Along the Pacific Northwest Coast, Raven is a creator and major culture hero who brings light to the world and shapes culture. Tobacco is widely used in the rituals of Native American tribal traditions as a potent spiritual "medicine." The list of plants and animals with religious significance could go on and on.

Here is what must be remembered to this point: Native American tribal traditions, though different from one another, are nonetheless similar in some respects. These traditions are directed toward the creation of a meaningful life for the people within a specific landscape that has been sanctioned by a tradition based on primordial events recorded in stories. Native American tribal traditions foster a closeness to and respectful interdependence with the natural world.

Shamanism

Health and healing are common concerns of tribal traditions. Some of these traditions, such as the Navajo, use health and healing to address almost all concerns. Some traditions, especially those in the Arctic and down the Pacific Northwest Coast into California, practice shamanism. Caution is needed when using the term *shaman*. Many have used it to name any religious or spiritual specialist. The term comes from tribal cultures in Siberia and refers to individuals who use ecstatic techniques—that is, it designates those who know how to enter into a trance. Through trances shamans enter the spiritual world to seek help in resolving human problems, most often illness.

The Pomo, a California tribe, is one group that continues to use shamans. These individuals, often women for the Pomo, sing and shake long rattle staffs in preparation for entering a trance. Kneeling beside the sick person, the shaman then breathes rapidly while blowing incessantly on a bird-bone whistle. Eventually the shaman's body begins to quiver and convulse, showing that she or he has entered into trance.

After entering a trance the shaman examines the body of the sufferer by passing a quivering hand over it. This locates the illness, believed to be a malevolent object—a bone, a worm, an arrow, an insect—that has intruded into the body. These objects are often thought to be "shot" by witches. The shaman sucks out this evil object. As it enters the shaman's body, there is a noticeable convulsion. The shaman spits the object in the fire or in a bowl of water to destroy it. In some cultures the Shaman actually displays for all to see the object that has been removed.

Another form of illness treated by shamans is conceived as the loss of the life form, sometimes called the soul. The Salish people of the Pacific Northwest engage troupes of shamans who ritually paddle canoes in search of the lost life form; that is, they dramatize this journey by sitting in a canoe in the healing lodge. They recover the life form in dramatized ritual battles and then paddle back to return it to the sufferer.

Ecstatic techniques are used in North America to find lost objects or relatives, to learn of the future, to ensure success in hunting, and to conduct the deceased to the land of the dead. Shamanism always involves the use of ecstatic techniques by an individual to call upon forces in the spiritual world to intervene in human affairs.

An individual is often called by a powerful vision or dream to enter a shamanic career. A persistent theme in these dreams, as well as in the initiatory rituals, is the aspiring shaman being stripped to a skeleton and reconstituted as a shaman. This theme suggests that a shaman gains power through a death and rebirth experience. Still, shamans require extensive training beyond these initiatory experiences.

Perhaps because Native American tribal traditions are shaped by an essential connection with a specific landscape and by an authority structure based on telling stories of primordial events, it may appear that these traditions do not change, that they do not have histories. But extensive changes often take place in these tribal traditions. Native Americans are not helpless recipients of changes brought on by others. Because many of their traditions bear the responsibility for the ongoing creation of the world, Native Americans often creatively manage their own histories. There is no greater evidence of this than the fact that so many tribal traditions not only have survived but continue to thrive in the face of half a millennium of almost constant onslaught by powerful visitors from other lands.

NATIVE AMERICAN CHRISTIANITY

When Columbus met Native Americans, all their religions were tribal traditions. One of his first observations of these new peoples was that he believed they could be easily Christianized. Missionaries soon began their work in this new land. Today not a single tribal tradition has escaped the influence of Christianity. Many Native American communities today are primarily Christian. Many other communities have extensively incorporated Christian elements into tribal traditions. Others, particularly those forced to become Christian, secretly continued their own tribal traditions while publicly practicing Christianity. The discussion of several cultures will exemplify these several types of Native American Christianity.

The Pueblo Peoples of the Southwest

Though it is often thought that American history moved across the continent from east to west and that American religious history began with the founding of Jamestown in 1607, one of the first meetings between Native Americans and Europeans was at Zuni in present-day New Mexico. The conquest of Mexico led to explorations north into the American Southwest. The first Franciscan missionaries attempted to establish themselves among the pueblo peoples by 1580. Santa Fe was a provincial capital city in 1610, a decade before the *Mayflower* sailed. Franciscan missionaries accompanied Spanish explorers, and by the early seventeenth century, mission churches had been built in pueblos throughout the Southwest. These churches are the largest build-

ings in most pueblo villages. The church in the village of Acoma, which sits high atop a mesa, required the forced labor of hundreds of pueblo people to hand-carry the building materials to the mesa top, including many enormous roof support beams from trees cut as far away as a hundred miles. Pueblo peoples were forced, sometimes on punishment of beatings or even death, to be baptized and to practice Christianity publicly. Missionaries discouraged the practice of the tribal traditions and even destroyed pueblo ceremonial paraphernalia such as altars, costumes, and masks. Little wonder this treatment did not endear Christians and Christianity to pueblo peoples.

Although the people were forced to practice Christianity, the tribal traditions of these pueblos survived and persisted by going underground. These practices became so secret that almost nothing is known about the religions of several pueblos still apparently quite vital today. This public practice of Christianity complemented by the secret and private practice of tribal traditions is sometimes called "compartmentalization."

As the centuries have passed, missionaries have become far less oppressive of Native American tribal traditions. Although the compartments remain, with less pressure the pueblo antagonism toward Christianity has diminished. Christianity has earned a meaningful place in the lives of many pueblo people today, complementing their tribal traditions.

The Yaqui

Among the most creative interactions between tribal traditions and Christianity are those of the Yaqui, who currently live in several Arizona communities. The Yaqui lived in present-day Sonora at the time of the conquest of Mexico. For a long time they effectively resisted Spanish influence. Finally, in 1617, they invited Christian missionaries (who were Spanish) to live among them. Almost overnight the Yaqui willingly transformed their culture and religion, taking on many Christian forms. In 1767, after more than a century, under pressure from the Mexican government, which was demanding economic and social change and rejecting everything Spanish, the Yaqui asked the missionaries to leave. In the century that followed, however, even without the presence of missionaries, they continued to practice and develop traditions that had distinctive Christian forms.

The Mexican government finally conquered the Yaqui in fierce military engagements and dispersed the culture. Some formed communities in southern Arizona. By the beginning of the twentieth century they began once again to practice their traditions. Central among these is the elaborate ritual process that unfolds during the forty days of Lent. Elements of the Christian Passion can be recognized in this ritual, but they are interpreted as representing the universal struggle between good and evil. The evil forces are portrayed by soldiers dressed in black known as *Pilates* and by groups of masked figures known as *Chapayekas*. Holy Week, the climax of this ritual season, includes the capture of the church by the evil forces, the crucifixion of Jesus (represented as an icon), and the return to the church of the good. The final struggle between good and evil occurs on Easter Saturday. An effigy figure of Judas is placed in the center of the plaza that extends in front of the Yaqui church. Midmorning the Pilates and Chapayekas march into the plaza in two long lines, prepared to assault the church and return to power. At the signal of the ringing church bell, the evil forces rush the church, which is defended by children and old women armed with flower petals and green leaves representing the transformed blood of Christ. These prove to be stronger weapons, and evil is repelled. The masked figures leave their swords, daggers, and masks at the foot of the Judas effigy and rush to the church to rededicate themselves to Christ and the good. Judas is torched, and as he, along with all the masks and swords, explodes into fire, the whole Yaqui village erupts into fiesta.

Native American Christian Communities

Throughout America today there are Native American communities that are primarily Christian, peoples who have little or no practice of tribal traditions. These Christian communities often have distinctive tribal designations. Others are identified generically as Indian, without tribal designation, especially in the large Native American communities in many cities. Although Americans of European ancestry introduced Christianity to Native Americans, Native American clergy and leaders have increasingly taken over the leadership of churches in these communities. Many young Native Americans have trained for Indian ministry in institutions such as Cook Christian Training School in Phoenix. Native American Christian communities are frequently fundamentalist in their theology, conservative in their practice, and often revivalistic and evangelical.

As Native Americans became Christian, they gained a certain freedom from being the objects not only of missionization, but also of academic scrutiny. As Christians they no longer seemed unknown or exotic. As a result very little is known about most of these communities. What are these religions? How are they related to tribal traditions? A scholar named Thomas McElwain did a study that gives us some hints. He studied Christian hymns that had been translated from English into Seneca for the 1834 publication of a Seneca Christian hymnal. He simply translated the Seneca back to English, examining especially the words in Seneca used for God. He found that the hymns express the religious ideas of Seneca tribal traditions much more than those of Christian theology.[4]

Many Native American Christian communities have responded innovatively to the pressures of Christianization, being able at once to continue older tribal traditions or ideas in new forms (and forms that have little compatibility with their own), to incorporate some aspects of the invading traditions, and coincidentally to diffuse the pressures of conquest and the intrusion of academic studies.

NEW RELIGIOUS MOVEMENTS

For Native Americans, religion is essential to life and cultural identity. In performing rituals and telling stories, Native Americans discover and create the meaning of life in the world. Religion provides some of the tools needed to go through the cycle of life, to hunt and grow food, and to deal with life's crises.

Throughout American history Native Americans have suffered wars, epidemic diseases, and forced displacements. They changed their way of life when horses, sheep, and new weapons were available from Americans. A never-ending progression of technologies, from electric appliances to pickup trucks, has introduced irreversible change to Native American cultures. The way Native Americans govern themselves has changed too. When they were forced as nations to negotiate with U.S. federal and state governments, Native Americans were compelled to develop new political and legal organizations, tribal councils, and governments that have little resemblance to former tribally distinct methods of governance. Literacy, schooled education, missionization, and the ceaseless treatment of Native Americans as objects of academic study, often motivated by the belief that these cultures were soon to become extinct, have forced many changes. Often outsiders invented images of Native Americans that served as standards by which the lives of actual individuals have been measured. These images, whether negative (the bloody savage) or positive (the noble savage) were always inventions. Notably, Native Americans have often consumed and reproduced these discourses, shaping Native American cultures to correspond with what others expect of them.

Crisis Movements

Sometimes the cumulative pressure of these intruding forces reached crisis proportions, and the Native American response often took the religious form of crisis movements. These movements, led by a visionary or prophet, helped strengthen threatened cultures. They commonly required Native clothing, language, hunting, and cultivation, while consciously rejecting American clothing, English language, schooled education, Christianity and missionaries, the use of alcohol, metal tools, and firearms. Finding themselves living in strange territories, with no way to continue practicing the ways of life that distinguish them, Native Americans have followed visions of those who saw the cataclysmic end of this world and the return of a former world, a world before European influences.

By the beginning of the nineteenth century, Seneca culture was facing a major crisis. Seneca people had been drawn away from Seneca ways through Christianization, education in schools, employment for wages, and the use of alcohol. A Seneca man named Handsome Lake typified the people at the time. He was an alcoholic and no longer knew how to be Seneca in a traditional sense. He fell ill, and many thought he had died. As he lay motionless in his bed he had a vision in which he received good news about the future. He brought new life to the Seneca by introducing a new religion based on his vision. Though there were difficult times ahead for Handsome Lake and for the Seneca, this religious movement, born of crisis, eventually became established and continues to serve the Seneca people.

During the nineteenth century many Native American cultures were pushed to the limits of their abilities to survive. The transcontinental railroad was completed. The great herds of buffalo were destroyed. Native Americans were confined to reservation lands on which they could not hunt or farm. Many Native American cultures began to face the possibility of extinction.

Throughout the northwestern United States during the last half of the nineteenth century, many crisis movements arose.

Among the most widespread was the Ghost Dance movement of 1890. A Paiute man named Wovoka had a vision that foretold the cataclysmic end of the world as it had become, followed by a return of the world that existed before the Europeans came. Those Native Americans who practiced the rituals of the movement and lived according to its tenets believed they would survive the cataclysm, that the dead humans and animals would return, and that the land would be renewed. The Ghost Dance ritual was a circular dance in which dancers fell into trances and often saw visions of the dead journeying back to the world of the living.

The Ghost Dance movement ended in the tragic massacre by U.S. troops of hundreds, including many women and children, at Wounded Knee at the end of December 1890.

The Native American Church

Peyote, a small hallucinogenic cactus, has long been used in ritual in Native American cultures in Mexico, especially in the area where the cactus grows. Late in the nineteenth century, a new religion with distinct ritual forms involving the ingestion of the cactus began to spread northward into Texas and through the Plains. Early in the twentieth century, in an effort to use this hallucinogen legally, the religion was formally constituted as the Native American Church. Comparing the use of peyote to the Christian sacrament of the Eucharist, Native Americans, though not at the time considered U.S. citizens, mounted a legal defense based on protection under the law of the free practice of religion. Though the legal battles continue, the Native American Church has thrived and by mid-twentieth century was widely practiced not only by Plains tribes, but also by many others.

Native American Church meetings are all-night singing and prayer meetings. They may be held in any form of lodge, although the Plains *tipi* is the most popular. Built on the floor of the lodge is a crescent-shaped altar carved from tip to tip with a design of the peyote road. This road represents the life lived according to the direction of the peyote spirit. A large peyote button, representing Chief Peyote or the peyote spirit, rests on the center of the altar. A water drum provides the rhythmic accompaniment for the singing. A beaded staff, feather fans with beaded handles, and gourd rattles are other ritual implements used in the meetings.

The meetings begin at sundown and end at dawn. Meetings are called for specific purposes: the illness of a member of the community, the celebration of a special event, even the preparation of a student for school examinations. A leader, known as the road chief, begins by stating the purpose of the meeting and inviting everyone to direct prayers to this need. Throughout the night peyote songs are sung—often in a Plains language, regardless of what tribe is singing the songs—to the accompaniment of rattle and drum. The beaded staff is passed around the meeting, and the person holding it becomes the singer. The drum, fan, and rattle are also passed. Periodically peyote is passed and eaten by the members. While members may experience visions, particularly increased intensity of colors and other sensations, the primary purpose is to increase concentration and the sense of community. It should be noted that peyote is not eaten to induce intense individual hallucinogenic experiences. Native American Church communities are often very conservative. The Native American Church is effective in the treatment of drug and alcohol abuse.

The Native American Church is distinct from tribal traditions in that it is practiced by Native Americans from many tribes. It can incorporate elements of Christianity; for example, the peyote spirit may be identified as Jesus. Passages from the Christian Bible may be incorporated in the ritual. Unlike Native American Christianity, however, peyote religion was not introduced by Europeans. Like tribal traditions, the Native American Church is distinctly Native American. The Native American Church need not threaten individual cultural identities. Indeed, there are often tribal variations in the ritual practice. The Native American Church links Native Americans together, forging a common identity out of their shared history of oppression.

NATIVE AMERICAN SPIRITUALITY

Early in the nineteenth century, faced with the displacement from ancestral lands by the American westward expansion, a Shawnee man named Tecumseh and his brother Tenskwatawa fought for Native American survival. They believed that cooperation among the various native cultures would provide more effective resistance than the separate efforts of many tribes. Military and political strength was the foremost concern, but there was also a vision of a common Indian religion. This perspective marks a shift from trying to accommodate the European American presence to the acknowledgment that Native Americans, despite significant cultural differences, held more in common among themselves than they did with those who were threatening their existence.

Especially since the middle of the twentieth century leaders have described what distinguishes all Native American peoples. These distinctive traits are religious in character, but the term *spirituality* will be used here to emphasize that the view is self-consciously anti-Western. The term *religion* denotes Christianity to many Native Americans; the term *spirituality* avoids this connection while suggesting an attitude of respect and reverence toward every aspect of life.

Notably, the rise of Native American spirituality has been associated with the print medium. Those who have shaped it are those who have written, or at least whose words have been written and published. There is perhaps some irony in this, but it has also made Native American spirituality the most known and accessible of all forms of Native American religions. The movement has served to mediate between mainstream American culture (whose primary access to other cultures is through print) and tribal cultures (which remain exclusively oral). No single book has been more important to the rise of Native American spirituality than *Black Elk Speaks,* recorded and developed by the non-Indian author John Neihardt. The extent of Neihardt's contribution has given rise to considerable controversy (see sidebar), yet many Native Americans see this book as equivalent

Black Elk

The Lakota man called Black Elk became a Christian after a traditional childhood that included visionary experiences. John Neihardt, a poet, traveled the northern plains looking for material to enrich his epic poem "A Cycle of the West." In 1930 he met Black Elk and they talked. Based on those conversations, yet heavily shaped by his own view of Native Americans as tragic figures willingly sacrificing themselves to the progress of U.S. expansion, Neihardt wrote *Black Elk Speaks* (1932). While scholars have shown that much of this work is Neihardt's construction and the book conveniently omits mention of Black Elk's life and work as a Christian, many Native Americans have embraced it as a sacred narrative. The late Vine Deloria Jr. referred to it as the Native American holy book. Hundreds of college classes throughout the United States use this book to teach traditional Native American religions.

to a holy book. *Black Elk Speaks* is complemented by *The Sacred Pipe,* in which Black Elk tells Joseph Epes Brown about the seven rites of the Oglala Sioux. Many other Native Americans have participated in the development of Native American spirituality. Vine Deloria Jr., schooled in Christian theology and the law, has written books widely read by Native Americans and other Americans alike. The fiction of Leslie Silko, N. Scott Momaday, and Sherman Alexie has shown that one of the spiritual centers of Native American traditions is storytelling.

Those Native Americans most influential in developing Native American spirituality have retained close contact with their specific tribal traditions. In describing their own tribally based spirituality, they have seen themes, images, and concerns common among all Native American peoples.

Native American spirituality encourages the continuity of tribal traditions, but more so the embracing of a common Indian identity. Native American spirituality exists in an arena of intense awareness of the crises and difficulties Native Americans face. Native Americans share a history of oppression and a pride and confidence in their heritage that has given them the strength to survive.

Understandably, the tenets of Native American spirituality are expressed largely in opposition to majority American culture. Native American spirituality condemns the very things its proponents identify as distinctive of most Americans: capitalism and the accompanying materialism, rational thought and literacy, political and economic policies that encourage the exploitation of the land and peoples, and Christianity. Native American spirituality builds upon its ancient roots in the American soil and a spiritual way of life that reveres the land as a mother, often formalized as Mother Earth, and respects as kin all plants and animals, indeed, all of nature. This perspective strongly holds that Native American spirituality not only is superior to the religion and culture of most Americans, but that it also holds the promise for saving the whole of America from a course of destruction.

Native American spirituality encourages the continuity and revitalization of the stories and rituals of tribal traditions. It has virtually no distinctive mythology apart from tribal traditions, though in its place is an extensive body of anecdotes, stories, and literature about Native American oppression and mistreatment by European Americans, and about the apparently foolish and destructive ways of these oppressors. Native American spirituality has embraced pipe ceremonies and sweat lodge rites. The dancing, singing, drumming, and ceremony of pow-wows have become the principal form of expression for many Native Americans.

Native American spirituality is widely popular among non-Native American peoples. This popularity is at once a backlash against what are considered negative aspects of our American heritage and a sign of respect for Native American religions.

Though it may seem that Native Americans are largely gone, a people of movies and books, it must be remembered that today millions of people identify themselves as Native Americans. Further, as we have learned in this chapter, Native Americans have rich and diverse cultures, including many forms of religious practice.

Notes

1. Diamond Jenness, "The Carrier Indians of Bulkley River," *Bureau of American Ethnology Bulletin*, no. 133 (Washington, D.C., 1943): 540.
2. Knud Rasmussen, *The People of the Polar North: A Record* (London: Kegan Paul, Trench, Trubner & Co., 1908), 99–100.
3. Adapted from Pliney E. Goddard, *Navajo Texts*, Anthropology Papers, vol. 34 (New York: American Museum of Natural History, 1933), 164.
4. Thomas McElwain, "'The Rainbow Will Carry Me': The Language of Seneca Christianity as Reflected in Hymns," in *Religion in Native North America*, ed. Christopher Vecsey (Moscow: University of Idaho Press, 1990): 83–103. See also James Treat, *Native and Christian: Indigenous Voices on Religious Identity* (New York: Routledge, 1996).

STUDY QUESTIONS

1. Discuss the stereotypes often associated with Native American religious traditions. How has reading this chapter changed your understanding of Native American religious traditions?

2. What are the four predominant categories of Native American religions in today's America? How do they function? What do you see as the important characteristics distinguishing these categories? How are they similar?

3. Native American languages are not written languages, at least not in their original forms. What do you see as the implications, positive and negative, of an oral tradition versus a written tradition? What would you gain from your religious tradition if your language were only oral? What would you lose from your religious tradition?

4. What is a story? Why is "story" important for any religious tradition? The Native American tradition? Describe or create a religious story from your religious tradition that functions like a story in the Native American religious tradition.

5. Explain how Native American art can be described as having a religious function. Give examples of Native American art and describe its role in the religious lives of its people.

6. Religious ritual plays a significant role in the lives of Native Americans. Define ritual. How would you distinguish ritual from habit? Describe at least two rituals from Native American religious traditions and discuss their functions.

ESSAY TOPICS

The Role and Function of the Shaman in Native American Religious Traditions

Native American Art: Exploring a Religious Tradition through Images

Native American Religious Traditions and Christianity: Conflict and Compromise

WORD EXPLORATION

The following words play significant roles in any discussion of Native American religious traditions and are worth careful reflection and discussion.

Tribe	Native American	Peyote
Oral Tradition	Medicine Person	Shaman
Sacred Rite of Passage	Ritual	Crisis Movement

FOR FURTHER READING

Beck, Peggy V., and Anno L. Waiters. *The Sacred: Ways of Knowledge, Sources of Life.* Tsaile, Ariz.: Navajo Community College Press, 1977.

Capps, Walter H., ed. *Seeing with a Native Eye.* San Francisco: Harper & Row, 1976.

Gill, Sam. *Native American Religions: An Introduction.* Belmont, Calif.: Wadsworth Publishing Co., 1982; rev. ed., 2004.

Silko, Leslie. *Ceremony* [a novel]. New York: Viking, 1977.

Talayesva, Don C. *Sun Chief. The Autobiography of a Hopi Indian.* New Haven, Conn.: Yale University Press, 1942.

WEB SITES

http://www.hanksville.org/NAresources
  Index of Native American resources on the Internet

http://www.wsu.edu/~dee/NAINRES.HTM
  The Native American Anthology: Internet Resources

http://www.sacred-texts.com
  The Internet Sacred Texts Archive

PART TWO

Christian Foundations of American Religions

2

Protestant Christianity in the World and in America

MARTIN E. MARTY

1509	French-Swiss reformer John Calvin born
1513	John Knox, reformer in Scotland, born
1517	Martin Luther posts theses that stimulate reform of the church; symbolic beginning of the Continental Reformation
1529	The label "Protestant" invented at the Diet of Speyer in Germany
1559	Puritans seek to reform Anglican Church in England
1607	First English settlement, with Anglican Church, in Virginia
1620	Pilgrims settle Plymouth Colony in Massachusetts
1622	Native Americans react in Virginia; colonial tensions grow
1630	Puritans establish Massachusetts Bay colony
1654	Jews arrive from Brazil after exile within Europe
1726ff.	First Great Awakening in colonies
1776–1789	Independence, formation of United States, with a Constitution that mentions God; "Fathers" were mainly Protestant
1784	Methodists, reformers within Anglicanism, organize in Baltimore
1801	Cane Ridge Revival in Kentucky kicks off Second Great Awakening
1844	Methodists split over slavery, as do many denominations (the Southern Baptists and American Baptists have still not reunited)
1870–1900	Great age of Protestant missionary work
1906	Pentecostal beginnings
1908	Federal Council of Churches created to promote ecumenism
1910ff.	Prime years of "the Social Gospel"
1942–43	"Fundamentalists" and "Evangelicals" organize
1948	World Council of Churches involves American churches
1951	Federal Council of Churches, largely Protestant
1956ff.	Protestants participate in civil rights movement
1970s	Evangelical Protestants emerge as a political force
2008	Protestants no longer a majority group; down to roughly 50 percent of all Americans

Taking Roll Call of Protestants

Suppose you rang a bell and exactly one hundred students responded to form an assembly. Suppose they represented a precise sample of adult America. If you were to ask them (as you probably would not in public), "What is your religion?" you would find that about fifty of the hundred would say that they are Protestant. If people in the United States engaged in holy wars the way people did in other times and still do in some other places, you would be very worried if you were one of the two or three Jews in the assembly. You would be concerned if you were one of the much larger but still outnumbered group of twenty-five Catholics. Things could be especially bad for you if you were one of the ten who said that you had "no religion."

Not to worry—as they say nowadays when they want us to be at ease—because those fifty Protestants would never be able to form a single team to gang up on you. First of all, they have no reason to be angry with you; most of them have many friends who are not Protestant, and they would not want to hurt their friends. Even more of them would not consider religion the main reason to take sides on anything; race or income would more likely define who is "in" and who is "out."

There are two even better protections for the fifty percent of Americans who do not say that Protestantism is their religion. First, American law and custom make holy war difficult to carry out, and also irrelevant. Over two hundred years ago, in the Bill of Rights, the founders distinguished between citizenship and religious belief. Some say they thus "separated church and state." This means, among other things, that religious majorities cannot use the law to take action against minorities and that minorities are protected. Along the way, Americans have also developed some habits of tolerance. These are not perfectly consistent habits, but very seldom does someone suffer or die in America because of a religious issue.

The other reason for protection, one that will help you understand your or your neighbor's Protestantism, is this: Protestants differ very much from one another. It would be hard to get them to agree on everything. Who would give marching orders? For what purpose would they attack? Only some of the adults would call themselves simply Protestant when asked. Instead, sixteen of them would say their religion was Baptist. Baptists form the largest group of white Protestants, and more than half of the African Americans in your assembly would also say they are Baptist. Further down the line, seven of these one hundred Americans would be Methodist, five Lutheran, three Presbyterian, and so on.

A Glance at the Map and the Landscape

These numbers give you some idea of what your neighborhood would look like religiously if it were a perfect miniature of the whole United States. Few neighborhoods, however, are good miniatures. You might be living and attending school in Rhode Island, for instance, where sixty out of a hundred people are Roman Catholic and few Protestants are in sight. Or you might get an opposite and wrong picture of American Protestantism if you live in South Carolina, where only six out of a hundred people are Catholic and almost all the people say their religion is Protestant.

Most people do not look different from others because of their religion. Your neighborhood more probably looks like it does because of the buildings on its landscape. If we think of Protestants as a species, we will want to track them to their habitats. If they are active in practicing their faith, they are likely to be found, at least occasionally, in a church. Although some Protestants worship in homes or rented spaces, most go to specific buildings for which they or people who came before them have paid. These take all kinds of forms. On the heights above Harlem, for example, we find the Episcopal Cathedral of Saint John the Divine, which was begun over a century ago and will probably never be finished; the funds for a project of this scale are simply not available. Even unfinished, it is the largest Gothic cathedral in the world. You would feel very small under its great vaults and arches. If you have traveled to Europe or know your architecture, you would think while in this cathedral that you were in a Catholic building of the Middle Ages. You would imagine the same thing on the heights of Washington, where another huge Gothic beauty often called "Washington National Cathedral" towers.

Just a few blocks from the cathedral in Harlem, you might find a Protestant church located in a storefront. The congregation would be largely made up of black or Hispanic citizens—many Mexican or Puerto Rican people whose grandparents were Catholic have now turned Protestant. You would see folding chairs, perhaps a stand for a Bible, a piano, a cross—and a crowd, since these humbler places often attract large congregations.

A few blocks from the cathedral in Washington you will find Protestant church buildings that look like those on calendars or greeting cards that make America look like a New England village: simple but stately, white or brick meetinghouses with plain windows. If you want to portray a rural midwestern or southern landscape, you will probably show, somewhere in the distance, a typical steeple with some bells in it.

From this variety of habitats, you will see that the style of the architecture does not set Protestants apart or help you to group them. The abundance of buildings suggests, however, that they do gather to worship God and to meet one another for an hour or two most weeks. After meeting, they disperse. We have to find other ways to help account for the remaining 166 or 167 hours of the week.

PROTESTANTISM ALPHABETIZED IN DENOMINATIONS

Try the Yellow Pages of the phone book in the section called "Churches." Although the list includes, for example, synagogues and mosques, most of these listings will be of Protestant denominations. ("Denomination," by the way, is a word invented to help us keep track of all the groups without saying anything good or bad about them. If you want to keep Protestant friends, don't say they belong to this or that Protestant "sect." *Denomination* is a neutral term.)

Protestant denominations run alphabetically from A, not to Z, but assuredly to U, V, and W. The number of listings may dazzle you; it also makes a point about Protestant varieties. We mentioned those sixteen Baptist citizens. In a large city like Chicago it takes four pages, twenty-four columns of small print, just to provide names, addresses, and phone numbers of the Baptist congregations. Most remarkably, they come in fourteen varieties, including "Independent-Fundamental," "Missionary," "Free Will," and "Southern" (even though Chicago is a northern city!). These individual churches often have colorful names—not just "First Baptist," but also "Cristo En La Ciudad," "Acme," "Aimwell," "Eureka," "Jordan River," "Original Rising Star," and "Traveler Rest." Protestants usually get to name their own churches, and they like these names to suggest what they cherish, which helps them feel at home.

So far all you would know from this quick tour is that many of your classmates and neighbors (and perhaps you yourself) call themselves Protestant, and that they come in a wide variety of denominations and do things—we mentioned only worship, so far—at an equally wide variety of places called churches. If this were all that Protestantism meant, we would have done no more to help explain America to most Americans than if we said there were many kinds of locusts or automobiles, without saying why they exist, what they do, who fears them, or who has good hopes for them. The rest of this chapter will discuss the meanings of Protestantism.

Looking Backward to Explain the Present

When you set out to explain what life in a group of people means, you have to look backward to determine why they exist as a group, where they came from, and how they got here. Thus if you see people in military uniform, you need to know their country and why that country stations troops where it does. If they are in very old uniforms, you might find that this is a civil holiday and they are going to reenact an old battle. If you see a woman in a long white dress with a man in a tuxedo and they are heading from a Protestant church to a limousine, you will have to understand the customs, handed down from the past, that lead people to dress that way and to go to such places in order to get married.

Many Americans at the end of the twentieth century are Protestant and go to Protestant places to do Protestant things, whatever they are. They have been doing this since the beginning of the seventeenth century, and what they do now is partly explained by why and when they came here. It is important to learn this, because the white Protestant ancestors of so many people today had most of the thirteen original American colonies pretty much to themselves, both in numbers and especially in having the power to set the terms for life around them.

Protestants do not have that kind of power in the nation today, but the nation is what it is today partly because they once had that kind of power. They may not know their own background; they probably take it for granted and would be surprised to learn the details. Whether or not you are Protestant, you will soon know something of that background and history, and you will begin to have an advantage over those who cannot explain why so many things today are as they are. Most of us Americans are not used

to looking at our past to explain our present, and few of us have learned to look for the deposits, traces, and legacies left by religious forces. These pages are an exception that we like to think of as an opportunity.

Setting the Stage: the European Backdrop

Let's call what follows "The Protestant Drama." Thinking of it that way—and its story is dramatic—allows us to get behind the American scene for a prelude, a plot before the scene unfolds. This is necessary because Americans did not invent Protestantism; they imported it from Europe and tried to spread it to Native Americans just as, eventually, they found themselves sharing it with people of African descent.

Europe was the original scene of operations. The opening event was a movement that today goes by the name of the Protestant Reformation. (There were also Catholic Reformations going on at the same time.) The word *reform* as we use it today usually has a moral ring. Not long ago, "correctional institutions" were called "reform schools." A young person whose life took the wrong form would be sent to such a place to be "reformed." This language may be familiar: "Young man, I want you to reform and be home by eleven o'clock every night; and keep your room straightened!" The term has other uses as well. A company that has a bad sales record might be called upon by its board to reform, which might mean to bring in new management or to design better ways to go about its business.

Reformation and the Birth of Protestantism

Almost five centuries ago in Europe, especially in northern Europe and the British Isles, leaders began to claim that the Christian church of their day, what we call the Roman Catholic Church, needed moral reform. It had to straighten out, bring in new management, and go about its business in better ways. In those days, Catholicism was not something you would find in a long listing of choices, the way you do in the Yellow Pages today. For a thousand years it had been a monopoly in Europe. Catholic Christians fought to keep their rivals, the Muslims, from taking over Europe, a battle that did not end until 1492—the year Columbus sailed—when Muslim armies were defeated in their European stronghold in Spain. (Had the Muslims prevailed, you would probably see mosques, not churches, across the American landscape.)

For hundreds of years Catholic Christians had also kept Jews from expanding their communities, moving about freely, or having religious influence. Often they persecuted and killed Jews; at best they segregated them in close communities, which in Italy began to be called *ghettos*. By the way, in the same year of Columbus, 1492, Spain expelled Jews and sent them into hiding and refuge. Europe was not to be Muslim or Jewish; it was to be Christian.

For some time after 1492 it was equally clear that Europe was also not supposed to be Protestant. The word was not even invented until 1529, when some "re-formers" of Catholicism presented a document that used the word "protest." (Protestants by and large do not like their name, since it sounds defensive and negative. That is partly why they more often say they are Baptist or Lutheran or Methodist than Protestant. But in the history books and to the polltakers, they are also Protestant.)

Catholic Christianity took mainly two forms. In Eastern Europe, from Greece through Russia, it was called Orthodox. You will find various Orthodox churches in the Yellow Pages, but fewer Orthodox peoples came to America than did Roman Catholic and Protestant peoples. The Eastern churches by and large ignored the Protestant Reformation and the Catholic reactions to it. What we call Western or Roman Catholicism—Roman because it was governed by and obedient to the bishop of Rome, the pope—was the subject of attack by reformers.

Today it is hard to picture how strong the Catholic hold was on Europe. For a thousand years its popes, bishops, and priests had a monopoly on formal religion. They even shared political power with kings, princes, and magistrates. Popes crowned emperors and emperors influenced popes. They might compete; they might argue; they might even go to war against each other. But they did not disagree on the basic idea that Christianity and the Church were necessary for running the state, for determining its laws, for blessing its battles. The Church was an owner of vast lands and wealth. It was represented in every village and in every corner of life. Priests did the marrying and burying and recorded the marriages and burials for the state.

The priests and their Church were corrupt, said restless parties in Bohemia, England, Germany, Switzerland, France, and the Netherlands. The leaders in these northern places could take advantage of local pride, of national goals, and of resentment against Rome, which was then often drawing wealth and power across the Alps to Italy. But even Catholics then, and especially now, admit that the Church needed reform. Priests often were corrupt. Monopolies become casual about the rights of people, and Catholicism was no exception. Often the common people were held in virtual bondage. They feared that if they displeased the Church they would be condemned to an eternity in hell. To get into heaven they believed they had to do what the Church wanted, often at great expense to themselves.

The Protestant reformers, including John Hus (1372–1415) in Bohemia, John Calvin (1509–1564) in Switzerland, John Knox (1513–1572) in Scotland, and most of all Martin Luther in Germany, did not make bad morals their main point of attack. When they said "straighten out!" they concentrated on the *teachings* of the Church. They all agreed that not the pope, but the ancient sacred scriptures that they called the Bible should be the authority in religion.

Catholicism made demands on people who wanted to be right with God. The reformers in turn said that people would be free only when they realized that Christian faith meant God was generous, gracious, and gift-giving, the assurer that they could be "saved" without earning their way to heaven in the life to come. Eventually the protests led the reformers to walk away from the Roman Catholic Church or to be expelled from it.

A Variety of Established Official Protestant Churches

Soon there were churches called Reformed, Lutheran, Anglican (after "England") or Episcopal, or Presbyterian (because they were ruled not by a pope but by presbyters, elders who were not official ministers). The Protestant Reformation was not complete, however, at least not by the standards of most later Protestants. The leadership did not do what America's founders did. They did not "separate church and state"; they basically changed management! When a king or a prince converted from Catholic to Protestant, as kings and princes did in England, Scandinavia, and elsewhere, all the people were expected to follow. Protestants, like Catholics, persecuted Jews and tried to punish dissenters. These dissenters were usually Protestants who rebelled against Protestantism, reformers who wanted to go further with reform. Still, reform did go far enough that the Bible and not the pope became the authority in these places. Preachers did preach that God's grace mattered and that human good works followed only because people loved God and not because they had to please him.

The Rise of Protestant England

After Columbus, it looked as if the Americas would be Catholic. From 1492 until 1607 almost all the settlers in what Europeans called the New World were from Spain and Portugal. Catholic France was also beginning to move toward settlement, and it later colonized parts of what is now Canada. Protestant princes and kings were still busy gaining power, purging Catholics, and developing nationalism. These processes were slow on the European continent. But during that American Catholic period, Protestant England was growing powerful and ambitious. The British began exploring, and their entrepreneurs were looking for a place in which to invest. America beckoned.

Some English Christians, hoping to convert Native Americans and lead them to heaven, which they did not think Catholic missionaries were doing, said they wanted to turn North America into a vast mission field. Some critics said that the English were never serious about converting or serving the people they called the Indians or natives or savages; they only talked about saving them in order to keep a good conscience about plundering their lands. Motives of nations are usually quite mixed, and plenty of motives went into the English mix.

Episcopal Virginia and the South

The English were sure, however, that they were destined to settle in America and that where they did, they and their official religion, no longer Roman Catholic but Anglican Catholic or Episcopalian, would go with them. They settled first in Virginia. Most of the Virginians and then the Carolinians went to America for reasons of investment and economy. They soon forgot about educating and saving Indians, especially after these Native Americans rose up in a bloody rebellion one spring day in 1622. As investors and not as exiles fleeing from repression, many of them did not think much about religion at all, but when they did, they thought Protestant. They brought along chaplains and ministers or priests, and from the first they held worship services. Before long they made the Episcopal church the legal monopoly in Virginia and elsewhere. They passed laws forcing people to go to church and to follow Episcopal teachings and practices.} Fortunately, many would say, they were not good enforcers of these laws, so there was not much persecution. But the law still gave Episcopalians great privilege.

In those early years of settlement a prophet would have predicted that in the future every religious, church-going American would be Episcopalian and that the laws would be dominated by the Episcopal leadership and its will. Yet fewer than two out of a hundred Americans today call themselves Episcopalian, and even in Virginia only three out of a hundred citizens do (as opposed to thirty who call themselves Baptists!). Many things happened to prevent an Episcopal takeover. The first and most important of these, however, resulted from the rise of another party in English Protestantism, a party that settled New England and had more influence on the later United States.

That rival did not extinguish Episcopal influence. Remember the cathedrals towering over Manhattan and Washington? They are Episcopal, but both of them, especially the one in Washington, are used by the nation at large for non-Episcopal events (such as burials of admirals and presidents, or celebrations of military victories and the return of peace). Episcopalians do not dominate anywhere, but they tend to be represented everywhere, North and South. Most of the southern colonial founders of the nation, people named Washington and Jefferson, Mason and Madison, were Episcopalians. Many of America's wealthy and educated people have been Episcopalian, so they make up a disproportionate share of the *Who's Who in America* list. They were soon outnumbered and out-influenced, however, by their rivals to the north.

NEW ENGLAND AND THE PURITAN NORTH

These rivals were called the Puritans. It seems to be a habit for Protestants to breed generations who feel that others have not gone far enough. Puritans were British Protestants who after around 1559 argued that Episcopalianism was too much like the Roman Catholicism it had left: it looked too formal and ceremonial, and felt too heartless and routine. Puritans wanted a religion that moved the people's hearts as much as it reached their heads or controlled their conduct. They also expected more strict observance of the faith, and promoted the notion that Christians had a covenant with God that God and they had to keep. God would be their God and they would be God's people. God would be gracious and they had to be disciplined. Many of these Puritans felt uncomfortable or were even persecuted in England. They tended to be educated people, middle class, ambitious, and restless about their own future security and their children's faith. They had to act upon their need to establish a pure community and their desires to worship freely. One of their leaders, Francis Higginson (1588–1630), made it clear that they were not saying farewell to the Church of England but in the New World they wanted to advance the work of reformation, which they were not able to do in the English context.

Before they could take action, however, they saw the rise of a more radical party. Remember the word about Protestant logic: there is always someone who will go further. You know the people who went further, because we call them the Pilgrims. In their black suits and dresses, with their silver buckles and trusted guns, they now appear on cardboard table decorations on Thanksgiving Day. Schoolchildren sing about the "land where our fathers died, land of the Pilgrims' pride." High school students know about them through Nathaniel Hawthorne's *The Scarlet Letter,* or through attacks on them for being too strict and stuffy, or even because of later persecution of witches at Salem. Students are also taught to admire them as people of conviction who worked to express their liberty.

These "Pilgrims," which is what they called themselves, were Puritans who became

"Congregationalists," which meant they allowed for no authority—no popes, no bishops, no presbyters—beyond the local congregation. The familiar New England "town meeting" was their ideal for the way to address concerns of church and state. They did not even need ministers, though in time some were welcomed. These independent English people first took refuge in the Netherlands, but found their children adopting what they thought were the worst practices of their neighbors. They needed a place apart and sailed, as you know, on the *Mayflower* and some successor ships. They settled in a place they called Plymouth in 1620. Ten years later the more moderate Puritans settled Massachusetts Bay at Boston, and some of their party later branched off to found Connecticut, which absorbed the earlier New Haven colony.

These lovers of liberty essentially loved their *own* liberty. They were sure that they were God's elect people, chosen as the people of Israel had been of old. They read the Hebrew Scriptures, which they called the Old Testament, and saw themselves in the plot. They passed laws they thought were influenced by the laws of Moses. (Jews have a right to say that their scriptures had a great influence on early America, not because there were many Jews here but because the Puritans found it easier to make their laws match the Ten Commandments of their Old Testament than Jesus' Sermon on the Mount from their New Testament.) Puritans liked to talk about living by a covenant with God. They did not welcome Jews, Catholics, Episcopalians, or anyone but their own kind. The liberty they wanted was the liberty to be themselves, to have things their own way, to set up a new Israel, a new Zion in the wilderness.

Eventually they were to lose out, too. The stricter Pilgrims of Plymouth were outnumbered and did not prosper as did the Puritans of Massachusetts Bay, who kept attracting English Puritans and who did prosper and propagate. But that did not mean that strictness disappeared from Protestantism. Soon a new group of dissenters came along to complain that even Puritanism was turning formal and routine. Where was the heart? they asked. People could no longer assume that their children would automatically inherit the religion of their parents.

Each individual had to make a choice, a decision for God, a response to Christ. People had to "own" the covenant. In language more familiar now than then, they had to be "born again," starting over, as it were, as new beings no matter how evil they had been from birth. They had to form vital congregations of their own. One group thought that baptizing children, pouring water over the heads of infants who did not know what was happening to them, was a kind of magic, a mere routine. These people would baptize only adults who converted and spoke up for themselves. They called themselves Baptists.

THE BAPTISTS AND METHODISTS MOVE SOUTH AND WEST

Baptists from England had already settled in Rhode Island when the new Baptists in Massachusetts and Connecticut started splitting the Puritan Congregational churches. Others moved south, spreading quickly through the backcountry of Virginia and the Carolinas. Here was a kind of democratic faith, one that appealed to emotions and the desire for community. When America west of the Appalachians opened up for settlement, at least in the South, these Baptists surged across the mountains and won converts. Today, Baptists predominate in nearly every county in the South (except in the southernmost portions of Florida, Louisiana, and Texas, and in the Southwest).

Back in England another Protestant party set out to reform the Episcopal church. Guided by a reformer who wanted to be holy and perfect, John Wesley (1703–1791), they eventually went their separate way as Methodists. Many Methodists came to America, and after the American Revolution they

The Protestant Parties and Schisms

While Roman Catholicism has maintained unity under the Pope, Protestantism has never been organized in a form that assures unity. The Reformation in Europe took on many different characters in various nations and locales, and the Protestant churches it spawned led to a pattern of schisms and separations. In the United States some of these occurred in divisions between "Northern" and "Southern" church bodies, along lines of sectional conflict in the Civil War.

The division into parties that is most notable today is between what has come to be called "mainline Protestantism" and "evangelicalism." The mainline dominated in public life until the latter half of the twentieth century. In many respects the line between the two camps is blurry, since they often share denominational names (e.g., the conservative Southern Baptist Convention and the more progressive American Baptist Churches) and most beliefs. Yet in the public realm the divisions are more visible and clear. The roots of the change came in the invention in the 1920s of fundamentalism as a reaction to modern trends in denominations. In the 1940s fundamentalists themselves split, and the more moderate ones began to refer to themselves as evangelicals. Both groups were seen as uninterested in political expression and organization.

When the United States Supreme Court ruled against government-sponsored prayer in public schools in 1962 and 1963 and ruled to permit abortion, the fundamentalists and evangelicals changed their ways and mobilized to support their vision of "Christian America," "family values," and various militancies. The favor shown political evangelicals, including the more extreme groups that made up the new "Christian Right," made them among the most active political movements in American life and had enormous influence in the Republican Party from 1980 well into the twenty-first century. Meanwhile, mainline Protestants, experiencing some decline, while not losing interest in public policy, did not work to mobilize voters as did the evangelicals.

spread across the South and West. Not as democratic as the Baptists, they used superior organization—they had bishops, superintendents, and ministers who "rode the circuit" to gain converts—to become rivals to the Baptists. From the middle colonies they won what we might call the north of the South and the south of the North; their greatest contributions on the map of American religion run from Baltimore and environs, where they were organized in 1784, to Kansas and the Great Plains in general, though they are well represented in most parts of America. The nineteenth century also saw the rise of at least two large black churches, the African Methodist and the African Methodist Episcopal Zion. The Methodists were the largest Protestant body for more than a century.

That these Baptists and Methodists influenced America is obvious to anyone who knows the history of slavery and abolition. In the South they were generally for slavery; in the North they often opposed it. Both churches split before the Civil War, and the Baptists never came back together. The same two denominations had a big role in reform movements, most notably Prohibition (1919–1933), which forbade the sale of alcohol in America. (Many of them still oppose the drinking of alcohol, but they have given up trying to pass laws prohibiting others from doing so.)

Baptists believe very much in liberty and human rights. They helped produce the separation of church and state in America and continue to work for human freedom. President Jimmy Carter was a Southern Baptist who said his faith moved him to work for human rights in other nations, even where such intervention caused complications in his foreign policy. Methodists, especially Methodist women, helped gain suffrage for women and were active in political and social causes. They long represented one of the great success stories in American Protestantism because of their rapid growth and influence in the society. In the 1960s, however, they began to decline in membership and influence.

Varied Influences from the Middle Colonies

Between the Episcopal South and the Puritan Congregational North were several "middle colonies," whose Protestantism still influences America. These colonies, unlike the other nine, never did set up ("establish") by law an official church for which everyone had to pay taxes. In Pennsylvania, a radical Protestant group led by William Penn, the quiet and pacifist (peace-loving) people called Quakers, wanted a "holy commonwealth" in which Native Americans, Quakers, and anyone else would be free to follow the Spirit. The Quakers were soon outnumbered. But they acquired such a reputation for their witness for peace and a passion for ethical living that they have had an influence beyond their small numbers. To the backcountry of Pennsylvania came non-English-speaking Protestants, not all of them welcome. These included small Baptist-type groups from Europe such as Mennonites and Brethren, people of peace who were disturbing to their neighbors because they were so different, set apart and apparently unworldly. Today a small group of these, the Amish, is best known. A much larger group were the Lutherans from Germany, whose descendants now make up the third largest Protestant group, thanks also to later immigrations to the Midwest in the nineteenth century.

Dutch of Reformed background settled New Netherland, especially New Amsterdam, today's New York State and New York City. They wanted an established church, but for purposes of trade and commerce they found themselves having to tolerate others. By 1654 they saw the settlement of Jews (fugitives from Spain in 1492, who came now fleeing Brazil and looking for new opportunity) and many other peoples and religious groups. Perhaps because they found that

they could not enforce a religion and had to make room for everyone, these New Yorkers were the "winners" in determining the future shape of America. Today we call American society "pluralist," which means, as the expression goes, "any number (of religions, in this case) can play"; many groups coexist, and all are free to worship as they please.

From Scotland and the Scotch-Irish lands came the Presbyterians, a hardy breed of people who were ruled by elders; who hated Anglicans in the British Isles; whose leaders loved true doctrine; and whose poor people spread from Philadelphia to the unsettled lands just east of the Appalachians. From there they poured forth into the West with the Baptists and Methodists, if in lesser numbers. Like the other groups, they split between North and South, but recently they have come together. Not officially established, they nonetheless became part of "the establishment." If many U.S. presidents were Episcopal, many others were Presbyterian, as were people of wealth and influence. As Presbyterians moved west, they built colleges, spread literacy, promoted reform legislation that had to do with temperance, education, and the like, and in general also exerted influence beyond their numbers.

Awakened America, Enlightened America

You can see that beginnings have much to do with outcomes in the American Protestant drama. With that in mind, we now examine two more events in colonial times that gave shape to America and continue to influence us today. The first event was later called the "Great Awakening." For several decades before the American Revolution, from New England to Georgia, local pastors stirred their people with vigorous prayer and preaching and saw many conversions. Traveling revivalists also upset establishments and fired up hearts and minds. These revivalists got the public talking about religion, and many converted to their churches. It is hard to measure such an event precisely, but the Awakening seemed to spread ideas of freedom of choice, the need for personal decision, and the premium upon individual liberty. Some historians think that these "awakened" people, being democratic in their antiestablishment outlook, provided much of the energy and many of the soldiers for the Revolution, the call for independence and the birth of the United States.

How does the Awakening affect us today? It helped spread the notion that religion is not something one inherits (as a Jew does by being a child of a Jewish mother) or acquires with the territory (as Catholics and earlier Protestants did, before church and state were "separated"). Religion is rather a matter of choice. Today some Jews try to convert people of Jewish inheritance to be "practicing Jews." Many Catholics know they have to stir people who were baptized Catholic if their faith is to make a difference in their lives. The evangelizing Protestant groups, who call for a "born again" experience, grow faster than those who do not. If Americans consider religion a matter of heart more than head, of choice more than inheritance, they do so in part because of habits acquired in the Great Awakening.

At the time of the Revolution, a new kind of Protestantism was being born in England and among the educated and elite people in the colonies. Scholars call this movement the Enlightenment. Those who welcomed its light were anti-Catholic—as were most of America's founders, George Washington being a rare partial exception—but they also feared the power of those Protestant ministers who insisted that to be a good citizen one had to be a converted church member who made and obeyed laws based on God's revealed will as recorded in the Bible. These Protestant churchgoing people— among them Thomas Jefferson, James Madison, George Washington, and John Adams—respected the Bible and the central Christian figure, Jesus, but they believed that God was revealed in (note the capital letters) Nature and Reason and Law. These were available to all thoughtful people of

goodwill. No religion should be established or forced on people. These Enlightened statesmen linked up with Baptists and other "outsider" Protestants to attack insiders. Through the First Amendment they ensured that the United States Congress would "make no law respecting an establishment of religion, or prohibiting the free exercise thereof." It was this act that Jefferson somewhat too dramatically called the erection of a "wall of separation between church and state." There was no wall, or, if there was, it was always porous. But this distinction, however incomplete, was something Catholics in the Middle Ages and official Protestantism in the colonies had not known.

From the time of the First Amendment, Protestants, and eventually Catholics, Jews, and others, were free to compete for the soul of America. This did not mean that they always engaged in fair and friendly competition: rivalries and hostilities at times were fierce. Some Protestants feared that this free market in religion would mean the end of churchgoing and the moral influence of faith. To their surprise the opposite happened. People *liked* to be persuaded rather than coerced; they chose freely, but they chose. Protestants in the United States are far more active in their churches than are their counterparts in Europe. These voluntary churches set up voluntary organizations to educate, spread their moral vision, and reform America. Much of the tradition of voluntarism in America, evidenced today by the energy put into United Way or the Red Cross, can be traced to these Protestant voluntary groups. To this day, most of the hours and dollars Americans donate are donated through religious groups, many of them Protestant.

THE IMPORTANCE OF BELIEFS IN PROTESTANTISM

Americans, not content to hear that a group performed services long ago, like to ask, in effect: What have you done for me lately? Informally, non-Protestants ask this of Protestants. That Protestants dominated and largely shaped colonial America and then kept control, power, or influence as America turned more secular (which here means less dependent upon religion for public choice) and more pluralist, tells us much but not everything about today's Protestantism. To understand those fifty out of a hundred people who call themselves Protestant or members of Protestant churches, we have to look at what is going on now. We already said that most Americans are not highly history-minded, and many Protestants know less about their own history than you just read in these few pages. So, what have they done lately? What are they doing now?

They are believing.

To understand a faith, a set of religious organizations, you have to ask why it exists. What do its adherents think about reality? A faith would not exist or would never survive if it did not successfully convince its followers to look at the world in a different way than if they did not believe and belong. In most respects, Protestants and Christians as a whole are just like everybody else. When they are sick, they go to a physician and want high-tech medicine. When they want to know the weather, they do not go to a magician; they consult a meteorologist, who may have a slightly better record than did ancient readers of signs in the sky. When they vote, they usually do not like it if religious voices are too noisy telling them how to vote or whom to elect. They use the same technological logic that their neighbors do to run computers, fill prescriptions, or invest in the stock market, and with about the same record of success and frustration. Sometimes, especially if they call themselves liberals or modernists—a distinct minority—they are so much like everyone else that the faith cannot hold the interest of its members, especially the young. That is partly why those who stress the differences, people called evangelical or Pentecostal or fundamentalist, seem to have stronger groups and grow more successfully.

To understand faiths we have to talk about beliefs and worldviews. Do not expect anything neat here. There are so many scores of Protestant denominations because their leaders and members differ on beliefs. Within these denominations there are endless varieties. Lacking a pope who has final authority to decide about doctrines, and depending on a Bible they can interpret so many ways, Protestants will not agree on the details—or perhaps even many of the essentials—of teachings. They may even differ on how important beliefs themselves are.

THE ROLE OF CREEDS

If you want to understand Jews, you do not ask which doctrines or dogmas or tenets they believe. Jews deal more with a story than a doctrine. Muslims will respond by reciting laws rather than by listing dogmas. Catholics can provide precise lists of what the official church sets forth as beliefs, but to the average Catholic it is a faith made up of scores of practices. Some Protestants, such as Quakers, resist the idea of doctrine. Most Baptists, Disciples of Christ, or members of the Churches of Christ—movements from the nineteenth century that claim to be dependent on the New Testament alone—will say that to determine faith, the Bible, not creeds (formal statements of faith), is all one needs, can have, or should have.

Lutherans, Episcopalians, Presbyterians, and many others will tell you, however, that they believe the Bible, but that they also interpret it using creeds. These belong to the whole catholic church (but not *Roman* Catholic, mind you!) of which they are a part. They also supplement these creeds with documents from the Reformation era. For Lutherans this means the Augsburg Confession, for Episcopalians the Thirty-Nine Articles, for Presbyterians the Westminster Confession, and so on.

If you go into a Lutheran or Episcopal or Presbyterian church, don't expect the members to be able to tell you all about these confessions and articles. Just because the guidebooks say that these are official or charter documents that help define the church, this does not mean that they are best sellers or even that they are read at all by most congregants. Scholars in the seminaries debate them, and sometimes during a quarrel between factions in a church both sides will claim these creeds. But they exert their influence in subtler, more diffuse, and often half-forgotten ways.

In this introduction to Protestantism, we cannot hope to detail all the particular teachings. We can only offer some illustrations. For instance, two of the original parties, the Lutheran (now fifth largest in American Protestantism) and Calvinist-Reformed-Puritan (in combination the most influential), both believe that God is gracious and all-powerful. But Lutherans start by asserting that God is gracious; whatever else they say, including anything about God's power, they will say in such a way that grace remains central, that God's loving initiative is primary and talk about God's power is secondary. Ask them whether God, being all-powerful and all-knowing, "knew" or "destined" in advance who would be the elect people, and they will say that because God is gracious, those who respond in faith and care about the answer can deduce that God somehow elected them. Ask the Calvinist the same question, and he or she may very well say that God did elect or foreknow outcomes. Should that not terrify someone who may not have been selected? Not really. Remember, says the Calvinist, God is also a God of grace, so you should feel confident in God's love. Neither of these teachings is "neat"; neither seems fully logical to the outsider. But to those who share these faiths, they match the reality the believers find in the Bible, their hymns, their prayers, their hearts, and their lives.

THE ROLE OF THE BIBLE IN PROTESTANT BELIEF

What can be said about Protestant doctrine? Here we have to paint with a very broad brush, leaving details to others or to your further inquiry. Two things to be said right off

are that Protestantism is a branch of Western Christianity, as opposed to the offspring of Eastern Orthodoxy, and it is that part of Western Christianity that rejects the authority of the pope at Rome and all that goes with his office. For the rest, things remain wide open. Let's look at the broad outline.

Protestants make much of their Bible, which includes the Hebrew Scriptures, which speak to Jews but which Christians reinterpret until Jews hardly recognize them—think what calling *your* book the "Old Testament" (or "Covenant") would do to a faith! Protestants also rely on the New Testament, the four Gospels telling the stories of Jesus and the earlier letters of Paul the apostle and others who spread the word of Jesus and told Asians, Europeans, and North Africans what Jesus meant. Most Protestants believe that these Testaments are *somehow* inspired by God, which means they are set apart from merely human documents. A large conservative minority even says that they are "inerrant"—free from error or infallible, that a loving God would have taken care to preserve the original manuscripts from any mistakes, even in trivial details of geography. Most Protestants say that the Bible speaks with God's authority, which God risks in a world where there are many changes and accidents, arguments and interpretations. The more liberal among them acknowledge that they use their own reason and experience to connect the witness of the Bible to their lives.

GRACE, FAITH, AND GOOD WORKS IN PROTESTANTISM

Most Protestants stress that God, being gracious, chooses to show love and favor by wanting to include all people in the divine reach, to "save" them all from whatever limits or ails them—their shortcomings or sins, their death, or "the devil," by which they mean everything from a literal figure to the forces of evil.

God shows this grace through Jesus Christ. His disciples called him "rabbi," which means "teacher." This rabbi taught, did wonders, attracted a following, and was put to death. Christian anti-Semitism arose from the fact that in the Gospels, the people responsible—alongside the Romans, who carried out the execution—were, like Jesus, Jews. Today the historic accusations that Jews were "Christ-killers" tend to be remote memories for most Protestants. Official Protestantism seems to do what it can to revise interpretations so that the Gospels will not be used against Jews. Most Protestants today are taught that not Romans, not Jews, but they themselves, through their own faults, in effect "put Jesus Christ on the cross."

Most Protestants believe that Jesus' death was not the end of his story. Somehow—don't expect agreement on detail—the story continues with the announcement that Jesus was "raised from the dead," resurrected; God did a new thing through this Jesus, who comes to be called "the Son of God." Protestants believe that their death will not be the end of their story, either; with Jesus, they will be part of a new creation, a new life. This does not mean that they do not fear dying. They just have a sense—which may range from vague to precise—that their dying does not end the reach of God's love to them.

Along with their biblical grounding and the story of grace and faith in Jesus Christ, the teacher, victim, and risen one, Protestants have any number of other doctrines that flow out of the logic of these basic ones. To take one major illustration: whoever observes Jews, and Catholics, and Muslims in action knows that to them the conduct of life, both as a people and as individuals, is extremely important. Protestants often like to say that those three and some other faiths are "legalistic," motivated by fear of a judging God whom the followers have to please. But don't accept that statement categorically. Some good advice: when you want to know what someone believes, ask him or her. Don't depend on even the most sincere attempts to represent others, and certainly do not be content with caricatures. God—the same God, many Protestants will say, for all the faiths just mentioned, faiths that are their kin—is seen as loving and gracious in all of them.

In many arguments, however, Reformation-era Protestants and their heirs found that wherever law and legalism ruled, they defined themselves best, not as people who did not care about "good works" or morality, but as those who simply wanted to relocate where efforts to follow God's ways came in. They insisted that doing good did no good, so far as being right with God was concerned, *before* one experienced grace. Doing good was always good for its own sake, of course. It helped one's neighbor and made for healthy citizenship. But in Protestant faith, the doing of good was to flow from the experience of grace. Because God has shown love, the believer, after receiving divine gifts, puts those gifts to work, empowered to love and serve others.

THE PRESENCE OF GUILT AND MORALISM

However much Protestants say that theirs is a religion of grace, of gifts, of the receipt of love, they do not always act accordingly. Many of them have heard and believe the message of grace, but they still feel and act guilty. As Protestants continue the Reformation, they have to keep reminding themselves that when they push guilt on their own faithful believers, they are contradicting themselves. Some Protestant youth react and rebel because they have felt the hand of repression or guilt. Others may become moralistic and legalistic; that is, they act as if Protestant church life is essentially a matter of being handed a list of dos and don'ts, which make impossible demands and leave them unhappy. Again, their teachers will ordinarily tell you that such an approach is based on a misunderstanding of the grace of God, but they are aware that the impulse to turn faith into a matter of responding to commands is very strong, and that makes it difficult to keep grace central in Protestantism.

From all this it is clear that Protestants do not believe that all is well for humans if and as they live their lives apart from faith in God. That is part of their worldview. This does not mean that most of them believe you must be a believer or a Christian or a Protestant or their kind of Protestant to be a good citizen. They will usually vote for their party or the candidate with their political viewpoint over a fellow church member. Nor do they think that only Protestants are moral or virtuous or capable of doing good. Most of them link up freely with non-Protestants for good causes, and admire people of any faith or no faith who feed the hungry, bring peace, provide housing, take care of the ill, and so forth. They argue instead that, as fortunate as these expressions of good may be, they do not bring peace to the restless heart, answers to the deepest questions of life, a sense of authority or identity, or an experience of being "saved," the way faith in the God of the Bible and grace through Jesus Christ bring these. The human, in old-fashioned but still vivid terms, is a sinner and needs God's help.

ALL BELIEVERS ARE PRIESTS: A HIGH VIEW OF LAYPEOPLE

Another Protestant teaching that somehow persists is that all believers are equal before God. When Protestant founders set out to reform the Roman Catholic Church—and even today, after much Catholic reformation—they saw that the clergy had a special status, a special set of rights, a special closeness to God that, in the eyes of these Protestant critics, made laypeople into second-class citizens of God's kingdom. (Remembering our rule to let faiths speak for themselves, we have to say that Catholics will not all and always regard that view as being accurate or up to date.) Protestants assert that all believers are "priests," that all people have equal access to God. The parents washing diapers,

the homemakers taking out the garbage, the people behind the plow or at the computer, the laypersons reading the prayer book, are as deeply involved in holy callings or "vocations" as are monks and priests and nuns.

HOW PROTESTANTS GOVERN THEMSELVES

Not all Protestants have put this democratic belief into practice in their organizations. Democratic forms of church life can produce great pressure for conformity. Some denominations vote on the truth or falsehood of doctrines, and thus look much like Catholics when their councils of bishops agree in collegial concord with the pope. Because almost all denominations have professional, ordained ministers or clergy, and because so many of them function well in their roles, there tends to be general respect for the offices of the clergy. Protestants call these "minister," sometimes "preacher," often "the Reverend," or, to symbolize a warm leadership role, "pastor." But when showing such respect, the laity are not to become second-class citizens.

Protestants govern themselves in many different ways. For instance, Episcopalians (and some Lutherans), like Orthodox and Roman Catholics, believe that their leaders, their bishops (which means "overseers"), receive some aspects of their authority when other bishops engage in a rite of "the laying on of hands." They believe that this rite has continued in unbroken succession ever since Jesus laid hands on his first disciples or apostles and gave them authority. Methodists, as in today's large United Methodist Church, or Lutherans in the also large Evangelical Lutheran Church in America, have bishops as well. But they see the bishop's office not as essential but as being *beneficial* to the life of the church. Presbyterians have presbyters, or lay elders; and Congregationalists of the Puritan tradition (now usually part of the United Church of Christ), along with Baptists, insist that congregations are the main seat of authority. They may link up for common practices, however, in "synods" or conferences or even through bureaucracies that have no official doctrinal support.

Unity and Dissent

Speaking of the point where faith, practice, and government meet leads us to the ecumenical movement. This movement, begun around 1910, tried to address the issue of too many Protestantisms, too much competition and divisiveness, too little interaction between Protestants and other Christians. From it issued in 1908 a Federal Council of Churches; in 1951, a National Council of Churches; and in 1948, a World Council of Churches. These ecumenical or unitive organizations do not attract as much attention in the churches or the public press as they used to, but the ecumenical spirit lives on. Protestants are unimaginably closer to one another than they were before they began to federate or form cooperative councils.

If there has been an ecumenical movement to bring Protestants together, there also have been movements away from traditional Protestantism. The Church of Jesus Christ of Latter-day Saints has added The Book of Mormon to the Bible as a basis for their faith. The Mormons share many aspects of Protestant life; but they believe that God is a physical being who once was a human and that humans can become godlike in the life to come, and those beliefs keep them at a distance from conventional Protestants. Later in the nineteenth century came Christian Science, a movement stressing spiritual healing. Jehovah's Witnesses appeared at about the same time. This was and is a group that stands entirely apart from all others, whom they consider to be opposing the purposes of Jehovah God. The Witnesses' particular views of the return of Christ and their zealous mission work set them apart. Much of what we are saying about Protestant life and worship does not apply to them. Yet their founders were all Protestant, and many almanacs and encyclopedias list them with Protestantism.

Rites of Worship

If beliefs or doctrines in endless detail are not vivid to most Protestant church members, one must look elsewhere to find them doing characteristic or distinctive things. A natural place to look is where we started, in the buildings to which the Yellow Pages served as a guide. Their collective habitats more often than not are churches, where a chief activity is worship.

Protestants believe that one of their duties and delights is to come together to praise God. They believe in the doctrine of creation, or, better, they believe that a divine creator made and makes the billions of stars in the billions of galaxies, and has a hand in the ongoing creation of the present world and of all life in it.

Most Protestants square their belief in continuing creation with modern science, with evolution. Fundamentalists and some other conservative parties believe that the two are opposed. Because they are quite vocal about what is taught in respect to origins of the universe, the world, and humans, they draw more attention than does the majority. But both wings believe that they are to show wonder in the face of the created order and the Creator. God, whom Jesus addressed as "Father," is the Creator. As Jesus prayed to the Father, they will sing or say praises to the Creator. That openness to a personal God who hears prayer, who welcomes praise, who wants people to gather, is a mark of most Protestants.

(Here we should say that some offsprings of the Protestant impulse, notably in the Unitarian Universalist Association, are uneasy about being called Christian. One wing of that body, whose ancestry is largely New England Congregational, defines itself as humanist. It gathers for meetings, messages, and worship, too, but does not focus on a personal God, and makes a point of expecting great freedom of expression, whether directed to God or not.)

Most Protestants gather for worship and praise. Roughly one-third of the people who call themselves Protestant and one-half of those who are on the church rolls will tell pollsters that they worshiped last weekend. Almost all did so on Sunday, but some Seventh-day Adventists and Seventh-Day Baptists hold Sabbath or Saturday worship. Protestants have some disadvantage in calling for people to gather for worship. Orthodox and Catholic Christians believe that something goes on in church that cannot go on elsewhere. Their view of the presence of Christ in the bread and wine of the Eucharist or Mass or Last Supper—a rite they believe Christ instituted the night before he died—means that you have to be there to get the full benefit of what is offered. Some Protestants, notably many Episcopalians, believe the same. Many others have a view that Christ is thus present, but they cannot as clearly make the point that something is missing if one is not present for this "presence."

This means that Protestants are always being urged or are urging one another to go to church. Many of them see church as a kind of voluntary association, a gathering of like-minded people who choose to come together for common purposes. When the polltaker comes by to ask whether one can be considered a good Christian if he or she does not worship regularly, the vast majority of the clergy will say "no" but the vast majority of the people—except in very conservative bodies—will say "yes," though regular churchgoing certainly is important. Some might charge that the clergy have a vested interest in having good crowds. It gives them power and assures the support of their institutions. But the belief goes deeper than that. Most Protestant leaders agree with Orthodox and Catholic teachings that the church of Jesus Christ is a body, a communion, a reality, a people, before an individual finds it advantageous to join.

Protestantism has just enough of the classic Jewish sense of a "people," as well as the classic Catholic sense that there is a community called the body of Christ, to make churchgoing vital. It also has a heavy dose of individualism that seems to make churchgoing part of a buyer's market, a bargain, a free choice. Despite some confusion over these conflicting claims, the presence of tens of millions of Protestants in worship each week astonishes visitors from Protestant Europe, where attendance is low. It may also astonish visitors from Protestant sub-Saharan Africa or Oceania, where the percentage of believers who worship regularly may be much higher.

On whatever grounds, the invitation to gather for worship pulls congregations together, and there one best sees Protestantism in action. The rest of the time religion often seems to be a private affair, rarely visible and not always spoken up for. But behind stained-glass or storefront windows, inside sanctuaries, in front of a cross in a picnic grove, or wherever Protestants gather, they may take for granted that what they do there is obvious. To a visitor, whether another kind of Christian, an unbelieving inquirer, a Jew, a Muslim, a Hindu, or a Buddhist, the rites and practices may seem very mysterious.

READING OF SCRIPTURES AND PREACHING

A Jew might find it easiest to understand Protestant worship because it derives from the synagogue. The reverent reading of the Scriptures is a major element in worship. Someone then applies what is read to life today, in the act called *preaching*. This person, specially trained and usually an ordained minister, rises to face the group and give voice to a shared faith. The preacher—formerly always a man but now, except in a couple of large conservative groups, quite possibly a woman—takes the Bible reading and applies it to life. The speaker may display good voice or bad, exact grammar or imprecise syntax, some excellent points and some meanderings, but somehow the people conceive of this elaboration of Scripture as "the preaching of the Word of

God." They like to have it applied to their daily living. In some churches the sermon will be more of a lecture, something like comment on current affairs or a book review. But that is still the exception.

To get a sense of what is intended in preaching, one should attend a black church, a Baptist, Methodist, or other congregation in the African American tradition. There will be little talk about a doctrine of biblical inerrancy or authority, but it will be clear that the Bible is the authority. The Bible provides a kind of scenario or script for the life of the people. The congregation, one might say, seems to be part of the plot, and everything is made contemporary. One expects to find Pharaoh in City Hall, or false prophets promising peace when there is no peace down the street. Martin Luther King Jr. and others in the succession of black leaders have played the role of a Moses, pointing to a Promised Land. God is on the move, they say, and the people will do well to take part in that movement. Here is liberation from oppression. Here is dignity for those who are usually trampled. Here is hope for the hopeless. Such preaching took rise in times of slavery and provided meaning in the worst of segregation times. Even among upper-middle-class blacks, where the forms of worship might be a bit more staid and discreet, preaching is likely to first address the people *as* a people, and then as individuals who need to experience grace and make new resolves.

PRAYER, PRAISE, AND SONG: THE GIVING OF GIFTS

Along with the preaching there is prayer, which seems to be common to most religions wherein a personal God is addressed. The prayers may be very formal, inherited from books of grand style and refined by centuries of usage. They can also erupt from the heart and be brought forward by people who are present. Nothing is too trivial, because nothing in the life of faith is trivial: the congregation is asked to pray for a young woman in military service and in harm's way; for a

couple who had a child; for those fighting addiction and trying to free themselves from substance abuse. The prayers then reach out to the overlooked, the homeless, hungry, and despised. Protestants also take from Jesus the signal to love their enemies, and are taught to pray for them. Prayers and praises often take the form of songs, by choirs, soloists, or the whole congregation. With a few passive exceptions, Protestants say theirs is a singing church. Spirituals and gospel music in black denominations; plainsong and chorales and Victorian anthems and folk music—all mix in various Protestant groups.

Most Protestant worship will include an offering, the bringing forward of money gifts. To grudging members or suspicious visitors this may look like money-grubbing by solid and greedy institutions. To people who have caught on to what is going on, this is more than an act of survival, of self-support, of a means to keep the building heated and lit and the ministers paid, the organ in tune and the hymnals in shape, the roof from leaking and the windowsills painted. It is even more than a means to provide seminaries to train ministers and publishing houses to spread the word; more than an instrument to support works of charity and mercy, to buy blankets and food for refugees, or to support development where there is threat of famine.

The giving is conceived as an act of worship, usually an expression of what is called *stewardship*. Protestants who grasp this concept say that in their stewardship they are acknowledging that God is the source of whatever they have; they have it on loan, as it were. By turning back part of it, they show that their possessions do not rule them, that they are free, that they can part with what dominates many lives and becomes an idol. This is the ideal, of course, and the reality may often differ from it.

RITES AND SACRAMENTS

Although Sunday is the big day of the week for most Protestants, they tend to celebrate other special days. Only a few groups, which see the festivals as inventions of Catholicism, avoid churchly observance of Christmas, the birth of Christ, and Easter, his resurrection. Many take note of certain seasons, such as the four weeks of Advent for the preparation for Christmas, or the six weeks of Lent, a serious time in which people ready themselves to follow the story of Jesus' death and resurrection. Many also recognize certain heroes, heroines, and saints, though they do not pray to these saints.

Two special rites or sacraments stand out. We have already referred to both. Although a few groups, such as Quakers, avoid sacraments, almost everyone else baptizes. Protestants disagree over whether or not to baptize infants, and whether baptism must be by immersion in water. They also differ over its meaning. It is somehow the initiation rite that begins or deepens the Christian life. Those who baptize infants see it as a pure act of God's grace that initiates a lifelong growth in grace. Adult baptism depends upon a conscious profession of choice, a decision of faith.

The night before Jesus died, according to the Gospels, he had a supper with his disciples. This is celebrated in the Lord's Supper, Holy Communion, or the Eucharist, which means thanksgiving. Protestants see this variously as a memorial, an observance, a deepening of faith, a spiritual union with Christ, or an actual if special form of presence of the same Jesus Christ who is also present in the preached Word of God. Some Protestants, such as the Disciples of Christ and many Episcopalians and Lutherans, commune every week; others enjoy this sacrament less frequently.

WOMEN, CHILDREN, AND YOUTH

The congregation is likely to have more women than men, though there are many elements in Protestantism that have appealed especially to men. Some women have accused this faith of being so interested in production, achievement, aspiration, and dominance that it has a "macho" cast. They argue—and many men agree—that its male adherents must recover the freedom to be vulnerable, to heal because one understands suffering, to stay close to the processes of life that women as mothers know so well, and to celebrate the poetry of faith. The women's movements have affected Protestantism considerably. Some women have disdained Protestantism for being patriarchal. Most believing Protestant women who want to change things have stayed around to help reform the churches, and their reinterpretations of the Bible and of Christian themes bring not only controversy but vitality to Protestantism.

As for the young, before, during, or after worship they may be in Sunday school or church school. There the simpler biblical stories become a part of their lives. They may have handiwork and craft projects that help make the landscape of Israel, the scene of Bible stories, vivid for them. Elsewhere in the same building, high school-aged members may be pursuing more advanced studies, often discussing how to apply biblical teachings to their own lives as they take on more responsibility. What does the church have to say about sexuality and marriage, about drugs and lifestyles, about the choice of careers and professions, about morals and ethics? These Protestant young people are also likely to have banded together in various organizations, some of them extremely successful and dynamic and some of them, to say the least, less so. There they gather for recreation, retreat, performing service, studying, and eating mountains of pizza. (Pizza is a borrowing from the Italian Catholic world that is now universal among younger Protestants, as casserole dishes at church suppers seem to be among older ones.)

EXTENSIONS OF PROTESTANT LIFE

In that parenthesis we tucked the clue that Protestant church life is not all supposed to be grim. Those who leave it behind tend to dismiss it as dull, dour, and boring. Those who stay with it find many of their best friends and most profound attachments there. In the loneliness of the modern city an alert Protestant congregation will have a young adults' social group where people meet, sometimes to find their marital partner but more often to find their friends. They laugh and work together. Then tragedy strikes; one in their number is abused or deserted or stricken with illness. Where the laughs had been, there come tears, or gentle gestures of support. Protestantism is by no means unique in offering this benefit as part of its package. But where it does not find a way for people to enjoy each other's company and to find means of bonding, it does not stand much chance of being vital or even surviving. Protestantism intends to be a faith that moves from weekend and sanctuary to weekday and workday and play time.

PROTESTANT INDIVIDUALISM IN POLITICS AND ECONOMICS

Protestantism is usually defined as a faith that appeals to individualists. When Martin Luther (1483–1546), in a moment that lives in Protestant mythology, thundered to the emperor that he would not abandon his stand unless convinced by Scripture and sound reason, he was standing for the idea that no pope, no authority, no collection of people, can take responsibility for each person's faith. This means that each person has to be equipped to make decisions. For that reason, Protestantism tended to promote literacy, having been born at about the same time as movable type and the printing press. Now it was possible to put the Bible into the hands of the people and to expect them to read it. Protestantism became a kind of religion of the printed page, and some parts of it have trouble making sense of the electronic age. Other parts—one thinks of those that are represented by televangelists—have become masters of electronic media. But the printed page has been the base of the spread of Protestant ideas.

Those ideas permeate the culture. A moment ago we mentioned individualism. The belief in what one scholar calls "the exalted individual" carries far beyond the encounters between a reformer and an emperor or a pope. It reaches far outside the sanctuary of a church. In colonial America, when the evangelists told backcountry people that they should decide about the truth of faith no matter what the official established preacher said, they started spreading the contagion of freedom. Some of these converts resented the Congregational or Episcopal church, for which they had to pay taxes even if they opposed it. When the time came to decide on independence from England, many of them carried this resentment into the political realm, along with the intoxicating idea that they had a responsibility to be free.

One should not make *too* much of that kind of connecting between religion and political and economic life. Human motives are too tangled and church memberships too varied to let us trace all such connections. But where they exist, they do suggest how many aspects of life the faith is to touch and direct. When Protestants of the Enlightenment and Protestant dissenters linked to promote freedom through the Bill of Rights, they bought into a logic that made Protestant support of slavery—and Protestantism was long the main support system for the idea of slavery—into a travesty. In England, evangelical Protestants were major players in the abolition of slavery; in America, the record was mixed. But blacks in slavery and as free persons found ideas of individualism ready at hand in their biblically based Protestant faith and their local Protestant congregations.

This individualist idea carried over into economic life as well. One great scholar, Max Weber (1864–1920), looking at Switzerland, Germany, and England, decided that modern economics, with its support of capitalism, had roots in Protestantism, especially in Calvinism. He spoke of "the Protestant Ethic," an idea that remains controversial; rivers of ink have been spent on books supporting or demolishing it. After all, there were capitalists in Venice before there were Protestants. There are capitalists in Japan, which is largely unmoved by Protestant Christianity.

Weber was not all wrong, however. In Protestantism, for better and for worse, religion came to be a matter of choice. One read the Bible and chose not to stay Catholic. One made up one's mind and decided to follow the preaching of this revivalist and not that one. One worked through the Yellow Pages and found a congenial denomination and then chose which form the expression of faith took. In a similar way, one chose independence and freedom in politics. Along came Adam Smith (1723–1790), whose *Wealth of Nations* appeared in 1776, the very year of American independence. He did not make his case for capitalism on Protestant grounds, and Protestant social thinkers have always found fault with his ideas. But some of what he observed matched many Protestant ways of doing things. One assessed situations, made calculations, used one's judgment, decided to be a steward, and then invested. The investment might be the long day's work or the money one needs to become an entrepreneur.

THE SOCIAL SIDE OF PROTESTANTISM

The majority of Protestants in America—and elsewhere, as exuberant forms of Protestantism spread throughout Catholic Chile and Guatemala, for example—are supportive of individualism, enterprise, competition, and capitalism. But there are other points of view within Protestantism. The Puritans were not simply economic individualists; their New England towns lived with a sort of planned economy. For a hundred years Protestants in movements such as the Social Gospel or Christian Socialism, while not endorsing the violence and class warfare that went into Marxism-Leninism, did advocate workers' cooperatives, some nationalization of industry, some limits on private property, and considerable support for the welfare state. This social preaching was probably always a minority voice, belonging to theologians, elected or appointed leaders, journalists, and the like.

But it too had some biblical basis and some effects in the political world.

PROTESTANTISM IN THE PUBLIC WORLD

Our foray into economics shows how controversial Protestantism can be when it leaves the sanctuary. Some Protestant denominations, notably Quakers, Mennonites, and Brethren, are "peace churches" that promote pacifism in the face of war. Other Protestants, in the old establishment style and often through nationalistic instincts, have been quite militaristic, ready to go whenever conflict attracts American energies.

Why pay attention to Protestantism, then, if it is so divided on such an issue? On every issue? It cannot be because Protestantism as a whole has an answer or The Answer. Although some of its task forces, boards, and bureaus sometimes give the impression that they speak for the church (and are on occasion even authorized to do so), most members pay little attention or resist if they think that such speaking is unrepresentative or even wrong. Many members do, however, show that they welcome the act of designating people who are supposed to have special competence to take on special tasks. These people make studies and try to set the terms for teaching, for speaking to the churches. When truly crucial issues appear, Protestants may put their energies to work in the public arena. Thus much of the historically white Protestant movement eventually linked up with black Protestant civil rights leaders—many of whom were clergy—to promote legal changes. But such moments of agreement are rather rare.

Take an issue which tears America apart today: abortion. The polltaker finds that 10 or 20 percent of the people believe it is always wrong. About the same percentage believes that only choices, not lives, are at stake: "A woman's body is her own to do with what she wants." Some fundamentalist churches are entirely in the former camp and some liberal ones are almost entirely in the latter. But the vast majority of Protestant churches and believers are in the company of the perhaps 70 to 80 percent of Americans who have problems of conscience with and moral distaste for abortion but who can envision numerous circumstances in which women must be free to choose it. Therefore it is hard for any commission to speak *for* the church body in helpful ways. And the speaking *to* each such body has to be so full of qualifiers that it may not settle much. Still, the exercise of discussing abortion, euthanasia, addiction, and health care practices is something most Protestants feel is urgent and, overall, beneficial, even if it does not leave their churches at peace.

THE PROTESTANT PARTIES AND SCHISMS

Several times we have referred to "liberal" or "modernist" Protestantism, on the one hand, and "conservative," "evangelical," or "fundamentalist," on the other.

These are imprecise and fluid categories. About ten percent of United States citizens are nonreligious in their self-definitions. In the remaining three fourths of polled Americans, which means non-Catholic America, Protestants dominate over Jews, Muslims, Eastern Orthodox, and the like.

Today they are conventionally divided into two groups, "mainline" and "evangelical." The mainline refers to the long-dominant denominations like the United Church of Christ, Presbyterian, Episcopal, United Methodist, Baptists (other than Southern Baptists), Evangelical Lutherans, and Christian Church, Disciples of Christ. African American Protestants do not fit the two categories well; in many respects, most are identified in interest with the mainline. In piety, however, many are "evangelical."

"Evangelical" has generally prospered in the last three decades while the mainline has experienced some loss. Evangelical can include fundamentalists, more moderate evangelicals, Pentecostals, Southern Baptists and some conservative Protestant denominations.

Many evangelicals like to think of themselves as "the old-time religion," but historians will say that, although these groups have roots in earlier conservative Protestantism, they took their present shape in this century as a reaction to modernity. They saw liberal and modernist Protestants saying that evolution was "God's way of doing things," and that the Bible did not have to be inerrant to carry authority. They thought some liberals were getting too worldly, too much like everyone else. So they reacted. They reached for what they considered to be "the fundamentals"— the inerrant Bible, and literal beliefs in Jesus' being born of a virgin, or that he would physically come to rule for a thousand years and end world history as we know it.

If modernists started finding too much to like in other religions and thought that God would save more or less everyone, so they could stay at home or engage in humanitarian missions, these reactive parties insisted that God would condemn those who condemned themselves by being unbelievers. For this reason they evangelize, meaning they spread God's good news and try to make converts. Pentecostals, most of whom trace their origin to revivals in California in 1906, believe that God the Holy Spirit is immediately available to them. They stress divine healing, and they speak or sing in languages that are unintelligible but which they interpret. At the very least, they want to provide an alternative to most Protestantism, which they think lacks fervor and commitment.

The fundamentalist-evangelical-Pentecostal movements and the liberal-moderate-modernist flanks came to a kind of schism in the twentieth century and now engage in a less-than-peaceful coexistence. Now that they are no longer united in anti-Catholicism, that not being a part of any large Protestant movement today, they have nothing around which to coalesce. They might struggle for control of the same church body, as fundamentalist Southern Baptists did when they took power from traditionally conservative Southern Baptists. Some fundamentalist, evangelical, and Pentecostal Christians choose to work chiefly outside denominational patterns. They have their own moderate spokespersons, such as Billy Graham, and their own celebrities, such as the televangelists. This company of Protestants, while prospering, has undergone drastic changes. For instance, until around 1975 they were seen as being largely "otherworldly," and not interested in politics. In a dramatic reversal they entered the political order and became the most vocal and potent religious-political force.

Because mass media often misrepresented them, evangelicals, fundamentalists, and Pentecostals fought back with television stations of their own or by boycotting programs they did not like. Because they disagreed with *Roe v. Wade,* the U.S. Supreme Court decision permitting some abortions, they worked for a constitutional amendment to counter it. Because they disagreed with court decisions ruling out Bible reading and school prayer, they carried on battles for "Creationism" in the science class and for amendments that would allow for prayer. Some built Christian schools of their own.

THE EXPRESSIONS
OF PROTESTANTISM
CLOSE TO HOME

It would be misleading, however, to suggest that either the elites of liberal Protestantism who make statements on public affairs which so many of their own fellow members ignore or the vocal leaders of New Christian Right Protestantism who gain the limelight represent the main agenda of most Protestants.

For most Protestants in your school, as elsewhere, church life extends first and foremost to home and personal life. When they cannot make sense of chaos, they try to find the hand of the God of Moses and Abraham and Jesus active in the confusing plot of history. When they feel guilty or oppressed or lonely, they believe that by supporting each other, by praying and speaking up, they can make Jesus Christ somehow vivid and can recognize his presence. When they fear disease, suffer illness, or face death, they expect

the Bible stories they learned, the sermons they heard, the songs they sang, the prayers they prayed, and the company they kept at church to comfort and be with them. They expect to be challenged to do good works even as they expect to complain about the institutional church or organized religion.

THE PROTESTANT
REFORMATION CONTINUES

If Protestants protest against the Protestant churches, including their own; if they think the reformers did not complete the task and that the church needs more reform—they are simply acting as Protestants are supposed to. This chapter would not be complete if somewhere we did not use a scholarly sounding term that makes one stop to stumble and, perhaps, to think. The early Protestants insisted, in Latin, that *ecclesia semper reformanda,* the church was always in need of being reformed.

Today's Protestants and their leaders still believe that, though they may find this belief uncomfortable when applied to themselves. They know that they are never supposed to sit back and think they have come to the fulfillment of the kingdom of God. But they do not like to have their own members point out how far short they have fallen, how much they need to do to see more unfolding of what they believe God's purposes to be. They find it easier to criticize Catholics and Jews, Muslims and Hindus, Buddhists and "secular humanists" or unbelievers, than to apply the Word of God critically to their own enterprises.

If Protestants are to be true to themselves, however, they must be ready for further protest and reform. They have had such ideas since their very beginnings, and they never know when, in the midst of routine organized church life, when everyone looks comfortable and smug, someone will come along and say "Thus saith the Lord!" and convince them to follow. That is why no chapter on Protestantism can present the final word. There is change every day. There is supposed to be.

STUDY QUESTIONS

1. How do you explain the "variety" that is called Protestantism? Give specific examples of the characteristics that have contributed to such variety. In light of such difference, does tolerance exist among different denominations? If so, how do you explain this tolerance? Be specific.

2. Explore what is meant by "The Protestant Drama." Who are its characters? What is its plot? Historically, how does the drama begin and develop?

3. What is Protestantism's relationship to Catholicism? What were the theological issues that led to the formation of the Protestant church? Develop, in particular, the role of the priest, the Bible, and how one is "saved" in discussing the Protestant Reformation.

4. Discuss the development of the earliest Protestant church in the United States. What were the motives behind the Protestant church's early development in this country?

5. Describe the historical and theological development of Puritanism in the United States. What are the major contributions of Puritan thought to contemporary Protestantism? To American government?

6. What is the Great Awakening? Why is the element of religious choice so crucial to understanding it? Do you see any connection between the Great Awakening in early American religious history and the development of the New Religious Right in the United States today?

7. What significant, if not unique, role do the Bible, the church, the "priest," grace, good works, faith, and guilt play in a Protestant's theology? What is "uniquely" Protestant about each of these theological issues? Give specific examples of these issues at work in contemporary Protestantism.

8. Define Protestant individualism. Is there a "social" side to Protestantism? If so, describe its function in society. If not, defend your position. What influence has Protestant individualism, as well as its social dimension, had on American politics?

ESSAY TOPICS

Jonathan Edwards: Puritan Spokesperson

The Protestant Sacraments: Baptism and Communion

The Bible Belt: Protestantism in the South

Going West: The Protestant Missionary Movement

The Great Awakening, Its Leaders and Its Theology

Protestantism and American Politics: Strange Friends?

WORD EXPLORATION

The following words play significant roles in any discussion of American Protestantism and are worth careful reflection and discussion.

Denominationalism	Ministers	Good Works and Faith
The Protestant Work Ethic	Protestant Individualism	The Great Awakening
Politics	Free Will	The Bible
Puritanism	Creeds	Guilt
Reformation	Pentecostalism	

FOR FURTHER READING

Balmer, Randall. *Mine Eyes Have Seen the Glory: A Journey into the Evangelical Subculture in America*, 4th ed. New York: Oxford University Press, 1989, 2006.

Blumhofer, Edith, and Joel A. Carpenter. *Twentieth Century Evangelicalism: A Guide to the Sources*. New York: Garland, 1990.

Handy, Robert T. *A Christian America: Protestant Hopes and Historical Realities,* 2d. ed. New York: Oxford University Press, 1984.

Hutchison, William R. *Between the Times: The Travail of the Protestant Establishment in America, 1900–1960*. New York: Cambridge University Press, 1989.

Marty, Martin E. *The Protestant Voice in American Pluralism*. Athens, GA: University of Georgia Press, 2004.

WEB SITES

http://protestant.christianityinview.com/
    Introduction to Protestant beliefs and history

http://www.theopedia.com/Reformation
    Basic information and timeline of the Protestant Reformation

3

The Religious World of African Americans

PETER J. PARIS

1619	Twenty African slaves arrive in Jamestown, Virginia
1740	Many slaves convert to Christianity during George Whitefield's religious revivals
1770	Crispus Attucks, former slave, among first to fall in Boston Massacre
1777	Vermont first state to abolish slavery
1787	Richard Allen, Absalom Jones, and others withdraw from Methodist Church in Philadelphia when forcibly removed from "whites only" section
1794	Richard Allen founds Bethel African Methodist Church in Philadelphia
1816	African Methodist Episcopal Church becomes first black denomination
1821	African Methodist Episcopal Zion Church founded in New York City
1831	Nat Turner's slave rebellion in Virginia
1842	Holy Family Sisters organized in New Orleans as one of first all-black Catholic religious orders
1863	Emancipation Proclamation frees all slaves in the United States
1865	Thirteenth Amendment outlaws slavery in the United States
1875	Congress passes civil rights bill banning discrimination in public places; overturned by Supreme Court in 1883
1895	National Baptist Convention of the U.S.A. founded
1906	Interracial Azusa Street revival in Los Angeles sparks growth of Pentecostal Christianity
1930	Wallace D. Fard creates Nation of Islam in Detroit
1957	Southern Christian Leadership Conference founded; Martin Luther King Jr., president
1965	Malcolm X assassinated less than a year after formal break with Elijah Muhammad and embrace of Sunni Islam
1968	Martin Luther King Jr. assassinated
1989	Barbara Harris elected the first woman bishop in the Episcopal Church
2000	Vashti Murphy McKenzie becomes first woman bishop in African Methodist Episcopal Church
2009	Civil rights activist Rev. Joseph Lowery, cofounder of the Southern Christian Leadership Conference, gives benediction at President Barack Obama's inauguration

The African American churches are the oldest and most important institutions in their communities. Some scholars claim that they predate the African American family because the latter had no independent existence during the period of slavery. Since African American religion has always been predominantly Christian in character, this essay will center largely on its gradual development from the time of slavery up to the present day.

The Context of Slavery

Unlike the vast majority of white Americans, African Americans did not come to this country voluntarily. Rather, they arrived on these shores in chains. Their descendants are the survivors of the Atlantic crossing historians refer to as the "middle passage." Packed like sardines in the humid bellies of slave galleys, these African peoples experienced indescribable suffering. Continuously exposed to the nauseous stench of feces, vomit, and vermin and the putrid smell of death, countless thousands perished en route. Those who survived the middle passage were delivered to the auction block in the slave marketplace, where they were sold like commodities to the highest bidder. Unlike the European settlers who came voluntarily to this country in search of freedom and wealth, Africans came in bondage, condemned to a life of misery and suffering.

In 1619, one year before the arrival of the *Mayflower,* twenty African slaves aboard a Dutch man-of-war were put ashore in Jamestown, Virginia. The American slave trade is said to have begun when the captain of that galley decided to trade his slaves for food. Yet this was not the first time Africans had arrived on these shores. Many of the earliest explorers and settlers brought domestic slaves with them. In fact, evidence shows that Christopher Columbus's cargo included African slaves.

Ruthlessly uprooted from their families and tribes, these African newcomers to this country suffered the unspeakable nightmare of slavery for two and one-half centuries.

Ironically, slave traders and owners were often devout Christians who saw no contradiction between their religion and the practice of owning slaves. Their deep conviction that African peoples were not fully a part of the human race meant that they felt no moral obligations toward them whatsoever. In fact, they viewed the slaves as part of their livestock; hence, they had a legal right to do with slaves whatever they wished.

As a result, the slaves were forced to labor from sunrise to sunset with minimum food and lodging. They inherited at birth a social status that excluded them from liberty. Any infractions of the rules could result in such arbitrary punishments as whipping, torture, disfigurement, or death. Slave women suffered the additional violence of constant rape and wanton abuse. Further, their children could be wrenched from them at any time and sold so far away that no possible trace of them could ever again be found.

Ironically, the colonial states institutionalized this cruel and treacherous system at the beginning of their history. Although the quest for freedom had inspired both the American Revolution and the new Constitution of the Republic, the system of slavery was left intact for nearly another century. This tragic historical fact has plagued the destiny of all Americans, both white and black, ever since. A lingering legacy of white racism remains deeply rooted in the American psyche and culturally ingrained in all of its institutions. As a result, white and black Americans alike have been shaped both morally and religiously by the experience of slavery and the enduring presence of white racism.

African American Spirituality

Throughout the seventeenth and much of the eighteenth century, African slaves had no other choice than to continue their own cultural traditions in this alien land. No rapid assimilation to the American cultural ethos was possible for them. Yet their white owners repudiated and disallowed all African cultural practices. Whenever the slaves were discovered engaging in such activities they were severely punished. Consequently, in underground locations African traditions were preserved and the substance of African American religion was born.

Not surprisingly, very few Africans became Christians during the first century of American slavery due in large part to two principal reasons. First, the Euro-American view that Africans were subhuman implied that the latter did not possess souls; hence, no effort was made to convert them to Christianity. Second, these Euro-Americans who believed differently about the nature of African humanity feared that if slaves participated with whites in a common religion, they might soon want to extend the notion of religious equality to the sphere of civil equality and thereby threaten the security of the slave system.

As a result, throughout much of the seventeenth and eighteenth centuries, African slaves were repulsed by Christianity because they viewed it as the religion of slave owners and, hence, not as a resource for the well-being of slaves. Their early rejection of Christianity reflected the African understanding that a people's religion is synonymous with their lifestyle. In other words, they believed that a people's lifestyle mirrored their religion and vice versa.

The African understanding that religion is synonymous with life implies that all life is sacred. Thus, unlike Western peoples, Africans (then and now) had no appreciation for the Western idea of secularization. The rejection of Christianity by the African slaves did not mean that they had no religion. On the contrary, African peoples have always believed that religion permeates every dimension of human life. Similarly, they have believed that religion serves the good of its devotees and is strongly opposed to its enemies. Thus, the slaves had no difficulty in viewing slave-owning Christianity as inimical to the well-being of slaves. Accordingly,

slave narratives are replete with descriptions of the disrespect that slaves expressed toward their masters' religion, which they experienced as an evil force intending their moral and spiritual demise.

Due to the circumstances of their departure from Africa, the American slaves had no choice but to leave their cultural artifacts behind. Yet they brought with them to these shores the spiritual substance of their culture, deeply embedded in their collective self-understanding. Gradually, these people shaped a new world of spiritual and moral meaning by appropriating and interpreting various elements in their new environment in accordance with their African understandings. Thus, the condition of slavery did not cut them off from their ultimate source of meaning, God, whom they knew by many names and who was for them the source and ground of all their religious and moral values.

Thus, despite the massive suffering endured for centuries of slavery, the acculturation of the Africans to their new environment did not result in a total loss of their former religious and moral understandings. On the contrary, African slaves were able to preserve many of the formal features of their most fundamental spiritual beliefs and moral values. This astounding accomplishment was due to their ability to make many of the Euro-American cultural expressions, including Christianity, serve as vehicles of cross-cultural transmission—a feat that involved no small amount of creative ingenuity.

Gradually, the slaves designed creative ways of expressing African meanings and values through the cultural forms of Western songs and stories. By amalgamating various African and Western elements, the African slaves adapted many of their traditional religious beliefs and practices to Christianity. Eventually, this process led to the birth of a peculiar hybrid religion that we call African American Christianity—which, incidentally, cannot be understood apart from the history of slave-owning Christianity and the response of the slaves to it.

THE CONCEALED CHURCH

Sometime around the middle of the eighteenth century, a growing number of slave owners had been persuaded by Christian missionaries to believe that slaves who converted to Christianity adapted more agreeably to the conditions of bondage than those who did not. Most slaveholders at the time opposed such a prospect because they assumed that if slaves experienced ecclesial equality in church membership they would aspire to civil equality as well. After they became convinced, however, that both civil law and local custom had long established the fact that the conversion of slaves to Christianity implied no change in their civil status, many gradually relaxed their opposition to slave conversions for at least two reasons: (1) their own personal conversion to Christianity sometimes caused them to view the evangelization of their personal slaves as an expression of their Christian compassion; (2) they gradually became convinced that the slave system would function more efficiently because converted slaves would likely cultivate the virtues of truth-telling, honesty, and patience, the lack of which among slaves constituted a persistent disciplinary problem. Thus, by the middle of the eighteenth century the membership of many white churches included slaves, because white slave owners were unwilling to permit racially separate associations, fearing possible slave involvement in abolitionist activity (activity designed to abolish the institution of slavery). However, most whites believed in the natural inferiority of Africans and therefore resented any semblance of equality that might be implied by slave membership in their churches. This led to the practice of relegating slaves to segregated spaces within white churches; for example, they had separate seating arrangements, received Holy Communion only after all whites had been served first, and had neither voice nor vote in matters of church governance. In spite of these restrictive conditions, however, some of the slaves gained considerable status as preachers and were praised by both whites and blacks for their oratorical excellence.

More often than not, however, special services were designed for the slaves in which the substance of the preaching consisted of the following basic tenets: (1) that the Bible admonishes slaves to obey their masters and be content with their condition in this world in the hope of eternal salvation in the world to come; (2) that slave ideas about freedom are signs of the devil's temptation; (3) that both diligence in their work and punishments for laxity are pleasing in God's sight; and (4) that forgiveness for wrongdoing lay not only with God but also with the slave owner.

Although slaves willingly participated in the worship services in order to experience some relief from the drudgery of forced labor, they were not fooled by the content of the instruction. Rather, they listened carefully and critically to the reading of the Scriptures and, in time, they discerned resources within the biblical teaching that led them to adopt an alternative understanding of Christianity to that proclaimed by the slave owners' preachers, namely, that God is the divine parent of all peoples and, hence, all are equal in God's sight.

This major turning point in the history of African American religious devotion occurred when slaves heard the biblical story of the exodus concerning Israel's deliverance from bondage. They quickly discerned that Israel's God had taken the initiative in that liberating event. The story had an indelible effect on the African slaves because it enabled them to see clearly that, contrary to the teaching of the slave owners' preachers, the biblical God identified with the Hebrew slaves and stood alongside them in opposition to their oppressors. This new understanding, which they embraced enthusiastically, portrayed God as the liberator of all oppressed peoples and opposed to all who are bent on maintaining oppressive sociopolitical systems. Henceforth, this view of God underlay the African American view of humanity.

As with the people of Israel, the exodus story has always been of paramount importance to African American Christians because it connotes a living and caring God who not only sees, hears, and knows about human suffering but willingly chooses to become actively engaged in liberating activity. The slaves gradually made the story of the exodus their own, and from one generation to the next they compared each of their major leaders to Moses and actually renamed them after him. For example, African Americans called each of the following Moses: Harriet Tubman, Sojourner Truth, Richard Allen, David Walker, and Frederick Douglass, to mention only a few.

Let us not suppose, however, that the slaves discovered this alternative understanding of Christianity under favorable conditions. Rather, their only alternative was to gather late at night for secret meetings in the brush. These meetings were subversive in nature because they provided the context in which slaves could reflect on their condition apart from the watchful eyes of their overseers. In these secret places an alternative understanding of Christianity was born, nurtured, celebrated, and proclaimed. Thus, concealed from the eyes and ears of the slave owners, the religion of African Americans emerged as a force strongly opposed to the theological and moral foundations of the slave system. Not surprisingly, in one way or another, everything that emanated from the religion of African Americans expressed their desire for freedom and their hope for a better day. Clearly, this entailed considerable ingenuity on their part, given the many severe proscriptions against such views.

SPIRITUALS

The so-called spirituals, which constitute slavery's most lasting legacy to America and the world at large, tell the story of suffering and triumph, of endurance and transcendence, of history and eternity. Composed by "unknown bards" of long ago, these songs contain the substance of African American Christianity. They represent the spiritual strivings of an oppressed people in their efforts to persevere in the midst of daily threats to life and limb. The imaginative power and creative skill demonstrated in the countless spirituals manifest the transcendent capacity of the human spirit.

Ironically, the destiny of the spirituals has not been confined to the restrictive world of the slave but has become woven into the fabric of America's distinctive cultural contribution to the world. Emerging out of the spirit of an oppressed people, these songs tell the universal story of agony and pain, but not that alone. They also tell of the faith and hope of suffering souls. Through the activities of poetry, music, and song, the slaves expressed and preserved their humanity against astounding odds. Interestingly, these activities comprise some of the slaves' earliest forms of resistance to their hostile environment.

Through spirituals the slaves proclaimed their faith and hope in a God whom they believed would deliver them from bondage because this same God had also befriended and liberated the Israelites from slavery. They were confident that what God had done for the people of Israel, God would also do for them. Hence, their songs were not about suffering alone but also about their faith in a God of deliverance and their hopes for freedom both in this world and in the world to come. For obvious reasons, however, all indicators of their desire for freedom had to be concealed by the use of code words that usually conveyed more than one meaning. For example, on the one hand, the spiritual,

Go down Moses,
Way down in Egypt's land,
Tell ole Pharaoh,
To let my people go.

could be viewed as an effort to make a song out of a biblical story. Yet, on the other hand, it could be viewed symbolically as a longing for a contemporary Moses to rise and do likewise. Similarly, the spiritual,

Steal away, steal away,
Steal away to Jesus;
Steal away, steal away home,
I ain't got long to stay here.

could be interpreted, on the one hand, as a meditative longing for a heavenly home. Yet, on the other hand, it could be understood as a mournful announcement of a forthcoming escape.

The slaves sang songs that spoke of ultimate justice for those who perpetrate injustice, and sometimes not without a bit of humor:

Rich man Dives, he lived so well,
When he died he found a home in hell.

Yet there were also songs that spoke of equality in heaven in such a way that the heavenly vision implied a severe criticism of the structures of injustice that shaped the daily lives of all the slaves. For example, slaves had no shoes as a rule, and robes and crowns were the inheritance of rulers alone. However, contrary to the beliefs of their slaveholders, they believed that in heaven everybody would have the freedom to walk wherever they wished and there would be no barriers of race, class, or other circumstance—everybody would have not only shoes but also robes and crowns. Why? Because all are children of God and, hence, brothers and sisters one and all. Again, the subtle humor of the slaves should not be missed as it appears in the line, "Everybody talking about Heaben ain't a-gonna there"—a double entendre unmistakably aimed at Christian slaveholders.

I've got shoes, you got shoes
All God's chillun got shoes
When I get to Heaben, gonna put on
  my shoes
Gonna walk all ober God's Heaben.

Refrain

Heaben, Heaben,
Everybody talking about Heaben

Ain't a-gonna there
Heaben, Heaben,
Gonna walk all ober God's Heaben.

I've got a robe, you got a robe
All God's chillun got a robe
When I get to Heaben, gonna put on
  my robe
Gonna walk all ober God's Heaben.

Refrain

I've got a crown, you got a crown
All God's chillun got a crown
When I get to Heaben,
gonna put on my crown,
Gonna walk all ober God's Heaben.

Refrain

The themes about which the spirituals speak are numerous even as the spirituals themselves are. They cover a broad expanse of the human spirit; their imagery is rich beyond belief; their symbols are filled with experiential meaning pointing always beyond the immediate circumstances of pain and suffering to a final resting place in the divine resolution. Heaven was viewed as a place of belonging—a home—and like every genuine home, it was thought of as a place where persons are made whole in both body and soul. Yet the focus of so many spirituals on heaven should not be viewed merely as otherworldly but also as a concealed way of criticizing a present situation of pain and suffering by depicting a contrasting vision of hope and promise.

African American Christians have always been convinced that the substance of the religion of the slaves is authentic Christianity, a gospel that they believe was corrupted and rejected by whites through the practice of slaveholding. This true gospel centers on the parenthood of God and the kinship of all peoples under God. Since kinship implies the equality of persons in community, the kinship of all peoples under God implies God's opposition to those who threaten or destroy the equality of God's people.

This religious vision was born in slavery; nurtured, developed, and protected in the secret meeting places of the slaves; and later institutionalized in the independent African American church movement, which began among freed slaves immediately following the American Revolution.

The religion of African Americans has constituted the one ongoing positive force in their history from the earliest times up to the present day. It has both saved the people from falling victim to fatalism and despair and given them theological grounds for their claim that suffering will end because God is on their side and desires their deliverance. Such a collective hope enables a people to dream of possible alternative worlds; such dreams formed the bedrock of black preaching from one generation to another. Clearly, all of this was implicit in the great "I Have a Dream" speech of Martin Luther King Jr., the twentieth century's most celebrated embodiment of the African American Christian tradition.

THE INDEPENDENT AFRICAN AMERICAN CHURCH MOVEMENT

The independent African American church movement was started soon after the American Revolution by freed slaves in northern cities. The founders of these churches, unwilling at first to form racially separate organizations lest they be viewed as racists, eventually agreed that the choice to separate themselves from the white churches was not a racist act but rather a religious and moral refusal to comply with the racist practices of whites that robbed them of their human dignity in the house of God. Convinced that compliance with racism compromised their understanding of the Christian faith because it forced them to deny the parenthood of God and the kinship of all peoples, these freed slaves felt obligated both theologically and morally to separate themselves from such blasphemy and establish alternative churches that would institutionalize these principles.

African American Denominations by Size			
Name of denomination	U.S. Membership in 2008	Ranking in Size Among All Denominations in the U.S.	Year founded
The Church of God in Christ	5,499,875	5th	1897
National Baptist Convention, U.S.A., Inc.	5,000,000	6th	1895
National Baptist Convention of America	3,500,000	8th	1915
African Methodist Episcopal Church	2,500,000	11th	1816
Progressive National Baptist Convention, U.S.A., Inc.	2,500,000	11th (tie)	1961
African Methodist Episcopal Zion Church	1,443,405	19th	1821

Thus, the independent African American churches came into existence as a prophetic response to the condition of slavery and racism. It had become abundantly clear that the white churches provided the theological and moral foundation for the degradation of African peoples. Consequently, African American Christians rebelled and their churches emerged as institutional symbols of that protest.

The African American churches suffered considerable persecution and severe restrictions during much of their existence. The most severe oppression, however, occurred during times of slave revolts, the most notable of which were the Gabriel Prosser uprising in 1800, the Denmark Vesey revolt in 1822, and the Nat Turner rebellion in 1831. Following those insurrections, African American church meetings were banned because they were viewed as the seedbeds for sedition.

The African Methodist Episcopal Church

The African Methodist Episcopal (A.M.E.) Church was the first independent African American denomination in the United States. It dates from 1787, when Richard Allen, Absalom Jones, and others withdrew from St. George's Methodist Church in Philadelphia because they had been forced from their knees while praying in an area of the church that was closed to blacks. In 1793, Allen bought a blacksmith shop and converted it into the Bethel Church, the first church owned by African Americans. The legal struggle to function as an independent church was formidable. Yet Allen and his supporters persisted and finally gained legal control over their property and independence over their internal affairs. From these meager beginnings, the African Methodist Episcopal denomination was formed in 1816, and Richard Allen was ordained as an elder and consecrated as its first bishop.

The African Episcopal Church

Interestingly, Absalom Jones, one of the persons who left St. George's Methodist Church with Richard Allen, was later ordained the first African American Protestant Episcopal priest. In 1794, he became the pastor of the St. Thomas African Episcopal Church. Thus, the independent African American church movement had expanded to include Episcopalianism.

The African Methodist Episcopal Zion Church

Like the A.M.E. Church, the African Methodist Episcopal Zion (A.M.E.Z.) Church also had its origins in the late eighteenth century, when a group of African Americans, led by an ex-slave, Peter Williams, separated from the John Street Methodist Episcopal Church in New York City. Again, the separation was sparked by the discriminatory practices of the white church, which included the refusal to ordain African Americans.

The Christian Methodist Episcopal Church

Although the circumstances of its origins differed from those of its northern predecessors, the A.M.E. and the A.M.E.Z. churches, the Christian Methodist Episcopal (C.M.E.) Church was born in the post-slavery South. Originally called the Colored Methodist Episcopal Church, this church separated from the Methodist Episcopal Church, South, after the 1844 split in white Methodism over the issue of slavery. In 1954 the denomination decided to change the term "Colored" in its name to "Christian" to retain the initials C.M.E. while also signaling its nonracial, universal character. Like its northern counterparts, the C.M.E. Church's separation from the white Methodists was a declaration of independence from the demeaning status of racial segregation within the white church.

Independent African American Baptist Churches

During the latter half of the eighteenth century a number of independent African American Baptist churches came into existence in various northern and southern cities. The first such church in North America was the Silver Bluff Baptist Church, founded in 1787 in Savannah, Georgia.

Prior to emancipation, virtually no African American Baptist church in the South and very few in the North enjoyed full independence. Rather, they were all dependent to some extent on the patronage of white Baptists, who displayed no small amount of ambiguity toward them. On the one hand, they did not want to share equal membership with either slaves or ex-slaves; on the other hand, they did not want African Americans to have their own independent churches. It is an understatement to say that a varied and complex history attends each of these semi-independent African American Baptist churches and, especially, the story of their gradual pilgrimage toward full independence.

National Baptist Convention, U.S.A., Inc.

Being radically congregational in their church polity, these African Baptist churches soon linked themselves together into regional associations, which were characteristically abolitionist and intensely active in the so-called Underground Railroad (an effective support system for aiding and abetting slaves bent on escaping from their bondage). Various efforts to form a national convention of African Baptists eventually culminated in 1895 in the establishment of the National Baptist Convention, U.S.A., Inc., which continues to be the largest convention of African Baptists anywhere in the world. Its membership presently is estimated in excess of five million.

National Baptist Convention of America

In 1915, the National Baptists suffered a split over an internal problem concerning the control and ownership of its publishing house. This division resulted in the formation of the National Baptist Convention of America (NBCA), which has a membership estimated at 3.5 million.

National Missionary Baptist Convention of America

In 1988 the NBCA suffered a split, with 25 percent of the membership opting to form the National Missionary Baptist Convention of America.

Progressive National Baptist Convention, U.S.A., Inc.

In 1961 the Progressive National Baptist Convention, U.S.A., Inc., came into existence as a result of a split within its parent body, the National Baptist Convention, U.S.A., Inc. This split centered on the alleged authoritarian leadership of President J. H. Jackson, who also opposed the strategies and tactics of nonviolent resistance. Under the leadership of the Rev. Dr. Gardner C. Taylor, such notable ministers and civil rights leaders as Martin Luther King Jr., Martin Luther King Sr., Benjamin Mars, Ralph Abernathy, and a number of others joined together to form the new convention with its motto, "Unity, Service, Fellowship, Peace." Its present membership is estimated to be 1.2 million.

The Church of God in Christ

Unlike the African Methodist and Baptist churches, the Church of God in Christ is a twentieth-century phenomenon that did not originate from a white denomination but from an interracial Pentecostal movement begun by a black minister and from which whites later withdrew. This movement was led by William J. Seymour, who conducted the so-called Azusa Street Revival in Los Angeles between the years 1906 and 1909. Out of that event emerged several Pentecostal denominations, of which the Church of God in Christ is the largest with a membership of 5.5 million.

Black Churches within White Denominations

Many predominantly white Protestant denominations (i.e., Episcopalian, Lutheran, United Church of Christ, Presbyterian, United Methodist, Mormon) along with Roman Catholicism have varying numbers of African American congregations within their denominational structures.

Women Leaders

During the twentieth century, women have emerged as founders and leaders of a growing number of African American churches. Until fairly recently few African American churches permitted women to be ordained. Although the number of ordained women has steadily increased, prejudices against their leadership have not decreased appreciably. For these and other reasons, many women have founded independent churches. The most notable of these is the Mount Sinai Holy Church of America, Inc., founded by Bishop Ida Robinson in 1924 in Philadelphia. Bishop Robinson later ordained several women as vice-bishops and elders.

Personal Voices: Amanda Smith

As African American churches grew in membership after the Civil War, new opportunities opened for women preachers and evangelists. In this excerpt, popular New York–area evangelist Amanda Smith reminisces about her call to preach.

It was in November, 1869. God had led me clearly up to this time confirming His work through me as I went all about—sometimes to Brooklyn, then to Harlem, then to Jersey City. All this was among my own people, and our own colored churches, though I often went beside to old Second Street, Norfolk Street, Willett Street, Bedford Street, and to different white Methodist churches, to class meetings and prayer meetings; but very little with white people, comparatively. The most I did was among my own people. There were then but few of our ministers that were favorable to women's preaching or taking any part, I mean in a public way; but, thank God, there always were a few men that dared to stand by woman's liberty in this, if God called her. Among these, I remember, was Henry Davis, Rev. James Holland, Rev. Joshua Woodland, Rev. Joseph H. Smith, and Rev. Leonard Patterson, and others—but it is different now. We have women deaconesses, and leaders, and women in all departments of church work. May God in mercy save us from the formalism of the day, and bring us back to the old time spirituality and power of the fathers and mothers. I often feel as I look over the past and compare it with the present, to say: "Lord, save, or we perish."

As the Lord led, I followed, and one day as I was praying and asking Him to teach me what to do. I was impressed that I was to leave New York and go out. I did not know where, so it troubled me, and I asked the Lord for light, and He gave me these words: "Go, and I will go with you." The very words he gave to Moses, so many years ago.

(An excerpt from chapter 11 of *An Autobiography: The Story of the Lord's Dealings with Mrs. Amanda Smith, the Colored Evangelist.* In the public domain.)

Protesting Racism

In spite of their denominational differences, African American churches are united by their common rejection of racism, which they consider to be the paramount sin of the white churches. Most importantly, they have never had policies of exclusion or segregation based on race or ethnicity. In fact, every independent African American church that chose to separate itself from its white counterpart, from the time of the American Revolution to the present day, did so as a religious and moral protest against institutionalized racism. By deliberately removing themselves from the public racism practiced by the white churches, African American churches gave birth to the civil protest tradition that continues to characterize their life and mission. The independent African American churches emerged especially, however, out of the desire to institutionalize Christianity in a nonracist form.

The independent African American church movement provided a place in which the people could worship God as they pleased, and in which it could serve the needs of the people in accordance with their own desires and choices. Faithful devotion to the principle of racial justice enabled these churches to construct alternative religious institutions with the unique aim of serving the well-being of African Americans in every dimension of their lives. This holistic approach and the nonracist character of the African American churches constitute the unique features of African American Christianity. Unlike any institutions in the larger white society, African American churches have made a theologically grounded nonracist principle the center of their associational life.

We must note, however, that the vast majority of African Americans have always opposed racism. That is to say, they have always abhorred any policies of exclusion based on the principle of race. This has been a predominant cultural ethos within the African American community from the earliest times to the present day. This nonracist principle has been nurtured and preserved continuously by the churches, which have been the primary societal institutions in the African American community. As such, they have been the custodians of the community's most basic values and especially its opposition to every form of white racism.

Thus, whenever African Americans become racist in attitude or practice, they betray the cultural ethos of their community and alienate themselves from it. Consequently, such leaders rarely attract much popular support.

Agencies for Social Organization and Cohesion

The African American churches have been and continue to be the primary institutions owned and controlled by African Americans. Because no area of life is excluded from their purview, they have always exercised multifaceted roles in the African American community. Being the only independent institution dedicated to the maintenance and enhancement of the community's well-being, the role of the African American churches has been analogous to that of governments. Historically no other institution primarily served the good of the African American community. Theologically and morally legitimized by all African Americans, the churches not only founded schools, colleges, seminaries, hospitals, publishing houses, newspapers, insurance companies, banks, countless social clubs, and so forth; they institutionalized the most basic moral values of the community and provided the role models for community leadership. In fact, for generations African American churches were the training ground not only for church leaders, but also for political, civil rights, and educational leaders. Further, many professional singers, musicians, and other artists got their initial support, encouragement, and promotion from the churches. In short, throughout the nineteenth and much of the twentieth century, the African American churches had a role in virtually every good thing that occurred in the lives of their people.

Sociologists have referred to the churches as the primary agencies for social organization and social cohesion following emancipation. Clearly, one basic reason why the African American churches have flourished is their unadulterated commitment to the good of the African American community. They alone provided African Americans with opportunities for leadership, achievement, self-esteem, and racial pride. They alone enabled the people to gain a positive sense of identity as individuals and as a group. Thus, one cannot overemphasize the importance of the principles of autonomy and self-determination embodied in the African American church movement because they alone enabled African Americans to gain a significant measure of freedom from the control and domination of whites.

FOUR TYPES OF AFRICAN AMERICAN CHURCHES

Regardless of denominational differences, African American churches can be classified in four major types based on the style of their ministry: pastoral, prophetic, political, and nationalist. It is important to note, however, that these styles are not mutually exclusive. That is to say, any particular church may exhibit the features of each style, although most likely one particular style will predominate at any given time.

The Pastoral Type

The pastoral type of ministry is the oldest, having emerged during slavery, many generations prior to the rise of the independent churches. Its function has been to proclaim the grace of God to all, regardless of circumstance, and, especially following emancipation, to assume a positive view of the nation's fundamental goodness. While condemning all forms of racism, these churches have tended to believe that the vast majority of white Americans do not approve of racism. In other words, they have tended to believe that racism is not a systemic problem but, rather, is due to the prejudicial attitudes of a few. Further, these churches have always abhorred societal conflict, which they view as the precursor of bitterness, hatred, and violence. Optimistic in outlook, they have consistently challenged blacks to be more self-respecting, industrious, honest, thrifty, self-reliant, morally virtuous, and hopeful that a better day will surely dawn because of God's providence. Accordingly, they have concentrated their energy primarily on saving souls and nurturing their people in the survival skills of patience, hope, and goodwill toward their oppressors.

The theological and moral substance of the African American churches was formed in the concealed churches of the slaves. Although the many and varied secret gatherings that comprised this concealed institution often served to aid and abet the efforts of slaves to escape, their primary purpose was to celebrate the goodness of God and to encourage one another through supportive communities in which the principal activities were praying, preaching, singing, and testifying. Clearly, these meetings concentrated on serving the intra-associational needs of the members, which, in turn, strengthened their moral and spiritual capacities. In fact, the goal of these meetings was to help the people nurture moral virtues and spiritual devotion, both of which were thought to be necessary for the preservation of their humanity. This objective has continued to characterize the ethos of many contemporary African American churches, especially those whose members are daily threatened by the devastating constraints of poverty and racism. Those whose lives are constantly being diminished need the moral support derived from close relationships with others who have had similar experiences. The character of this ministry is largely communal in nature; the people help and sustain one another as they all seek to develop the capacity to face personal suffering constructively. These churches may rightly be called "spiritual support groups." Acts of praying, singing, and testifying manifest signs of the transcendent spirit that helps them overcome adversity. This community attributes its life to the grace of God and, hence, it seemingly never ceases "praising God."

The political expression of this pastoral type of African American ministry has often been labeled accommodationist, that is, submissive to the design of racism. An alternative view is that the resiliency of the human spirit is such that African Americans constantly devised creative and subtle ways of resisting their oppressors, especially the latter's definition of them as genetically inferior to whites. As a consequence, African Americans often assumed a posture of accommodation that was more form than substance. As a defense mechanism, African Americans have tended to conceal their beliefs and feelings from whites. This tendency has often resulted in deceptive activity, such as speech and actions calculated to please their overseers while hiding their true feelings. In that way, blacks resisted the demand to participate in their own dehumanization. Hence, what might seem on the surface to be accommodationism in fact enabled many to submit partially to the racist practices while concealing alternative viewpoints.

The Prophetic Type

Prophetic ministry is characterized by its courage in proclaiming the justice of God by publicly condemning all forms of racial injustice. Accordingly, these churches boldly criticize the white churches for straying from what they consider to be the authentic biblical understanding of humanity. Similarly, they charge that by its support of racist practices the nation has betrayed the values of its founders, as immortalized in the Declaration of Independence and the Constitution.

Although both the pastoral and prophetic traditions appeal to common sources of legitimation, that is, Scripture, tradition, and experience, those in the prophetic tradition believe that redemptive ends necessitate direct conflict with the perpetrators of injustice. As we have seen, the dominant ethos of the pastoral churches is celebrative worship expressed in dynamic preaching, vibrant song, and rhythmic music. In contrast, the dominant ethos of the prophetic churches is that of social ministry, often labeled "protest activity," in the service of enhancing social justice. Like the pastoral type, however, it also relies heavily on a liturgical pattern of powerful preaching coupled with exuberant music and song.

This prophetic church ministry originated with the birth of the independent African American church movement in the last decade of the eighteenth century. The civil rights struggles of the post-emancipation period are deeply rooted in the abolitionist tradition that was born in the Negro convention movement of the 1830s (an annual convention of all African American leaders concerned with evaluating the state of the race). Amid much debate and controversy over strategies and tactics, this protest tradition has been at the heart of these prophetic churches. In fact, the relationship between the churches and civil rights activities has been so close that many scholars have wrongly concluded that the black church is little more than a political organization promoting racial justice. Frederick Douglass, W.E.B. Du Bois, Martin Luther King Jr., and Jesse Jackson represent some of the greatest leaders to emerge from the prophetic type of ministry. Various abolitionist societies as well as the National Association for the Advancement of Colored People, the Southern Christian Leadership Conference, and numerous other groups were virtually spawned and nurtured by these prophetic churches.

The mutual interdependence and cooperation of the pastoral and prophetic churches were graphically demonstrated in the mass rallies of the civil rights movement under the leadership of Martin Luther King Jr. On those occasions the atmosphere was continuously charged with the testimonies and prayers of the faithful, the moving beauty of the spirituals, the guttural exuberance of the gospel music, and the persuasive oratory of dynamic preaching. These provided the means by which blacks were woven together into a harmonious whole imbued with a common mission, which they zealously affirmed. Thus folk artists and professional musicians, civil rights leaders and welfare recipients, movie stars and rural farmers, poor and middle-class people sang, prayed, joined hands, and marched together in their quest for a racially just social order. And many whites joined with blacks in that movement and thereby expressed their belief in and commitment to the struggle for a common humanity.

The Political Type

During the brief period of the Reconstruction, following the Civil War, African American churches were fully engaged in electoral politics through voter education and registration. Many clergy and laypersons were encouraged to run for political office. During the periods of exclusion from political participation, both before and after Reconstruction, the pastoral and prophetic black churches served as training grounds for the day when African Americans would assume their rightful place in electoral office.

Due to their institutional primacy in the community, African American churches have provided meeting places for virtually every forum concerning the welfare of the black community. Further, the democratic style of congregational governance in the vast majority of African American churches, together with the prudential style of pastoral leadership on matters concern-

ing the well-being of the community, readied many African Americans for the practice of democratic politics in the nation's governments. Similarly, the long protest struggles of the churches for civil rights also prepared the way for black participation in electoral politics. Clearly, both the pastoral and prophetic styles of ministry have been and continue to be strongly supportive of black participation in elective office.

The Nationalist Type

The nationalist type of ministry stands apart from the mainstream of the African American Christian tradition. Unlike that mainstream tradition, which believes that racial justice can be realized in the nation through various kinds of reforms, the nationalists claim that America is incurably racist; hence, they believe that every attempt to rid the nation of racism is destined to failure. This implies that African Americans cannot rely on white allies in their quest for racial justice. Rather, they must rely on themselves alone. Hence, a major focus of the nationalist type of ministry is to inculcate within the people a strong sense of racial identity and self-respect that were lost as a result of slavery and its aftermath. The nationalist churches also believe that the necessary enlightenment of the race can only occur through racial separation and the development of racial pride and self-determination through a renewed appreciation for African values.

Elements of this nationalist tradition can be found in virtually every period of African American history but most clearly in the vision of such historical figures as Martin Delaney, Bishop Henry McNeal Turner, Alexander Crummell, Edward Wilmot Blyden, and Marcus Moziah Garvey, all of whom encouraged African Americans to return to Africa and aid the process of decolonization there. All of these figures claimed that the liberation of Africa was a necessary condition for the liberation of African Americans, and each advocated the importance of African American agency in Africa's liberation from colonialism. The African missionary enterprises of the independent African American churches also reflected this nationalist orientation.

Many of the marks of this nationalist type of ministry are evident in the nascent black theology movement. This movement began with the 1969 publication of James H. Cone's book *Black Theology and Black Power,* a Christian defense of the political ideology of black power and a prophetic demand that liberation from racial injustice be the goal of every authentic theology. The black theology movement initially aimed its prophetic challenge at the so-called conservative African American churches, the racist practices of the white churches, and the theological curricula of white seminaries. Its impact on the study of religion in America and abroad has been considerable, as can be seen by the number of African American religious studies courses presently offered in universities and seminaries as compared with virtually none twenty years ago.

In addition, the black theology movement has had a decisive impact on the practical life of the African churches in South Africa, where their opposition to constitutional racism (apartheid) desperately needed theological categories that would enable them to rebut the theological justification of apartheid provided by the Dutch Reformed Church. Accordingly, black theology enabled many in South Africa to construct a contextual theology with which to proclaim a prophetic message of liberation and to act courageously for its realization.

Thus, the nationalist type of ministry differs from the pastoral, prophetic, and political types by the primary importance it gives to racial identity, self-respect, African heritage, and the principle of self-determination. In short, this type maximizes the positive values implied by the distinctiveness of African heritage. Its adherents adamantly deny all accusations of advocating "reverse racism." Their principal aim has always been that of liberating the race from every vestige of racial inferiority that was bequeathed to them by white racism.

CONCLUSION

Since the social situation of African Americans has always been circumscribed by white racism, their churches have always struggled to maintain and enhance the humanity of the race by providing the necessary space for all sorts of activities in the social, economic, political, and religious spheres of life. That is to say, the internal life of the churches provided African Americans the opportunity for association and expression denied them by the white world.

More specifically, the black churches have struggled to create a world of harmony wherein the virtues of justice and respect permeate communal life. In their religious life, African Americans have sought to justify the principles of freedom, liberty, and equality as harmonious with God's will. Most importantly, they have placed their trust primarily in the biblical God, whom they believed to be free from racism. Further, they have tended to evaluate all political activity in terms of its commensurability with God's nonracist will.

In short, the religion of the African American churches has always viewed freedom as both a religious and a political goal. For the most part, black churches have viewed their quest for black liberation as a contribution to the liberation of all. Although the black churches were implicated occasionally in slave revolts, in general they were committed to nonviolent resistance long before the term was popularized by Martin Luther King Jr. Clearly, the African American churches have enriched the nation's public realm by keeping alive issues of social justice related to public responsibility and the rights of citizenship by exposing all forms of racial hypocrisy and injustice. In this respect, they have been the conscience of the nation.

The black churches emerged on the stage of history as a response to the public issue of racism that had been firmly established both politically and religiously at the beginning of the Republic. Consequently, their life and mission have aimed at effecting alternative ways of living in a racially just world. The independent African American church movement of the late eighteenth and early nineteenth centuries represents the religious institutionalization of that aim.

The abolition of legalized racism (i.e., racial segregation and discrimination) in the 1960s marked the successful culmination of the civil rights movement, which was the political arm of the African American churches. Civil rights legislation bestowed upon African Americans their long awaited citizenship rights. Unfortunately, a residue of cultural and psychological racism continues to function in the decision-making processes of most of the nation's institutions. In recent years, however, African American electoral politics has received strong support from the churches because its political agenda gives high priority to the role of government in protecting civil rights and effecting economic justice through full-employment policies and the abolition of poverty both at home and abroad.

POSTSCRIPT ON NON-CHRISTIAN RELIGIONS

African American religion is no longer exclusively Christian. A number of non-Christian groups have emerged in many urban areas during this century. Of these Islam represents the largest group, with a U.S. membership estimated at two to three million total, with approximately one million of those Muslims being African American. Various forms of Islam constitute viable alternatives to African American Christianity, especially among African American males, many of whom are readily attracted to Islam's teaching and discipline.

During the Great Depression two extraordinary developments occurred in African American religion under the leadership of two charismatic personalities, namely, the Father Divine Peace Mission Movement and Bishop Grace's (widely known as "Daddy Grace") United House of Prayer for All People. Both leaders claimed that they were divine.

In addition, various other religious groups were founded at about the same time, the most notable being Prophet Cherry's "Black Jews" (who claimed that they were the only authentic Jews) and Elijah Muhammad's "Black Muslims." All of these groups were founded by self-educated charismatic personalities who had recently migrated to the North from the southern states.

More recently various immigrants from Africa and the Caribbean have transplanted many of their traditional religions to American soil. Many of these have attracted African American members.

STUDY QUESTIONS

1. What is the "middle passage"? Why do you think that the middle passage is important for understanding the religious world of African Americans?

2. Why did few Africans become Christians during the first century of American slavery? If African slaves believed that religion is synonymous with lifestyle, what was the African slave's initial introduction to the Christianity of the white person?

3. How did African slaves maintain their religious and moral understandings of the world within the context of a new religious environment? In the contemporary African American community, do you still see "African religion" in the context of Christianity?

4. How did the "concealed church" of African American slaves differ from the white churches of their owners? What biblical message was most preached to the slaves in the white church? What was the religious message of the "concealed church"? Why might we describe this message as subversive?

5. What are the religious messages of spirituals? What symbols from traditional Judaism and Christianity are used to address the African slave's situation? What historical observations can we make about slavery by reading and listening to spirituals? Why do issues of suffering and freedom play such crucial roles in these songs?

6. Why might African American religion be considered a religion of hope? How has this theme of hope and religion manifested itself not only in the religion of African American slaves but also in this century's civil rights movement?

7. How did the independent African American church movement develop historically? What were the theological and moral underpinnings of its establishment? Name several of the founders of the independent movement. What were their specific contributions to the African American religious tradition?

8. Why has the African American church become such a critical institution in the lives of African Americans? What role has it played, and does it continue to play, in the life of the African American social community, in education, and in the business world? What contributions has the African American church made to white America, its government and its churches?

ESSAY TOPICS

Spirituals: Their History and Theology

African Religions and Their Influence on American Christianity

The African American Preacher: A New Moses

The Slave and Christianity: Paternalism or Liberation?

The Political Dimensions of African American Religion

WORD EXPLORATION

The following words play significant roles in any discussion of the religious world of African Americans and are worth careful reflection and discussion.

Sacred	Concealed Church	African Spirituality
Secularization	Slavery	Spirituals
Acculturation	Middle Passage	Independent African American Church

FOR FURTHER READING

Cone, James H. *Black Theology and Black Power*. Maryknoll, N.Y.: Orbis Books, rev. ed., 1997.

Lincoln, C. Eric, and Lawrence H. Mamiya. *The Black Church in the African American Experience*. Durham, N.C.: Duke University Press, 1990.

Paris, Peter J. *The Social Teachings of the Black Churches*. Philadelphia: Fortress Press, 1985.

————. *Black Religious Leaders: Conflict in Unity*. Louisville, Ky.: Westminster John Knox Press, 1991.

Raboteau, Albert J. *Slave Religion: The "Invisible Institution" in the Antebellum South*. Oxford: Oxford University Press, 1978, 2004.

Sernett, Milton C. *African American Religious History: A Documentary Witness*. Durham, N.C.: Duke University Press, 1999.

Wilmore, Gayraud S. *Black Religion and Black Radicalism*. Maryknoll, N.Y.: Orbis, 1983, 1998.

WEB SITES

http://www3.amherst.edu/~aardoc/menu.html
   The African American Religion Documentary History Project

http://docsouth.unc.edu/neh/religiouscontent.html
   North American slave narratives

http://www.digitalhistory.uh.edu/black_voices/black_voices.cfm
   Personal voices of African Americans through history

4

The Catholics in the World and in America

ANDREW M. GREELEY AND PAUL MURRAY

313	Emperor Constantine legalizes Christianity in Roman Empire
324–325	Council of Nicaea defines doctrine regarding the divinity of Christ
354–430	St. Augustine of Hippo, theologian and overarching influence on Western church
451	Council of Chalcedon defines doctrine regarding divine and human natures of Christ
480–ca.546	St. Benedict, founder of Western monasticism
1054	The "Great Schism" between Byzantium and Rome
c.1182–1226	St. Francis of Assisi, founder of Order of Friars Minor (Franciscans)
c.1170–1221	St. Dominic, founder of the Dominicans (Friars Preachers)
1491–1556	St. Ignatius of Loyola, founder of the Society of Jesus (Jesuits)
1515–1582	St. Teresa of Ávila, mystic and Carmelite reformer
1545–1563	Council of Trent reforms church governance and pastoral practice
1500s	Inauguration of Franciscan missions in Spanish American territories
1600s	Inauguration of Jesuit missions in French North American territories
1789	Pope Pius VI appoints John Carroll first bishop of the United States
1820s–1920s	Catholic immigrants enter United States in large numbers, including Irish, Germans, Italians, and Poles
1869–1870	First Vatican Council declares papal infallibility
1919	National Catholic Welfare Conference founded as instrument of policy and activity at national level
1950s to present	Spanish-speaking immigrants enter United States in large numbers
1960	John F. Kennedy, first Catholic president of the United States
1962–1965	Second Vatican Council updates Church's image and practice in modern world and declares religious freedom
1968	*Humanae Vitae*, encyclical of Pope Paul VI, opposes artificial contraception
2001	Formation of United States Conference of Catholic Bishops, the instrument of national coordination and outreach of the American bishops

Catholicism is a very old religion. It can be recognized in its present shape at least as far back as fifteen hundred years. It has penetrated, one way or another, most of the world. It has adjusted to many different cultures and appears in many different forms. It has learned much about the ways of human nature and society and hence claims a certain kind of perennial wisdom. It defines its boundaries as both extensive and permeable, including among its members anyone who has not formally left. It has at various times in its history been the only patron of arts and literature and is responsible for preserving drama, music, sculpture, painting, and literature through the troubled centuries after the end of the Roman Empire.

Yet in this country Catholicism is seen as a religion of immigrants, often poor and illiterate immigrants—more than two out of five Catholics are either immigrants or the children of immigrants. Although Catholics were among the first to explore the land that is now the United States—as such names as St. Augustine, St. Petersburg, San Antonio, San Diego, San Francisco, and Los Angeles (the Pueblo of Our Lady, Queen of the Angels) reveal—most Catholic families in the United States are descendants of immigrants who came in the last great European immigration at the turn of the twentieth century, and half of all new immigrants today are Catholics.

Catholicism, then, is a very old, complex, and often sophisticated religious tradition in the world, but a rather new and often, it seems, rather simple religious manifestation in this country, one whose chief goal seems to be to protect the religious faith of immigrants while they are becoming successful in American society. It is sometimes hard for Americans who are familiar with the tolerant and mature Catholicism of, say, Italy or France, to comprehend how Catholicism in this country is the same religion.

WHO AND WHERE
ARE THE CATHOLICS?

About a quarter of the American population is Catholic; of this number, half attend church regularly (at least several times a month) and another quarter attend at least once a month. Fifteen percent of those who are raised Catholics leave the Church—about half of these for another religion (usually at the time of marriage) and the other half for no religion at all.[1] This loss has been canceled out by those who convert to Catholicism and by immigration. Indeed, the proportion of the country that is Catholic may be increasing slightly because of immigration.

Five major ethnic groups account for 80 percent of the Catholic population: Irish, German, Italian, Polish, and Hispanic (which includes Mexican, Puerto Rican, and Cuban, each with its own Catholic tradition).[2] Catholics are concentrated in the big cities and suburbs of the Northeast and North Central regions of the country—most notably Boston, New York, Newark, Philadelphia, Baltimore, Pittsburgh, Cleveland, Cincinnati, Detroit, Chicago, Milwaukee, St. Louis, and Minneapolis/St. Paul. There is also a substantial Catholic population, much of it Hispanic, around the southern and western rim of the country—Miami, New Orleans, San Antonio, Santa Fe, Albuquerque, San Diego, Los Angeles, and San Francisco.

When Catholic immigrants first came to America, many people thought that they would never adjust to American life and become successful Americans unless they abandoned their religion and their ethnic customs. The Irish were thought to be brutal and superstitious drunks, the Italians (according to the National Immigration Commission) to be innately criminal, and the Poles to be inherently ignorant and incapable of education. This notion of Catholic inferiority persisted for a long time.

Despite these beliefs, shared by many of the "best minds" in America, Catholic immigrants and their descendants have been remarkably successful. The average education and income of Catholics are higher than those of Baptists and Methodists, about the same as those of Lutherans, and somewhat less than those of Episcopalians and Presbyterians. Irish Catholics are the most affluent and best-educated gentile ethnic group in America, and Italians are not far behind.

As long ago as the first decade of the twentieth century the proportion of Irish Americans who attended college was above the national average. Polish and Italian Americans caught up in the years immediately after World War II, and are now also slightly above the national average. Only Jews and Episcopalians are more likely than Catholics to attend college today.

Catholics are also at the national average of 2 percent in the proportion who might be considered intellectuals: artists, musicians, writers, and scholars. Moreover, the Catholic intelligentsia attends church services not only more often than do other intellectuals but even more often than do Catholics who are not in the 2 percent that could be classed as intellectuals.

These paradoxes—a church for immigrants who are no longer immigrants, a church for the poor who are no longer poor, a church for the uneducated who are now well educated, a worldwide and complex church that has been simplified to adjust to a new society—explain not only the tensions inside Catholicism today, but also why it is often difficult for non-Catholics to understand Catholicism.

Who is Catholic anyway—the poor Mexican celebrating the Festival of Our Lady of Guadalupe or the Irish professor who makes fun of the pope but goes to mass every day? The answer is that both are Catholic, and between them there are a lot of other types of Catholics. A good rule of thumb for an outsider is that if you think you have finally figured Catholics out, you've almost certainly got it wrong.

Are younger Catholics drifting away from the Church, especially given its current internal chaos and confusion, evidenced by the obvious tendency of Catholics to obey Catholic rules selectively? It does not seem that they are. Religious affiliation and devotion for all Americans correlates with age—the rates go down in the middle and late teens, bottom out in the middle twenties, and then slowly climb to a plateau like that

of the parental generation in the early forties. The curve of the relationship between age and church attendance (and prayer) is the same for Catholics as it is for others. There was a slight increase during the 1970s in the proportion of Americans with no religious identification; but that increase, a result of people marrying later or never marrying, leveled off by 1980, and Catholics were no more affected by it than was anyone else.

American Catholics indeed dissent from certain Catholic doctrines; in 1963 half accepted the Church's teaching on birth control. By 1974 that proportion had fallen to about one-tenth—for clergy as well as laity—and has not increased since then. However, this dissent, though it may have affected frequency of church attendance and financial contributions (half of what they were in 1960, adjusted for inflation), has not lessened Catholic affiliation.

In summary, American Catholics are successful urban immigrants who are loyal to their church despite some disagreement with its leaders. They have adjusted to the changes in the Catholic Church since the Second Vatican Council in 1962 with remarkable ease.

ORGANIZATIONAL CHART

According to canon (or church) law, the basic unit of the Catholic Church is the diocese. Above it stands the pope and below it the parish and the people. The bishop is the key person in the Church, speaking to the local church for the universal and to the universal Church for the local. This canonical definition came into being when there was only one parish in each city, the cathedral was the parish church, and the bishop was the parish priest. In fact, from the empirical point of view of most Catholics, the parish and the parish priest *are* the Church. If they like their parish priest and think he's doing a good job (especially in liturgy—that is, worship and preaching), most Catholics are content with their church.

In many dioceses, parishes are organized into deaneries or vicariates, but the deans and vicars have little real power in comparison with the bishop. Moreover dioceses are organized into archdioceses, but the only power an archbishop has over his "suffragans" (bishops) is that he presides at their meetings. Since the Second Vatican Council, in most countries there is a national conference of bishops that holds meetings, passes laws, maintains a national bureaucracy, and tries to collect voluntary taxes from the various dioceses. But the United States Conference of Catholic Bishops, for example, has no authority over what a local bishop does and can neither supervise him nor enforce its rules on him.

In most countries there is also a papal nuncio or an apostolic delegate (the former if the country has formal diplomatic relations with the Vatican, as the United States now does) who is the pope's representative and supervises in his name the Church in that country.

The papal representative, the national conference, and the individual bishops report to Rome (called *ad limina*, the "doorway" of Peter) every five years. This normally means they report to the Roman Curia, which might be thought of as both the pope's cabinet and his personal staff. There has been some debate in recent years about the relationship between the bishops and the Roman Curia. The Roman Curia's version in practice is that the bishop is a bureaucrat in their service. But others, including many bishops, hold that the pope, as Bishop of Rome, governs the whole Church together with his brother bishops (though he is not dependent upon them) and that the Roman Curia ought to work for the bishops and be responsible to them.

A Synod of Bishops was established by the Second Vatican Council to meet every three years with the pope and advise him about problems within the Church. Some bishops hoped that this Synod eventually would become the highest governing body of the Church and that the Roman Curia would be subordinate to it. In fact, however, the Synod is itself now firmly under Roman Curial control and many bishops have lost interest in it.

It must be said candidly that many American bishops, even some of the more conservative ones, privately resent the occasional and, as they see it, arbitrary interference of the Roman Curia in their work, though they would never dare to say so in public.

In addition to the diocesan structure of the Catholic Church, there are many communities of men and women religious, some of whom are relatively independent of local bishops and do the specialized work of the Church, such as education, medical care, and missionizing. The most famous orders are the Jesuits, the Benedictines, the Dominicans, the Franciscans, and the Carmelites;[3] the last three include both male and female groups—indeed, many of each. They are usually governed by a "general" (now often called "president"), who may live in Rome, and by the Congregation of Religious, a part of the Roman Curia.

HOW THE CHURCH ACTUALLY WORKS

This elaborate and well-defined structure may create an initial impression of a tightly organized monolith in which orders are passed down from the pope to the local parish by a centralized power elite that has control over everything that happens in Catholicism. Nothing, in fact, could be further from the truth. Partially because of principles[4] and partially because of inefficiency, the Church leaves enormous power in the hands of the local bishop and the parish priest. Occasionally it might elect to intervene directly in the affairs of a diocese or a religious order, especially in the case of a financial scandal, though usually only after the harm has been done. Generally, however, the parish priest can do pretty much whatever he wants, if he doesn't mind an occasional complaint letter sent to Rome or an occasional phone call of reprimand from the local chancery office (the bishop's staff and cabinet).

Nothing better illustrates the radical decentralization and pluralism of the Catholic Church than its financial procedures.

There is no consolidated budget for the whole Church, for the various national conferences, or even for the individual dioceses.[5] Rome does not really know what the Jesuits, for example, are doing with their money, or what the American Church is doing with its money. No one beyond the local diocese oversees its financial workings. A bishop has almost no control of how the religious orders and their institutions spend their money. Each Catholic high school and college, for example, has its own budget. Moreover, the bishops' control of the finances of local parishes is dependent upon the pastor's willingness to submit accurate reports.

One might say that this system maximizes local freedom and autonomy. One might also say that it is chaotic and invites corruption. One might also say that, given the flawed nature of the human condition, it works on the whole not too badly. One cannot say, however, that this is the way a highly centralized power structure works.[6]

Catholicism, therefore, is a mysterious combination of centralized control and local freedom, a system which has worked fairly well for centuries and does not seem likely to change in the near future. This governance style can be illustrated by the issue of young women acting as acolytes (those who light the candles) at the Eucharist (worship service). The Vatican forbids this practice, not as a matter of Catholic doctrine, but as a matter of disciplinary practice, probably because it fears that such young women might think they have a chance to be priests someday. In the United States, however, women who may be indifferent to the possible ordination of women are often infuriated by what they take to be intolerable discrimination against their daughters. (The daughters don't particularly like it either, to put it mildly.) So the rule is evaded or ignored in many, probably most, American Catholic parishes. Some bishops, but by no means all, have written letters to their priests asking that the rule be kept. Such instructions are usually disregarded; most priests would much rather face an occasional complaint

from a chancery bureaucrat than the wrath of their women parishioners.

A working compromise has emerged: there are no women acolytes (and perhaps no women distributing Holy Communion when there are enough priests available) at those times when a bishop visits the parish. That way the bishop is not personally embarrassed by being forced to witness what he knows is going on anyway, and no one can complain to the Vatican that he tolerated by his presence that which is forbidden.

Whether or not one approves of such a flexible style of governance, in which theoretical rules are sometimes interpreted out of existence to respond to local circumstances, this is the way the Catholic Church normally operates in the real (as opposed to the "organizational chart") world. For many non-Catholics this description—which you will not find in any official Catholic textbook—might come as a shock. They have always heard the "organizational chart" explanation and are astonished to hear that in reality the Catholic Church is not the massive, centralized monolith that they thought it was. They are also amazed that practices in one Catholic parish (in dealing with cases of remarriage after divorce, for example) may differ dramatically from the practices of the neighboring parish, and that Catholics now "shop" among parishes to find a parochial style and solutions that are responsive to what they think are their needs.

In fact, however, it has always been that way. What is different today is that the variety and the freedom of the local Catholic communities is more public, to the joy of "liberal" Catholics and the dismay of "conservative" Catholics. It is precisely this astonishing grassroots variety and flexibility that has enabled American Catholics to remain Catholic on their own terms during the troubling last half century of Catholic history. In this decision to be Catholic, but on their own terms, American Catholics (and those in the British Isles, too, for that matter) have merely caught up with how the Catholics of continental Europe have been living for years, if not for centuries. The argument here is not that this is the way they ought to live, but that this is the way they do live, for the most part with serene consciences.

A Democratic Church?

It is often said, especially by bishops who feel that they have to say it, that the Catholic Church is not a democracy. This statement is ambiguous. It describes the current organizational chart of Catholicism pretty well, though as we have seen it is less accurate in its description of how Catholicism works in practice. As a historical generalization, however, it is utterly false.

For much of the first thousand years of Catholic history bishops, including the Bishop of Rome, were elected by the vote of their clergy and people. Several popes who are also saints said that it was a grave sin for bishops to be selected any other way. Pope Leo III, for example, wrote (in elegant Latin), "He who presides over all should be chosen by all."[7] The cardinals, who were then the parish priests of Rome, would gather in St. Peter's Cathedral to nominate a new pope. They would then bring him out on the balcony for approval by the people. If the crowd cheered, he was crowned. If they booed, the cardinals would go back and try again.

Most of the great medieval orders still elect their own leaders, either for life, as in the case of the Benedictine abbot, or for limited terms (three years for a Dominican provincial). Moreover, no major statement from a pope or a council was issued without words such as "with the assent of the whole Christian people." It was even argued that such decisions were not valid without the assent of the people.

Thus the governmental structure of the Catholic Church was once far more democratic than it is today, indeed almost riotously democratic. There is no theological reason why it could not become that again. Indeed, a democratization of Catholic Church structure would return the Church to more traditional and more orthodox practice.

Cardinals and Monsignors

A word should be said about two common honorary offices in the Church: the monsignor and the cardinal.

In the United States, a monsignor is usually a priest who for one reason or another is awarded with an honorary office as a member of a papal household.[8] The office carries no special power but it does provide strikingly colorful robes. It is awarded much less frequently than it used to be.

A cardinal is technically the pastor of one of the parish churches of Rome (though in fact a vicar almost always carries out the work for him) and, in a remnant of ancient practice, is designated as one of the papal electors until he reaches his eightieth birthday. In current Church law there can be only 120 cardinals under eighty years of age. Beyond his occasional role as a papal elector, the cardinal theoretically has no powers besides those given to him as a bishop, Curial official, or (in a few cases) priest.[9] However, the prestige of the office, its long history, its striking robes, and the pope's frequent use of cardinals as close advisers make it potentially a very powerful position indeed.

The Catholic "Story"

The crucial question with which this essay began, however, remains: Why have this large international institution in the first place? Why have popes and cardinals and monsignors and Jesuits and Dominicans and Franciscans? Why is Catholicism so different from other Christian denominations, which don't seem to need all this fancy stuff? What does it all have to do with God and human relationships to God?

The answer to that question goes beyond organizational structure and theological differences to the root of religion itself. Catholicism pictures the relationship of God to the world and of humans to God differently than other forms of Christianity. Its picture is not completely different, but sufficiently

American Catholics and the Arts

Do religious beliefs make a difference in how people live? Does Catholic "imagination" have real life consequences? Sociological investigation of several behavioral areas, including family, sexuality, community, and the arts, suggests that religion does yield perceptible differences.

The concept of Catholic imagination draws from the work of theologian David Tracy, who noticed a fundamental difference in outlook between Catholic and Protestant theologies. Catholic theologians stress the nearness of God to the world; that is, the world reveals and brings humans into contact with God through, for example, family, sexuality, community, and art. Experiences in these areas show what God is like.

Protestantism, as known through its classic theological works, presents a different outlook, one that emphasizes God's distance or absence from the world. While family, sexuality, and community are also important from this perspective, they are not in themselves ways of knowing what God is like.

Reducing each outlook to a word, one might say that Catholicism emphasizes the "immanence" of God, while Protestantism emphasizes God's "transcendence." Does this theological difference yield an observable difference in, for example, interest in the fine arts? Despite the fact that American Catholics are not popularly known for their involvement in the arts, sociological data indicate strong Catholic interest in the arts.

Examination of data from the 1993 General Social Survey of the National Opinion Research Center, shows the following (in percentages):

Respondents	Catholics	Protestants
say they like opera	27	19
say they like classical music	55	47
report attending a dance performance in last year	24	15
report attending a music performance in last year	21	13
report attending a visual arts performance in last year	47	35
report attending a fine arts performance or exhibition in last year	56	44

All of these results are statistically significant. That means the differences between Catholic and Protestant populations in fine arts activities are not attributable to chance alone. There really is some behavioral difference between these two populations. Religious outlook, including "sacramental imagination," does make a difference in the choices that people make and how they conduct their lives. This finding does not mean that Catholics are better than Protestants or vice versa. It does mean, however, that to understand these populations it is necessary to take religion into consideration.

(For more information see "Catholics and the Fine Arts," at www.agreeley.com.)

so to produce a distinct approach to religious behavior.

Religion is poetry before it becomes prose. It is experience, image, story, ritual, and community before it becomes doctrine, code, and cult. Because we are rational creatures, we must reflect on our religious poetry and translate it into prose. Poetry is open to many different interpretations, so it is necessary to have some kind of community that can examine new interpretations critically to make sure they do not depart from the tradition of the story. Nonetheless, religion originates in and takes its power from its poetry, experiences, images, stories, rituals, and communities. If one wants to know why one religion is ultimately different from another religion, one must examine the different poetries of these religions. The Catholic "story" of God and humankind is somewhat different from that of other denominations. One might not like the conclusions that come from this different story and, when one hears the story itself, one might not find it particularly appealing. However, the point here is that if one wishes to understand Catholics, one ought to know the story; and if one wants to be friends with Catholics, one ought to listen to the story, not necessarily with approval, but at least with sympathetic understanding.

In brief, the Catholic story (which explains such things as votive candles, rosaries, medals, saints, a large international organization, and a papacy) is that the world tells us what God is like and that we respond to the God who is revealed to the world, not merely as individuals, but as members of communities.

THE CATHOLIC EXPERIENCE

Unlike some other Christian religious denominations, Catholicism experiences the world as "grace-full." It is not afraid to say that all the creatures of the earth and all the experiences of human life are hints of what God is like. The world is sacramental in the sense that it is a metaphor for God—it gives us a hint of what God is like. Catholicism is not worried about contaminating God by comparing God to creatures and human experiences.

Perhaps the reason for this approach to God is that in its very earliest years Catholicism, filled with the optimism that came from its memory of the Easter experience, appropriated everything it thought was good, true, and beautiful in paganism and turned these adoptions to Christian purpose. If a pagan city had a special goddess to protect it, when the city became Christian it was awarded to a Christian saint whose life was thought to be a story of God's love. If a symbol told a pagan story of the return of spring (like the Brigid cross in Ireland) it was turned into a Christian symbol of Jesus the light of the world. If a pagan goddess was responsible for taking care of poets, she would be replaced by a Christian patron with the same duties (thus was the Irish goddess Brigid converted to St. Brigid). If another symbol told the story of the divinity's protection of fertility (as did the so-called Irish cross with its union of male and female symbols), then it was converted into a symbol of God's life-giving love. If washing in water was a rite of initiation into pagan cults, so baptism would come to be a rite of death and rebirth for new Christians.[10]

The argument here is not that one should accept this version of the relationship between God and world, but rather that one should understand how Catholicism tends to experience that relationship. Obviously it has its weaknesses, most notably a tendency to superstition and a mixture of Christianity and paganism that is called folk religion. But the alternative, Catholics would argue, is a much less "grace-full" and hence a far bleaker world, a "God-forsaken world" instead of a "God-full" world.

CATHOLIC IMAGERY

Because the Catholic experience is of a world filled with God, Catholic imagery tends to be sacramental. "Grace is everywhere," as the novelist Georges Bernanos writes at the end of his classic *The Diary of a Country Priest*.

The Seven Sacraments of Catholicism

Sacrament	Meaning	When performed
Baptism	Baptism represents the new life and cleansing power that is available through the sacrifice of Jesus Christ. Baptism frees people from the stain of original sin and allows them to receive sanctifying grace.	Catholics can be baptized, usually by pouring water over the head, from infancy on up through adulthood. If a baby is being baptized, parents may select "godparents" to welcome the child into the community of faith. Baptized adults who convert to Catholicism from another Christian denomination don't usually need to be rebaptized.
Confirmation	Confirmation is a sacrament of initiation that welcomes a Catholic into a deeper level of understanding and celebrates the training and knowledge he or she has attained. Confirmation honors the role of the Holy Spirit in building a strong faith.	Customs vary, but in the U.S., the usual age for confirmation for those born into the Catholic faith is around twelve or thirteen. Confirmands make promises of faith before their families and the bishop.
Communion/ Eucharist	Catholics believe that the Eucharist, or communion meal, is the "real presence" of Christ and not merely symbolic or a memorial of the Last Supper. When Catholics eat the bread, they believe it is miraculously transformed into the physical body of Jesus Christ.	The Eucharist is what makes a Catholic mass a mass. Mass is performed daily in some parishes, weekly in others. To make it official, the elements of bread and wine must be blessed by a Catholic priest, although laypeople can help with serving. Only baptized fellow Catholics are invited to partake. Children begin to receive communion around age seven.
Reconciliation	Reconciliation is made possible when Catholics confess their sins in person to a priest and feel genuine sorrow. The priest offers absolution, or an assurance of God's forgiveness.	Some Catholics confess weekly, as used to be the standard expectation; others, less often. Confession typically happens in a private confessional booth in a parish church. It is entirely confidential.
Ordination (Holy Orders)	Men take special vows to be deacons, priests, or bishops in the Church. They must be ordained before they can perform the mass, baptize a baby, or preside over other sacraments.	Ordinands take vows depending on the office to which they are being ordained. A bishop lays hands on their heads to confer priestly authority.
Anointing the Sick	This sacrament imparts a special grace to soothe the spirit of an ill person, and also absolves unconfessed sin.	Formerly called "extreme unction" or "last rites," this ritual used to be commonly performed only when death was imminent, but it is now more common at all stages of serious illness. A priest or bishop uses consecrated oil to anoint the recipient's forehead.
Marriage	Marriage serves as a reminder of God's faithfulness and his commitments to humanity. For Catholics, marriage is a vocation, or an opportunity to serve God.	Some Catholic weddings are performed with mass and some without, typically on a weekday or Saturday. A priest or deacon must be present. For marriage to be considered a sacrament, both parties must intend for the marriage to be permanent, promise to be faithful to each other, and be open to the possibility of children.

The realities and experiences of human life are not exactly what God is, but they are not totally different either. God lurks everywhere, revealing goodness and love. Catholic imagery says that God is like fire and water, birth, eating and drinking, the moon, the sun and the stars, the human body, and sexual love. Such notions may seem dangerous to others because of the risk of idolatry, but to Catholics they are wonderful hints of what life means.

The Church says that some events are Sacraments with a capital "S" because they are such powerful hints of what God is like. Thus the Eucharist, a common meal eaten with friends, does not make all family meals holy. Rather it is holy and Jesus comes to us in a special way in this reenactment of his last meal with his followers because all family meals are potentially graceful and potential hints that our relationship with God is familial.

The fact that the Church has declared marriage a Sacrament does not make human sexual passion holy. Rather it is precisely because human sexual love between permanently committed partners is a hint of God's passion for us and hence enormously holy that it becomes a Sacrament.

Everything is holy. Some things become especially holy because Jesus has confirmed their holiness and made them rich and deep sources of grace.[11] Hence birth (Baptism), life cycle (Confirmation, Ordination, Sacrament of the Sick), and reconciliation (Confession, or the Sacrament of Reconciliation, as it is now called) complete the list of Catholicism's seven Sacraments. But in the Catholic imagination they can become especially holy because everything is holy.

The most distinctive of Catholic symbols is that of Mary the Mother of Jesus, a hint of the mother-love of God. It tells the story of a God who loves us with the power of a father and the tenderness of a mother,[12] of a God who organizes the whole of creation and who gives life and nurturance. Catholics don't confuse God with Mary (and are astonished at the persistent argument of others that they do).[13] Rather, in Mary they see revealed the maternal love of God, and they respond to that love. Anyone who has ever been a mother or been held in the arms of a mother knows that the passionate and tender love of a mother for the child she nurses is a hint of how God loves us. Any religion that has such an image of God's love will have powerful and durable appeal to humankind.

Catholicism has no trouble finding hints of God in such things as devotion to the saints, statues, medals, the changing cycles of the year, art, and music. Naturally abuses of all these good and holy things is possible, but Catholicism does not reject their sacramentality merely because of the possibility of abuse.

The Catholic sacramental imagination makes the world a more lovely and reassuring place—perhaps flawed in many important ways, but not inherently evil. This imagination results in the Catholic story.

THE CATHOLIC STORY

Others may think of the world as inherently evil and of human nature as fundamentally perverse. That may be their story, and it may well more accurately describe human existence. Such a story may have a deeper sense of tragedy and a greater awareness of irony. Others may claim to stare unflinchingly at the cross of the crucified Jesus and see the only true revelation of what God is like. Catholicism claims that it too is aware of irony and tragedy in creation, but it is more aware of hope and grace. It believes deeply in new beginnings, second (and third and fourth and higher-order) chances. It knows about tragedy, but it still believes in happy endings—eventual happy endings anyway. It may seem too lighthearted a religion with all its parties and celebrations, but at least in its best moments it insists that joy and not grief, comedy and not tragedy, are the best explanations of the human condition.

Two quotations sum it up. The first is from Hilaire Belloc, an English Catholic poet of a half-century ago, in one of his "Cautionary Verses":

Wher'er the Catholic sun does shine,
There's always music and laughter and
  good red wine,
At least I've found it so,
Benedicamus Domino![14]

But every Catholic knows that it is not always so. Sometimes there is no laughter, the music is awful, and the wine is sour. So, from St. Teresa of Ávila: "From silly devotions and sour-faced saints, libera nos, Domine!"[15]

CATHOLIC COMMUNITY

Precisely because it believes that human relations are sacramental, the poetry of Catholicism thinks that all human communities reveal God, however imperfectly. In the Catholic story, human groups do not impede our relationship with God; they enhance and support it. We relate more fully to God with the help of others than when we try to do it by ourselves. Individual prayer is necessary and wonderful, but it is far more effective when it is sustained and supported by communal prayer. Hence the Catholic community, organized however imperfectly by the Church institution, is a sacrament of God, especially in the experience of the local parish community.

This element in the Catholic story may be the most offensive to those who say that they don't need a pope, a church, a parish, or a community to relate to God. They can do it by themselves. That is clearly a very different religious story and a better one to those whose story it is. A Catholic response to this point of view (which it would think of as the most rugged of rugged individualism) is that humans don't live by themselves and don't relate to anyone else (including the most intimate lover with whom one shares life) in isolation from the rest of humankind, so it seems strange that they would prefer to deal with God in this way.

CATHOLIC RITUAL

Religious rituals re-enact the story, re-present the images, re-create the experiences, and re-new the community that is constituted by the religious tradition. Therefore Catholic rituals tend to be exuberant, at least when carried out properly. They are rituals of grace, of a present God rather than an absent one, of sacramental imagery, and of stories with hopeful and hence happy endings.

For many this exuberance is too much. They prefer sober, restrained, self-controlled, even somber rituals (Catholics might call them dour). They believe that life is much too serious a business for all the celebration (especially when the celebration is mixed with paganism as at Christmas and Easter). They are entitled to that taste if it is more in keeping with their own religious story, but they should realize that Catholics have a different religious story and rituals that are consistent with that story.

CONCLUSION

What seems so strange to many other Americans about Catholic doctrines, organization, behavior, and practices is not the result necessarily of ignorance, superstition, idolatry, or perversion, but rather of a slightly different religious story. Like all other Christians, Catholics believe in God and Jesus and the Bible. That they may approach these beliefs in a somewhat different fashion is the result of the fact that they tell the Christian story from a somewhat different perspective.

Whether it is a better or worse, richer or poorer story is for everyone to decide for themselves. In order to understand Catholics, however, you must know they have this slightly different story. And to be friends with Catholics it helps to try to hear this story as they hear it, from the inside.

Notes

1. This rate has not changed since 1960.
2. Of the other groups, the largest are the French Canadian, either in New England or as "Cajuns" of Louisiana and Texas, and the Portuguese in New England (including immigrants from the Azores and the Cape Verde Islands). In addition to the "Roman" Catholics, those whose rite (customs, especially the format of the Mass) follows that of the Church of Rome, there are other "Eastern" or "Greek" or "Uniate" Catholics whose rites follow ancient customs different from those of Rome but who remain in communion with the Roman rite. In the United States the largest group are the Ukrainian Catholics, whose churches were suppressed by Stalin but restored by Gorbachev. At one time their Eucharist (Mass) was in Old Slavonic and married men were ordained as priests. Now the liturgy is in English and somewhat different in format (as well as longer) than the Roman Mass. In the United States the ordination of married men is not permitted, much to the offense of the Ukrainians. A patriarch presides over each of these rites, the pope being the patriarch of the Roman rite.
3. Founded, respectively, by St. Ignatius of Loyola, St. Benedict, St. Dominic, St. Francis of Assisi, and St. Simon Stock.
4. The Catholic social principle of subsidiarity says that nothing should be done in any human organization at a higher level that cannot be done just as effectively at a lower level. This principle has been enshrined by name in the charter of the European Community, though it now seems to be ignored by most American Catholic social theorists, who are committed to ever more government intervention.
5. Not consolidated in the sense that the various high schools, colleges, universities, religious orders, and hospitals (for example) are included.
6. What, it may be asked, about the vast wealth of the Vatican? In fact, the Vatican's endowment is not any larger than that of a small-sized Catholic university such as Georgetown. Despite its income from the annual Peter's Pence collection (which is reportedly diminishing each year), the Vatican has been forced to operate at an ever-increasing budget deficit. Should it sell all its "treasures," including the Vatican Museum and the Sistine Chapel? Income from such sales would not notably enhance the Vatican's endowment, and it is not clear what the worth of Michelangelo's frescoes would be, even if they could be peeled off the walls of the Sistine.

   What about all the Catholic property in the big cities? Some of the empty parish "plants" (from which Catholics have moved to the suburbs) may look rich and might cost large sums of money to replace. But their resale value is minimal because no one has any use for a secondhand Catholic church. In fact, subsidies to keep the buildings from falling apart and the school open (for a heavily non-Catholic student body) mean that the "plant" has no real value and indeed is a negative asset—it costs a lot more than the income it produces.

   The Catholic Church may look rich; it may even seem to be rich to some of its leaders. In fact, it is poor, poorer perhaps than it ought to be given its size and, in the United States, anyway, the relative affluence of its membership.
7. "Qui praesidet super omnes, ab omnibus eligatur." The Latin verb *eligo*, it should be noted, is the root from which the word *elect* comes.
8. A fact which has led some priests, usually not monsignors, to say that their empurpled colleague is nothing more than a papal broom sweeper.
9. Some men who were not priests have been named cardinals in the past. It is even possible, according to some, for a layman to be named a cardinal. A laywoman? Not yet anyway!
10. Catholicism in its best moments has always had the courage to adapt foreign cultures to its religious poetry. At other times, it has turned its back on such adaptation, most notably in the sixteenth and seventeenth centuries on adaptations in China, India, and Ethiopia.
11. Note that this is "pre-theological" talk, poetry before prose. Precise theological reflection on the poetry of the Sacraments can be found in any standard Catholic theological book.
12. The image of God as mother as well as father has always been part of the Catholic tradition and was expressed again by Pope John Paul I.
13. Catholics wish that others would listen to them when they talk about the Mother of Jesus, instead of imposing their own preconceptions on that devotion.
14. "Let us praise the Lord!"
15. "Deliver us, Lord!"

STUDY QUESTIONS

1. List four or five characteristics that you believe best describe Catholicism. Compare with a classmate. Have you agreed or disagreed with this chapter?

2. Which major ethnic groups account for the make-up of American Catholicism? How is such diversity considered a contributing factor in what the author describes as the religious "paradox" of American Catholicism?

3. What is the organizational structure of the Catholic Church? Is the structure hierarchical? How so? What roles do persons in the organization play? Which role does the author believe is most representative of the Church? Why?

4. What disagreements have begun to take place between American Catholicism and Catholic doctrine coming from Rome about the role of women in the Church? About birth control? How, in light of such differences, can American Catholicism remain Catholic?

5. What are the roles and functions of the two honorary offices, cardinals and monsignors, in the American Catholic Church? How do these roles relate to the priestly positions in other religious traditions with which you are familiar?

6. What does "sacramental" mean in the Catholic religious tradition? How does the sacramental experience inform the ways in which Catholics relate to the world? Name the seven sacraments of the Catholic Church. What functions do they play in defining social order for Catholics?

ESSAY TOPICS

Women in the Catholic Church

The Historical Development of the Papacy

The Development of Catholicism in the United States

American Catholicism and Native Americans

American Catholicism and American Politics: John F. Kennedy, the First Catholic President

WORD EXPLORATION

The following words play significant roles in any discussion of Catholics in America and are worth careful reflection and discussion:

Ritual	Pope	Rome
Madonna	Canon Law	Sacrament
Priest	Parish	Religious Orders

FOR FURTHER READING

D'Antonio, William V., James D. Davidson, Dean R. Hoge, and Mary L. Gautier. *American Catholics Today: New Realities of Their Faith and Their Church*. Lanham, Md.: Rowman & Littlefield Publishers, Inc., 2007.

Day, Dorothy. *The Long Loneliness*. New York: HarperOne, 1952, 1996.

Dolan, Jay. *The American Catholic Experience: A History from Colonial Times to the Present*. Notre Dame, Ind.: University of Notre Dame Press, 1992.

Greeley, Andrew. *The Catholic Imagination*. Berkeley, Calif.: University of California Press, 2001.

Massa, Mark S. *Catholics and American Culture: Fulton Sheen, Dorothy Day, and the Notre Dame Football Team*. New York: Herder & Herder, 2001.

WEB SITES

http://www.vatican.va/
    Official Web site of the Holy See, with full texts of major church documents

http://www.nccbuscc.org/
    Official Web site of the American Catholic bishops

http://woodstock.georgetown.edu/links/
    Jesuit institution at Georgetown University with list of Catholic links

http://www.cta-usa.org/
    National organization of Catholics withextensive related links

5

The Religious World of Latino/a-Hispanic Americans

JUSTO L. GONZÁLEZ AND CARLOS F. CARDOZA-ORLANDI

1769　Franciscan missionary Junipero de Serra establishes first Christian mission in California

1810　El Grito de Dolores (the Cry of Dolores)—battle cry of the Mexican War of Independence; war with Spain lasts until 1821

1819　United States buys Florida from Spain; most Spanish-speaking people move to Cuba

1845　United States attempts "voluntary annexation" of Texas, resulting in war with Mexico

1857　Constitution of Mexico reconfiscates Mexican landholdings from Catholic Church and works toward separation of Church from state government

1898　Strong expansionist sentiment motivates U.S. involvement in Spanish-American War

1906　Azusa Street Revival in Los Angeles primary catalyst for spread of Pentecostalism

1917　Inhabitants of Puerto Rico become statutory U.S. citizens when President Wilson signs Jones Act

1959　Cuban Revolution overthrows U.S.–backed dictatorial governments of previous decades

1962　United Farm Workers Organizing Committee, led by Cesar Chavez, initiated as independent organization; in 1965 secures a national table grape boycott

1963　Bracero Movement ends, forcing Latin American migratory workers to leave the U.S.

1994　North American Free Trade Agreement established between Canada, Mexico, and the United States

2003　Hispanics become largest minority group in the U.S., with 37.1 million people

A Long and Varied Tradition

Can you name the four countries in the Western Hemisphere with the largest Spanish-speaking populations? Mexico is clearly the largest. Then come Argentina, Colombia, and . . . the United States! Yes, this country has the fourth-largest Spanish-speaking population in the Western Hemisphere, and it is about to become the third. Thus, if you yourself speak Spanish, or if you

---

What's in a Name? Hispanic-Latino/a

During the 1970s, the term *Hispanic* was adopted by the U.S. government to identify people of Latin American or Spanish-speaking descent. The term softened racial connotations and emphasized origin and family background. In recent years and in many circles, the term frequently used is *Latinos/as* in order to emphasize the Latin American and Caribbean background, although the term does not include those in the region whose primary language is not Spanish—i.e., Brazilians. Currently, both terms are officially used by the U.S. government. These terms have acquired interesting regional usages. For example, in the northeast the term *Hispanic* is the most common, while *Latino/a* is mostly used in the southwest. To be Latino/a also has a political force that is beyond language and reclaims culture and gender as resources for personal and communal identity. In some academic circles, the terms are either interchangeable or brought together—Hispanic-Latino/a.

---

have several classmates who do, you are not an exception. On the contrary, if you live in an area where you never hear Spanish, you are indeed an exception. The 1990 census recorded just over 22 million Hispanics in the United States out of a total population of 249 million. Of these, roughly 64 percent had traditional ties with Mexico, 10 percent with Puerto Rico, 5 percent with Cuba, and 21 percent with other countries.

But the Hispanic population has doubled since then. According to the United States Census, as of July 2006 there are 44.3 million Hispanics out of a total population of 299 million. Latino/a-Hispanics represent more than 15 percent of the total population of the United States, with a growth rate of almost 25 percent, which is more than three times the growth of the total population. Moreover, while California, Texas, and Florida are the states with the most Latino/a-Hispanics between 2000 and 2006, Arkansas, Georgia, and South Carolina are the three states with the highest Latino/a-Hispanic growth during the same period. The most reliable demographic information points not only to significant growth but to a redistribution of the Latino/a-Hispanic population to the southern United States. Of these, 64 percent have traditional ties with Mexico, 9 percent with Puerto Rico, almost 8 percent with Central American countries, 3.4 percent with Cuba, and 19 percent with other countries.

How did this come about? Obviously, in recent years there has been a great wave of immigration. But the story is much longer than that. In fact, the first European language to be spoken in what is now the United States was not English but Spanish. As you know, the Englishman Sir Walter Raleigh tried to found a colony in Virginia in 1584, but it failed. Jamestown Colony was founded in 1607, and the Pilgrims arrived at New England in 1620. By that time, the Spanish had explored much of the continent and had even founded cities that are now part of the United States.

Naturally, the explorers came first. Juan Ponce de León landed in Florida in 1521. Between 1539 and 1543 Hernando de Soto reached the Mississippi River and crossed Arkansas and part of Oklahoma. In 1540 Francisco Vásquez de Coronado led an expedition that explored much of what is now Texas, Oklahoma, and Kansas. A few years later, another expedition from Mexico reached Oregon.

Then came the settlers. After a number of failed attempts by other Spaniards, some as far north as the Carolinas, Pedro Menéndez de Avilés founded St. Augustine, Florida, in 1565. Santa Fe, now the capital of New Mexico, was founded in 1610. If you ever visit one of those cities, you will be able to see many signs of their Spanish heritage. At first, the United States did not include any permanent Spanish settlements, only the thirteen former British colonies on the eastern seaboard. However, as the country expanded, it came to include many people whose language was Spanish. For a long time, there were tensions between the United States and Spain over Florida. In 1819, the United States finally bought Florida from Spain. At that time most Spanish-speaking people living in Florida chose to leave and settle in Cuba, but some remained.

The largest geographical expansion of the United States into Spanish-speaking territories, however, took place at the expense of Mexico. First was the independence and eventual annexation of Texas. One of the conditions on which Mexico insisted before granting independence to Texas, and to which the United States agreed, was that Texas would remain an independent republic and would not become part of the United States. In 1845, however, through a joint act of Congress, Texas was made part of the United States.

That also was the year when the famous phrase "manifest destiny" was coined, to refer to the historic task of the United States to encompass all the land "from sea to shining sea." This involved occupying Oregon, whose possession the British disputed, and all Mexican territories directly west of the original thirteen colonies. The Oregon matter was settled through diplomatic channels; the other, by force of arms. The war with Mexico did not last long. It ended in 1848, through the treaty of Guadalupe Hidalgo, which stipulated that for $15 million the United States would purchase from Mexico the present states of New Mexico, Arizona, California, Utah, Nevada, and part of Colorado. Also, by

the same treaty, Mexico agreed to accept the annexation of Texas by the United States.

Even after the treaty of Guadalupe Hidalgo had moved the border to the Rio Grande, Mexicans continued their age-old tradition of moving freely north and south across the river. They had families on both sides of the border, so they would cross back and forth in order to find jobs, or simply to go visiting. Then, around 1880, as railroads established closer links with the East, the territories that the United States had acquired became part of the national economy and began requiring a larger labor force. This in turn meant that more people moved from Mexico to the United States than the other way around.

Although you may have heard much about the patrolling of the border and about immigration laws, the main factors governing Mexican and other Latin American migration have been the relative economic and political conditions on both sides of the border. When things have been good in the United States and bad in Mexico, there has been a veritable flood of immigration, no matter what the law may have said or what the border patrol may have done. When things have been good in Mexico and not so good in the United States, immigration has practically stopped.

Between 1909 and 1929, it is estimated that about one million Mexicans—roughly one-tenth of the entire population of Mexico—migrated to the United States. This was the time of the Mexican Revolution, which caused great hardship for many people. It was also a time of economic expansion in the United States. Then came the Great Depression, and Mexicans ceased coming to a country where there was no work. Furthermore, throughout the Southwest there was a widespread sentiment that "Mexicans" were taking jobs that belonged to "Americans," and as a result almost half a million "Mexicans"—many of whom were born in the United States—were deported, as you may have seen in the movie *Mi Familia*. Later the situation changed again. Farmers in the United States needed laborers, and arrangements such as the Braco Treaty were made so that farm workers could come from Mexico. Although in theory they were allowed to come to the United States only temporarily, many stayed. Eventually this program was legally discontinued. Whenever there was a shortage of farm laborers, however, other similar means—some legal and some not—have been found to provide farmers with the laborers they required by bringing them across the border. More recently, when vast reserves of oil were discovered in Mexico and the price of oil was high, immigration into the United States slowed to a trickle, only to accelerate again when the price of oil dropped and the Mexican economy came to the verge of collapse.

Similar factors have also governed immigration from other Spanish-speaking places. Puerto Rico became an American territory in 1898, and its inhabitants became American citizens in 1917. Therefore, they can travel freely between Puerto Rico and the mainland without passports or other documents. After World War II, Puerto Ricans began migrating to the mainland in vast numbers. As in the case of Mexico, those numbers have depended mostly on the economy of the island.

The case of Cuba is similar. In the second half of the nineteenth century, when Cuba was still a Spanish colony, many Cubans went into exile in Tampa and Key West, and their descendants still live there. Since Cuba's independence in 1902, migration to the United States—particularly to Florida—has depended on the political and economic conditions in Cuba. Large numbers of Cubans fled to southern Florida after the revolution of 1959, led by Fidel Castro.

More recently, as war, unrest, and economic collapse have shaken countries in Central America and elsewhere, immigrants from those countries have come to the United States in large numbers. In the late 1970s and early 1980s, for instance, economic conditions in the Dominican Republic became desperate and many Dominicans settled in New York and neighboring areas. By the mid-1980s,

civil war and human rights violations in El Salvador and Guatemala uprooted hundreds of thousands of people, and more than half a million settled in southern California.

In short, Hispanics in this country are both recent immigrants and descendants of people who have been here for centuries. The ancestors of some Hispanics were here even before the country itself existed. In many cases, they did not come into the country; rather, the country engulfed them. Although many are recent immigrants, almost three out of four Hispanics are native citizens of the United States. At the same time, they are preserving their language and cultural identity. Thus, three out of four Hispanics, even those whose families have been here for centuries, still speak Spanish, although most also speak English.

Even more, Latino/a-Hispanics represent one of the youngest population sectors of the nation, with a median age of approximately twenty-seven years for both males and females. Latino/a-Hispanics are a force in the United States, both in the present and in the future.

THE RELIGION OF THE EARLY SETTLERS

Obviously, the Spanish language is no more native to this land than is English. Both languages are here because of a long history that involves immigrants coming here from Europe and, in the case of Hispanics, also from other Spanish-speaking countries in the Western Hemisphere. Elsewhere in this book you have studied how this affected the original Americans, who lived here long before Columbus; you have also studied how the English language and the religious traditions of Britain were brought here. Now, in order to understand the traditions and religious life of Hispanics, we must say a word about the Spanish who first came to these lands.

These people came from Spain to the Western Hemisphere—to what is now both Latin America and the United States—for a number of reasons. Many were following dreams and legends: Ponce de León came to Florida in quest of the "fountain of youth," and the early explorers of the Southwest were looking for the Seven Cities of Cíbola. Some hoped to get rich through mining or trade; others were simply curious. But in almost every case, even among those who were dreaming of youth, gold, and power, there was also a strong religious motivation. That is why so many of the cities they founded bear names of saints: San Antonio, San Agustín, San Francisco, Santa Mónica, Santa Paula, San Juan, and so on. (You may wish to look in the index to an atlas of the United States to see how many names of cities and places begin with San or Santa.)

Spain was a deeply religious country. Isabella and Ferdinand, who ruled there at the time of Columbus, were given the title of "Los Reyes Católicos"—the Catholic Sovereigns. Their Catholicism, however, was of a very special kind. In 711 Spain had been invaded and conquered by the Moors, who were Muslims. Soon, however, small Christian kingdoms had emerged in the north. For several centuries Christians, Muslims, and Jews had lived together. There were frequent wars between various rulers, Christian as well as Muslim; but in such wars religion seldom played a crucial role. Indeed, quite often a Christian ruler would make an alliance with a Muslim counterpart in order to make war against another Christian neighbor. Even El Cid, the famous warrior who later was depicted as a great Christian champion, on occasion fought on the side of the Moors and against other Christians—his very title, "Cid," comes from an Arabic word meaning "lord." This historical period of Jewish, Christian, and Muslim coexistence is called the period of *convivencia* (to live together) and marks an interesting era of religious and cultural exchange.

Then, shortly before the time of Columbus, things changed. The northern Christian kingdoms—particularly Castile—decided to undertake a great crusade against the infidel, who must be expelled from the peninsula. In their view it was the task of Christians in Spain to unify the country under one crown and one faith. They would look back at their history and see it, not as it had really been, but as a great "Reconquista"—reconquest—against the Moorish invader. They felt God had given them this task, and in order to accomplish it they had to be faithful to God and to the Christian religion.

In 1492, just a few months before Columbus sailed, the last Moorish stronghold in Spain, Granada, had fallen to the armies of Ferdinand and Isabella. The terms of surrender included a number of guarantees for the Moors and their customs. But these were soon forgotten, and by 1502 all Moors living in Spain were ordered to either convert to Christianity or leave the country. In 1492, just about the same time that Columbus sailed, some 200,000 Spanish Jews had been forced to leave under similar circumstances. It mattered little that these Muslims and Jews considered themselves Spanish, or that they had lived in Spain for generations. (Remember, the Moors had been in Spain roughly twice as long as English-speaking people have lived in what is now the United States.) They were not Christians, and there was no place for them in Spain, whose "manifest destiny"—especially after the birth of Protestantism a few years later—was to uphold true, pure, Catholic Christianity.

This combination of Catholicism and nationalism was also the main reason why the Inquisition became so powerful in Spain. It was feared that some Muslims or Jews who had declared themselves Christian and accepted baptism might in fact be practicing the old religion in secret. Anyone who did not eat pork was suspect. In Seville, an officer of the Inquisition would climb to the top of the cathedral tower on Saturdays and take note of any chimney where no smoke could be seen—perhaps the inhabitants were Jews keeping the Sabbath and should be investigated.

Conquest and Protest

Then God seemed to place a new challenge before Spain. Across the ocean, vast new lands were "discovered"—lands ripe for conquest, exploitation, and Christianization. These three motives—conquest, exploitation, and Christianization—went hand in hand. At times, it is difficult to distinguish among them. When Spanish explorers met a native ruler, they were supposed to read to him a strange document called the *Requerimiento*—a Spanish word whose meaning is somewhere between a request and a demand. This document claimed that Christ had been made absolute ruler over the entire world, that he had given his authority to the pope as his representative on earth, and that the pope in turn had given these lands to the Spanish crown. Those who heard the *Requerimiento* were invited to accept these facts and submit to their new masters. If they refused—or if they simply did not understand what was being said, usually in Spanish—they became rebellious subjects, and therefore those reading the document to them were free to take military action against them, to take their lands, and to enslave them. Strange as it may seem, the regulations regarding the reading of the *Requerimiento* were enacted by well-meaning people who thought they were protecting the rights of the native inhabitants!

Another indication of the manner in which Christianity was brought to these lands is the system of *encomiendas*. The word *encomendar* means "to entrust." Therefore, an encomienda was a group of natives who were "entrusted" to a Spanish settler in order to be taught the rudiments of Christianity. In exchange for that service, which they had not requested, and for their keep, which they could easily earn in their traditional occupations with much less work, the natives were to work for the settler—the *encomendero*. Again, those in Spain who issued laws regarding the encomiendas thought that they were doing what was right and apparently believed that through this system they were truly serving and protecting the "Indians," as Native Americans were mistakenly called.

Needless to say, both the *Requerimiento* and the encomiendas were very much abused. In theory, they were means to make certain that the native inhabitants of these lands were treated justly. In fact, they functioned as excuses for violence and exploitation.

Most Spanish settlers, and even most religious leaders, were convinced that this was a proper and just way to do things. They were used to judging everything by European standards, and therefore they had very little appreciation for the native people, their culture, or their family lives, all of which were being destroyed.

There were, however, others who saw things very differently. At first these were mostly Dominicans, and later also Jesuits and Franciscans. These are all religious orders whose members have vows of poverty—they cannot own anything. For that reason, they were often used as the vanguard of missionary work. Many lived among the native people (as you may have seen in the movie *The Mission*), so they could understand the tragic side of the conquest—that people were dying, families were being broken up, and entire tribes were being wiped out. Some missionaries endeavored to go out into Native American territory far ahead of the soldiers and settlers, to help the people organize themselves into towns that they hoped would provide a greater chance of survival. That was the origin of many of the "missions" in the West and Southwest. Others responded by raising their voice of protest.

These voices of protest in Spanish (and Portuguese) America are one of the bright points in the history of the Christian church. At a time when most people, including just about all the top leaders of both church and state, were convinced that Spain was leading the world in doing God's will, these people thought otherwise and said so quite plainly, even at great personal risk. Antonio de Montesinos, a Dominican priest in Hispaniola (the island that is now Haiti and the Dominican Republic), preached the first sermon on this topic. Among many other very harsh things, he said:

> Tell me, by what right do you wage such detestable wars on these people who lived mildly and peacefully in their own lands, where you have consumed infinite numbers of them with unheard-of murders and desolations? Are they not men? Do they not have rational souls? Are you not bound to love them as you love yourselves? How can you lie in such profound and lethargic slumber? Be sure that in your present state you can no more be saved than the Moors or Turks who do not have and do not want the faith of Jesus Christ.[1]

Hundreds of others protested similarly. Probably the most famous is Bartolome de Las Casas (see sidebar), who spent a lifetime traveling back and forth between Spain and the colonies. He would lobby in Spain to have laws enacted for the protection of the Native Americans and then would come back to the colonies to try to have them enforced. When the settlers found a way to get around the new laws, he would hurry back to Spain and try to plug whatever loopholes there were. Others voiced their protest by refusing to give Communion to those who had taken lands from the native people—which was just about everybody who owned any real estate. These dissenters persisted even when they were ordered by higher church authorities to give Communion to the settlers. Many were silenced and sent back to Spain. Others were murdered. But still the protest continued. Eventually, even in the famous University of Salamanca, in Spain, there were some who questioned the legitimacy of the conquest. Some say that Charles V himself, moved by all these voices of protest, for a while con-

sidered canceling the entire colonial enterprise. Whether that claim is true or not, its very existence is an indication of the extent of the protest against the injustices that were being committed.

Thus, the Christianity that came to Spanish America was marked by contrasts that today we find striking. It was intolerant

---

Bartolome de las Casas (1484–1566)

De Las Casas, a Dominican priest, returned all the way to Spain to protest the inhumane treatment of native peoples in the Caribbean and the Americas, arguing that Native Americans had souls (a radical thought at the time) and that they deserved Christian teaching, not slaughter.

Now in God's name consider, you who read this, what sort of deeds are these, and whether they do not surpass every imaginable cruelty and injustice, and whether it squares well with such Christians as these to call them devils; and whether it could be worse to give the Indians into the charge of the devils of hell than to the Christians of the Indies. . . . the Spaniards of the Indies have tamed and trained the strongest and most ferocious dogs to kill and tear the Indians to pieces.

Listen and see, all you who are true Christians, and also you who are not, whether such deeds have ever been heard of in the world; to feed the said dogs they take many Indians in chains with them on their journeys, as though they were herds of swine; and they kill them, making public butchery of human flesh; and one says to the other, "lend me a quarter of one of these villains to give to my dogs to eat, until I kill." It is as though they were lending a quarter or pork or of mutton.

---

and authoritarian. It found ways to justify wanton war, cruelty, and exploitation. Yet many within it raised voices of protest and criticized the entire colonial enterprise with a firmness that had no parallel in the British colonial enterprise—or, later, in the United States' continued conquest of Native Americans' lands, which destroyed and uprooted entire tribes.

A Mixture of Cultures and Traditions

There was much more contact between Europeans and Native Americans in the Spanish colonies than in the British colonies of North America. There were many reasons for this. For example, the Spanish came earlier and settled in the areas where gold and precious metals were most abundant. They needed the native inhabitants to work in the mines. In contrast, British settlers in North America came later, and they came to farm. In order to farm, they needed land; therefore, the native inhabitants were simply pushed farther and farther west. Also, very few women came from Spain in the early stages of the conquest, so there was more intermarrying of races. As the native population dwindled in many areas and slaves were brought from Africa, the practice of mixed racial unions continued. Later immigrants came to Latin America from various parts of Asia—especially China and Korea—and their genes too were added to the pool. Today's Hispanics in the United States represent that entire history. Therefore, today you may find some "Hispanics" who look like Africans, some who look like Europeans, some who look like Native Americans, some who look like Asians, and many who look like a mixture of two or more of these. What makes them "Hispanic" is not race but the Spanish language and the culture and traditions that have resulted from all this mixture.

This mixture of cultures can also be seen in the field of religion. Most of the early Spanish missionaries thought that whatever religion was already here was of the devil and should be entirely rejected. Similarly, they also felt that the religions of the Africans and Asians were demonic and threatened the security of the European establishment. Yet matters were not that simple. Native and African peoples had dances and other ceremonies for just about every occasion—planting, harvest, building, birth, puberty, marriage, death, rain, drought, and so on. The missionaries saw that they could use some of those traditions to communicate and teach their faith. Thus developed hundreds of religious customs in which to this day one can see the mixture of the native, African, and European elements.

For example: When Queen Isabella heard that the "Indians" in the Caribbean bathed every day, amid much shouting and celebration, and seemed to make a ritual out of it, she gave instructions that such an ungodly custom should be stopped. (What she objected to was not so much the ritual as the bath itself. It is said that she once took a bath, and felt that it was a terrible sin!) But then the island of Puerto Rico was consecrated to St. John the Baptist, and on his feast day it was customary to reenact the baptism of Jesus. The native people took that as an opportunity to practice their tradition of communal public bathing, which had always had religious significance for them. To this day, on the feast day of St. John the Baptist, thousands of Puerto Ricans wade into the sea, even with their clothes on, in a celebration that may look like a wild party but has religious overtones that go back for centuries.

Naturally, Native Americans also played an active role in combining their traditions with those of the newcomers, sometimes even hoodwinking the missionaries. In a city in Bolivia, for example, the parish priest of a small church dedicated to Saints Peter and Paul commissioned one of his parishioners to make statues of these two saints. After several weeks, the man arrived with two statues. They were so large that they could not be put inside the church, so they were placed at each side of the entrance. The priest was delighted to see people flocking to pay their respects to Peter and Paul. It is only recently that scholars have discovered that "Peter and Paul" were in fact ancient images of local deities, which the supposed sculptor had taken from their original setting and moved to the church. No wonder so many people came to pay their respects. Eventually, even in the minds of those who knew the true origin of the statues, the two Christian saints became confused with the ancient gods.

Another example of the same phenomenon: In several places, altars built with native labor have been found to contain images of ancient gods, which the workers apparently hid there when the church was being built, so that they could continue coming before such altars and worshiping in good conscience.

A similar pattern developed with the coming of slaves from Africa. They too brought their religion with them. It was part of their identity and an important means of psychological survival. When they were forced to become Christians, they often did so by equating their traditional gods with Christian saints. In some areas, the ancient god of entrances (in the Yoruban pantheon, for example, *Ele-qua*), was equated with St. Peter, who was always depicted with keys. St. Barbara, the patron saint of artillerymen, became the same as Chango, who ruled over thunder. The old practices of healing with herbs and potions continued and, because some of them seemed to work, slowly made their way among people who were not necessarily of African descent. (That is why to this day, in some areas of Miami and New York, you may find *botanicas*—stores where medicinal herbs are sold jointly with all kinds of ingredients for potions that are supposed to have medicinal and even magical powers.)

PROTESTANT CHALLENGES AND GROWTH

Independence from Spain came for most Latin American countries in the early nineteenth century. With independence came the Protestants, mostly from Britain and the United States. A few came as immigrants, but most came as entrepreneurs or as missionaries. The entrepreneurs built railroads, factories, and various sorts of trade and industry. The missionaries brought new ideas, not only about the meaning of Christianity, but also about how the church and the society ought to be organized. Many were convinced that Protestantism and democracy were two sides of the same coin. As they saw it, Latin America's worst problems stemmed from its Roman Catholic tradition. To them, Roman Catholicism was obscurantist, authoritarian, and reactionary. To some degree they were right, for by that time much of Latin American Roman Catholicism had indeed become reactionary. (It is important to understand that the nineteenth century was a time of great upheavals in politics, as well as astounding scientific discoveries that challenged many traditional notions. While Protestantism tended to go overboard in accepting many "modern" ideas, Roman Catholicism tended to reject them. In more recent times, both traditions have taken a more balanced approach.) In contrast to what they saw as an authoritarian and antiquated Catholicism, Protestant missionaries insisted on people reading the Bible for themselves, on freedom of expression, and on a more democratic form of church government—although many of the missionaries who spoke of such a democratic ideal were rather reluctant to give up their own power in the churches they had founded.

Protestants also came to what is now the American Southwest, especially after the area became part of the United States. At that point, most major Protestant denominations decided that God was opening a door for their missionary work in the area, and they began work among the Hispanic population there. What was done there was similar to what took place in Latin America, except that it was done in an area where Hispanics were rapidly losing control of the land, the economy, and their own future.

Protestantism came to the Hispanic world claiming to be a purer form of Christianity than Catholicism. Any practice that could not be found in the Bible was to be rejected—at least that was the theory. What in fact happened was that anything that was not practiced by Protestants in the countries where the missionaries came from was declared to be "Roman" and "unbiblical." Candles, robes, incense, and crucifixes were out. So was the practice of wearing black for mourning, or of *novenas* for the dead—the custom of meeting for nine days after someone's death to remember them and to pray for them. Even Ash Wednesday and Lent were often decried as unbiblical. But pianos, pews, and Christmas trees were acceptable, and no one seemed to remember that they too are not in the Bible.

Finally came the great Pentecostal wave. Stemming mostly from a great revival that took place at a church in Azusa Street in Los Angeles early in the twentieth century, it rapidly spread throughout the world, but especially into Latin America and among Latino/a-Hispanics in the United States. The movement has taken many shapes among Hispanics and Latin Americans. In some countries, it has resulted in independent denominations with hundreds of thousands of members. There are also thousands of small independent churches. Some tend to be very otherworldly and shun any social or political activity. Others are very much involved in organizing their communities for self-improvement, and for empowering the people to oppose various systems of oppression. Therefore, any generalization would be wrong.

Pentecostalism clearly has hit a nerve among Latino/a-Hispanics. Today, Pentecostals form the second-largest religious group among Hispanics in the United States, after Roman Catholics. Although some Pentecostal Hispanics are members of North American denominations, many are members of denominations that began in Latin America and then spread to the United States. Even many of those who belong to North American denominations have been converted through their connections with Latin America. This is true, for instance, in the greater metropolitan area of New York, where several of the largest

Pentecostal churches were founded by pastors or by members moving to the United States from Puerto Rico.

RELIGION AND IDENTITY

Today in any major city in the United States one can find a variety of religious practices and traditions among Hispanics. On the surface these practices and traditions may seem to have very little in common, but they are fundamental to the identity of a people who have often wandered in exile, and whose identity has sometimes been denied by the dominant culture. At the same time, however, these religious expressions also reflect much of the dominant culture. Thus, while from the perspective of that culture they may seem alien, something brought from Latin America, from the perspective of Latin America they often seem very much influenced by North American culture and religious traditions.

You may find, for instance, Spanish-speaking synagogues. In some of those synagogues you will find Sephardic Jews—descendants of those who were expelled from Spain in 1492—who still speak Spanish very much as it was spoken back then.

You also will find other Jews who went to Latin America from central Europe or from Germany, many fleeing from Nazism, and who have now come to the United States. A number of these Jews consider themselves both Jewish and Hispanic; they are also very much citizens of the United States and participants in much of the common culture of this nation.

You will also find a number of Catholic traditions and practices that are closely tied to people's identities. Among these are the *posadas*, the healings at *El Santuario de Chimayó*, and the devotion to the Virgin of Guadalupe.

The posadas—literally, "lodgings,"—are an ancient tradition that became quite popular in Mexico and in what is now the American Southwest, and is still practiced in various parts of the United States. Traditionally, they begin on the evening of December 16 and continue for nine evenings in a row until Christmas Eve—although there are now many variations on this. Each evening, people set out with Mary and Joseph, seeking lodgings. "Mary and Joseph" may be an actual young girl riding a donkey, with an actual young man leading it, or they may be statues that the people carry. The procession goes from house to house, asking for lodging in traditional songs and being told, also in song, that there is no room. Finally, they arrive at a prearranged place, where they are told that there is lodging. They all go in, and there is a celebration that usually includes food, songs, prayers, a rosary (a prayer to the Virgin Mary), and often a piñata. The crowds grow larger each day, so that the posada on Christmas Eve is often a big affair that ends at the church or at some public place that can accommodate a large crowd.

The posadas are lots of fun. But more than that, they have become very important for people who have had to move repeatedly looking for work, many of whom do not have legal papers for residence in the United States, while others, even those who are citizens by birth, are often told in many different ways that they are foreigners. In such a situation, it is comforting and strengthening to remember that Jesus too had difficulty finding a place, that he was born away from home, and that thereafter he was an exile in Egypt.

El Santuario de Chimayó is probably the most visited church in New Mexico. Originally built on a sacred Native American site where a crucifix appeared, it has welcomed people to pray for healing and miracles. With time, the "powers" of the crucifix shifted to the *posito*, a sacred sand pit from which the crucifix sprang, and today thousands of people take a pilgrimage to take with them a bit of the sacred dirt. This is another example of more recent exchanges between Roman Catholicism and Native American religions. The veneration of the Virgin of Guadalupe celebrates a story that

takes place shortly after the conquest of Mexico by the Spaniards. The story, in a nutshell, tells of a poor Indian, Juan Diego, and his conflict with the learned and powerful bishop of Mexico. According to the story, the Virgin Mary appeared to Juan Diego and gave him some instructions for the bishop, who refused to pay any attention to what the Indian had to say. After repeated attempts by Juan Diego to instruct the bishop, the Virgin provided proof that Juan Diego was telling the truth by imprinting her own image on the apron in which Juan Diego was carrying flowers to the bishop. When the bishop saw the miraculous image, he repented and did as Juan Diego told him. A large church was built where the Virgin had appeared, and the miraculous apron was enshrined in it.

Some may see in this nothing but superstition. Yet what we have here is the story of the vindication of Juan Diego and others like him, to whom people of power and prestige, like the bishop, pay no attention. For that reason, among Catholic Hispanics, especially those of Mexican or Mexican American descent, the Virgin of Guadalupe—who is understood to be the Virgin Mary as she appeared to Juan Diego—has been a sign of empowerment and vindication for the oppressed native inhabitants of these lands, and in general for all the poor and the downtrodden. Her image was on the first national flag of Mexico. For the same reason, when in 1962, under the leadership of Cesar Chavez, Mexican American farm workers and others began a long struggle for the right to unionize, the Virgin of Guadalupe was one of their most powerful symbols.

Many such celebrations and stories contain much that is Native American in origin. Indeed, the hill of Tepeyac, where the Virgin of Guadalupe is said to have appeared to Juan Diego, was also a place where an ancient goddess was worshiped—and there are elements of those ancient traditions in much that is done today at Tepeyac in celebration of the Virgin.

RECENT DEVELOPMENTS

In recent times, a reform has taken place in Roman Catholic worship. Until a few years ago, the mass had to be said in Latin, even if the people did not understand a word of what was being said. With the new directives of the Second Vatican Council in the 1960s, the mass was translated into the languages of the people, including Spanish. In ancient cathedrals such as those in San Antonio and Santa Fe, where Spanish had long been the language of the people, the mass was said in Spanish for the first time. This renewed people's interest in the mass. A number of Hispanic musicians began composing new music for the mass, exploring some of the ancient native traditions to see how they could be related to Catholic worship. The result has been astounding. If you want to go to mass at the church of San Juan de los Lagos, in San Antonio, you had better arrive early or you will not be able to get in. Once in, you may be surprised to hear mariachis playing tunes that are typically Mexican and that convey the meaning of the mass with amazing freshness and vigor. You may be even more surprised to see a group of dancers wearing costumes that look very much like those of the ancient Aztecs, decorated not only with feathers, but also with images of the Virgin of Guadalupe. Above all, you will notice that, although the mass has lost the somber tone it had when it was said in Latin, it has become a very significant and enriching worship experience for those who participate.

In other sections of the Hispanic American community, you may hear drums beating in rhythms that are clearly African. If you approach, you may find yourself in a *bembé*—a religious celebration that has deep roots in Africa. Most everybody will be dancing to the rhythm of the drums, which will be so catchy that you will have difficulty standing still. There may be religious symbols about. If you do not come from that tradition, you may recognize some Christian symbols, such as the cross or perhaps the image of a saint, but others will be quite foreign. In some cases, you may see offerings of grain and animals. People will dance, and dance, and dance—sometimes for three days and nights without stopping. If you attend these rituals often enough, you will come to recognize that different rhythms are used for different occasions. If you stay long enough in one of them, you may see someone who "gets the saint": that person will fall to the ground in spasms, roll his or her eyes back, and perhaps speak words of wisdom on his or her own behalf or on the community's. Then the person will be so exhausted that he or she will have to be carried to another room to rest.

If you think you are a little sophisticated, you may look upon all this with a bit of disdain, telling yourself that it is primitive and has no place in the modern world. But if you stop to think about it you may realize that these people are trying to come to grips with the mystery of life; that they are celebrating rituals that somehow connect them with a distant past that is half forgotten and has been denied them; that they are celebrating their common heritage and mourning their common lot; that they are making a statement that religion has to do not only with the soul and the mind, but also with the body; that rhythm and music, just as much as logic and speech, are God-given and may be used to worship God.

In the same city where you find a Spanish-speaking synagogue and a bembé, and where Catholics celebrate the posadas, you probably can also find a Hispanic Pentecostal church. Even if you do not belong to this tradition, you will again find much that will be familiar from other experiences, especially if you understand the language. The church will look like most Protestant churches, though perhaps less ornate. There will be no images, usually no stained-glass windows, and probably no organ— depending mostly on the financial resources of the church. There will be pews, a railing, and a pulpit that will be the focus of attention. Perhaps there will be a few scriptural verses inscribed on the wall—a custom that may remind you of some Jewish synagogues or Muslim mosques. There will be music—lots of music, with pianos, guitars, tambourines, maracas, and synthesizers. If you have attended an evangelical church you will recognize many of the hymns whose lyrics have been translated from English. Others may be quite different, with rhythms that sound like something you would expect in a secular setting. People will sing loudly, clapping and swaying to the rhythm of the music. At times, the place may seem as noisy as a baseball stadium during a World Series. Some people may be shouting, "Alleluia" and others "Amen," while still others may be praying their own prayers out loud.

If you are an outside observer, you will probably conclude that there is much here that is similar to what you could see in a synagogue or in a Catholic church—especially as far as the words are concerned—but that there is also much that reminds you of the bembé: the rhythm, the noise, the willingness to release oneself to the consciousness of the group. If you are used to

---

Pentecostal Worship Practices Among Latino/a Immigrants

While many mainline Christian communities debate issues of Latino/a immigration and some serve immigrant communities by providing the basic needs for immigrants as they cross the border and live in American cities and suburbs, Pentecostal and charismatic independent churches seem to be the location for the religious vitality of immigrant communities. New hymns and songs that tell the story of immigration and religious experience are abundant in Pentecostal or charismatic communities. Many of these hymns and songs are spontaneously performed in worship services, claiming God's work in the life of the immigrants and serving as "testimony" for the nurturing of the community.

In addition to hymns and songs, immigrant Pentecostal and charismatic independent Christian communities create new ritual practices and modify their moral and legal codes. Healing practices and services, particularly in times of incredible harassment and persecution from governmental authorities, are common in congregations. People pray for the Holy Spirit to heal illnesses and provide comfort so that they do not need to go to the public health care system. These congregations sometimes "suspend" their usually tight moral family codes, allowing unmarried couples to have some level of participation in the congregation. Many of the assigned tasks for those whose family configuration is not traditional are teaching the children during Sunday school, singing, and helping with cleaning and small programs. No major role, like public prayer, serving the Lord's Supper, and prayers for healing are assigned.

It is no surprise for members of these congregations to have prayer requests for family members crossing the border. Pastors and congregational leaders will create "chains of prayer"—assign members of the congregation to pray and fast daily—during the entire week when a family member or friend of a congregant is crossing the border. Moreover, the congregation celebrates the safe arrival of the immigrant to U.S. territory. If the new immigrant arrives to the congregation, an exuberant celebration welcomes the stranger(s). The congregation praises God and celebrates God's intervention on behalf of the immigrant during the dangerous journey.

Though Pentecostal and charismatic Latino/a congregations experience vibrant religious practices, they also experience uncertainty and displacement. Tougher laws against immigrants generate more movement among Latino/a immigrants as they seek less hostile environments where they can settle. Consequently, church rosters and membership roles are irrelevant. Frequently, members will not provide much personal detail. These congregations lean towards a fluid-member participation and do not follow or fit the mainline denominational structures for churches.

more sedate worship services, you may even be shocked and decide that this is not true worship at all. If so, you may try conveying that opinion to one of the members, and she might respond that she does not understand how you can get so excited over a football game but then hear the story of Jesus and not jump up and down. Perhaps she has a point worth considering.

She might also tell you that in order to understand what the people there are celebrating, you have to listen to their "testimonies." Testimonies, in which people stand up and give an account of what God has done for them, are an important part of most Hispanic Pentecostal services. In this particular service, this woman would tell you, you might hear the testimony of a young man who had been unable to free himself from his drug addiction until he came to church. Now, through prayer and with the support of the rest of the community, he can finally say that he is free of his habit. Another may speak of how her child was ill, and how she had no money for medicines; but the congregation prayed for the child and it was cured. Still a third would speak of how he was unemployed, and how through prayer and the support of the community he was able to survive and then to find a job. In short, these people, many of whom have found themselves in desperate situations, are celebrating a newly discovered life. This new life is not only spiritual, but also communal, and in many cases even economic. As with the other places you would have visited, you would be witnessing religion at work in affirming people's identity and empowering them to deal with the adversities of life.

In urban centers like New York, Chicago, Washington, Dallas/Ft. Worth, and Los Angeles, many Latino/a-Hispanic Americans now embrace Islam. Finding religious grounding in the family structure, in the disciplined spirituality, and in their own ancestry—both from Spain and Africa—Hispanic Americans are shaping the Muslim religion. It is not strange to find a Latina Muslim with great devotion to Mary. It is equally important to Latino/a-

Hispanic Americans to carry out disciplined lives, rejecting the vices of this world—very similar to a Pentecostal religious code. The growth of Latino/a-Hispanic Muslims in the United States is evident in the fact that in Puerto Rico there are five Sunni mosques and that in the U.S. mainland a growing number of Islamic centers are catering to the needs of Latino/a-Hispanics.

Among middle and upper-middle class Latino/a-Hispanic-Americans, there are practitioners of different Buddhist traditions. Though many Hispanics of Asian ancestry continue to have connections to their original religious traditions, many non-Asian Latino/a-Hispanic Americans keep deep affinities with their Roman Catholic traditions while practicing Zen and Tibetan Buddhism.

WHAT MAKES IT ALL LATINO/A-HISPANIC AMERICAN?

By now you may be wondering if there is any unity at all to the Hispanic American religious life and experience. What is it, after all, that allows us to speak of "Hispanic American religious life," as if there were something common to it? In this chapter, we have met Jewish, Catholic, Protestant, and Muslim Hispanic Americans, as well as some whose religious practices still reflect much of their Native American, African, and Asian ancestry. If there had been more space to go into further details, you would also have met Hispanics with many other beliefs.

Obviously, the most important element common to all Hispanics, no matter what their particular religion, is the Spanish language and cultural tradition. People are Hispanic not because of their race but because of their culture and traditions. Genetically, Hispanics are various mixtures of European, African, Native American, and even Asian ancestry. It is the language and all the traditions and social conventions that go with it that make us Hispanic. It is also the history, for we all somehow partake of the history of the original inhabitants of America, of the

Spanish invaders, and of slaves who were brought from Africa. That is why some Hispanics speak of themselves as "the race that is not a race," while others prefer to speak of a *raza cósmica*—a "cosmic race."

Once you begin to understand that common history and culture, you may also begin to see commonalities cutting across many of the varying religious practices that we have been discussing. I have already mentioned that the writings on the walls of a Pentecostal church are reminiscent of many ancient synagogues and mosques in Spain. And there is much similarity between the mood of a Pentecostal service and that of a bembé—or even a mariachi mass.

In some cases, ancient traditions lead to religious practices that cut across denominational lines. For instance, for most Hispanics, Catholic or Protestant, Christmas Eve and Epiphany (January 6) are much more important than Christmas Day. If you grew up in a non-Hispanic Christian household in the United States, Christmas probably was the big family day, and much of the excitement of Christmas had to do with Santa Claus and presents. Among Hispanics, both Catholic and Protestant, the big family day is Christmas Eve, when the family gets together for a late meal. Many traditional Catholic families then attend a midnight mass at which they celebrate the birth of Jesus.

The other important day is January 6, which in the Christian calendar is usually called Epiphany, but in most Hispanic households is called "Kings' Day." That is the day the "Three Kings"—the three wise men—bring gifts to children. Hispanic Christian children know the Three Kings by name and await them as eagerly as many other children await Santa Claus. Some households leave out straw for the Kings' camels. Many set up nativity scenes a few days (often nine days) before Christmas Eve, with figures depicting Mary, Joseph, the shepherds, angels, and all the animals at the manger. The Child is not placed in the manger until Christmas Eve. Slowly, the wise men appear on the horizon, until they arrive on January

6. That morning children get up to find the goodies that the Kings have left, under the bed or in some other convenient place.

This is one of the many traditions that make us *Hispanic* Americans. But we are also Hispanic *Americans*. We are part of a society and a culture that has its own traditions. In the old days, after going to mass late on Christmas Eve, we could sleep late on Christmas morning. Santa Claus never came to Latin America, or to the American Southwest, until commercial interests got him there. Now, however, Santa is also part of our common tradition, and we no longer get to sleep late on Christmas morning! But the children are the winners, for they get presents on Christmas *and* on Kings' Day.

This is a symbol of what it means to be a Hispanic American. Hispanics belong to a tradition that has deep and long roots in this country. As Americans, we share in a wider culture that draws from many a tradition. Sometimes these two seem to be in conflict. Most of the time, however, they enrich each other.

As to the wide variety of religious expressions among Hispanics, perhaps that too is part of what it means to be an American. In the Spain of Ferdinand and Isabella, none of those various religious expressions would have been tolerated. Here in the United States, they are all tolerated and celebrated. Some may think that this is because religion is not important, that it makes no difference. But the opposite is true: The reason why we tolerate and even celebrate such a variety of religions is precisely because religion is so important, because it touches each of our lives so deeply, and because its contributions to society are so valuable. If we do not allow all to bring their contributions, we shall all be the losers.

Notes

1. H. McKennie Goodpasture, *Cross and Sword: An Eyewitness History of Christianity in Latin America* (Maryknoll, N.Y.: Orbis, 1989), 11–12.

STUDY QUESTIONS

1. How did Spanish-speaking people come to reflect such a large percentage of the American population? Be sure to name several significant events in American history that brought this about, and to distinguish between recent immigrants and descendants of persons who have been here for centuries.

2. What influence did Spain have on the development of the religion of the earliest Spanish-speaking settlers in America?

3. What role did the Spanish-speaking church and its priests play in resisting the "conquest, exploitation, and Christianization" by Spain of the Americas? Why does the author call this resistance one of the "bright points in the history of the Christian church"? How did the priests who practiced such resistance suffer?

4. Why was there more contact between Europeans and Native Americans in the Spanish colonies than the British colonies of North America? What effect did this mixture of cultures have on the religious development of the colonies? Give two examples of how Native Americans made Spanish Christianity acceptable to their own religious traditions.

5. What conflicts developed between Catholicism and Protestantism soon after the Spanish colonies established independence from Spain? Describe several details of this conflict.

6. What is the "Pentecostal wave" that began in Los Angeles in the early twentieth century? What was its impact on Hispanic Americans?

7. Why is it wrong to assume that Hispanics belong to any particular religion? Why is such an assumption often made?

ESSAY TOPICS

The History of Pentecostalism in the Hispanic Church

The First Spanish Missions in the Americas

The Religious World of Hispanic America: Unity and Diversity

Spain and the Christianization of America

Religious Story: The Virgin of Guadalupe

WORD EXPLORATION

The following words play significant roles in any discussion of the religious world of Hispanics in America and are worth careful reflection and discussion.

Hispanic	Pentecostalism	Latin America
Manifest Destiny	Bembé	*Posadas*
Requerimiento	Virgin of Guadalupe	The Catholic Sovereigns
Encomiendas	Moors	

FOR FURTHER READING

Avalos, Hector. *Introduction to the U.S. Latina and Latino Religious Experience.* Boston: Brill Academic Publishers, 2004.

Espín, Orlando O. and Miguel H. Díaz, eds. *From the Heart of Our People: Latino/a Explorations in Catholic Systematic Theology.* Maryknoll, N.Y.: Orbis, 1999.

González, Justo L. *Mañana: Christian Theology from a Hispanic Perspective.* Nashville: Abingdon, 1990.

Gutierrez, David, ed. *The Columbia History of Latinos Since 1960.* New York: Columbia University Press, 2004.

Maldonado, David, ed. *Protestantes/Protestants.* Nashville: Abingdon, 1999.

Romero, C. Gilbert. *Hispanic Devotional Piety: Tracing the Biblical Roots.* Maryknoll, N.Y.: Orbis, 1991.

Valdez, Margarita, ed. *Tradiciones del Pueblo: Traditions of Three Mexican Feast Days in Southwest Detroit.* Detroit: Casa de Unidad Cultural, 1990.

FILM

Mi Familia; Walkout (HBO production); *El Norte; Un día sin mejicanos (A Day without Mexicans)*

WEB SITES

http://ilarioba.tripod.com/
Eleda.Org, dedicated to the study of the *Lukumí* religion, or *Santería.*

http://www.sandiego.edu/theo/Latino-Cath/index.php
Center for the Study of Latino/a Catholicism

http://www.latinotheology.org/
Web site for the *Journal of Hispanic/Latino Theology*

6

Orthodox Christianity in the World and in America

JAROSLAV PELIKAN AND JOHN McGUCKIN

862	Mission of the brothers Cyril and Methodius to the Slavic nations
1054	Schism between Rome and Constantinople (Great Schism)
1204	Fourth Crusade sacks Constantinople and desecrates its churches
1503	Fall of Greece and its Churches to Islamic rule
1737	Orthodox liturgy first celebrated in the Western Hemisphere by Russian Naval chaplains in Alaska
1768	First Orthodox congregation established in America by a Greek colony in Florida
1794	First official (Russian) Orthodox mission at Kodiak, Alaska
1840	Ivan Veniaminov, pioneering Russian missionary to Alaska, consecrated as Bishop Innocent of Sitka (later, Saint Innocent)
1864	Holy Trinity Church established in New Orleans by Greek Orthodox
1890–1914	More than 350,000 Greek immigrants seek greater economic opportunity in America
1900–1930	Serbian, Romanian, Ukrainian, Albanian and Syrian Christians found their own Orthodox communities in America
1917	Russian Revolution. Bolshevik atheist government hostile to the Orthodox Church; clergy and monastics in Slavic countries dominated by Russian communism martyred; Russian churches in America left without leadership
1922	Greek Orthodox Archdiocese of America founded
1925	Ecumenical meeting at Stockholm involving Orthodox churches
1964	Mutual reconciliation of Pope Paul VI and Patriarch Athenagoras of Constantinople at Jerusalem; denunciations made against each other by the churches of Rome and Constantinople in 1054 symbolically lifted
1970	Foundation of the Orthodox Church in America (OCA) as an independent body from out of the former Russian (Greek Catholic) Metropolia Church
1989	Progressive collapse of Communist stranglehold on Orthodox Church life in Russia and Eastern Europe; revival of Church life
1994	Ligonier meeting gathers Orthodox bishops and leaders from many traditions
2000s	U.S. Orthodoxy grows more from conversion than immigration

Their onion-domed churches dot the hills of Pennsylvania coal country and the mill towns of New Jersey and Ohio; in Tarpon Springs, Florida, their Greek priests bless the fleet of the sponge fishermen in the colorful ceremonies for the annual opening of the season; and, about as far away from Tarpon Springs as anyone can go and still be in the United States, Kodiak and Sitka, Alaska, are connected by way of their traditions, which date to the Russia of the Czars, to the Judeo-Christian traditions shared by most other Americans. There are about four million Eastern Orthodox Christians in the United States, with ties of varying firmness binding them to mother churches in Greece, the Middle East, and the Slavic lands of Eastern and Central Europe. They have a long and turbulent history of their own in the New World, and they are increasingly visible as a vital force within American religion.

The first time some of you encountered Orthodox Christianity may have been through the luminous discourses of Father Zossima in Dostoyevsky's *Brothers Karamazov,* or through the liturgical pageantry in the coronation scene of Modest Mussorgsky's *Boris Godunov,* or through the haunting faces and figures of icons from Mount Athos or icons by Andrey Rublyov (ca. 1350–ca. 1430) in a book on art history. Or perhaps you read a spy novel in which a Western operative in Moscow, despite his flawless Russian, blew his cover at the dinner table, by making the sign of the cross Western-style, from left to right rather than from right to left ("always ending at the heart," as my late mother used to say). But as Orthodox Christianity throughout the United States has finally begun to emerge from its various language ghettos, its system of religious belief and practice has also begun to claim its proper share of serious attention from other American religious groups, from the American public, and sometimes even from the American media.

Depending on how one elects to count them and on how seriously one takes their recurrent schisms, past and present, there are as many as twenty-five or more jurisdictions of Orthodox Christians in the United States. The very names of the American types of Orthodox Christianity, as usually listed in standard almanacs, are instructive echoes of their immigrant origins. Of these, the major ones are, in alphabetical order: the Albanian Orthodox Diocese of America; the American Carpatho-Russian Orthodox Greek Catholic Church ("Carpatho-Russian" or "-Rusyn," from what was once called Ruthenia, part of Czechoslovakia between World War I and World War II, and now forming western Ukraine); the Antiochian (formerly Syrian Antiochian) Orthodox Christian Archdiocese of North America; the Bulgarian Eastern Orthodox Church; the Coptic Orthodox Church; the Diocese of the Armenian Church of America; the Greek Orthodox Archdiocese of North and South America; the Orthodox Church in America (formerly Russian Orthodox Greek Catholic Church of North America); the Romanian Orthodox Archdiocese of North America and Canada; the Serbian Eastern Orthodox Church; the Syrian Orthodox Church of Antioch; the Ukrainian Orthodox Church in America; and the Ukrainian Orthodox Church in the U.S.A.

This bewildering, almost kaleidoscopic array of names, some of which have changed over the years, and the ongoing disputes between the groups in both ecclesiastical and secular courts, often in terms of who is the legitimate heir to properties, indicate the quest for religious identity that persists among American Orthodox. It also indicates the continuing need to struggle to achieve some sort of stronger unity within Orthodox America before being able to work on the problems of unity with other Christians or even with Orthodoxy throughout the world. It would be unfair, however, to exaggerate this problem (part of the multiethnic heritage of immigrant communities), because about three-fourths of all the Orthodox believers in the United States belong to either the Greek Orthodox Archdiocese of North and South America or to the Orthodox Church in America.

THE HISTORICAL ORIGINS
OF ORTHODOX CHRISTIANITY

Orthodoxy was called "a new and unknown world" by an outstanding Russian Orthodox poet and lay theologian of the nineteenth century, A. S. Khomyakov (1804–1860). But as Khomyakov was the first to insist, this "new world" is in fact very old, and it deserves to be better known in the West. For Eastern Orthodox Christianity is, in a very real sense, as old as Christianity itself. At the first Pentecost in Jerusalem fifty days after Easter, described in the second chapter of the Acts of the Apostles and often called the birthday of the Christian Church, many nations of the Mediterranean world were represented among the converts: "Parthians, Medes, Elamites; inhabitants of Mesopotamia, of Judaea and Cappadocia, of Pontus and Asia, of Phrygia and Pamphylia, of Egypt and the districts of Libya around Cyrene; visitors from Rome, both Jews and proselytes; Cretans and Arabs" (Acts 2:9–11). Almost every one of these (with the major exception of Rome, of course), indeed almost every Christian center referred to by name anywhere within the pages of the New Testament, belongs to Eastern Christendom—Jerusalem, Antioch, Alexandria, Athens, Corinth, and many others (many of them now bearing other names as a result of later conquests, especially by Muslims). In each of those centers, moreover, Orthodox Christianity has had a more or less unbroken history since the first century C.E.

During the centuries of Christian history when Eastern and Western Christendom were still maintaining some sort of communion with each other, moreover, the religious and spiritual balance of trade—liturgically, culturally, and theologically—was predominantly from East to West. Most of the major Christian theologians before Augustine (d. 430) wrote in Greek (as did, for that matter, most of the major heretics): Ignatius of Antioch, Irenaeus of Lyons, Clement of Alexandria, Origen, Athanasius, Basil of Caesarea, Gregory of Nazianzus, Gregory of Nyssa, Cyril of Jerusalem, and Cyril of Alexandria, to name only a few. All seven ecumenical councils of the "undivided Church" were held in Eastern territory: the First Council of Nicaea (present-day Iznik, Turkey) in 325; the First Council of Constantinople (present-day Istanbul, Turkey) in 381; the Council of Ephesus in 431; the Council of Chalcedon (present-day Kadiköy, Turkey) in 451; the Second Council of Constantinople in 553; the Third Council of Constantinople in 680–681; and the Second Council of Nicaea in 787. Christian monasticism began in the East and only eventually moved West, and the same was true of Christian mysticism, Christian philosophy, and much of Christian art. And Greek was the language not only of Paul's epistles to the Greek cities of Corinth, Philippi, and Thessalonica, but also of his epistle to Rome, a city where the Eucharist was celebrated in Greek (not Latin) until the mid-fourth century. Even the sayings of Jesus, which originally were probably spoken in Aramaic, a Semitic language, were written down and preserved in the Gospels through the medium of Greek, from which they have been translated into nearly two thousand languages (including Semitic languages). "Ex Oriente lux," according to the Latin proverb: the light rises from the East (sometimes the proverb has been amplified with the addition, "ex Occidente lex": law comes from the West).

It was appropriate to put the phrase "undivided Church" into quotation marks in the preceding paragraph, because implicit and explicit forms of disunity can be found regardless of how far back in time our historical study goes. The official schism between East and West, with its fateful consequences for both, did, however, change things in a fundamental way. Like most divorces, it was a consequence of estrangement, which turned into alienation, which turned into hostility, which turned into separation. When the official and legal separation finally did come, the idea of a unified Church had long since died among the people. Textbooks of history, including Edward Gibbon's *History of the Decline and Fall of the Roman Empire,* have traditionally dated the schism from 1054, when spokesmen for the two churches exchanged writs of excommunication. Others have marked the date earlier, to the ninth century. At the beginning of that century, on Christmas Day in the year 800, the pope crowned the king of the Franks, Charles (Charlemagne), as Roman emperor, despite there already being a Christian Roman emperor in Constantinople, who claimed authority also over the upstart West. As has happened so often, and not only in East-West relations, this political schism had its counterpart in the ecclesiastical schism. Later in the ninth century, as we shall note in greater detail later, East and West clashed over the mission to Moravia of the two brothers, Saints Constantine-Cyril and Methodius, in 862.

For my part, I have always been inclined to accept the view of many Orthodox scholars that the real break came in the year 1204, when the Western Christian armies on the Fourth Crusade, ostensibly bent on the liberation of the Holy Land and the Holy Places, sacked Christian Constantinople, desecrating its churches and establishing a Latin empire (until 1261) and forcibly "reuniting" the Latin and Greek churches, though in fact they were dividing them, perhaps permanently. Temporary reunions, notably the one at the Council of Florence in 1439, have all proved to be short-lived. The attendance of Orthodox clergy at the ecumenical Stockholm Conference of 1925, however, marked a gradual change in attitude on both sides, and such significant gestures as the embrace of Ecumenical Patriarch Athenagoras and Pope Paul VI at their meeting on the Mount of Olives in 1964 or the many ecumenical meetings between Pope John Paul II and Patriarch Bartholomew of Constantinople, have reawakened hopes that someday there may still be a reconciliation between Eastern and Western Christendom after so many centuries of bitter conflict.

Above all, however, it has been in America that Orthodoxy has come to play a significant ecumenical role, partly because of its new situation in the New World and partly because of the ecumenical rediscovery of other Christians that has played a large part in the history of almost every denomination in the twentieth century, especially on American soil. Ecumenical hopes are also fueled by the very large measure of doctrinal and spiritual harmony between the Orthodox and Catholic traditions.

HOW EASTERN ORTHODOXY CAME WEST

Eastern Orthodoxy came to the Western Hemisphere by traveling east. Although the very first Orthodox believers to arrive in colonial America were probably the members of a Greek colony in Florida in 1768, the institutional beginnings of Orthodox Christianity came a few decades later and many thousands of miles away, on Kodiak Island, Alaska, in what was then Russian territory. It was in Alaska that the Divine Liturgy of the Orthodox Church was celebrated, apparently for the first time anywhere in the Western Hemisphere, by naval chaplains of the Russian Orthodox Church on July 20, 1737. With the establishment of partial control of the Czar over Alaska, permanent settlements of Orthodox Russians came to Alaska. There was a growing conviction among some of them, partly for commercial and political reasons but also partly for spiritual reasons, that their Christian and Orthodox faith should be brought to the natives of the region. The Metropolitan of the Russian Orthodox Church for Novgorod and St. Petersburg, Gabriel Petrov, commissioned ten Russian monks to undertake the Kodiak mission. The monks landed at Kodiak on September 24, 1794, which is observed as the founding date of American Orthodoxy.

The Orthodox mission in Alaska nourished two of the earliest Christian saints of any faith tradition in America. One was the monk St. Herman of Alaska, who worked there for forty years until his death in 1837. The other was Bishop Innocent, whose name as a layman had been Ivan Venjaminov, bishop of Sitka (1840) and eventually of Moscow (1868); his saint's day is observed according to the calendar of the Orthodox Church on October 6. As Paul D. Garrett, historian of American Orthodoxy and biographer of Innocent, has said of him, he was "a true 'Renaissance man'" who "traveled widely for fifteen years in Unalaska and Sitka, personally helped the people build churches, mastered their languages (translating and writing in Aleut), and provided the first detailed scientific description of the region," before being called back to Russia. (I once had the unforgettable experience in Alaska of attending an Orthodox liturgy celebrated by an Aleut priest with a Tlingit congregation and choir, who chanted the responses in Church Slavonic—although I was the only Slav in the room!) Alaska Orthodoxy continued after the purchase of the territory by the United States in 1867; thus Orthodox Christianity can lay claim to a history in North America that has persisted, though not without serious interruptions, for more than two centuries.

These origins are extremely important for the self-definition not only of the Orthodox believers in Alaska who are Native Americans, such as Eskimos, Aleuts, and Tlingits, but also for that of all Orthodox Christians in North America whatever their ethnic origins may be. Nonetheless, the majority of the Orthodox population in the Western Hemisphere must, of course, trace their own roots to far more recent arrivals. This is not the place to recount the entire history of the immigrations from Eastern Europe to America during the nineteenth and twentieth centuries, except perhaps to point out that even in a time that celebrates "cultural diversity," most history books continue to be preoccupied with the English-speaking population of America and to manifest an interest in other groups primarily after they, too, become English-speaking. As a result, the vast body of historical source material in languages other than English, including the several languages of Eastern Orthodox Christianity, remains largely unknown even to many scholars.

It was especially in the thirty years or so prior to World War I, and as a result of the political and economic upheavals in Russia and the Balkans, that Orthodox Christians began to come to America in large numbers from Russia, Greece, Serbia, Romania, Austria-Hungary, and the Near East. As sociological-historical studies with such titles as *Has the Immigrant Kept the Faith?* (Gerald Shaughnessy, 1925) have repeatedly shown, it has been true of immigrant religious groups as widely separated, both geographically and spiritually, as Sicilian Catholics and Finnish Lutherans that "when you leave the language, you leave the church." But Orthodox Christians in America have experienced their own special version of this phenomenon. Because they had no centralized authority anywhere in the world that could legislate their organizational and liturgical life for them—even in the Old World, much less in the New World—Orthodox Christians were free to evolve here, particularly after their separation from their original countries in the aftermath of World War I into the linguistic and jurisdictional Tower of Babel evidenced by the catalog of forms of Orthodoxy listed at the beginning of this chapter. The great-grandchildren of Greek, Russian, and Syrian immigrants now find themselves united in their Orthodoxy but separated from their fellow Orthodox by the bonds of their ancestral language, which has increasingly become a foreign tongue for them also. That situation becomes all the more ironic in the light of the ancient Orthodox emphasis on celebrating the Divine Liturgy in the language of the people, in contrast to the traditional Western Catholic insistence on the use of Latin in the mass.

The traumatic effects of the Bolshevik Revolution of October 1917 made themselves felt with dramatic force in the Orthodox Christianity of the New World. After the fall of Constantinople to the Seljuk Turks in 1453, Moscow had increasingly assumed a place of importance and influence, becoming a patriarchate in 1589 by the action of the Ecumenical Patriarch of Constantinople, Jeremias II. Moscow was sometimes called "Third Rome"—superseding Old Rome as the "First Rome," which fell to heresy, and New Rome (Constantinople) as the "Second Rome," which fell to Islam—which serves to symbolize a considerable shift of Orthodox power to Muscovite Russia. But with the ascendancy of the atheistic Communists, Moscow was in the control of the avowed enemies not only of Orthodox Christianity but of all religions, including Judaism and Islam. There was, consequently, a new wave of emigration of Orthodox Christians to the West.

A unique feature of this emigration, by comparison with earlier ones, was that these refugees included many artists and intellectuals, and among these many scholars and theologians. Through their work in such cultural and intellectual centers as Paris, Prague, and Oxford, the knowledge of the Orthodox artistic and literary heritage, as well as its liturgical and theological heritage, was broadly disseminated in the West for the first time. Of special importance for us has been the work of Orthodox émigrés on American soil, above all that of Georges V. Florovsky (1893–1979), who left Russia in 1920, taught in Prague from 1922 to 1926, and then in Paris at the Orthodox Theological Institute of Saint Sergius from 1926 to 1948, before coming to America. While teaching at Saint Vladimir's Orthodox Seminary (1948–1955), Union Theological Seminary (1955–1956), Harvard Divinity School (1956–1964), and Princeton University until his death in 1979, Father Florovsky became for many American scholars (including myself) a mentor and guide to Orthodox history, theology, and spirituality; and by his books (see "For Further Reading" at the end of this chapter) he continues to instruct others.

DISTINCTIVE FEATURES OF ORTHODOX CHRISTIANITY

Throughout its history, Orthodox Christianity has had certain qualities by which it continues to be identified by its adherents and by outsiders. To those Americans who are accustomed to being able, at best, to recognize some of the major differences between Roman Catholicism and Protestantism, or perhaps even some of the differences among some of the bewilderingly many species of Protestantism, Orthodox Christianity poses a particularly challenging problem. As has already been noted, Rome is the one significant exception to the historical observation made earlier, that most of the major centers of early Christianity are now identified with Eastern Orthodoxy; and that exception has often been taken to be the defining principle of Orthodoxy. To many Americans, whether Jewish, Christian, or secular, therefore, Orthodox Christianity is to be defined as a Christianity that is somehow neither Roman Catholic nor Protestant. In fact, of course, this is neither fair nor accurate, for reasons that should become clear to anyone after even a brief examination of a few of the distinctive features of Orthodox Christianity.

Orthodox Worship

The most imposing of these features is undoubtedly Orthodox worship. Within Judaism, "Orthodoxy" refers chiefly to matters of religious observance; within Protestantism, to matters of doctrine, especially perhaps to the doctrine of the inspiration of the Bible. Neither of these criteria, particularly the second (though with the emphasis on the Trinity and the Incarnation, rather than on biblical inspiration), is altogether absent from the definition of Eastern Orthodoxy, but neither of them is exclusive. One of the roots of the name "Ortho*doxy*," the Greek word *doxa*, may sometimes mean "opinion, teaching," but it also means "glory." In the Slavic word for Orthodoxy, Pravoslavie, *slava* means "glory," too, so that Orthodoxy/Pravoslavie means the proper method of rendering glory, right worship, and consequently the right way of teaching about the One to whom the glory is rendered. This, for Orthodox dogma, is what is meant by the doctrines of the Trinity and the Incarnation.

According to an ancient chronicle of Kiev (capital of modern Ukraine), when a delegation of pagan Slavs came to Constantinople in the tenth century and visited the massive Church of Hagia Sophia (Holy Wisdom), which had been constructed by Emperor Justinian in the sixth century, they reported: "We knew not whether we were in heaven or on earth. For on earth there is no such splendor or such beauty, and we are at a loss how to describe it. We only know that God dwells there."

Already a century earlier, in 862, the two previously mentioned brothers, Saints Constantine-Cyril and Methodius, originally from Thessalonica, had come from Constantinople to the Slavs of Moravia. Unlike the Western missionaries, who in Christianizing most of Europe brought with them the Latin Mass instead of creating a form of worship in the language of the people, these "apostles to the Slavs" translated the Divine Liturgy into Slavonic, inventing an alphabet in the process; the present-day alphabet of Eastern Slavs such as Russians, Ukrainians, Bulgarians, and Serbs is still called Cyrillic, though it was probably not the alphabet that St. Cyril created, which is usually called Glagolitic (from *glagol,* the Old Slavic word for "word"). In the latter half of the ninth century, the Slavonic liturgy of Cyril and Methodius occasioned a bitter conflict with German Catholic missionaries, who had been working among the Slavs in Latin, and the case was appealed to Rome. The pope confirmed the legitimacy of the appointment of Methodius as archbishop of Moravia, but despite an initial friendliness to the Slavonic liturgy Rome ultimately decreed that Latin must be used.

The Slavic Christian world, alone among the major ethnic groupings, was thus divided into two camps, with consequences that are still visible, for example, in the present-day conflicts between Orthodox Serbs and Croatian Catholics in the former Yugoslavia. On the one side were those Slavs who accepted the authority of Rome and surrendered the Slavic liturgy (Poland, Bohemia, Slovakia, Croatia); on the other side were those who adhered to the Slavic liturgy but lost the tie to the pope (Russia, Ukraine, Byelorussia, Serbia, Bulgaria). This ancient liturgy, whether in Slavonic, Greek, or Arabic, has constituted the form of Orthodox worship.

Immediately upon stepping into an Orthodox church building, of whichever tradition it may be, the visitor will be struck by how different in atmosphere it is from any other house of worship, Christian or non-Christian. To begin with the most obvious difference from other Christian church buildings, there are no pews (although chairs are often provided for the elderly and infirm), so that even during a very long service, such as the Easter vigil of several hours' duration, worshipers are expected to remain standing. If such a visitor witnesses a church service, even a wedding or a funeral, the difference of atmosphere will become much more pronounced. From its beginning the Orthodox Christian liturgy has sought to emphasize simultaneously two opposite poles of faith: God's distance and majesty, and God's nearness and accessibility. God the Almighty is transcendent over heaven and earth and humanity—indeed, transcendent over all the language, including the language of Orthodox liturgy and doctrine, with which mortals seek to describe the awesome mystery of the Holy One. At the same time, the Holy One is near and accessible to us through the ultimate mystery of the Incarnation of the Son of God, "God the Word," in the birth, life, death, and resurrection of Jesus Christ, and therefore through the "mysteries" (the Orthodox term for "sacraments") celebrated by the Church in its liturgy. As the divinely chosen instrument of the Incarnation, the Virgin Mary occupies a unique place also in the liturgy:

she is *Theotokos*—"the one who gave birth to the one who is God"—and in that sense, though only in that sense, the Mother of God. The Council of Ephesus decided in 431 that it was inadequate to call her only *Christotokos,* "bearer of Christ," as though she were not the mother of the entire person of the incarnate God-man, divine as well as human.

Worship and song are inseparable in many religions, but the ancient Byzantine chant—in Greek or Church Slavonic, but now also in English—dominates Orthodox worship, there being no service that is only spoken. Although song is so central to Orthodox worship, most Orthodox churches do not include musical instruments. Igor Stravinsky (1882–1971), though an Orthodox Christian, composed a Roman Catholic Mass in Latin because, as he explained to Robert Craft, "I wanted my Mass to be used liturgically, an outright impossibility so far as the Russian Church was concerned, as Orthodox tradition proscribes musical instruments in its services." Although many Protestant theological seminaries have been able to carry on their work of training clergy for centuries without having a professor of church music on their faculty, that would be unthinkable at an Orthodox seminary. So powerful is the Church Slavonic chant of the Russian Orthodox Church that in the twentieth century it became part of the secular concert repertoire, with several choirs in Europe and the United States, including choirs completely made up of non-Slavs, carrying it far beyond the sacred precincts of the church to the music hall and the recital stage. That process has been abetted by the popularity of masterpieces by several composers in the Russian Orthodox tradition, notably the *Vespers* of Sergey Rachmaninoff (1915) and various sacred works of Dmitry Bortnyansky (1751–1825) and Pyotr Ilich Tchaikovsky (1840–1893).

Orthodox Tradition

Another characteristic of Orthodox Christianity, evident in its liturgy but expressed throughout its faith and life, is its profound sense of tradition. It is true of all Christians, perhaps of all believers everywhere, that when they pray they do so with an awareness of the presence and power of all who have believed before them, sharing in what one ancient Christian creed calls "the communion of saints." For an Orthodox Christian, that awareness is heightened by a church calendar on which every day is dedicated to a particular saint, and by a liturgy in which not only the saints of Israel and of the New Testament, but also the ancestors of the faith throughout Christian history, are remembered and honored. Upon stepping into an Orthodox church, moreover, that casual visitor we spoke of will see pervasive evidence of the communion of saints in the icons—characteristically Eastern pictures of Christ, of the Virgin Mary, and of other saints—prominently featured on the "iconostasis," a wall dividing the altar area from the main part of the church.

There was, in the "iconoclastic controversy" of the eighth and ninth centuries, severe religious and political conflict over the legitimacy of employing such pictures, in the light of the prohibition against images in Exodus 20:4 (which Orthodox Christians, together with most Protestants, count as the Second Commandment, although Roman Catholics and Lutherans do not): "Thou shall not make unto thee any graven image, or any likeness of any thing that is in heaven above, or that is in the earth beneath, or that is in the water under the earth." The outcome of the controversy, at the Second Council of Nicaea in 787, was the reinstatement of the icons. This took place through a characteristic combination of political and religious forces, but the rationale for it was the argument that the coming of the very Son of God in human flesh had fundamentally altered the meaning of the Second Commandment. What was now pictured in an icon was not an idol of pagan mythology, but part of the history of Jesus' sojourn on earth, either during his own human lifetime or in the careers of his disciples and saints. Significantly, the anniversary of that

What Is an Icon?

Among Orthodox Christians, icons are described as being "written" rather than painted or carved; that is because they are designed to communicate. . . . [Icons] are designed to be doors between this world and another world, between people and the Incarnate God, his Mother, or his friends, the saints.

   If a door is to do its job, it must have throughput in two directions. As we move toward an icon, it moves toward us with a warm and precise Christian content—if we understand the language that it speaks. The primary purpose of an icon is to enable a face-to-face encounter with a holy person or make present a sacred event, but icons are also "theology in color."

   . . . A religious icon can be of Christ, the Virgin Mary, an angel, or a saint; it can be of an event from the Old or New Testament, or of a saint's life. It is painted on a wooden panel that is small enough to be portable, and placed on a shelf in someone's home for domestic devotion. Icons like that were made by the thousands and were an enriching focus of devotion for countless thousands of Christians, from famous theologians to the so-called "simple faithful."

   . . . To the Orthodox Christian a holy icon is an image that is made according to the iconography of the Orthodox Church and has been blessed by an Orthodox priest with the proper prayers. When you see an icon in an art gallery, can you tell? Perhaps. A picture that has been blessed does not glow with holy light; its status is hidden. Orthodox Christians will tell you that a holy icon is a picture made by a believing craftsman. When you see an icon, can you tell the painter was a sincere believer? Sometimes. There have been thousands of craftsmen working in and beyond the Byzantine Empire since the fourth century. If their personal faith flickered low they could still have followed the proper iconography and produced good, or at least adequate, work. On the other hand, an icon infused with prayer will have an indefinable "plus" quality that may come across even to a not particularly spiritual beholder.

(From *Sacred Doorways: A Beginner's Guide to Icons*, by Linette Martin [Brewster, Mass.: Paraclete Press], xv–xvi, 3, 5. © 2002 Joe Walton Martin. Available from Paraclete Press, http://www.paracletepress.com.)

reinstatement is observed as the "Sunday of Orthodoxy" at the beginning of Lent.

Orthodox Doctrine

The Orthodox reverence for tradition, moreover, comes to voice not only in liturgy but in doctrine. This reverence is expressed in the opening words of the most important creedal affirmation of Christian faith about the relation between the divine and the human in the person of Jesus Christ, an affirmation shared also by most Western Christians, adopted at the Council of Chalcedon in 451: "Following the holy fathers." This formula could serve as the motto for much of what Orthodoxy is and does, for how it prays, what it teaches, and how it lives in the world. Again, while it is probably true that every religious group affirms the authority of tradition—even if it

is only the tradition of formally rejecting the authority of all tradition!—Orthodox Christianity is based on a special form of such authority. On the one hand, there is no central figure in the Orthodox hierarchy whose office possesses the right to speak on behalf of the entire Church, as the Bishop of Rome does in the Roman Catholic Church. On the other hand, Orthodoxy does not reject that centralized structure in the name of the Protestant principle (as the seventeenth-century Anglican, William Chillingworth, formulated it) that "the Bible, and the Bible alone, is the religion of Protestants." To Orthodox Christian believers, supreme authority attaches to the Bible only as it has been interpreted by tradition. Specifically, tradition has been set down for all time in the doctrines decreed by the previously mentioned Seven Ecumenical Councils of the Church, which took place between 325 and 787. To be on the same level with the decrees of those councils, a doctrine would have to be in harmony with that tradition and would have to be legislated by a body of comparable authority. The political situation of Orthodoxy today, with all of its ancient patriarchates and most of its other major centers in the control of governments hostile to it, has sometimes all but paralyzed its capacity to respond to opportunities or to crises, as well as its ability to formulate "the faith once delivered to the saints" (Jude 3) against the major heresies of the time, such as Marxist dialectical materialism.

It is in the intersection of liturgy and doctrine that one of the most persistent differences between Eastern and Western Christendom appears. To the words of the Nicene Creed, "[We believe] in the Holy Spirit . . . who proceeds from the Father," the West added: "and from the Son," in Latin ex Patre Filioque. In one way, this difference may well seem, even to a sympathetic observer, to represent an unwarranted prying into the impenetrable mystery of the inner life of God. Therefore, such an observer might conclude that both sides are wrong if they claim to understand that mystery which is denied to mortals, indeed to all creatures and even to the angels.

At another level, however, this Western addition to the original text of the Creed as shared by all is taken by Orthodox Christians as manifest proof of the tendency of the Western Church to ignore both the authority of ancient tradition and the collegiality of the Church as a whole, with all its bishops, in contradiction also to the explicit statement of Christ in the New Testament (John 15:26): "the Spirit of truth, which proceedeth from the Father."

At yet another level, the two theological theories may be said to involve two distinct ways of affirming (and safeguarding) the oneness of God in the face of the Christian doctrine of the Trinity: either by saying that both the Son of God and the Holy Spirit proceed from the Father, who is thus the single Source of both (the Eastern version); or by saying that the Holy Spirit, in proceeding both from the Father and the Son, unites them in the single Godhead (the Western version). The need to protect the oneness of God against an interpretation of the Trinity as teaching "three Gods" is affirmed by all: the Nicene Creed opens with the formula "We believe in one God" before it goes on to say anything about either the Son or the Holy Spirit.

Another difference of doctrine is considerably less abstract, and it is, as so often in Orthodoxy, expressed more in the language of worship and prayer than in theological speculation. Although both Eastern and Western Christians believe, with all Christians, that the human race was saved through the works performed by Jesus Christ, crucified and risen, there is between East and West a difference of emphasis so profound as to become substantive. In speaking about how Christ saves, the West has used the metaphors of sacrifice (Christ as the Lamb of God, who takes away the sin of the world) and of vicarious atonement (Christ as the one whose sinless death satisfies the violated justice of God over human sin). The Orthodox way of speaking and praying about Christ as Redeemer, while also invoking the biblical concept of sacrifice, emphasizes instead the theme of "Christ as Victor": sin, death, hell, and the devil hold the human race captive, until Christ the Son of God, coming as a human being through the Incarnation, engages them in conflict through his death on the cross and triumphs over them through his Resurrection. "Thou host," the Liturgy of St. John Chrysostom prays, "trampled down death and overthrown the devil and given life to the world." To attend one of the Easter services in an Orthodox church is to see in action this emphasis on Christ as Victor and to sense its difference from Western ways, a difference that is not an official matter of dogma but that deeply touches the life of Orthodox Christian faith.

Orthodox Church Organization

As is already clear from its definition of doctrinal authority, the conception of church organization in Orthodoxy is also distinctive. Like Roman Catholicism—indeed like ancient Christianity in both East and West until the Protestant Reformation—it affirms a hierarchical structure. Orthodox Christians recognize deacons, priests, and bishops (the latter category being further subdivided into ordinary bishops, archbishops, metropolitans, and patriarchs). But that structure is not seen as a pyramid in its design, with one bishop at the apex. Rather, as Metropolitan Kallistos Ware has phrased it, "the Orthodox Church is a family of self-governing Churches. It is held together, not by a centralized organization, not by a single prelate wielding absolute power over the whole body, but by the double bond of unity in the faith and communion in the sacraments."

Within the family of Orthodox churches, a special position of honor is accorded to the Patriarch of Constantinople, who carries the title of "Ecumenical Patriarch," and a special position is accorded also to the other ancient Patriarchates of Jerusalem, Alexandria, and Antioch; but these are positions of honor rather than of jurisdiction. Much honor is also afforded to the patriarchs of Russia and Romania for the antiquity as well as the size and importance of the national churches over which they preside. The clash between the Eastern and the Western churches over the Moravian mission in the ninth century, described earlier, was indeed provoked by the issue of liturgical language; but coming when it did in the already stormy history of relations between Rome and Constantinople, it quickly became an issue also of jurisdiction and authority. The same Council of Chalcedon in 451, whose phrase "Following the holy fathers" has served here as an epitome of the Orthodox view of tradition in matters of doctrine, also spoke, in its famous (or infamous) Canon 28, on the question of jurisdiction: "Following in all things the decision of the holy fathers [from the Council of Constantinople in 381] . . . we also enact and decree . . . equal privileges to the most holy throne of New Rome [Constantinople] . . . with the old imperial Rome." Old Rome and its bishops never accepted that canon, despite its having been solemnly legislated by an Ecumenical Council. The gradual development of papal monarchy in the Middle Ages, combined with the loss of all four Eastern Patriarchates to Muslim conquest, helped to bring about the estrangement, separation, schism, and mutual excommunication recounted earlier.

The large Orthodox churches of Greece, Russia, Ukraine, Romania, Serbia, and Bulgaria all have administrative self-rule, as do the smaller churches of Albania, Cyprus, and Poland, and even the tiny Church of Sinai (whose membership may be as small as one hundred). This feature of Orthodox church administration—especially in combination with the emphasis on using the language of the people in the liturgy—has enabled each Orthodox church to develop its own special relation with its national culture and to avoid homogenizing all the Orthodox churches into a single organization.

But that great advantage has been transformed into a distinct disadvantage in the New World, as the catalog of Orthodox jurisdictions in the United States indicates. Orthodox observers themselves have noted, with a rather grim sense of irony, that the flexibility that allows the Orthodox Church of Sinai to have its own local control does not seem to apply to the thriving Orthodoxy of the United States and Canada. Part of the same irony is that, although Orthodoxy for more than a millennium had differentiated itself from Roman Catholicism by worshiping God in the languages of its several peoples rather than in the language of ancient Rome, Orthodox congregations in the Western Hemisphere went on worshiping in the languages of ancient Greece, Syria, or Moravia—and this at a time when, as a result of the "Constitution on the Sacred Liturgy" of the Second Vatican Council (1962–1965), Roman Catholic congregations in America and elsewhere had begun to use English and other vernaculars. In the New World, ancient forms and ancient languages can constitute an obstacle for the generations born in the United States. The jurisdictional question of self-determination and the liturgical question of the language of worship were obviously connected, so that the establishment of the Orthodox Church in America in 1970 out of the former Russian Orthodox Greek Catholic Church of North America entailed also the transition from Old Church Slavonic to English. In the parishes of the Greek Orthodox Archdiocese, moreover, and despite the canonical rupture occasioned by the creation of the Orthodox Church in America, bilingual services have been evolving, though rarely towards a wholly English liturgy.

The Question of Church and State

Throughout much of the history of Orthodoxy, the question of ecclesiastical jurisdiction has been closely related to the question of church and state. The existence of Constantinople as the capital of a Christian empire, indeed the name itself, testified to the historic importance of the conversion of the emperor Constantine (d. 337). For more than eleven hundred years, the Christian emperor and the Christian church maintained there a relationship that was sometimes amicable and sometimes adversarial, but was always close. A similar pattern of coexistence has characterized the Orthodox relationship to the state in the Kingdom of Greece and in most of the Orthodox churches in Czarist Russia, the Kingdom of Serbia, and the Kingdom of Bulgaria. But when conquest from without or revolution from within put an end to one or another of these political regimes, this coexistence meant that the national church, too, was in jeopardy. During the many centuries of its dependence on a Christian monarch, Orthodoxy had not developed the patterns of self-government—an independent canon law, an international organization, and a long-range strategy of political activity—that had come

to characterize Roman Catholicism. Already in the seventh century, the Patriarchates of Jerusalem, Antioch, and Alexandria had come under Muslim rule; in 1453 Constantinople itself followed, and then Athens in 1503. But the Orthodox pattern of church-state relations and the very way of life and faith identified as Orthodox faced an even graver threat in the twentieth century.

ORTHODOXY AT THE BEGINNING OF THE TWENTY-FIRST CENTURY

A religion whose central features are liturgy, tradition, and dogma and whose organizational structure has tied it closely to the political regime must seem a museum piece to many, especially to activist American Christians, one of whom, Walter Rauschenbusch (1861–1918) identified sacramentalism, asceticism, and dogma (all three of them typically Orthodox) as the three forces that "deflect" Christianity from its primary responsibility for "Christianizing the social order." Therefore, when the Bolshevik Revolution of 1917 declared war on all religion, but in particular on Orthodox Christianity, there were more than a few voices heard who said, in effect, that Russian Orthodoxy was only getting its just reward. Though less shocking than the indifference of American Christians to the events that were to take place in Nazi Germany two decades later, this dismissal of Orthodoxy became standard in American textbooks and sermons. From time to time, as accounts of the terror reached the West, above all in the three volumes of Aleksandr Solzhenitsyn's *Gulag Archipelago, 1918–1956*, readers also received glimpses of the heroism and faith of Orthodox believers, both clergy and laypeople. Since the overthrow of communism, however, the picture of those seven decades has become clearer. Although there is practically no Orthodox believer alive in Eastern Europe who was baptized before the Bolshevik Revolution, and although the sacramental life and the religious instruction of the Orthodox Church operated under enormous handicaps even during those times when they were not being subject to overt persecution, Orthodoxy has survived.

Through the patient but stubborn continuity of what Russians sometimes call "the church of the grandmothers," Orthodoxy has demonstrated that it does not need to be sitting in the lap of a friendly "Christian" government to promote the obedience of faith, and that the qualities denounced as "reactionary" by its critics, both Christian and non-Christian, are the ones that can sustain it in a time of troubles and can outlast its persecutors. Meanwhile, the decades of communist oppression have also been responsible for a generation of what are now being called in Russian "neo-martyrs," who showed themselves to be worthy successors of the Three Men in the Fiery Furnace (Daniel 3) and of the Martyrs of the Catacombs. Such revolutionary changes in the Orthodox world, especially in combination with the radically altered ecumenical climate, must have far-reaching effects on American Orthodoxy at the beginning of the twenty-first century.

The new situation in the former Soviet Union presents the Orthodox here with an opportunity similar to that envisioned by Winston Churchill when, speaking on June 4, 1940, he looked to a future in which, "in God's good time, the New World, with all its power and might, steps forth to the rescue and the liberation of the Old." Material relief and spiritual solidarity, books and liturgical needs, exchange students and communications technology—all of these are elements of that new opportunity for American Orthodox. Conversely, the fall of communism in the late 1980s evoked the less-than-edifying picture of various Western denominations scrambling for Russian and Eastern European proselytes, instead of looking for ways to support and strengthen those who have survived difficult times.

These opportunities would seem to add new urgency to the imperative for American Orthodoxy to put its own house in better order. To quote Paul D. Garrett, "the essential unity of the Orthodox church, in spite of conflicts and paradoxes, is still evolving. But if unity comes and the false accretions finally fall away, it will be in America." And now that Orthodoxy is more free in other countries than it has been for generations, American Orthodoxy faces the prospect of recovering a unity across national boundaries to match the unity across the centuries that has always been one of its most priceless treasures.

STUDY QUESTIONS

1. How do you explain the rich diversity of Orthodox Christianity in America, particularly in light of the various names of the American forms of Orthodox Christianity?

2. Why does Orthodox Christianity lay claim to being as old as Christianity itself? What connection does Orthodox Christianity have to the New Testament church?

3. According to the author, when did the schism take place between Western and Eastern Christianity? What were the causes of the split?

4. What were the reasons for Orthodox Christianity's spread to America? Trace its historical development and growth.

5. What are the characteristics and functions of the following distinctive features of Orthodox Christianity? (a) Orthodox worship; (b) Orthodox tradition; (c) Orthodox doctrine; (d) Orthodox church organization; and (e) Orthodox church and state relations.

6. What chief differences in practice and doctrine do you see between Orthodox Christianity, Catholicism, and Protestantism?

ESSAY TOPICS

The Schism between East and West

The Religious Art of Orthodox Christianity

Elements of Worship in Orthodox Christianity

Settlement in Alaska: The First Orthodox Christians in America

Emperor Justinian and the Church of Hagia Sophia

Orthodoxy in Eastern Europe after the Fall of Communism

WORD EXPLORATION

The following words play significant roles in any discussion of Orthodox Christianity in America and are worth careful reflection and discussion.

Schism	Theosis	Iconography
Hagia Sophia	Christ as Victor	Theotokos
Orthodoxy	Constantinople	Divine Liturgy

FOR FURTHER READING AND REFERENCE

For some of the reasons already pointed out, the number of works in English about Orthodox Christianity has lagged significantly behind those dealing with other major religious traditions in America. Nevertheless, it is possible to go a long way toward acquiring a solid grasp of the issues and developments described here, even if one does not read Greek or Russian.

There are several general introductions to Orthodoxy in English, each of which has a bibliography for deeper and more detailed reference. Among these, J. A. McGuckin, *The Orthodox Church: An Introduction to Its History, Doctrine and Spiritual Culture* (Oxford and New York: Blackwell-Wiley, 2008) is an important resource; so too the less detailed study by Kallistos [Timothy] Ware, *The Orthodox Church* (Harmondsworth: Penguin Books, 1964). Alexander Schmemann, *The Historical Road of Eastern Orthodoxy,* translated by Lydia W. Kesich (New York: Holt, Rinehart & Winston, 1963), and John Meyendorff, *The Orthodox Church: Its Past and Its Role in the Best Today,* 3d ed., translated by John Chapin (Crestwood, N.Y.: Saint Vladimir's Seminary Press, 1981), analyze the problems and opportunities in the light of Orthodox history. John Meyendorff, *Byzantine Theology: Historical Trends and Doctrinal Themes* (New York: Fordham University Press, 1974), and Jaroslav Pelikan, *The Spirit of Eastern Christendom (600–1700)* (Chicago: University of Chicago Press, 1974), which is Volume 2 of the five-volume *The Christian Tradition: A History of the Development of Doctrine,* cover the development of Orthodox thought and teaching in the period of its transition from the history it shares with the West to the emergence of the modern period. For that modern period, the most authoritative treatment in any language is now available in English: Georges Florovsky, *Ways of Russian Theology,* translated by Robert L. Nichols, Volumes 5 and 6 of his *Collected Works* (Belmont, Mass.: Nordland Books, 1979–1987). Florovsky discusses all the major thinkers, placing them into the context of Russian intellectual, literary, and religious history. The pages of *The Greek Orthodox Theological Review* and *Saint Vladimir's Quarterly* are an ongoing documentation of American Orthodoxy as it works to define itself.

The best brief introduction to the history of Orthodoxy in America is the succinct but substantial essay by Paul D. Garrett, "Eastern Christianity," in *Encyclopedia of the American Religious Experience,* edited by Charles H. Lippy and Peter W. Williams (New York: Charles Scribner's Sons, 1988), 1:325–344. Garrett has also written *Saint Innocent, Apostle to America* (Crestwood, N.Y.: Saint Vladimir's Seminary Press, 1979). The broader context of the work of St. Innocent is outlined in Gregory Afonsky, *A History of the Orthodox Church in Alaska (1794–1917)* (Kodiak, Alaska: Saint Herman's Theological Seminary, 1977). Constance J. Tarasar and John H. Erickson have edited *Orthodox America, 1794–1976: Development of the Orthodox Church in America* (Syosset, N.Y.: Orthodox Church in America, 1975). The cultural, literary, and religious significance of the Russian emigration after the Bolshevik Revolution is described by Nicholas Zernov, *The Russian Religious Renaissance of the Twentieth Century* (New York: Harper & Row, 1963).

There are histories of most of the major and minor Orthodox groups on American soil. George Papaioannou, *From Mars Hill to Manhattan: The Greek Orthodox in America under Athenagoras I* (Minneapolis: Light and Life, 1976), concentrates on the experience of the Greek immigrant community. Gerald J. Bobango, *The Romanian Orthodox Episcopate of America* (Jackson, Mich.: Romanian-American Heritage Center, 1979), is an introduction to one of the lesser-known groups. Jaroslav Pelikan, *Confessor Between East and West: A*

Portrait of Ukrainian Cardinal Josyf Slipyj (Grand Rapids: Wm. B. Eerdmans, 1990), is a portrait of the largest group of Eastern Rite Catholics in America. The essays in Volumes 8 and 9 of the *Collected Works* of Georges Florovsky (see above), *Ecumenism: A Doctrinal Approach* and *Ecumenism: A Historical Approach,* both published in 1989, benefit from the author's personal experience as the leading Orthodox participant in the ecumenical movement and from his scholarship on all periods of Orthodox history. His thought and work have been treated with great sympathy and understanding in a monograph-length article by George Huntston Williams, "Georges Vasilievich Florovsky: His American Career," *Greek Orthodox Theological Review 11* (1965): 7–107.

WEB SITES

http://orthodoxeurope.org/page/10/1.aspx
   The online Orthodox Catechism

http://www.oca.org
   Official site of the Orthodox Church in America

http://www.goarch.org
   Official Web site of the Greek Orthodox Archdiocese of America

Part Three

Other Monotheistic Traditions in America

7

Judaism in the World and in America

JACOB NEUSNER

1654	Jewish community founded in New Amsterdam (New York)
1658	Newport, R.I., Jewish community founded
1712	First public synagogue in Berlin
1760	Death of Baal Shem Tov, founder of Hasidism
1789	U.S. Constitution guarantees freedom of religion
1790s	Jews receive full citizenship in France and Holland
1815	Polish Constitution omits Jewish rights
1825	Jews granted full citizenship in state of Maryland
1847	Birth of Solomon Schechter, leader of Conservative Judaism in the United States
1866–1868	Emancipation of Jews of Switzerland and Austria-Hungary
1870	Unification of Italy; ghettos abolished
1873	Founding of Union of American Hebrew Congregations (name changed in 2003 to Union for Reform Judaism)
1881	Beginning of mass immigration of East European Jews to the United States, Britain, Canada, Australia, South Africa, and Argentina
1882	Bilu Movement—beginning of Jewish immigration into Palestine
1885	Pittsburgh Platform of Reform Rabbis renounces hope to return to Zion; affirms reason, progress
1886	Jewish Theological Seminary founded in New York City to train Conservative rabbis
1896	Herzl publishes *The Jewish State*, urging creation of Jewish State to solve problem of anti-Semitic politics in Europe
1897	Zionist movement founded at Basel, Switzerland
1909	Tel Aviv founded as first Hebrew-speaking city since ancient times
1933	Hitler becomes Chancellor of Germany; Jews begin to lose rights
1935	Nuremberg Laws in Germany; Jews lose all rights
1938	Every synagogue in Germany burned down on Nov. 9
1939–1945	Deportation to death camps and mass starvation; massacres of Jews of Europe. Nearly six million Jews put to death
1943	Warsaw ghetto revolt

1945	World War II ends; Jews in displaced persons camps
1948	Palestine partitioned; State of Israel created in Jewish part
1967	Jerusalem reunited; ancient Temple wall recovered for Jewish veneration
1972	First woman ordained a Reform rabbi at Hebrew Union College-Jewish Institute of Religion
1973	Yom Kippur War calls into question messianic spirit generated in 1967 and intensifies messianic hope associated with State of Israel and Jerusalem
1982	Invasion of Lebanon; Christian Lebanese massacre of Palestinian women and children precipitates moral crisis in State of Israel
1984	First woman ordained as a Conservative rabbi by the Jewish Theological Seminary of America
1996	U.S. Reform rabbis (Central Conference of American Rabbis) vote to conduct same-sex marriages and to exclude from Reform religious schools children who simultaneously attend Judaic and Christian religious schools
1996	Religious-political parties in the State of Israel win more than 20 percent of the vote for Israeli parliament (Knesset) and take over major ministries of state
1999	United Synagogue of Conservative Judaism asks congregations to recommit themselves to keeping kosher, observing the Sabbath, and attending synagogue regularly
2000	Senator Joseph Lieberman, an Orthodox Jew, is Al Gore's choice for running mate
2002	*Wall Street Journal* reporter Daniel Pearl murdered by terrorists in Pakistan

I grew up three things: (1) a boy in West Hartford, Connecticut, and therefore a New Englander; (2) a native-born American, son and grandson of native-born Americans, and therefore very patriotic; and (3) a Reform Jew. The toughest moment of my young life, therefore, came when I discovered that the Pilgrim Fathers about whom we studied in third grade—founders of the first three towns of Connecticut, Hartford, Windsor, and Wethersfield—weren't Jewish; they attended a church, which wasn't the same thing as our Temple on Farmington Avenue (which, I thought the most beautiful building in the world, where surely God lived), and didn't even take Hebrew class when they went to Sunday school the way I did. But I got used to the idea that I was different from other kids in some ways; I remained a proud New Englander—America was the only country I could imagine and I made my peace with the fact that the Congregation-

alists who founded Connecticut had ample place for me, too. I decided I liked things as they are, and me as I was—and am.

American Jews make their peace with lots of things; they are different in religion but the same as other people in most other ways of life. They are Jewish, but not so Jewish that they can't be as American as everybody else. In a country with a Christian majority, where the celebrations of Christianity divide the year, American Jews respect their neighbors and enjoy their goodwill as well. The secret of the Jews in America and Canada is that, although they are different, they love being exactly what they are.

You probably have Jewish neighbors and friends. A 2007 study from Brandeis University estimates that there are now slightly more than six million Jews in the United States (just under half of all the Jews in the entire world). They live in all fifty states, adding up to less than two percent of the

American people. Close to half of the Jewish population is found in the Northeast, with large populations in the South and the Far West as well. Wherever you live in this country, you are likely to know Jews and realize that Judaism is widely practiced.

Most American Jews live pretty much the way other Americans do. It is estimated that, because of intermarriage between Jews and non-Jews, more than seven million Americans live in households in which there is at least one Jewish member. One study showed that 28 percent of married Jews are wed to non-Jews (who are called "gentiles"), and another 4 percent are married to converts to Judaism. A very high proportion (88 percent of Jews surveyed) said that they would accept the marriage of their child to a non-Jew. About 72 percent of Jews live in homes that are entirely made up of Jews.

Jews come in all shapes, sizes, and colors, so just by looking at a person you cannot tell whether or not he or she is Jewish. Jews do not form a single racial group or ethnic group. There are black Jews—the late Sammy Davis Jr. is among the more popularly known black Jews—and they generally find a welcome in synagogues. (The State of Israel recognized as authentic Jews the dark-skinned "house of Israel" of Ethiopia and undertook heroic efforts to save nearly the entire community from massacre during the wars there.) There are blond Jews and brown-haired Jews, rural Jews and urban Jews, rich Jews and poor Jews. American Jews live in most localities and are found in all social and economic groupings.

It is not easy to tell a Jew from a gentile, except in one important way: most Jews believe in one religion: Judaism. Of the approximately six million Jews in the United States, about three-quarters, or about 4.5 million, define being Jewish as a matter of religion. So while Judaism is not the religion of a single people, most Jews are a people with a single religion. But you should not take for granted that because someone you know is Jewish, that person practices Judaism. There are also many Judaisms in North

America, just as there are many Christianities, and the differences between Reform, Orthodox, Reconstructionist, and Conservative Judaisms are as real as the ones that separate the Catholic from the Protestant, or the Latter-day Saint, or Mormon, from a member of the Unification Church.

And clearly, there are many Jews who do not identify "being Jewish" with "being religious" or practicing a Judaism. Jews form a set of ethnic groups, and those Jews who practice a Judaism form a religious group. But if you practice Judaism the religion, you automatically have a place among the Jews, an ethnic group. So Judaism is the religion of one people, although not all Jews belong to one and the same religion, Judaism, or to any religion at all.

Most Christians know three things about Judaism. First, it is the religion of the Old Testament. Second, it is the religion into which Jesus Christ was born, in which he lived, and which he practiced to the day of his death. Third, Jews do not "accept" Jesus, meaning they are not Christians. These three statements are true, but they are only part of the story. Left out of the picture of Judaism is most of what Jews believe, since the prevailing portrait is negative—"they don't believe this, they don't do that"—and misses what makes Judaism a living religion for millions of Americans.

The three things that make Judaism a living religion are represented in the words _God_, _Torah_, and _Israel_. These are the native categories of Judaism. To put it differently, the name, in Judaism, for the religion of Judaism is "the Torah." The Torah is given by God to "Israel," which is not the contemporary State of Israel but the Israel that is holy and loved by God. Israel is made holy by the Torah and defined by the Torah. Clearly, just as there are Jews who are ethnic and Jews who are ethnic and also religious, so the word "Israel" stands for both a worldly, political fact, and also for the children of Abraham, Isaac, and Jacob, to whom God through Moses gave the Torah: a holy people, comparable to the church as "the mystical body of Christ." This problem of understanding the ambiguity of the word "Israel," which refers to several things, not some one thing, will be discussed in a moment.

GOD, TORAH, AND ISRAEL

The God of Judaism is the one and only God, who created heaven and earth, who governs our lives with mercy and justice, and who revealed the Torah to Moses at Mount Sinai.

The "Torah," a Hebrew word taken to mean "revelation" of Judaism, is God's will and word to humanity. The Torah includes the Ten Commandments (Exodus 20) as well as many other commandments that God has given to Israel, the holy people.

God's word comes to "Israel." Who, and what, is this "Israel"? In Judaism, "Israel" is defined as the children of Abraham, Isaac, and Jacob, who assembled before Mount Sinai to receive the Torah from God, and their descendants through all time, including all of those, anytime and anywhere, who join them at Sinai by accepting the Torah. The word "Israel" also refers to a particular land, which in Judaism is called "the land of Israel," and which today corresponds to the State of Israel, created in 1948. The "Israelites" of the ancient Hebrew Scriptures or Old Testament bear two other names, Hebrews and Jews. Hebrews take their name from the Hebrew language; Jews are the descendants of that part of ancient Israel that survived the destruction of the Northern Kingdom of ancient Israel in 722 B.C.E. In general, "Israelites," "Hebrews," and "Jews" may be used interchangeably, but in this country most are comfortable with the designation "Jews." The citizens of the present-day State of Israel are called "Israelis," to keep them distinct from the ancient Israelites of Old Testament times.

As a living religion—not merely a naysayer to some other religion—Judaism thrives in American homes and synagogues. The first American synagogue was built in New York City in 1654, when Jews fleeing from Brazil and the Spanish Inquisition reached American shores. In our own day, Judaism also draws Jews from home and synagogue to pilgrimages to distant lands as well. Judaism makes life meaningful for millions of Americans.

WHERE JUDAISM LIVES: HOME, SYNAGOGUE, PILGRIMAGE

To understand the religion of Jewish Americans, you have to go to the home and the synagogue, and you also have to travel with Jews to distant places, because that is where Judaism lives: at home, in the synagogue, and on pilgrimages.

Home

Some of the most important moments in the life of Judaism take place in the home. In the United States and Canada nearly all Jews celebrate a festival meal at Passover. At the festival of Passover, which coincides with the first full moon after the vernal equinox, Jewish families gather around their tables for a holy meal. At this meal Jews, seeing themselves as the contemporary "Israel" of whom the Scripture speaks, retell the story of the exodus from Egypt in times long past. With unleavened bread and sanctified wine, they celebrate the liberation of slaves from Pharaoh's bondage. What is important is that Jews don't merely recount an event from their ancestors' remote history. They see themselves today as personally freed by God from the slavery of Egypt:

> For ever after, in every generation, *every Israelite must think of himself or herself as having gone forth from Egypt* [italics added] . . . We were slaves of Pharaoh in Egypt and the Lord our God brought us forth from there with a mighty hand and an outstretched arm. And if the Holy One, blessed be He, had not brought our fathers forth from Egypt, then we and our descendants would still be slaves to Pharaoh in Egypt. And so, even if all of us were

full of wisdom, understanding, sages and well informed in the Torah, we should still be obligated to repeat again the story of the exodus from Egypt.

Another passage of the Passover liturgy says:

This is the promise which has stood by our forefathers and stands by us. For neither once, nor twice, nor three times was our destruction planned; in every generation they rise against us, and in every generation God delivers us from their hands into freedom, out of anguish into joy, out of mourning into festivity, out of darkness into light, out of bondage into redemption.

This sense of being "Israel" in the here and now, the representatives in today's America of the Israel to whom God spoke at Sinai, is made explicit:

For ever after, in every generation, *every Israelite must think of himself or herself as having gone forth from Egypt.* For we read in the Torah: "In that day thou shall teach thy child, saying: All this is because of what God did for me when I went forth from Egypt." It was not only our forefathers that the Holy One, blessed be He, redeemed; us too, the living, He redeemed together with them.

Why does Passover mean so much to American Jews? The Jews are a minority, small in numbers. They are different, and difference can be difficult to take. To be different—whatever the difference—requires explanation; it may provoke resentment or create tension demanding resolution and pain requiring remission. Treating difference as destiny, Passover celebrates the family of Israel and is celebrated by the families of Israel.

The Passover rite is not the only occasion on which your Jewish friends and neighbors turn their homes into holy places. The rite of circumcision—in Hebrew, *berit milah*—commonly takes place in the home. This covenant of circumcision involves the surgical removal of the foreskin of the penis of male Jews eight days after birth in commemoration of the covenant made by Abraham with God. The marriage rite happens as often at home as in a synagogue. The festival of Tabernacles—in Hebrew, Sukkot—commemorating the first full moon after the autumnal equinox, is celebrated at home by building a temporary shelter covered with leafy boughs, under the stars, and eating meals there. The December festival of dedication—in Hebrew, *Hanukkah,* the feast of lights—in remembrance of the salvation of Israel in the time of the Maccabees in the second century B.C.E. when pagans tried to destroy Judaism, takes place through the lighting of candles in the home.

There are dietary laws, observed by some Jews at home, fewer of them outside of the home, involving the food laws given in the book of Leviticus (not eating pork, shellfish, and eating only meat that has been humanely slaughtered). These laws identify food that is *kosher,* or fit and suitable for Jews. Keeping these laws is another way in which the home is made into a holy place, where God is worshiped and where God's will, in the Torah, governs.

Synagogue

The synagogue, or temple, is the other location in which Judaism takes place. Synagogue buildings in the United States take many forms, from New England colonial, as in Worcester, Massachusetts; to Moorish, as in San Francisco; to Gothic, as in the Temple Emanu-El in New York City. But if you walk into any synagogue in the world, the first thing you will see is the holy ark, in which the scrolls of the Torah are kept. That fact tells you how the place of worship is made holy: through the public reading of the scrolls of the Torah, which takes place on the Sabbath, the day of rest (Saturday), and (in abbreviated form) Monday and Thursday as well. In an Orthodox, Conservative, or Reconstructionist synagogue you will notice that men and boys cover their heads with a skullcap, called in Hebrew a *kippah,* and in Yiddish a *yarmulke.* This covering of the head is a sign of humility and respect in worship. Many Orthodox males keep their heads covered at all times.

The synagogue in any American town or city is a place of study of the Torah, a place of prayer in community, and a place of gathering. Study of the Torah translates into "Jewish education." Most synagogues maintain schools for young people that meet on Sunday morning and several afternoons a week as well; many also maintain ambitious adult education programs. All synagogues conduct Sabbath and festival prayer, and many have daily worship too. All synagogues bring people together for occasions of meeting and renewal. Israel, the Jewish people, form a strong community; Jews enjoy one another's company and share concerns, commitments, and responsibilities. Associating with other Jews forms an important part not only of the life of the Jews as an ethnic community, but also of the expression of their religion. (In contemporary European Judaism, that is the main function of the synagogue. In the United States there are Jewish community centers, in addition to synagogues, which bring together all elements of the Jewish community, whether religious or secular.)

The synagogue fills to capacity during the New Year (in Hebrew, *Rosh Hashanah)* and the Day of Atonement (in Hebrew, *Yom Hakippurim),* a period of ten days in the autumn that marks the beginning of the holy season three weeks prior to the autumnal equinox. The holy season comes to a climax in the Festival of Tabernacles. During this season, the community assembles for rites that are, in fact, intensely personal and private. The New Year and Day of Atonement define a penitential season, a time of stocktaking, when, in the language of the faith, God judges each person and decides on the future of us all. The prayers that are said speak of what happens to me, but use the language of "we" and "us" and speak about the entire holy people, Israel, which stands before God for judgment.

The prayers recited in the synagogue define the individual and holy Israel together; a pilgrim people, seeking to worship the God of all humanity. On the New Year, which is called "the birthday of the world," God asserts sovereignty, as in the New Year Prayer:

> Our God and God of our Fathers, Rule over the whole world in Your honor . . . and appear in Your glorious might to all those who dwell in the civilization of Your world, so that everything made will know that You made it, and every creature discern that You have created him, so that all in whose nostrils is breath may say, "The Lord, the God of Israel is king, and His kingdom extends over all."

Since people have been told what God requires of them, they are judged:

> On this day sentence is passed upon countries, which to the sword and which to peace, which to famine and which to plenty, and each creature is judged today for life or death. Who is not judged on this day? For the remembrance of every creature comes before You, each man's deeds and destiny, words and way.

The liturgy creates a dramatic moment. These are strong words for people to hear. As life unfolds and people grow reflective, the Days of Awe seize the imagination: I live, I die, sooner or later it comes to all. The call for inner contemplation implicit in the mythic words elicits deep response.

We see that Judaism, a religion of one holy people, presents a vision of all humanity; it is not particular but universal in its concerns. It also is very personal, dealing with sin, atonement, and reconciliation. The most popularly practiced public rite of Judaism is the rite of atonement, which takes place in the autumn and occupies what are called in this country "the High

Holy Days" and in Judaism, "the Days of Awe." The most personal, solemn, and moving of the Days of Awe is the Day of Atonement, _Yom Kippur,_ the Sabbath of Sabbaths. It is marked by fasting and continuous prayer. On it, the Jew makes confession:

> Our God and God of our fathers, may our prayer come before You. Do not hide yourself from our supplication, for we are not so arrogant or stiff-necked as to say before You. . . . We are righteous and have not sinned. But we have sinned.
>
> We are guilt laden, we have been faithless, we have robbed. . . . We have committed iniquity, caused unrighteousness, have been presumptuous. . . .
>
> We have counseled evil, scoffed, revolted, blasphemed.

The Hebrew confession is built upon an alphabetical acrostic, as if by making certain every letter is represented, God, who knows human secrets, will combine them into appropriate words. The very alphabet bears witness against us before God. Then:

> What shall we say before You who dwell on high? What shall we tell You who live in heaven? Do You not know all things, both the hidden and the revealed? You know the secrets of eternity, the most hidden mysteries of life. You search the innermost recesses, testing men's feelings and heart. Nothing is concealed from You or hidden from Your eyes. May it therefore be Your will to forgive us our sins, to pardon us for our iniquities, to grant remission for our transgressions.

A further list of sins follows, again with a line beginning with each letter of the alphabet. Prayers to be spoken by the congregation are all in the plural: "For the sin which we have sinned against You with the utterance of the lips. . . . For the sin which we have sinned before You openly and secretly. . . ."

The community takes upon itself responsibility for what is done in it. All Israel is part of one community, one body, and all are responsible for the acts of each. The sins confessed are mostly against society, against other people; few pertain to ritual laws. At the end comes a final word:

> O my God, before I was formed, I was nothing. Now that I have been formed, it is as though I had not been formed, for I am dust in my life, more so after death. Behold I am before You like a vessel filled with shame and confusion. May it be Your will . . . that I may no more sin, and forgive the sins I have already committed in Your abundant compassion.

While much of the liturgy speaks of "we," the individual focus dominates throughout. The Days of Awe speak to the heart of the individual, telling a story of judgment and atonement. So the individual Jew stands before God; possessing no merits, yet hopeful of God's love and compassion. The power of the Days of Awe derives from the sentiments and emotions aroused by the theme of those days: What is happening to me? Where am I going?

Answers to these questions come not only from the synagogue, but also from the home. But just as the home forms a principal setting in which the public life of Judaism takes place, so the synagogue makes ample place for events in personal life. The most important is the celebration of the maturing of young women and men. At the advent of puberty the community, along with the family, celebrates the young person's becoming responsible, specifically, for keeping the Torah, in Hebrew, _bar mitzvah_ (for males) or _bat mitzvah_ (for females); _mitzvah_ means one who is responsible to carry out religious duties. The religious rite is simple. At any synagogue service, when the Torah is read aloud to the community, various persons are called to say a blessing before each reading. On the occasion on which a young person reaches the age of religious responsibility, that person is called to the Torah and says the blessing. In addition, the bar or bat mitzvah will also be given the honor of reciting the *haftarah,* which is a passage from the Prophets (the Old Testament books of Joshua, Judges, Samuel, Kings, Isaiah, Jeremiah, Ezekiel, or the Twelve Minor Prophets). Family assembles from far and wide, and, in North America, chances are many Christian and other gentile friends of the young person and family will participate in the celebration.

Pilgrimage

A journey undertaken for religious reasons, to a holy place, or a place rich in memory, is called a *pilgrimage.* In ancient times, Judaism called upon people to leave their homes and come to the holy Temple in Jerusalem, where animal sacrifices were prepared, as set forth in the Torah in the books of Leviticus and Numbers; the fat was burned on the altar, and the meat was eaten by the pilgrim. Three times a year, on Passover, Pentecost (in Hebrew, *Shavuot,* held fifty days after Passover to commemorate the revelation of the Torah to Moses at Mount Sinai fifty days after the exodus from Egypt), and Tabernacles, people would leave their villages and make the trip to Jerusalem, a vast assembly of holy Israel in its holiest place. The Temple was destroyed in 70 C.E. by the Romans, who then controlled the Land of Israel (later on called Palestine) and suppressed a Jewish rebellion against their rule. The destruction of the Temple brought an end to animal sacrifice as a form of worship in Judaism. It also canceled the possibility of pilgrimage. Three generations later, in 135, in subduing a second war against their rule of the Land of Israel, the Romans even prohibited Jews from entering Jerusalem, their holy city.

Events in our own century have once more made pilgrimage into a major expression of Judaism. The most important was the reestablishment of the Jewish state in the Land of Israel in 1948. This was the work of Zionism, a political movement begun in 1897 to bring all Jews who needed a home

and a refuge together in the ancient Land of Israel and there to found the State of Israel. In half a century Zionism succeeded in its goals. But between 1948 and 1967, Jerusalem was divided between the State of Israel and Jordan, with the Judaic holy places in Jordanian hands. At the end of the Six Day War, when the Arab countries surrounding the State of Israel tried to destroy the Jewish state, the Israelis retook the eastern sector of Jerusalem from the Jordanians and reopened the holy places of Judaism (as well as of Christianity and Islam) to everybody. From that time onward, the western wall of the ancient Temple of Jerusalem, which had survived the destruction in 70, became the principal center of pilgrimage for Jews throughout the world. Many American Jews have made the pilgrimage to the wall, and most American Jews take a deep interest in the welfare of the State of Israel and its people. That concern, political as much as ethnic and religious, persuades American Jews to accept their share of responsibility for sustaining the State of Israel as the refuge for all Jews who need a home.

For some Jews in recent times the pilgrimage to Jerusalem takes a detour through Poland and other places in Central and Eastern Europe. To understand the route you have to remember that the State of Israel came into being because of the Holocaust, the systematic, well-organized, and efficient murder of millions of Jews in Europe as part of Germany's war effort in World War II, particularly from 1941 through 1945. In the recent past, therefore, one form of the expression of Judaism has called people to visit sites at which Jews were murdered. The Germans built death factories, in which thousands of people were gassed and their bodies then cremated, day after day, so people—including many Germans today, who have sincerely repented the crimes of World War II—come to pray, remember, and cry. From Auschwitz, near Cracow, in Poland, where millions of Jews died only because they were "Israel," the holy people, the pilgrims' path ascends to Jerusalem.

Many American Jews are descendants of those who came in the mass migration between 1880 and 1920 from the lands of Eastern Europe, Poland, Russia, White Russia, Ukraine, Hungary, Bohemia, Moravia, and Slovakia, as well as Germany. When the immigrants came to America, many changed their names in order to cut ties to the past and start anew. As a result, many American Jewish families cannot even name the victims of the Holocaust to whom they were personally related. But all identify with the experience of Holocaust and the heroism of emerging from death camps to found a state; that is why the age of pilgrimage opens roads that lead from Cracow to Jerusalem.

So much for the life of Judaism in the world today. Now to define the faith in its classical and normative writings: the Torah.

DEFINING JUDAISM: WHAT IS THE TORAH?

You now know that Judaism is the account of the way of life and the worldview set forth by (1) God in (2) the Torah given to Moses at Mount Sinai to (3) Israel, the holy people. So you may define "Judaism" as God's will conveyed in the Torah to Israel. From the viewpoint of Judaism, when the Torah is properly explained, people who practice Judaism, who are called "Israel," therefore know what God has to say to them and wants them to do. If you look in the Old Testament or in other holy books of Judaism, however, you will not find the word *Judaism*. When the faithful wish to refer to the faith, they use the word *Torah*. Torah refers to God's revelation to the holy people, Israel, through Moses at Mount Sinai, which is described in the Old Testament book of Exodus. Judaism teaches that this revelation of the Torah at Mount Sinai was in two forms, one written and one oral.

The Written Torah

Included in the Torah is, to begin with, the Pentateuch or the Five Books of Moses: Genesis, Exodus, Leviticus, Numbers, and Deuteronomy. In addition, the written Torah comprises two other parts: the Prophets (listed earlier) and the Writings, which are Psalms, Proverbs, Job, Song of Songs, Lamentations, Qohelet ("Ecclesiastes" in the Christian Old Testament), Ruth, Esther, Daniel, Ezra, Nehemiah, and Chronicles.

The Oral Torah

Judaism maintains that the Torah was given ("revealed") by God not only in the written form—that is, in what the Christian world now knows as the Old Testament—but also in oral form. The oral tradition was handed on from master to disciple, from Moses to Joshua, and onward to the sages who flourished for centuries to come. The Torah therefore stands for an enduring revelation by God to Israel, the holy people who stood at Sinai. When the scroll of the Torah—the Five Books of Moses—is read in worship services, a blessing prior to the reading says, "Blessed are you, Lord, our God, ruler of the world, who has chosen us from among all peoples and has given us the Torah. Blessed are you, Lord, who gives the Torah."

The story of the oral Torah is contained in a few words of a document called the *Sayings of the Founders* (in Hebrew, *Pirqé Avot*), a writing of about 250 C.E. read in the synagogue, chapter by chapter, as a principal part of Torah study. *Avot* 1:1–2 tells us,

Moses received Torah at Sinai and handed it on to Joshua, Joshua to the elders, and the elders to the prophets. And the prophets handed it on to the men of the great assembly. They said three things: "Be prudent in judgment. Raise up many disciples. Make a fence for the Torah." Simeon the Righteous was one of the last survivors of the great assembly. He would say: "On three things does the world stand: On the Torah, and on the Temple service, and on deeds of loving kindness."

This statement is striking for three reasons. First it claims that there is a tradition from God's revelation to Moses at Sinai that continues beyond the figures we know in the Holy Scriptures of ancient Israel ("the Old Testament"), specifically, Joshua and the Prophets. The "men of the great assembly" and Simeon the Righteous stand in the chain of tradition from Sinai, but they are not figures out of the Old Testament. It follows that there is another part of the Torah that is orally formulated and orally transmitted. The second claim is that this other Torah comes down through the relationship of master to disciple, who then becomes a master. The third striking fact is that what is stated is not a citation of Scripture but a saying that stands on its own. Simeon's saying is part of that Torah from Sinai, for example, but it does not refer to or quote Scripture.

Certainly the single most important figure in the chain of tradition from Sinai onward is Hillel, a sage who flourished at about the same time as Jesus, and to whom is attributed a statement strikingly like the Golden Rule: "What is hateful to yourself, do not do to anybody else. That is the whole of the Torah. All the rest is commentary. Now go learn." Both the teaching of Hillel and that of Jesus in the Golden Rule—"Do unto others as you would have them do unto you"— state in other language the commandment of the Torah at Leviticus 19:18: "You shall love your neighbor as yourself," and many great sages of Judaism have maintained that that statement summarizes the whole of Judaism. A further statement in Hillel's name (*Avot* 1:13) forms the foundation of the morality of Judaism:

If I am not for myself, who is for me?
And when I am for myself, what am I?
And if not now, when?

The collection of sayings gathered in the *Sayings of the Founders* appears now as part of the most important holy book of Judaism after the written Torah, the Mishnah, a philosophical law code written down about 200 C.E.

Scripture, which Judaism calls the written Torah, and the Mishnah, which Judaism knows as the first document of the oral Torah, received extensive commentaries. Books of the written Torah, such as Genesis, Exodus, Leviticus, Numbers, and Deuteronomy, were given extensive commentaries, called in Hebrew *midrash* (plural: *midrashim*). The Mishnah too was given its extensive commentary, called in Hebrew a *talmud* (plural: *talmudim*). There are two *talmudim*, the Talmud of the Land of Israel (ca. 400 C.E.) and the Talmud of Babylonia (ca. 600). The fact that the written Torah and the Mishnah are treated in precisely the same way—that is, are read in a close and careful manner so as to discover their meaning for the world today—proves that the Mishnah enjoyed a unique position as part of the Torah. The two *talmudim* then provided an authoritative explanation of what the oral part of the Torah meant and how it was to be observed.

To sample the kind of religious writing we find in the Mishnah, let's consider the single most important statement of that book. What makes this statement important is that it defines who is, and who is not, "Israel"—that is, who does or does not gain "a portion in the world to come," meaning the resurrection of the dead and eternal life beyond the grave. Judaism has its dogmas, for example, that God is one and that God gave the Torah. Here is how "Israel" is defined, together with some of its key dogmas:

Mishnah-tractate Sanhedrin 11:1–2

A. All Israelites have a share in the world to come,

B. as it is said, "your people also shall be all righteous, they shall inherit the land forever; the branch of my planting, the work of my hands, that I may be glorified" (Is. 60:21).

C. And these are the ones who have no portion in the world to come:

D. He who says, the resurrection of the dead is a teaching which does not derive from the Torah, and the Torah does not come from Heaven; and an Epicurean.

Here is the rule of the Mishnah that defines who is, and who is not, a Jew, that is, "Israel, the holy people." It does so by explaining who belongs and who does not: "All Israel" will not die but will rise from the dead at the end of days; then those who do not "have a portion in the world to come" will not be part of Israel in the resurrection. Excluded are those who deny the resurrection of the dead, or deny that the Torah teaches that the dead will live, those who deny that the Torah was given by God ("does not come from Heaven"); and those who deny the principles of the faith ("an Epicurean").

The notions of "the world to come" and "the resurrection of the dead" clearly refer to the end of time; the Torah teaches that in the end of days, God will rule over all humanity, and life as we know it will be succeeded by eternal life. The belief that Jesus Christ was raised from the dead corresponds to this conviction and was taken by his followers to indicate that the end of days was at hand and the rule of God ("the Kingdom") beginning. This passage asserts that every Israelite has a share in the world to come, meaning that each will rise from the dead and live forever in the Holy Land.

The Babylonian Talmud reference to this passage begins with two questions in mind: Is the rule of the Mishnah fair? How, on the basis of the written Torah, do we know the fact taken for granted by the oral Torah, namely, that the resurrection of the dead will take place and that the Torah itself says so? First comes the justification of God's way:

Babylonian Talmud Tractate Sanhedrin Folio Pages 90A–B

I.

A. [With reference to the Mishnah's statement, *And these are the ones who have no portion in the world to come;*] Why all this [that is, why deny the world to come to those listed]?

B. On Tannaite authority [it was stated], "Such a one denied the resurrection of the dead, therefore he will not have a portion in the resurrection of the dead.

C. "For all the measures [meted out by] the Holy One, blessed be he, are in accord with the principle of measure for measure."

What someone denies shall be denied to that person; hence, it is only fair that someone who does not believe in the resurrection will not live when the dead are raised up. But where in Scripture do we find that fact? The Talmud proceeds to many pages of proofs, among which the following provide a taste of the discussion:

IV.

A. It has been taught on Tannaite authority:

B. R. Simai says, "How on the basis of the Torah do we know about the resurrection of the dead?

C. "As it is said, 'And I also have established my covenant with [the patriarchs] to give them the land of Canaan' (Ex. 6:4).

D. "'With you' is not stated, but rather, 'with *them*,' indicating on the basis of the Torah that there is the resurrection of the dead."

V.

A. *Minim* [believers, sectarians, sometimes identified as Jews who believed in Jesus as the Messiah, hence, Christian Jews] asked Rabban Gamaliel, "How do we know that the Holy One, blessed be he, will resurrect the dead?"

B. He said to them, "It is proved from the Torah, from the Prophets, and from the Writings." But they did not accept his proofs.

C. He said to them, "From the Torah: for it is written, 'And the Lord said to Moses, Behold, you shall sleep with your fathers and rise up' (Deut. 31:16)."

D. They said to him, "But perhaps the sense of the passage is, 'And the *people* will rise up' (Deut. 31:16)?"

E. He said to them, "From the Prophets: as it is written, 'Thy dead men shall live, together with my dead body they shall arise. Awake and sing, you that live in the dust, for your dew is as the dew of herbs, and the earth shall cast out its dead' (Is. 26:19)."

F. They said to him, "But perhaps that refers to the dead whom Ezekiel raised up."

G. He said to them, "From the Writings, as it is written, 'And the roof of your mouth, like the best wine of my beloved, that goes down sweetly, causing the lips of those who are asleep to speak' (Song 7:9)." . . .

L. [The *minim* would not concur in Gamaliel's view] until he cited for them the following verse: "'Which the Lord swore to your fathers to give to them' (Deut. 11:21) to them and not to you, so proving from the Torah that the dead will live."

We see how the Talmud of Babylonia has faithfully expounded the Mishnah's teaching, so forming an expansion and explanation of the oral Torah's claim. What it tries to do in particular is explain the faith, and its particular point is to show that the teachings of the oral part of the Torah—for example, about the resurrection of the dead—derive from and are validated by the written part of the Torah. That is why so many verses of Scripture, the written part of the Torah, are cited in this passage.

We see that Judaism sets forth a number of theological dogmas of fundamental importance. The first concerns the belief that the Torah is revealed by God ("comes from heaven"), that there is the world to come, and that the resurrection of the dead will take place at the end of time. Another concerns the unity of God. A third maintains that God is made manifest in the Torah. A fourth is that God wants humanity's love ("You will love the Lord your God with all your heart"), and a fifth is that Israel, the holy people, is made holy by various religious obligations, or commandments, that God has assigned to them. Living the holy life in this world will lead in time to the advent of the Messiah, the end of days, and the resurrection of the dead. These theological dogmas, set forth in the Mishnah and the Talmud, come to expression in the prayers that are recited in the synagogue as much as in the documents of the Torah that are studied in the schoolhouse. They define Judaism.

JUDAISM IN AMERICA OR AMERICAN JUDAISM? SEGREGATION AND INTEGRATION

If you ask your Jewish friend or neighbor, Do you believe in the resurrection of the dead? chances are that the answer will be negative. For what the books say and what the people actually believe are two different things. Just by reading the books of the Torah, you cannot describe Judaism as it flourishes in North America, even though Jews refer to those holy books and revere them. Religions don't live in books but in the lives of people working together, so if you want to describe a religion, you can't just find out "what Judaism believes," but have to ask, "What do people do, because they practice Judaism?"

If you know Jews, you probably realize that different families observe Judaism in different ways. Chances are that in your community there are Conservative synagogues and Reform temples, and there may be an Ortho-

---

Opinion: "Charity Is an Individual Responsibility"

Among Jews and Christians, there is much confusion about the Bible's preferred course for addressing the needs of poor Americans, the dominant assumption being that support for the impoverished is a public responsibility.

Recently, the issue came up in the Seattle suburb where I live. Our local weekly newspaper reported that a tent city for the homeless was to be set up in a church parking lot. In the article, a representative of the city government explained preemptively that the church had every right to do this, and so, like it or not, the rest of us had no grounds for complaint.

Apart from the legal question, an implicit moral challenge was being issued: Anyone who did grumble couldn't be a very good Christian, or Jew.

In a subsequent issue of the paper, a letter to the editor appeared making a wonderfully biblical point. I was proud that this lone voice of protest belonged to a Jewish woman. Given the modern Jewish weakness for socialism, I was also surprised.

Would it not be better, she asked, if instead of setting up the tent city, members of the church invited individual homeless people to live with them? That would be so much more personal and loving. It would also provide these needy individuals with role models: functional, successful families, a setting they may never have experienced, perhaps accounting for the dysfunction in their own lives that resulted in their being homeless. Graciously, the writer did not mention that this would not impose an unwanted cost on the rest of who do not belong to the church and who may feel very ill at ease having an encampment of transients as neighbors.

This personal approach is exactly what the Bible commends to us. I can find nowhere in Scripture where the nation or the city is directed to compel generosity to the impoverished. Nor is a city like ours commanded to assume the responsibility (and dangers) created by someone else's generosity.

While society in general is indeed obliged, it is understood that the society is composed of individuals, bearing individual moral responsibility.

The book of Leviticus turns this ethos of charity into legislation: "If your brother becomes impoverished and his means falter in your proximity, you shall strengthen him . . . so that he can live with you." (25:35) Live with you, it says—not in a tent city, nor in shelters funded by money taken by the government from other people.

The prophet Isaiah was echoing the Pentateuch when he told the Jews living in his time, "Surely you should break your bread for the hungry, and bring the moaning poor [to your] home; when you see a naked person, clothe him and do not hide from your kin." (58:7) The emphasis on a personal relationship with the poor is unmistakable, not a pole's-length interaction as in the model of charity through taxation—or of inviting the poor to camp out in a parking lot adjacent to other people's homes.

(David Klinghoffer, "Charity Is an Individual Responsibility," *The Forward* [July 18, 2007], http://www.forward.com/articles/11179.)

---

dox shul as well. All three words refer to the same thing, a building where people gather for prayer, study, and fellowship. But each word speaks of a different kind of Judaism. In fact, there is no single, uniform Judaism here or anywhere else in the world. Like Islam and Christianity, Judaism comes to everyday expression in more than one way. Just as we know about Roman Catholic and Protestant and Orthodox Christianity or Sunni and Shiite Islam, so we recognize that there are Reform, Conservative, Reconstructionist, and Orthodox forms of Judaism, and within Orthodox Judaism there are many subdivisions as well. To make sense of them all, you have to start with a single question, which every form of Judaism answers. When we know the answers, we can make sense of the differences.

Segregationist and Integrationist Judaisms

The question that allows us to sort out different Judaisms is, Should Jews live not only among gentiles, but also with them, or should Jews live all by themselves? The Jews who believe that they should be fundamentally different from everyone else segregate themselves in as many ways as they can. Those who believe that Jews should be fundamentally like everybody else, except for some specific, religious differences, integrate themselves.

For many centuries Jews believed that they should live entirely in their own framework, in line with the prophecy of the gentile prophet, Balaam, "For from the top of the mountains I see him, from the hills I behold him; lo, a people dwelling alone, and not reckoning itself among the nations" (Num. 23:9). Living throughout Europe, North Africa, and the Middle East, speaking the languages of the countries where they dwelled, most Jews preferred a segregated existence. Long before Christian Europe imprisoned Jews in ghettos, where they were required by law to live, Jews preferred to live in Jewish streets or neighborhoods, near synagogues for example, since traveling long distances on the Sabbath is forbidden. In 1787, the American Constitution accorded to all white males full rights of citizenship; in 1789, the French revolution proclaimed the same. Jews then had to decide whether or not they wished not only to live among gentiles, but also with them as part of a nation other than holy Israel, God's people.

Segregationist Judaisms

From that time to the present, some Jews have freely chosen to live a life that, in most ways, separates them from everybody else. They choose to speak a Jewish language, in the United States preferring Yiddish, a language based on medieval German with many Hebrew, Polish, and Russian words in it spoken only by Jews. Their sense of the holiness of Israel required them to wear clothes that were distinctively Jewish; to eat only food that was kosher in a very strict sense, and hence not to eat at a gentile's table under any circumstances; to live in mostly Jewish neighborhoods; to study only the sacred books of Judaism; to buy goods and services only from other Jews; and, in general, to live that wholly segregated life that much of Israel, the Jewish people, had lived for many centuries. In the world today, such Jews are numerous in most of the largest cities of the United States and Canada—New York City (especially Brooklyn) and Montreal, for instance—some major cities in Europe (Antwerp is one), and in the State of Israel (Jerusalem and Bené Beraq, for instance, as well as in neighborhoods of every Israeli city).

All segregationist Judaisms are Orthodox in their fundamental affirmations, but not all Orthodox Judaisms are segregationist. What makes a Judaism Orthodox is the belief in the literal truth of the Torah, written and oral, and the commitment to practice the requirements of the Torah in every detail, both the ritual and the ethical teachings, as the way of carrying out God's will. Segregationist Judaisms believe that the only way to carry out the Torah is to live separate from both other Jews and also gentiles. Integrationist Orthodox Judaism, as well as all other integrationist Judaisms, maintains that Jews can live by the Torah and also share the common life of modern society.

Hasidic Judaism

Segregationist Jews do not agree among themselves on numerous important questions. Some of them belong to groups that are called "Hasidic." Others reject the basic doctrines and practices of that subset of Judaisms. A Hasidic Judaism believes that a holy man, or *tsaddiq* in Hebrew, stands in a special relationship to God, and takes shape around a particular holy man, believed to convey God's special blessing to his followers. The most important Hasidic Judaism is Lubovitch Hasidism, with its center at 770 Eastern Parkway in Brooklyn, New York, and with adherents in nearly every Jewish community in the world. Its principal figure, Rabbi Menachem Schneerson, died in 1994, but the disciples continue to revere his teachings. Lubovitch Judaism lives wholly in accord with the rules that all Orthodox Judaisms follow, which derive from the written and oral Torah as interpreted for all Jews through time. But they revere, in addition, teachings of their own group, and especially those of their rebbe. In his service they call on Jews who are in prisons; they find their way to the most remote places of the world where Jews are located and try to win them to the service of God in the way in which they serve God. They are the single most successful Judaism when it comes to winning formerly secular or isolated Jews to the Judaic religion as they define it.

Yeshiva Judaism

Not all segregationist Judaisms fall into the classification of Hasidic. Another type altogether is centered on *yeshivas*, or places in which people spend some or all of the day studying the Torah, and particularly the Talmud. These communities flourish in North America, Europe, and the State of Israel. The segregationist Judaism formed around a yeshiva will focus on the study of the Talmud of Babylonia, its commentaries and codes, and will involve its members in intense relationships of study and prayer. Some members of the community will devote their entire lives to Torah study, and others—very often, their wives—will support them to do so. Like monastic communities, the yeshivas, with their masters and disciples, will aim at forming centers of holy living, quite distinct from the world outside. Such yeshiva communities flourish in Boston, New York City, Baltimore, Chicago, Los Angeles, and elsewhere in the United States, and in Montreal and Toronto, in Canada, among many places.

Integrationist Judaisms

Integrationist Judaisms include Orthodox, Reform, Conservative, and Reconstructionist groups. Broadly divided among themselves in both theology and practice, all integrationist Judaisms concur that the Jews can and should live lives like those of their neighbors, differing only in some ways. All maintain that Jews should study secular as well as religious books. All agree that Jews may wear the same kinds of clothing as gentiles, pursue the same kinds of careers, speak the same language, and in most (though not all) ways, live the same kinds of lives. True, there may be some "insider-words," often from Yiddish, such as *kosher* or *maven*. But these words circulate everywhere and end up in common use. In that way, all integrationist Judaisms differ from all segregationist ones. But to know one integrationist Judaism from another, we have to turn from questions of how Jews are supposed to live their lives to those concerning what Jews are supposed to believe. Differences of doctrine separate one integrationist Judaism from another.

Orthodox Judaism

Among Jews who live integrated lives among gentiles, a small number observe the rules of the Judaism of the dual Torah precisely as these are kept by all of the segregationist Judaisms. If you live in a big city, Los Angeles, Chicago, or Miami, for instance, you probably know Jews who go to school with you but bring their own, kosher food; who play baseball with you but will not travel to games from sundown on Friday through sundown on Saturday. If you go to France, England, or Germany, you will find that most Jews in those countries identify with Orthodox synagogues. The leading voice of Judaism in Great Britain is the Chief Rabbi, who is the leader of Orthodox Judaism, as well as a major figure in British religious life.

These Jews call themselves "Orthodox." (The word *orthodox* means "right doctrine.") They will belong to Orthodox synagogues, where the prayers are said entirely in Hebrew, where women and men sit apart from one another, and where the classical writings of the Torah are expounded in terms familiar through the ages. But they are integrationist in that they do not center their lives on a yeshiva, or on a rebbe, and so they may be distinguished from those who do. Orthodox Judaism is diverse and includes segregationist and integrationist, Hasidic and non-Hasidic, and yeshiva-centered and synagogue-centered types. But all Orthodox Judaisms concur that the entire Torah, oral and written, comes from God, in exactly the words in which we now have it, and that everything in the Torah happened exactly as it is said to have happened.

Orthodox Judaisms, whether segregationist or integrationist, enjoy the support of approximately 13 percent of Jews in the United States, a small but growing number. The majority of American Jews are integrationist; according to the National Jewish Population Survey conducted in 2000–2001, 34 percent are Reform, 26 percent Conservative, and 2 percent Reconstructionist. The largest synagogues in most Jewish communities are Reform or Conservative; the Orthodox ones, though numerous, are smaller in membership. The reason for this is that the vast majority of Jews in America have formed for themselves a Judaism that is distinctively American. It is thoroughly integrationist, so that few Jews keep the dietary laws, and fewer still keep them in such a way that they cannot eat with gentiles. While Jews in numbers attend synagogue services on Friday evening or Saturday morning, they drive to synagogue, so that they are not limited to homes within walking distance of a synagogue. Nearly all Jews provide their children with a secular education, and most of them send their children to public or secular schools, not to yeshivas or to Jewish parochial schools that combine religious and secular education as Roman Catholic or Lutheran parochial schools do.

So the vast majority of Jews in America want to be Jewish in a way that permits them, also, to be an integral part of the American society and culture (however these may be defined).

Reform Judaism

Reform Judaism is the largest branch of Judaism in the United States, and the most successful of the integrationist Judaisms. It is on the basis of total integration that Reform Judaism sets forth its reading of the Torah. In matters of doctrine and practice, Reform Judaism affirms that the Torah is holy, but reads it as the work of people of a given time and place. The holy way of life taught in the Torah is binding, with special reference to what is relevant to the everyday world in which Jews live. Above all, what God wants is for us to "do justice, love mercy, and walk humbly with God," that is, ethics takes the highest priority in Judaism.

The American Reform rabbis, meeting in Pittsburgh in 1885, issued a clear and accessible statement of their Judaism. The initial, forthright formulation of Judaism as integrationist and not segregationist still holds true, not only for Reform, but in its ideal of integration, for most American Jews today:

> We recognize in the Mosaic legislation a system of training the Jewish people for its mission during its national life in Palestine, and today we accept as binding only its moral laws and maintain only such ceremonies as elevate and sanctify our lives, but reject all such as are not adapted to the views and habits of modern civilization. . . . We hold that all such Mosaic and rabbinical laws as regular diet, priestly purity, and dress originated in ages and under the influence of ideas entirely foreign to our present mental and spiritual state. . . . Their observance in our days is apt rather to obstruct than to further modern spiritual elevation. . . . We recognize in the modern era of universal culture of heart and intellect the approaching of the realization of Israel's great messianic hope for the

establishment of the kingdom of truth, justice, and peace among all men.

The Pittsburgh Platform takes up each component of the system in turn. Who is Israel? What is its way of life? How does it account for its existence as a distinct, and distinctive, group? Israel once was a nation ("during its national life") but today is not a nation. It once had a set of laws that regulated diet, clothing, and the like. These no longer apply, because Israel now is not what it was then. Israel—in America at least—now forms an integral part of Western civilization. The reason to persist as a distinctive group was that the group had its work to do, namely, to realize the messianic hope for the establishment of a kingdom of truth, justice, and peace. For that purpose, the nineteenth-century founders of Reform Judaism held that "Israel"—meaning the people—no longer constitutes a nation. It now forms a religious community. Long before the creation of the State of Israel in 1948, Reform Judaism redefined its views and affirmed that the Jews form not only a religious group but a "people." For instance, in 1937 the Reform rabbis, meeting in Columbus, Ohio, reframed the notion of "Israel" to make room for Zionism, the movement that saw the Jews as a nation and that ultimately created the State of Israel. At the same time, the Reform rabbis affirmed the basic concept that Jews live not only among gentiles, but with them. This formulation of Judaism today speaks for the largest group of American Jews.

Conservative Judaism

Most communities of Jews are divided between Reform temples and Conservative synagogues. The differences do not strike outsiders as very weighty. On most basic questions, members of Reform temples and Conservative synagogues concur. Differences on religious observance among ordinary folk, not rabbis, will be trivial. Their rabbis may differ, since Conservative Jews who do not observe dietary laws or the Sabbath and festivals expect that their rabbis will, while Reform Jews do not. Indeed, Conservative rabbis will refer to the Talmud of Babylonia and the later commentaries and codes for precedents on questions of Jewish observance, and they make every effort to keep the faith in a manner not strikingly different from the way in which Orthodox rabbis and some Orthodox laypeople do. Consequently, some suppose that Conservative Judaism is best described as Orthodox rabbis serving Conservative synagogues made up of Reform Jews, and that formulation is not unfounded. Conservative Judaism was the most numerous and influential Judaism in the United States in the middle of the twentieth century, but at the end of the century, Reform Judaism had replaced it.

Reconstructionist Judaism

A distant third in numbers, after Reform and Conservative Judaism, Reconstructionist Judaism emphasizes a naturalist theology, meaning a theology that defines God entirely in this-worldly terms ("God is the power that makes for salvation," so "what makes for salvation is God"). Reconstructionism is the most ethnic of Judaic religious systems, because it treats the Jewish people as the center of interest, and the values and beliefs of the people as the source of authority. It took shape in America as a naturalist, this-worldly Judaic system, originally within Conservative Judaism. Only in the recent past has it attained recognition as a distinct Judaism.

Gentiles and Judaism

Anti-Semitism

Whether segregated or integrated, Jews find themselves the object of hatred. The murder, by Germany and its allies, of nearly six million Jews in Europe between 1933 and 1945 points toward the persistence of hatred of Jews called "anti-Semitism." That hatred is a form of racism that attributes negative traits to all Jews. For many centuries, the New Testament's picture of the conduct of Jews in the time of Jesus and Paul—themselves also

Jews—led people to call Jews "deicides," or "Christ-killers." In the aftermath of the murder of European Jewry, the Christian churches have repudiated that charge.

The National Socialists, or Nazis, claimed that the Jews bore racial traits that accounted for the evil in the world and should be murdered ("exterminated" like vermin), and this was called "the final solution to the Jewish problem." In this country, some maintain the stereotype that Jews love money (more than most people) or that they are excessively clever. Imputing to an entire group of people traits such as these is seen by most people as unfair, untrue, and unintelligent, so for most Jews anti-Semitism is not an everyday problem. They find themselves accepted, and a mark that they are right is the very widely held agreement—approximately 88 percent—among gentiles that they would accept the marriage of a child of theirs with a Jew or that they would "vote for a Jew for president." Specific incidents of anti-Semitism notwithstanding, American society accepts Jews as normal and entirely ordinary members of society.

Gentiles in the Life of Judaism

Since most Jews in the United States opt for an integrated life, and since most gentiles accept this, we cannot find it surprising that many gentiles find a place within the Jewish community. Sociologist Barry A. Kosmin comments, "There is integration into American society that makes intermarriage more possible. On the other hand, a more tolerant, pluralistic society allows you to continue to maintain your traditions even in an intermarriage." One study found that in families in which all members are Jews, 86 percent attend a Passover seder; where there is a mixed marriage, 62 percent do. Only 18 percent of families in which both parents are Jewish will have a Christmas tree, whereas 80 percent of those in which one is a Jew and the other a gentile will have one. Where both parents are Jewish, 41 percent of families belong to synagogues; where there is an intermarriage, 13 percent do. Since 1985, 52 percent of Jews to marry have married gentiles; before 1954, the figure was 9 percent. This does not mean Judaism is done for in America. It means that Judaism is changing under conditions of integration.

Jewish Americans or American Jews: Neither or Both?

When we study Hinduism or Buddhism in America, what we learn about is Hinduism and Buddhism; these world religions have only recently arrived on the American scene, and we do not yet know much about how the challenges and opportunities of life in this country will shape these ancient religions. And although Protestant and Roman Catholic Christian religions have shaped America, so has America shaped them. Hence we learn as much about America as we do about Christianity when we study about Protestant and Roman Catholic Christianity in America. Judaism falls somewhere in between.

Most Jews in the United States see themselves as Jewish Americans—a Jewish species of American, different in religion alone. A smaller number regard themselves as American Jews—that is, a particular kind of Jew, but not different in any important ways from other Jews. Both are deeply American in their loyalties and commitments, but each has a quite distinctive theory of what it means to be an American. In the climate of a country open to difference but united in political institutions and loyalties to "one nation, under God, indivisible," American Judaism flourishes in diverse forms—segregationist and integrationist alike—because America accepts and even nurtures diversity. So the very diversity of American Judaism itself expresses the character of the shared life and social dreams of this country. But that diversity is possible to begin with because America stands on foundations of a national consensus. And one plank in the American platform is that there is room for every religion the world has known, and every version of that religion. That is what "one nation, under God" means.

STUDY QUESTIONS

1. What do you think the author means when he says that "while Judaism is not the religion of a single people, the Jews are a people with a single religion"?

2. What are the three things that make Judaism a living religion? How does each function within Judaism?

3. What roles do home, synagogue, and pilgrimages play in the religion of Jewish Americans? What religious functions take place in each of these locations and activities? How would you compare these "places" of religion in Judaism to "places" of religion in other traditions you have studied?

4. What is the difference between the written Torah and the oral Torah? Is it an important distinction? Why?

5. What do you see as the relation between the Torah and the Christian Old Testament? How are they similar? How do they differ?

6. Compare and contrast segregationist Judaism with integrationist Judaism. What are the reasons for Jews choosing to embrace either policy? Are there religious disagreements among members within each tradition? Why does such diversity within traditions suggest strength of commitment as opposed to fragmentation?

7. Why do you think anti-Semitism exists? What stereotypes should we avoid to help us prevent anti-Semitism? What evidence suggests that Jews and gentiles within the United States are developing even closer and more harmonious relations?

ESSAY TOPICS

The Relationship between Conservative, Orthodox, Reform, and Reconstructionist Judaism

The Role of the Torah in Judaism

The Holocaust and the Jewish Religion

The Religious Dimension of the Synagogue: Design and Function

Sacred Days of Judaism: Origin and Function

WORD EXPLORATION

The following words play significant roles in any discussion of Judaism in America and are worth careful reflection and discussion.

Jews	Bar Mitzvah	Hebrew
Temple	Yahweh	Scroll
Torah	Mitzvah	Yarmulke
Synagogue	Shavuot	Rosh Hashanah
Holocaust (Shoah)	Anti-Semitism	Yom Kippur

FOR FURTHER READING

Glazer, Nathan. *American Judaism*. 2nd ed., rev., with a new introduction. Chicago: University of Chicago Press, 1989.

Neusner, Jacob. *Death and Birth of Judaism: The Impact of Christianity, Secularism, and the Holocaust on Jewish Faith*. New York: Basic Books, 1987. Second printing: Lanham MD, 2000: University Press of America.

Sachar, Howard Morley. *A History of the Jews in America*. New York: Knopf, 1992.

Sachar, Howard Morley. *A History of the Jews in the Modern World*. New York: Knopf, 2005.

Wenger, Beth S. *The Jewish Americans: Three Centuries of Jewish Voices in America*. New York: Doubleday, 2007.

WEB SITES

http://www.urj.org
   Official site of the Union for Reform Judaism

http://www.jewfaq.org
   FAQ about Judaism, including beliefs, holidays, and practices

http://www.chabad.org
   Information about ultra-Orthodox Judaism

http://www.uscj.org
   Official site of the United Synagogue of Conservative Judaism

8

Islam in the World and in America

JOHN L. ESPOSITO

ca.570	Birth of Muhammad
610	Muhammad receives first revelation, commemorated as "Night of Power and Excellence"
620	Muhammad's Night Journey to Jerusalem
622	Emigration (*Hijrah*) of Muslim community from Mecca to Medina; first year of the Muslim lunar calendar
632	Muhammad's final pilgrimage to Mecca, farewell sermon, and death
632–661	Rule of Four "Rightly-Guided" Caliphs, formative period for Sunnis
8th–9th c.	Formation of major Sunni law schools
1095–1453	Crusades
11th–12th c.	Rise of Sufi orders
1187	Saladin and Muslim forces reconquer Jerusalem
1281–1924	Ottoman Empire (Middle East, North Africa, portions of Eastern Europe)
1453	Fall of Constantinople/Istanbul, capital of former Byzantine Empire, to Ottomans
1483–1857	Mughal Empire (South Asia)
1501–1722	Safavid Empire (Iran)
1897–1975	Elijah Muhammad, leader of the Nation of Islam in the United States
1964	World champion boxer Cassius Clay joins Nation of Islam; takes name Muhammad Ali; in 1975, converts to Sunni Islam
1965	Malcolm X assassinated at a religious rally
1965	Changes in U.S. immigration laws pave way for larger immigration of Muslims, primarily from Middle East and South Asia
1975	Wallace D. Muhammad (later changed to Warith Deen Muhammad) succeeds father Elijah Muhammad and brings followers into conformity with mainstream Sunni Islam
1978–1979	Islamic Revolution in Iran
1979	Soviet Union invades Afghanistan
1979	Militants seize Grand Mosque in Mecca
1990–1991	Saddam Hussein invades Kuwait; Persian Gulf War
1995	Welfare (Refah) Party wins parliament; Dr. Necmettin Erbakan becomes Turkey's first Islamist prime minister

1997	Mohammad Khatami, progressive cleric, elected president of Islamic Republic of Iran
1998	U.S. Embassies in Tanzania and Kenya bombed by Muslim militants
1999	Abdurrahman Wahid, head of major Islamic organization, Nahdatul Ulama, elected president of Indonesia
2001	9/11 terrorist attacks in New York City initiate U.S.-led war against terrorism
2002	Islamic candidates win parliament in Bahrain; Turkey's Muslim-oriented Justice and Development Party (AKP) sweeps parliamentary elections; terrorist attack by Islamic militants at nightclub in Bali, Indonesia
2003	U.S.-led invasion of Iraq and overthrow of Saddam Hussein
2005	Iran's reformist President Muhammad Khatami succeeded by hardliner Mahmoud Ahmadinejad
2005	Muslim Brotherhood candidates win Egyptian parliamentary elections; vocal oppositional bloc controls one-fifth of the parliament
2006	Keith Ellison, Minnesota lawyer, becomes first American Muslim elected to U.S. Congress

In the aftermath of the September 11, 2001, terrorist attacks in New York and Washington, D.C., a basic knowledge of Islam has become essential for every American. With 1.2 billion Muslims globally, including fifty-six Muslim-majority countries, Islam is the second-largest of the world's religions. Although the number of Muslims in the United States is a contested figure, there are likely between four and six million Muslims now living in America, making Islam the third-largest U.S. religion. Therefore, it is no longer appropriate to think of Muslims as those people in the Middle East or Africa or Asia. Islam, like Judaism and Christianity, is a major religion in America.

Islam suffers from a number of misconceptions and stereotypes. For example, although many Arabs are Muslims, most Muslims are not Arab. The majority of the world's Muslims are not Arab but Asian and African. The largest Muslim communities are found in Indonesia, Bangladesh, Pakistan, India, and Nigeria rather than Saudi Arabia, Egypt, or Iran.

Muslims worship the same God who is revered by Christians and Jews.[1] Muslims also recognize the biblical prophets. They especially consider Moses and Jesus to be great prophets who received revelations from God. Like Judaism and Christianity, Islam began in the Middle East. Moses, Jesus, and Muhammad were all born there. Like Judaism and Christianity, Islam also spread throughout much of the world. Islam is truly a world religion that embraces people of many races and languages.

WHAT DOES ISLAM MEAN?

The word *Islam* means "peace" and "submission" to God. Just as Jews use the greeting "Shalom" (peace), Muslims say "Assalam wa alaykum" (peace be upon you) whenever they meet a friend or say goodbye. Many Muslims say "In the name of God the Merciful and Compassionate" each time they begin to speak, read, write, or do just about anything. Muslims, like most religious people, believe in peace and compassion and indeed are raised from an early age to associate these qualities with God and their religion.

The word *Muslim* means one who submits to God's will. The term *Islam* really reflects not only a religion, but also a way of life and a community. Islam puts heavy emphasis on one's community. To be a Muslim is not just an individual activity; it is a community identity and responsibility. Every Muslim, regardless of his or her race, sex, and tribal, ethnic, or national background, is also considered to be a member of a worldwide community of believers, called the *ummah*. They are bound together by a common faith in God and God's prophets.

Like Judaism and Christianity, Islam includes a number of communities or branches. The two major groups are Sunni Muslims, who comprise about 85 percent of Muslims, and Shii (or Shiite) Muslims, who account for 15 percent of the world's Muslim population. Despite their differences, all Muslims share a common faith in Allah (God) and follow the teachings of their prophet, Muhammad. In addition to their shared belief in God and his prophets, Muslims share the practice of daily prayer, concern and responsibility for the poor, and an emphasis on community and family.

GOD AND GOD'S MESSENGER

Just as Moses in Judaism and Jesus in Christianity hold a special place as messengers and models for their communities, Muslims believe that Muhammad is the revealer of God's will for two reasons. First, he received God's message, which was later written down. This message is the Quran, which is Islam's scripture, like Christianity's Bible and Judaism's Torah. Second, the way Muhammad lived his life is used as an example for believing Muslims today. As you can see, there are many links between Judaism, Christianity, and Islam. In fact, from a Muslim's point of view it is more correct to speak of the Judeo-Christian-Islamic tradition.

Muslims, like Jews and Christians, believe that there is one God, whom Muslims call Allah, the Creator, Sustainer, and Judge of the universe. Although one can come to know God through the wonders of creation, Muslims believe that God's will was revealed to a long series of prophets or messengers, first to Adam, Abraham, Noah, and Moses, then to Jesus, and then to Muhammad, the final prophet. Muhammad is of key importance to Muslims as a living

example of the "ideal Muslim," the model for all to learn from and copy. Many Muslims are named after the Prophet; in some countries all males have the name Muhammad as one of their names. Not surprisingly, Muhammad's birthday is celebrated as a great feast.

Muhammad (570–632 C.E.) was born in Mecca, a commercial, cultural, and religious center in Arabia. An orphan raised by his uncle, he worked as a caravan manager, traveled extensively, and eventually married Khadija, the woman who owned the caravan company. Muslim tradition tells us that he was very happily married and was a well-respected businessman, known for such honesty and trustworthiness that he was often called upon to mediate disputes. He was a pious man who often spent time in meditation and reflection. At the age of forty, Muhammad had an experience that would change his life. In fact, Muhammad's experience would affect the lives of hundreds of millions of people across the world and throughout history.

Muhammad liked to withdraw from time to time to be alone and reflect. One day he heard a voice which commanded him, "Recite!" Muhammad was stunned and confused. Was he hearing voices? Was there something wrong with him? Frightened and bewildered, he responded that he had nothing to recite. The angel Gabriel again commanded him to recite. Finally, the words came to him: "Recite in the name of your Lord who has created, created man out of a germ-cell. Recite for your Lord is the Most Gracious One Who has taught by the pen, Taught man what he did not know!"

Muhammad began to receive a series of revelations from God through the angel Gabriel. Like the biblical prophets, Muhammad spent many years communicating the message he received from God, calling upon the people to repent their sinful ways and to return to the worship of the one true God. These revelations continued for approximately twenty-two years until shortly before Muhammad's death at the age of sixty-two.

Muhammad served as a moral conscience for his community, warning that God would judge people for their pagan practices and social injustices. Like the biblical prophets, he was rejected by many who saw him as a threat to their beliefs and lives of privilege. He was a reformer who seemed like a revolutionary to them.

The leaders of Mecca persecuted Muhammad and his followers. As a result, in 622 an event occurred that proved pivotal in Muslim history. Muhammad and a group of his followers moved to a nearby city, Medina, where he established and governed the first Muslim community. Muslims date their calendar from the year that the Muslim community was established in Medina rather than the year that Muhammad was born or the year that he received the first revelation of the Quran.

Muhammad was both a religious and a political leader, a prophet and a statesman. His charismatic authority was so strong and overpowering that much of Muslim practice came to be identified with him. After Muhammad's death, narrative stories (called "traditions," or *hadith*) preserved accounts about the Prophet's example, what he said and did, which is called his *Sunnah*. These stories or traditions covered everything from Muhammad's advice about prayer, fasting, marriage and divorce, diplomacy, and holy war, to his teachings and example. During the early centuries of Islam, collections of these traditions (which mushroomed into the thousands) and biographies of the Prophet became sources of guidance for Muslims as they struggled after his death to better understand what it meant to be a good Muslim.

ISLAM: A WAY OF LIFE

Islam is considered a total way of life for the religious community. For many in America who are raised with the idea of the separation of church and state and the sense that religion is a private affair, Islam can seem confusing, especially since Islam does not

have a "church" to preserve and promote its beliefs. Islam, like Judaism, responds to this challenge through Islamic law and the activity of its religious scholars, or *ulama*. When Muhammad died and the community no longer had the Prophet to guide it and resolve its problem, many Muslims felt the need to define more clearly what it meant to be a Muslim and how Muslims should live. If being a Muslim meant submission to God's will, and if eternal reward in heaven or punishment in hell was dependent upon following God's law (*shariah*), then it was important to know what that law required. This became even more of an issue as Islam spread across the world, absorbing peoples in different regions who had different laws and customs and encountering new situations, problems, and questions.

Unlike Christianity, Islam does not have a pope or group of bishops to determine what people are to do or believe. Answering the question, "What should a good Muslim be doing?" became the job of the ulama, scholars who devoted their lives to study, debate, and spelling out as fully as possible God's law. The ulama were like the great theologians of Christianity and rabbis of Judaism in this regard, and they became the teachers and guardians of Islam.

Of course, the starting point for developing Islamic law was to look at the teachings of scripture, the Quran, and the life or example of the Prophet. Since these sources did not offer specific answers for every situation, Muslim scholars relied upon their personal interpretation and opinion to determine God's will in a given situation. For example, the ulama have prohibited the use of drugs by pointing out their similarity to alcohol, which the Quran explicitly bans.

Depending on where a Muslim is born, he or she follows the regulations or guidelines of a specific Sunni or Shii school of law. Islamic law covers all aspects of religious life, including prayer, fasting, and pilgrimage, but also all aspects of social life, ranging from marriage, divorce, and inheritance to self-defense and warfare.

Sufism

In the eighth century, Sufism (Islamic mysticism) developed as a reform movement within Islam. Like Islamic law, the Sufi path developed to limit the arbitrary power of the caliph and the growing wealth and materialism of Muslim society that accompanied the expansion and growing power of the Islamic Empire. The term *Sufi* derives from *suf*, the Arabic word for "wool," because the first Sufis wore coarse woolen garments. While many believed that Islamic law, the ideal blueprint for Muslim life and society, would suffice to counter the excesses of imperial lifestyles and luxuries, Sufis found emphasis on laws and duties alone spiritually insufficient. Instead, they emphasized an "interior" path of asceticism and meditation with devotional love in their quest for direct, personal experience of the presence of God. The reformers did not reject the world so much as dependence on the things of this world. Desiring a more faithful return to the purity and simplicity of the Prophet's time, men and women pursued a path of self-denial and good works.

Sufism spread in the twelfth century and later swept across much of the Islamic world. Sufi orders became the great missionaries of Islam, and Sufism became integral to everyday popular religious practice and spirituality. Their tendency to adapt to local non-Muslim customs and practices, and their strong devotional character, helped them to become a popular mass movement. Sufism continues to exert great influence within the Muslim world and in the West.

THE FIVE PILLARS OF ISLAM

Profession of Faith (*Shahada*)

No matter what country they live in, all Muslims share certain basic beliefs and practices. These are called the five pillars of Islam. The first and foremost pillar is the profession of faith, which is called the *shahada.* Muslims proclaim: "There is no God but God and Muhammad is the Prophet (or messenger) of God." This statement expresses the essence of Muslim faith: faith in the one true God

and recognition that Muhammad is the last in a long line of prophets, all sent to communicate God's message to the world. When a Muslim pronounces these words of belief, he or she formally becomes a member of the Muslim community.

Like Jews and Christians, Muslims believe that God communicates to the human community through prophets. Professing that Muhammad is the final messenger of God implies acceptance of the Quran as the literal and final revelation from God. For Muslims, the Quran represents the very words of God that were sent down through Muhammad to guide humankind. Although Muslims believe that God also sent revelations to the Jews through their scripture or Torah, and to the Christians in Jesus' message or New Testament, they believe that over time foreign ideas and beliefs corrupted the original revelations to Jews and Christians. Thus, the Quran was revealed to Muhammad and contains the final, uncorrupted, and complete message from God.

Prayer or Worship (*Salat*)

The second pillar of Islam is prayer or worship (*salat*). Muslims worship God five times each day. At designated times throughout the day and night, in whatever country they are in, whether they are at home, in the office, or on the road, Muslims stop to face Mecca and to worship God. Their prayer is preceded by a ritual ablution, which includes the washing of the hands and face. Both physical and spiritual cleanliness, purity of body and spirit, are required for approaching God and reciting God's holy word in prayer. When performing the salat and reciting God's revelation, Muslims believe that they are in the presence of their Lord.

Muslims may pray alone or in a group. If in a group, since there is no priesthood in Islam, one of the worshipers serves as the prayer leader (*imam*), guiding the movements and recitation. Prayer consists of a series of prostrations before God. Muslims stand, then kneel and touch their foreheads to the ground, and then stand again. Throughout, they recite verses from the Quran.

On Friday, Muslims are expected to perform the noon prayer in a congregation. Like the Sabbath (Saturday for Jews and Sunday for Christians), this is a special time when the community comes together at a mosque. In American communities most Muslims are not able to pray at their mosque on Friday because they have to work. Many will gather on Sunday to worship and socialize as a community. During the congregational prayer, the imam is especially important because the imam supervises the rows of worshipers and coordinates the recitation and prostrations. People tend to dress up to go to their local mosque, and a preacher delivers a sermon. The sermon usually begins with the recitation of a passage from the Quran, which provides the subject for the sermon. Depending on the personality and style of the preacher, the sermon is often presented in a dramatic style. At other times, it may sound more like a scholarly lecture, exhorting the faithful to obey and follow God's commands. The imam relates relevant Quranic passages and traditions of the Prophet to issues in Muslim life.

Almsgiving (*Zakat*)

Just as the obligation to pray has an individual and a community dimension, so too almsgiving (*zakat*), the third pillar of Islam, is an individual obligation that instills and reinforces a sense of community identity and responsibility.

Islam teaches that because God is the creator of the world, all wealth ultimately belongs to God. Human beings are caretakers who are given an opportunity to share in and use that wealth. The pursuit and accumulation of wealth by Muslims has always been recognized as an acceptable and indeed noble endeavor. After all, Muhammad was himself a businessperson, as was his wife, Khadija, who owned the caravan business for which he worked. Throughout history, merchants and traders have been a respected class among the leaders in the Muslim community, providing support for religious institutions and activities. Thus, for example, they were effective missionaries, bringing the message of Islam along with their business interests to India, Southeast Asia, and Africa. Often, Muslim religious leaders have had close family ties with the merchant class and have themselves, like Muhammad, been engaged in business or land ownership.

Although wealth is a legitimate reward for one's labors, it also brings responsibility. From earliest times, charity has been recognized and strongly encouraged in Islam. Individuals may perform such actions as often as they wish. However, in addition to voluntary concern and care for others, Muslims also came to recognize a corporate responsibility; it is the duty of all who are financially capable to pay an annual 2.5 percent wealth tax to address the needs of less fortunate members of the community.

Integral to the mission and message of Muhammad and one of the major concerns of the Quran is the welfare of the poor and oppressed. This passage emphasizes his message: "Who denies religion? It is the person who repulses the orphan and does not promote feeding the poor. Woe to those who worship but who are neglectful, those who want to be noticed but who withhold assistance from those in need" (Quran 107:1–7). Payment of the zakat is an act of worship; it is a way that Muslims thank God for their material success and well-being. Many passages in the Quran and in the teachings of the Prophet Muhammad emphasize socioeconomic justice. Exploitation of the poor, weak, women, widows, orphans, and slaves and the hoarding of wealth are condemned. All Muslims belong to a broader community, so it is not surprising that Islam emphasizes the obligation of the more successful and prosperous members of the community to share their wealth with those who are less fortunate.

Fasting (*Sawm* or *Siyam*)

Once a year, all adult Muslims who are physically able fast during the month of Ramadan. Fasting (*sawm* or *siyam*), the fourth pillar of Islam, is a special time for reflection and discipline. It is a time to thank God for his blessings, repent and atone for one's sins, discipline the body and strengthen moral character, remember one's ultimate dependence upon God, and respond to the needs of the poor and hungry. For one month, each day from dawn to dusk Muslims abstain from eating or drinking anything, even water. The Islamic calendar is a lunar calendar, so over the years Ramadan falls during different seasons. When it occurs in the summer months, fasting can be especially difficult for those who live in very hot climates and must fast while they work. In such countries, it is often common to start work very early in the morning in order to finish by early afternoon.

The rigors of daytime fasting are offset at dusk when families come together for a quick, light meal to break the fast. This meal is popularly called "breakfast." Breakfast is then followed by a round of visiting and a full late-night meal with family, friends, or neighbors. Muslims will retire quite late in the evening only to rise early enough before sunrise to have a full meal before they face another day of fasting. In some parts of the Muslim world, special foods and desserts are served only at this time of the year. Similarly, many go to the mosque for evening worship, followed by a special prayer recited only during Ramadan. Ramadan is a time for many other special acts of piety, ranging from reciting and reflecting on the entire Quran over the course of the month to looking after the needs of the poor.

Near the end of Ramadan (on the twenty-seventh day), Muslims commemorate the "Night of Power and Excellence," the night when Muhammad first received God's revelation. Finally, the month of Ramadan comes to a close with a grand celebration, the Feast of Breaking of the Fast (*id al-Fitr*).

This joyful celebration is similar to Christmas or Hanukkah, as families come from near and far to celebrate together, wear their finest clothing, feast, and exchange gifts in a three-day affair that sometimes stretches into a week or more.

Pilgrimage to Mecca (*Hajj*)

The last pillar of Islam is the pilgrimage, or *hajj*, to Mecca. Every Muslim who has the health and financial ability is obliged to make the pilgrimage once in his or her lifetime. In many faiths, devout believers travel to the sacred cities of their faith—Jews and Christians to Jerusalem; Catholics to Rome, Fatima, and Lourdes; Hindus to Benares; and Sikhs to Amritsar—where they commemorate and often ritually reenact important moments from their sacred history. So too in Islam, once each year almost two million Muslims journey to Saudi Arabia, to the cities of Mecca and Medina, to perform the hajj. They come by plane, boat, car, and on foot. Men and women, rich and poor, black and white, from America, Asia, Africa, Europe, and the Middle East, descend upon Saudi Arabia during the last month of the Muslim calendar. Pilgrims come with awe and great excitement as many fulfill the dream of a lifetime. They return to their spiritual roots, the very land and sites where much of the early Muslim community's history unfolded. It was here that Abraham, regarded as the first prophet of purer monotheism, and his son Ishmael are reported in the Quran to have built the *Kaba,* the "House of God." This cube-shaped structure houses the black stone that tradition says was given by the angel Gabriel to Ishmael as a sign of God's covenant with Abraham and, by extension, with the Muslim community. This is also where Muhammad was born, received God's revelation, proclaimed his message, established and guided the Muslim community, and died.

As pilgrims from all over the world near Mecca, their excitement erupts into joyous shouts of "I am here, O Lord, I am here!"

Whatever their backgrounds and social class, all are equal before God. Fine clothes, jewelry, and perfume are set aside. All don the simple garments of the pilgrim; men and many women wear two seamless white sheets, a sign of their purification as well as a symbol of the unity and equality of the Muslim community. During the pilgrimage, participants visit sacred sites associated with Abraham, Ishmael, and Muhammad and ritually reenact and commemorate sacred events.

The pilgrimage ends with one of the great feasts or holy days of Islam, the Feast of Sacrifice (*Id al-Adha*), also known as the Great Feast. The feast commemorates God's command to Abraham to sacrifice his son, Ishmael. In the Bible, Abraham is commanded to sacrifice Isaac. Just as God in the Bible ultimately permitted Abraham to sacrifice a ram instead of his son, so too Muslims at the conclusion of the hajj sacrifice animals (sheep, goats, camels) in memory of Abraham's willingness to sacrifice his son at God's command. The animal sacrifice serves as a symbolic reminder to the faithful of their declaration that they too are willing to sacrifice what is most important and precious to them. Whatever meat is not consumed is distributed to the poor. The Feast of Sacrifice is celebrated across the Muslim world.

At the end of the pilgrimage, many pilgrims visit the mosque and the tomb of Muhammad in Medina before returning home. For many Muslims the special character of this moment is remembered by sharing their pilgrimage experience with family and friends and by preserving it through some memento. Many commemorate this milestone in their lives with a picture of the Kaba in their home or office. In some parts of the Muslim world, people paint a picture of the Kaba on the front wall of their house. Other pilgrims symbolize the significance of this event in their lives by placing the noun designating one who has made the hajj, *hajji*, before their given name, as in Hajji Muhammad Ali.

THE WORLDWIDE COMMUNITY OF MUSLIMS

Wherever Muslims may live, however devout or nonobservant they may be, most are acutely aware of their common bond with other Muslims throughout the world. They share a common faith and a common sense of a rich and vibrant early religious history: the spread of Islam in its first centuries and the creation of Islamic empires that extended from North Africa, across the Middle East, to Southeast Asia. Islamic empires brought with them the development of a rich Islamic civilization that made major contributions to the arts and sciences. Muslim scholars contributed to the development of algebra (which comes from the Arabic *al-jabr*), as well as to medicine, astronomy, philosophy, and literature. This brilliant legacy is part of the history and identity of all Muslims wherever they may live and however diverse their national origins.

Because Muslims belong to the *ummah*, a worldwide faith community, they are concerned about what is happening to their Muslim brothers and sisters in other parts of the world. Thus, events as widespread as the invasion and occupation of Afghanistan by the Soviet Union in 1979, the Iranian Revolution of 1978–1979, the plight of Muslims in Palestine and Kashmir, or the condition of Muslims in Europe and America capture the attention of many Muslims worldwide.

THE ISLAMIC REVIVAL

Perhaps the most visible sign of the vitality of contemporary Islam is the Islamic revival or resurgence. Too often, it is mislabeled "Islamic fundamentalism"[2] and simply equated with radicalism and violence. In fact, in many parts of the world in recent years, many Muslims have become more conscious of their Islamic faith and identity, and this religious reawakening has expressed itself in a variety of ways in Muslim life. The contemporary revival of Islam may be seen both in personal and in public life. Many Muslims have become more religiously observant, expressing their faith through prayer, fasting, and Islamic dress and values. This is reflected in an increase in the number of mosques, religious schools, and organizations. Not only has mosque attendance increased, but also a growing number of Muslim women, both overseas and in the United States, choose to wear Islamic dress, in particular a headscarf, or *hijab,* as a sign of modesty.

The belief that Islam is a total way of life has led some to want to create and live in a more Islamically oriented society and state. Islam has reemerged in politics both in highly visible and in more subtle ways. While many in the West are familiar with some of the more explosive examples, from the Iranian revolution to Saddam Hussein's call for a holy war in the Persian Gulf crisis of 1990–1991, these are headline events that often obscure or ignore a far more pervasive change in Muslim societies.

There is a great diversity of opinion and activity among the world's Muslims. While some leaders and movements have turned to violence to achieve their goals, the majority of Islamic activists wish to live peacefully in societies that are more firmly grounded in their faith and that are socially just. Their organizations call upon those who were born Muslim to become better or more observant Muslims and to work to transform their societies. They emphasize education in order to produce a sector of society that is well-educated but oriented toward Islamic, rather than secular, values. Many are graduates of the best universities in their countries or in the West, professionals in law, medicine, teaching, business, or engineering. The social dimension of this movement can be seen in the growth of Islamic schools, banks, student groups, publishing and media, and social welfare agencies (hospitals, clinics, legal aid societies).

Islam today is a vibrant faith in which Muslims, like all religious peoples, seek in diverse and sometimes conflicting ways to adapt their lives and religious tradition to the changing realities of modern life. This vitality and diversity may be seen not only in the traditional countries of the Muslim world, but also in America.

MUSLIMS IN AMERICA/ AMERICAN MUSLIMS

Muslim Immigration

Although Islam is a world religion, for many years the presence of Muslims in the West was small enough to go unnoticed. They often existed in Western societies that consisted predominantly of Christians as well as small Jewish communities. However, today that situation has changed remarkably. In France, Islam is the second-largest religion; in England and the United States, Islam is the third-largest religious community. It is estimated that by the year 2020 the number of American Muslims will surpass that of American Jews. These changes raise many questions for non-Muslims and Muslims alike. Who are these Muslims? How did they get here? What does it mean to be an American Muslim?

As we have said, there are approximately four to six million Muslims in the United States, and more than 1500 mosques are spread across the country. We have often been unaware of the Muslim presence because many Muslims have kept a low profile, preferring, like many immigrants before them, to blend in and be accepted. Others have sought to avoid special notice and harassment in an America that has often portrayed Islam as a violent religion, thus forgetting that like any other religion or ethnic group, Islam and Muslims represent great diversity.

About two-thirds of the American Muslim population consists of immigrants or descendants of Muslims who came to America from overseas. (The remaining one-third are African American converts to Islam plus a smaller number of white American converts.) Waves of Muslim immigrants began to come to America in the late nineteenth century and have continued to do so into the twenty-first century. At first, they were primarily laborers from Syria, Jordan, and Lebanon; then came Palestinian refugees who fled or were homeless after the creation of Israel in 1948. In recent decades, Muslim immigration has included well-educated Muslims who fled oppressive regimes in Egypt, Iraq, and Syria, or who came from South Asia seeking a better life. Like most immigrants from Italy, Ireland, Poland, the former Soviet Union, and other countries, many Muslims were concerned with economic survival. Many lived among other Muslims and attempted to assimilate rather than to stand out in society. Others came with the intention of striking it rich and returning home. Few were anxious to emphasize their differences by preaching Islam, seeking converts, or building mosques.

Large numbers of Muslim students have come to America since the late twentieth century from countries extending from Sudan to Indonesia—for example, from Egypt, Tunisia, Algeria, Saudi Arabia, Kuwait, Iran, Iraq, Pakistan, Bangladesh, and Malaysia. Muslim students now can be found at universities across the country. America provides an environment in which these students can share their faith and ideas. The freedom in America enables them to explore political ideas that would be impossible in their own countries, as well as to come to know about the teachings of Muslim leaders from other parts of the Islamic world.

African American Muslims

During the first half of the twentieth century a number of American blacks converted to Islam and established communities or movements. The most prominent of these was Elijah Muhammad (formerly Elijah Poole) and his Nation of Islam. Combining an emphasis on hard work and a strict moral code with an insistence on black separatism, the Nation of Islam promoted its ideas by opening temples and mosques in many poor urban neighborhoods and recruiting its members especially from the younger generation.

Elijah Muhammad's message of black separatism, with its denunciation of "white devils," created suspicion and fear among many white Americans, as well as Muslim immigrants, all of whom regarded it as a radical organization. However, in the black community the message proved extremely effective and had a significant impact not only among the poor, but among a growing number of students and professionals. Cassius Clay (born 1942), the heavyweight boxing champion of the world (1964–1967, 1974–1978, 1978–1979), drew headlines across the world when he joined the Nation of Islam, taking the name Muhammad Ali.

Another prominent convert was Malcolm X (1925–1965), who learned about the Nation of Islam in prison and subsequently became one of its most prominent ministers. In the mid-1960s Malcolm X made the pilgrimage to Mecca, where he saw and experienced Islam as a universal community of believers that was blind to differences of color and race. He returned from that experience rejecting the notion that the white race was inherently evil. He sought to preach an Islam that was more consistent with mainstream Muslim belief and practice, and therefore broke with Elijah Muhammad. In 1965, Malcolm X was assassinated at a religious rally. Two members of the Nation of Islam were subsequently charged and convicted of his murder.[3]

After the death of Elijah Muhammad in 1975, his son, Warith D. Muhammad, succeeded him. Warith subsequently rejected the separatist teachings of his father and brought many of his other teachings into line more closely with Islamic belief and practice. By 1985, he had integrated his organization into the worldwide Muslim community. However, a minority of African American Muslims, under the leadership of Louis Farrakhan, still retain the name Nation of Islam along with its separatist outlook.

Challenges Facing Muslims in America

As our discussion demonstrates, there is as great a diversity among Muslims as there is among other religious communities in America. Not only do Americans come from different countries and races, but we relate to and practice our faith in differing ways. For some Muslims, like members of other faiths, being a Muslim is part of their social and cultural background. However, they may not practice their faith regularly. Some pray or go to a mosque only on religious holidays, in the same way that some Christians celebrate only Christmas or Jews commemorate only Passover. Others are quite observant, praying regularly and living according to their faith. Still others, emphasizing that Islam is a total way of life, struggle to implement their faith in their public as well as private lives, in state and society.

Like all peoples and communities who have come to the United States as a minority, Muslims face special problems. Because America is predominantly Judeo-Christian in its origins and population, it is sometimes easier for Christians and Jews to practice their faith, although some Muslim religious holidays have become recognized and honored

---

Hijab and the Single Girl

For Americans, the *hijab* looks repressive and may serve as symbolic proof of the stereotype that Muslim women are oppressed. For American Muslims, the *hijab* represents the eye of the storm, with the storm being how American Muslims are interpreting the Qur'an and bringing their own perspectives to it. To some, wearing *hijab* is a way of showing physically a preservation of traditional Islam, as it was practiced in the country from which the immigrants came, or to show that they are serious about being Muslim. I have no doubt that conservative Muslims' hearts are elated when they see a young woman wearing *hijab*, as if that proves that Islam is surviving in the United States. To others, wearing *hijab* is an act of devotion, a way of serving God.

So where did *hijab* come from? Though there are accounts of head-covering in pre-Islamic Arabia (which would explain why Catholic nuns wear, in essence, *hijab*, not to mention that it is shown in practically every representation of the Virgin Mary), the Islamic basis for *hijab* is a few Qur'anic passages. The first asks that men and women be modest in their appearance and lower their gaze when with the opposite sex. The majority of the world's Muslims have come to interpret this to mean that women should cover their heads when out in public. The second passage instructs that men and women should cover their heads while praying. Some Muslims read this and come to the conclusion that since everything they do in life is a prayer and/or in service to God they should always cover their heads.

I have a few problems with seeing *hijab* as a Qur'anic requirement, the main one being that, if the above interpretations are true, men are severely, disproportionately, excluded from the *hijab* requirement, particularly in the United States. The modesty passage is directed to both men and women, as is the prayer passage. In addition, the modesty passage does not necessarily suggest covering one's head. It actually specifies arms and chest. Furthermore, if everything we do is an expression of prayer, men as well as women should be required to wear *hijab* as there is no exception in the Qur'an. (It does not say "Only women's actions count as prayer.") Finally, if the whole point of wearing *hijab* is *not to attract attention* to oneself, *hijab* in America certainly does not serve that purpose. Instead, it epitomizes the phrase "sticking out like a sore thumb."

(Asma Gull Hasan, *American Muslims: The New Generation* [New York: Continuum, 2002], 35–36).

by schools and in the public square. Attending Friday congregational prayer and taking a break to perform the salat during working hours are sometimes difficult. Because Muslims should not drink alcohol, eat pork, or eat meat that has not been slaughtered in a properly Islamic way (similar to Judaism's strict preparation of kosher foods), attending social functions or eating at restaurants can sometimes be awkward. However, things are changing rapidly. Muslim chaplains have been recognized by the armed services and in the prison system. Muslim religious leaders have joined Christian and Jewish chaplains to recite an opening prayer for sessions of the U.S. Congress.

Life in America also brings with it new situations and challenges. For those who come from Muslim societies that emphasize strong religious and family values and modesty in dress, life in a more secular and pluralistic American society can contribute to tensions and changes in values and outlook. American coed schools, dances, beaches, and social events may challenge traditional values. The greater sexual freedom in the West can bring out the tension and contradictions between living in a new society and abiding by one's religious values. Although socializing with non-Muslims is not a problem for Muslims, dating and intermarriage can be; however, intermarriage is becoming more common.

In the face of adversity, Islam in America has proven to be a dynamic faith. As a result of their experience, Muslims are constantly demonstrating the flexibility of their faith. Incorporating American customs, Islamic centers often include not only the mosque, but also a Sunday school where children study their religion, and a social hall for community events that range from bake sales to featured speakers. Those mosques that can afford it often have a professional religious leader (imam). In addition to his role in the Muslim world, where he would look after the mosque and lead the prayers, an imam in the United States also often performs such duties as counseling, social work, and public relations. Most American Muslims have become integrated into American society politically and socioeconomically. Muslims are present in the professions from local store owners to corporate leaders as well as teachers, professors, lawyers, and physicians. In 2006, Keith Ellison, a lawyer from Minneapolis, Minnesota, became the first American Muslim to be elected to Congress.

Islam and September 11

Given the fact that Osama bin Laden, the al-Qaeda, and the 9/11 terrorists who crashed planes into the World Trade Center and the Pentagon all called themselves Muslims, questions about the relationship of Islam to politics, violence, and terror have arisen.[4]

During recent decades, many Muslim countries have faced a large, restless younger generation; unemployment; housing shortages; unequal distribution of wealth; and corruption. At the same time, globalization and increasing Western influence are seen by many as political, economic, military, and cultural threats. These elements have influenced the growth of Islamic political (fundamentalist or Islamist) movements.

In response, many rulers have appealed to Islam to enhance their legitimacy and mobilize popular support. At the same time, Islamically motivated social organizations have been created to provide much-needed educational, medical, legal, and social services. Political movements that range from conservative and reformist to radical extremist have emerged in many states.

As a result, in the 1990s, Islamically oriented candidates became the prime minister of Turkey (Dr. Necmettin Erbakan), the deputy prime minister of Malaysia (Anwar Ibrahim), and the president of Indonesia (Abdurrahman Wahid). Others have held cabinet-level positions and have been elected to office in countries as diverse as Morocco, Egypt, Sudan, Lebanon, Turkey, Pakistan, Yemen, Kuwait, Malaysia, and Indonesia. In other nations, action has moved outside the political system. Violent extremists, in nations such as Morocco, Iraq, Saudi Arabia, Pakistan, and the Phillipines, have posed a direct threat nationally and internationally.

Governments have responded in diverse ways to the reassertion of religion in politics. In North Africa, the king of Morocco has combined his Islamic pedigree as a descendant of the prophet Muhammad with a modest reform agenda that has included parliamentary elections. Tunisia and Algeria have pursued more secular paths, repressing Islamist parties that challenge their rule. In contrast, Iraq's Saddam Hussein, while oppressing his own population also threatened the stability of governments in the Middle East. The invasion and occupation of Iraq in 2003 ended Saddam's rule but also led to an insurgency that increased widespread violence and acts of terrorism across Iraq.

Egypt's Hosni Mubarak, an ally of the United States, has battled and largely suppressed violent extremist groups. The Mubarak government has also tried to control the media and more tempered critics including the Muslim Brotherhood, which in the past several decades has pursued a path of nonviolent opposition.

Merely embracing Islam has not proven to be a political panacea. Saudi Arabia has been rocked by threats and challenges: the seizure by militants of the Grand Mosque in Mecca in 1979; dissident religious leaders who demand stricter observance of Islamic belief; and extremists like Osama bin Laden and the fifteen September 11 Saudi hijackers who not only called for the overthrow of the Saudi government but also engaged in international terrorism. In contrast to Saudi Arabia, Iran's clergy-dominated republic has had a "limited" political system that permits political parties and regular municipal and parliamentary elections in which women serve as candidates and vote. However, in elections in 2005, President Muhammad Khatami, a reformer, was succeeded by Mahmoud Ahmadinejad, a more militant leader whose statements and policies again led to Iran's being regarded as a threat.

However different their governments, many Muslim countries face the same long-term issues of authoritarianism, legitimacy, security, and terrorism. Secularists argue for the separation of religion and the state; Islamic reformers call for greater democratization in the name of Islam; rejectionists believe that Islam is incompatible with democracy. Those who maintain that Islam is incompatible with democracy include both moderate and militant Muslims. Accommodationists use Islamic concepts such as consultation (*shura*) between ruler and ruled, community consensus (*ijma*), and the right to reinterpret (*ijtihad*) religious traditions to justify popular political participation.

At the same time, as 9/11 and subsequent terrorist attacks in Europe and across the Muslim world have demonstrated, religious extremist organizations and movements exist in many societies. Like Osama bin Laden and al-Qaeda, they "hijack" their religion, using it to justify violence and terrorism and calling for a jihad against their own societies, America and Europe. Jihad, for example, is an important concept in Islam with multiple meanings. Jihad means to struggle or exert oneself in the path of God. A primary meaning is the struggle to lead a good life, to be virtuous. Jihad also refers to the right, often duty, to defend Islam or the Muslim community from oppression and injustice. However, extremists manipulate its meaning, arguing that they are fighting oppression and injustice, that they are waging a holy war against the enemies of God. They regard all who disagree with them—whether Jews, Christians, or other Muslims—as enemies who are to be fought and killed. They ignore other clear teachings of the Quran and Islamic law that forbid killing noncombatants.

THE FUTURE OF ISLAM

At some point in the twenty-first century, Islam will become the second-largest religion in America, as it already is in Europe, and will continue to be an important presence and force in Muslim societies. Extremist Muslims, like Jewish, Christian, and Hindu extremists, are a minority, though a dangerous minority.

As in the past, Islam will continue to be the fastest growing religion in many parts of the world and will take diverse forms, depending upon local political, social, and cultural contexts. The vast majority of mainstream Muslims, like their non-Muslim counterparts, will continue to lead constructive and productive lives informed by their faith. However, the perpetuation of authoritarian regimes, lack of freedoms, and repression of human rights will foster the concomitant feelings of powerlessness. The inability to address deep-seated issues and grievances within the political process will create discontent and instability and serve as a breeding ground for extremist movements.

For more than fourteen centuries, Islam has been a dynamic and expansive faith, providing inspiration and meaning to the lives of many. Today, that dynamism is seen not only abroad, but also by the significant presence of Islam in America. Like Jews and Christians before them, and indeed all religious peoples, the vast majority of Muslims struggle to preserve their faith and religious identity within America's pluralistic society. The presence and participation of Muslims in America adds to the tapestry of nationalities and faiths that have come to constitute the richness and diversity of America.

Notes

1. Throughout this chapter, I have drawn on my previous work, especially *Islam: The Straight Path,* 3d ed. (New York: Oxford University Press, 2004).
2. See, for example, John L. Esposito, *Islam and Politics,* 3d ed. (Syracuse, N.Y.: Syracuse University Press, 1991); and Esposito, *The Islamic Threat: Myth or Reality?* (New York: Oxford University Press, 1992).
3. For more about Islam in America, see Yvonne Y. Haddad, *A Century of Islam in America* (Washington, D.C.: Middle East Institute, 1986); Yvonne Yazbeck Haddad and Adair T. Lumis, *Islamic Values in the United States* (New York: Oxford University Press, 1987); and *The Muslims of America,* ed. Yvonne Yazbeck Haddad (New York: Oxford University Press, 1991).
4. See John L. Esposito, *Unholy War: Terror in the Name of Islam* (New York: Oxford University Press, 2002); and Esposito, *What Everyone Needs to Know about Islam* (New York: Oxford University Press, 2002).

STUDY QUESTIONS

1. Why is it important for Americans to have an understanding of Islam?

2. How is Islam similar to Judaism and Christianity? Name several major differences between these religious communities.

3. Who is Muhammad? Give a brief biographical description. What role does he play in the development of the Islamic religion? Name a figure in Judaism and in Christianity to whom Muhammad is similar.

4. What are the five pillars of Islam? How do they function in a Muslim's understanding of religious life?

5. What role does the month of Ramadan play in the practice of Islam? How is fasting believed to contribute to the Islamic way of life?

6. What is the goal of the religious pilgrimage in the Islamic faith? How is it similar to "faith journeys" in other religious traditions?

7. Why did Muslims come to America? When and how did the African American Muslim community develop in the United States?

8. What is Malcolm X's relation to the Nation of Islam? Why did Malcolm X believe that Islam represented an important religious experience for the African American community?

9. What problems do Muslims face in America? How has the Muslim community grown in light of such diversity?

ESSAY TOPICS

The Life of Muhammad

The Quran: Sacred Scripture of Islam

Malcolm X and the Nation of Islam: Religious Alternatives in the African American Community

Mecca: Holy City of Islam

WORD EXPLORATION

The following words play significant roles in any discussion of Islam in America and are worth careful reflection and discussion.

Allah	Quran	Pilgrimage
Ramadan	Elijah Muhammad	Mosque
Muhammad	Mecca	Imam
Theocracy	Islam	Jihad

FOR FURTHER READING

Abdo, Geneive. *Mecca and Main Street: Muslim Life in America After 9/11*. New York: Oxford University Press, 2006.

Bukhari, Zahid, John L. Esposito, et al., eds. *Muslims' Place in the American Public Square: Hopes, Fears and Aspirations*. Walnut Creek, Calif.: AltaMira Press, 2004.

Esposito, John L., *Islam: The Straight Path*, revised 3rd ed. New York: Oxford University Press, 2005.

____. *What Everyone Needs to Know About Islam*. New York: Oxford University Press, 2002.

Nyang, Sulayman. *Islam in the United States of America*. Chicago: Kazi Publications, 1999.

Smith, Jane. *Islam in America*. New York: Columbia University Press, 2000.

WEB SITES

http://www.islam.com
  Portal for the teachings, practices, and sacred texts of Islam

http://www.islam101.com
  History, beliefs, rituals, and prayers

http://www.usc.edu/dept/MSA/quran/
  Compendium of searchable Muslim texts, including multiple translations

9

The Bahá'í Faith in the World and in America

MIKE McMULLEN

1817   Birth of Baha'u'llah, prophet-founder of the Bahá'í Faith

1863   Declaration of Baha'u'llah as "Manifestation of God" on the outskirts of Baghdad, Iraq

1892   Death of Baha'u'llah and assumption of 'Abdu'l-Baha, his eldest son, as leader of Bahá'í community

1893   First mention of Bahá'í Faith in the U.S. at Columbia Exposition's World Parliament of Religions in Chicago

1894   Thornton Chase, first American to convert to the Bahá'í Faith

1909   Formation of "Bahá'í Temple Unity," organization formed to build the Bahá'í House of Worship in suburban Chicago

1911   'Abdu'l-Baha visits major U.S. cities

1921   Death of 'Abdu'l-Baha and assumption of Shoghi Effendi Abbas, his eldest grandson, as leader of the Bahá'í Faith

1925   First election of the National Spiritual Assembly of the Bahá'ís of the United States and Canada

1929   First Bahá'í summer school established in Eliot, Maine, called "Green Acre Bahá'í School"

1944   Dedication of the Bahá'í House of Worship in Wilmette, Illinois

1957   Death of Shoghi Effendi

1963   First election of the Bahá'í Universal House of Justice, the supreme governing body of the Bahá'ís of the world

1985   Publication of "The Promise of World Peace," definitive statement by the Bahá'í Faith on the elimination of prejudice and need for lasting global peace

1992   World Congress of the Bahá'ís of the World, New York City, commemorates centenary of the death of Baha'u'llah

1992   Publication of Kitab-i-Aqdas, the most important text in Bahá'í scripture

1997   Establishment of Regional Bahá'í Councils

2007   Actor Rainn Wilson (*The Office*) publicly discusses Bahá'í membership

2009   Bahá'í Faith claims five million members worldwide

The first exposure of Americans to the Bahá'í Faith was in 1893 at the first World's Parliament of Religions in Chicago, often seen as the beginning of the modern ecumenical movement fostering dialogue among the world's faith traditions. While the Parliament, held in conjunction with the Columbian Exposition, had a decidedly "Protestant" bias, many people who traveled to Chicago from all over the United States and the world would get their first exposure to "Eastern" religions, such as Hinduism, Buddhism, and Islam, by meeting swamis, monks, and imams.

The Columbian Exposition was held in 1893 to commemorate the four-hundredth anniversary of Columbus making his voyage to the New World. Representatives from Europe, Africa, India, Asia, South America, the Middle East, and the Caribbean showcased their culture, art, architecture, science, and technology, as well as religion, all in a spirit of cooperation and crosscultural dialogue. As such, the World's Parliament of Religions, as part of the wider Exposition, was an appropriate venue for the first public mention of the Bahá'í Faith in America—a religion whose explicit aim is to foster unity and eliminate racial, religious, and national prejudice. Bahá'í scripture declares that "the world is one country, and mankind its citizens." The World's Parliament of Religions represents one of the first times in human history that the world's faith traditions gathered in peace as an expression of global citizenship and ecumenical cooperation. Increasing immigration immediately before and after the 1893 event was making the United States the most ethnically, racially, and religiously diverse nation on the planet. In concert with these demographic changes, the Bahá'í Faith emerged in America with a message of racial unity some sixty years before the modern American civil rights movement, with a message of gender equality some twenty-five years before women in America were given the right to vote, and a message of global order and world government some fifty-five years before the United

States would help charter the United Nations. The Bahá'í Faith was a new religious voice ahead of its time in a country undergoing dramatic social change. It is appropriate, therefore, in this early attempt at religious unity and cooperation, that the Bahá'í Faith, which claims a unity among all the world's faith traditions, would get its first U.S. hearing at such an event. The message of the Bahá'í Faith was particularly revolutionary when it came to the United States in 1893 because it is one of the few, if not the only, of the world religions that explicitly deals with issues of racism. Bahá'í scripture states that racism is "the most vital and challenging issue" to face America, and the resolution of its cancerous effects is required to usher in the kingdom of God. When the Bahá'í Faith came to America, our society was only three decades past the Civil War and Reconstruction, and Jim Crow segregation was firmly entrenched throughout the South. By 1909, Bahá'ís were spreading the message of racial unity in places like Atlanta, risking their lives by holding racially integrated meetings, and eventually promoting interracial marriage while it was still formally illegal. Through all this, Bahá'ís claim their motivation to be spreading the message of Bahá'u'lláh and building the kingdom of God.

Since then, the Bahá'í Faith has experienced slow, steady growth as Bahá'ís spread their message of one God, one religion, and one humanity. At the core of Bahá'í belief is the idea that the one God who created the universe has been the author of one universal and unified religion. This one religion, however, was revealed by God in stages throughout the history of humanity through prophets whose appearance at different times and cultures has been misinterpreted as opposing and rival religious civilizations. The purpose of these historical installments of God's religion, Bahá'ís claim, is to educate humanity about spiritual reality, to establish ethical civilization, and to unite larger and larger collections of humanity until the goal of a unified human race at peace is realized. Far from being mistakenly labeled a

"Persian religion," the Bahá'í Faith claims millions of members worldwide (with the largest number in India), including nearly 144,000 followers in the United States.

RACIAL UNITY

According to the Bahá'ís, no religion in the world more directly addresses the issue of race than does theirs, and none is more relevant to the challenges facing the American social order than the Bahá'í Faith. This is because racial unity and the unity of humanity is the primary goal of the Bahá'í Faith. Bahá'ís claim that every religion was sent by God to unify and organize larger and larger segments of humanity, starting with the family and moving on to the clan, tribe, and nation. The purpose of the Bahá'í Faith is to unify all of humanity into one family (considered the culmination of social evolution on this planet), which can be done only by eliminating racism in all of its forms.

The most important way that Bahá'ís in America live out their "global citizenship" and the "oneness of humanity" is in their promotion of racial unity with the goal of "unity in diversity." Bahá'ís strive for racial unity not only within their own community, but as a general societal goal as well. Promoting racial unity and the Bahá'í Faith often go hand in hand. What is distinctive to this religious movement is the *explicit* manner in which Bahá'ís connect local race unity efforts and their global worldview. Bahá'ís declare that the elimination of all forms of prejudice is a fundamental requirement to achieve global unity and peace. The "oneness of humanity" is probably the key social principle that Bahá'ís champion, and the greatest demonstration of the oneness of humanity is found in the promotion of racial unity and elimination of racial prejudice. Promoting racial unity is a local expression of thinking globally. To learn how to advance racial unity locally and throughout the United States, Bahá'ís draw from (1) the example of `Abdu'l-Bahá, and (2) the guidance of Shoghi Effendi.

The Example of `Abdu'l-Bahá

`Abdu'l-Bahá (the son of founder Bahá'u'lláh and head of the Bahá'í Faith from 1892 to 1921) made a trip throughout Europe and North America in 1911–1912. While in America, he traveled from New York to San Francisco, teaching his father's religion and preaching about the desperate need for Bahá'ís to practice racial unity among themselves.

While in Washington D.C., `Abdu'l-Bahá upset Washington's racially segregated protocol by inviting a young black lawyer, Louis Gregory, to sit at his right hand in the seat of honor at a dinner reception. Louis Gregory—then a new Bahá'í—went on to become one of the most prominent travel teachers of the Bahá'í Faith in U.S. history. Gregory traveled throughout the South spreading the message of racial unity. It was through the encouragement of `Abdu'l-Bahá during his 1912 trip that Gregory and a British woman—Louisa Mathew—got married after a long friendship, becoming the U.S. Bahá'í community's first interracial couple. Throughout `Abdu'l-Bahá's trip, he frequently spoke about the positive influence interracial couples would have on the elimination of racism in America.

While in the United States, `Abdu'l-Bahá spoke to the fourth annual meeting of the NAACP about racial unity, undoubtedly because of the influence that Louis Gregory had within black intellectual circles.[1] The importance of `Abdu'l-Bahá as the "exemplar" of the Bahá'í Faith, in part, stems from his willingness to take a stand for racial unity, even upsetting socialite Washington, D.C., in the process. Bahá'ís thus turn to `Abdu'l-Bahá as a model for their behavior.

The Guidance of Shoghi Effendi

The second resource that Bahá'ís draw from is the guidance Shoghi Effendi (the great-grandson of Bahá'u'lláh and head of the Bahá'í Faith from 1921 to 1957) sent in a letter to the U.S. Bahá'í community in 1938, reminding them of the absolute necessity for Bahá'ís to embrace racial unity, and which has since been published in the book *The Advent of Divine Justice*.[2] The criticism of the American Bahá'í community Shoghi Effendi expressed in this letter has left an indelible impression on the American Bahá'í identity, and still challenges the Bahá'í community more than seventy years after its initial writing.

In one section, titled "The Most Challenging Issue," Shoghi Effendi told the American Bahá'í community in 1938, "As to racial prejudice, the corrosion of which, for well nigh a century, has bitten into the fibre, and attacked the whole social structure of American society, it should be regarded as constituting the most vital and challenging issue confronting the Bahá'í community at the present stage of its evolution."[3] He sent this message during a period in U.S. Bahá'í history when Bahá'ís themselves were making accommodations, especially in the South, to Jim Crow segregation laws. Shoghi Effendi censured the American community, calling it to a different standard. After forewarning them that "a long and thorny road, beset with pitfalls, still remains untraveled, both by the white and negro exponents of the redeeming Faith of Bahá'u'lláh," and recalling the example set by `Abdu'l-Bahá when in America (see above), he said:

To discriminate against any race, on the ground of its being socially backward, politically immature, and numerically in a minority, is a flagrant violation of the spirit that animates the Faith of Bahá'u'lláh. The consciousness of any division or cleavage in its ranks is alien to its very purpose, principles, and ideals. . . . If any discrimination is at all to be tolerated, it should be a discrimination not against, but rather in favor of the minority, be it racial or otherwise.[4]

In addition, Shoghi Effendi explained that both whites and blacks have responsibilities in eradicating prejudice.

Let the white[s] make a supreme effort in their resolve to contribute their share to the solution of this problem, to abandon once for all their usually inherent and at times subconscious sense of superiority, to correct their tendency towards revealing a patronizing attitude towards the members of the other race. . . . Let the negroes, through a corresponding effort on their part, show by every means in their power the warmth of their response, their readiness to forget the past, and their ability to wipe out every trace of suspicion that may still linger in their hearts and minds. . . . Let neither think that anything short of genuine love, extreme patience, true humility, consummate tact, sound initiative, mature wisdom, and deliberate, persistent, and prayerful effort, can succeed in blotting out the stain which this patent evil has left on the fair name of their common country.[5]

The willingness to tackle the problem of racism is one of the characteristics of the Bahá'í community that has most appealed to many of its converts, and certainly is one of the most widely communicated aspects of the Bahá'í message. It is the confidence Bahá'ís express in the eventual establishment of racial unity that distinguishes those with a Bahá'í worldview, from non-Bahá'ís, who are skeptical about the complete eradication of prejudice in a world filled with neo-Nazis, race riots, and ethnic cleansing.

HISTORY

The Bahá'í Faith is considered one of the "newest" of the world's religious traditions, and grows out of an Islamic context. To get a sense of why Bahá'ís consider this a "modern" religion appropriate for the times, it is helpful to have a brief understanding of its origins in Iran and history. Bahá'í history has two major founding figures: the Báb and Bahá'u'lláh. Bahá'ís claim that the appearance of the Báb fulfills many of the expected prophecies in the Shi'ite Islamic tradition, and that Bahá'u'lláh fulfills the expected prophecies of *all* the world's religious traditions at the same time: for example, Bahá'u'lláh is the fifth incarnation of the Buddha for Buddhists, the messiah for the Jews, and the return of Christ for Christians. Thus, according to Bahá'ís, Bahá'u'lláh is the expected prophet of all the world's religions who will usher in the kingdom of God. The Bahá'í Faith was anticipated historically when in 1844 a Persian merchant named Siyyid `Alí-Muhammad, known to Bahá'ís as the Báb ("the Gate" in Arabic) began to reveal new religious teachings. The thrust of his message was to herald the coming of "One Whom God Will Make Manifest," a prophet of greater importance who would lead humankind into a new era of peace. Thus, many Bahá'ís compare the function of the Báb to that of John the Baptist, who heralded the coming of Christ. The Báb attracted a substantial following from Shi'ite Muslims, arousing the suspicions and distrust of Islamic authorities, especially the Islamic clergy. In an effort to crush the religious movement after a period of persecution and imprisonment, the government of Persia executed the Báb in 1850, which almost destroyed the new religious movement. The Báb had not revealed when the "One Whom God Shall Make Manifest" would come, but had indicated the time would be soon.

One of the most ardent followers of the Báb was Mírzá Husayn-`Alí, a Persian whose family was part of the governing class of the country. His leadership role within the Bábí movement revitalized and invigorated the new religion after the death of the Báb. His social position protected him at first from the persecutions of the Persian authorities, but as fervor increased, he too was imprisoned. Bahá'ís believe that while he was in prison in Tehran from 1852 to 1853, God revealed to Mírzá Husayn-`Alí that he was the "One Whom God Will Make Manifest" prophesied by the Báb, whose teachings would inaugurate the long-awaited kingdom of God. Persian authorities exiled Mírzá Husayn-`Alí, his family, and fellow-Bábís to Baghdad, thus beginning a lifetime of imprisonment. While in Baghdad, he took the title Bahá'u'lláh ("The Glory of God" in Arabic), and announced that he was the one promised by the Báb, whereupon the vast majority of Bábís pledged allegiance to Bahá'u'lláh and his authority as a new religious leader.

In 1863, the group of Bahá'ís (the new name given to the followers of Bahá'u'lláh) were banished from Baghdad and sent to Constantinople (now Istanbul) and then to Adrianople (now Edirne) in Turkey. Finally, in 1868, the group was exiled permanently to `Akká, Palestine, the prison-city of the Ottoman Empire (near present-day Haifa, Israel, the location of the Bahá'í World Center). Here, as in the other cities of his banishment, Bahá'u'lláh carried on his ministry, wrote prolifically the texts that partially comprise Bahá'í scripture, and met with pilgrims who traveled to `Akká to see the man whose message was spreading throughout Persia and the Middle East.

For nearly a quarter century, Bahá'u'lláh lived first in the prison-city of 'Akká, and then later was allowed to live outside the city walls under house arrest (he was never permitted to travel). He and his family suffered many hardships during this time: hunger, disease, assassination attempts, despair, and even the death of Mírzá Mihdí, Bahá'u'lláh's son. Throughout it all, Bahá'u'lláh was the source of the exiles' strength and faith. He wrote, gave talks, received guests and later pilgrims, and began the process of mapping out his vision of global order, all from his prison cell. Accounts of believers record that some would travel by foot from Iran, only to be denied entrance to 'Akká and an audience with their Beloved. So great was their faith that those who could not attain the presence of Bahá'u'lláh would be satisfied with seeing his arm as he waved from a narrow window in the house he occupied.

While in exile, Bahá'u'lláh wrote nearly 15,000 documents—what Bahá'ís call "Tablets," which range in length from a few pages to book-length treatises on philosophy, law, ethics, spiritual life, and personal conduct. Bahá'ís claim that Bahá'u'lláh's writings are unique in the history of the world's religions, because Bahá'u'lláh is the first Manifestation of God to actually write his own scripture, unlike in previous dispensations where stories, parables, or laws were written down years or even decades later. Sometimes, Bahá'u'lláh would dictate the verses Bahá'ís believe he received from God to an amanuensis (or secretary), and then proofread what had been written for accuracy. The majority of Bahá'u'lláh's writings are preserved in an archive at the Bahá'í World Center in Haifa.

When Bahá'u'lláh died of natural causes in 1892, he left behind a growing movement, and a will and testament that named his eldest son, 'Abdu'l-Bahá ("Servant of the Glory" in Arabic) his successor and the authoritative interpreter of Bahá'í writings. After the Young Turk revolution in 1908, all political and religious prisoners of the Ottoman Empire were released, thus freeing 'Abdu'l-Bahá to begin establishing his father's covenant: the institutionalization of the Bahá'í Administrative Order as communicated through Bahá'u'lláh's writings.[6]

DOCTRINE

Progressive Revelation and Universal Ideology

In order to understand the universalizing goal of Bahá'í ideology and its promotion of global order and solidarity, one must understand the central ideological concept for Bahá'ís: progressive revelation. Bahá'ís' vision of global unity includes the ideological claim that all of the world's major religions are only evolutionary stages in God's plan to educate and unify the whole planet—in effect, there is only *one* religion, but it is revealed by God in distinct historical stages. Bahá'ís claim that the *spiritual* truths of all religions are the same; religions *appear* to be in conflict due to the *social* laws that differ because of the need throughout history for new moral and social codes by which larger segments of humanity are unified. Bahá'ís call the founders of the world's major faith traditions "Manifestations of God," which include Abraham, Krishna, Buddha, Zoroaster, Moses, Jesus, Muhammad, the Báb, and most recently, Bahá'u'lláh.

Thus, Bahá'ís believe that religious knowledge as recorded in the world's holy scripture is revealed incrementally throughout history and educates humanity according to its collective ability. Bahá'ís are confident that their ideology and institutions can bring about global unity, claiming that Bahá'u'lláh shows how all the religions are logically and progressively linked. In fact, Bahá'ís assert that Bahá'u'lláh is not only the return of Christ as expected by Christians, but that his life fulfills the messianic expectations of all the world's faith traditions. Bahá'u'lláh also condemns discrepancies in prophecy or conflict among religious ideologies as human-made misinterpretations. Differences in the social laws reflect the different requirements for social and moral solidarity of the age in which they were revealed.

Bahá'ís do admit, however, that there are differences in the content (but not the function) of the message brought by the "Manifestations of God." For Bahá'ís, there is a twofold function of religion: the spiritual education of individuals, and the social solidarity of humanity through various laws and institutions. Examples of *spiritual laws* governing Bahá'ís are laws that regulate daily prayer, fasting, sexual morality, abstinence from drugs and alcohol, marriage, and burial. Examples of *social laws* and principles that establish the foundation of a global civilization include the founding of a single auxiliary language that every person on the planet would learn; a world government that includes a global executive, legislature, and court system; collective security and the reduction of the nations' armaments; the elimination of racism, sexism, and prejudice; the reduction in the extremes of wealth and poverty; and universal education.

Thus, Bahá'ís consider that God's revelation to humanity has been evolutionary, teleological, and progressive. Bahá'ís believe that the solution to the problems of the modern age is global unity based on the recognition of one common faith that fulfills the prophecies of all the world's functionally equivalent, yet historically specific, religions. Bahá'ís do not think that theirs is the *last* stage of religious evolution for humanity—only the *latest*—but cite Bahá'u'lláh's statement that a full one thousand years will pass before the next Manifestation will appear.

Who Is Considered a Bahá'í?

Most Bahá'ís acknowledge a basic three-stage process in crossing the threshold into the Bahá'í world, inaugurating a lifetime deepening process as "world citizens." Bahá'ís do not use discourse such as "becoming saved" when accepting the Bahá'í Faith (as in some Christian denominations), but most Bahá'ís would acknowledge the day on which they finally, often after years of investigation, "declared" their Bahá'í identity.

Becoming a member can be roughly divided into three stages. The first is belief in Bahá'u'lláh. This involves acceptance of the idea of progressive revelation, with Bahá'u'lláh being the latest Manifestation sent from God to humanity. Bahá'í theology states that in truly accepting Bahá'u'lláh, one of necessity must accept all the other Manifestations of God. Thus, one not only must acknowledge Bahá'u'lláh, but also accept Abraham, Krishna, Buddha, Moses, Zoroaster, Christ, Muhammad, the Báb, and Bahá'u'lláh all as *equal* messengers from God.

The second stage is "declaration." This second, more formal step, is administrative in nature. Over the last seventy years, this has become the most formalized aspect of Bahá'í membership. In declaring, one signs a card that states, "In signing this card, I declare my belief in Bahá'u'lláh, the Promised One of God. I also recognize the Báb, His Forerunner, and `Abdu'l-Bahá, the Cen-

ter of His Covenant. I request enrollment in the Bahá'í Community with the understanding that Bahá'u'lláh has established sacred principles, laws, and institutions which I must obey." Upon declaration, one is assigned a Bahá'í number signifying one's status as a full-fledged Bahá'í with the right to attend Nineteen-Day Feasts, vote in elections, and contribute to Bahá'í funds (discussed below).

The third stage for a Bahá'í begins a lifelong journey in personal transformation and socialization according to Bahá'í principles. This process also involves participating in the Administrative Order through voting, and, if called upon by one's fellow Bahá'ís, to serve on the Local Spiritual Assembly. It also involves personal and collective deepening, or systematic study of Bahá'í scripture.

Distinctions Between Bahá'ís and Non-Bahá'ís

Bahá'ís make the distinction between the "old" world order and "new" or "Bahá'í" world order. This concept highlights the fact that the worldview of Bahá'ís, while universal and global, also differentiates between what is true and what is false. To be a Bahá'í, in part, means that one identifies with the divine mission envisioned for the Bahá'í Faith: to lay the foundation for a global civilization based on a common religious worldview and ecclesiastical authority. But to succeed in that enterprise, Bahá'ís must patiently wait for the disintegration of the old world order, while they themselves build the framework (the Bahá'í Administrative Order) for the new world order. The boundary between Bahá'ís and others, in part, lies in their ability to foster and inculcate new world order thinking. Bahá'ís would say that racism, sexism, partisan politics, and ignorance all were part of the old order of society. The new world order emphasizes the Bahá'í values of universal peace, spiritual education, and unity in diversity.

It is this division of the world into "old" and "new" worldviews that shapes the relationships Bahá'ís will have with the non-Bahá'í world. Bahá'ís seek out and collaborate with other groups that pursue similar principles upon which the new world order will be based. Examples include issues like racial unity (collaboration with other groups celebrating the Martin Luther King Jr. national holiday); universal education (helping to establish community literacy programs); or the use of consultation to solve disputes (neighborhood conflict resolution programs). This division of the world into old and new paradigms is also the rationale for why Bahá'ís refuse to support political parties or platforms: partisan politics is not only divisive, but part of the old world order, which is beyond repair. Bahá'ís therefore focus their energies in two directions. The first is outward, in the teaching efforts to spread the news about the Bahá'í revelation. Partnership with groups that share similar goals is considered by Bahá'ís part of the teaching process. The second is inward, fostering the growth and maturity of local and national Bahá'í communities for the expanding role Bahá'ís presume will be theirs in the future, as secular or old world order conditions deteriorate around the planet. Bahá'ís feel that by building up their own local, national, and global institutions, and making the world aware of their beliefs, they will be one of if not the only viable model for social life as the conditions of the secular society steadily worsen. [7]

PERSONAL PRACTICES

A Bahá'í's personal and collective life is divided up into daily devotional requirements, and also monthly and yearly festivals that conform to specific laws of Bahá'u'lláh and the dictates of the Bahá'í calendar. Ritual sustains the values and solidarity of a religious community. This is certainly true of Bahá'ís, as their rituals reinforce the authority and global worldview of the Administrative Order and link them to the global center of their faith. While organizational structure and ideology provide the scaffolding and motivation to link *local community* with *global society*, ritual observance gives Bahá'í institutions the everyday practices that enact its global doctrine.

The Daily Devotional Life of Bahá'ís

In the *Kitáb-i-Aqdas* ("The Most Holy Book"), the main scripture written by Bahá'u'lláh, he has enjoined his adherents to follow a daily regimen of prayer and scripture reading, as well as periodic contributions to Bahá'í Funds, fasting during the month of 'Alá', and if financially able, a pilgrimage to the World Center in Haifa.

Prayer

Bahá'ís have available to them hundreds of prayers written by the Báb, Bahá'u'lláh, and 'Abdu'l-Bahá, which are used in private devotion as well as recited at Bahá'í gatherings. One common denominator for nearly all American Bahá'ís is possession of a prayer book. The prayers found in Bahá'í prayer books are addressed to God, but Bahá'ís are free to pray directly to Bahá'u'lláh or any of the other Manifestations of God. Prayers are usually arranged by topics, found in prayer books under headings such as "aid and assistance," "family members," "detachment," "spiritual qualities," "firmness in the Covenant," "protection," "steadfastness," or "success in teaching." Some of the more popular prayers have been set to music and are sometimes sung at Bahá'í gatherings. Prayers are read at the beginning of every Bahá'í gathering, whether it is a worship gathering, a meeting to plan the next teaching campaign, or an administrative meeting.

Bahá'u'lláh has also enjoined upon Bahá'ís daily obligatory prayers, before which ablutions must be performed (washing of the hands and face). To perform obligatory prayers, Bahá'ís must face the Bahá'í World Center in Haifa. Bahá'ís can choose between the Short Obligatory Prayer (to be said between noon and sunset); the

Medium Obligatory Prayer (to be said in the morning, at noon, and in the evening); or the Long Obligatory Prayer (to be said once in twenty-four hours). During the Medium and Long Obligatory prayers, certain genuflections must be performed (similar to Muslim prayers), involving bending down with one's hand resting on one's knees, raising one's hands "in supplication," and bowing one's forehead to the ground.

Fasting

Part of a Bahá'ís' devotional life is to follow the provisions in the *Kitáb-i-Aqdas* for the month of Fasting (the month of `Alá', lasting March 2 to March 20, the last month in the Bahá'í year). It is enjoined upon Bahá'ís between the ages of fifteen and seventy. Like Muslims during Ramadan, Bahá'ís fast from sunup to sundown, refraining from eating, drinking, and smoking (although unlike Islam, believers are not required to abstain from sexual relations during the fast). Those who are ill, pregnant, traveling, or engaged in arduous labor are exempt from fasting. The purpose of fasting, according to Bahá'ís, is to purify the soul and turn one's attention to God.

Reading the Writings

Bahá'ís are enjoined to read daily from Bahá'í scripture and meditate on what they read—a process done in private or collectively with others and known as "deepening." Typical deepenings involve Bahá'ís sitting in a circle and taking turns reading from scripture. People give their interpretation or understanding of a particular passage, and sometimes lively discussions ensue.

Pilgrimage

The World Center in Haifa is at present the pilgrimage destination for Bahá'ís from around the world. Bahá'ís must receive permission from the Universal House of Justice (UHJ) to come on pilgrimage—in part to make sure only Bahá'ís with their administrative rights are allowed to go and in part to accommodate pilgrims in the limited quarters. While on pilgrimage, Bahá'ís visit the Shrines of Bahá'u'lláh and the Báb, the gravesites of `Abdu'l-Bahá and his sister, as well as the various institutions of the Bahá'í Faith on Mt. Carmel above the city of Haifa (such as the International Teaching Center, the Archives Building, and the Universal House of Justice). No particular attire is required for Bahá'í pilgrimage (unlike the Muslim *hajj*), although some Bahá'í pilgrims wear their national/ethnic dress at formal occasions during their stay as a celebration of Bahá'í "unity in diversity."

Fund Contributions

Bahá'ís are also, as in other religious organizations, encouraged to contribute money to their faith. Non-Bahá'ís are not allowed to give any money to Bahá'í projects, nor are Bahá'ís who have lost their administrative or voting rights. It is considered a spiritual bounty as well as a duty to give money to Bahá'í Funds. Bahá'ís consider their projects—whether a health clinic in the developing world or the House of Worship in Illinois—to be "gifts to the world" from the Bahá'í Faith. It is thus a privilege reserved only for Bahá'ís. There are local, national, and international Bahá'í Funds that support Bahá'í projects at all levels of the Administrative Order.

WORSHIP

A Bahá'í's daily life is governed by the personal laws given to the Bahá'í community by Bahá'u'lláh, but the organizational participation of the average Bahá'í is dictated by the rituals of the Bahá'í calendar. Bahá'í theology states that whenever new Manifestations of God appear to humanity, they bring with them a new calendar to institutionalize a new pattern of worship, festivals, and holidays. In the future, Bahá'ís say, the Bahá'í calendar, which was first proposed by the Báb and sanctioned by Bahá'u'lláh, will become the accepted global standard for dividing the year.

The Bahá'í year is divided into nineteen months each with nineteen days (totaling 361), with the insertion of "Intercalary Days" (four in an ordinary year, five in a leap year) between the eighteenth and nineteenth months to adjust the calendar to the solar year. Each month (and each day of the month) is named after an "attribute of God"—virtues that Bahá'ís are supposed to acquire throughout their lives (examples include "Glory," "Mercy," "Loftiness," or "Knowledge").

The Nineteen-Day Feast

On the first day of each Bahá'í month, Bahá'ís gather for the Nineteen-Day Feast, which is the central worship experience in the Bahá'í Faith and which only Bahá'ís are allowed to attend. The Nineteen-Day Feast consists of three loosely structured parts: (1) a devotional period, where the writings and prayers of the Báb, Bahá'u'lláh, and/or `Abdu'l-Bahá are read, as well as passages from other holy scripture (such as the Bible or Qur'an); (2) an administrative period, where the chair of the Local Spiritual Assembly leads community-wide consultation on important issues facing the community; and finally (3) a social portion, involving fellowship and refreshments. Sometimes, several Local Spiritual Assembly (LSA) jurisdictions will all meet together for what is known as a "Unity Feast," which non-Bahá'ís are welcome to attend (in which case the administrative period is omitted).

The administrative portion is in some ways the most important aspect of a Feast. Participants brainstorm new local teaching or service projects. A treasurer's report updates members on the financial health of the community. Someone usually updates the community on future activities, deepenings, or social events. Sometimes, individuals will give reports on teaching trips they have recently taken, or relate a story they heard concerning successful teaching taking place in other parts of the world. Recommendations that require official approval are referred to the LSA for consideration. In a sense, each Feast represents a mini-Town Hall meeting, where Bahá'ís can have input into community governance and exchange information. Most Feasts are accompanied by a letter from the Bahá'í National Center in Evanston, Illinois, informing local communities of decisions made by the National Spiritual Assembly (NSA) or of global activities of interest to the Bahá'í world. Feasts are usually held in members' homes, although some communities own or rent a building designated as the "Bahá'í Center." It is usually the "host" or "hostess" of the Feast who prepares the refreshments, and chooses the readings from the Bahá'í Writings (since there are no clergy). This reinforces the "democratic" nature of Bahá'í collective ritual, as individual community members are each given the chance to shape the devotional services. Attendance at the Feast is encouraged but not obligatory. Nor can the LSA prescribe any sanctions against Bahá'ís who do not attend the Feast.

Holy Days and Special Event Days

Holy Days tend to take on two distinct moods: one festive and celebratory, the other reverent and somber. For example, the festivals of Ayyám-i-Há (or Intercalary Days, right before the month of Fasting) or Naw-Rúz (the Bahá'í New Year on the spring equinox) are bright, joyful occasions, with many Bahá'ís bringing "seekers" to introduce them to Bahá'í hospitality at its best. Bahá'í homes might be decorated with balloons and banners, and festive music from all the world's cultures is played. Ayyám-i-Há is also a period of exchanging gifts and doing charitable work. On the other hand, the Ascension of Bahá'u'lláh, commemorating his death on May 29, 1892, has a more subdued atmosphere, evoking reverence and veneration among Bahá'ís for the founder of

Bahá'í Houses of Worship

Bahá'í Houses of Worship (sometimes referred to as Bahá'í Temples) play a special role in the institutional life of the Bahá'í community. The term in Arabic, *Mashriqu'l-Adhkár*, literally means "the Dawning-place of the mention or remembrance of God." (In addition, a Mashriqu'l-Adhkár can be any room or building reserved for devotions, meditation, and prayers; it also can refer to the heart of the sincere believer.)

While Bahá'ís envision a Bahá'í House of Worship (HOW) in every local community in the future, at present there are only seven completed HOWs in the world. Similar to the philosophy of a dispersed plan of expansion for the global Bahá'í movement where growth was not concentrated in any one national or ethnic community, Bahá'í HOWs are distributed on each continent except Antarctica, reflecting the global vision of Bahá'í theology. HOWs exist in Kampala, Uganda; Sydney, Australia; Frankfurt, Germany; Panama City, Panama; Tiapapata, Samoa; Delhi, India; Ishqabad, Turkmenistan (destroyed in an earthquake); and one is under construction in Santiago, Chile. The eighth, in the United States, is in Wilmette, Illinois, and in the area is the Bahá'í National Center and meeting place of the National Spiritual Assembly. The Wilmette HOW is listed in the National Register of Historic Places in the United States.

Bahá'í temples share similar architectural elements, some specifically mentioned in Bahá'í scripture. All Houses of Worship are circular in shape, with nine sides and a central dome. No pictures, images, or statues can be exhibited in the temple, and no musical instruments are allowed. Bahá'ís say that only the human voice can befittingly sing or chant the Word of God during devotions (although music is allowed at other Bahá'í celebrations). No sermons or pulpits are permitted. All the seats in the auditorium face the Shrine of Bahá'u'lláh outside of Haifa, Israel—the world headquarters of the Bahá'í Faith. In the HOW in Wilmette, the phrase "O Glory of the All-Glorious" is depicted in Arabic calligraphy at the top of the central dome, and verses (in English) from the writings of Baha'u'llah adorn the nine walls.

In the future, Bahá'ís say that when every city has a Bahá'í temple, surrounding the House of Worship will be subsidiary institutions such as hospitals, travelers' hospices, schools and universities, and homes for the elderly. All of these institutions will be open to people of all religions, as is each HOW.

---

their faith. It is held at 3 A.M., the recorded time of Bahá'u'lláh's death.

The other principal collective rituals in the Bahá'í calendar are the ten Holy Days and six special event days that commemorate specific occasions in Bahá'í history, or celebrate the global vision of the religion. Non-Bahá'ís are always welcome at any of the Holy Day or special event celebrations (Bahá'ís are encouraged to bring their friends who are "seekers"). In the Bahá'í calendar, the numerous Holy Day celebrations, with the exception of Naw-Rúz and Ayyám-i-Há, are related to the lives of the Báb, Bahá'u'lláh, and 'Abdu'l-Bahá. On nine of the holy days, work is to be suspended.

The following are Holy Days observed by Bahá'ís:

*Feast of Naw-Rúz (Bahá'í New Year), March 21

*Feast of Ridván (Declaration of Bahá'u'lláh's mission): April 21, April 29, May 2

*Declaration of the Báb, May 23 (same as 'Abdu'l-Bahá's birthday)

*Ascension (death) of Bahá'u'lláh, May 29

*Martyrdom of the Báb, July 9

*Birth of the Báb, October 20

*Birth of Bahá'u'lláh, November 12

Day of the Covenant, November 26 (celebrating Bahá'u'lláh's covenant with his followers)

Ascension (death) of `Abdu'l-Bahá, November 28

Ayyám-i-Há, or Intercalary Days, February 26–March 1

* indicates work to be suspended

And these are special event days given secondary importance:

Race Unity Day, second Sunday of June

International Day of Peace, third Tuesday of September

Universal Children's Day, first Monday of October

United Nations Day, fourth Tuesday of October

United Nations Human Rights Day, second Sunday of December

World Religion Day, third Sunday of January

Holy days and special event days are important for Bahá'ís' collective life, for several reasons. First, unlike the Nineteen-Day Feast, these festivals are open to non-Bahá'ís; in fact, Bahá'ís are encouraged to bring their non-Bahá'í friends and relatives to experience the best in Bahá'í hospitality. Second, since there is very little if any prescribed way to celebrate these events, Bahá'ís can celebrate their doctrine of "unity in diversity" by incorporating multicultural dances, skits, poetry readings, music, and food into the festivity. Finally, these holidays remind Bahá'ís of special historical events in the founding of their faith: holy days that mark the birth, death, and proclamation of the "central figures" (the Báb, Bahá'u'lláh, and 'Abdu'l-Bahá) of early Bahá'í history. The special event days were established to promote Bahá'í ideals, such as universal human rights, world peace, and racial unity. While primarily celebrated by members within their faith, Bahá'ís hope that special event days gain an acceptance and recognition in the wider society. For example, local Bahá'í communities often seek city mayors or state governors to formally declare the second Sunday in June to be "Race Unity Day," and publicize the event with a picture in the local newspaper of Bahá'í representatives and government officials shaking hands and displaying a signed document.

HOW BAHÁ'ÍS GOVERN THEMSELVES

To understand the Bahá'í Faith in America as well as the world, it is important to review the hierarchical authority in the Bahá'í religion. This is because Bahá'ís consider their form of religious governance to be the only one designed by the founder of the religion. Bahá'ís frequently point out that nowhere in the Bible can you find Christ discussing bishops, priests, ministers, deacons, or church structure. This, Bahá'ís claim, has in part led to the misunderstandings and divisions we see in Christianity. The same is true of all other faith traditions. However, Bahá'ís emphasize that Bahá'u'lláh told his followers how to set up and govern the religion after his death, making it unique and less prone to error and schism.

The Bahá'í Faith seeks to be a global religion and to instill a "world-embracing" identity upon its adherents. They do this by creating a combination of top-down authority and bottom-up democratic empowerment, which Bahá'ís define as their "Administrative Order." The Administrative Order is able to link a local community with a global organizational structure. The growth of the Bahá'í Faith, and its rise as a truly *global* social movement, continues today through the institutionalization of a network of structures at the local, national, and international levels of social life. This expansion to every corner of the globe has taken place through methodical, detailed blueprints called "teaching plans."

Bahá'ís consider their ecclesiastical organization to be unique in the world, in part because it was designed, Bahá'ís claim, not only to be the model of world unity, but also because Bahá'u'lláh was the first Manifestation of God to deliberately design the organization that would outlive him. This is significant for Bahá'ís, considering that Bahá'u'lláh strictly forbade the formation of clergy in the Bahá'í Faith. As part of the ideology of progressive revelation, Bahá'ís believe that humanity has developed beyond the need for a special class that monopolizes religious knowledge. Bahá'ís claim that the lack of clergy protects their faith from being corrupted by the power that accrues to one individual. In the Bahá'í Faith, no one Bahá'í (theoretically) has any authority over anyone else. Instead, all religious authority lies in councils, which operate at all levels of society.

Bahá'í authority resides in a series of democratically elected "spiritual assemblies" at the local, national, and international levels of social life. These assemblies constitute the core of the Bahá'í World Order, and the focus of all the teaching plans for growth. Each year, wherever there are at least nine adult Bahá'ís (age twenty-one and older) within a recognized municipal boundary (such as a city or county), an election is held to form a Local Spiritual Assembly (LSA) of nine members, which constitutes the foundation of local Bahá'í community life. Every community member votes for nine individuals, and the nine receiving the most votes become LSA members—this is true of Bahá'í elections at all three levels of the structure.[8] (If there is a tie for the ninth spot, administrative law dictates that the position goes to the individual who is a "minority" in the community—a form of electoral "affirmative action.") Local elections take place the first day of the twelve-day Festival of Ridván, held April 21–May 2 each year.

In all Bahá'í elections, there is no electioneering, nominating, campaigning, or proposed slate of candidates—this is expressly forbidden in Bahá'í scripture. Rather, Bahá'í elections are to be held in an atmosphere of reverence and spirituality. Each Bahá'í is given a list of all Bahá'ís in that jurisdiction who are at least twenty-one years old and have their full administrative rights (which have not been removed as punishment for serious infractions of Bahá'í law). Members are then asked to prayerfully consider their selections. Each Bahá'í marks nine names, and the nine names that receive a plurality of votes are elected to that spiritual assembly.

Usually the first weekend in October, Bahá'ís in America attend their Unit Convention, an administrative meeting where a National Delegate is elected—the first step in the formation of the National Spiritual Assembly (NSA), the next higher level in this branch of the Administrative Order. Units are composed of somewhat arbitrary groupings of several LSA jurisdictions. These two elections—the April Ridván festival and the October Unit Convention— are the two democratic rituals in which all Bahá'ís have a chance to participate; indeed, they are viewed as spiritual obligations for members.

The elected National Delegates then go to the National Convention (held in Wilmette, Illinois, near the Bahá'í National Center) in May to elect the (NSA)—again, a nine-member body that oversees Bahá'í activity within a nation or region. Often, the National Delegates will return to their districts and hold a meeting to report on the decisions made at the National Convention (the proceedings are also summarized in the monthly publication of the NSA, *The American Bahá'í*, sent to every Bahá'í household in the United States). Unlike officials or representatives in many electoral systems, Bahá'í delegates or assembly members are not bound to "represent" the choices of their "constituents"—rather, they are elected based on spiritual character to vote their own conscience.

Finally, once every five years, the members of all the NSAs in the world gather at the Bahá'í World Center in Haifa, Israel, to elect the nine-member Universal House of Justice (UHJ), the highest authority in the Bahá'í world. The first UHJ was elected in 1963, a few years after the death of Shoghi Effendi.

None of the *individuals* who are elected to the assemblies have any authority—only the decisions arrived at through consultation by the *institution* are authoritative. Again, Bahá'ís are not allowed to "run" for office, since Bahá'u'lláh strictly forbade campaigning in his writings. Instead, Bahá'ís are instructed to vote for any Bahá'í who is eligible based on his or her spiritual character.

Bahá'u'lláh promised Bahá'ís that decisions made by the UHJ are divinely guided and infallible. Although the UHJ cannot change any law revealed by Bahá'u'lláh, it is empowered to legislate on all matters not covered in Bahá'u'lláh's scriptures. Subsequently, Bahá'ís believe that through the collective decisions of the institution (again, not theoretically based on any charismatic authority or individual revelation) of the UHJ, the Bahá'í world, and eventually the global civilization which will supposedly be generated from Bahá'í institutions and laws, is assured of divine guidance until the appearance of the next Manifestation of God. Thus, Bahá'ís believe that infallible authority and guidance flow from the UHJ.

More recently, the UHJ in 1997 established a new institutional level: the Regional Bahá'í Councils (RBC). Administratively, they exist between the local and national Spiritual Assemblies. The RBCs are elected yearly by the members of all LSAs in the regional jurisdictions (there are currently seven RBCs in the United States). The function of RBCs is to coordinate teaching activity in their region and to aggregate the resources of multiple local communities for larger teaching projects. They also allow for the decentralization of decision making in large national communities.

The Administrative Order and Global Expansion

Since Bahá'u'lláh declared his mission over 130 years ago, the Bahá'í Faith has seen rapid development. In 1992 the *Encyclopedia Britannica Book of the Year* reported that the Bahá'í Faith had established "sig-

nificant communities" in more countries and territories than any other independent religion with the exception of Christianity. Its fastest growth has been in the developing world. The *World Christian Encyclopedia*[9] indicated that from 1970 to 1982 the Bahá'í Faith grew at an average rate of 3.63 percent, compared with 2.74 percent for Islam, 2.3 percent for Hinduism, 1.67 percent for Buddhism, 1.64 percent for Christianity, and 1.09 percent for Judaism. In 2002, the *Encyclopedia Britannica* revised its figures, claiming that there were then more than seven million members of the Bahá'í Faith around the globe. The organization's own statistics are more modest: There are approximately five million Bahá'ís worldwide, established in 235 countries and independent territories and represented by over 2,100 ethnic groups on the planet. Their literature has been translated into 802 languages, and they have established 32 independent publishing trusts, 6 radio stations, 950 schools, and 1,300 literacy and socioeconomic development projects throughout the world. [10]

The period of most intensive growth came at the beginning of the 1950s, coinciding with the worldwide increase in transnational institutions and globalization.[11] In 1954, some 94 percent of the world's Bahá'ís lived in Iran, the land of its birth. By 1988, only 6 percent lived there. It is estimated that in 1963, at the end of the Ten-Year Plan, there were approximately 400,000 Bahá'ís worldwide, that number expanding to 3.5 million in 1985, and more than five million today (a 43 percent increase since 1985).[12]

Four major reasons can account for this rapid expansion:

1. *Systematic plans.* The Bahá'í Faith has grown through a series of calculated teaching plans first developed by Shoghi Effendi, the great-grandson of Bahá'u'lláh and head of the Bahá'í Faith from 1921 to 1957, and then by the UHJ since 1963. In each of these cases, and especially since the plans became "glo-

balized" in the Ten-Year World Crusade 1953–1963, there have been numerical goals of new local and national assemblies, new believers, publishing trusts, and so forth.

2. *The status and mission of the "Pioneer."* When Bahá'ís volunteer to go "pioneering" (the term for Bahá'í missionaries), they travel to various parts of the world to evangelize and establish local assemblies. Their goal is for these assemblies to eventually become self-supporting from among indigenous believers. Bahá'í pioneers attempt to recruit new adherents and assist in the development of LSAs. Thus, Bahá'í pioneers consider themselves part of a larger, divinely ordained project of building the kingdom of God.

3. *Grassroots construction of the Administrative Order.* Shoghi Effendi set out to erect the Administrative Order from the ground up, using blueprints in the writings of Bahá'u'lláh and `Abdu'l-Bahá. Enough LSAs had to be established in a nation or region in order for an NSA to be elected according to the scripturally defined rules. And enough NSAs had to be established before the UHJ could be formed.

4. *Ideological principles.* Finally, in addition to organizational features, the very ideology of the Bahá'í Faith has also contributed to its attraction and growth. Bahá'ís claim that the ideological elements of the Bahá'í Faith have affinity in a variety of cultural settings (such as eliminating prejudice and discrimination against women, reducing poverty, and emphasizing universal education). The greatest concentration of Bahá'ís globally is in India, where the Bahá'í emphasis on equality and unity in diversity has resulted in a relative breakdown in caste divisions among Bahá'ís.[13]

CONCLUSION

Bahá'ís in America and throughout the world teach their message of global and religious unity in two ways. First, they build up their Administrative Order from the grassroots, establishing local Spiritual Assemblies in cities and communities around the world. Each is linked to the World Center located in Haifa, Israel, and attempts to set an example of how a diverse humanity can live, work, and serve others in harmony and unity. Second, they grow by "teaching the Cause of God" through individual initiative, media campaigns, prayer services and discussion groups. The teaching activity of Bahá'ís in America constitutes most of the public awareness that others might have of the Bahá'í Faith. Through all this, Bahá'ís hope to unify humanity "one heart at a time."

In the United States, Bahá'ís have made their biggest impact in spreading their message of racial unity—which they point to as the most serious social problem faced by a pluralistic nation such as ours. Bahá'ís, therefore, do not distinguish between teaching fellow Americans about the Bahá'í Faith, and spreading the message of racial harmony and the unity of humanity. Bahá'ís say that although currently steeped in stupefying materialism, the American society will best lead the world by being the first nation to achieve racial peace and true fellowship among all races, ethnicities, and nationalities.

Notes

1. Gayle Morrison, *To Move the World: Louis G. Gregory and the Advancement of Racial Unity in America* (Wilmette, Ill.: Bahá'í Publishing Trust, 1982).

2. Shoghi Effendi, *The Advent of Divine Justice* (Wilmette, Ill.: Bahá'í Publishing Trust, 1963).

3. Ibid., 28.

4. Ibid., 29.

5. Ibid., 33–34.

6. For more details of Bahá'í history, see Shoghi Effendi, trans., *The Dawn Breakers* (New York: Bahá'í Publishing Committee, 1932); Shoghi Effendi, *God Passes By* (Wilmette, Ill.: Bahá'í Publishing Trust, 1995); J. E. Esslemont, *Bahá'u'lláh and the New Era* (Wilmette, Ill.: Bahá'í Publishing Trust, 1970); William S. Hatcher and J. Douglas Martin, *The Bahá'í Faith: The Emerging Global Religion* (San Francisco: Harper & Row, 1985); Peter Smith, *The Bábi and Bahá'í Religions: From Messianic Shi'ism to a World Religion* (Cambridge: Cambridge University Press, 1987); Robert H. Stockman, *The Bahá'í Faith in America, Vol. 1* (Wilmette, Ill.: Bahá'í Publishing Trust, 1985); and Taherzadeh, *The Covenant of Bahá'u'lláh* (Oxford: George Ronald, 1992).

7. For more on Bahá'í doctrine, see William S. Hatcher and J. Douglas Martin, *The Bahá'í World Faith: The Emerging Global Religion* (San Francisco: Harper & Row, 1985); Peter Smith, *The Bábi and Bahá'í Religions* (Cambridge: Cambridge University Press, 1987); Richard W. Thomas, *Racial Unity: An Imperative for Social Progress* (Ottawa: Bahá'í Studies Publications, 1993).

8. The number nine appears regularly in Bahá'í symbols, and is explained in Bahá'í writings: "Nine is the highest digit, hence symbolizes comprehensiveness, culmination; also, the reason it is used . . . is because 9 has the exact numerical value of 'Bahá' (in the numerology connected with the Arabic alphabet) and Bahá' is the name of the Revealer of our Faith, Bahá'u'lláh" (in Helen Hornby, *Lights of Guidance: A Bahá'í Reference Guide* [New Delhi: Bahá'í Publishing Trust, 1983] 416).

9. See David B. Barrett, ed., *World Christian Encyclopedia: A Comparative Study of Churches and Religions in the Modern World* (New York: Oxford University Press, 1982).

10. All statistics from *The Bahá'ís: A Profile of the Bahá'í Faith and Its Worldwide Community* (New York: Office of Public Information, Bahá'í International Community, 1994).

11. See Malcolm Waters, *Globalization* (New York: Routledge, 1995) for more on economic, political and cultural/religious globalization trends.

12. See Peter Smith and Moojan Momen, "The Bahá'í Faith 1957–1988: A Survey of Contemporary Developments," in *Religion*, 19:63–91.

13. See Margit Warburg, "Conversion: Consideration Before a Field-work in a Bahá'í Village in Kerala," in *South Asian Religion and Society*, ed. Asko Parpola and Bent Smidt Hansen (London: Curzon Press, 1986); W. Garlington, "The Bahá'í Faith in Malwa," in *Religion in South Asia*, ed. G. A. Oddie (London: Curzon Press, 1977).

STUDY QUESTIONS

1. How do Bahá'ís link the oneness of God, the oneness of religion, and the oneness of humanity?

2. What role does the Nineteen-Day Feast play in Bahá'í worship? How is the Nineteen-Day Feast distinctive compared to church, synagogue, or mosque services?

3. What role do race unity efforts play in promoting the Bahá'í vision of the "oneness of humanity"?

4. How does the Bahá'í Administrative Order combine both democratic participation as well as hierarchical authority? How do the two branches of the Administrative Order function together?

5. Compare the personal practices of Bahá'ís with those of other religious faiths. What is similar? What is distinctive?

6. What does the Bahá'í doctrine of "progressive revelation" imply about the possibilities of religious cooperation?

ESSAY TOPICS

The Bahá'í Administrative Order

The Life of Bahá'u'lláh, the Prophet-Founder of the Bahá'í Faith

The Importance of the Nineteen-Day Feast to Local Bahá'í Community Life

The Universal and Global Themes in Bahá'í Doctrine

WORD EXPLORATION

The following words or phrases play significant roles in any discussion of the Bahá'í Faith in America and are worth careful reflection and consideration.

Bahá'u'lláh	'Abdu'l-Bahá	Shoghi Effendi
Universal House	National Spiritual	Local Spiritual
of Justice	Assembly	Assembly
Administrative Order	New World Order	Old World Order
Nineteen-Day Feast	Progressive Revelation	Racial Unity
Manifestation of God	Messianic	

FOR FURTHER READING

Bowers, Kenneth E. *God Speaks Again: An Introduction to the Bahá'í Faith*. Wilmette, Ill.: Bahá'í Publishing, 2004.

Dahl, Gregory C. *One World, One People: How Globalization is Shaping Our Future*. Wilmette, Ill.: Bahá'í Publishing, 2007.

Etter-Lewis, Gwendolyn and Richard Thomas. *Lights of the Spirit: Historical Portraits of Black Bahá'ís in North America, 1898-2000*.Wilmette, Ill.: Bahá'í Publishing, 2006.

Khan, Janet A. and Peter J. *The Advancement of Women: A Bahá'í Perspective*. Wilmette, Ill.: Bahá'í Publishing, 2003.

Lepard, Brian D. *Hope for a Global Ethic: Shared Principles in Religious Scriptures*. Wilmette, Ill.: Bahá'í Publishing, 2005.

WEB SITES

http://www.bahai.org
  International Web site of the Bahá'í Faith

http://www.usbnc.org
  Administrative Web site of the Bahá'í of the United States

http://www.media.bahai.org
  Bahá'í Media Library with extensive photos

http://www.bahaiprayers.org
  Selection of Bahá'í prayers

PART FOUR

More Recent Arrivals

10

Hinduism in India and in America

GERALD JAMES LARSON

Ca. 3000–1500 B.C.E.	Indus Valley Period
Ca. 1500–600 B.C.E.	Brahmanical Period
Ca. 600 B.C.E.–300 C.E.	Buddhist and Shramanical Period
Ca. 300–1200 C.E.	Classical Hindu Period
Ca. 1200–1757	Muslim Period
Ca. 1757	Modern Period Begins
1840s	American writer Henry David Thoreau reads Hindu sacred texts and praises Bhagavad Gita's "sanity and sublimity"
1893	Hindus achieve recognition at World's Parliament of Religions in Chicago
1900	An estimated 1,700 Hindus live in America
1907	Riots in Bellingham, Washington, attempt to force Indian Americans, including Sikhs and some Hindus, out of working in the local mills
1947	Indian independence; creation of separate nation of Pakistan
1965	U.S. immigration laws change to permit more non-Europeans to come to America; Hinduism begins rapid U.S. growth
1965	International Society for Krishna Consciousness founded
1976	First North American Hindu temple dedicated in the suburbs of Pittsburgh, Penn.
1981	Malibu Hindu Temple dedicated in California
1983	*Hinduism Today* estimates approximately 400,000 Hindus in the United States
2004	U.S. State Department estimates just under 1.5 million Hindus in the U.S., or one-half of one percent of the population
2007	Rajan Zed becomes first Hindu to lead a prayer in the United States Senate, which is briefly disrupted by angry Christian activists

PEOPLE OF INDIA
IN THE WORLD TODAY

People from India live in all fifty of the United States and now represent the fourth-largest Asian ethnic minority (after Chinese, Japanese, and Filipinos). According to the 2000 U.S. Census, there are about two million "Asian Indians," people from India or people of Asian Indian descent, living in the United States. This is more than double the 815,447 recorded in the 1990 census. The largest concentrations of Asian Indians are in the states of New York and California and in such major urban areas as New York City, Chicago, Los Angeles, Houston, Philadelphia, and the San Francisco Bay area.

Many of the people from India who have settled in the United States are highly educated and prosperous and have become prominent in such areas as medicine, law, engineering, aerospace research, business, and the arts. More than five thousand Asian Indians in America hold faculty positions (especially in the sciences and engineering) in American colleges and universities, and many have become department chairs or directors of programs.

There are also sizable populations of Asian Indians elsewhere in the world today, including Canada, the United Kingdom, Europe, the Caribbean, South America, the Middle East, Africa, the Indian Ocean islands, and elsewhere. Asian Indians, in other words, can be found almost everywhere in the world.

India itself has an established population of 1.3 billion in 2008 making it the second most populous nation in the world after China.[1] Given the present growth rate and the relative youthfulness of India's population (40 percent under the age of fifteen), the population of India may surpass that of China early in the twenty-first century.

When speaking about Asian Indians, therefore, we are speaking about a sizable percentage of the population of our planet (currently 16 percent, but rapidly advancing toward 20 percent). We are also speaking about people of great diversity and remarkable contrasts. Whereas Asian Indians living in the United States and other industrialized Western nations (and to some extent those living in the Persian Gulf region) are for the most part highly educated and prosperous, the same does not hold true for Asian Indians elsewhere in the world, for example, in South Africa, Malaysia, or, of course, in India itself.

India is made up of twenty-eight states and seven Union Territories, ranging from Jammu and Kashmir in the far north (in the cold foothills of the Himalayas, bordering Tibet and China on the east and Pakistan on the west) to Tamil Nadu in the far subtropical south (almost reaching to Sri Lanka). Eighteen official languages are recognized in addition to English. Hindi is spoken by about 40 percent of the population, mainly in those highly populated northern states sometimes referred to as the "Hindi Heartland." English is spoken by about 3 percent of the population.

The Anthropological Survey of India has identified the staggering number of 4,599 distinct communities in India, and as many as 325 languages in 12 language families and 24 different scripts. Nevertheless the survey also found that an "all-pervasive sense of Indianness" prevails through the linguistic, cultural, and ecological diversities of the communities of the country.[2]

At this point you may well be thinking, What about religion? Why aren't you telling us about Hindus and Hinduism? My answer is that I have been writing about Hindus and Hinduism. The most important thing to learn about Hindus and Hinduism is that being religious for Hindus has very little to do with what they think or believe; put another way, it has very little to do with "orthodoxy," or correct belief and doctrines. There are, of course, some common beliefs or characteristics that pertain to most Hindus, which we will look at later in this chapter, but there is overall a remarkable freedom and tolerance for almost all religious points of view (including agnosticism and atheism). Being religious for the Hindu, rather, has much more to do with behavior and action, or what is sometimes called "orthopraxy"—correct action. The Hindu has basic duties and responsibilities in terms of personal cleanliness (ritual bathing), eating habits (what kind of food is to be eaten, who prepares it, and with whom it can be eaten), family relations (obligations to siblings and parents), marital practices (when and whom one can marry), regional associations (including caste associations), and the manner in which one can choose and interact with friends. In other words, Hindus are engaging in a kind of "religious" talk when they tell you about their family, their occupations, the regions in India from which they come, the groups to which they belong by birth or choice, the native languages they speak, and the sorts of food they eat. Moreover, as your Hindu friends describe all of this, you will be struck not only by how different their views and ideas can be, but also by the great range of differing duties and responsibilities that they follow depending upon the regions and groups from which they come. The rules are by no means the same for everyone. While you will come to realize that there are many ways of being "Hindu," you will also note an "all-pervasive sense of Indianness." This somewhat strange juxtaposition of radical diversity or tolerant pluralism along with an "all-pervasive sense of Indianness" is basically what it means to be a Hindu.

HINDU, HINDUNESS, INDIAN, AND INDIANNESS

At this point you might be tempted to think that "Hindu" simply means "Indian" or "Asian Indian." In other words, you might be tempted to think that Hinduism is the name of a culture, civilization, or ethnic identity rather than a religion as such. To some extent, you would be right—much of what it means to be Hindu is related to the simple fact that one has been born in India into a Hindu family. However, such a simple equation of Hindu or Hinduness with Indian and Indianness is not by any means the full picture, for there are many Asian Indians who are not Hindu and deeply resent being called Hindus. The Sikhs, for example, refuse to be absorbed into Hinduism, and Indian Muslims make up a significant minority. The actual breakdown of major religions in India, according to the population totals of the 1991 census, is roughly as follows:

Hindu	80.5%
Muslim	13.4%
Christian	2.3%
Sikh	1.9%
Buddhist	0.8%
Jain	0.4%
Other	0.5%

The "Other" category includes Parsees, Jews, Animists, and other traditions, all of which together are only one-half of 1 percent. There is, thus, a clear overlap between Asian Indian and Hindu, but it is equally clear that we cannot equate the two.

THE DEVELOPMENT OF HINDUISM IN INDIA

Unlike most historic religions, such as Christianity, Islam, and Buddhism, Hinduism has no human founder and no datable beginning in time or history. In an important sense, one might well say that Hinduism has no beginning; it just emerges out of the ancient earth of South Asia. If you have ever seen a banyan tree with its aerial roots that grow down from its branches into the soil to form additional trunks, thereby spreading in all directions in a bewildering complexity of formations, then you have a good metaphor for thinking about Hinduism.

The development of Hinduism occurs over many centuries and is incredibly dense and complex, so it may be helpful if we identify certain distinct periods in order to organize the discussion. Altogether it is useful to identify six such fundamental periods for the development of Hinduism: the *Indus Valley Period* (ca. 3000–1500 B.C.E.), the *Brahmanical Period* (ca. 1500–600 B.C.E.), the *Buddhist and Shramana Period* (ca. 600 B.C.E.–300 C.E.), the *Classical Hindu Period* (ca. 300–1200 C.E.), the *Muslim Period* (ca. 1200–1757 C.E.), and the *Modern Period* (ca. 1757–present).

The Indus Valley Period
(ca. 3000–1500 B.C.E.)

The Indus Valley civilization flourished from the third through the first half of the second millennium B.C.E. in the region of the Indus valley and in the area known as the Punjab. It was a sizable civilization, covering as much as half a million square miles (including what is now Pakistan and much of northwest India as well). Very little is known about the origins of this civilization or about its end.

Excavations of the two large urban sites, Mohenjo-daro and Harappa, have yielded some intriguing clues about the culture and religion of the Indus Valley civilization. Each city, for example, had a large artificial hill or citadel with what appear to be sizable official buildings (possibly governmental or religious, or both). There was also in Mohenjo-daro what appears to be a large, rectangular bathing area in the main part of the citadel area with steps leading down into it, suggesting some sort of ritual bathing practice (not unlike the ritual bathing "tanks" connected to Hindu temples in later Indian culture). The cities themselves are rather sophisticated in design, with carefully planned streets and houses facing away from the street.

In terms of artifacts, archaeologists have uncovered what appear to be phallus-shaped stones and crude terra-cotta female figurines, suggesting some sort of fertility cult and belief in a Mother Goddess. The Indus Valley language has not yet been deciphered, so scholars can only guess what this civilization's religion and culture were like. But it is intriguing to entertain the possibility that prominent features in later Hinduism may indeed be traceable ultimately all the way back to the third millennium B.C.E., and possibly earlier to the village cultures that go back to time immemorial.

The Brahmanical Period
(ca. 1500–600 B.C.E.)

Sometime in the early part of the second millennium, semi-nomadic tribes who had been living in the steppeland that ranges from Eastern Europe to Central Asia began to undertake extensive migrations. These migrations may have been occasioned by famine, some sort of natural disaster, or an epidemic. Whatever the reasons, some tribes migrated west, finally finding their way to Europe and becoming the ancestors of the Greeks, Romans, Celts, and Teutons. Other tribes remained in the steppeland region, becoming the ancestors of the Baltic and Slavonic peoples. Still others migrated south and east, moving first into Persia and then into present-day Afghanistan, and Baluchistan (a desert region in western Pakistan), and finally into the Indus Valley region. The tribes intermarried with the indigenous population and developed into a ruling elite. They called themselves Aryas or Aryans (meaning "noble ones"), and those Aryan tribes that reached ancient Persia and India are known as Indo-Iranians or Indo-Aryans. These migrations did not occur all at once. There were probably waves of migrating Indo-Aryan tribes over a period of some years.

In the middle of the second millennium (ca. 1500 B.C.E.) these Indo-Aryan nomadic tribes developed a number of cultural characteristics that were to determine the development of later Indian civilization and Hinduism: (1) a form of the Sanskrit language called simply Old Indic (or Vedic Sanskrit), later to develop into the classical language of India known as classical Sanskrit; (2) a patrilineal system of organization that centered around the three social functions of priests (Brahmins), warriors, and food-gatherers, later to develop into what we now know as the caste system; (3) an elaborate ritual system of sacrifice on open-air altars involving offerings of milk, honey, clarified butter (ghee), and animals, together with imbibing a sacred drink that brought about hallucinogenic effects; and (4) the worship of an elaborate pantheon of sky, atmospheric, and earth gods.

In order to perform the ritual sacrifice, the Brahmins had to master an extensive body of what can be called sacred "utterances," including hymns, chants, and ritual instructions. These liturgical utterances (not yet written texts, since writing was not extensively used until many centuries later) are referred to as the Vedas, from the root meaning "to know." In other words, the Vedas are what the Brahmins had to know in order to perform the ritual sacrifice. Originally there were three basic ritual collections. Somewhat later a fourth set of sacred utterances was added.

The purpose of the ritual sacrifice was to propitiate and "feed" the gods. In return the gods would assist their Indo-Aryan devotees with long life, much cattle, and earthly happiness. This reciprocity between gods and Brahmins maintained the cosmic order. Interestingly enough, in this early Brahmanical Period, gods other than Vishnu and Shiva, who nearly a millennium later would emerge as principal gods in classical Hinduism, were preeminent. The tendency in this Brahmanical Period was to move away from personal gods in the direction of speculative abstractions, which put ever greater emphasis on the importance of the Brahmins both for the performance of ritual and for the interpretation of its meaning.

Over the next thousand years the Indo-Aryan nomadic tribes spread over all of north India, intermarrying with the indigenous population and becoming a settled agricultural people. During this thousand-year period many important changes occurred. The sacrificial ritual became much more complex and came to be divided into two

basic types: (1) great public rituals involving as many as seventeen priests and three sacred fires and lasting for several days and in some instances up to two years; and (2) home-based oblations into a single fire in the domestic hearth. Also related to the domestic rituals were the life-cycle rituals, from twelve to sixteen rites of passage, including the marriage ritual, the ritual for conceiving a male child, a birth ritual, a name-giving ritual, and so forth. Whereas most of the Indo-Aryan families were able to maintain the home-based rituals, only the rich could afford the great public rituals.

As the rituals became more complex and expensive, the Brahmin priests became more specialized in one or another aspect of the ritual process. Long commentaries were composed (first orally but eventually written down) explaining the rituals, called *Brahmanas* ("pertaining to the priestly function"). Specialized schools developed in centers of learning just outside the towns in various parts of north India. The products of these schools were called *Aranyakas,* or "forest-books." Finally, the priests began to speculate on the deeper meaning of the ritual process and even began a kind of elementary philosophizing about the relation of the ritual to the cosmos and to the human community (mainly to the priestly community, but to the ruling Kshatriya or warrior community as well). These early speculative and proto-philosophical reflections came to be collected in a group of compositions called *Upanishads* (meaning literally "to sit down near" the teacher or guru and to learn the special, secret teaching). Upanishads were being composed already in the ninth and eighth centuries B.C.E. and continued to be composed well into the first centuries of the Common Era. The Brahmanas and Aranyakas are somewhat older, reaching back to the eleventh and even the twelfth century B.C.E. The Vedic verse-collections, the Brahmanas, the Aranyakas, and the Upanishads are referred to collectively as the Veda or *shruti* ("scripture"—literally "that which has been heard"). These Vedas are considered to be eternal and to have been intuited or "seen" by the ancient Rishis ("seers") and thus not to have a human origin ("not derived from men," or *apausheya*).

The Buddhist and Shramana Period (ca. 600 B.C.E.–300 C.E.)

With the Buddhist and Shramana Period, we begin to see some reactions against the all-powerful priestly religion of the Brahmins, as well as the first manifestations of two other kinds of spirituality that will prove to be as important in later Hinduism as ritual sacrifice, namely, ascetic or disciplined meditation (*yoga*) and focused or single-minded devotion (*bhakti*) to a personal god. We also see some important new literature taking shape toward the end of this period: the *Dharmashastras* (law books) of the Hindus and the two great epics of India, the *Ramayana* and the *Mahabharata*, the latter of which contains the most important religious text of classical Hinduism, the *Bhagavad Gita* (Song of the Lord).

The term *Shramana* is from the root *shram*, meaning "to exert oneself" or "to practice austerities." The search for inner truth, the turn toward meditation and self-searching, and the pursuit of yoga were found not only among some of the Brahmin priests, but also among all of the non-Brahmanical mendicant groups that began to appear in north India sometime around the sixth century B.C.E. These groups did not accept the authority of the Brahmin priests, nor did they accept the validity of the Brahmanical sacrificial system. Rejecting also the sacred literature of the Brahmins, they formed their own separate communities and represent the first examples of the monastic life in ancient India.

There were many such Shramana groups, but two in particular eventually developed into independent religions in ancient India: the Jains and the Buddhists. The founder of the Jain tradition was Vardhamana, also known by the honorific epithet Mahavira

("Great Hero"). He was born into a warrior (Kshatriya) family and lived in the sixth century B.C.E. (ca. 549–477 B.C.E.) in northeastern India, in the region of the Gangetic plain in what is now the state of Bihar. He practiced rigorous asceticism and organized a Jain monastic community. Jain comes from the word *jina,* meaning "conqueror." Both monastic and lay Jain communities have existed in India throughout the centuries. There are about 5.2 million Jains in contemporary India and between seventy and a hundred thousand who live in the United States today.

The founder of the Buddhist tradition was Gautama the Buddha (the "awakened" or "enlightened" one). Also from a warrior (Kshatriya) family, Gautama (ca. 563–483 B.C.E.) was an older contemporary of Mahavira and lived in the same region of the Gangetic plain. Since there is a separate chapter of this book on Buddhism, suffice it to say here that the Buddhist tradition was also a mendicant tradition with a focus on meditation that enables a monk to attain enlightenment and eventually release (*nirvana*) from the frustrations of ordinary life. Unlike the Jains, however, the Buddhists followed a much more moderate regimen of yogic meditation, which they called the Middle Path, a middle way between sensuous indulgence, on the one hand, and extreme asceticism, on the other.

The new traditions of the period shared a profound dissatisfaction with the older sacrificial cult of the Brahmins and represented a new spirituality focusing on the interior life and the practice of yoga. They were probably also profoundly dissatisfied, or at least frustrated, with certain social changes occurring at this time: the development of cities, the development of a monied economy, and the rise of an imperial state that would become the first to rule all of India (the Mauryan Dynasty, which ruled from 322 to 183 B.C.E.).

The other development of importance in this period is the first appearance of devotional cults, specifically the Shaiva (devotees of Lord Shiva) and V<u>aishnava</u> (devotees of Lord Vishnu) traditions. Although both Shiva and Vishnu were known in the older Vedic religion and are sometimes mentioned in the Upanishads, they were clearly not dominant figures. It is in the Buddhist and Shramana Period that we first see the emergence of devotion, or bhakti, to a personal god, and it appears that these devotional cults were originally outside the Brahmanical sacrificial framework, as were the Shramana groups themselves. Shiva, Vasudeva-Krishna, Narayana, Rama, and many other later Hindu deities probably all began as local heroes or local deities outside of the Brahmanical tradition, their origins in some instances possibly even predating Indo-Aryan times. They begin now, however, to become major cults. The making of images and image worship (*puja*), the appearance of temples (possibly influenced by the Buddhist building of *stupas*, or burial mounds, for relics of the Buddha), the practice of pilgrimage (again probably due largely to the Buddhist custom of making pilgrimages to certain sacred places), singing devotional songs, observing certain religious festivals, and so forth, all now emerge as important religious practices that go considerably beyond and to a large extent supplant the old Brahmanical sacrificial cult.

The Classical Hindu Period (ca. 300–1200 C.E.)

The Brahmanical reaction to all the developments of the Buddhist and Shramana Period was not rejection or condemnation but rather, to whatever extent possible, assimilation and accommodation. This can be seen in the new literature shaped in Brahmanical circles toward the end of that period, from about 200 B.C.E. to about 300 C.E. This new literature attains its final shape or redaction in the first centuries of the Common Era.

This new literature as a whole is referred to as literature "worthy to be remembered"

(*smriti*) in order to distinguish it from the literature that is considered to be authentic "scripture" (*shruti*), that is, the Vedas (including the Upanishads) that we have already discussed. Interestingly enough, however, even though Hindus only accept the

---

Bhagavad Gita

Written sometime in the first century CE, the Bhagavad Gita *is Hinduism's classic text of popular devotion. Here, the god Krishna teaches Arjuna, the warrior-prince, that single-minded devotion (*bhakti*) is the way to obtain release from the cycle of samsara (suffering and rebirth):*

Whoever with devotion offers me leaf, flower, fruit, water, that, presented with devotion, I accept from him whose self is pure. Whatever you do, O son of Kuntî, whatever you eat, whatever sacrifice you make, whatever you give, whatever penance you perform, do that as offered to me. Thus will you be released from the bonds of action, the fruits of which are agreeable or disagreeable. And with your self possessed of [this] devotion, [this] renunciation, you will be released [from the bonds of action] and will come to me. I am alike to all beings; to me none is hateful, none dear. But those who worship me with devotion [dwell] in me, and I too in them. Even if a very ill-conducted man worships me, not worshipping anyone else, he must certainly be deemed to be good, for he has well resolved. He soon becomes devout of heart, and obtains lasting tranquility.

(Text translated in 1882 by Kâshinâth Trimbak Telang; in the public domain.)

Vedas as authentic scripture, in fact, most of the basic ideas and practices of classical Hinduism derive from the new *smriti* literature. In other words, Hindus for the most part pay little more than lip service to the Vedic scripture. The most important dimensions of being Hindu derive, instead, from the *smriti* texts. The point can also be made in terms of the emerging social reality. Whereas the *shruti* is taken seriously by a small subset of Brahmins, the *smriti* are taken seriously by the overwhelming majority of Hindus, regardless of class or caste identity.

This new *smriti* literature includes the following:

1. The great epic of India known as the *Mahabharata*, the story of a great war between two branches of a family (the Kurus and the Pandus) that establishes the ancient kingdom of India. The *Mahabharata* includes within it the most popular and beloved text of the Hindu tradition, the *Bhagavad Gita* ("Song of the Lord"), which features the teachings of the famous Lord Krishna, an incarnation or "descent" (*avatara*) of the mighty god Vishnu, who fights on the side of the victorious Pandas against the evil Kurus;

2. A second epic known as the *Ramayana*, a story of another great war, this time between Lord Rama, another incarnation of the mighty Vishnu, and the great demon, Ravana, who had kidnapped Rama's beloved wife, Sita, and carried her off to his fortress in the far south (present-day Sri Lanka), from which captivity Lord Rama rescues her with the help of a mighty army of monkeys led by the beloved monkey god, Hanuman;

3. A group of texts called *Puranas* ("Old Tales"), repositories of the great myths and legends of classical Hinduism, dealing with how the world came to be, and with the beloved stories and tales about the three high gods of classical Hinduism, Brahma, Vishnu, and Shiva; and

4. A group of law books called *Dharmashastras*, the most famous of which is the "Law-Book of Manu," which provide detailed discussions of such matters as the proper purposes of life, the stages of life, the caste system, and the manner in which the community is to be governed.

All of these texts receive their final form and general acceptance by the larger Hindu population in this Classical Hindu Period, the period of the full flowering of classical Indian civilization. In this period one can properly begin to use the terms "Hindu" and "Hinduism." Classical Hinduism now shows itself as an artful synthesis of ritual action, disciplined meditation, and devotional piety. It is shaped on one level by the old Brahmanical religion of ritual sacrifice, and on another level by the Shramanical and non-Brahmanical religious traditions of meditation and devotion deriving from the Buddhist and Shramana Period. It resonates as well as the spiritual rhythms of the old Indus Valley civilization and the archaic village spirituality of the fourth and fifth millennia B.C.E. Clearly "Hinduism" is not simply one entity or tradition. It is a synthesis of many traditions.

Gods and Goddesses

There are, of course, many gods and goddesses in classical Hinduism, but most Hindus think of the various gods and goddesses as manifestations of one ultimate truth. Classical Hinduism combines the old Vedic notion of the Brahman, the Ultimate or Absolute, with the notion of a plurality of forms that the Ultimate or Absolute assumes, three of which are central in the everyday beliefs and practices of Hindus: Brahma, the creator god; Vishnu, the preserving god; and Shiva, the destroying god. Brahma, Vishnu, and Shiva taken together are referred to as the "three basic forms" of the Ultimate or Absolute.

The Absolute or Ultimate also assumes female forms. Shri or Lakshmi is the goddess of abundance, often linked with Vishnu. Durga or Kali is the awesome power of the Great Goddess, able to devour the demonic and evil forces in the world. She is often linked with Shiva. Sometimes the Absolute or the Ultimate assumes an androgynous form, a composite of male and female, known as the "Lord whose half is woman" (Ardhanarishvara).

The Ultimate is boundlessly various, and so too are the cultic forms that everyday puja, or worship, takes. The devotees of Lord

Vishnu, together with his many incarnations or descents (*avataras*)—the two most important of which are Lord Krishna (the divine hero of the *Mahabharata*) and Lord Rama (the divine hero of the *Ramayana*)—are called *Vaishnavas* ("followers of Vishnu") and have numerous temples and shrines through the subcontinent for their puja. Well over half of all Hindus are followers of one or another form of Vaishnavism (including devotees of Lord Krishna and Lord Rama). Devotees of Shiva, whose mythology and ritual prescriptions are set forth primarily in the Puranas, are called *Shaivas* ("followers of Shiva") and have numerous temples and shrines for their puja throughout India, especially in Tamilnad in the south, West Bengal in the north, and Kashmir in the far northwest. About one-third of all Hindus are Shaivites. Devotees of the goddess, whether Kali or Devi or Durga, are called *Shaktas,* a term which means something like "followers of power," referring to the power (*shakti*) of the goddess to create and sustain the world, to destroy the demonic, or to bring an end to all things.

Karma, Rebirth, and Strategies for Release

The endless cycles of unfolding time and the boundless variety of living forms are controlled not by the gods and goddesses, as one might anticipate, but by a process of principle known as *karma*. Indeed, even the gods and goddesses are governed by karma. The term *karma* means "action" and refers to the simple principle that one's life is governed by one's own continuing behavior or practice. In other words, what one does governs what one will become, not only from the perspective of human life but from the perspective of the entire hierarchy of living forms. Moreover, just as one passes through various stages of life, so too death is only one more stage. After death, in other words, there will be rebirth, to be followed in due time by another death, to be followed by another rebirth, and so forth. Through endless cycles of recurring time,

depending upon one's karmic heritage or trajectory, one might come to be embodied in any number of life forms. There is a beginningless cycle of continuing transmigration or rebirth (called *samsara*) that parallels the seemingly endless cycles of unfolding time. These endless cycles of our karmic trajectories are frustrating and painful, and there is a deep urge within all living things to be free or to be released from these endless cycles of recurring rebirth.

The human life form, though painful like all other life forms, is nevertheless potentially liberating, since it can exercise a good deal of control over an unfolding karmic trajectory, whereas nonhuman life forms are largely victims of a mechanical unfolding of effects. By disciplined meditation that leads to correct insight or wisdom (known as the "discipline of knowledge," or *jñana-yoga*), by disciplined meditation that allows one to become engaged in ordinary life but not to be attached to the fruits of one's actions (known as the "discipline of action," or *karma-yoga*), or, finally, by disciplined devotion to a chosen deity who will aid the devotee in the quest for release (known as the "discipline of devotion," or *bhakti-yoga*) the human being can begin to control his or her own karma and to move toward "release" (moksha) from the endless cycles of recurring transmigration and rebirth. These three types of yoga are discussed at great length in the *Bhagavad Gita*. The *Bhagavad Gita* is known and beloved by all Hindus, and the process of karma and rebirth together with the various strategies of yoga have been widely accepted by all Hindus down to the present time. If there is any one text that comes near to embodying the totality of what it is to be a Hindu, it would be the *Bhagavad Gita*.

The Four Purposes of Life, the Four Stages of Life, and the Four Castes

Classical Hinduism also involves a complex variety of rules and regulations regarding social life. These are set forth in the group of *smriti* texts called "law books," or *Dharmashastras*. Certain general principles or categories were devised that provide an overview of Indian social life as a whole.

The "four proper purposes of human life" refer to certain basic activities that all people can or ought to pursue: (1) Dharma ("law," "duty," "custom"), the pursuit of one's duty, including all of the general and specific social obligations related to one's place in the family and community; (2) Artha ("wealth," "work," "business"), the pursuit of worldly advantage—in other words, making a living, pursuing an occupation, including not only everyday life in the family and local community but also the proper political functioning of the kingdom or state; (3) Kama ("desire," "pleasure"), the pursuit of one's legitimate erotic and aesthetic activities, including sexuality, play, recreation, the arts, and literature; and (4) Moksha ("release," "salvation"), the pursuit of spiritual practices, such as ritual meditation (yoga), and devotion (bhakti), in order to attain release from the continuing round of rebirth and transmigration.

The "four proper purposes of life" are correlated with the "four stages of life," or *ashramas*: (1) Brahmacarin ("pursuing sacred knowledge"), the stage of being a student, when a young person lives in the home of the guru and learns about the tradition; (2) Grihastha ("householder"), the stage of becoming married, raising a family, and fulfilling one's basic social responsibilities in the community; (3) Vanaprastha ("forest-dweller"), the stage of retirement from ordinary family life and social obligations, when one begins to think about the ultimate goal of Moksha; and (4) Sannyasin ("abandoning," "renunciation"), the final stage, when one renounces all worldly attachments and becomes a naked, wandering ascetic in pursuit of Moksha. The stages are a matter of personal choice, and most Hindus go only as far as the first two.

Finally, the "four proper purposes of life" and the "four stages of life" are correlated with the four groups of castes, or *varnas* or *jatis*. The word *caste* is from the Portuguese word *casta*, meaning "breed," "race," or "kind." The word was first used by the Portuguese, when they came to India in the sixteenth century, in order to describe the peculiar social groupings that they noted among the people of India. There were groups of families (1) having the same name; (2) intermarrying with one another; (3) following the same occupations; (4) following certain elaborate rules and restrictions about eating, drinking, and exchanging with other groups; and (5) arranging themselves in each area in certain hierarchical orderings.

There are actually hundreds of *jatis* or "birth groups" in India, but an overall classification is fourfold: (1) Brahmins (priests), the highest castes, made up of those collections of families considered the purest and most learned among the people of India; (2) Kshatriyas ("warriors"), the next highest castes, made up of those collections of families with primary responsibilities in the areas of governance and maintenance of social order, especially the function of kingship; (3) Vaishya ("belonging to the people"), those collections of families involved in commerce, business, and ordinary economic productivity; and (4) Shudra ("servile"), the lowest castes of servants or those collections of families who serve the higher castes. The highest three castes are referred to as "twice-born" (*dvija*), since they are eligible for initiation into sacred learning; in other words, they are permitted to learn about the Vedas. The lowest castes of Shudras are not permitted to study the scriptures. In addition to this hierarchical fourfold grouping, there is yet another grouping that is even lower than the Shudras, namely, the "Untouchables" (*asprishya* or *candala*). These are collections of families considered to be polluted because they are involved in such activities as cleaning human waste areas, removing dead animals, tanning, and so forth. The Untouchables usually live in segregated areas outside of a main village or town.

What is distinctive about the caste system, in contrast to a class system, is that for the most part there is almost no mobility. While there has been more flexibility and mobility among caste groupings in various parts of India than was originally thought, the more rigid, modern system of caste probably developed during the long centuries (ca. 1200–1750) of Muslim dominance in India.

The Muslim Period
(ca. 1200–1757 C.E.)

Contact with Islamic culture occurred as early as the middle of the seventh century, largely through Arab traders coming to the west coast of India across the Arabian Sea. Some military forays into India by Muslim armies began as early as the eighth century. By the beginning of the thirteenth century the Turko-Afghan Muslim descendants of Mahmud established the Delhi Sultanate that ruled north India for the next three centuries (1206–1526). The Delhi Sultanate was succeeded by the famous Mughal dynasty, which lasted from 1526 to 1858 and reached its highest point under the famous Emperor Akbar (1556–1605).

Islamic rule was sometimes harsh and uncompromising. For the most part, however, the Muslim rulers accommodated themselves to the larger Hindu culture, if only because they were greatly outnumbered overall and very much in need of Hindu support. Particularly under the Emperor Akbar, an open-minded and tolerant attitude toward other religious traditions, including Hinduism, prevailed, at least among the court elite. Among the elite there emerged an interesting blend of Perso-Islamic and Rajput-Hindu traditions and styles. Discussions about religion were regularly held in the Hall of Worship with the emperor himself presiding.

Akbar's great-grandson, Dara Shikoh (1615–1659), a follower of one of the Sufi mystical orders, was also a student of Hindu philosophy and mystical practices. However, his brother Aurangzeb, who was emperor from 1658 to 1707, had Dara Shikoh executed in 1659, mainly for political reasons but with the "religious" excuse that Dara Shikoh had become too influenced by heretical Hindu ideas. In any case, with the coming of Aurangzeb's leadership, the period of accommodation between Islam, Hinduism, and other religious traditions came to an abrupt halt, and thereafter Islamic orthodoxy was enforced in court circles.

It must be said overall, however, that any compromise or accommodation between Islam and Hinduism during the centuries of Muslim domination hardly went beyond a very small elite in court circles. Generally speaking, Islam and Hinduism have barely coexisted in India over the centuries. The mutual hostility and suspicion that the two communities have for each other eventually brought about the partition of the subcontinent at the time of independence in 1947 (into India and Pakistan). Even now, barely a half a century after independence, deep distrust continues between the communities in India as well as throughout the South Asian area.

In the Muslim Period, Hindus put great emphasis on preexisting traditions such as vegetarianism, nonviolence (*ahimsa*), and the veneration of the cow as a symbol of divine benevolence, all notions of ritual purity that clearly differentiate the Hindu from the Muslim. Throughout the Muslim period the various Hindu monastic orders also continued to consolidate their traditions and practices. They even developed "militant" orders, groups of Yogis equipped with weapons and trained in martial arts to defend the monastic institutions against the encroachment of Muslim bands or hostile Hindu groups.

Of much greater significance for the development of Hinduism in the Muslim Period is the remarkable increase in bhakti, or devotional Hinduism. This growth is undoubtedly related in important respects to the growing presence of Islamic traditions, especially the Sufi devotional mysticism that was spreading rapidly across north India through the medium of the various regional languages. It is difficult to determine whether Sufi devotional mysticism influenced Hindu bhakti or vice versa. It could well be that Sufi devotionalism and Hindu bhakti have a natural affinity for one another and that, therefore, there was simply a broadbased mutual interaction between these traditions in the sixteenth century and after. The devotional focus of the Sikh religion, founded by Guru Nanak (1469–1539), on one transcendent God and its rejection of the caste system owe much to Islamic Sufi ideas, while its incorporation of Hindu devotional songs in its sacred scripture (called the *Adi Granth* or *Granth Sahib*, the "Book of the Lord") shows clear influence from the Hindu bhakti side. In the final analysis, however, Sikhism is itself a distinct religious tradition that differs from both Islamic Sufism and Hinduism.

The Modern Period
(ca. 1757–present)

Although the Mughal Dynasty survived until 1858, by the mid-eighteenth century it was a dynasty in name only and proved an easy mark for European traders and adventurers (Portuguese, Dutch, French, and British) who came to the subcontinent in the sixteenth and seventeenth centuries. Already in the early decades of the eighteenth century the Mughal empire was breaking up, with local *nawabs,* or "provincial governors," becoming de facto rulers in their areas. The 1757 defeat of Nawab Siraj-ud-daula of Bengal and his army of fifty thousand troops at the hands of Sir Robert Clive of the British East India Company with only eight hundred British troops and some two thousand *sepoys* (native recruits) is usually cited as the beginning of the Modern Period in the history of the subcontinent.

At first, the British controlled little more than what is now Calcutta and some surrounding regions of Bengal and Bihar, and their interest in India was almost totally commercial. Within a century, however, as a result of certain strategic military victories

together with carefully crafted diplomatic alliances with local rulers, the British controlled almost the whole of the subcontinent with only small numbers of troops. With the British, of course, came all of the forces of modernization: the involvement of the subcontinent in the world economy; new patterns of education (at least in the main urban areas with the introduction of English education after 1813); new bureaucratic and legal structures; new philosophical ideas such as humanism, liberal democracy, and Enlightenment rationalism; and new religious ideas through the aggressive work of all sorts of Christian missionaries.

Reactions among Hindus to the encounters with modernity were complex and multidimensional. On one level, there was a rapid and positive response, especially in urban centers such as Calcutta, Bombay, and Madras, to English education, government service, and new economic opportunities. A new Indian elite began to emerge, made up largely of English-speaking members of the upper castes, in such fields as modern trade, manufacturing, civil service, commercial agriculture, and the newly emerging professions of law, journalism, and education. Indeed, some of the present-day descendants of this new elite are the very Asian Indians that one is likely to find in today's America. On another level, there was widespread dislike, even revulsion, against evangelical Christian missionizing. On still another level, many English-educated Indians opted not only for the new language and the resulting benefits to career and personal wealth, but also for Western ideas such as liberalism, representative democracy, and social reform.

Likewise on the level of religion, Hindus responded to modernity in complex and multidimensional ways. By the beginning of the nineteenth century and thereafter, some significant innovations began to appear on at least two distinct levels. First, a reformist and nationalist recasting of Hindu values and traditions culminated in the emergence of India as a modern, secular nation-state. Second, a revisionist and internationalist recasting of

Hindu values and traditions culminated in the export of a variety of Hindu guru-cults to the West, especially to the United States. Both levels can be characterized as "Neo-Hindu" in the sense that they reflect distinctly new elements being introduced into what we have called the classical Hindu synthesis as a result of the impact of modernity and the encounter with Western civilization.

Neo-Hindu Reformist and Nationalist Movements

A variety of reform movements emerged both before independence (1947) and after, representing political strategies ranging from radical extremism to moderate reformism. Perhaps the most famous reformist and nationalist movement in the Modern Period is the Ramakrishna Mission, established by Swami Vivekananda (birth-name Narendranath Datta, 1862–1902) in Bengal, and named after the Bengali spiritual teacher or holy man Ramakrishna (birth-name Gadadhar Chatterjee, 1836–1886), who was Vivekananda's guru. Ramakrishna spent his entire adult life as a priest in a temple devoted to the goddess Kali in the district of Dakshineshwar, near Calcutta. He had a number of extraordinary mystical experiences and over the years attracted a small band of followers, one of whom was Narendranath Datta, later to be given the spiritual name Vivekananda (meaning "whose bliss is discrimination"). After Ramakrishna's death, Vivekananda made a pilgrimage around India and determined, finally, to propagate the spiritual message of his guru. Vivekananda developed and taught a simplified version of monistic Vedanta philosophy and combined those ideas with a program for social action and social reform for modern India. He attended the World Parliament of Religions in 1893 in Chicago as a representative of Hinduism, and his considerable oratorical skills made a deep impression in the popular press and in certain liberal religious intellectual circles. He traveled widely in the United States and made

a number of American converts. In 1897, after his return to India, he established the Ramakrishna Mission in India, along with a series of Vedanta Societies in the United States, Europe, and Latin America.

Mohandas Karamchand Gandhi (1869–1948) was born in the western region of Gujarat, studied law in England (1888–1891), practiced law for twenty-one years in South Africa (1893–1914), and then returned to India to lead the nationalist struggle for independence from the British. He was primarily a political leader, but his political work was inextricably linked to his reformed and nationalist Neo-Hindu vision that stressed (1) the oneness of all religions; (2) the pursuit of nonviolent noncooperation against the British as a political strategy, or what he called "truth-force" or "grasping truth" (*satyagraha*); and (3) the cultivation of nonviolence (*ahimsa*) in all conflict situations. He detested the inequities of the caste system, especially "untouchability," and he thought that the spiritual life was essential to political life. Although he never founded a religious group as such, it can be said that he rallied an entire nation to his Neo-Hindu vision of reform and nationalism.

Despite their varying political orientations and strategies these Neo-Hindu reformist and nationalist movements had in common (1) a primary focus on developing among the people of India a self-confident national awareness that would provide a solid foundation for India as a modern nation-state; (2) the reform of outdated, parochial, and superstitious Hindu practices; (3) the rejection of the caste system; (4) female emancipation; (5) the improvement of social conditions for the poor; and (6) economic progress for the entire nation. These groups contributed incalculably to the identity of the modern Indian nation-state.

Neo-Hindu Revisionist and Internationalist Movements

There also emerged among other Neo-Hindu groups what can be called a revisionist and internationalist impulse. "Revisionist" and "internationalist" imply ideas and practices that have clear antecedents in older patterns of Hindu spirituality but are designed to appeal not only to Asian Indians, but to a broad-based international audience as well. Common features of these "export" brands of Neo-Hinduism include (1) devotion to a deified guru; (2) total obedience to the will of the guru; (3) the practice of one or another type of yoga; (4) the claim that all religions are basically valid; (5) the claim that one's national or ethnic identity has no bearing on the practice of the particular Neo-Hindu tradition; and (6) a tendency to de-emphasize social work or political activity of any kind.

Some of the better known of these export brands of Neo-Hinduism include:

1. The Self-Realization Fellowship in Los Angeles, founded by Paramahamsa Yogananda (birth-name Mukunda Lal Ghosh, 1893–1952), a Bengali *sadhu,* or "holy man," who first came to the United States to attend a conference in Boston in 1920 and then remained to establish his Self-Realization Fellowship in the same year. Today the Self-Realization Fellowship maintains eight temples throughout the western United States and has its international headquarters in Los Angeles.

2. The Center of Satya Sai Baba (birth-name Satya Narayan, b. 1926), a non-Brahmin from Puttaparthi in the state of Andhra Pradesh in South India, who at the age of fourteen declared himself to be a reincarnation of the Shirdi Sai Baba, a holy man from Maharashtra who died in 1918. Alleged to be a great healer, he has a purported following in India of two to three million. Currently Satya Sai Baba maintains three major centers in the United States (Los Angeles, San Francisco, and Phoenix).

3. The Spiritual Regeneration Movement or Transcendental Meditation (TM), founded by Maharishi Mahesh Yogi (birth-name Mahesh Prasad Varma, b. 1911) in the 1960s. TM centers are found throughout the United States and Europe. The international headquarters of the movement is in Switzerland. The Maharishi teaches a simple technique of sound-meditation. The devotee is given a sacred *mantra,* or sound, and then told to meditate one-half hour to an hour every day.

4. The International Society for Krishna Consciousness (ISKCON), founded in the 1960s by A. C. Bhaktivedanta Prabhupada (birth-name Abhay Charan De, 1896–1977), a Bengali businessman from Calcutta who became a Vaishnava monk. Also known as the Hare Krishna movement, the Society's followers can be seen on street corners in many American cities, chanting "Hare Krishna, Hare Rama," the basic mantra of the group.

5. The Siddha Yoga ("Discipline of Spiritual Fulfillment") Movement, founded by Swami (Baba) Muktananda (1908–1982), is currently based at an Ashrama in South Fallsburg, New York, and an Ashrama in India at Ganeshpuri, Maharashtra (near Bombay). Since the death of its founder in 1982, the movement has been led mainly by a young woman, Guru-mayi Cidvilasananda. The movement is a blend of classical and Tantric Yoga practices, emphasizing the importance of *shakti* ("power" or "divine energy"). Followers believe that shakti can descend suddenly (a process called *shaktipat*) into a devotee by the mere presence or touch of the guru.

Although all of these and other Neo-Hindu revisionist and internationalist movements have some connection with traditional Hindu spirituality, all have clearly moved away from a specifically Indian identity. They are all international movements with sizable followings throughout the world.

HINDUISM IN
TODAY'S AMERICA

Currently there are hundreds of Hindu temples in the United States, divided evenly between the eastern and western regions of the country. Many of these are quite small centers, some being little more than converted private homes. Others, however, are major temple complexes. For example, the

Lord Venkateshwara Balaji Temple in Malibu Canyon near Los Angeles is an authentic South Indian (primarily Vaishnava) temple. Artisans and priests were brought from India for the actual planning and construction of the temple, and priests from India continue to assist in the temple's ritual operations. In 2007, Hindus in suburban Atlanta dedicated a $19 million temple that is the largest of its kind in the United States—at least for the time being.

Basic Types of Hinduism in America

A broad, general perspective would suggest five basic types of Hinduism in America:

1. Secular Hinduism
2. Non-sectarian Hinduism
3. Bhakti or Devotional Hinduism
4. Reformist-Nationalist Neo-Hinduism
5. Guru-Internationalist-Missionizing Neo-Hinduism

Most Asian Indians that you meet in the United States will probably fit into one of these broad, general types. By "Secular Hinduism" we mean those Asian Indian Hindus who do not identify with any particular beliefs or practices of traditional Hinduism but who at the same time have never chosen to be in any other religious grouping. Among Asian Indian Hindus in today's America many would be of this secular variety (especially highly educated, professional Asian Indian adult males). "Nonsectarian Hinduism" refers to those Asian Indian Hindus who do not identify with any particular branch of Hinduism, but who practice a broad, eclectic form of Hinduism that relates to the regions and castes of India from which they come. Most of these Hindus would come from the high or "forward" castes, mainly Brahmin. "Bhakti or Devotional Hinduism" includes those Asian Indian Hindus who would identify themselves with a particular sectarian tradition, Vaishnava, Shaiva, or Shakta, all of which have been described earlier in the chapter. By "Reform-

ist-Nationalist Neo-Hinduism" we mean those Asian Indian Hindus who are followers of groups such as the Ramakrishna Mission. Finally, "Guru-Internationalist-Missionizing Neo-Hinduism" incorporates those Asian Indian Hindus who are followers of groups such as the Transcendental Meditation movement or the Hare Krishna movement. What distinguishes the two types of Neo-Hinduism is that the Reformist-Nationalist type maintains a primary interest in the native homeland of India and is not especially mission-minded, while the Guru-Internationalist-Missionizing type has a broadly internationalist perspective and actively seeks converts from outside the Asian Indian population.

Basic Beliefs of Hindus in America

As we have stressed throughout this chapter, there is no specific, required set of beliefs for a Hindu. An American Hindu organization, however, known as the Himalayan Academy, has set forth what it calls Nine Beliefs of Hinduism, as a general summary of Hindu views largely accepted by all of the types of Hinduism in America (with the exception, of course, of Secular Hinduism).[3]

The nine beliefs are as follows:

1. That there is "one, all-pervasive Supreme Being";
2. That there are "endless cycles of creation, preservation and dissolution" (that is, a cyclical view of time and history);
3. That "all souls are evolving" toward or seeking "Moksha" or "liberation";
4. That there is a "law of cause and effect" known as Karma;
5. That there is "reincarnation";
6. That there are "divine beings and forces" that require "temple worship" and "personal worship," or puja, in the home;
7. That there is a need for an "awakened Master of Sat Guru" (that is, a reliable, personal teacher) for one's personal and ethical life;

How Should "Hindu Religion" Be Taught?
The California Textbook Controversy

Recently, the State of California has debated the manner in which "Hindu Religion" or "Hinduism" should be taught in public schools. Since 1991 the State of California has included teaching about the world's religions as part of its sixth-grade curriculum on ancient civilizations. According to state standards, religions are to be presented in a fair and balanced manner. Religious diversity is to be respected, and care must be exercised not to be insensitive to the religious beliefs of various groups.

Textbooks are reviewed and revised approximately every six years, and community groups are invited to comment about the various textbooks before they are approved for use. Community groups are allowed to suggest editorial changes, or minor alterations or clarifications in the textbook presentations, which the California State Board of Education is free to accept or reject.

From the beginning of the process in 1991, the journal *Hinduism Today* raised questions about the quality of the textbooks, as did some Jewish and Muslim community groups. Many of the editorial changes suggested by Jewish and Muslim readers were adopted by the State Commission, but Hindus did not take serious action for fourteen years. In 2005, two Hindu groups (the Vedic Foundation and the Hindu Education Foundation) decided to take action, because many Asian Indian Hindu families felt that the textbooks did not portray the Hindu religion in a positive manner. Too much emphasis was being placed on the rigidities of the caste system, and the Hindu notion of God and/or Brahman was not carefully described. Also, the families said that the textbooks were full of factual errors, and they proposed some 170 editorial changes to correct these errors. A committee of the California Department of Education, one of whose members is the distinguished South Asian historian Dr. Shiva Bajpai, reviewed the suggested changes and approved them for inclusion in the revised textbooks.

In December 2005, however, Dr. Michael Witzel, a professor of Sanskrit Studies at Harvard University, intervened in the review process, arguing that many of the proposed edits were inappropriate and that they advocated highly conservative and ideological Hindu views that were not representative of Hindu religion. Accepting the changes, according to Dr. Witzel, would lead to an "international educational scandal."

The State Board of Education then examined the proposed edits further, and invited Dr. Witzel and other scholars to comment. After additional meetings, Dr. Witzel and Dr. Bajpai compromised by accepting many of the suggested changes, but the issue continues to be debated, and a Hindu group called California Parents for Equalization of Educational Materials has filed suit in state court. The suit, which is still pending, objects to what the group considers to be derogatory descriptions of Hinduism and a bias in favor of biblical indoctrination for sixth-grade students.

Although the specific details regarding the controversy are well worth exploring further, for our purposes, you might wish to ask the following questions:

1. Is it possible to present the beliefs of the world's religions in a fair and balanced manner?
2. If so, who decides what is fair and balanced? Should Boards of Education listen primarily to academic experts or to devout believers in a particular religion?
3. Does teaching about religion in public schools violate the principle of the separation of church and state?

8. That "all life is sacred" and that one should pursue "*ahimsa* or non-violence"; and

9. That "no particular religion teaches the only way to salvation above all others, but that all genuine religious paths are . . . deserving (of) tolerance and understanding."

Basic Practices of Hindus in America

Generally speaking, Asian Indian Hindus, with the exception of the followers of Secular Hinduism, center their religious life around three kinds of practices: personal or family worship or puja in the home; determining crucial times or seasons for important activities (astrology or horoscopy); and celebration of important festivals or holidays.

Personal or Family Worship in the Home

Almost every Asian Indian Hindu home will have a special room or at least a shelf or special place for daily worship and meditation (puja). Usually the puja room will have statues or color pictures of various deities (gods and goddesses) and gurus (teachers). The deities and teachers will usually be from the region in India from which the family comes (West Bengal, Maharashtra, and so forth), but also frequently include such universal Hindu figures as Vishnu, Lord Krishna, Lord Rama, Shiva, and Ganesh, for example. Candles and incense will be burned, usually at set times (dawn, evening, and so forth), and prayers will be uttered, interspersed with periods of quiet meditation and sometimes even one or another kind of yoga practice. In most Asian Hindu families, the mother is in charge of the puja room and the daily and seasonal devotional practices in the life of the family.

Astrology and Horoscopy

For many traditional Hindus and Neo-Hindus, all important events in the unfolding life of the family and community—family planning, a major journey, the marriage of a child, the building and dedication of temples, and so on—will only be undertaken after having determined the appropriate time by consulting a professional astrologer or casting horoscopes. Most Asian Indian Hindu families in America use Western traditions of astrology, but some also follow traditional South Asian horoscopy. Astrology is an important component in the family's planning, especially in determining marriage. Most Asian Indian Hindu marriages, even among the followers of Secular Hinduism, are arranged marriages, and many Hindu families will have horoscopes cast for the proposed bride and groom and for determining the day and specific time of the wedding. This is an important legacy of the traditional caste system, and even Neo-Hindus who reject the traditional caste system continue to practice the tradition of arranged marriages and the casting of horoscopes.

Celebration of Important Festivals and Holidays

Important festivals or holidays that many Hindus in America observe include:

1. "Worship of the Goddess Sarasvati," a special festival for scholars, teachers, and students celebrating the great goddess of learning;

2. "Shiva's Night," a special festival day for Shaivas but celebrated by many other non-Shaiva Hindus as well;

3. "Holi," named after the demon-goddess Holika, a raucous fertility festival in which Hindus pour colored water or paint on one another and exchange humorous erotic obscenities and jokes;

4. "The Ninth Day for Rama," celebrating the birth of Lord Rama;

5. "The Guru's Full-Moon Day," a festival that honors the particular guru of the Hindu devotee;

6. "The Bracelet-Tying for Protection," a festival when brothers commit themselves to protecting their sisters, symbolized by having their sisters tie a special bracelet around their brothers' wrists;

7. "The Eighth Day for Krishna," the festival celebrating the birth of Lord Krishna;

8. "The Fourth Day for Ganesh," a celebration in which businesspeople, students, artisans, and others implore Lord Ganesh (the elephant god) for blessings on their work;

9. "The Nine Nights" celebration (mainly for Bengalis) Durga Puja, or the worship of the goddess Durga, who overcomes the buffalo-demon (the symbol of evil), or celebrating (for Vaishnavas devoted to Lord Rama) the great struggle between Lord Rama and the demon Ravana;

10. "The Tenth Day," celebrating the final victory of Lord Rama over the demon Ravana;

11. "The Festival of Lamps," involving the lighting of candles or colored lights or lamps signifying the reappearance of the sun and prosperity after the long rainy season.

CONCLUSION

This brings to a conclusion our telling of the story of Hinduism. It is an incredible story, containing some of the oldest forms of religion known to humankind, as well as some of the newest. Hinduism is boundlessly various in its myriad forms and yet bears an unmistakable coherence in patterns of ritual performance, the pursuit of quiet mediation (yoga), and the exuberant expression of passionate devotion (bhakti).

Notes

1. Judith E. Walsh, *A Brief History of India* (New York: Checkmark Books, 2007), 287.
2. Gerald James Larson, *India's Agony Over Religion* (Albany: SUNY Press, 1995), 11.
3. Nine Beliefs of Hinduism, published by the Himalayan Academy, 3575 Sacramento Street, San Francisco, CA 94118.

STUDY QUESTIONS

1. What does "being religious" mean for the Hindu? How does Hinduism's emphasis on correct action differ from other religious traditions you have studied?

2. What are the six fundamental periods for the development of Hinduism? What are the defining characteristics of each of these periods? How is the historical development of Hinduism different from that of other religious traditions?

3. What do most Hindus think of the concepts of gods and goddesses? What are the names of three or four well-known Hindu deities? What roles do they play in the Hindu religion?

4. What are the "four purposes of life" in the Hindu religion? How do these purposes function to describe the Hindu's understanding of living in the world?

5. What are the "four stages of life"? How do these stages function to describe the Hindu's understanding of living in the world?

6. What are the four divisions of castes in Hinduism? How do they function to describe the Hindu's understanding of living in the world?

7. What were the reactions, particularly among Hindus coming to America, of their encounter with the modern world? Socially? Religiously?

8. Who is the most famous reformist of the Hindu Modern Period? What were his contributions to Hindu social and religious development?

9. What are the five basic types of Hinduism in America? Give a brief description of each. What are the nine basic beliefs that serve to define American Hinduism?

10. Name and describe some of the important festivals or holidays observed by Hindus in America. Are these festivals similar in function to other religious festivals you have studied? In what way?

ESSAY TOPICS

Hinduism and Modernity: Conflict and Assimilation

The *Bhagavad Gita*: Sacred Text of Hinduism

The Gods and Goddesses of Hinduism

Karma and Rebirth: Two Fundamental Principles of Hinduism

The Hindu Pilgrimages: Four Purposes, Four States, Four Castes

Hinduism in America: Beginnings and Growth

WORD EXPLORATION

The following words play significant roles in any discussion of Hinduism in America and are worth careful reflection and discussion.

Hindu	Vaishya	Shiva
Ritual	Shudra	Samsara
Sanskrit	Brahmin	Moksha
Upanishads	*Bhagavad Gita*	Temple
Veda	Yoga	Vishnu
Kshatriyas	*Mahabharata*	

FOR FURTHER READING

Klostermaier, Klaus K. *A Survey of Hinduism.* 3rd. ed. Albany: SUNY Press, 2006.
Larson, Gerald James. *India's Agony Over Religion.* Albany: SUNY Press, 1995.
Smart, Ninian. "The Indian Experience: Classical Hinduism," in *The Religious Experience.* Upper Saddle River, N.J.: Prentice Hall, 1996, 87–114.

WEB SITES

http://www.hindumandir.us/
    List of Hindu temples and mandirs in America

http://www.us-hindus.com/
    Principles and practices of Hinduism

http://www.sanatansociety.org/hindu_gods_and_goddesses.htm
    Hindu gods and goddesses

http://www.hinduamericanfoundation.org/
    Official Web site of the Hindu American Foundation

II

Buddhism in the World and in America

MALCOLM DAVID ECKEL

5th c. B.C.E.	Life of Siddhartha Gautama, the historical Buddha
3rd c. B.C.E.	Reign of King Asoka; introduction of Buddhism to Sri Lanka
1st c. C.E.	Development of Mahayana Buddhism in India
2nd c. C.E.	Introduction of Buddhism to China
8th c. C.E.	Introduction of Buddhism to Tibet and Japan
12th c. C.E.	Disappearance of Buddhism in India
1853	First Buddhist temple in San Francisco
1875	Helena Petrovna Blavatsky and Henry Steel Olcott found the Theosophical Society in New York
1880	Blavatsky and Olcott travel to Sri Lanka and become champions of Sri Lankan Buddhism
1893	World's Parliament of Religions in Chicago; arrival of Asian missionaries in North America
1899	Buddhist Mission to North America, forerunner of Buddhist Churches of America
1927	Zen temple founded in Los Angeles, soon followed by one in San Francisco
1945	Incorporation of the Buddhist Churches of America
1950s	D.T. Suzuki, Alan Watts, and others begin the popularization of Zen in America
1960	Daisaku Ikeda, third president of Soka Gakkai, visits America and encourages the growth of Soka Gakkai
1965	Change in immigration policy leads to a surge in immigration from Asia
1972	Seung San, Korean monk and Zen master, establishes Buddhist center in Providence, Rhode Island
1973	First visit by the Dalai Lama to the West
1974	Founding of Naropa Institute in Boulder, Colorado, as a center for the study and teaching of Tibetan Buddhism
1975	Founding of the Insight Meditation Society in Massachusetts
1978	Founding of the Buddhist Peace Fellowship
1988	Founding of Hsi Lai Temple in Hacienda Heights, California, representing the Fo Guang Shan movement in Taiwan
1991	Founding of *Tricycle: The Buddhist Review*
2001	Followers of the late Chögyam Trungpa build nation's largest Buddhist stupa near Red Feather Lakes, Colorado
2006	Two Democrats, Mazie Hirono (Hawaii) and Hank Johnson (Ga.) become first Buddhists ever elected to U.S. Congress

If you have never thought of religion without thinking of God, or if you think that a religion has to have clear boundaries that separate insiders from outsiders, then you will be intrigued and challenged by your encounter with Buddhism. For over two thousand years in Asia, and more recently in Europe and North America, the Buddhist tradition has brought joy, consolation, and meaning to human life without affirming the existence of a personal God. It has found ways to exist side by side with other religious traditions without many of the great conflicts that have plagued religious life in the West.

Buddhism arose in India, and the largest concentrations of Buddhists in the world can still be found in Asia. In some places, as in Tibet, Sri Lanka, and Thailand, Buddhism is clearly the dominant tradition; in others, such as China, Korea, and Japan, Buddhism has not necessarily dominated the culture but has had a deep impact on the way people think through religious questions and deal with the religious crises in their lives.

As the Buddhist tradition spread across Asia, it spawned many different varieties, and a surprising number of these varieties have made their way to North America. The most visible Buddhist community in some parts of the United States is a group known as the Buddhist Churches of America (BCA). The BCA brings together a venerable Japanese tradition of devotion to the Buddha Amida (the Buddha of Infinite Light) with many of the trappings of modern American religious life, from a Buddhist Sunday school to the Young Buddhist Association. In many communities in America you can find, for example, centers for the practice of Zen, the Japanese version of an ancient discipline of seated meditation; centers of the Nichiren Shoshu of America (NSA), devoted to meditation on a Buddhist text known as the Lotus Sutra; Insight (Vipassana) Centers for meditation that is derived from the Buddhist practice of Southeast Asia; and centers for the study of the different varieties of Tibetan Buddhism. The list seems almost endless.

Even if we could name all the centers of Buddhism in America, we still would not begin to exhaust its influence on American cultural life. For a hundred years or more, Buddhist values have left their mark on the American cultural landscape. Japanese attitudes toward nature significantly affected the way American painters and architects visualized the landscape as early as the nineteenth century. The countercultures of the 1950s and 1960s echoed the strains of Jack Kerouac's *Dharma Bums*. Bruce Lee brought the meditative tradition of the martial arts into American living rooms. Now you can hear echoes of Buddhist values almost everywhere you look. The rock group Nirvana took its name from the Buddhist ideal of release from the cycle of transmigration, and the title of their album "Nevermind" is a direct reflection of the important Buddhist concept of "no-mind." Whether Americans have really understood Buddhist values is a question you may want to ask yourself when you have finished this chapter, but there is no doubt that Buddhism has crept into our culture in surprising and delightful ways.

If Buddhism is so varied and has influenced American culture so widely, what makes it "Buddhist"? It would be wonderful to point to a single doctrine or practice that we could identify as the "essence" of Buddhism. But Buddhists have been uncomfortable with any language suggesting that things have "essences." They insist that everything changes and nothing has any permanent identity, least of all a movement as complex and as varied as the one we call "Buddhism." It is better not to look for a single essence, but rather for a center of gravity or for lines of force around which Buddhist people have oriented themselves as they struggle to give meaning, depth, and texture to their lives. For centuries the most basic point of orientation has been the story of Siddhartha Gautama, the founder of the Buddhist tradition.

The Contrast Between "Ethnic" Buddhism and "Convert" Buddhism in America

It is common to group the varieties of American Buddhism in two categories: "ethnic" Buddhism, in which the traditions and practices serve as a way of maintaining the ethnic identity of an immigrant community, and "convert" Buddhism, in which American-born converts adopt Buddhist ideas and practices and adapt them to an American way of life. This distinction is useful is two ways. It calls attention, first of all, to the incredible ethnic diversity of American Buddhism, from the foundation of the first Chinese temple in San Francisco in 1853 to the proliferation of Southeast Asian Buddhist temples across America after the liberalization of American immigration laws in the 1960s and the end of the Vietnam War. It is important to understand that, for many Asian communities in America, the practice of Buddhism connects them to their tradition and honors their identity as a people, whether they are Chinese, Japanese, Thai, Burmese, Khmer, Vietnamese, Lao, or from one of the other distinctive Buddhist communities of Asia.

This distinction is useful also to call attention to the process of conversion that has been part of the spread of American Buddhism since the late nineteenth century. One of the most important milestones in this process was the World's Parliament of Religions in 1893, when religious teachers from many of the religious traditions of Asia brought their teachings to this country and began to attract groups of followers. But the process began even earlier as small groups of Americans traveled to Asia and became fascinated with Buddhist teachings. Two of the most important of these were Helena Petrovna Blavatsky and Henry Steel Olcott, two founders of the Theosophical Society, who traveled to Sri Lanka in 1880, became champions of Sri Lankan Buddhism, and helped formulate a distinctively "modern" Buddhism. This process of conversion picked up steam after the Second World War as Zen Buddhism, Tibetan Buddhism, and other forms of Buddhist practice became popular with Americans who had become disenchanted with their own religious traditions or who saw in Buddhism a way of dealing with the pressures of modern life.

But the state of American Buddhism is now far more complex than this simple distinction is able to express. As the different ethnic Buddhist communities have evolved and welcomed American converts, they have been transformed in a way that mirrors the diversity of American culture at large. The Jodo Shinshu tradition, for example, came to America from Japan in 1899 as the Buddhist Mission to North America. In 1945 it was incorporated as the Buddhist Churches of America. In 1964 it gave rise to the Institute of Buddhist Studies in Berkeley, California, which functions as a degree-granting Buddhist seminary affiliated with the Graduate Theological Union. The line between ethnicity and conversion is dissolving with the creation of new forms of Buddhist life and practice. It also is becoming more and more difficult to distinguish someone who has "converted" to Buddhism from someone who has not. Is a Catholic monk who practices Zen meditation any less Catholic for having adopted a Buddhist practice? The same question could be asked of any Americans who adopt Buddhist ideas or practices in any aspect of their lives. Buddhism has now become part of the shifting process of religious exploration and transformation that is affecting all areas of American religious life.

THE BUDDHA

From a modern Western perspective, the history of Buddhism begins with the story of a man named Siddhartha Gautama who lived about five hundred years before the Common Era in a small kingdom in the foothills of what is now southern Nepal. Buddhist tradition tells us that this man was born into a princely family and raised in a palace. He married, had a child, and then, in his early thirties, saw four sights that burned into his consciousness an image of the decay and death that stalks human life. He saw a sick person, an old person, a corpse, and finally an ascetic who was attempting to leave this suffering behind by renouncing the pleasures of ordinary life. Siddhartha decided to follow the example of the ascetic and abandon the princely life. He left the palace, gave away his princely ornaments, cut off his hair, and took up the life of a wandering holy man on the roads of northern India. Legends tell us that he studied with a series of teachers and starved himself until he was reduced almost to skin and bones. Siddhartha found, however, that strict denial of the pleasures of the body did not produce the insight he was seeking. He decided instead to take up a balanced discipline known as the Middle Path, where he would seek neither pleasure nor pain. On the Middle Path, he began finally to make progress. He sat down under a tree called the Bodhi Tree and, after a series of temptations, broke through to the realization that he no longer was subject to the suffering of human life. He became, in other words, a Buddha—someone who has been "enlightened" or, more accurately, someone who has "woken up" from the sleep of ignorance that binds people in the suffering of this world.

Most of the details of the Buddha's story come from traditions and legends that are now very difficult to confirm. Yet there is little doubt among scholars of Buddhism that something like this actually happened: there was a man who was raised in a princely setting, left it behind, and achieved a breakthrough that became the basis of a great world religion. But if you ask Buddhists where the story of the Buddha really begins, it is not just with the birth of Siddhartha Gautama. It has to be traced back many lifetimes to his career as a future Buddha, or *bodhisattva* (a Buddha-to-be), when he laid the groundwork for his eventual awakening by performing acts of generosity, moral courage, and self-sacrifice.

Buddhists tell a story, for example, about a time when the bodhisattva was born as the leader of a herd of deer. The herd was being hunted mercilessly by the king of a neighbor-

ing kingdom. To limit the king's cruelty, the deer agreed that they would make a regular sacrifice of one of the herd. When the time came to give up a particular doe who was about to give birth to a fawn, the bodhisattva, as the leader of the herd, offered to present himself to the king in the doe's place. The king was so impressed by the deer's willingness to sacrifice himself that he agreed to stop hunting and guarantee the herd's safety. The story is simple and is meant to appeal to ordinary people who do not have the chance to imitate the example of the Buddha's renunciation, but the themes of self-sacrifice are very similar. Not everyone has the chance to become a monk and formally renounce attachment to this world, but even the simplest and most worldly people can be called on to make great sacrifices to help others. To become a Buddha, Siddhartha Gautama had to leave the palace—to give up what he once was and become something new—but he also had to prepare for that final renunciation with acts of generosity and self-sacrifice in previous lives. These images of generosity and renunciation, both great and small, have colored Buddhist life throughout its history.

The stories of the Buddha's previous lives bring us face to face with an aspect of Indian religion that is difficult to fathom, but is crucial for anyone who wants to understand the ideal of renunciation that motivates so much of Indian religious life. Buddhism is rooted in the Indian doctrine of *samsara,* a word that we translate as "reincarnation" or "transmigration," but it literally means a "wandering" from one life to the next. Sometime in the centuries that preceded the life of the Buddha, Indian thinkers began to imagine that human existence involved not just a single life followed by a possible reward in heaven, but a series of lives stretching into the past without beginning and potentially into the future without end. The fate of a soul as it wanders through the forest or over the stormy sea of *samsara* is determined by its *karma,* its actions. People who perform good actions are rewarded in future lives, perhaps even by being reborn in the heaven of one of the myriad Indian gods, and people who perform bad actions are punished with birth as an animal, an insect, or an inhabitant of one of the Indian hells. But all the results of action, both good and bad, slip away, so that the gods eventually fall back down into the human realm, and the animals eventually rise to take birth as human beings.

To understand the impact of the doctrine of reincarnation it is important to grasp two points. First, the doctrine is *fundamental*. In the West ideas of reincarnation hover on the fringes of established religious traditions: they are options that people feel free to take or leave. But in India the doctrine of reincarnation has the status of a basic assumption. It poses a problem that generations of Indian religious thinkers have attempted to solve. What makes the doctrine of reincarnation so problematic? As thoughtful religious figures pondered the implications of reincarnation in the centuries that preceded the life of the Buddha, they came to feel not only that reincarnation was fundamental but that it was enormously *burdensome*. As they looked back into the past and forward into the future, not for just one or two lives but for many, many millions of lives, they saw reincarnation as the frustration of all human hopes and desires. No matter how delightful pleasures might be, they were doomed eventually to slip away.

This sense of disillusionment with the endless cycle of death and rebirth was what gave the story of the Buddha's career its urgency and power. Siddhartha Gautama set out to find the solution to the problem of reincarnation, and the teaching that grew out of the experience of his awakening mapped a way for others to follow as they struggled to find their own passage through the forest and across the ocean of death and rebirth. Buddhists have elaborated the teaching, or the Dharma, of the Buddha with great eloquence and doctrinal sophistication. But the Buddha's Dharma is not meant to satisfy idle curiosity or serve as an intellectual game. It is meant to chart a path out of suffering and into an experience of freedom from the endless cycle of rebirth.

DHARMA: THE BUDDHA'S TEACHING

After the Buddha experienced his awakening, Buddhist tradition tells us, he rose from his seat under the Bodhi Tree and walked to a Deer Park in Varanasi (the same park that was associated with his earlier life as the king of the herd of deer). In the Deer Park he met some friends, and he sat down and told them of his awakening. This act of teaching is called the first "turning of the wheel of Dharma" and has come to represent the moment when the Buddha set the Buddhist tradition in motion. The Dharma is symbolized by a wheel, and the wheel has become the symbol of Buddhism. The words spoken by the Buddha on this occasion, as tradition has preserved them, are surprisingly simple, but they contain many of the insights that set the Buddhist tradition apart from other great religions of the world.

The content of the Buddha's first sermon is divided into *Four Noble Truths*: the truth of *suffering*, the truth of the *origin* of suffering, the truth of the *cessation* of suffering, and the truth of the *path that leads to* the cessation of suffering. The first of these truths is expressed by saying "all is suffering," a claim that has given the Buddhist tradition an unjustified reputation for being the most pessimistic of the world's religions. As one commentator said, if Buddhists mean what they say, they should go around with the world's longest faces. Like many important religious claims, however, the truth of suffering needs to be interpreted.

Buddhist tradition says that the claim "all is suffering" can be understood three ways. First, there is an obvious sense in which some things are simply painful. To be run over by a bus or crushed by a raging elephant is painful, and that pain is a form of suffering. There is a second form of suffering that comes when you become too attached to something that brings pleasure. If you try to hold on to things that bring great satisfaction, they eventually bring pain. Even the most satisfying things begin to change and slip away, and, if you cannot let them go, they cause pain. This kind of pain is the suffering that comes from change. The third kind of suffering is more difficult to grasp. Buddhists say that "pleasurable" things can cause suffering even while they bring us pleasure, because the idea of "pleasure" is based on a misconception about the nature of reality. The objects that we consider pleasurable or painful are no more than a series of "conditioned states," and the idea of "pleasure" or "pain" is something that we in our ignorance and desire impose upon them.

Buddhist texts often use the example of a vehicle or a cart to reflect on the doctrine of suffering and the vision of reality that lies behind it. To bring the example up to date, we could say that the experience of suffering is like the American experience of an automobile. If you drive a new car into a telephone pole, the feeling you have in your bones is the first kind of suffering. If you take the car home, live with it for a while, and watch rust creep slowly up the door panels, the sensation of satisfaction turning slowly to disappointment is the second kind of suffering. The third kind of suffering lurks within the experience of satisfaction itself. When you drive the car out of the showroom door and imagine that it is an object that brings you great pleasure, the pleasure itself is a subtle form of pain. It clouds the mind and prevents you from seeing reality as it truly is.

Is the truth of suffering pessimistic? Not necessarily. There is still plenty of room to smile and take quiet delight in something like a new car as you watch it change. You can still put the top down on a sunny day, drive it through the landscape, and feel the wind blowing in your hair. But the Buddhist analysis of suffering contains a clear warning against attachment—against the desire to freeze these moments of satisfaction and not let them go—and it forces a person to look carefully at the moments of satisfaction and cut through the illusions that make many objects of desire seem more satisfying than they really are.

According to the *Second Noble Truth,* suffering comes from desire, and desire comes, through a complicated mental process, from *ignorance*. Like suffering, the concept of ignorance has more than one meaning. To see the world without ignorance you have to be able to recognize things that are palpably painful. You have to see the car when it is bearing down on you and step out of the way. You also have to realize that the satisfaction you feel when you see it glistening in the sunlight is constantly changing. You have to enjoy it while you can and then let it go. You also have to realize that, while it glistens, it is nothing but a combination of plastic, steel, chrome, and glass. There really is nothing to call "car" apart from this combination of constituents, and the constituents themselves are constantly decaying and evolving into other things.

The idea that there is no car apart from an evolving combination of parts is an example of the famous Buddhist doctrine of *no-self*. From the time of the Buddha, it seems Buddhists have claimed that nothing has any permanent identity. What we imagine to be its "self" is nothing more than an illusion we impose on an arbitrary and changing flow of events. This illusion is just as true of the driver as it is of the car. What we think of as being our "selves" is nothing more than a combination of thoughts, feelings, memories, and conscious states, all of which are in a continuous state of change. We can speak in a practical way about ourselves being the "same" personality from one moment to the next, just as we can say that the fire burning in the fireplace is the "same" fire from one moment to the next. But the truth is that we are changing, just as the fire is burning, and the "sameness" we attribute to ourselves is nothing more than a convenient fiction that helps us get on with the process of living.

Sometimes people ask why Buddhists seem to pay so much attention to abstract questions of identity or selfhood, when the

Buddha was concerned with the practical issue of relief from suffering. The answer is that *wisdom*, a deep understanding of no-self, starts the process of unraveling the chain of suffering. It begins to put out the fire of the personality and leads to the peace that Buddhists associate with the *Third Noble Truth*, the truth of *cessation* or *nirvana*. Nirvana is the definitive end of the cycle of reincarnation. It is difficult for people who pride themselves on being active and busy to sympathize with the traditional Buddhist concept of nirvana. Instead of busyness, it speaks of quiet and cessation. Instead of a constant drive to create and succeed, it speaks of an impulse to take a bit of what we think of as existence and let it slip away. The word nirvana refers literally to a "blowing out," as if the fire of the personality could be allowed to flicker out like the dying flame of a candle.

To understand Buddhist approaches to the concept of nirvana, it is important not to wish away the negative aspect of the concept but to confront it directly. If you assume, as Buddhists have, that life in the cycle of reincarnation has been going on from a time that had no beginning, and that the job of each individual ultimately is to bring the cycle to an end, then cessation, extinction, and stopping are positive images. They convey a sense of peace and serenity that cuts through the constant frustration of life. To touch the spirit of nirvana in your own experience you might simply imagine what goes through your mind when you crawl out of bed in the morning and begin to face the day. Is your job to do what God is pictured as doing in the Jewish or Christian scriptures—to look into the primordial chaos of the day and make something new come into being?—Or is it to look closely at the fire of existence that has been burning from time without beginning and allow some of it to burn away? If you choose the second option, you will find yourself becoming more meditative, more focused on the quiet moments of experience—the silent spaces between heartbeats—and you will feel some of the distractions of ordinary experience begin to slip away. This is not nirvana, but it is a step in that direction, and it introduces you to the basic Buddhist practice of meditation.

The practice that we call meditation is part of the *Fourth Noble Truth,* the path to the cessation of suffering. Standard outlines of the path speak of it as having eight parts (the "noble eightfold path"), beginning with "right understanding" and proceeding through "right action" and "right livelihood" to "right mindfulness" and "right concentration." But the easiest way to get a sense of how Buddhists have put the insights of the noble truths into practice is to divide the practice of the path into three categories: moral conduct, concentration, and wisdom. Traditionally, Buddhists have observed five moral precepts: no killing, no stealing, no lying, no abusing sex, and no taking of intoxicants. Concentration has to do with the practices of mental discipline that we usually associate with meditation. A very common type of concentration is to sit down in a stable posture and concentrate on the movement of the breath. As thoughts and distractions rise in the mind, you observe them, let them gently pass away, and bring your concentration back to the movement of your breath. The practice of the moral precepts and the practice of concentration both allow the negative tendencies that afflict the mind and body to pass gently away so that the mind can begin to see clearly the flow of phenomena that make up ordinary experience. Finally, you infuse this clear mind with the wisdom, or the awareness of no-self, that unravels the chain of reincarnation.

SAMGHA: THE BUDDHIST COMMUNITY

When the Buddha taught the four noble truths to the small band of friends who gathered around him in the Deer Park in Varanasi, he set in motion a historical movement that eventually carried his teaching through much of Asia. The Buddha himself spent about forty years wandering the roads of northern India, preaching his Dharma and gathering followers into the community that constituted his *Samgha,* a word that sometimes is translated as "church." The community split naturally into two categories. There were *monks* and *nuns* who followed the Buddha's example by giving up their possessions and their normal social responsibilities to seek nirvana, and there were *laypeople* who followed the Buddha's basic precepts, but who did not engage in the acts of renunciation that would bring them directly to nirvana.

In time, this two-part division of the community produced a pattern of life that is duplicated in different ways throughout the Buddhist world. There are monasteries where monks study and teach the Dharma, and there are laypeople who support the monks and gain "merit" that will help them in future lives. In the countries of Southeast Asia, such as Thailand, Sri Lanka, and Burma, this relationship between the monks and the laypeople is expressed most vividly in the morning begging rounds, when the monks in a monastery go out into the surrounding villages with their begging bowls and beg food at the homes of their lay supporters. Monks are not allowed to eat after noon and cannot keep food from one day to the next, so each day begins with this basic ritual. The monk begs and the layperson gives, each one demonstrating a sense that

---

Who and Where Are the Buddhists in the United States?

Here's a conundrum as tricky as a Zen koan: how many Buddhists are there in the United States? Because Buddhism has no central record-keeping organization and because there are so many different kinds of Buddhism in the United States, it is difficult to ascertain accurately just how many Buddhists exist in this country. Making this even more challenging is the fact that some Buddhists self-identify as Buddhist *and* something else: there are "Jew-Bus" (Buddhist Jews) and Buddhist Christians, for example.

Still, it is possible to make an educated guess. Conservative estimates state that there are at least a million Buddhists in America, and possibly far more. In 2004, the U.S. State Department's International Religious Freedom Report estimated that two percent of the American population is Buddhist, which would mean approximately six million people. Columbia University scholar Robert Thurman has similarly guessed at five to six million Buddhists in the United States.

In 2008, however, the Pew Forum on Religion and Public Life reported that 0.7 percent of its survey respondents identified themselves as Buddhists. If that statistic is representative of the nation as a whole, it would put the total number of Buddhists in America at just over two million.

The Pew findings are also interesting in what they say about the demographics of American Buddhism. More than half of American Buddhists are white (53 percent), while a third are Asian or Asian American (32 percent). Buddhists as a group are highly educated: 74 percent have gone to college, and more than a quarter have advanced degrees. Most American Buddhists are converts (73 percent); almost half live in the western United States; and the majority (70 percent) do not have children living at home.

Perhaps most interesting are the Pew survey's revelations about Buddhist Americans' ideological leanings. They were the most liberal of any of the religious groups surveyed, with 50 percent identifying themselves as liberal (compared to 20 percent nationally), and 82 percent saying that they believed homosexuality should be accepted by society (compared to 50 percent nationally). And although Buddhism is, traditionally at least, a nontheistic religion, only 19 percent of American Buddhists say they do not believe in God.

people have to let go of the things of this world to achieve the goals they seek.

Another pattern of action associated with the life of the Buddha is a practice of worship, although Buddhist worship has a shape that makes it different from the worship you find in most other religious communities. Stories about the end of the Buddha's life tell us that the Buddha's supporters asked him how they should treat the remains of his body after his death. He made it clear that he expected monks to concentrate on following his example: to venerate him, as Buddhists say, through his Dharma Body rather than through his physical form. But he advised his lay supporters to cremate his body as they would the body of a great sage or a king, and erect a shrine to hold his ashes. This shrine, known traditionally as a *stupa*, could then be the focus of the actions that constitute worship (*puja*), the offering of flowers, water, or fragrant ointments and the lighting of lamps. The Buddha's possessions and the relics of his cremation were divided into several parts shortly after his death. They have subsequently been subdivided and fought over in so many different ways that it is difficult any longer to trace their history, but they still serve as the focus for some of the most important shrines in the Buddhist world. In northwest India there used to be a famous shrine that housed the Buddha's begging bowl, but the shrine succumbed to one of the many barbarian invasions of India. In the town of Kandy in Sri Lanka there still is a famous temple dedicated to the Buddha's tooth. The tooth relic is paid daily homage and brought out once a year to serve as the focus of an elaborate festival.

For someone who looks at religion through Western eyes, the most intriguing aspect of Buddhist worship is that it does not need to involve anything like a belief in God. To venerate the Buddha as the Dharma Body requires only that you follow the Buddha's example. To worship the Buddha's relics requires only the belief that they have been infused with a certain power. The Buddha himself may long since have disappeared.

There has been ambiguity in the Buddhist tradition about whether the Buddha lingers in some indefinable state after his death. But it is clear that the Buddha should not be considered a substitute for God. For centuries Buddhists have resisted the idea that the universe is governed by a creator god. There is nothing but a cycle of reincarnation and a man whose example made it possible for his followers to find their way out. In this respect Buddhism is genuinely an atheistic religion, a religion that does not presuppose the existence of God.

This does not mean, however, that Buddhists do not worry about the "gods" and spirits. In India and Southeast Asia, different kinds of supernatural beings play as much a part in the cycle of reincarnation as human beings. They are not the God of Christianity, Judaism, or Islam: they are not the creators of the world and they do not occupy their positions forever. They rise and fall in the scale of reincarnation just as human beings do. But they do have extraordinary powers to cause illness or to bring good luck, and they need to be treated with care. In Thailand many families have special "spirit houses" in their family compounds to serve as homes for the spirits. There also are ritual specialists who control access to the spirits and preside over the rituals of spirit possession and exorcism.

Many people ask whether the "spirit cults" in Buddhist countries are genuinely Buddhist. The question is difficult to answer without raising some hard questions about what we mean by religion. The gods and spirits do not know the way to nirvana, so they play no role in the Buddha's quest for nirvana. But they are an essential part of the religious life of the people in countries that consider themselves Buddhist. Is the worship of gods and spirits Buddhist or not? Some would say no. But there is a strong tendency these days to look for religion in the things people actually do—to look for American religion, for instance, not just in the pages of the Bible but in the celebration of Halloween and the Fourth of July. By this measure, the worship of the spirits and gods in Buddhist countries is just as much a part of "Buddhism" as the quest for nirvana. It is one of the religious actions that Buddhist people perform to deal with uncertainty and give meaning to aspects of their lives that otherwise might seem out of control.

MAHAYANA:
THE GREAT VEHICLE

After the Buddha's death, his teaching gradually spread across the countries of Asia. Wandering monks brought the Dharma to regions that had never heard of the Buddha. Within a few centuries, the teaching spread from its birthplace in northern India up into the northwest and down into the south. Buddhist missionaries also began to carry the Dharma beyond India to the countries of Southeast Asia, so that the tradition was well established outside the Indian subcontinent before the beginning of the Common Era. By the second century C.E. Buddhist teaching had made its way through Afghanistan and across the Silk Road, and had begun its long and productive relationship with the religious traditions of China and the rest of East Asia. As the teaching spread it also began to change. There were many small sectarian movements within the community in the first few hundred years after the Buddha's death, but none was more important or changed the face of Buddhism more dramatically than the movement that is called Mahayana, the "Great Vehicle."

The best way to understand the depth of Mahayana's impact on Buddhist life is to see it as a radical reinterpretation of the story of the Buddha. The texts that refer to themselves as Mahayana began to appear about four centuries after the Buddha's death and spoke of a "second turning of the wheel of the Dharma," a second major event when the Buddha initiated a new teaching. This new teaching shifted attention back from the final life of the Buddha toward the previous lives that prepared for the Buddha's nirvana—the lives, in other words, when the

being who was to become the Buddha was a bodhisattva. The texts of the Mahayana spoke of the bodhisattva as an ideal that Buddhists should follow in order to imitate the example of the Buddha. This may not seem like an important change. After all, the tradition had always spoken of bodhisattvas as beings who were on the way to becoming Buddhas. But it made an enormous difference for people to begin thinking of the bodhisattva as the model of what a Buddhist should be. For one thing, it meant that a person did not have to become a monk to be an ideal practitioner of the Dharma. Laypeople could be just as good bodhisattvas as monks, and in some situations they could even be better. It also meant that Buddhist practice could no longer focus exclusively on the virtue of wisdom. The Mahayana still thought that it was important to see reality clearly, but it also was important to put that insight into practice—to act, as the deer king did, for the welfare of others. The bodhisattva ideal was a marriage of two virtues, wisdom and compassion. It combined the reflective virtues of the monastic life with the active virtues of a layperson.

The changes in the Mahayana did not stop here. The new movement also had a profound effect on the devotional relationship Buddhists had with the Buddha. Buddhists had always been able to "worship" the Buddha in one form or another, but the Mahayana opened up a whole new range of possibilities for worship and devotion. People began to think of bodhisattvas not just as human beings who struggled along in this world to follow the Buddha's example, but as celestial beings who, from many lifetimes of dedicated discipline, had developed the power to help others in extraordinary ways. Among the greatest of these celestial bodhisattvas was Avalokitesvara ("The Lord Who Looks Down"), the bodhisattva of compassion, who vowed to help creatures when they fell into danger. Avalokitesvara's compassion was crystallized in the *mantra* (a sacred phrase) *om mani padme hum.* Tibetans have understood the words of this mantra as meaning "O, the jewel in the lotus," but the meaning of the mantra (like the meaning of many religious phrases) lies less in the reference of the words themselves than in the function of the phrase as a whole. Mahayana Buddhists speak the mantra to invoke the power of Avalokitesvara's compassion. In Tibet, a country that is particularly devoted to Avalokitesvara, the mantra is carved on rocks, written on flags, and inscribed in prayer wheels so that with every spin of the wheel the country is filled with the limbs of Avalokitesvara's compassion. In China Avalokitesvara took female form as Kuan-yin, the mother of compassion, who functioned in many ways like the Virgin Mary in Roman Catholic countries. Pilgrimage sites grew up in places where people had visions of Kuan-yin, and temples were dedicated to her worship.

Mahayana texts also began to speak of a multitude of celestial Buddhas who had completed the long and arduous discipline of the bodhisattva path and achieved their awakening, not in this world (as Siddhartha Gautama had), but in the realms of the heavens. As part of their practice of the bodhisattva path, they had vowed to transport believers to their heavens if the believers had faith in the power of the Buddha's compassion. One of the most important of these celestial Buddhas was Amitabha ("Infinite Light"), known in Japan as Amida. Amida is associated with a heaven known as the Pure Land and, like Avalokitesvara, has crystallized his compassion in a powerful phrase. In Amida's case, however, it is simply his name. To touch the power of Amida, you can chant the phrase *namu Amida Butsu* ("homage to Amida Buddha") with faith and, by some accounts, Amida will appear at your deathbed surrounded by thousands of bodhisattvas to transport you to the Pure Land. I once asked a priest in the San Jose temple of the Buddhist Churches of America, the organization that represents Pure Land Buddhism in this country, what he thought was the most important thing for a young Buddhist to take with him when he went off to col-

lege. He said that it was this phrase, called the *nembutsu*, the chant of Amida's name. These words contained the essence of Amida's compassion.

The new emphasis on compassion changed the mood of the Buddhist tradition in remarkable ways. No aspect of ordinary life was so humble that it could not somehow be affirmed as part of a person's gradual pursuit of the bodhisattva path. But no change was more remarkable than the change that took place in the Mahayana vision of reality. In the earlier tradition, reality was viewed as a stream of momentary phenomena. Everything from the gods in their heavens to a blade of grass was undergoing a process of change, and nothing had a "self" that endured from one moment to the next. The philosophers of the Mahayana took a close look at the so-called "moments" that made up this process and asked whether they were any more real than the continuous "selves" they seemed to make up. The answer was no. The Mahayana philosophers claimed that nothing was ultimately real, including the moments that seemed to make up the stream of reality. The Greek philosopher Heraclitus once argued that, because everything changed, you could not step into the same river twice. Without being aware of him, of course, the Mahayana philosophers took Heraclitus a step further: they argued that you could not step into the same river once. The result was the *doctrine of emptiness,* which states that everything is illusion or is "empty" of any identity.

The doctrine of emptiness has struck many people as carrying the negative approach of the doctrine of no-self to a logical extreme and shattering all the distinctions that give life its meaning, from the distinction between you and me to the distinction between the world of reincarnation and nirvana. But the doctrine's effect on life in the Mahayana, paradoxically, was exactly the opposite. If there ultimately is no distinction between you and me, then it makes just as much sense for me to act like a bodhisattva and work for your welfare as it does for me to work for my own. And if there is no difference between the world of reincarnation and nirvana, then I can realize freedom from suffering right in the midst of suffering itself. All I have to do is see suffering for what it really is (and for what it is not). Emptiness is the glue that holds the bodhisattva practice together, and it is the realization that makes each moment of experience a possible mirror of the Buddha's awakening.

The doctrine of emptiness is beautifully reflected in the tradition of meditation that, in its Japanese form, goes by the name of Zen. This style of meditation is now so popular in America that you can find books to teach yourself everything from Zen in the traditional art of flower arrangement or the martial arts to the art of motorcycle maintenance or tennis. But Zen arose historically in China (under the Chinese name of *Ch'an*) as a combination of Indian monastic meditation and a form of Chinese contemplation associated with Taoism. It was simple, down to earth, and focused on the emptiness that can be revealed in a single moment of experience. Zen practice often involved long periods of study, with meditation sessions extending from early morning long into the night. It also involved intense intellectual struggle with the cryptic questions, called *koans,* that Zen teachers posed to stop the mind in its tracks and push students through to moments of awakening—questions like "Does a dog have Buddha nature?" or "What is the sound of one hand clapping?" But the most attractive and accessible expressions of Zen ideals often appear in the arts, when an artist or a poet seems to capture, in a single moment of experience, the sense of stillness in motion that lies at the heart of Zen awakening. The Japanese poet Basho crystallized this sense in a single three- line poem that is justly famous as an expression of the spirit of Zen.

Old pond
Frog jumps in—
Sound of water!

CONCLUSION

The values of the Mahayana had little enduring impact in the countries of Southeast Asia, such as Sri Lanka, Burma, Thailand, and Cambodia. There the people seemed quite content to pass on, under the name *Theravada* ("Teaching of the Elders"), the values of an earlier time in the development of the Buddhist tradition. But the more northerly countries of Asia, China, Japan, Korea, and Tibet were deeply influenced by the Mahayana.

In India itself, the Buddhist impulse eventually ran its course and died out for reasons that are difficult fully to explain. The great monasteries that dominated Indian Buddhist life came under intense pressure from two directions between 900 and 1200 C.E.: they were threatened from the outside by Muslim armies and from within by a lively movement of popular Hindu devotion that seemed to steal Buddhism's vitality and diminish its importance in Indian religious life. But Buddhism has not ceased to be a vital force worldwide. With about 350 million people identified as Buddhists in the countries of Asia, it continues to have a crucial role in shaping the religious life of the world, and it has grown constantly in importance in modern America. Many people in the United States identify themselves formally as Buddhist (see sidebar), and echoes of Buddhist values can be heard in many areas of American cultural life.

Behind all of the modern variations in the Buddhist tradition, behind the processions of monks that wind through the fields of Southeast Asia to beg their daily food, behind the parry and thrust of a Japanese swordsman, behind the lines of children in a California temple who chant to invoke the compassion of Amida, sits the figure of the Buddha, a man whose serenity and quiet smile have for centuries symbolized the human aspiration for peace in the midst of suffering and the wisdom to see through the illusions of this world.

STUDY QUESTIONS

1. How does Buddhism's understanding of a personal god distinguish it from many other religious traditions?

2. In what ways has the Buddhist tradition influenced American cultural life over the years?

3. Why is it difficult to point to any one religious practice or doctrine to decide what it means to be Buddhist?

4. Who is the Buddha? Give a brief biographical sketch of his life. What role does he play in the development of Buddhism?

5. Define karma. How does the Buddhist understand karma and the religious life? What is karma's relationship to reincarnation?

6. What is Dharma? Why is it symbolized by the wheel?

7. What are the Four Noble Truths of Buddhism? What is the importance of each in the religious life of the Buddhist?

8. Describe the doctrine of emptiness. How does it relate to the meditative practices of other religious traditions you have studied?

9. What role do gods play in the Buddhist tradition? How does this differ from other traditions you have studied?

ESSAY TOPICS

The Life and Thought of Gautama, the Buddha

The Four Noble Truths and the Buddhist Spiritual Journey

Buddhism and Suffering

Zen and the Doctrine of Emptiness

WORD EXPLORATION

The following words play significant roles in any discussion of Buddhism in America and are worth careful reflection and discussion.

Gautama	Reincarnation	Nirvana
Buddha	Dharma	Mahayana
Bodhisattva	Karma	Zen
Suffering	*Samgha*	

FOR FURTHER READING

Fields, Rick. *How the Swans Came to the Lake: A Narrative History of Buddhism in America*. Boulder, Colo.: Shambhala, 1981.

Lopez, Donald S. Jr. *The Story of Buddhism: A Concise Guide to Its History & Teachings*. San Francisco: HarperOne, 2002.

Prebish, Charles S. and Kenneth R. Tanaka, eds. *The Faces of Buddhism in America*. Berkeley: University of California Press, 1998.

Seager, Richard Hughes. *Buddhism in America*. New York: Columbia University Press, 1999.

Tweed, Thomas A. and Stephen Prothero. *Asian Religions in America: A Documentary History*. New York: Oxford University Press, 1999.

WEB SITES

http://www.pluralism.org
  Web site of the Pluralism Project at Harvard University

http://www.buddhanet.net
  Buddhist e-zine, directory of meditation centers, and links

http://www.sacred-texts.com/bud/index.htm
  Sacred texts of Buddhism, including sutras and dharma talks

12

East Asian Religions in Today's America

ROBERT S. ELLWOOD AND MARK A. CSIKSZENTMIHALYI

551–499 B.C.E.	Traditional dates of Confucius
300 B.C.E	Date of earliest discovered manuscript of the *Dao De Jing*
184	Religious rebellions in China seed Daoist religious tradition
193	Construction of temple in Pengcheng marks mass Buddhist conversion
638	Construction of first Nestorian Christian Church in Chang'an
741	Japanese Emperor Jito Shomu starts a provincial Buddhist temple system
1272	Nichiren begins his exile and the development of his own Buddhist sect
1838	Namayama Miki, founder of Tenrikyo, has her first revelation
1870 C.E.	The Meiji Emperor makes Shinto Japan's official state religion
1949	Mao Zedong's revolution begins the People's Republic of China (PRC)
1951	D. T. Suzuki tours U.S. universities, popularizing Zen Buddhism
1959	The PRC takes control of Tibet
1960	First chapter of Soka Gakkai established in United States
1966	Vietnamese monk Thich Nhat Hanh meets Martin Luther King Jr., persuading him to denounce the Vietnam War
1976	The end of the ten-year Cultural Revolution leads to gradual relaxation of restrictions on religious practice. Dharma Realm Buddhist University founded in Ukiah, California
1979	Deer Park Monastery in Wisconsin founded in the Tibetan tradition
1988	Opening of the Hsi Lai Buddhist Temple in Hacienda Heights, California
1999	The PRC bans the Falun Gong religious sect; members establish the Falun Dafa Information Center in New York
2006	Yu Dan publishes the best-selling book *Reflections on the Analects of Confucius* in the PRC

In a suburb east of Los Angeles, amid shopping malls and upscale homes with pools and gardens, a spectacular bit of old China rests atop a scenic hill. The Hsi Lai ("Coming to the West") Buddhist Temple, built by a Buddhist organization in Taiwan, is a dramatic token of the presence of East Asian religion in America today. Its ornate eaves turn upward, and its high steps are worn by the continual coming and going of worshipers. The worshipers, largely in family groups, come to bow and light sticks of incense placed in huge pots as they pay respects and offer prayers, perhaps on behalf of a deceased relative.

These practices are different from those of many other American religious groups, in which spiritual life tends to be more focused on public ceremonies. Although there are rites at Hsi Lai that center around chanting sutras or Buddhist scriptures and formal offerings of flowers and fruit, the conspicuous "life" of the temple, as in traditional China, is the continual coming and going of small groups of worshipers with their own purposes. That this is a distinctive style of religious life is also indicated by the intermingling of students and sightseers who, unless they have journeyed to East Asia, have never seen anything quite like this unforgettable temple.

The Hsi Lai Temple has two great halls. The outer hall is the hall of *bodhisattvas,* individuals once human but now virtually godlike who, after tremendous effort, have attained perfect wisdom. With wisdom they have perfect compassion as well, for anyone truly wise will understand that, in a universe in which all beings are interrelated, what you do to another you do to yourself as well; therefore, compassion or sympathetic love is the only absolute ethical value.

Along with wisdom and compassion, bodhisattvas have "skill in means," or in knowing how to put compassion into practice effectively. Their unlimited wisdom shows them how things work down to the subtlest levels. They can do things—come in various guises, make things appear out of

nowhere—that look to the ordinary eye like miracles. Technically, however, these things are not magic but the manipulation of subtle laws of causation known only to holders of supreme wisdom.

In the outer hall are huge gilded images of five different bodhisattvas, all human but godlike, waiting to receive prayers. They stand on the borderline, so to speak, between this ordinary world—"the world of red dust," the Chinese call it—and the golden world of Buddhas and bodhisattvas, with their marvelous powers and winning compassion. The central one is Maitreya (Sanskrit; Mi-lo in Chinese), the popular and familiar portly, smiling lord of the coming paradisiacal Buddhist world.

Across an enclosed courtyard is the Buddha-hall, higher up and deeper in that golden realm. Present on the vast main altar are three large Buddhas, or enlightened beings. In Mahayana Buddhism—the form of Buddhism practiced in China, Japan, Korea, and Vietnam—a Buddha is not just the historical person who began the religion. There are countless Buddhas known and unknown throughout the depths of space and time, awesome minds able to comprehend the cosmos and whose meditations sustain worlds and galaxies. The Buddha-hall contains statues of three of the known Buddhas: the historical Buddha in the center; to the left Amitabha, a compassionate Buddha best known as the giver of salvation after death in his "Pure Land" to all who call upon him in faith; and on the right the healing Buddha.

The walls of this Buddha-hall are covered with a striking display of tiny Buddha images, like reflections of the cosmic Buddhas in the Buddhas of every world—and in the Buddha-nature in every person, for Mahayana says that we are all Buddhas, all enlightened, but that many of us don't realize it.

The majority of the neatly dressed men and women and the lively children coming to this temple and this hall, like the majority of worshipers in any holy place, perhaps do not consciously reflect on the deeper points of their faith. They are content to sense here the presence of something sacred, something that lifts them for a moment out of the everyday grind, and at the same time links them to family, community, and roots in a faraway land. Here they can hear language, see smiling Buddha-faces, smell incense, and on certain occasions even taste foods that bring back other days and other vistas in a country of rivers, mountains, rice paddies, and numberless temples like this one. For some, it may have been grandparents or great-grandparents who knew that country, but it still helps them feel a connection with their past.

Several miles away, in a modern American city, is a church of Tenrikyo, the "Religion of Heavenly Wisdom," one of the so-called new religions of modern Japan. The arrangement of its altar is similar to that of Shinto, the ancient Japanese religion of many local gods and shrines that goes back to prehistoric times, even before the coming of Buddhism to the island nation around the sixth century C.E. But whereas Shinto worships many deities, Tenrikyo has but one, the Creator of the world, Oyagami "God the Parent." This Father/Mother God was revealed to Nakayama Miki,[1] a peasant woman, in the nineteenth century. She composed a scripture under God's inspiration describing the making of the world, and taught her followers beautiful dances that pantomime that creation story; they are still performed as major acts of the religion's worship in order to call humankind back to its true origins.

This altar contains no image, for divinity in the Tenrikyo and Shinto tradition generally does not take human form. Instead there are three simple cabinetlike shrines. When they stand open for worship, they reveal the gleaming mirrors that in Japan betoken the presence of *kami* (gods). On tables in front of these four shrines are stacked attractive piles of fruits and vegetables and bottles of rice wine as offerings. The shrine to the right, always open, is dedicated to the founder of the faith; in front of it are two red lanterns because Nakayama Miki always wore red to indicate her difference from other human beings. The shrine to the left is dedicated to the ancestors of Tenrikyo faithful—this faith, like most in Japan, has found a way to incorporate the veneration of ancestors, an important constituent of the East Asian spiritual mentality. The largest shrine, in the center, is dedicated to Oyagami.

In Japan an entire town of some fifty thousand people, Tenri-shi, is dedicated to this faith. It contains Tenrikyo schools from kindergarten through college, the religious headquarters, and extensive hostels for pilgrims. The main feature is a vast temple complex centered around an upright pillar, the Kanrodai, located at the spot where, it was revealed to Nakayama Miki, the creation of the world commenced. Once a month, around the base of this pillar, the leaders of the faith perform Tenrikyo's most solemn rite, the sacred dance commemorating this event. In Tenrikyo churches across the world, similar rites are held on the same day. They begin with music from the gongs and reedy flutes of classical Japan, and with prayers and offerings by richly robed priests. The rite concludes with a portion of the sacred dance, showing God's search for lost humankind, and the symbolic wiping away of the spiritual dust or pollution that causes human error and suffering.

Neither of these two institutions is solely concerned with worship. In 1991, the University of the West was created by the order that runs the Hsi Lai Buddhist Temple, and today several hundred students attend its campus in Rosemead, California. The Tenri University was founded in 1925 and is located in the Nara section of Japan, but has always specialized in language teaching, in part as an aid to its missions. In Japanese religions, as in Confucianism, educational mission is part and parcel of institutional religion.

These vignettes should give something of the flavor of East Asian religion. It is colorful, with ornate temples and worship involving prayer, offerings, and often incense and dance. It is strongly linked to family, both living and departed, and to community. It includes both ancient religions, such as Buddhism, and religious movements started in modern times by charismatic figures, often women like Nakayama Miki.

The Major Religions of East Asia

The major religious traditions of East Asia are Buddhism and Confucianism, both of which have profoundly influenced all East Asian societies; Daoism (the following of the Dao or "Way," the all-embracing course of the universe, which has philosophical, mystical, and magical dimensions, sometimes spelled "Taoism") in China; and Shinto, the ancient polytheistic "Way of the Gods" in Japan. These are joined by many new religions such as Tenrikyo and Falun Gong (see sidebar). Because most East Asians who are religious (many today in the People's Republic of China and other parts of East Asia are not) have relationships with two or more traditions—being both Shinto and Buddhist in Japan, or embracing Confucianism, Daoism, and Buddhism in China—religious membership figures for this third of humanity are virtually impossible to obtain or assess.

Many manifestations of East Asian religion, to be sure, have arrived on our shores. The personal spiritual quest for one's own Buddha-like enlightenment is important to many. It may be typified by the rows of monks in seated meditation in a Zen[2] Buddhist monastery, seeking to still the activity of the ordinary "monkey mind" in order that the enlightened mind may arise. There are Zen temples of Chinese, Japanese, Korean, and Vietnamese background in the United States.

In Hawaii I once visited a family ceremony celebrated by a Daoist priest, who stood dramatically robed before an altar, calling up higher and higher celestial beings until he stood before the Great Dao, the uni-versal Path or Way, itself. Many American cities and towns today have centers where one of the East Asian "martial arts," such as Japanese karate, Chinese kungfu, or Korean tae kwon do, are taught. These are not in themselves religions, but they are influenced by values borrowed from Daoism and Zen.

All East Asian society has been profoundly influenced by Confucianism, the tradition of ethical teachings combined with rituals started by the great sage Confucius. In traditional China there were Confucian temples and rituals, particularly in connection with centers of government, and these rites are still performed in Korea and Taiwan. But by far the most important influence of Confucian values has been in the arena of family life and society. Confucianism, with its high regard for education, tradition, hard work, loyalty to one's family and benefactors, and its emphasis on cooperation rather than individualism, has made East Asia what it is. Both communism as it is practiced in the People's Republic of China and the ethos of the highly successful corporations of Japan and South Korea largely reflect various applications of Confucian values under other names. East Asian American families are also frequently noted for the same emphasis on education, family cohesiveness and cooperation, and traditional values—sometimes to the point of tension with their younger, more "individualized" members over issues such as marriage or going into the family business versus striking out on one's own.

Confucianism today is not so much a separate religion as a set of values and a way of life that speaks through the ethical ideals of virtually all East Asian religions, and through East Asian educational and family systems as well.

Most forms of Confucianism have reinforced the hierarchies that were part of the early Chinese society in which it formed. In the twentieth century, however, New Confucian philosophers attempted to accommodate the tradition to more egalitarian values. Today, what Boston University's Robert

Falun Gong

Founded by Li Hongzhi in May 1992, the Falun Gong movement consciously combines elements of different Chinese religions. For example, the movement's symbol, the Falun (dharma wheel), is described by its founder as a combination of Daoism and Buddhism: "The Daoist Yin-Yang and the Buddha's Dharma-wheel both have their reflections in the Falun." It began as an officially sponsored association dedicated to proving the efficacy of *qigong* (literally "working *qi*" an important traditional Chinese medicine technique) under the auspices of the China Qigong Scientific Research Association. Li broke with the association in 1996.

Falun Gong is characterized by the cultivation of a Falun, located at the lower abdomen. As an intelligent entity of high-energy substance, the Falun automatically absorbs energy from the universe and relieves the body of bad elements. The rotation of Falun synchronizes with the revolution of the universe. It has the same characteristics as and is a miniature of the universe. Falun is constantly rotating, putting the practitioner in a state of cultivation twenty-four hours a day.

Falun Gong became internationally known after thousands of its followers staged a sit-in at Zhongnanhai, the Beijing residence compound of the leaders of the Chinese Communist Party, on April 25, 1999. They sought official recognition as a means of bypassing government restrictions on their group. This show of political will worried a leadership aware of China's long history of revolutionary movements that were initially based on popular healing arts. They imposed a ban on the practice of Falun Gong and ordered the arrest of many of its leaders beginning in late 1999. A central theme of the government's information offensive against the group was Li Hongzhi's alleged resistance to scientific medical practice.

Adherents of the Falun Gong religion have found a foothold in the Chinese diaspora, and also in the United States, especially in California. Many Asian businesses distribute the *Epoch Times*, an anticommunist newspaper connected with the Falun Gong organization, and the group maintains a sophisticated Web presence. The group claims over a hundred million adherents worldwide.

Neville has called "Boston Confucianism" has brought historians of Chinese Confucianism into dialogue with Anglo-American philosophy to create a hybrid unique to the United States. Beginning as an informal network that included Neville's colleague John Berthrong and Harvard University's Tu Weiming, the Boston Confucians have attempted to draw out aspects of traditional Confucianism that may be used as resources for ethical practice in today's societies.

ASIAN RELIGIONS IN THE UNITED STATES

Who are the followers of Asian religions in the United States? According to the 2000 U.S. Census, there were 4,306,157 Americans of East Asian descent: 2,432,585 Chi-nese, 796,700 Japanese, and 1,076,872 Koreans. The figures would be larger if they included persons of partial or unacknowledged East Asian ancestry.

Not all of these persons practice a traditional East Asian religion. Some, especially Koreans, have become Christians. Reliable figures for the religious affiliations of East Asians are impossible to obtain, since the U.S. Census does not ask religious questions, the religious groups involved are very disparate and keep very different kinds of records, and many East Asians observe traditional religious practices only in a family, not an institutional, context. A very rough guess might be that half of Americans of East Asian descent maintain some kind of significant link to the traditional religions of their homelands.

On the other hand, more than a few Americans who are not of Asian descent have also become involved with an East Asian religion. Sometimes it has been through a personal spiritual quest, sometimes through marriage, sometimes as a byproduct of an interest in, say, meditation or one of the martial arts. Commitments range from entering a Zen monastery to taking class or doing practices on a level that does not preclude primary adherence to another faith. Presbyterians have stilled and focused the mind like the wise men of the East as they have striven for budo[3] black belts, and Roman Catholic monks and nuns have meditated with Zen masters. Again figures are elusive—under a hundred thousand might be a conservative guess—and are less significant than the general cultural and even political impact these East Asian religions have had in America. On that score one need only mention the influence of Zen on the "Beat" writers of the 1950s, especially Jack Kerouac and Gary Snyder. Daoism, through the martial arts mystique, has made a diffuse but discernible impression on popular culture through such vehicles as the *Star Wars* and *Ninja Turtles* movies. Confucianism, believed by many in Europe and America in the eighteenth century to have molded a virtually ideal rational, nonsectarian society in China, helped inspire both the U.S. Constitution and, later, the civil service examination system. As early as 1771, Benjamin Franklin called for closer study of China in the preface to the first volume of the American Philosophical Society's *Transactions*.

China: Daoism and Confucianism

We should now look at the history and teaching of the major East Asian religions that have influenced Asian American life. Let's begin with China around 500 B.C.E. by the Western calendar. This was the time known as the period of the Warring States,

for it was a time of recurrent conflict among various feudal lords, accompanied by great cruelty. As is usual in such situations, the suffering was greatest of all for the common people, as armies campaigned and looted back and forth through their villages.

Not surprisingly, perhaps, the Warring States period was closely followed by the period of the Hundred Philosophers, for people began asking, What went wrong? How can we get society back on the right course again? Or if we cannot, how can a person nonetheless live a personally meaningful and worthwhile life in such times? Many answers were given, but only two are of particular interest to the study of East Asian religion. One is that of Confucius (551–479 B.C.E.), the other that of the more legendary Laozi, the "Old Man," whose book, the *Dao de jing,* "The Book of the Way and Its Power," is the fountainhead of the tradition known as Daoism.

Both traditions had one thing in common. They were concerned with the Dao (Tao in older transliterations), the Way or Path down which the universe is moving, and how human life can best get in harmony with it. But they held differing ideas about where it can be found. For Confucius and the Confucians, we human beings are social creatures. For us, therefore—however it may be with sharks or trees or other entities—the Dao is found in society. The supreme human good is a good society, and it is through the interrelationships on which good societies depend that true virtue is expressed.

Thus Confucianism taught that the family, the bedrock of the social order, and above all "filial piety," the relationship of parents and children, is where virtue is first learned, and is its most important locus. By being filial children and benevolent parents, people acquire those virtues that will also make the larger society humane and the state benign. All right relationships, whether parent and child or sovereign and subject, entail "mutuality," recognition that there are obligations on both sides. *Li,* or ritual, such as the rituals of mourning for deceased relatives, is very important to Confucian society because it gives persons an opportunity to "become what they are," that is, to act out the part society has given them, whether ruler or servant, parent or child.

Confucianism, in other words, depended on the formal promulgation and enactment of ethical principles. It tended to hold that although persons were good and inclined by nature to do right, they were unformed and needed the benefit of education and example to become effective members of a well-running social order. The way to get the corrupt society back on track was to follow the example of the ancient sage-emperors whom Confucius, as a deeply principled conservative, always exalted. One should be a scholar-statesman who embodies virtue in teaching and action, whether it is immediately rewarded or not, by promoting both rites and justice, and if necessary remonstrating against those in power if they fail to set a like example.

The *Dao de jing* and Daoism took an opposite tack. To them, as to many romantics in the West, society was fundamentally artificial and corrupt. The way to get in touch with the Dao was not with other people amid social convention. It was in rapport with nature and, especially for the poets and artists who tended to find their spiritual path in Daoism, through contact with their inner being, the place from which dreams and visions stream.

The *Dao de jing* did not forget the state and the social order. But it idealized a small and simple society, and it held up as its model the leader who leads by indirection, hardly even letting his name be known, so that when the society achieves something the people will say, "We did this ourselves."

Daoism is also a term that refers to a set of later religious traditions that were only marginally influenced on the *Dao de jing*. Beginning in the second century C.E., around the time that Buddhist influences from India became more common in China,

a set of social movements that promised healing and salvation to their followers borrowed Daoist themes and terminology to describe their methods and goals. In truth, early medical and spirit-medium traditions were just as influential on these religious traditions as the *Dao de jing*, which was read and chanted by some of these followers. As the centuries went on, the Daoist religious traditions developed esoteric teachings, added texts supposedly revealed by the spirits, developed their own alchemical traditions, and began an ascetic tradition parallel to that of Buddhism.

For the great majority of Chinese, both in China and in America, the Confucian and Daoist strands of their spiritual culture are not mutually exclusive. In fact, it is said that the traditional Chinese gentleman was a Confucian at work and a Daoist on vacation. The sober Confucian principles of diligence, rectitude, and loyalty upheld him on the job, while away from it he could permit himself the pleasures of nature, art, fantasy, perhaps the spiritual luxury of a retreat in a well-situated Daoist monastery, and even of assessing the prospects of his own immortality. Chinese American communities also reveal both sides. The Confucian quality of Chinese attitudes toward family, business, and education are well known. Yet a glimpse at the art in Chinese homes and shops, or a glance into a Chinese temple, reveals the magical world of Daoism, with its wizard-like hermits and immortals, its mysterious martial-arts powers, and its gentle poetry of love and nature.

In some places in the United States, such as Hawaii and parts of California, there are old, traditional Chinese temples which, like many in China itself, feature both Buddhist and Daoist elements. On the Daoist side, there may be such godlike immortals as the Jade Emperor, Ruler of the Heavens, and Mazu, "Queen of the Sea" and protector of sailors. In traditional homes one may find the Kitchen-God, to whom offerings are made at the end of the year, when this familiar deity is said to present his report to the Jade Emperor on the family with which he resides.

The annual offering to the Kitchen-God is one aspect of the Chinese New Year, which in traditional China was the most important annual holiday. Another prominent New Year's custom is the dragon procession. A great paper dragon is paraded through the streets mobilized by numerous human feet. The dragon represents yang, the force associated with maleness, the sun, day, growth, and expansion—and therefore the first half of the year, when the crops are growing and days are getting longer. According to Daoism, humans desire to harmonize with what the Dao is doing, which at this time of year is accentuating the yang force. (At midsummer, when the Dao is shifting to yin, the energy associated with femaleness, night, moon, gathering-in, harvest, and shortening days, the famous Chinese lion-dances are held, for that animal is the patron of yin.)

JAPAN: TRADITION
AND MODERNITY

In Japan, the primordial religious stratum is Shinto. No one can visit Japan and fail to see, in mountain strongholds, in traditional villages, and in the heart of modern industrial cities, the graceful gates called *torii* that span the entrance to a Shinto shrine. The path going through the gates will lead to a simple but well-proportioned building with a mirror and *gohei* (zigzag strips of paper) in front to mark the presence of deity, an eight-legged offering table, and massive doors sealing off the chamber where the kami-presence dwells. The kami venerated in these shrines are limited deities, for the most part patrons of particular families, communities, and areas, but they are deeply interfused in lives of those who worship them.

The Shinto shrine has a tranquil, natural atmosphere. But Shinto is also noted for its colorful matsuri, or festivals. Every shrine of any size has an annual *matsuri,* full of traditional festivities, like carnival or mardi gras in Latin societies. Some matsuri draw

visitors from all over Japan and around the world.

There are no regular Shinto shrines in the United States except in the states of Hawaii and Washington, which have large populations of Japanese descent, though modest shrines in homes and businesses may sometimes be seen elsewhere. However, as we have noted, some of the new religions of Japan have altars and worship with marked Shinto overtones.

One of the more interesting of contemporary religious phenomena, the Japanese new religions have emerged more or less parallel to the emergence of Japan as a modern nation. As many as one-fifth of all Japanese now belong to one of the new religions. Most began as special revelations to their founders, often women and persons of humble background, such as Nakayama Miki of Tenrikyo. They have characteristically emphasized healing, belief in the coming of a new paradisiacal world, and a simple practice that transmits the faith's power; they also usually have simple but definite processes for entry, modern organization, and (like Tenrikyo in Tenri City) imposing centers for pilgrimage.[4]

Besides Tenrikyo, several other Japanese new religions have established themselves in America. One of these is Konkokyo, which was founded in 1859 when a farmer, Kawate Bunjiro, received what he believed to be a commission from God to initiate a ministry of mediation between the divine and the human. Although this religion draws substantially from Shinto, it is monotheistic, worshiping one God. A distinctive practice is *toritsugi,* in which a minister gives formal counseling through a mediation rite that has been compared to confession in the Catholic Church.

The Omoto ("Great Source") movement began officially in 1892 with revelations given to a peasant woman, Deguchi Nao, who had undergone extremes of deprivation and suffering in her life, and who was told that God was now bringing in a new and better age. Her son-in-law, Deguchi Onisaburo, a man of great religious creativity, subsequently developed the religion much more fully with new teachings about the spirit world, healing, the sacred importance of art, and the power of the mind. He also took on the role of social critic, even challenging the position of the emperor in a time of rising nationalism in Japan, and thus brought persecution and considerable reduction of numbers to Omoto in the 1920s and 1930s. However, other movements carried on various aspects of the Omoto tradition, and these are represented in the United States.

Sekai Kyusei Kyo, often translated "Church of World Messianity," was founded by Okada Mokichi, a follower of Omoto, on the basis of revelations he had beginning in 1926. It emphasizes belief in a coming paradise, and also a healing practice called *jorei*, which involves channeling light through a cupped hand. There are several World Messianity churches in the United States with both Asian American and western members. A daughter religion of World Messianity, Mahikari ("True Light"), founded in Japan in 1960, has a similar practice involving the channeling of light and has been relatively successful in both Europe and North America.

Seicho no Ie, the "House of Growth," was founded in 1930 by another onetime follower of Omoto, Tasniguchi Masaharu. Influenced substantially by an American "New Thought" or "Positive Thinking" faith, the Church of Religious Science, Seicho no Ie stresses the power of mind, affirming that good thoughts can bring one health, happiness, and success. It has an American church headquarters in California and publishes a widely circulated inspirational magazine.

The PL Kyodan ("Perfect Liberty Order") was organized by Miki Tokuchika in 1946, on the basis of a series of prewar movements. It is not a direct offshoot of Omoto, but was undoubtedly influenced by Deguchi Onisaburo's stress on the importance of art. One of its basic precepts is that "Life is Art," meaning that one should express oneself through one's life as an artist does through art. PL churches, which teach the importance of balance to works of art, sponsor sports and educational centers and perform beautiful rituals. They also have a formal practice for receiving spiritual guidance in writing from a leading teacher. PL has several churches in the United States predominantly but not entirely Japanese American in membership.

Several of the new religions are based in Nichiren Buddhism and are discussed later.

BUDDHISM

How can we understand Buddhism in a way that helps us understand what it is in East Asia and among East Asians in America? In its heart Buddhism can be seen as a spiritual path that has to do with the mind, with consciousness, and with the relation of the individual mind to the infinite universe. It says that by stilling the mind in meditation we can cut through all the attachments and barriers that hobble the mind and make us unhappy. One can transcend all of the mind's limitations and join it to the universal. Then we have all the compassion, wisdom, and power of the universal, like the Buddhas and bodhisattvas at the Hsi Lai Temple.

The Mahayana Buddhism of East Asia puts particular emphasis on the Buddhas and bodhisattvas. It points out that even in our own imperfection, even given our own inexperienced efforts at meditation or the bodhisattva path, we can receive the help of those much further ahead of us and in a deep sense become one with them. What they have attained through immensely profound meditations over countless aeons, we can share in by their grace. So it is that Mahayana temples present their rows of such transcendent Buddhist figures and teach the worth of simple prayer and faith.

The Enryakuji temple complex on Mount Hiei, just outside Kyoto, Japan, is an example. Its many different temples, set amid deep, meditative woods, all represent varied angles on the Buddhist mystery. There is a temple to Dainichi, the "Great Sun Buddha,"[5] the personified essence of the universe whose unfathomable meditations sustain all things, a Buddha perhaps especially attuned to the perspective of mystics and philosophers. There is one to Kannon,[6] the so-called "Goddess of Mercy," actually a bodhisattva who expresses wisdom and compassion by answering simple prayers like a deity in heaven, appealing to the religious needs of more ordinary folk.

Down the road looms a shrine to Amida,[7] the Buddha of faith. Amida is the central personality of "Pure Land" Buddhism who has vowed to bring all who call upon his name in pure faith to that paradise realm, from which entry into ultimate nirvana is easy, after death. Everywhere in East Asia, Pure Land Buddhism is popular among the laity because it makes salvation accessible to everyone through the help of another who has realized ultimate wisdom, compassion, and power, not just to those priests and monks who have leisure to do it "on their own."

Finally, in a woodsy nook is nestled a little temple to Fudo,[8] his black figure as fierce as other Buddhas are serene. Fudo's countenance is wrathful, he holds a sword and lasso, and he is poised against a backdrop of flames. But this fearsome warrior is entirely on the side of righteousness, for his rage is directed against error and the enemies of the Buddha's good teaching. Fudo's style of Buddhist commitment may call out especially to those of activist, samurai-like temperament.

Buddhism in China

This Indian faith first appeared in China around the first century C.E., apparently brought by traders and teachers from Buddhist kingdoms in central Asia, visitors who had traveled along the fabled Silk Road to the teeming cities of Han China. (It may also have reached South China by ships from India and Southeast Asia about the same time.) It did not become an important presence, however, until after the fall of the

Confucianist Han Dynasty in 220 C.E. For more than three centuries thereafter, China was disunited and old ways were to some degree discredited. It was a good time for a new faith from outside to present itself as a serious alternative, and Buddhism did. Its ideals of universal compassion, monasticism, other-worldly salvation, and karma all challenged Confucianism's family-centered values. Many persons of means embraced Buddhism, endowing temples, monasteries, and works of mercy such as orphanages and hostels for travelers.

Buddhism was criticized for allegedly undermining loyalty to family and the state by putting religious celibacy and personal enlightenment first, and for being an imported, non-Chinese religion. It was sometimes persecuted. But by the Middle Ages a general pattern was worked out by which Buddhism accommodated itself to the Chinese system. Monks maintained filial piety by taking their teachers as surrogate parents, and by praying for their family's departed. Confucianism reasserted itself as the ideology of the state and the elite, while Buddhism and Daoism—often, as we have seen, intermixed—were tolerated as the religions of the masses.

Buddhism in traditional China took both monastic and lay forms. Monasteries were generally run along Chan (Zen) lines, except in those extreme northern and western areas where Buddhism of the esoteric Vajrayana (Tibetan and Mongolian) type was to be found. In Chan cloisters monks devoted themselves to a quiet round of labor, as in the gardens and kitchens, of some study, and of long hours of seated meditation together with sutra-chanting and other rituals. A similar pattern can be found in various Zen centers in the United States today. The priests of old China's many thousands of local temples were usually trained in monasteries, then released and assigned to local temples, which they maintained and where they provided religious services.

Popular or lay Buddhism, on the other hand, generally centered around Pure Land, the honoring of O-mi-to (Amitabha) Buddha, along with worship of Kuan-yin, the bodhisattva that expressed the compassion of O-mi-to. It also gave much attention to funerals and memorial services for the dead; these family obligations consumed much of the priests' time, as well as the money of the bereaved families. From this cult also stemmed admonitory teachings, graphically illustrated in temples and popular prints, about reincarnation, judgment, and Buddhist hells and purgatories for various sins. Whether portraying the horrors facing the damned or the wonders of the Pure Land, Buddhism was the religion especially concerned with the afterlife and its mysteries.

Buddhism in Japan

Buddhism spread from China to Korea, and then from Korea to Japan. The traditional date of its arrival in Japan is 532 or 552, and the traditional story of its coming is rather interesting. According to an ancient Japanese chronicle, the king of one of the small states into which Korea was divided at that time wanted to make an alliance with the emperor of Japan. As part of his approach, the Korean ruler, full of Buddhist enthusiasm, sent his Japanese colleague an image and scripture of the new faith, together with a letter stating that all the other nations of the region worshiped the Buddha and asking why Japan alone did not.

The Japanese sovereign, intrigued but unsure what to make of the unusual gifts, turned to his council. The prime minister, of the ambitious Soga clan, urged acceptance of Buddhism, saying this would make Japan as up-to-date as the other nations. But two other ministers, of the Nakatomi and Mononobe families, both houses with traditional Shinto priestly responsibilities, advised caution instead, saying that the ancient kami of Japan would be angered if this foreign god were honored.

The ruler, with a certain wisdom, resolved the matter in this way. He told the Soga that, since they had recommended the new cult, they should venerate the Buddha image experimentally and see what happened. Not long afterward a pestilence broke out, and the Shinto loyalists were quick to put the blame on kami anger at the intruding deity. As a consequence, the image was thrown into a river. But then fire destroyed a part of the palace, and now reproach went the other way. In time the controversy degenerated into civil war. The Soga eventually emerged victorious in the 590s and established Buddhism as a national religion.

But the test between Shinto and Buddhism did not result in the complete suppression of one religion by the other. Then, as so often right down to the present, the Japanese psyche was divided between an eagerness to learn and accept all it could from the outside world, and a no less compelling need to preserve something ancient and highly distinctive in its own soul, something often represented by Shinto and its native gods.

It is interesting to observe that Buddhism came in force to Japan at just about the same time Christianity was doing the same in Britain and other parts of northern Europe, and that Shinto was, broadly speaking, much the same kind of religion as the polytheistic faiths of pre-Christian Europe, the worship of Zeus or Minerva, Wotan or Thor. But whereas Christianity effectively abolished or drove underground the older gods, the Shinto kami instead achieved a kind of harmonization with the Buddhas and bodhisattvas. Shinto shrines shared the same precincts with Buddhist temples, and various theories proposed that the kami were there as students or guardians of the Buddha's dharma. Some even said the kami were the same as the Buddhas or bodhisattvas, but in native Japanese dress, so to speak. The two faiths coexisted in this way until the nineteenth century, when, for nationalistic reasons, Shinto and Buddhism were again separated.

In the seventh and eighth centuries Buddhism was a great vehicle for cultural development in Japan. The government sent promising young priests to China to study in various leading monasteries, and these priests brought back not only sacred texts and mystic practices, but also practical arts, such as printing, and fresh perspectives on government and education, including those of Confucianism.

In 794, when the government was established in the new city of Heian (modern Kyoto, still the center of traditional Japanese culture), new forms of Buddhism emerged that not only combined Shinto and Buddhism more effectively than before, but also combined the popular and aristocratic forms of Buddhism. The principal schools were Shingon and Tendai Buddhism, denominations that still number their followers in Japan in the millions, and both of which have churches in the United States. Tendai and Shingon both represent the complex Mahayana Buddhism we have already discussed; the Mount Hiei monastery is in fact the headquarters of Tendai. Shingon, more in the tradition of Vajrayana Buddhism with its use of powerful meditations on particular Buddhas and bodhisattvas, and its use of chants and hand gestures (mantras and madras), also has a many-templed headquarters, on Mount Koya.

The pattern of Japanese Buddhism changed significantly in the Kamakura period (1185–1333), which followed the Heian period. Most Japanese Buddhists today belong to Buddhist denominations that arose in this era. The Kamakura era commenced when the samurai, or warrior class, based in the north seized effective control of the country from the old imperial court and the Fujiwara family, which had dominated Heian politics and society. Regarding the old capital in Heian (Kyoto) as effete, under the leadership of the Minamoto house they established a new center of government in Kamakura, on Sagami Bay not too far from modern Tokyo. Although they did not dare depose the emperor, who was regarded as sacred, the Minamoto had

him designate their leader as shogun—a sort of military dictator—who ruled in the sovereign's name from Kamakura.

The new order had important religious as well as political consequences. Indeed, what happened next has sometimes been called the Kamakura Buddhism Reformation, and in some ways it paralleled the Protestant Reformation in Europe three centuries later.

The new samurai class—and with them a rising merchant class, as well as the peasants, who in these troubled times had at least relatively more influence—wanted a simpler, more clear-cut religion than that offered by Shingon and Tendai. Like Martin Luther in Europe, they were preoccupied by the question, How can I be sure that I am saved? They wanted an assurance of salvation that was just as accessible to the warrior on the field of battle, the merchant in his shop, or the farmer in his rice paddies as it was to the priest or monk with time and expertise to undertake the deep but complex meditations of the older schools. Again like Luther, they found the answer in forms of simple faith that undercut the ideological and institutional underpinnings of the existing forms of Buddhism.

The new forms tended to be easy but exclusive, teaching that all that one needed was a single, simple, sure key. They can be thought of as simplifications and popularizations of Buddhism. Although these new denominations had earlier roots, they came into their own as separate religious movements in the Kamakura era.

Pure Land Buddhism

The first was Pure Land or Amidist Buddhism, founded as a separate movement by Honen (1133–1212) and his disciple Shinran (1173–1262). Their respective denominations, Jodo-shu (Pure Land School) and Jodo Shinshu (True Pure Land School), are both found in the United States, and the latter, as the Buddhist Churches of America, has been the largest and best-established form of Buddhism among Japanese Americans.

Pure Land centers on the Mahayana cosmic Buddha Amitabha (Amida in Japanese), whom we met as one of the three Buddhas in the Hsi Lai Temple and in Chinese Pure Land. Pure Land in Japan, as in China, is based on simple faith in the original vow (*Hongan* in Japanese; hence many temples have this expression in their names) of Amida to bring all those who call upon his name to the Pure Land or Western Paradise after death. But Honen and above all Shinran, with a radical thrust typical of the Kamakura spirit, taught Pure Land as a single exclusive practice. It is expressed in the *Nembutsu* ("Remembering the Buddha"), as the chant *Namu Amida Butsu* ("Hail Amida Buddha") is called. This chant is all that is needed for salvation. Shinran, like Luther, gave up his monastic garb and married, realizing that if the simple faith of the Nembutsu is sufficient, celibacy, monasticism, meditations, elaborate rites, and the rest of traditional Buddhism are superfluous. He further denied that any particular number of recitations of the Nembutsu is required—once may be enough—because we are not saved by anything we do, but by the grace of Amida received through simple faith.

Pure Land Buddhism was a popular movement in medieval Japan, spread not only by the two founders, but also by wandering evangelists who preached faith and taught spectacular Nembutsu dances. In the end the two schools became large and established denominations boasting fine temples with married, and often hereditary, clergy. (Although Jodo Shinshu paved the way, now clergy in virtually all forms of Japanese Buddhism can be married.)

Nichiren Buddhism

Nichiren Buddhism follows the teachings of Nichiren (1222–1282), a fiery prophet who insisted that the Lotus Sutra, one of the great Mahayana texts, is the supreme expression of the Buddha's teaching and the one and only version of Buddhism for our day. His disciples are divided into two denominations, Nichiren-shu and Nichiren Shoshu. The former sees him as a bodhisattva or priest mentioned in the Lotus text, and as such a radical new teacher for the era beginning with his life. Nichiren Shoshu sees Nichiren even more radically as a Buddha for the new age (said to have begun in 1052), presenting a new dispensation based on the Lotus Sutra.

Nichiren Buddhism has two central focuses in practice. First is the *Daimoku*, the chant *Namu Myoho Rengi Kyo,* "Hail the Marvelous Teaching of the Lotus Sutra." Repeated constantly by Nichiren believers, it is thought to have extraordinary power. For them it is the single, simple, sure key characteristic of Kamakura Buddhism. Second is the *Gohonzon,* a diagram calligraphed on white paper containing the names of leading bodhisattvas and Buddhas in the Lotus Sutra, with the Daimoku in large characters down the center; it is the major object of worship on Nichiren altars both in temples and in homes.

Nichiren Buddhism displays both dynamism and exclusivism. Nichiren himself promoted his truth enthusiastically, and he denounced other forms of religion with no less vigor. His movement has presented itself as the one and only true form of Buddhism for our day, promoting the Daimoku in good times and in bad. This has been particularly true of the movement known as Soka Gakkai, a lay organization within Nichiren Shoshu. Begun in the 1930s, its founders were harshly treated by the militaristic Japanese regime of those days, but it came into the postwar era with a good reputation for its refusal to compromise with militarism. It advanced the Nichiren faith by promoting the healing, this-worldly benefits of chanting, by forming highly organized block and precinct cell-groups, by means of popular music concerts and energetic youth work, and even by establishing its own political party. By such means Soka Gakkai spread so phenomenally in the 1950s that it was sometimes called "the fastest growing religion in the world." Its aggressive tactics, though often criticized, have made Nichiren Shoshu the largest single religious denomination in postwar Japan.

Soka Gakkai also brought Nichiren to America. The first chapter of Soka Gakkai in America was established in 1960 in California. It quickly became Nichiren Shoshu of America (NSA), later Nichiren Shoshu Academy, and grew at a remarkable rate in the fertile spiritual climate of the 1960s. NSA claimed some 200,000 American followers by 1970, predominantly non-Asian Americans. While the number of active members is probably much lower, it has undoubtedly made an impact, especially among young people and in the entertainment industry, with its colorful rallies and its claims for the power of chanting.

NSA meetings I have attended in California have suggested anything but the ethereal meditative image Buddhism holds for many people. Here were energetic, personable youths chanting the Daimoku together over and over at a rapid clip, then doing cheerleader-type yells and jingles on behalf of the cause, and finally giving testimonials on behalf of how chanting had brought them better grades or better jobs. The feeling was overwhelmingly of a modern, streamlined Buddhism for the rock 'n' roll era—but one which produced in its own way an inner confidence and joy corresponding to the inner peace of older meditative varieties.

Two other modern Nichiren movements that have come to America are Rissho Kosei Kai and Reiyukai. Both emphasize Buddhism for the laity and group counseling activities and are predominantly Asian American in constituency.

Zen Buddhism

The third form of Kamakura Buddhism, Zen, is probably the best known in the West. It was supported in the Kamakura

and several subsequent eras primarily by the samurai class, including some shoguns. The best Zen masters taught, and themselves exemplified, a stern monastic and meditative discipline that favorably impressed the warriors as matching their own ideals of rigorous self-control. In addition, the famous Zen-related arts—the tea ceremony, flower arrangement, gardens, and of course the "martial arts"—enabled the new upper class to exercise its own pretensions to gentility.

These two "wings" of Zen are not as far separated as it might appear on the surface. Zen emphasizes that we all have the Buddha nature within us, as do all things. Ordinarily it is woefully obscured by our out-of-control passions, attachments, and lack of mental concentration. But long hours of *zazen*, seated Zen meditation, can bring the "monkey mind"—as Zen people sometimes call it—under control. Further, the skillful tactics employed by a seasoned Zen master can lead to a radical breakthrough, sometimes called *satori* ("surprise"), into enlightenment. Stories of such breakthroughs focus on the famous one-on-one interviews between masters and disciples, and may include use of the *koan*, the Zen riddles ("What is the sound of one hand clapping?" "What was your face before you were born?") intended to bring the ordinary rational mind up against its limits, and even the "shock therapy" of shouts and slaps celebrated in Zen lore.

With the realization of the unstained mind comes freedom—freedom of expression; freedom to see the same Buddha nature everywhere; freedom to "be here now," to live in the fullness of the present. So it is that a Zen adept makes and serves tea with the simple grace of one who is fully at home with himself and what he is doing. The Zen artist sees a bird on a branch and captures it in a few seemingly spontaneous strokes of the brush that find the eternal Buddhahood within that frail creature. With a shout and a single sure lunge, the Zen swordsman hits his mark. This discipline and freedom can be illustrated by a music student's hard, disciplined practice of a piece on the piano over and over, until the day comes when it just flows out; she does not need to think "put this finger here, put that one there," but it "plays itself" masterfully without thought, and no doubt sounds far better than ever before.

In the two dozen or so Zen centers in America, one can see Zen meditation practiced by persons of diverse backgrounds. The posture is properly the cross-legged lotus, or some approximation of it; this gives one a sense of balance and stability. As one sits, a proctor walks back and forth with a stick, ready to tap anyone who nods back into mindfulness. Zazen meditators may focus their minds inwardly on counting breaths, on pure awareness, or on one of the koans that bring one to the limits of the rational mind and beyond it into cosmic freedom. From time to time, they may go in for an interview with the *roshi,* or Zen master, who will give advice and perhaps ask them to demonstrate the meaning of the koan on which they are working. A satisfactory answer would be less a verbal analysis of it than a spontaneous gesture that showed, in a leap or a shout, the freedom of a breakthrough to satori.

Tibetan Buddhism

Other Americans, both Tibetans and others, follow the demanding but rewarding practices of Vajrayana, the school of Buddhism for which the Himalayan nation of Tibet is famous. Its leader, the Nobel prize-winning Dalai Lama, has brought world attention to his land and his faith. Vajrayana puts particular emphasis on the importance of serious practitioners receiving initiations from lamas (teachers/priests) in well-qualified lineages. To prepare for initiation, disciples are taught to do numerous prostrations and chants; further practice includes deep and powerful visualizations of

Buddhas and deities and complex but colorful ceremonies. Tibetan centers of several schools can be found in most major American cities.

Deer Park, a Buddhist monastery in Oregon, Wisconsin, is an example of a modern Tibetan monastery. Founded in 1979 by Geshe Sopa, a retired professor from the nearby University of Wisconsin at Madison, the Kalachakra Temple at Deer Park has weekly religious services, as well as celebrations on major Tibetan Buddhist holidays, drawing both members of the local Tibetan community and also visitors from across the Midwest. The Fourteenth Dalai Lama is a frequent visitor to Deer Park, often in conjunction with an ongoing project to measure the physiological dimensions of Tibetan meditation with Dr. Richard Davidson of the University of Wisconsin. By monitoring the neurological and bodily correlates of monks during meditation, the project is using science to explore the nature of religion. Although some see work like this as reducing practice by ignoring aspects of it that cannot be measured, it has influenced the way that Tibetan Buddhists in America explain and understand their own practices.

CONCLUSION

East Asian religions are today a part of American life, and are followed by Americans of virtually every background. They have also had an influence on American life through many media—such as poetry, architecture, cinema—that extends far beyond their number of official adherents.

In the twentieth century and continuing in the twenty-first, the United States and the very different societies of East Asia have found themselves in increasing interaction. Whether through the tragedy of war or the more benign means of economic interaction, tourism, and cultural exchange, Americans and East Asians have found their lives and nations more and more intertwined. In this situation the religions of East Asia located in the United States have a very special role. By familiarizing themselves with these outposts of East Asia, Americans of all backgrounds, whether or not they are personally drawn to these religions, can learn about East Asia on levels inaccessible by most other means, make East Asian friends, and prepare themselves and their country for the pluralistic world of the twenty-first century.

Notes

1. In Japanese and most other East Asian languages, the surname—Nakayama, in this case—comes first.

2. This tradition, emphasizing meditation and enlightenment in the midst of everyday life, is called *Chan* in China, *Son* in Korea, and *Thien* in Vietnam.

3. *Budo* is Japanese for the way of the warrior (i.e., the "martial arts"), including such traditional forms as karate ("empty hands"), kendo ("way of the sword"), kyudo ("way of archery"), aikido ("way of harmonious energy"), and others. All these have developed a strongly spiritual dimension, emphasizing the cultivation of a quiet and clear consciousness for the sake of full concentration on the immediate present, direct intuitive action, and balancing one's breath and vitality. Acting in profound unity with the energies of the universe is stressed. Especially in aikido, nonaggressive practices are accentuated. Many in both East and West study budo primarily as spiritual/physical exercise with little intent of making warlike use of these skills. (Ninjutsu, the "art of invisibility," that is, of the ninja, "invisible or secret person," much popularized in America through films and other means, is not regarded as a spiritual path by followers of other martial arts because of its stress on violence rather than on harmony with the way of the universe. Perhaps the Ninja Turtles will lead to changes here!)

4. New religious movements have also appeared in China and Korea. A Korean movement that has attained quite a bit of publicity is the Unification Church, popularly known as the "Moonies," founded by the Rev. Sun Myung Moon, a Korean minister. Although it has incorporated some elements of Korean shamanism, it is essentially a Christian movement presenting unconventional views of the role of Christ and suggesting that a new coming of Christ, perhaps in the person of Moon, may be imminent. This new religious movement is addressed in another chapter.

5. Dainichi is the same figure called Vairocana in Sanskrit.

6. Kannon is Kuan-yin in Chinese, Avalokitesvara in Sanskrit.

7. Amida is O-mi-to in Chinese, Amitabha in Sanskrit.

8. Fudo is Pu-tung in Chinese, Acala in Sanskrit; these names all mean "The Immovable One." Fudo is technically not a Buddha or bodhisattva but one of five Myo-o or Maha-devas, "Wondrous Kings," who are manifestations of Dainichi, or Vairocana. Their mission is to protect truth and combat evil.

STUDY QUESTIONS

1. How has Confucianism influenced East Asian thought, particularly regarding family life and society? Give specific examples.

2. What are examples of East Asian religion's influence on American Christianity? Be specific.

3. How would you define the Dao? How did Confucius and the Confucians differ from Laozi in their understanding of the Dao?

4. How do you understand the East Asian religious idea of yin and yang? What are some examples you see, perhaps from your own religious tradition, in which opposites work to create a balanced life?

5. What are the several Buddhist movements that have come to and established themselves in America? By what practices and rituals do they distinguish themselves?

6. Why do you think Zen Buddhism has had such a popular appeal in America?

ESSAY TOPICS

Exploring the Lives of Confucius and Laozi

Popularizing Zen in America: *Zen and the Art of Motorcycle Maintenance*, by Robert Pirsig

The NSA and Its Development in America

Women and the Religions of East Asia

Japanese Gods

WORD EXPLORATION

The following words play significant roles in any discussion of East Asian religions in America and are worth careful reflection and discussion.

Confucius	Zen	Yin	Shinto
Laozi	Omoto	Yang	Dao
Confucianism	Kami	Daoism	
Dao de jing	Shrine	Chinese New Year	

FOR FURTHER READING

Buddhism in America

Fields, Rick. *How the Swans Came to the Lake: A Narrative History of Buddhism in America.* Boulder, Colo.: Shambhala, 1981.

Numrich, Paul. *Old Wisdom in the New World: Americanization in Two Immigrant Theravada Buddhist Temples.* Knoxville: University of Tennessee Press, 1996.

Prebish, Charles. *Luminous Passage: The Practice and Study of Buddhism in America.* Berkeley and Los Angeles: University of California Press, 1999.

Tweed, Thomas A. and Stephen Prothero, eds. *Asian Religions in America: A Documentary History.* New York: Oxford University Press, 1999.

Chinese Religion

Ch'en, Kenneth K. S. *Buddhism in China: A Historical Survey.* Princeton, N.J.: Princeton University Press, 1964.

Neville, Robert Cummings. *Boston Confucianism: Portable Tradition in the Late-modern World.* Albany: State University of New York Press, 2000.

Thompson, Laurence G. *Chinese Religion: An Introduction.* Belmont, Calif.: Wadsworth, 1969.

Japanese Religion

Earhart, H. Byron. *Japanese Religion: Unity and Diversity.* Belmont, Calif.: Wadsworth, 1982.

Ellwood, Robert S., and Richard Pilgrim. *Japanese Religion: A Cultural Perspective.* Englewood Cliffs, N.J.: Prentice-Hall, 1985.

WEB SITES

http://www.falundafa.org
   Falun Gong's English-language Web site

http://Website.leidenuniv.nl/~haarbjter/falun.htm
   Barend ter Haar's page of Falun Gong resources

http://www.deerparkcenter.org/
   Deer Park Monastery (Wisconsin)

http://www.sgi-usa.org/
   Soka Gakkai

http://www.tibet.com/DL/
   Tibetan Government-in-exile online resources about the Dalai Lama

http://academics.hamilton.edu/asian_studies/home/TempleCulture.html
   Thomas Wilson's Confucianism image collection

PART FIVE

Made (Or Re-Made) in the U.S.A.

13

World Religions Made in the U.S.A.: Apocalyptic Communities— Seventh-day Adventists and Jehovah's Witnesses

DELL deCHANT

1782	William Miller born
1827	Ellen G. White (née Harmon) born
1843–1844	Time range given in Miller's apocalyptic prophecy
1844	Ellen G. White's first visions
1849	William Miller dies
1852	Charles Taze Russell born
1863	"Seventh-day Adventist" movement officially established
1869	Joseph Franklin Rutherford born
1874	Adventist missionaries sent to Europe
1874	Prophesied apocalypse in Witness tradition (first of many)
1879	Russell begins publishing *Zion's Watchtower and Herald of Christ's Presence*
1914	Prophesied apocalypse in Witness tradition
1915	Ellen G. White dies
1916	Charles Taze Russell dies
1931	"Jehovah's Witnesses" officially adopted as name of Russell-Rutherford group
1942	Rutherford dies
1975	Prophesied apocalypse in Witness tradition
1993	Branch Davidian tragedy in Waco, Texas
2005	*National Geographic* feature story cites the Adventists' health practices as beneficial to longevity

In recent years Americans have heard more than a few media reports about tragic occurrences involving religious communities whose doctrines and practices seem unusual. The two most well known events of this type in recent American history were the 1993 tragedy at Waco, Texas, involving the Branch Davidians and the agencies of the United States Government, and the equally regrettable 1997 event at Rancho Santa Fe, near San Diego, where thirty-nine members of the Heaven's Gate movement took their lives. Similar incidents include the death of over five hundred persons associated with the Ugandan group, Restoration of the Ten Commandments of God, in March 2000; the suicides of participants in the Solar Temple in Canada and Switzerland, in 1994; and the death of over nine hundred persons at the People's Temple in Jonestown, Guyana, in 1978.

These were national and international tragedies and when they occurred the press was ablaze with reports about the occurrences and the peculiar religions that in some way contributed. Closer to home, nearly all of us have heard or read about local persons whose religious principles and practices bring them into violation of civil law or the sometimes stricter law of public opinion. Because they stand out as different, all too often these persons and their religions are wrongly associated with the groups involved in the tragedies noted above.

Perhaps we have heard of local persons refusing to salute the flag of the country, repeat the pledge of allegiance, or stand for the national anthem at some public function. We might recall reports about high school students raising objections to traditional Christian invocations before graduation ceremonies or baseball games, and parents who do not allow their children to have blood transfusions or medical care for religious reasons. Some of our colleagues may not attend a public event because it is their sabbath, and we might have friends who do not celebrate traditional holidays—especially Christmas, Easter, and Halloween. Across the street we might have good neighbors who reject our earnest entreaties to support a particular candidate or political cause because political activity is contrary to their religious beliefs. While these persons certainly stand out from the mainstream of our society, they would no more willfully harm themselves, their children, or others than would other average citizens.

All of us have doubtless been exposed to sensational national and local media reports about religious communities and individual participants that challenge our traditional sensibilities and legal codes. Yet few of us realize that persons deeply committed to the ideals and practices of these religions are our vocational colleagues, employers, employees, neighbors, and friends. Although few of us (demographically) are likely to join an alternative religious tradition, many people find inspiration and spiritual refreshment in such groups. Some of us may also find that these groups are harshly criticized by other denominations, attacked in the media, and challenged by the government.

In this regard, it is helpful to remember that most "mainstream" religions of today were once alternative religious communities, which advocated religious doctrines and customs that were decidedly different from those in the cultures where they emerged, became established, and eventually flourished. Judaism, Buddhism, and Christianity are historic examples of this. Others of more recent origin include Baptists, Methodists, the Church of Jesus Christ of Latter-day Saints, and Pentecostals. In their historical moments of origin, and indeed up until the present day, these more well-known traditions and their participants have been attacked, culturally and religiously persecuted, and vilified in certain societies.

It is healthy for us, as students of religion, to ask about differences and similarities between familiar religions of the past, which many of us practice, and the new religions of today. It is also of primary importance for all of us to realize that many contemporary religions were born and bred in the United States, have since grown into international religions, and today not only struggle for acceptance in nations far distant from their origin but also in their native land. This chapter centers on two world religions "made in the U.S.A." that exemplify the challenges and successes of America's contribution to the global religious ecology. Other chapters in this book will consider additional world religions that originated in America: the Church of Christ, Scientist (Christian Science) and Theosophy (chapter 14); New Thought (chapter 15); the Church of Scientology (chapter 16); and the Church of Jesus Christ of Latter-day Saints (chapter 18). Our specific focus here will be on the Seventh-day Adventist Church and the Watch Tower Bible and Tract Society (Jehovah's Witnesses).

A YOUNG AMERICAN ENCOUNTERS AMERICA'S YOUNG RELIGIONS

The Seventh-day Adventists came into our family life because of a local Adventist church's openness to other religious communities using their sanctuary on Sundays. I remember my parents debating the virtues and demerits of a congregation of my mother's religion meeting at a Seventh-day Adventist church. My father was a fairly nonreligious person, although he had been raised in an intensely religious family, which had produced preachers for the previous five generations. His family was originally affiliated with the Reformed Church, but later in life he became a Lutheran and still later a Methodist. My father's chief concern was that the Adventists were "not Christian." He also had concerns about my mother's religion, which had begun as a schismatic sect of Christian Science. He referred to both groups as "cults," and cited a sermon by a famous radio preacher he listened to occasionally. My parents' discussions concerned the Adventists convening their religious assembly on Saturday, leaving Sundays open for other groups to use the facilities; their belief that we are living in the "last days"

before the end of time; and their opposition to smoking and alcohol consumption. My father considered the prohibitions "religious meddling," but my mother found them healthy guidelines. Neither of my parents found the belief about the "last days" consistent with their own. This type of belief is technically referred to as apocalypticism and is found in many Christian groups, especially those of recent origin. Ultimately my mother's religious community found sanctuary in the religious home of the Adventists and there they celebrated their Christian tradition in the church of a Christian community that for many other Christians is decidedly "non-Christian." My parents' debate about the Adventists was my first introduction to a world religion born in the United States.

Like many, perhaps most, Americans, my introduction to the Watch Tower Bible and Tract Society (Jehovah's Witnesses) occurred when members of this community appeared unexpectedly at the door of our home. The only other religious visitors we had were a local Baptist minister and two young men from the Church of Jesus Christ of Latter-day Saints; the minister and the Mormon missionaries visited only once. Delegations of Witnesses, on the other hand, came by many times. Like the Adventists, the Witnesses expressed a firm belief that the present world was going to end very soon and only the Witnesses would survive. Unlike the Adventists, the Witnesses affirmed that the end would come in what was then the very near future, specifically 1975. Neither of my parents felt comfortable with the Witnesses' apocalypticism, but my father was particularly annoyed by the spirited commitment of the local evangelists. I remember him saying, "Don't they know that we are not interested—we're Lutherans." That did not seem to bother them. If my father was home when the Witnesses called, they usually departed early and left only their publications, *The Watchtower* and *Awake!*, for which my father would give them some money. If my mother was present when the Witnesses came by, she welcomed them in, offered them coffee (which my mother loved but which they refused) and involved them in dialogue about the Bible and various religious myths and rituals. She was interested in their appeal, and she seemed to genuinely enjoy their presence; I think this was due to her appreciation of the intensity of their faith. The visits were always cordial and at times actually quite friendly. She remained unconvinced of the "scientific" basis of their doctrine and she interpreted the Bible very differently than they.

As a youth, what struck me most about the Witnesses who visited our home was their conservative dress, the fact that young people (my age, 8–12) accompanied their parents on their evangelistic missions, and that these people seemed to very sincerely believe their religious teachings—especially those about the end of the world. I remember listening to my mother's conversations with the Witnesses and reading *The Watchtower* and *Awake!* In spite of my father's concerns, I could not help finding the Witnesses and their beliefs fascinating, even though they were different from those of my family. What I had trouble understanding was why children my age joined their parents in missionary activity since such activity would have been not only unusual to most of my peers but actually taken to be quite bizarre. Only years later did I realize that Witnesses involve young people as part of their mission to culture because they believe strongly that family members should participate together in religious service and all Witnesses, regardless of age, are called to preach. In fact, every baptized Witness is an ordained minister.

Turning now to the specific forms and shapes of America's contribution to the world's religious ecology, we are immediately struck by the overwhelming scope of our inquiry. The study of America's new religions is indeed a vast and somewhat daunting task, if for no other reason than the fact that there are so many of them—hundreds at least, if not thousands. America is not only the world's leader in industrial production, it is the decided leader in religious production as well. Although some other nations seem to be catching up (Japan, Nigeria, and Brazil, for example), our lead is comfortable and most likely continuing to grow. In fact, even limiting our study to the two traditions of this chapter suggests the considerable range and diversity of America's new religions.

The Adventist tradition alone numbers more than eighty different incorporated groups, of which the Seventh-day Adventists is the largest. Groups related to or derived from the Jehovah's Witness movement (itself usually classified as a subgroup of the Adventists) number more than a dozen. These numbers increase substantially when one adds to the count "related groups" that are entirely independent and self-sufficient, which lack official institutional identity, but nonetheless have historical or doctrinal affinity with one of these groups. Thus, from these two traditions alone, we can explicitly specify nearly one hundred different religious communities, but there are certainly many more. This much being given, our inquiry into "Religions Made in the U.S.A." must not only proceed with caution and extreme discretion, but it must also be limited. Due to these considerations, our study will be restricted to the root traditions already introduced, their history, primary beliefs, and current manifestations. Certain important sectarian expressions will be noted, but the focus will remain on the primary carriers of the systems.

The Seventh-day Adventist Church

Both Seventh-day Adventists and Jehovah's Witnesses trace their origins to the apocalyptic prophecies of a New England Baptist, William Miller (1782–1849). We will consider the Jehovah's Witnesses later, but for now let us give our attention to the "mainstream" of the tradition—the Seventh-day Adventists.

Although he lacked formal seminary education, William Miller was a serious student of the Bible. He was keenly interested in apocalyptic texts, particularly the book of Daniel and the book of Revelation. On the basis of his careful study of the book of Daniel, he became convinced that the return of Jesus, or Second Advent, would occur sometime between March 21, 1843, and March 21, 1844. The event would be cataclysmic; evil and evildoers would be destroyed, the dead resurrected for judgment, and the faithful taken to heaven. The expectation of such an event is typical of apocalyptic groups, which often refer to it as the "cleansing."

Miller quickly began preaching about his belief in the Second Advent and soon attracted a large following. So powerful was his influence that his followers were called Millerites. When the Second Advent did not happen in March of 1844, the biblical calculus of the apocalypse was reworked and a new date established—October 22, 1844. It is not unusual for apocalyptic prophecies to include designation of precise dates; this of course leads to revisions when the event does not occur.

By the time the new date was announced, Miller had attracted followers from many Protestant groups. Estimates suggest that there were as many as 100,000 Millerites in the country in October 1844. It is reported that as the prophesied date drew near, some Millerites sold homes and property, settled financial affairs, and then patiently awaited the Second Advent. While there are no confirmed reports, folklore has it that many dressed in white garments and stood on their housetops on October 22, awaiting the return of Jesus.

When the predicted event failed to occur, the Millerites were devastated and most disillusioned followers left the movement, returning to their former religions. The failure of the prophecy came to be known as "The Great Disappointment." Not all Millerites abandoned the belief in a Second Advent, however, and from the scattered remnants of Miller's movement a new and enduring tradition emerged, the Seventh-day Adventists.

Although Miller based his prophecies solely on his study and interpretations of the biblical texts, the same cannot be said of the person most responsible for the growth and development of the Adventists, the prophet Ellen G. White (née Harmon 1827–1915). It was White, the daughter of Millerites, who in the same year as the Great Disappointment had the first of her many visions. Among her early visions in 1844 was one of Adventists ascending to heaven. In the course of her life, she would have over two thousand visions, which would come to be accepted by Adventists as "inspired counsels from the Lord." Many of these, such as the vision of 1844, proved decisive to the development of the new religion.

Among those associated with White, two important doctrines developed. The first was the belief that the prophetic event of 1844 was an error only with regard to the place specified for Jesus' return. Turning again to the Bible for guidance, but also doubtless inspired by White's vision of Adventists ascending to heaven, this small group of former Millerites came to believe that rather than returning to earth, Jesus had actually returned to the inner sanctuary (the "Most Holy Place") of the heavenly temple in 1844. According to their belief, the heavenly sanctuary had to be cleansed prior to the "cleansing" of earth. Upon completion of the heavenly task, which would happen soon, Jesus would then return to earth to begin the earthly task. Miller had been right after all; he simply had misunderstood the fullness of the message. Jesus was still going to return soon, but the exact date could not be known. To this day, the belief in the imminent return of Jesus is a central belief of Seventh-day Adventism, although a specific date is never given.

The second major doctrine the group established was the specification of the seventh day of the week (Saturday) as the Sabbath. This practice was already followed by some Millerites and other Christians, most notably the Seventh-day Baptists. White and her followers accepted it as a biblical directive; one further reinforced by another

What Is Apocalypticism?

Although the two religious communities explored in this chapter are relatively recent arrivals on the world's religious scene, the apocalyptic worldview that nourishes them has been around for over two thousand years. Scholars generally trace the origins of apocalyptic beliefs to a religious visionary in ancient Persia, Zoroaster (628–551 BCE). The word itself is derived from the Greek word for "reveal," and what is being revealed in this case is the process through which the world will be transformed through divine intervention.

Apocalypticism is found in various religious systems, although it is most prominent in the monotheistic traditions, especially Christianity and Islam. Although there is considerable variation in apocalyptic beliefs, the dominant theme is the imminent transformation of the world, which results in the establishment of a perfect world, typically after a cataclysmic struggle between cosmic forces of good and evil. In American popular culture, this theme is often expressed in abbreviated aphorisms and catchphrases, such as "The End of the World is at hand," "The End Times are upon us," and "Judgment Day will soon begin." Such phrases are oversimplifications of apocalyptic beliefs, most of which are quite detailed and highly complex. Nonetheless, they do suggest the sense of impending transformation that is common in all forms of apocalyptic belief; and it is here that the apocalyptic groups differ from others in their respective traditions.

In general, the monotheistic faiths believe that there will be a transformation of the world, initiated by God. Broadly speaking, such beliefs are based in what scholars refer to as "eschatology," another word of Greek origin that refers to teachings about the "last things." Such teachings deal with the same subjects and issues as those that concern the apocalyptic communities: God's transformation of the world, the elimination of evil, the establishment of a new and perfect world, and so on. The key difference, however, is that mainstream religious groups tend to treat such teachings as relevant to a future time, while apocalyptic groups view them as critically important right now and right here. For them, the grand struggle between good and evil, God and the adversary, righteousness and perdition is about to begin or has already begun. For them, the judgment of the world is at hand. So, in addition to the other apocalyptic phrases that have entered popular culture, one other that members of apocalyptic communities would suggest is equally important is the question "Are you ready?"

vision, in which White saw Jesus and the Ten Commandments, with the fourth (on keeping the Sabbath holy) illuminated with a supernatural light. The doctrine of the seventh-day Sabbath, together with the belief in the Second Advent, became the cornerstones of the movement. Together, these two beliefs not only distinguish Seventh-day Adventists from other Christians, serving as the basis for the name of their tradition, they also stand as primary elements of their faith. For Adventists, the second coming of Jesus is soon to occur and the proper observance of the Sabbath is a necessary part of their preparation for this event.

On the foundation of these two primary teachings, and with the inspiration of Ellen White's visions, the Seventh-day Adventist Church was born. By 1850, the Whites were publishing *Review and Herald*, a periodical promoting Adventist beliefs. When it was officially organized in 1863 there were already over one hundred congregations identifying with the movement. Under White's charismatic leadership, the new church grew rapidly, especially in western states. She and her husband traveled widely, promoting the new religion, holding "Sabbath Conferences," and advocating improvements in education, health care, and diet. Following White's lead, Adventists have continued to express great interest in education and health reform, and their dietary practices are among the strictest of all Christian groups. In 1872 White took the Adventist message to California and by the end of the century she had traveled to Europe and Australia.

Even before White's travels to Europe, the Adventists had begun missionary activity outside of the United States, sending their first missionary to Europe in 1874. By 1900 there were Adventist missionaries active on all continents. Wherever they went, Adventists not only brought their apocalyptic and seventh-day Sabbath doctrines, they also brought educational institutions and health care facilities. Today Seventh-day Adventism counts more followers outside the United States than here, its nation of origin.

Adventist Teachings, Practices, and Cultural Impact

In matters of doctrine, Seventh-day Adventists affirm themselves to be Protestants and can be classified as "evangelical conservatives." Were an outsider to attend a typical Adventist Sabbath service, he or she would probably notice nothing particularly different from typical Protestant services—except perhaps the day of the week on which the service was held. Indeed in most respects, the Adventists are quite similar to many other Protestant communities. They believe in the Trinity, practice baptism by immersion, recognize the literal truth of the virgin birth of Jesus, and accept Jesus Christ as their personal savior. In their denial of predestination, they differ from those Protestants who derive their doctrines from Calvin. Like other Protestants, Adventists reject the sacraments of the Roman Catholic Church, the authority of the pope, and any mediating role for the church in the personal salvation of individuals. Aside from their seventh-day Sabbath, the only other major area of distinction from other Christians is their denial of eternal punishment in Hell for those who are evil and their belief in "conditional immortality." Both beliefs are derived from their understanding that there is no immortal soul and that at death people enter what is sometimes called a "soul-sleep" until the second coming of Jesus. At that time the dead will awaken to be judged, with the righteous receiving eternal life and those who are evil being annihilated.

Adventists accept a literal interpretation of the Bible, believing that its authors were inspired by God. Accepting it as the sole religious authority, they seek to conform their doctrines and lives to teachings found in both Testaments. In the New Testament they find the details of their apocalyptic doctrines, and in the Old Testament, especially the Ten Commandments, they find instruction for personal and social life. Their commitment to both parts of the Bible is reflected in their use of Daniel, an Old Testament book, to predict the return of Jesus, the Christian savior whose second coming is reported only in the New.

As already noted, the two oldest and most distinctive doctrines of the Seventh-day Adventists are those concerning the imminent return of Jesus and observance of the Sabbath on Saturday. Their belief in the return of Jesus is not unique. All Christians believe that Jesus will return sometime in the future, and throughout the history of Christianity certain groups have predicted that this would occur soon. Groups that affirm that the second coming will happen in the very near future are called apocalyptic. The specific form of the Adventists' apocalypticism is called millenarianism (or millennialism), a term derived from the belief that Jesus' return will be followed by a thousand-year period (the millennium) when his followers will live with him in heaven.

Millenarian groups differ considerably regarding details of the apocalypse and the millennium, and that is one of the reasons why there are so many different communities related to the Adventist tradition. The Branch Davidians, well known to most Americans due to the tragedy at Waco, Texas, in 1993, trace their roots to an Adventist schism in the 1930s. The Davidian movement itself is divided into several groups, all of which are apocalyptic. While they generally accept the more traditional Adventist beliefs about Jesus' second coming, they go further in adding details related to the restoration of the kingdom of David, the king of ancient Israel, upon whose throne some Christians believe Jesus will sit when he returns. Although Branch Davidians represent an extreme form of apocalypticism, and the militarism of the group at Waco is certainly contrary to the pacifism of mainstream Adventism, history reveals that some apocalyptic communities have generated radical subgroups, and at times violence, bloodshed, death, and war have resulted. It must be remembered, however, that apocalypticism can take root in a great variety of religious traditions; for example, Joseph Kibwetere, the leader of the Ugandan apocalyptic community in which over five hundred persons died in March 2000, grew up in the Roman Catholic Church and had been an administrator in the church's educational system.[1]

This short chapter does not allow full coverage of all the nuances in the Seventh-day Adventists' millenarian beliefs, but some of the more salient points can be sketched. Generally, the details of their millenarianism are derived from the New Testament, especially the book of Revelation. According to this belief, when Jesus returns he will battle Satan and his followers, while Jesus' true believers, including the dead (who have been resurrected), will ascend to meet him in the sky and then be lifted up to heaven. Unbelievers will be killed. Once in heaven, Jesus and his followers will reside there for the millennium while the earth remains a lifeless wilderness. At the end of the thousand-year period, Jesus and his followers will return to earth, where there will be a final battle in which Satan is defeated. At this time the wicked will be resurrected to receive their final judgment. Following the judgment, the earth will be cleansed by fire, annihilating evil forever, and then re-created by Jesus as an eternal paradise for his followers.

As apocalypticists, Seventh-day Adventists believe the return of Jesus is quite near. Using various passages from the Bible for support, they argue that current political, social, and economic conditions presage the second coming. For those who are prepared, the event holds no fear, but for those who are not, the consequences will be dire indeed. For committed Adventists, the primary focus of life is religion and the primary focus of religious life is preparation for the return of their Lord. This preparation takes many forms and requires the observance of rules that to outsiders may seem quite demanding, especially by standards of contemporary American society. For them, however, these very standards are indicative of the dire problems humanity faces today, problems that for the Adventists are portent of the last days of the world. Several Adventist teachings are of special note in this regard.

In keeping with their commitment to the Bible as the sole religious authority, early on Adventists adopted stances of extreme pacifism and nonparticipation in politics and government. These stances have changed significantly over time, and today Seventh-day Adventists are generally supportive of the government, although generally uninvolved, except in situations where they deem the state is infringing on religious liberty.

Their relationship with government was first tested in the Civil War when Adventists lobbied the government and eventually won the right to be recognized as conscientious objectors. Some members, however, did participate in the war and the church removed their membership. Conditions had changed by World War I, when Adventists were given church sanction to participate in military service as noncombatants in medical units; by World War II, Adventists comprised the largest single group of conscientious objectors serving as noncombatants in the military. In the midst of the Vietnam War, the church went even further, asserting that military service was a matter of personal conscience, that noncombatant service was preferred but active military service was allowed. Today military recruiters visit Adventist schools, Adventists volunteer for military service, and some two thousand participated in the Persian Gulf War. Adventist veterans of the Gulf War were given warm and supportive welcome when they returned, and many Adventists have served in recent years in conflicts in Iraq and Afghanistan.[2] While current events certainly indicate a change in the Adventists' position on military service, their fundamental beliefs continue intact and they remain adamantly committed to religious freedom and the separation of church and state. What their revised position on military service does tell us is that even for religions made in the United States, American culture changes religions just as religions change American culture. Still, among America's major religious groups they remain among the least active in politics and still strongly committed to the ideal of pacifism.

The focal point of the Adventists' resistance to government encroachment on religious freedom has been the affiliated Religious Liberty Association, which publishes the remarkable periodical *Liberty*. Initially the publication was devoted to specific challenges facing the Adventists, especially Blue Laws (which they felt resulted in making Sunday a legal Sabbath). Today *Liberty*, which has a circulation of about 200,000, includes articles about contemporary issues related to the separation of church and state, relations between different religious groups, and historical figures and communities who were persecuted for their faith.

Belief in the literal truth of the Bible and the teachings of the Old Testament has led Seventh-day Adventists to advocate strict observance of the Ten Commandments. We have already mentioned the Adventist recognition of Saturday as the Sabbath. In addition to recognizing the same Sabbath period (sundown on Friday to sundown on Saturday), in many respects the Sabbath activities of observant Adventists would seem quite like those of observant Jews. Adventists are directed to refrain from all labor on the Sabbath, attend religious services, pray, study the Bible, and generally reflect on the religious dimensions of life.

Not only do Adventists share the same Sabbath as Jews, they also recognize traditional Jewish distinctions between acceptable and unacceptable foods. Their commitment to observing Old Testament dietary laws is complemented by their dedication to healthy living, which from the time of Ellen White has been evidenced in the Adventists' great interest in health maintenance and health care. Although most Americans do not realize it, the origin of breakfast cereal can be traced to the Adventists, whose laymember, J. H. Kellogg, invented corn flakes as a healthy alternative to eggs and breakfast meats.

Still following White's directions, Adventists today are enjoined to abstain from tea, coffee, meat (especially pork), shellfish, alcohol, tobacco, hot condiments, spices, highly refined foods, and narcotics. A vegetarian diet is preferred but dairy products can be consumed. The Adventists find biblical support for their especially strict dietary codes in the New Testament statement that the body is "the temple of the Holy Spirit." For this reason exercise is also encouraged. Although such prescriptions were considered unusual when they were first introduced, today many medical experts consider them sound guidance for a healthy life, and increasing numbers of Americans are putting at least some of them into practice. In this way, the Adventists have been well in advance of the rest of society.

Not all of us may recall having met a Seventh-day Adventist, but their influence on American society has been significant. Today the church supports over 6,000 schools worldwide, including fourteen colleges and universities in the United States and Canada. It operates over 500 hospitals and clinics around the world and educates physicians, dentists, and medical support specialists. The church's humanitarian outreach knows no religious boundaries, and in times of need the church extends medical and material support to all who ask, including special disaster-relief units that can move into action at a moment's notice.

Its international work has brought improvement in living conditions to the developing world and to disadvantaged persons in industrial countries. So successful have its international missions been that in 2007 the church reported a global membership of over 15.4 million people, only ten percent of whom reside in the United States.

To the outsider, the Adventists may appear paradoxical. On the one hand, they believe in an imminent end of the world, while on the other they work tirelessly to improve the world of today. Still labeled a non-Christian "cult" by some Christians, they exemplify the Christian ideal of charity more thoroughly than many of their accusers. And although apolitical in their essential disposition to government, they have actively opposed the government through legal means in their tireless defense of religious liberty. Perhaps the best account for these paradoxes is found in the names of two programs they broadcast. Their radio program is called *Voice of Prophecy* and their TV program, *Faith for Today*. In a very real sense, the Adventists successfully accommodate both the voice of their prophecy, which claims the end of the world is near, and a vital faith for today, which demands they make themselves better people and their world a better place to live—until tomorrow comes.

Watch Tower Bible and Tract Society

Like the Seventh-day Adventists, the Jehovah's Witnesses can trace their roots to the apocalyptic prophecies of William Miller. Like the other made-in-the-U.S.A. religions, and even more so, the story of the Witnesses is a story of struggle, criminal and civil trials, public vilification and condemnation by other religions. Of all the world religions born in the United States, Witnesses have endured the most severe and long-lasting governmental persecutions, both here and abroad. They have also been the most persistent of apocalyptic groups, publicly proclaiming at least six different dates when the

end of the world would occur. Despite their persecutions and failed prophecies, they have survived and flourished.

The origins of the Witnesses can be found in the work of Charles Taze Russell (1852–1916). Russell was originally attracted to the teachings of an independent (non-Seventh-day) Adventist leader, Jonas Wendall, who had reinterpreted Miller's teachings to conclude that the Second Advent would occur in 1874. Inspired by Wendall's teachings, Russell soon formed his own Bible study group and began developing the unique doctrines that would come to characterize the Jehovah's Witnesses. When the prophecy of 1874 failed to bring the return of Jesus, Russell accepted a reinterpretation of the event offered by Nelson H. Barbour, which held that Jesus had indeed returned but in an invisible form. But Barbour, like other apocalyptic prophets, made a critical error, one that cost him the support of Russell; he predicted that believers would go to heaven in April 1878.

In 1879, Russell began his own movement, which initially took the form of a publication, *Zion's Watchtower and Herald of Christ's Presence*. The periodical, which included Russell's own teachings and prophecies, was originally sent to Barbour's followers. Like Seventh-day Adventism, Christian Science, and other new religions born in the United States, from their earliest days Jehovah's Witnesses have successfully utilized publications to further their mission. Within a year more than thirty groups had affiliated with "Pastor" Russell and in 1881 he sent missionaries to England. When Russell's movement was incorporated in 1884 as the Watch Tower Bible and Tract Society, it had already become a world religion.

The direct relationship of the Witnesses to Russell's followers is a matter of some debate, and although many of his teachings have been abandoned or modified, others remain of central importance. Most important, the organization he incorporated in 1884 and the "Russellite" groups associated with it served as the foundation for the movement that in 1931, under the leadership of Russell's successor, J. F. Rutherford, declared itself to be Jehovah's Witnesses.

It was Rutherford who was responsible for shaping the Witnesses into the movement that is today so well known to most Americans. Elected President of the group after the death of Russell in 1916, Rutherford was a lawyer by profession and had served briefly as a judge in Missouri. As Russell was known as "Pastor," Rutherford came to be known as "Judge." Ironically, he would be among the first of countless Witnesses brought before government judgment and sent to prison for his religious convictions. The specific charge brought against Rutherford and several other members of the group was sedition. This occurred shortly after his election as President of the Society during World War I, when Rutherford and the others advised young men to avoid military service.

Rutherford and his colleagues were imprisoned until the end of the war, and the government eventually dropped all charges on the eve of a second trial. When the Judge emerged from prison he quickly moved to reenergize the movement, which had suffered from his imprisonment and several of Russell's failed prophecies—the most recent giving 1914 as the date of the apocalypse. One of his first acts was to empower all Witnesses to be ministers, and today each baptized member is an ordained minister.

Rutherford also institutionalized the Witnesses' resistance to government authority. Today, Witnesses staunchly oppose any government laws and regulations believed to be contrary to the law of God as established in the Bible. For this reason Witnesses do not engage in political activity, refuse to salute the flag, and affirm neutrality in times of war. This does not mean that Witnesses are opposed to the government. They are not. What they oppose are government actions that cause them to compromise their faith. This nuanced position notwithstanding, Witnesses have suffered tremendously in times of war or periods of heightened nationalism, just as Rutherford

did in World War I. During World War II they were particular targets of the Nazis, who sent all they could find into concentration camps, while in America a report published in 1941 cited over three hundred "instances of mob violence in forty-four states" against Witnesses.[3]

Under Rutherford's leadership the movement became what he called "Theocratic Organization," which resulted in a more centralized corporate structure for the group and a more focused mission for its evangelists. All Witnesses were directed to promote the faith through distribution and sale of its publications. Rutherford went on the radio, vehicles equipped with loudspeakers traveled city streets, and the movement produced portable phonographs and records for use by local evangelists.[4] By the 1940s, after the death of Rutherford, the Witnesses abandoned the use of radio, loudspeakers, and phonographs in favor of the now distinctive door-to-door missionary approach. After the end of World War II membership increased dramatically, only to fall off again in the late 1970s due to yet another failed prophecy.

Jehovah's Witnesses' Teachings, Practices, and Cultural Impact

Unlike the Adventists, Jehovah's Witnesses do not consider themselves Protestants. In fact, they are quite critical of Protestants, and even more critical of Catholics. To Witnesses both traditions have fallen away from the true teachings of the Bible and actually are working in ways contrary to God. There was a time when Witnesses even denied their movement was a religion, since religion had come to mean something quite different from what they believed was their mission—to be witnesses to Jehovah in the world and to warn the world of the impending apocalypse. Suffice to say, the Witnesses' view of other Christian groups has had no small part to play in the massive and intense opposition they have received from both Protestants and Catholics.

Still, the Witnesses share common elements with many Protestant groups. First among these is its acceptance of the Bible as the inspired Word of God. The official Bible of the Witnesses is *The New World Translation of the Holy Scriptures*, a text produced by the movement. Although it contains the sixty-six books found in Protestant Bibles, it offers many unique variations—such as a version of the death of Jesus found in the Gospels that has him dying on a stake, not on a cross. All doctrines are derived from their interpretation of the Bible. They practice baptism by submersion, a variation of Communion once a year, and believe in the virgin birth of Jesus.

Their differences from traditional Christianity are significant for them as well as their Christian critics. Chief among the differences is their opposition to the Trinity and their conception of the nature and role of Jesus. Rather than the second person in the Trinity, Witnesses believe Jesus was the first of God's creations. He was not God and on earth he was entirely human. God also created Satan, who rebelled against him and became ruler of the world. This led to human sin, wickedness, and death. To end Satan's reign, God sent Jesus, whose death was a sacrifice that allows eternal life for persons of steadfast faith.

Witnesses' beliefs about God and Jesus form the foundation for their apocalyptic doctrines, which are similar in some respects to the Seventh-day Adventists. Unlike the Adventists, however, Witnesses have not hesitated to give dates for the Second Advent. Russell's most famous prophecy was for the beginning of the millennium in 1914. After this did not occur, he revised the date to 1918. Over their history, Witnesses have offered other dates, the most recent being 1975.

Russell's 1914 date is critical to contemporary Witness beliefs about the apocalypse and the status of believers. Again like Adventists, Witnesses believe in "soul sleep," and the judgment of the living and the dead at the time of Jesus' second coming. Those who have followed Jehovah faithfully will be allowed to live while those who have not will be annihilated in a great battle. Unlike the Adventist belief, those who have been accepted by Jesus will dwell on earth and restore it to the paradise it was prior to Satan's rule. This period will last for a thousand years (the millennium), at the end of which Satan will again return, tempt those who can be tempted, and then Satan and all evildoers will be finally destroyed. Those who have followed God will inherit the earthly paradise.

The most unique element in the Witnesses' version of the story concerns a distinction made between believers. For them there are two classes of believers, a heavenly (Elijah) class and an earthly (Elisha) class. The heavenly class numbers exactly 144,000, a figure derived from the book of Revelation; the earthly class includes all others. The heavenly class will rule the earth with Jesus from heaven, while the earthly group will be given "everlasting life" on the earth. According to the teachings of the Witnesses, the heavenly class was "sealed" in 1914, the date of Russell's original prophecy, with no additional persons being added. Thus today most Witnesses do not plan to go to heaven but instead look forward to life on the regenerated earth. As they happily await the advent of Jesus and the paradise of their imminent future, they steadfastly observe the strict teachings of their faith and tirelessly strive to tell others of this good news. This mission is absolutely required of all Witnesses for should they fail to communicate the message not only might others lose the opportunity to experience eternal life in paradise, they themselves could lose the opportunity as well.

Witnesses go about their lives guided by this understanding of the world and their mission. For this reason they are extremely devout in their religious practices, which are quite exacting. As noted earlier, all Witnesses are ordained ministers, and their life is as strict (if not stricter) than the lives of most religious professionals serving in other groups. Nearly all engage in door-to-door missionary work for many hours each month, attend Kingdom Hall (their congregational centers) several times a week, and generally refrain from all secular activities—aside from work. Due to their strict commitment to the Bible, Witnesses do not recognize or celebrate religious or patriotic holidays, refuse to salute the flag or sing the national anthem, and neither accept nor give blood. In all these ways Jehovah's Witnesses stand apart from other religions and the rest of society, yet in this way they remind us all that freedom of religion brings with it the necessity of diversity. In this regard it is well to remember that as the rest of America looks at the Witnesses and finds the intensity of their loyalty to their beliefs unusual, Witnesses look at other Americans and find their resistance to these very beliefs just as hard to fathom. In these differences we all identify ourselves as Americans, even if for some of us such an identification would violate our faith. It is a remarkable feature of America that here one can put one's religion above all other things—country, job, education, community, and society—and still be allowed to practice it freely. It has taken America a long time to realize this, and perhaps it is still not fully realized, but whatever progress has been made over the years is due in no small part to these followers of Jehovah who in their quest to witness God have demanded that other Americans witness their freedom to do so.

Like the Adventists, the doctrines and practices of the Jehovah's Witnesses distinguish them from other Christian traditions, but this is not what makes them such a distinct and notable movement. It is not so much their unique teachings per se but the intensity of their allegiance to them. Like the Adventists, the Witnesses are both apocalyptic and strongly supportive of religious liberty. In both instances, however, the Witnesses go further in their public commitment to their beliefs than their histori-cal predecessor. In fact, few religions rival the Witnesses in terms of sheer religious zeal. A 2007 report indicates that there are nearly seven million Witnesses worldwide-with over 101,000 congregations in more than two hundred countries. Wherever they are found, Witnesses conduct their door-to-door missionary work and disseminate their literature to all who will receive it. Annually, publications reach "well into the hundreds of millions," and the periodical *The Watchtower* is printed in over one hundred languages.[5]

That they have managed to grow in numbers and maintain this zeal in the face of nearly a century of equally zealous opposition from national governments, local communities, and other religions testifies to the power of the movement's teachings in the lives of its followers. It also testifies to the enduring virtue of America's commitment to religious freedom, for the Witnesses have tested this commitment more strenuously than most other groups and found, over time, that it is a commitment extended to them as well.

WHAT APOCALYPTIC RELIGIONS MADE IN THE U.S.A. TELL US

My first encounters with these two religions, which I shared earlier, are part of the story of my own life, part of my growing up in the United States. They took place more than forty years ago, but I remember them quite vividly. Each told me something new about myself, my family, and the world in which I lived. Through these experiences I learned firsthand about the remarkable religious diversity that is a feature of American society in which freedom of religion is an ideal. They also revealed to me marked differences between how believers in one tradition view those in another and how these differences can lead to increases in both understanding and acrimony.

Forty years later, I have discovered that my experiences as a young person were not all that different from most other Americans.

Encountering new and unusual religious traditions and individuals committed to those traditions is a common American experience, and for most of us probably part of our shared narrative of growing up in a pluralistic society. If anything, this is even more true today than when I was young.

The discovery of new and different religions is also part of the story of America and America's chapter in the story of the world's religions. Today we know that all the major world religions and most minor ones as well can be found here. In our public and private activities we are as likely to meet Hindus as we are Catholics, Buddhists as Jews, Muslims as Protestants. Since World War II America has become even more religiously diverse due to new immigration patterns as well as conversions of persons already living here.

Long before this time, however, important contributions to America's chapter in the story of the world's religions were being made by persons called Seventh-day Adventists and Jehovah's Witnesses. Together with the Mormons, Christian Scientists, and Theosophists, these persons embodied America's first new religions, and what made them new was not just that they were new to America but new to the world as well. These were indeed religions of the New World, as the Americas were once called, and their proponents affirmed that they were also religions preparing a way for an even more dramatic new world that was soon to come.

From the days of their origin and continuing on into the contemporary period, for many Americans these religions were their first and only encounter with religious diversity. Just as today may bring contacts with religions new to our land, for more than a century Americans have been encountering new religions that originated here. Then as now, these encounters bring both rewards and dangers. The rewards are growth in understanding and the societal health and cultural dynamism that comes with the appreciation of diversity. The dangers are those associated with bias, fear, and suspicion of those who are different. We are still learning how to maximize the rewards and minimize the risks; so too is the rest of the world. If America is doing better at this than other countries, it is perhaps due to the fact that we have been working at it longer and harder than most; and one of the reasons we have been doing so is because the freedom of our political system has allowed new religions to be born, mature, and thrive. With their success, Adventists, Jehovah's Witnesses, and other new religions have helped turn the ideal of religious freedom from a promise to a practical necessity. What these religions tell us is that just as "anyone can become a real American,"[6] so too have religions made in the United States become authentic religions of the world; and just as "America has the power to make its own all the religions of the world,"[7] so too can it share with the rest of the world uniquely American religions that long ago revealed both the rewards and risks of religious freedom. In their success these religions remind us all that the rewards are certainly worth the risks.

Notes

1. See Joshua Hammer, "An Apocalyptic Mystery," *Newsweek* (April 3, 2000), 46–47.
2. For information on the Adventists' changing positions on military service and data on Gulf War service, see Ronald Lawson, "Church and State at Home and Abroad: The Evolution of Seventh-day Adventist Relations with Governments," *JAAR* 64 (Summer, 1996): 270–311, esp. 285, 291, and 299.
3. From 1941 ACLU text, *The Persecution of Jehovah's Witnesses*, cited with commentary in Jerry Bergman, *Jehovah's Witnesses and Kindred Groups: A Historical Compendium and Bibliography* (New York: Garland, 1984), xxi.

4. Bergman, xxvi.

5. Citation of a number of texts printed from J. Gordon Melton, *Encyclopedic Handbook of Cults in America* (New York: Garland, 1992), 86; citation of a number of languages for *The Watchtower* from Bergman, xxvi–xxvii.

6. Jacob Neusner, "Introduction," in *World Religions in America*, revised and expanded ed. (Louisville, Ky.: Westminster John Knox Press, 2000), 5.

7. Ibid.

STUDY QUESTIONS

1. Discuss the importance of apocalypticism to Seventh-day Adventists and Jehovah's Witnesses.

2. Why (or why not) would participants in an apocalyptic religious community have a high degree of commitment to the beliefs and practices of their religion?

3. Compare and contrast Seventh-day Adventists and Jehovah's Witnesses. Be sure to take into consideration the roles played by the founders of these groups, their relationship with American society, and the keys to their success.

4. Why do you think Seventh-day Adventists and Jehovah's Witnesses have faced opposition from established forms of Christianity and the government?

5. Compare and contrast either Seventh-day Adventism or Jehovah's Witnesses with one of the other new religions presented in this book. Pick one of the following for your comparison: Church of Jesus Christ of Latter-day Saints, Christian Science, Theosophy, or Scientology.

6. Why do you think Seventh-day Adventists and Jehovah's Witnesses are growing and expanding today?

7. Comment on the role of Jesus in the two movements. In what ways do they reveal understandings of Jesus that are similar to traditional Christian understandings? In what ways do their understandings differ from traditional Christian understandings?

8. Compare and contrast the beliefs and practices of Seventh-day Adventism with those of Judaism.

9. Compare and contrast the work of Charles Taze Russell in founding the Jehovah's Witnesses with the work of a founder of another new religion presented in this book.

ESSAY TOPICS

Ellen G. White's Role in the Growth and Development of Adventism

Catholic and Protestant Reactions to Adventist Churches and Jehovah's Witnesses' Kingdom Halls

Role of Publications in the Growth and Development of Seventh-day Adventism and Jehovah's Witnesses

"Rewards and Dangers" of Religious Diversity Experienced when Encountering Seventh-day Adventists and Jehovah's Witnesses

The Lives of Ellen G. White and Charles Taze Russell

Professional and Personal Challenges of Seventh-day Adventists and Jehovah's Witnesses

The Cultural and Religious Impact of Seventh-day Adventism and Jehovah's Witnesses

WORD EXPLORATION

The following words play significant roles in any discussion of religion and society in America and are worth careful reflection and discussion.

Apocalyptic/Apocalypticism	Prophecy	Adventism
Resurrection	Soul-Sleep	Sabbath
Vegetarianism	Missionary	Pacifism
Davidians/Branch Davidians	Blue Laws	The Heavenly Class/
The Book of Revelation	Millenarianism	The Earthly Class
Kingdom Hall	The Second Coming	

FOR FURTHER READING

Bull, Malcolm and Keith Lockhart. *Seeking a Sanctuary: Seventh-day Adventism and the American Dream*. 2nd ed. Bloomington: Indiana University Press, 2006.

Franz, Frederick W. ed., *The New World Translation of the Holy Scriptures, rendered from the Original Languages by the New World Bible Translation Committee*. Revised ed. 1961. Brooklyn: Watchtower Bible and Tract Society of New York, 1961.

Holden, Andrew. *Jehovah's Witnesses: Portrait of a Contemporary Religious Movement*. New York: Routledge, 2002.

Morgan, Douglas, *Adventism and the American Republic: The Public Involvement of a Major Apocalyptic Movement*. Knoxville: University of Tennessee Press, 2001.

Numbers, Ronald L. *Prophetess of Health: Ellen G. White and the Origins of Seventh-day Adventist Health Reform*. Rev. ed. Knoxville: University of Tennessee Press, 1992.

Penton, M. James. *Apocalypse Delayed: The Story of Jehovah's Witnesses*. Toronto: University of Toronto Press, 1985.

White, Ellen G. *The Great Controversy Between Christ and Satan*. Mountain View, Calif.: Pacific Press Publishing Association, 1950. (Originally published in 1858.)

WEB SITES

http://web.archive.org/web/20060907005952/http://etext.lib.virginia.edu/relmove/
Religious Movements Homepage with links to religious groups

http://www.watchtower.org/
Jehovah's Witnesses Web site, with articles from *Watchtower*

http://www.whiteestate.org/books/gc/gc.asp
Ellen G. White's *The Great Controversy Between Christ and Satan*

http://www.WhiteEstate.org/
Official Ellen G. White Web site

http://www.adventist.org/
Official Web site of the Seventh-day Adventist Church

14

World Religions Made in the U.S.A.: Metaphysical Communities— Christian Science and Theosophy

DELL deCHANT

1821	Mary Baker Eddy (née Mary Morse Baker) born
1831	Helena Petrovna Blavatsky born
1866	Mary Baker Eddy's "fall on the ice" and subsequent healing
1875	*Science and Health* published
1875	Theosophical Society founded in New York City
1877	*Isis Unveiled* published
1878	Blavatsky and Henry Steel Olcott travel to India
1879	Church of Christ, Scientist officially organized
1883	Expansion of *Science and Health* to include *with Key to the Scriptures*
1881	*The Secret Doctrine* published
1891	Blavatsky dies, setting off a struggle for leadership
1895	Rival Theosophical Society of America founded by William Q. Judge
1907	Annie Besant becomes president of Theosophical Society
1908	Mary Baker Eddy begins *The Christian Science Monitor*
1910	Eddy dies at the age of 89
1940s	Popularity of Alice A. Bailey's books testifies to the influence of Theosophical ideas in the New Age movement
1970s	Mother Church engages in aggressive but largely unsuccessful attempt to attract new members through media and outreach
2008	Christian Scientists lobby the Massachusetts state legislature to have spiritual healing and practitioners covered by health insurance plans
2009	*Christian Science Monitor* moves to an online-only publication after 100 years in print

It is not uncommon today to hear or read about the New Age movement or religious communities that are referred to as "metaphysical." Beliefs and rituals associated with these groups have received significant public attention in American culture for the past few decades. While not all of the attention has been positive, some of these groups have continued to grow and their beliefs gain in popularity. We may even have friends and neighbors who attend a metaphysical church or identify themselves as New Agers. Long before these new and growing movements came on the scene, however, two American-born religions pioneered this religious terrain now well known to many and increasingly inhabited by average Americans. These two religions are Christian Science and Theosophy. Aside from their names, few Americans know much about either, yet since the late nineteenth century both groups have had a profound impact on religion in the United States and the world.

Although many people have heard of the "power of positive thinking" or studies reporting a connection between mental health and physical well-being, they may not know that more than a century ago Christian Science was promoting the belief in the power of the mind to heal the body. More precisely, it claimed that it was *Mind* that healed, for God was a universally present Divine Mind and through our minds we were spiritually unified with God. When we discovered our mental oneness with God, healing occurred. About the same time that Christian Science was making its bold assertions about mental healing, Theosophy was introducing and advancing equally novel concepts: that human beings were "sparks of divinity," dwelling in physical bodies, and prior to this life these "sparks" (our souls) had existed in other bodies. Aside from the small numbers of practicing Hindus and Buddhists in America at the time, few people knew much about this belief and fewer still took such a notion seriously. Today, this belief, known as reincarnation, is accepted by more than 20 percent of the American population,[1] and it is certainly well known to most Americans.

From Christian Science came a new religious text, *Science and Health with Key to the Scriptures*. The book became the foundation for Christian Science belief and practice, and soon enough the American mental healing movement, which William James would come to call America's "only decidedly original contribution to the systematic philosophy of life."[2] From Theosophy came a host of texts, including *Key to Theosophy*, a celebration of Asian religious systems, which Mahatma Gandhi reported as a powerful influence in sending him back to Hinduism.[3] Needless to say, it also served to introduce many Americans and Europeans to Hinduism for the first time. From Christian Science came the impetus for popular religious idealism, which has generated a host of new religions, most notably groups associated with New Thought. From Theosophy came the root beliefs of the contemporary New Age movement, which has influenced everything from politics to pop music. Perhaps most notably, from them both came the empowerment of women as religious professionals. Long before the more traditional religions confronted the question of female leadership, in fact long before women even had the right to vote in America, these traditions recognized women as religious officials, teachers, administrators, visionaries, and healers.

And so today, when we hear talk of "the power of positive thinking," we are hearing echoes of a belief first popularized by Christian Science; and when a friend offhandedly comments, "It must have been something I did in a previous life," we are hearing echoes of a belief first popularized in America by Theosophy. But the voices of these two movements are not just echoes. They still speak to us today, directly or indirectly inspiring countless persons around the world. Although quite different from each other, together these groups formed the foundation for what is called the "metaphysical movement."

Before going further it is important to understand a bit about how the term *metaphysical* is used by these groups and those who study them. The word itself literally means "beyond the physical" and most commonly is used in reference to a branch of philosophic inquiry that deals with questions related to ultimate reality and the basic categories of thought and experience. As it applies to Christian Science, Theosophy, and numerous other new religions (and as they apply it to themselves), its meaning is somewhat different, however. When used to describe religious communities, it refers to groups that share a general belief that the physical world is in some manner secondary to a higher spiritual world and that humans are in their truest essence part of the higher spiritual world. Additionally, they claim in various ways that knowledge of the higher spiritual world gives one power over the physical world. The Christian Science belief that our minds are part of a Divine Mind and the Theosophical belief that we are sparks of divinity are examples of the general tenor of metaphysical religious assertions. Needless to say, for many Americans such beliefs are unusual and perhaps difficult to grasp. This chapter will help you comprehend them more clearly, although, truth be told, for many readers they may still seem pretty unusual. Perhaps two stories from my own life can help you better understand what I mean by this.

MY FIRST ENCOUNTERS WITH CHRISTIAN SCIENCE AND THEOSOPHY

I first learned about the Church of Christ, Scientist, the way I suspect many people do—from someone disparaging its beliefs and practices. I could not have been much older than eleven or twelve when I heard a rather vivid attack on Christian Science and its founder, Mary Baker Eddy. The person delivering the attack was a respected community leader, and he made the particular point that Christian Science was neither Christian nor science. I remember that he

also noted that Christian Scientists did not endorse medical care and that this practice had led to the death of their children. Their opposition to medical care he deemed contrary to science and the consequences of this to their children's health he considered non-Christian. I recall being moved by the passion and rhetoric of what I now realize was a polemic. I do not remember any of the listeners taking exception with what he said. When I got home, I dutifully reported to my mother the powerful presentation and I mimicked the speaker's denunciation of Christian Science. My mother listened to my animated and parroted attack and then calmly but directly reported to me that she was alive because of Christian Science and that if it had not been for Christian Science I would not have been born. Talk about correction by one's elders! She had never spoken of Christian Science before that day. I later learned that although my mother was not a Christian Scientist, her own religion emerged from Christian Science and was strongly influenced by it. I also never brought the subject up again. In my adult life I have discovered that my mother's response is quite like that made by Christian Scientists to their accusers—generally calm, gentle, but nonetheless corrective and *direct*.

While my first exposure to Christian Science was vivid and dramatic, my first encounter with Theosophy was quite the opposite. Again, the connection came through my mother and her religion. Like Theosophy (as we will see), my mother's religion is syncretistic, which means its primary beliefs were derived from more than a single religious tradition. This characteristic is, incidentally, quite common in groups derived from Christian Science and Theosophy. Hers was also broadly tolerant of religious diversity and promoted appreciation of all religions. This being the case, people from various religious backgrounds routinely participated in services at her religious center. Some stayed on and joined, others left after a single visit—another characteristic of many New Age and "metaphysical" religions. Many, however, visited our home or were transported by my mother to and from religious services. On several occasions after the departure of one or another of my mother's co-religionists, she would observe, often in a whispered voice, that the person was "really a Theosophist" or "used to be a Theosophist." There were only a few people that she ever mentioned in this way, and, at the time, her classification of these folks made no particular impression on me. I do remember that they were all women who were quite a bit older than my mother— at least one could not drive—and all were very dignified and gracious. I recall nothing of their conversations with my mother, aside from the observation she would later make that the person was, or had once been, a Theosophist. The only other people I ever remember my mother identifying by religion or religious background were several individuals she classified as Spiritualists—again in a whisper. I later learned that there is an historical connection between Spiritualism and Theosophy; both believe in paranormal communication and the founder of Theosophy, Helena Petrovna Blavatsky, first attracted public attention for her study and defense of Spiritualism. Additionally, Theosophy, and to a lesser extent Spiritualism, are expressions of what is called *occultism*, which is derived from the Latin word for *cover* or *conceal*. In terms of religion, occultism refers to religious systems with beliefs in a supernatural reality accessible only to trained initiates who through practice can learn its secrets and thus gain insight and power. At the time of my introduction to living Theosophists, I did not know about the historical affinities between Theosophy and Spiritualism, and I certainly did not know about occultism. All I knew was that Theosophy and Spiritualism were religions that my mother spoke about with a hushed voice—as though it were some sort of secret, something to keep quiet about. Perhaps that was enough.

As we learned in our study of the Seventh-day Adventists and the Jehovah's Witnesses,

America's contribution to the world's religious ecology has been vast indeed. Those two movements alone can arguably be cited as the source for nearly one hundred distinct religious groups. In the case of Christian Science and Theosophy the number is even larger, even though Christian Science and Theosophy themselves are considerably smaller than the Adventists and the Witnesses.

Christian Science can be conservatively recognized as the root tradition of at least fifty-two other distinct religious groups— some of which are themselves quite large. In addition, one of these groups, the International New Thought Alliance (with no formal ties to Christian Science), includes dozens of independent religious communities with no official connection to any of the other groups. Groups related or directly derived from Theosophy number approximately fifteen, but the influence of Theosophy on many other groups far exceeds this number. Included among these other groups are some that could also be classified as New Thought and many (if not most) that identify themselves as part of the contemporary New Age movement. When New Age groups are added to the Theosophy list, which many scholars believe they should be, the numbers would easily swell into the hundreds, if not over a thousand.

Thus, at this point, as we direct our attention to the "metaphysical" religions "made in the U.S.A.," we must offer the same cautions and limitations noted in our chapter on apocalyptic communities. As with the Adventists and Jehovah's Witnesses, our study will be restricted to the root traditions already introduced, their history, primary beliefs, and current manifestations. Certain sectarian expressions will be noted, but the focus will remain on the primary carriers of the systems. Do bear in mind, however, that with Christian Science and Theosophy, their influence on the contemporary religious world, especially the world of new religions, far exceeds their current size today.

The Church of Christ, Scientist

In February 1866, a woman in her mid-forties slipped on a slick patch of ice in Lynn, Massachusetts. The woman's name was Mary Baker Patterson, but history knows her as Mary Baker Eddy (1821–1910), the "discoverer" of Christian Science and the founder of the Church of Christ, Scientist, another distinctively American contribution to the world's religions. Eddy, her followers, and the religion she established would come to be publicly condemned, immersed in scandals, socially vilified, and subjected to countless civil and criminal legal struggles. Her religion would also come to change America and the world, so much so that in 2006, *Atlantic Monthly* named her one of the one hundred most influential Americans of all time.

Why the turmoil? The answer is quite simple, actually. What Mary Baker Eddy did was directly and emphatically challenge the status quo of American culture. In both her religious teachings and in their practical application she called into question the authority of two of America's most venerable institutions—religion and medicine. In matters of religion she challenged both male dominance and the social power of male-dominated religions; in matters of medicine she challenged the belief that medical institutions hold a monopoly on healing. Even more, and perhaps even more fundamentally (and this is often overlooked), Eddy challenged one of the most primary presuppositions of the modern secular West—the material basis of reality. As she affirmed in the oft-quoted "Statement of Being": "There is no life, truth, intelligence, nor substance in matter. . . . Spirit is immortal Truth; matter is mortal error. Spirit is the real and the eternal; matter is the unreal and the temporal. Spirit is God and man [humanity] is His image and likeness."

Eddy came to her beliefs as a result of the "fall on the ice" and the miraculous healing that followed (see sidebar). The details of the healing are quite well known to Christian Scientists. After the fall, Eddy began to suffer extreme discomfort, which may have been internal bleeding. She was confined to bed and some in her company thought her condition was terminal. Shortly thereafter she was given a Bible, perhaps as a Protestant form of extreme unction—she had been raised a New England Congregationalist. Within three days she experienced a sudden healing predicated on her reading the story of one of Jesus' healings (in Matt. 9:1–8) and the realization that "Life in and of Spirit; this being the sole reality of existence." This was her "discovery," that she and all persons were part of God, God was the only life, and that the conscious (mental) realization of this reality would eliminate all adverse physical conditions. She then got dressed and entered the adjoining room to greet her amazed friends—many of whom thought she was soon to die. Mary Baker Eddy had healed herself through the use of her mind. This was the origin of what would soon become Christian Science, and through its success the "mental healing" and New Thought movements, popular religious Idealism, the American "metaphysical" tradition, and arguably the contemporary New Age movement.

Shortly after her healing, Eddy began writing and holding classes on mental healing based on her experiences and the beliefs behind them. In 1875 she published her writings in the book *Science and Health,* which was expanded in 1883 to include biblical interpretations, adding *with Key to the Scriptures* to the original title. Together with The Book of Mormon, *Science and Health with Key to the Scriptures* is certainly the most well known American contribution to the world's religious texts. It is wrong, however, to think that Christian Scientists give *Science and Health* equal standing with the Bible. They do not; instead they understand it as a textbook to be used to better understand the Bible and its meaning in their lives. Today *Science and Health with Key to the*

The Founding Myth of Christian Science

Questions about a religion's origins and formative influences are of great importance to our understanding of how a religion begins and develops. Such questions have been asked about all the major religions of the world, and there is often lively debate about how to best answer these questions. The same is true of younger religions like Christian Science and Theosophy.

It would seem that in the case of these younger communities, and perhaps unlike those that emerged in antiquity, the origins and formative influences would be easier to establish. After all, these groups came on the scene in the modern world, and their emergence was chronicled in both the mainstream press and their own publications. Unfortunately, however, the origins of these groups, like numerous other younger religions, are often fraught with controversy.

The case of Christian Science is a particularly good example of the sorts of disputes that often occur over the origins of new religions. As you may recall, the formative event in the emergence of Christian Science was Mary Baker Eddy's miraculous healing after a fall on a slick patch of ice. It was this healing that supplied the impetus to Eddy's mental healing system, which was soon systematized into the teachings of Christian Science. For this reason Eddy is recognized as the "discoverer" of Christian Science.

The account of Eddy's healing is what scholars of a religion term a *myth*, specifically a formative myth or a myth of origins. When used in this way, the term *myth* refers to a sacred narrative that communicates the truth of life and the world to believers. A myth is a story of powerful and profound meaning to the religious community that accepts it, giving the community a unique account of the truth of existence and each member a sense of being part of this truth. In the case of Eddy's fall on the ice and subsequent healing, Christian Scientists find a foundation for their beliefs and a vivid account of their unique relationship with God.

Soon after Eddy began her religious work, however, the sacred story of Christian Science was challenged. Critics and detractors claimed that her teachings were plagiarized, and she was accused of being a fraud. The dispute continues to this day among scholars trying to understand the origins and formative influences for Christian Science. For the Christian Scientist, however, there is no dispute. Such is the power of myth, and scholars are wise to respect this power even as they dispute the details of its origins.

Scriptures can be found in most bookstores in America and, of course, the numerous Christian Science Reading Rooms around the country.

The movement was officially organized as the Church of Christ, Scientist, in 1879. In 1882 its headquarters were moved from Lynn to Boston, where Eddy opened the Massachusetts Metaphysical College. Then as now, Boston was a major center of religion, medicine, and higher education in America. With the move, Eddy had taken her religion out of the frying pan and into the fire, for her religion challenged all three institutions. Her challenges to religion and medicine have already been noted, but with the founding of the college, she also challenged higher educa-

tion, for her graduates (mostly women in the beginning) were accorded sanction not just as religious professionals but also as healing technicians, entitled to be sanctioned as facilitators of spiritual healing. They were "practitioners"—a title that continues to be recognized as the most important religious office in Christian Science. Response from the Boston intelligentsia was swift. Christian Science was denounced as quackery, its healing methods deemed dangerous, and its "practitioners" seen as charlatans. Undaunted, Mary Baker Eddy continued in her mission to spread the gospel of Christian Science, and the new movement flourished. Today Christian Scientists worldwide see in the "Mother Church," located in the heart of Boston, not only one of the enduring monuments of American-born religion but a testimony to the virtue and success of their Christian tradition; and in "Mrs." (a term of endearment and honor) Eddy they find a figure acknowledged as the revealer of God's truth for this age.

Christian Science Teachings

Christian Scientists of today are strongly committed to the Bible and the teachings of Mrs. Eddy found in *Science and Health with Key to the Scriptures*. In principle and practice, Christian Scientists, like Adventists, consider themselves Protestants, although both they and other Protestants make numerous distinctions between mainline Protestant teachings and those of Christian Science.

Unlike the Adventists, Christian Science observers would find salient differences in Christian Science services and those of typical Protestant churches. They would also find some similarities, including prayer, the singing of hymns, and the use of the Bible. Foremost among the distinctions would be the absence of a preacher since Christian Scientists recognize only the Bible (KJV) and *Science and Health* as the "pastors" of the church. Rather than a traditional sermon, attendees hear readings from the texts of the "pastors," with biblical passages being complemented with passages from *Science and Health*. While this approach may be less dynamic than the traditional sermon delivered by a Protestant preacher, it is the normative and expected structure for Christian Scientists. There are two Readers in each church, and they are not allowed to depart from the words found in the texts of the "pastors." Services are filled with music, both vocal and instrumental solos, and hymns sung by the entire congregation from the *Christian Science Hymnal*. Major services are held on Sunday morning and Wednesday evening. A special feature of Wednesday services are "testimonials," in which believers report successes in life

due to Christian Science principles. These Wednesday testimonials would strike Protestant observers as mini-sermons, and there they might again find common ground.

Christian Scientists accept the divinity of Jesus as the son of God, and they regard his healings as the result of divine law. They accept the virgin birth of Jesus and the Trinity but, since God is the singular reality, they deny that God is "three persons in one." Rather they affirm that Life, Truth, and Love (their trinity) are the "triune Principle of God." Jesus is recognized as the exemplar of Christian Science, and he is often referred to as Master and Way-shower. Jesus does indeed "save," but he saves through his teachings, which all Christian Scientists are directed to follow.

Departing from the mainstream of the Christian tradition, Scientists do not believe that sin is elemental to the human condition; rather, it is seen as an error based on the belief that there is some other reality besides Divine Mind, which is a commonly used synonym for God. Others include Spirit, Principle, and Truth. In Christian Scientists' belief, God is the only reality, which leads them to the conclusion that matter is an illusion. Coming to the right understanding of the singular and all-pervasive reality of God frees one from sin (error) and its consequences—decay, sickness, and death. The true nature of humanity is spiritual and perfect, the "image" of God, and it is the work of the Christian Scientist to discover and express this true nature.

Aside from their unique beliefs about God, Jesus, and sin, the major areas of distinction between Christian Scientists and other Christians concern the proper interpretation of the Bible and the status of the material world. In these areas, Christian Science has been both celebrated and condemned. Its supporters have seen it as a new revelation while its critics have rejected it as a "dangerous cult."

Since the publication of *Science and Health with Key to the Scriptures*, Christian Scientists have recognized that the Bible is not a literal document, but rather a symbolic text designed to direct and guide individuals in spiritual matters. Using this method of interpretation, Christian Scientists find the Bible consistent with the doctrines of their faith. This approach offers a contemporary updating of a method of Biblical interpretation that had largely vanished since the rise of Protestant "literalism," although it was a common practice in the early church. Interpreting the Bible as a symbolic or metaphorical document is technically termed "allegorical"; and largely due to the pioneering work of Christian Science, several contemporary Christian groups interpret the Bible following this method, which they refer to as "metaphysical interpretation."

Christian Science Healing and Controversy

Probably the greatest controversies regarding Christian Science are related to its stance on medical treatment. This position is often misunderstood and misrepresented. In order to properly grasp the Christian Science position on medicine, one must first understand its most fundamental teachings about the nature of reality itself. In these teachings, Christian Science distinguishes itself from the majority of Americans—religious or not.

Simply put, Christian Scientists believe that God (Spirit, Divine Mind, Principle Truth) is the only reality and matter is its antithesis. Matter is thus the diametric opposite of God. Rather than recognizing matter as the basis of reality as do most people, Christian Scientists believe it to be unreal and belief in its reality as the most fundamental of errors. Such a belief is the primary source of all other errors, such as sickness, decay, and death. For Scientists, humans are the image of God and so we too are spirit, not matter; the great goal for the human race then is to overcome bondage to the illusory ("hypnotic") reality of matter. Sickness and death are consequences of the bondage to matter, and so healing becomes a demonstration of the truth of spirit over the illusion of matter.

Spiritual healing as practiced by Christian Scientists is "scientific" in that it is based on the application of universal law. In short, that law is that God alone is real and anything that is not of God (such as sickness) is unreal. Thus to facilitate healing, the Christian Scientist seeks to reach a clear understanding of the reality of God, and with the understanding comes the elimination of any specific ill. Success thus depends on the degree of the believer's spiritual understanding.

The problem with conventional medical care from the standpoint of Christian Science is the premise of medicine itself. Rather than God, medicine recognizes the opposite of God (matter) as the basis of reality, and it then reinforces the error by using material means, most notably drugs and surgery, to try to correct the error. The result is that the belief in the reality of matter becomes even more intense—even when medical treatment is successful.

For this reason committed Christian Scientists reject medical care, preferring instead scientific prayer, which they believe is the method used by Jesus in his healings. Practitioners often assist in the prayer activity by working to achieve the spiritual understanding necessary to overcome the particular physical challenge. It is important to mention that although spiritual healing is the ideal in Christian Science and all devout followers strive to follow it in practice, no one is condemned or ostracized for using medical care. For most Christian Scientists, medical care is simply not an option. While choosing this method over conventional medical care may seem surprising to outsiders, for many believers it is both a matter of faith and the most responsible action they can take.

Scientists are firmly convinced that their process is not only effective but proven. They have carefully documented and published accounts of thousands of instances where persons with medically incurable conditions have been healed through Christian Science.

Early examples of such testimonials are published in *Science and Health*. Moreover, they make a compelling argument when pointing out that medical treatment is by no means universally successful but the cultural evaluation of medicine is measured by its successes while the evaluation of Christian Science is usually measured by its failures.

Christian Science's Cultural Impact

Christian Science does not publish membership statistics, but indications are that its numbers are declining. Also, its members are getting older, with fewer converts and young families joining the movement. The Mother Church has experienced a serious financial crunch in recent years. Like the Seventh-day Adventist Church, however, the impact of the Church of Christ, Scientist, on American life has been distinctive and its presence today remains significant. While most Americans may not know much about Christian Science, its churches are found throughout America and the world. Reports from 2003 listed approximately two thousand congregations throughout the world, but some more recent estimates put the number as low as 1,000, with venerable Christian Science congregations closing their doors almost on a monthly basis. Since 1908 it has published *The Christian Science Monitor*, one of the nation's most highly respected daily newspapers, though in its centennial year of 2008 its financial difficulties led the *Monitor* to announce that it would cease being a print publication and become available only online. Other publications include *The Herald of Christian Science* (published in thirteen languages and braille), *The Christian Science Sentinel*, which features healing testimonials, and *The Christian Science Journal*. These and other church publications are made available at Christian Science Reading Rooms, found in most American cities.

Often found in busy downtown districts, these Reading Rooms function as appropriate symbols of Christian Science's presence in American culture. Serving as both centers of passive evangelism and shrines to an alternative vision of reality in the midst of our materialist culture, they reveal the success of this American-born religion and house its texts that quietly but emphatically deny the status quo. From the outside these inviting centers may not seem unlike the offices and retail centers around them, but inside the very basis of the surrounding culture is called into doubt; for there one finds books and periodicals that tell of a Christianity that denies the reality of sin and a science that denies the reality of matter. For many Americans such notions are neither Christian nor science; for believers, however, they not only are both, but Truth cannot be otherwise.

The greatest contribution of Christian Science to both American religious life and the world's religions can be found in the new vistas of religious expression it pioneered and first developed. From its beginnings, Christian Science has challenged traditional notions about the authority of medicine in healing and it has done so in the name of religion. Even more important, however, is its challenge to Christianity itself. Not only did Christian Science offer new interpretations of traditional Christian doctrines, such as humanity's innate sinfulness and the salvational role of Jesus, it also offered new ways of *doing* religion. Its pastors are books, its "sermons" are readings, its missionaries are periodicals, and its religious leaders are never ordained.

Foremost among these new ways was the support for female leadership, for this was one of the first major religious traditions in modern times officially founded and led by a woman, a woman who consciously and emphatically empowered other women to be religious leaders, a woman who established all the doctrines of a church that has endured the test of time, and a woman whose great work, *Science and Health with Key to the Scriptures*, is read today throughout the world. Since her work, other women have founded religious groups, some quite successful, and a number of traditional religions have allowed women to hold positions of religious authority. While these latter developments cannot be traced solely to the work of Mrs. Eddy, it was she who had the daring to do it first and the brilliance to do it well.

The Theosophical Tradition

In 1875, the same year that Mary Baker Eddy published the first edition of *Science and Health*, just down the road from Boston, in New York City, two unlikely partners founded the Theosophical Society. The unlikely partners were a Russian emigrant who had traveled the world, Helena Petrovna Blavatsky (1831–1891), and a former military officer who had fought in the American Civil War, Henry Steel Olcott. Drawn together due to a common interest in Spiritualism, Blavatsky and Olcott soon realized that the American public yearned to learn more not only about Spiritualism but also about the occult tradition and its mystical secrets of wisdom and power. Although Olcott played a major role in the movement, and the group's counsel, William Q. Judge, figured prominently in the development of its American branch, it was Blavatsky's charismatic style and her vivid expositions of an alternative to traditional Western religions that put Theosophy on the religious map of the world, bringing occultism out of the shadows and introducing it to mainstream culture.

At its founding, the Theosophical Society was essentially an intellectual salon, which met in Blavatsky's apartment to discuss esoteric religious beliefs, enjoy her company, and witness her displays of occult powers. Among the early members were Abner Doubleday, the inventor of baseball.[4] The Society initially affirmed three general purposes:

1. To form a nucleus of the Universal Brotherhood of Humanity without distinction of race, creed, sex, caste, or color

2. To encourage the study of Comparative Religion, Philosophy, and Science

3. To investigate the unexplained laws of nature and the powers latent in man

In terms of what it would become these aims appear rather modest, although it must be remembered that the comparative study of religion was still in its earliest academic stages at this time and psychic and occult realities ("unexplained laws of nature and powers latent in man") were hardly the stuff of popular inquiry and discussion. The first hint of the greater implications of Theosophy would come two years after the Society's rather inconspicuous birth. This was when Blavatsky's first book, *Isis Unveiled*, was published. The massive two-volume text offered an interpretation of the Western esoteric tradition with insights into the Kabbalah and the mystery religions of ancient Egypt and Greece. It is notable that the text makes few references to reincarnation, a belief that figures prominently in the later development of Theosophy. Even more notable, however, was Blavatsky's assertion that she had been guided in its composition by a spiritually advanced being who served as her spiritual master, or "mahatma." Such Masters became an important part of Theosophical belief. Blavatsky reported that she had been in contact with these Masters since her twenties and it was they who were the inspiration behind her writings. One common method of communication was through written messages left for Blavatsky in a special cabinet in her lodgings.

Although America would soon prove ready enough for Blavatsky's teachings, in 1878 she and Olcott traveled to India, stopping briefly in England to establish a branch of Theosophy there. They left the American work in the hands of Doubleday and Judge. Rather than traveling to Asia to spread a Western religious message, which had been the typical Christian model until that time, Blavatsky and Olcott went East in search of wisdom. The couple stayed in Bombay for a time but soon moved to Adyar, where they established a Theosophical center and an international headquarters. They also began a periodical, *The Theosophist*, which promoted study of

Hinduism and its sacred language, Sanskrit. Among those attracted to their work was Max Müller, the celebrated philologist and one of the pioneers in the academic study of religion. Müller praised them for assisting in the development of scholarship on Sanskrit but denounced them for supporting Hindu superstitions by giving esoteric meanings to the "Hindu scriptures."[5]

The people of India had no such reservations, and the couple were welcomed wherever they traveled. Not only did they celebrate Hinduism and promote the study of its sacred language, their behavior stood in marked contrast to that of the British colonial officials, who were often demeaning of India's cultural traditions. As noted earlier, no less a figure than Mahatma Gandhi found in Theosophy a powerful inspiration to return to the teachings of Hinduism. Gandhi himself was criticized by some of his coreligionists for distorting Hindu scriptures for much the same reason that Müller had criticized Olcott and Blavatsky; that is, for giving esoteric meanings to the sacred texts of Hinduism—especially the Bhagavad Gita.

Müller's criticisms of Theosophy were insignificant, however, compared to the devastating scandal that would soon engulf the movement. In 1884 Blavatsky and Olcott hastened to England to try to resolve problems related to the movement's first schism. In their absence the scandal erupted. Specifically, Blavatsky was accused of fraud by persons she had appointed to oversee activities at the Adyar headquarters. It was their charge that Blavatsky had directed them to "produce letters [from the Masters] fraudulently."[6] The claims were investigated by a representative from the recently formed (1882) Society for Psychical Research (SPR), which concluded that the accusations were true. In short, its findings concluded that there were no spiritual Masters, only a spiritual hoax perpetrated by Blavatsky. To this day supporters of Theosophy argue that the investigation was flawed, although in subsequent years some of Blavatsky's colleagues substantiated the findings. A century later, in

1986, the SPR "published an article refuting the portion of the report that dealt with the handwriting analysis," and further declared that the original report "did not represent the corporate opinion of the Society."[7] Still, the damage had been done and it seemed that as quickly as Theosophy had emerged it was in danger of collapse.

Turmoil and controversy swirled around the movement in the wake of the SPR investigation. This would be a common feature of the movement through the 1930s. Blavatsky remained the chief visionary until her death in 1891, her popularity seemingly unaffected by the charges of fraud. In 1888 she published her most famous work, *The Secret Doctrine*, which is generally recognized as the fullest expression of Theosophy's beliefs and arguably the most significant text of the modern occult movement. Blavatsky also remained active in the organizational development of Theosophy. In the last years of her life, she and Olcott came to an agreement that the ideals of Theosophy would be best advanced if Olcott continued to serve as its official head and Blavatsky led the elite Esoteric Section, whose purpose was to work closely with the Masters to advance the goals of spiritual evolution. Chief among these goals was preparation for an avatar, an incarnation of one of the Masters (Lord Maitreya), who would initiate a New Age of spiritual growth and earthly harmony.

When Blavatsky died in 1891, the movement was again rocked by controversy and schism. There were struggles for power between different branches of the society and within the various national organizations. The primary struggle was between the Esoteric Section, led by a young Blavatsky protégé, Annie Besant, and the American branch, led by Judge. In 1895 Judge declared independence from the Adyar headquarters, forming the Theosophical Society of America. Schisms occurred in other national branches and, again, it appeared the movement was in the process of disintegration.

Remarkably, the movement again survived the crisis, largely due to the work of

Besant, who assumed the presidency of the Society in 1907. Under her leadership the rival branches were brought into harmony and Theosophy began a process of expansion to all parts of the globe. The author of more than three hundred books and pamphlets, Besant furthered the occult dimension of Theosophy and together with a colleague (C. W. Leadbeater) claimed to have discovered the avatar of the New Age. This was the agent of the secret hierarchy that Blavatsky had been expecting; a young Indian boy, named Jiddu Krishnamurti. The advent of the Theosophical avatar was a worldwide sensation, at least within the alternative religious community, and membership in the Society soared. Besant founded the Order of the Star of the East as an umbrella organization to publicize Krishnamurti's activities, and she herself toured the world preaching about his mission and the coming of the New Age. As had happened before, however, the success spawned by the Krishnamurti sensation was short-lived, for in 1929 Krishnamurti renounced the claims that Besant had been making about him and disbanded the Star of the East. This event, coupled with renewed sectarian squabbles and the international depression of the 1930s, led to steep declines in membership. When Besant died in 1933, Theosophy had become less of a worldwide movement and more of a loose association of various organizations and individuals. It has remained so to this day, yet curiously, despite its lack of institutional size and power, the teachings of Theosophy continue to influence spiritual seekers around the world—many (perhaps most) of whom have probably never heard of the movement or its founder, the magus of contemporary occultism, Helena Blavatsky.

Theosophical Teachings, Practices, and Cultural Impact

As noted earlier, and like Christian Science, the importance of Theosophy to the world's religious ecology far exceeds its current size today. And even more so than Christian Science, its impact on religion and culture as a whole is best measured in terms of its influence on other groups rather than its own success as a religious movement. Although Theosophy today can claim a membership of, at best, a few tens of thousands, it can be properly cited as the direct or most significant source for over one hundred religious groups. The key to its influence can be traced to the appeal of Blavatsky's vision of an alternative reality and the movement's capacity to disseminate her teachings far beyond its immediate membership. From the vast and often quite technical body of Theosophy's teachings, certain major principles emerge. These will be the focus here. And while these are certainly primary elements of Theosophy's particular brand of metaphysical religion they are also central components of a host of other groups that have no formal ties to the movement. Thus, the selected Theosophical teachings presented here tell us not only about the beliefs of Theosophy but also a large collection of other religions for which it is the root tradition.

The Inner Quest and Personal Spirituality

Turning now to the teachings and practices themselves, it must be observed immediately that unlike other new religions we have studied in this text (Mormonism, Adventism, Jehovah's Witnesses, and Christian Science), the primary doctrines of Theosophy cannot be clearly or easily related to Christianity and most Theosophists would not identify themselves as Christians. Additionally, the ritual expression of Theosophy tends to be highly individualized and quite personal. While several groups derived from Theosophy do engage in formal rituals, individuals typically follow their own unique path to spiritual mastery. *The Secret Doctrine* supplies the guiding vision and supplemental texts suggest the general contours, but it is really up to the individual to internalize the teachings and develop an openness to the higher realities that lay back of and beyond the ordinary material world of time and space. These features should not lead one to think that Theosophists are escapists or antisocial. Most are active members of their communities, holding jobs, engaging in routine commerce, and entirely conversant with the social world around them. They may even attend religious services of more traditional religions, like my mother's friends. If possible, Theosophists will gather with others at a Theosophical center, called a lodge. There they will most likely visit with one another, listen to lectures on occult and esoteric subjects, and engage in dialogue and discussions. Still, the primary religious activity is not public, but very private, and best thought of as occurring in the consciousness of the individual. This emphasis on the individual spiritual quest has become widely popular today, and a vast array of new religions recognize it as one's primary religious activity. Needless to say, such an emphasis also has great appeal for a significant number of Americans who do not identify with any formal religion but nevertheless engage in a form of personal spirituality.

Universal Truth and Syncretism

As noted above, Theosophy does not identify itself as Christian; in fact, it identifies with no other existing religious tradition. While rejecting linkage with any specific religion, Theosophists would readily observe that the inner truth of all religions is essentially the same. It is this inner truth that they seek to discover, and which they believe the teachings of Theosophy disclose. They might further observe that the various creeds, laws, and dogmas of institutional religion limit the discovery of the truth of existence and foster discord and strife. As a corollary to this general belief in the essential unity of religious truth is the syncretistic character of Theosophical teachings. Like many new religions that followed it, the Theosophical worldview melds together elements derived from several different traditions. The extent of syncretism in Theosophy is remarkable,

and only a few of the features can be noted here. The dominant characteristics (reincarnation, karma, spiritual evolution, and a hierarchy of spiritual Masters) are derived from Hinduism, Buddhism, and ancient mystery religions. But major figures from virtually all the world religions are incorporated into the Theosophical system—most typically as spiritual Masters, such as those who communicated with Blavatsky and later other Theosophists. Prior to their initiation, the Masters had worked through the rigors of spiritual evolution and acquired power over the material world and its laws of space and time. Included in their number are persons like Confucius, Moses, Jesus, and the Buddha, to name a few.[8] The belief in spiritual Masters such as these is common in many New Age religions.

Reincarnation, Karma, and Spiritual Evolution

In our chapters on Hinduism and Buddhism we introduced the concepts of karma and reincarnation. Long before Westerners became interested in Hinduism and Buddhism as religious alternatives to traditional Western religions, Blavatsky and her fellow Theosophists had introduced and widely popularized the doctrines of reincarnation and karma. Again, guided by the syncretism of its system, theosophy explains that great religious leaders, already known to Westerners, had been reincarnated numerous times before they reached their exalted status as prophets, saviors, visionaries, and saints. Over these lifetimes, the future Masters worked through the law of karma and pursued their spiritual evolution through occult studies until they finally became part of the divine hierarchy that rules and guides the evolution of the earth. Moreover, the same process that the Masters followed is open to anyone with the courage and persistence to learn the secret mysteries articulated by Theosophy. We are, after all, each a "divine spark" and ultimately a part of God, typically called the Solar Logos in

Theosophy. The aim of spiritual evolution is, then, to reunify with God—to bring the "spark" back to the flame, so to speak. At the point of mastery, the individual no longer needs to reincarnate (as with moksha in Hinduism or nirvana in Buddhism) and may join the lodge of the spiritual Masters, called the Great White Brotherhood. While not all New Age groups share a belief in Masters, most believe in reincarnation, karma, and spiritual evolution, and they purport to supply their participants with the secret doctrines to hasten spiritual evolution.

The New Age and Beyond

Toward the end of her life Blavatsky came to the realization that a primary mission of the Esoteric Section was to work to prepare the way for the incarnation of one of the Masters. The expected Master was Lord Maitreya (who in traditional Buddhism is the Buddha of the future), and he would usher in a period of accelerated spiritual advance for the human race. Again, employing the syncretistic approach, Theosophy explained that Maitreya had previously incarnated as Jesus. The linkage of the Buddha of the future with the Jesus of the past was a particularly dynamic example of religious syncretism, for not only did it bring together two major savior figures, it also allowed for a much closer association of Theosophy with Christian apocalypticism. As we know, interest in the advent of the Master accelerated in the work of Blavatsky's heir, Annie Besant, who not only realized that Maitreya was soon to appear but actually recognized him in the young Indian boy, Krishnamurti. Although Krishnamurti turned out not to be the avatar (and left the movement), the belief in the imminent appearance of a Master persisted in the occult community, especially in groups that broke away from Theosophy or developed as part of the New Age.

In fact, the New Age movement proper is best traced to the work of a former Theosophist who reaffirmed and widely promoted the incarnation of Maitreya and the initiation of a period of enhanced spiritual development for humanity. This was Alice A. Bailey. Among her numerous books, the most significant in this regard are *Discipleship in the New Age* (vol. 1, 1944; vol. 2, 1955) and *The Reappearance of the Christ* (1948). Like Blavatsky and Besant, Bailey's books were produced in connection with a Master, and much that she and the Master had to say differed little from her illustrious predecessors. Bailey, however, had an evangelical fervor and put great emphasis on the need to form religious groups to hasten the incarnation of Maitreya. Moreover, she emphatically identified Maitreya as the Christ and warned that the current "planetary condition . . . proved to be so catastrophic in nature"[9] that it required his immediate return. In her urgent tone, evangelical fervor, and strong identification of Christ as the avatar of the New Age, Bailey's mission took on something of an apocalyptic character more often associated with Christian groups. For a time her work and organizations (most notably the Arcane School) were quite popular, and groups inspired by her writings continue to thrive throughout the world. More important, the vision she articulated has spawned a large assortment of other groups and inspired countless prophets of the New Age—many of whom may know nothing of Bailey or her work.

Bailey and the Arcane School are, thus, representative of Theosophy's second incarnation, the contemporary New Age movement. In fact, Bailey's writings and organizations can be seen as the definitive tap root of this movement and its historically unique marriage of occultism and apocalypticism. That Bailey may not be known to many New Age enthusiasts hardly diminishes her influence on the movement.

Today Theosophy and the groups directly related to it are largely unknown to most Americans even as key elements of their worldview seep ever further into American culture and younger, more dynamic expressions of occultism find greater favor with the public. While the relatively slight success of

Theosophy as a religious movement and its very low public profile today may lead one to deem the movement of little consequence, such a conclusion would be off the mark for it would overlook the impact of the Theosophical *tradition* on other religious groups and America's religious sensibilities.

This is not to say that there are not still plenty of practicing Theosophists or that the movement has reduced its outreach. If anything, Theosophical groups are probably publishing more than they ever have before and membership may be increasing slightly, although there are not vast numbers of Theosophists and, for that matter, there never have been. In fact, the movement never had more than twenty or thirty thousand members.[10] Still, at one time, it was easier to find Theosophy itself. There were more members of the various groups and local lodges. Blavatsky's books were much more popular than they are today. And the movement was more attractive to the media, albeit generally for its scandals, controversies, and sensational claims. In the early twentieth century it established a major alternative religious community in Point Loma, California. It supported the independence movement in India. Blavatsky's work inspired Gandhi, and Olcott is still revered in Sri Lanka for his promotion of Buddhism. That it is less well known today does not mitigate its historical significance but rather suggests, again, that its importance as a movement is something less than it once was. It still lives on, but its greatest vitality today is not to be found in its lodges, its publications, or even its revered texts, such as *The Secret Doctrine* or *Isis Revealed*. Thus, rather than looking to its outer forms and expressions, we must look elsewhere to find its vitality.

But where? Quite simply to its ideas and its vivid depiction of an alternative, occult-metaphysical vision of religion and life. Here the cultural impact and enduring vitality of this movement is decidedly found. And, in an important sense, this is especially fitting, since, after all, Theosophy has never been much interested in material reality but always what lay behind and beyond it—in the metaphysical and occult realms. That Theosophy was the first movement in America to illuminate these realms in a way that fascinated and attracted large segments of the American public is notable enough. What makes it important, however, is that the fascination has not ceased and today is more pronounced than ever. At the beginning of this section we considered Theosophy's role in popularizing reincarnation and karma. These are but two of numerous new and alternative religious concepts that first gained a foothold in American culture due to Theosophy. All around us we see the signs of its enduring presence.

When businesspeople consult their horoscope in the daily paper, most do not know that Theosophy helped introduce astrology to America in the 1890s. When TV airs the Psychic Friends Network, and people around the country dial up a psychic guide, few callers know that Helena Blavatsky was the person who popularized psychic phenomena. When we hear media reports of explorations in search of the sunken continent of Atlantis (or even its discovery!), the reports usually do not tell us that it was Blavatksy who first called America's public attention to the presence of that lost world—and other sunken continents as well. Of the millions who have read James Redfield's *The Celestine Prophecy*, which was on the *New York Times* bestseller list for over one hundred and fifty weeks in the 1990s, how many know that the spiritual odysseys of his characters take them into the same occult realms that Theosophy had begun to map a century before? And how many readers realize that the underpinnings of Rhonda Byrne's more recent runaway best seller *The Secret* can be traced back to some of Blavatsky's esoteric ideas? How far, then, does the cultural impact of Theosophy extend? It reaches from the musical *Hair* and its hit song, "Age of Aquarius," to Shirley MacLaine telling us about her past lives; from *A Course in Miracles* to the local music store's wide selection of New Age tapes and CDs; from hundreds of speakers delighting thousands of audiences on the New Age lecture circuit to reports that Ronald Reagan's wife had consulted astrologers in the White House; and finally from countless New Age religious groups, communes, churches, temples, and bookstores springing up around the country to the lives of average Americans who consider themselves more than physical beings but rather spiritual seekers in search of a divine reality that transcends this world. It is in expressions and pursuits like these that Theosophy lives on in today's America, its doctrines far less secret than ever before and its occult beliefs quite at home in an American culture where everyone belongs.

WHAT METAPHYSICAL RELIGIONS MADE IN THE U.S.A. TELL US

Like my first encounters with Seventh-day Adventism and Jehovah's Witnesses, my first experiences with Christian Science and Theosophy are part of the story of my own life, part of my growing up in America. They too told me new things about myself, my family, and the religious diversity that is such a natural part of our country, which affirms freedom of religion as an ideal.

Unlike my experiences with Adventism and Jehovah's Witnesses, I have come to learn that while most people discovered religious diversity at a young age, my childhood encounters with Christian Science and Theosophy were rather exceptional. There were not many Christian Scientists and Theosophists around at that time, and there are probably fewer now. And while today you are more likely than ever to have the happy opportunity to experience religious diversity at a young age, the chances that such an experience will bring you into contact with members of either of these movements are rather slight. On the other hand, you are quite likely to meet people who belong to religious groups that share many of the same beliefs as Christian Science or Theosophy. Perhaps this will be a member of a New

Thought center or a New Age meditation group, a student of *A Course in Miracles* or a member of the Universal Foundation for Better Living, a person who attends a Religious Science International church or a participant in the work of the White Eagle Lodge. Do not be surprised if when this happens you find their beliefs quite different and maybe a little strange, but remember they are just as committed to their beliefs as you are to yours—and maybe they find your beliefs a little strange as well.

As we have seen with other religions we have studied, when we first encounter beliefs and practices that we know little about they often seem strange, outlandish, and even threatening. In this regard, my observations at the close of the chapter on apocalyptic communities might be reviewed again, especially those concerning the rewards and dangers of encountering religious diversity. The rewards of such encounters are growth in understanding and cultural sophistication. The dangers are those associated with bias, fear, and suspicion of those who are different. It is to our advantage to learn how to maximize the rewards and minimize the risks, but doing so may be challenging.

This is certainly true in the case of new and emerging religions like Christian Science, Theosophy, and groups derived from both. By their very newness these religions seem strikingly different from those that are already well established, especially our own. Even more challenging may be encountering religions that are not only new but also relatively small, since their small number of adherents may signal an even greater degree of difference from the rest of us. This, then, is the context of our encounter with Christian Science, Theosophy, and all the many religious groups that are similar to them. Not only are these metaphysical religions new, they are also quite small compared to the other religions we are studying in this text. For this reason, perhaps these religions are the very most important ones for us to learn about since of all the religions we are considering in *World Religions in America* these may seem the most different from what most Americans consider "normal." Yet these religions are not only firmly rooted in American culture, they are also American in origin and have been nurtured by our nation's freedom, which fosters and safeguards the right of all people to practice their religion freely. And so as we seek to better understand Christian Science, Theosophy, and similar groups, we might indeed find something more than just another religion that is different from our own. We might find yet again, and perhaps more clearly than ever before, that, as Jacob Neusner states in the Introduction, "in America, there is no 'other.' Everyone is one of us."

Notes

1. Aidan A. Kelly, "Reincarnation and Karma," in *New Age Encyclopedia*, ed. J. Gordon Melton (Detroit: Gale, 1990), 384.
2. William James, *The Varieties of Religious Experience* (New York: New American Library, Mentor, 1958), 88–89. First published in 1902.
3. Martin Green, *Gandhi: Voice of a New Age Revolution* (New York: Continuum, 1993), 100.
4. Robert S. Ellwood and Harry B. Partin, *Religious and Spiritual Groups in Modern America*, 2d ed. (Englewood Cliffs, N.J.: Prentice Hall, 1988), 61.
5. J. Stillson Judah, *The History and Philosophy of the Metaphysical Movements in America* (Philadelphia: Westminster Press, 1967), 98.
6. Ellwood and Partin, 62.
7. J. Gordon Melton et. al., *New Age Almanac* (New York: Visible Ink Press, 1991), 17.
8. See Judah, 106.
9. Alice A. Bailey, *The Reappearance of the Christ*, as cited in Judah, 126.
10. Ellwood and Partin, 74.

STUDY QUESTIONS

1. Discuss the importance of idealism to Christian Science beliefs and practices.
2. Discuss the importance of Masters to the beliefs and practices of Theosophy.
3. Compare and contrast Christian Science and Theosophy. Be sure to take into consideration the roles played by the founders of these groups, their relationship with American society, and the keys to their success.
4. Why do you think Christian Science and Theosophy have faced opposition from established forms of Christianity and the media?
5. What gives Theosophy a more "international" flavor and Christian Science a more American flavor?
6. Why do you think Christian Science and Theosophy are so small today?
7. Comment on the role of Jesus in the two movements. In what ways do they reveal understandings of Jesus that are similar to traditional Christian understandings? In what ways do their understandings differ from traditional Christian understandings?
8. In what ways are these two religions "made in the U.S.A." similar to religions that have come to America from other cultures? In what ways are they different? How has being "made in the U.S.A." been an advantage to these groups and how has it been a disadvantage?
9. Christian Science and Theosophy were both founded by women. Comment on the significance of this fact in light of the other religions you have studied and the observations made in chapter 20, "Religion and Women in America."

ESSAY TOPICS

Catholic and Protestant Reactions to Christian Science Churches and Theosophical Lodges

Role of Publications in the Growth and Development of Christian Science and Theosophy

Personal Experience with Christian Scientists and Theosophers Reveal the "Rewards and Dangers" of Encounters with Religious Diversity

The Lives of Mary Baker Eddy and Helena Petrovna Blavatsky

Professional and Personal Challenges of Christian Scientists and Theosophers

The Cultural and Religious Impact of Christian Science and Theosophy

WORD EXPLORATION

The following words play significant roles in any discussion of religion and society in America and are worth careful reflection and discussion.

Idealism	Mental Healing	Testimonials
Divine Mind	New Thought	Allegorical Interpretation
The New Age Movement	Masters	Power of Positive Thinking
Syncretism	Occultism	Practitioner
Maitreya	Spiritual Evolution	The Great White
Jesus as "Way-Shower"	Reading Rooms	Brotherhood

FOR FURTHER READING

Albanese, Catherine L. *A Republic of Mind and Spirit: A Cultural History of American Metaphysical Religion*. New Haven, Conn.: Yale University Press, 2007.

Blavatsky, Helena Petrovna. *The Secret Doctrine: The Synthesis of Science, Religion, and Philosophy*. 3 vols. Wheaton, Ill.: Theosophical Publishing House, 1978. (Orig. pub. 1888).

Campbell, Bruce E. *Ancient Wisdom Revived: A History of the Theosophical Movement*. Berkeley: University of California Press, 1980.

Eddy, Mary Baker. *Science and Health with Key to the Scriptures*. Boston: First Church of Christ Scientist, 1991. (Orig. pub. 1875 as *Science and Health*).

Ellwood, Robert S. *Theosophy: A Modern Expression of the Wisdom of the Ages*. Wheaton, Ill.: Theosophical Publishing House, 1986.

Gomes, Michael. *The Dawning of the Theosophical Movement*. Wheaton, Ill.: Theosophical Publishing House, 1987.

Gottschalk, Stephen. *The Emergence of Christian Science in American Religious Life*. Berkeley: University of California Press, 1973.

Melton, J. Gordon. "The Case of Edward J. Arens and the Distortion of the History of New Thought." *Journal of the Society for the Study of Metaphysical Religion*, 2, no. 1 (1996):13–29.

Schoepflin, Rennie B. *Christian Science on Trial: Religious Healing in America*. Baltimore: Johns Hopkins University Press, 2003.

WEB SITES

http://www.tfccs.com
  Church of Christ, Scientist Web site

http://www.spirituality.com
  Christian Science Web site with selections from *Science and Health With Key to the Scriptures*

http://www.theosociety.org
  The Theosophical Society (America) Web site

http://www.blavatsky.net/blavatsky/blavatsky-links.htm
  Books by H.P. Blavatsky online

http://www.marybakereddylibrary.org
  Mary Baker Eddy Library with biography, selected texts, and photos

15

New Thought: A Quintessentially American Religion

DELL DeCHANT

1849   Emma Curtis Hopkins born
1879   Christian Science founded
1885   Hopkins's ministry in Chicago begins
1888   Divine Science founded
1889   Hopkins's first ordination service; Unity founded
1895   Hopkins's seminary in Chicago closes
1902   William James's *The Varieties of Religious Experience* published
1915   International New Thought Alliance founded
1920   Hopkins's *High Mysticism* published
1925   Hopkins dies
1927   Religious Science founded
1954   Religious Science schism (United Church of Religious Science and Religious Science, International)
1966   Association of Unity Churches established
1974   Universal Foundation for Better Living founded
1992   Television talk show host Oprah Winfrey promotes New Thought leader Marianne Williamson's book *A Return to Love*, which becomes a national bestseller
2006   Book and movie *The Secret* capitalize on New Thought ideas, including the Law of Attraction

For most New Thought participants, their current religious community is not the one into which they were born and in which they grew up. It is probably not the community in which they experienced their own rites of passage and attended weddings and funerals for others. It is not their parents' religion.

This is not just because New Thought is a new religion, although it has been around for only a little over a century, having been founded near the close of the nineteenth century. It has more to do with the type of people who discover New Thought and find hope and empowerment in its teachings.

Folks who belong to New Thought communities (often called churches or centers) typically become involved only after having tried other religions—often quite a few. Many of them would probably identify to some degree with the Annie Savoy character in the popular 1988 baseball movie, *Bull Durham*. In her famous address at the opening of the film, Annie tells us,

> I've tried all of the major religions and most of the minor ones. I've worshiped Buddha, Allah, Brahma, Vishnu, Siva, trees, mushrooms, and Isadora Duncan.
>
> I know things. For instance, there are 108 beads in a Catholic rosary and there are 108 stitches in a baseball. When I learned that I gave Jesus a chance. But it just didn't work out between us. The Lord laid too much guilt on me.
>
> I prefer metaphysics to theology. . . .[1]

Now, aside from the fact that Annie Savoy chose the "church of baseball" rather than a more typical religion, she sounds quite a bit like New Thought participants. Most of them have tried a wide array of religions, including many not historically found in America. Most began their religious lives as members of a Christian denomination. Some were very devout; others, less so; some, not at all. In this regard they are a typical cross-section of the American population.

Where they differ is that they did not stay in their original community. They also did not become religious dropouts or atheists. Instead, they became religious seekers.

When you get to know New Thought participants you will find that by and large they are people who do not like negativity, fear, and pessimism. And, like Annie Savoy, they especially do not like guilt. New Thought believers often cite the absence of teachings that promote guilt as a major reason for their involvement. Many come from traditions in which they report having felt burdened by guilt. For them, New Thought is a breath of fresh air—a reviving inspiration.

They come from all walks of life, all religious backgrounds, all races and ethnicities. The majority are middle-class whites, and there is a higher percentage of entrepreneurs in the movement than in the population as a whole. Above all, these folks have thought about religion and in many instances tried more than a few. Like Annie Savoy, they want metaphysics, not theology. They want the mystical quest, not the formal catechism; they want spirituality, not religion; they want the good in all religions, not an exclusive and exclusionary set of teachings. They want a religion that does good things for them, not a religion that calls them to service or sacrifice. In short, as noted previously, they seek to be uplifted and empowered, and for that they will sacrifice tradition, formal doctrines, comfort, and consolation. They know what they are looking for because they have shopped around America's religious marketplace and become quite aware of what they do *not* want in their religion; and like Annie Savoy, they have tried enough to know what they do want.

The Annie Savoy character is representative of the sort of person who finds, or more likely stumbles upon, New Thought. Such persons are not uncommon in America today. You may have had such feelings yourself or known others who have; perhaps one of your relatives, or even your parents or grandparents—especially if they are members of the "baby boom generation." In a study of the religious inclinations of the boomer generation (persons born between 1946 and 1964), sociologist Wade Clark Roof coined the term "seekers" for those who pursue religious experiences of a different order from those of their childhood.[2]

It is certainly true that the generation that entered young adulthood from the mid-1960s to the mid-1980s was exposed to a much wider array of religious options than those of earlier generations. During this period, American culture became aware of a number of new religious communities. Many originated prior to this period, but during these decades they became widely recognized and rather well established, despite their decidedly nontraditional beliefs and practices. Some of the more recognizable of these groups are Scientology, the Nation of Islam, EST, Neopaganism, Transcendental Meditation, the Unification Church, the Children of God, and Rajneeshism. Perhaps most prominent was a collection of groups broadly characterized as the New Age movement.

Besides these new (or newly discovered) religions, from the 1960s to the 1980s several classical Asian religions received considerable attention and attracted American converts—most notably Zen Buddhism, Tibetan Buddhism, and Sikhism. So, as the baby boomers were becoming adults they certainly had a wide array of religious options from which to choose, and a far wider array than earlier generations. Whether or not they were, as a whole, more inclined to pursuing new and alternative religious experiences than earlier generations is another matter and not of particular interest to the subject of this chapter.[3] What is of interest, however, is that such seekers have been a prominent part of the American religious scene since the nineteenth century, even if today there are more options than there were in earlier times.

Baby boomers may well be accurately understood as a generation of seekers, but as our chapters on the Latter-day Saints, apocalyptic communities, and metaphysical communities clearly reveal, there have been seekers (and plenty of them) in every American generation, long before the baby boomers came on the scene. As a personal aside, seekers of the baby boomer generation are of particular interest to me because I am one of them, and my own religious adventures are quite similar to those of other seekers. I do not believe this is particularly generational, however; my mother was also a seeker, and so was my grandfather, and so (incidentally) was the first member of my family who arrived in America in 1806. In each instance, members of this family (for various reasons) journeyed beyond their inherited religious tradition and discovered another religious community that they made their home. This may not be the family history of the majority of Americans, but it is more likely to be part of the story for Americans than for most other people in the world.

As we have seen throughout this book, America has been uncommonly hospitable to a wide range of religions, and it has been particularly productive in creating new religions. As a nation, it has been a religion-generating engine, and it has given seekers an abundance of options to consider in their individual quests. New Thought is among the more unusual of these options, and one that has always appealed to religious seekers (and especially baby boomers, of late). Curiously, it is both widespread and little noticed.

THE FOUNDER OF NEW THOUGHT

The story of New Thought begins in the late 1880s, at the point where Christian Science and other branches of the American mental healing movement parted ways. Like Christian Science and Theosophy, New Thought is part of the metaphysical tradition. New Thought has affinities with both of these earlier movements, although it is most similar to Christian Science in that it is a popular form of religious idealism with a focus on healing. As such, New Thought affirms that ultimate reality is mental, that the physical world and the life experiences of individuals are a consequence of mental conditions, and that all healing must first occur in the mind. Aside from sharing an idealistic worldview and a focus on mental healing, New Thought and Christian Science differ considerably, as will be explained a bit later.

As noted in the chapter on metaphysical religions, the well-known American philosopher William James referred to the mental healing movement, what he called "Mind-Cure," as America's "only decidedly original contribution to the systematic philosophy of life."[4] James devoted a significant portion of his major work, *The Varieties of Religious Experience*, to the Mind-Cure movement; and although he mentions New Thought only in passing, his analysis of Mind-Cure is a fine exposition of New Thought in its formative period.[5] To understand where New Thought came from, then, we need to know a little bit about Mind-Cure and Christian Science.

In the late nineteenth century, the Mind-Cure movement was comprised of a loose assembly of individuals who were committed to the principles of idealism as the basis of healing and general well-being in life. While some of these idealists aligned themselves with Christian Science when Mary Baker Eddy (1821–1910) founded the religion in 1879, many did not. Some considered themselves "independent" Christian Scientists, indicating their rejection of Eddy's approach. Others claimed inspiration from an even earlier mental healer, Phineas Parkhurst Quimby (1802–1866), with whom Eddy had been associated prior to the founding of Christian Science. Still others related their work to more recognized cultural figures, such as the Swedish mystic Emmanuel Swedenborg, the German idealist G. W. F. Hegel, or the American Transcendentalist Ralph Waldo Emerson.

By the time James made his pronouncement about the "original contribution" in 1902, both Christian Science and Mind-Cure were increasingly being rejected as the preferred self-reference by many mental healers. Replacing the earlier terms was a new concept and new religious identity, one that was especially suitable for the new century and what some believed was a whole new age for humanity. The new concept became the name of the movement, New Thought, and its origin can be traced to the work of a former protégé of Mary Baker Eddy, a visionary and evangelical idealist named Emma Curtis Hopkins (1849–1925).

Like others in the early New Thought community, Hopkins was a Christian Science renegade, a dissident who left the movement to pursue new religious horizons. A true American seeker long before the term came into cultural vogue, Hopkins left not only Christian Science but also Boston, the center of its religious influence. Joining many other Americans in the latter part of the nineteenth century, Hopkins moved westward, and it was in that great gateway to the west, Chicago, that she started the new religion that came to be called New Thought.

In technical terms, Hopkins's work in Chicago prompted a schism, a division within a religious community that leads to the formation of a new group, independent of the original community. Schisms are relatively frequent occurrences in modern religious communities, and many American religious groups emerged as the result of such divisions. In the case of the Christian Science schism that resulted in New Thought, Hopkins and her followers initially continued to refer to themselves as Christian Scientists, but they rejected control by Eddy's church and ignored Eddy's demand that her teachings were the sole religious authority for all Christian Scientists. This dogmatism was unacceptable to Hopkins and was a major factor in her leaving Eddy's movement, in which she had once held positions of some rank, including the editorship of the *Christian Science Journal*.

Hopkins was hardly alone in rejecting Eddy's authority. Others of note were Mary Plunkett, Augusta Stetson, and Ursula Gestefeld. Like Hopkins, each of these individuals had previously been affiliated with Eddy's movement, and each contributed to what would become New Thought. Hopkins, however, quickly became the dominant figure, and Chicago became the epicenter of the schism.

Hopkins was fired by Eddy in 1885, and by the following year she was already at work in Chicago, setting up an independent form of Christian Science. Like founders of other new religions, Hopkins's first major project was to create a school, the Emma Hopkins College of Christian Science, established in Chicago in 1886. By 1887, she had developed a national organization, the Hopkins Metaphysical Association, and begun publishing a periodical (*Truth*). The association claimed twenty-one affiliated communities, including groups in major cities such as San Francisco, Denver, and New York, as well the center of Eddy's movement, Boston. A convention of the association in Boston had an attendance of over a thousand.

There are many reasons for Hopkins's ascent and her central role in the formation of New Thought. She was a charismatic speaker with a magnetic personality, a dynamic teacher, and a talented organizer. In addition to these considerable talents, the fact that she was also a woman made Hopkins's work especially notable in late-nineteenth century America. Your textbook has noted several other women who made significant contributions to religion in America (Ellen G. White, Helena Petrovna Blavatsky, and Mary Baker Eddy), each of whom had talents similar to those of Hopkins. What makes all of these persons especially remarkable is that they were founders of religious movements in a time when women were marginalized in American society and barred from professional religious leadership positions in mainstream religious communities. All were audacious pioneers on the frontiers of American religious life. Quite literally, they did what women had never done before. This made them heroes for many Americans; certainly for many women yearning for greater opportunities, but also for plenty of men as well. Of them all, Hopkins was perhaps the most audacious.

What separates Hopkins from White, Eddy, and Blavatsky, and can be cited as the key reason for her central importance to the origin of New Thought and, in fact, her importance in American religious history, was an event of 1889. The year before, Hopkins had reorganized her school and reformulated its mission. Under a new name, the Christian Science Theological Seminary, Hopkins's school would now be dedicated to educating students for professional ministerial service. The decision was pivotal to the rise of New Thought as a religion because it offered a formal process through which persons could receive institutional sanction as professional clerics. As she herself declared, "[This] is not a business . . . it is a ministry."[6]

In 1889, the first class of twenty-two students graduated from the seminary, and on January 10 of that year, Emma Curtis Hopkins ordained them as ministers. Twenty of the ministers were women. With this ordination ceremony, Hopkins distinguished herself from the other female religious pioneers noted previously, for it marked the first time in American history (and possibly Western Christian history) that a woman had ordained women—or men for that matter.

Hopkins's ordination of ministers in the context of a seminary education established the religious basis of her work while also giving it cultural legitimacy. Persons who studied at her seminary now could pursue professional religious careers, carry the title of minister, preach, teach, and conduct religious services. The fact that the majority of these ministers were women certainly challenged the norms of the day, but there appears to have been no lack of seekers (both male and female) willing to accept the challenge. By 1893 Hopkins had ordained 111 persons and the seminary had an enrollment of 350 students.

Hopkins's decision to ordain ministers separated her work from the rest of the Mind-Cure movement, as well as from Eddy's Christian Science. Until the establishment of Hopkins's seminary and her ordination of ministers, Christian Science and independent mental healing groups had been lay movements. Eddy had recognized the offices of teachers and practitioners, and professional clerics from other communities participated in the mental healing movement, but Eddy's decision not to ordain ministers seems to have influenced other leaders in the Mind-Cure movement to do the same. With Hopkins's audacious decision, however, the emerging New Thought movement at once stood apart from all similar groups. Rather than a lay movement of teachers and practitioners, Hopkins's association was clearly a religious organization, dedicated to educating persons for the ministry, ordaining them for professional religious service, and empowering them to go forth to preach, teach, and establish churches. These ministers and the churches they established became the foundation for New Thought, a movement that offered America and the world a new gospel based on idealism, optimism, self-improvement, and the pursuit of happiness through mental healing. In this regard, to William James's earlier observation that this was an original contribution to "the systematic philosophy of life" can be added his characterization of the movement as "the religion of healthy-mindedness."[7] It was, for him, a quintessentially American religion.

Because of the success of her seminary, Hopkins became known within the New Thought movement as the "teacher of teachers," and nearly all of the first generation of New Thought leaders studied with her or with her students. From the long list of major figures taught by Hopkins, several are of special importance because they established the first distinctly New Thought organizations. These students are Charles and Myrtle Fillmore (cofounders of Unity); Kate Bingham, the teacher of Nona Brooks (a founder of Divine Science); Annie Rix Militz (founder of Homes of Truth); and Ernest Holmes (founder of Religious Science). These figures were but a few of the Hopkins students who began religious groups, but they are significant because their groups grew into successful religious movements—the core communities of New Thought.

Through the work of her students, Hopkins's teachings spread throughout America and soon to other countries as well. Following Hopkins's own plan, initially, her students established themselves as mental healers and leaders of study groups—healing and education always serving as the twin foci of New Thought. An early slogan of the movement was "We heal by teaching, and we teach by healing." If successful, the study groups became genuine religious communities, offering a full range of religious services. The leaders, after all, were fully vested religious professionals, ordained ministers trained to perform traditional religious rituals—marriages, funerals, christenings, and (of course) Sunday church services. In the early years, these communities were seldom referred to as churches (although most are today), but rather as societies, centers, and even temples.

By the early 1890s, several of Hopkins's students began to develop independent religious movements that rightly could be identified as denominations. These were networks of mental healers, teachers, and laypersons who identified themselves with a specific religious leader or organization. The first of these organizations were Divine Science and the Unity School of Christianity, both of which continue to this day, with Unity being the largest of all New Thought groups.

Unity, Divine Science, and other early movements were organized and developed in close accord with the model of Hopkins's Metaphysical Association. Central to their mission was mental healing and teaching religious idealism, with a national outreach developed through periodicals, correspondence courses, and texts. They tended to have few, if any, strict doctrinal structures, and affiliated groups operated with a high degree of autonomy. Soon enough, they opened educational centers to train their own teachers and ministers. Like Hopkins before them, her students began ordaining ministers and sending them out to establish communities dedicated to the study and practice of religious idealism, as variously interpreted by the Hopkins-inspired leaders.

No sooner had her students begun having large-scale success than Hopkins retired from public ministry. In 1895 she closed the seminary and moved to New York City. Until her death in 1925 she continued to lecture, meet privately with students and clients, and write. Her two most notable books are *High Mysticism* (1920) and *Scientific Mental Practice* (n.d.). Her importance to the birth of New Thought was not in her writing but in her recognition that the mental healing movement could be organized as a traditional religion. Before her work in Chicago, religious idealism had taken the form of Eddy's Christian Science or the rather amorphous Mind-Cure movement. The former was strictly organized but rejected traditional religious structures in

---

The Softening of New Thought Radicalism

In the early days of New Thought, its leaders were countercultural social activists, even radical by the standards of their day. Emma Curtis Hopkins, for one, championed workers' rights and strongly criticized the weak child labor laws of her time. Others supported women's suffrage (the right to vote), prohibition, and utopianism. Some called for the establishment of self-sufficient communities based on their religious beliefs. There were critiques of capitalism and strong hints of socialism. Some leaders advocated celibacy and vegetarianism as religious virtues. Occasionally publications contained rather harsh rhetoric directed toward various branches of mainstream Christianity.

This radicalism faded over time, and by the middle of the twentieth century New Thought had lost it radical edge. In texts published after 1960 one rarely finds anything particularly controversial. New Thought certainly maintained its distinctive form of idealism, which in principle challenged the basic principles of America's materialist culture; but its idealism was softened and in a sense domesticated. Rather than a countercultural movement, New Thought grew disengaged from larger cultural issues. It remained largely silent during the tumult of the 1960s, saying little about the Vietnam war, the civil rights movement, or the sexual revolution. One can only speculate about what Emma Curtis Hopkins would have said about these major social and political issues. One suspects, however, that it would have been more than her spiritual descendants had to say.

It was during the latter part of the twentieth century that the baby boom generation emerged, and with it came a renewed interest in New Thought. Somewhat ironically, members of this generation, which is popularly portrayed as revolutionary, found religious meaning in this rather quietistic movement. At the same time, new activist religious groups were developing into what has come to be called the New Age movement. Baby boomers were also attracted to the New Age groups, perhaps in even greater numbers than they were to New Thought.

Today, the New Age movement appears to have passed its crest and is in decline. On the other hand, New Thought has continued to grow, being larger now than in any previous period in its history. At one time some scholars suggested that the New Age movement would engulf New Thought, appropriating its more attractive elements and popularizing them in the context of its own system. Precisely the opposite has occurred, however; New Thought has appropriated the more attractive features of the New Age movement and incorporated them into its system. This is part of the dynamic and fluid nature of New Thought's syncretism. By giving up its more strident countercultural stance, while maintaining its openness to all religious beliefs, New Thought has allowed itself to be infused with new teachings, and with them, new believers. This very openness may turn out to be what is most "new" about New Thought.

its ecclesiastical offices and public religious services; the latter was entirely unstructured and highly individualized. Both stressed individual healing, therapy, one-to-one treatment and prayer, and highly unorthodox religious practices.

Hopkins did not abandon these features, except for the unorthodox religious practices. Her vision, however, was larger than what the others seemed to offer. It was nothing less than the transformation of consciousness and culture. For her, the way to do this was through religion as traditionally understood in American society and as close to the cultural norms as she (as a woman in the nineteenth century) could make it. She set her sights on the goal of changing the world, not by being radically different (but different enough) and not by being highly focused on the individual (but focused enough). The approach was successful in establishing a new religion, if not in changing the world.

NEW THOUGHT GROUPS TODAY

Today, Hopkins's vision is carried on in a widely varied spectrum of religious movements, independent religious communities, prayer and meditation groups, and the personal spiritual practices of countless individuals. Currently, the largest and most notable of New Thought organizations (in order of size) are Unity, Religious Science, the Universal Foundation for Better Living, and Divine Science, with the International New Thought Alliance serving as a voluntary association group with membership open to organizations and individuals.

Of this group, the largest and best known is Unity, which was founded in 1889 by a married couple, Myrtle and Charles Fillmore. Its sacred center is Unity Village, located just outside Kansas City, Missouri. Unity Village is the home of the Unity School of Christianity, an education and retreat center for the movement. Nearby is the headquarters of the Association of Unity Churches, which is independent of the school and facilitates

ecclesiastical operations. Unity recognizes the Bible and *Lesson In Truth*, by H. Emilie Cady, as its primary textbooks.

The second largest New Thought group is Religious Science, founded in 1927 by Ernest Holmes. A schism in the movement in 1954 led to the formation of Religious Science International, headquartered in Spokane, Washington. Holmes's original group is called the United Church of Religious Science, headquartered in Los Angeles. The central text of both branches of Religious Science is Holmes's New Thought classic *The Science of Mind*. Religious Science does not identify itself as explicitly Christian, although it uses Christian terms and concepts in its teachings.

The youngest of the major New Thought communities is the Universal Foundation for Better Living. It was founded in Chicago in 1974 by Johnnie Colemon, a Unity minister and former president of the Association of Unity Churches. Universal Foundation for Better Living closely adheres to the traditional teachings of the Unity movement, much more closely, in fact, than some communities in the Association of Unity Churches. Representative texts would be those of the cofounders of Unity, for example, *Christian Healing* or *Prosperity* by Charles Fillmore.

The oldest New Thought group is Divine Science, which traces its origin to 1888 in San Francisco. Several figures are associated with its founding, most notably Malinda E. Cramer and Nona Brooks. Brooks led the movement during its ascent to prominence from her church in Denver. Divine Science is in decline and is today represented by two organizations, Divine Science Federation International and United Divine Science Ministries, International. A classic Divine Science text is Cramer's *Divine Science and Healing*.

In addition to these distinct communities, the International New Thought Alliance serves as a general organization that seeks to advance New Thought principles throughout the world. Its origins can be traced to a conference in London in 1914, and it was formally established in 1915 in San Francisco. It is loosely structured, with membership open to all New Thought communities, religious professionals, and laypersons. Its "Declaration of Principles" serves as a generic New Thought creed. Acceptance of the "Principles" is required for membership. Centered in Mesa, Arizona, the Alliance is currently led by the longest-serving president in its history, Blaine C. Mays.

AN INITIAL ENCOUNTER WITH NEW THOUGHT

In the early days of New Thought, it was not uncommon for persons to have their initial contact with the movement though its literature, especially its periodicals. Although this is still true today, it is much more likely that one's first encounter with New Thought will be at a Sunday morning church service. New Thought churches (sometimes called centers) can be found throughout the country, and most larger cities will have a number of New Thought groups—in some instances two or more from the same branch of New Thought.

Because of the lack of strict doctrinal structures and the general openness of the movement and its various branches, there is considerable diversity in New Thought services and in the organization of their material environment. They also vary greatly in size, from communities of less than fifty (often called study groups) to others with membership in the thousands.

The composition of congregations will range from ones that are racially diverse to others that are far less so, with some being predominantly made up of persons of European descent and others comprised mainly of persons of African descent. Persons of all backgrounds, races, and ethnicities, however, are welcome in New Thought churches, and first-time attendees can expect a warm welcome. Women generally outnumber men, but only slightly so; family groups are common, and larger communities offer activities and classes concurrently

with services. Youth programs are featured on Sundays, and adult education classes are offered on Sundays as well as other days of the week.

Some groups meet in theaters, hotel conference rooms, and even other churches. A New Thought community that my mother belonged to for a time met in a Seventh-Day Adventist Church. More often, the groups meet in structures that they own and have dedicated to their religious work. These may be classical church structures, with steeples, stained glass windows, and pews. In such instances, the New Thought group has probably acquired the building from a more traditional Christian group, which has vacated the structure. On the other hand, they can be converted retail establishments, professional office centers, and personal residences. Religious structures commissioned and built by New Thought groups themselves usually lack the characteristic features of traditional churches (as noted above), and architectural styles and floor plans vary widely. The central Christian symbol of the cross will rarely be featured, although, as with so many other aspects of New Thought, there are exceptions.

On entering the meeting place, attendees may expect to find a bookstore, offering a wide assortment of popular culture religious literature, most of which would be classified in commercial bookstores in the areas of "self-help," "New Age," "esoteric," and "metaphysical." There are usually representative publications of the specific New Thought denomination, such as books, study guides, and periodicals, although as often as not, denomination-specific publications are far outnumbered by those of a more commercial nature. For general research purposes, it is informative to look for Bibles in New Thought bookstores. Those that offer them for sale may put a greater emphasis on mainstream Christian beliefs and generally be more theologically conservative. There will also be plenty of tapes, CDs, and DVDs for sale, some commercially produced, and others produced by the local community, featuring sermons of the community's leader. Many church bookstores also sell religious accouterments such as bumper stickers, slogan T-shirts, promotional pens, posters, and (revealing New Age influences) healing crystals, therapeutic oils, and incense.

Sunday services have the look and feel of Protestant services, although certain features will be absent or presented differently. Formal readings from the Bible are not the norm, nor are clerical vestments. Individual Bibles will not be available for congregants; candles will be infrequent; and communion using the traditional elements (bread and wine) are rare.

On the other hand, public prayers or religious affirmations spoken in unison are routine features of most New Thought services, as are sermons and formal collections of offerings. The Lord's Prayer is common (and often sung), but the words of the prayer in New Thought communities will be different from those in traditional versions of the prayer. The services will also last the standard norm of about one hour. Like most Christian churches, services will start with a greeting and welcome, perhaps a few announcements, and an opening hymn.

Similar again to other churches, music is a prominent element in New Thought services for all but the smallest study groups. Larger churches will have choirs, professional music directors, and soloists. Hymns are another feature shared with mainstream Christianity. These often follow the same arrangement as well-known Christian hymns, but the words may well be different. When singing hymns they know by heart, first-time attendees may be surprised when singing certain words and verses to find the rest of the congregation singing different ones. A good example of this is the well-known "Doxology," featured in many Christian churches. The traditional version (in this case, from a Presbyterian church) goes like this:

Praise God, from whom all blessings flow;

Praise Him, all creatures here below;
Praise Him above, ye heavenly host;
Praise Father, Son, and Holy Ghost.[8]

Many, if not most, Protestants would recognize these familiar lyrics. To the same melody, however, New Thoughters sing a hymn titled "Praise God That Good is Everywhere":

Praise God that good is everywhere;
Praise to the love we all may share,
The life that thrills in you and me.
Praise to the Truth that sets us free.[9]

Without going into excessive detail, a brief comparison of the two versions of this hymn reveals much about New Thought's similarities and differences from better-known forms of Christianity. First, the similarities: Both are about God, both are focused on praising God, and both offer important insights into the nature of God and humankind. The differences occur when the specific insights are considered. One important difference is found in the spatial imagery. The traditional version places God "above" and "creatures" (presumably including humans) "below." In contrast, the New Thought version praises God in the context of a good, which is found everywhere, and a love that is shared by all. The lyrics affirm a fundamental belief of New Thought, that God is both absolute good and omnipresent. Understanding God and the world in an above-below relationship is rejected.

God in the traditional version is recognized as the source of all blessings, which "flow" forth from him. In the New Thought version, God is still the source of blessings, but there is no sense of anything flowing forth from him into creation. Instead, existence itself is the blessing, and the good is already present because of God's omnipresence. There is no external being from which good things come. The good is already here as the fundamental essence of creation; and, as the New Thoughter would say, it just needs to be recognized.

Further, the traditional hymn affirms praise for the God "above," expressed in the form of the Trinity (Father, Son, and Holy Ghost). The Trinity is not included in the New Thought variation, although trinitarian concepts are recognized in various ways within the movement. Instead, the New Thought hymn affirms love, life, and freedom brought by "Truth" (another aspect of God). Where the focus in the original hymn is the believer's praise of God, per se, the focus of praise in the New Thought version is on the expression of God in the experience of the believer.

What is revealed in the similarities and contrasts between the two hymns is also found in other aspects of the worship service. Metaphorically, the tune is the same but the words are different; and the words are different because the religious orientation is different. In traditional forms of Christianity, the orientation is toward a God who stands above all creation as a sovereign being and who is worthy of praise because of the blessings he bestows. In New Thought the orientation is toward a God who is the principle of good that is already in all things, and that is expressed in experiences of love, life, and freedom.

As the service progresses, other hymns will be sung, of which the most well-known outside of New Thought is "The Peace Song," which begins "Let there be peace on Earth and let it begin with me." Unlike the "Doxology," "The Peace Song" is a regular feature in many New Thought churches, often sung at the end of services.

Another regular feature is an extended period of group meditation. This ritual activity may also be referred to as a treatment or prayer-treatment. The ritual is conducted by an experienced leader of the community, sometimes the minister, but more often a teacher, spiritual practitioner, or other lay leader. Meditations typically begin with the closing of eyes and follow with directions to relax the body, put aside outer thoughts, and look within. The ritual is usually accompanied by serene music and often includes a period or periods of silence. The leader speaks slowly and quietly about God (Spirit, Truth, Law, Love, Good), principles of idealism, the causative nature of consciousness, the spiritual essence of individuals, and so on. The idea here is that listeners in meditation will discover or rediscover these fundamental features of life, appropriate them in consciousness, and then bring them forth in their everyday experience during the coming week.

In comparison to meditation rituals used in Buddhism and South Asian religions, meditations in New Thought services are rather brief (three to five minutes, and ten minutes at the most), but for folks familiar with traditional Christian services, they will probably seem rather lengthy. For devout New Thought believers, however, it is time well spent and of precious value to their religious pursuits. A popular variation on the ritual is the "guided meditation," during which the leader takes meditators on an inner journey, using softly spoken words that describe vivid yet serene images and usually involving the visualization of happy experiences and achievement of desired goals.

As with mainline Protestantism, the center of the service will be a sermon delivered by the religious leader, usually an ordained minister. Most of these ministers have entered religious service as a second or third career, often coming to it after having been successful in other professions. It is unusual to find a New Thought minister in her or his twenties. Like good clerics in other religions, those who are successful tend to be nicely socialized, comfortable with people, sincere, caring, and generous with their time, as well as good speakers. As in other religions, the best will have dynamic personalities and be charismatic orators and genuine leaders who are politically astute. Those who are said to best embody New Thought teachings will be, on the whole, cheerful, optimistic in outlook, charming, never publicly negative, and empowering of others— the very embodiment of James's religion of healthy-mindedness.

The topics of Sunday sermons (often called lessons) will be diverse, as will delivery styles. Popular books on healing, self-help, and successful living are frequent topics, and a series of sermons over several weeks may be devoted to a single book. Classic New Thought texts are sometimes the basis of sermons, as are New Age books. In other instances, the sermon will explore a specific New Thought religious concept, such as the Law of Mind Action, Visualization, Denial and Affirmation, prayer-treatment, Substance, Mental Equivalents, and so on. Less frequently, ministers will focus their entire sermon on Christian scriptures, although passages from the Bible or references to Jesus are included in many sermons. Central themes common in New Thought sermons are success, happiness, prosperity, health, and overcoming difficulties.

Relatively few New Thought churches focus primarily on the Bible. In those that do, sermons will present and interpret passages in scripture in the context of New Thought beliefs and themes noted above. Interpretations of scripture will often follow the "metaphysical" method, which is the New Thought term for what in earlier times was called the "allegorical" method.[10] This approach, which was established initially by Christian Science, has continued and, arguably, been advanced in New Thought. Among the movement's important contributions to the rebirth of allegorical interpretation, the most notable is *The Metaphysical Bible Dictionary*.

Following the sermon is the collection of tithes and other offerings (often called "love-offerings"), affirmation of thanks for the gifts, a closing prayer or treatment, and a concluding hymn or solo. After the service, participants may linger to enjoy community fellowship, visit with friends, or shop for religious merchandise in the bookstore. As is typical of many religious communities in America, New Thought churches offer coffee and pastries after the service. In summary, Sundays at New Thought centers begin and end very much like Sundays at traditional Protestant churches. The services themselves will also have the look and feel of Protestant services, but when the details are examined (from the hymns, to the sermons, to the prayers) differences emerge.

THE RELIGIOUS IDENTITY OF NEW THOUGHT

What these differences tell us is that, despite appearances, New Thought is definitely not a branch of Protestantism. Although it has been identified as such, its affinities with the historic churches of the Reformation are tenuous at best. Luther and Calvin, along with their adversary, the sixteenth-century Catholic Church, would not have recognized it as Protestant. None would have hesitated to declare New Thought (even in its most Christian expressions) heretical. They would probably treat it as some variant of the ancient Christian heresy Gnosticism.[11] In fact, several contemporary critics of New Thought have classified it as such. This classification is not entirely unjustified, but it seems a bit of stretch; indeed, it is a bit more of a stretch than classifying Christian Science or Scientology as Gnostic, since New Thought is so much less hostile toward matter.

In America, however, the days when being a heretic (Gnostic or otherwise) made any difference to one's life and liberty have long since past. Today, American seekers of all generations can freely explore a vast array of religious traditions that in earlier times would have put their social standing, if not their very lives, in jeopardy. However, it is still not helpful to have one's religion labeled a cult, and for this reason, scholars of religion (especially New Religions) generally avoid using the term. It still shows up in the media and public discourse, and New Thought, like several other New Religions presented in this book, has had that label assigned to it by some. Even the power of that derisive term is fading today, however.

New Thought may be difficult to classify, but this is not entirely unexpected, owing to the movement's lack of formal doctrines and emphasis on individual religious freedom. Furthermore, like Theosophy (an earlier metaphysical religion), New Thought is a classic example of religious syncretism—the melding of beliefs from various traditions to form a new religion, distinct from all others. In addition to appropriation of teachings from other religions, it has originated its own specific beliefs and practices. Finally, the movement itself is made up of a number of independent communities that while sharing a core of foundational beliefs also offer distinct interpretations of those beliefs. In short, it is not surprising that classifications of New Thought are not consistent.

The list of various traditions that may accurately be cited as contributing to New Thought is rather lengthy, yet a small handful are of special importance. As noted above, and will be treated in more detail shortly, the major precursor of New Thought, and the greatest initial influence on New Thought, was Christian Science. New Thought developed in distinction to Christian Science under the leadership of Hopkins; it maintained the popular religious idealism of Christian Science but rejected major doctrines of the earlier movement. It was also influenced by New England Transcendentalism (especially the work of Emerson) and its notions of idealism, self-development, and the Over-Soul. From Swedenborgianism it derived (albeit in a greatly modified form) the concept of correspondences between the world of spirit (the ideal realm) and the material world (the world of appearances). Finally, from Vedanta (as developed in America by Vivekananda) it appropriated general notions of religious universalism. Besides these, there were many other influences, including Theosophy, Spiritualism, Hegelianism, and (of course) the earlier Mind-Cure movement.

While New Thought is rightly understood as a form of seeker religion, it is most appropriately included in the metaphysical family. New Thought is a younger member of this family of American-born religions, which includes older groups like Christian Science, Theosophy, and Spiritualism. Of the three other metaphysical communities, New Thought is most similar to Christian Science, chiefly due to their mutual emphasis on mental healing and acceptance of an idealistic worldview. Aside from this important point of congruence, there are major differences between the two groups. Thus, in order to better understand New Thought's primary beliefs, its differences with Christian Science should be noted first.

NEW THOUGHT BELIEFS AND TEACHINGS

There are numerous points of distinction between the two movements, but three are especially critical. These can be summarized in each group's understandings of three features central to the identity of each community: dogma, matter, and medicine. Unlike Christian Science, New Thought is nondogmatic. Where Christian Science follows the teachings of Mary Baker Eddy exclusively, New Thought is extremely flexible, accepting a wide range of religious teachings and beliefs, but all predicated on the principle of idealism. This rejection of dogmatism is easily traced to the initial schism, precipitated by Hopkins's interest in teachings not authorized by Eddy.

Although most New Thought groups have an affinity with Christianity (in widely varying degrees), teachings from all the major world religions (and many minor ones) are frequently cited in the groups' literature, religious classes, and sermons. In this regard, New Thought's syncretism is readily apparent, despite idealism serving as the foundation of its theology and worldview. This being so, New Thought communities will not generally endorse teachings that compromise its idealistic beliefs. Other than that, there is considerable range in the teachings presented under the banner of New Thought.

When visiting New Thought communities, one is just as likely to encounter teachings derived from Buddhism, New Age magi, and popular spiritual self-help gurus as those based in traditional New Thought beliefs. Some are profoundly Christian in orientation and put great emphasis on Jesus and the Bible, while others affirm a nondenominational status and refer to the Bible (if at all) no more so than other scriptures. New Thought is, thus, nicely positioned to appeal to contemporary religious seekers, as described earlier. On the topic of religious authority and dogma, in contrast to Christian Science's singular focus on the teachings of Mrs. Eddy, New Thought looks like a religious convenience store, offering one-stop shopping for the religious consumer.

When it comes to matter (the material world), New Thought takes a less hostile stance than Christian Science. As a form of idealism, New Thought does recognize the material world (at least in its current state) as falling short of perfection. This condition, however, is by no means permanent. Unlike Christian Science, New Thought has traditionally believed that the physical world can be uplifted, transformed, and perfected. Consistent with its belief in the omnipresence of God (the Good), New Thought affirms the essential goodness of all things, including the physical world. In fact, as we remember from the hymn presented earlier, for New Thought, "good is everywhere," and this good is a primary attribute of the omnipresent God. This being so, the existence of matter is not denied; what is denied is the belief that matter is limited and limiting. It only seems to be limiting when the higher reality of God (the Good) is forgotten or not recognized in the first place.

This latter point (forgetting or not recognizing the reality of God) is cited by New Thought as a cause of all limitation. We often experience challenges, so the teachings reveal, not because matter is an evil force or some sort of entrapping illusion, but rather because we have failed to recognize the presence of divinity (the Good) in some sort of material condition. Matter is problematic only to the extent that it is mistakenly believed to be absolute and the sole basis of reality. Rather than denying the reality of matter, New Thought is better understood as rejecting materialism—the belief that matter is primary. The distinction between the movements can be characterized in terms of idealism, with Christian Science affirming a radical or dualistic type of idealism and New Thought taking a more moderate or inclusive stance.

Directly related to its differing interpretation of the status of matter is New Thought's distinction from Christian Science on the role and status of medical treatment. Just as Christian Science rejects medicine as a religiously legitimate form of healing on the basis of its prior rejection of matter, so New Thought accepts medicine simply as another avenue though which the Good is manifest in life. All healings are spiritual healings for the New Thought practitioner, and God (the Good) works though the mind and hands of the surgeon just as readily as through the spiritual treatment of the mental healer. New Thought will remind, however, that all true and lasting healings are predicated on mental healing.

New Thought's distinction from Christian Science and the basis of its worldview as a whole is rooted in three foundational beliefs: (1) idealism; (2) God as Principle; and (3) the divinity of humanity. There are variations in terminology among the various New Thought groups in the presentation of these beliefs, but there is little disagreement about the basic conceptions. Each of these beliefs has been touched on previously in this chapter. They can now be explored in a little more detail and related to one another.

By this point, it is presumed that readers have a good working understanding of idealism in general and how it pertains to New Thought. It can now be further observed that New Thought's idealism is both *theoretical* (insofar as it is related to the understanding of God and the universe) and *practical* (insofar as it is understood to be used routinely by believers). Theoretically and theologically, New Thought's idealism affirms that the highest reality is mental. As in Christian Science, in New Thought a frequently used metaphor for God is Divine Mind.

The origin of all creation is this Divine Mind, which is always pure and perfect. At the practical level, it is believed that human beings are part of or have access to Divine Mind. When individuals fully recognize this truth in their own consciousness, they are able to manifest the reality of Divine Mind in their lives. This includes experiences of health, peace, love, prosperity, joy, and other assorted positive states and experiences. Following the idealistic principle, then, there is a causal relationship between consciousness and physical conditions, with the latter predicated on the former. A New Thought aphorism nicely captures this concept: "Like attracts like, like begets like; thoughts held in mind produce after their kind." It is not quite as simple as this, but this is the basic principle.

New Thought's idealism informs and supports its understanding that God (Divine Mind) is Principle, the foundation of all existence. As principle, God is also recognized as the all good, omnipotence, and omnipresence. Each of these concepts is evident in the New Thought "doxology," presented earlier, and throughout New Thought literature. A rather classic expression of the belief is one from the Unity movement: "God is good and God is all, hence there can be no *real* condition but the good."[12] As expressed in the form of mental treatment, a Religious Science text affirms, "I partake of the nature and bounty of the All Good and I am now surrounded by everything which makes life worth while."[13]

Although God is commonly used in New Thought and sometimes personalized (as Father, Mother, or Father-Mother), God is most fundamentally the principle of being—similar to Brahman in Hinduism. God is not a being but rather the fundamental reality of the universe. This being so, God is present in all things, but also present in the spaces between things, and the spaces between the spaces. God as Principle is at once the Law of creation, the Substance (another New Thought concept) from which all things are made, and Order that harmonizes the cosmos. Besides Mind, Law, Substance, and Good, numerous other synonyms for God express ideal and perfect states. Among those commonly used are Truth, Love, Health, Life, Wisdom, and Spirit.

As a corollary to the belief that Divine Principle is all good, New Thought denies the reality of evil, claiming that logically, the nature of God precludes evil as a real force in the universe. The only *real* condition is the good. This belief follows the same reasoning as a traditional explanation for evil, called the "instrumentalist" response. The response offers an explanation for the seeming contradiction of having a God who is omnipresent, omnipotent, and omnibenevolent (all-present, all-powerful, and all-good) and also having evil in the world. It argues that that which appears evil is not evil in itself but rather an *instrument* for a greater good to come. New Thought further claims that that which appears evil is merely an error in human thinking and understanding. It is a consequence of the failure of individuals, families, communities, and ultimately the entire human race to recognize the reality of God (the All Good) in some event or experience or to harbor thoughts of limitation, fear, and even evil itself. New Thought's foundational idealism, thus, traces all material and physical conditions back to consciousness (thoughts, ideas, and beliefs). To the degree that consciousness is attuned to the reality of the All Good, limitations are minimized; to the degree that it is not, they prevail. There is no acknowledgement of an evil power or entity in this belief system, only errors in thinking. Moreover, New Thought affirms that those errors can be overcome.

This brings us to New Thought's beliefs about humanity, and it is here that the movement's emphasis on encouragement and empowerment are most clearly expressed. It is also here that New Thought most clearly departs from traditional forms of Christianity.

As noted above, like everything else in creation, humanity is believed to be one with Divine Mind. This may be understood as the human mind being an extension of Divine Mind or humanity being first and foremost a divine idea within that Mind. However it is conceived, the foundational notion is that the essence of humanity is divine, one with the All Good, and pure and perfect. The spiritual essence of humanity is variously referred to as the Christ Mind, superconsciousness, "the Spiritual Principle in man," or other exalted expressions. Oneness with Divine Mind or a divine idea within that Mind is the essential identity of all persons. Jesus is typically recognized as having fully realized this conscious oneness and expressed the Christ Mind in his life.

Jesus is, thus, seen as the great revealer of New Thought principles. Typically, he is seen to be at once humanity's greatest teacher and its foremost guide in living. New Thought groups differ in their emphasis on Jesus, and some recognize similar religious significance in figures such as the Buddha or Krishna, but few will ignore him, and most will celebrate his life and teachings. In New Thought, however, the stress is not on Jesus, but rather on the Christ, the principle of perfection within all persons and the divine identity of humanity itself. Jesus is significant for having realized and expressed this perfection, as well as for teaching others how they may do it too. In short, for New Thought, Jesus saves not by his death and vicarious atonement, but by his life and demonstration of the divine identity of humanity. His mission was not to take away sin or the divine punishment for sin (for in New Thought there is no sin), but rather to teach others how to discover their own inner perfection and then how to bring that perfection into manifestation.

Jesus is recognized as a singular individual, but the Christ Mind is the true essence of all people. As such, humanity is divine, without original sin, and not destined to fall short of perfection. The problem (or challenge, as New Thoughters would say) is that, despite our innate divinity, we do fall short of perfection. We do get sick, grow old, and die. We lose jobs, fail to reach our goals, have family difficulties, and suffer through natural and human-made disasters. Granted, the New Thought gospel would say, but these unpleasant events and tragedies need not occur. That they do indeed happen is not the consequence of the essential nature of the universe or of human beings—the essential nature of both, after all, is divine, perfection, the All Good. Their cause is simply the result of human beings not recognizing that essential nature. The goal for humanity in New Thought is to achieve that recognition fully. When that occurs, the physical/material world is uplifted, becoming reflective of its divine nature.

In this regard, human beings are seen as co-creators with God or the self-knowingness of Divine Mind. New Thought calls persons to this higher realization of their nature and role in creation as agents of the Good. This may occur at the personal level, in specific instances of empowerment, or it may occur in the context of larger issues and causes. New Thought affirms that the results of this realization are positive experiences for individuals, communities, and even the world: healing, greater happiness, success, and peace of mind.

On the other hand, to the degree that persons do not fully realize the reality of the All Good or the presence of the Christ mind within themselves, even ignore or reject it, less desirable conditions occur—pain, sickness, failure, poverty, and assorted other ills. These undesirable conditions are a consequence of their limited thoughts. Because the universe is first and foremost mental, all material and physical conditions are a consequence of prior mental states—thoughts, ideas, and beliefs. Limited thoughts produce limited conditions, positive thoughts produce positive conditions, and thoughts in harmony with Divine Mind produce perfection.

NEW THOUGHT RITUALS

New Thoughters are not Pollyannas. They do not naively ignore physical and material hardships, disasters, illness, financial crises, physical injury, or any of the terrible acts that humans do to one another. They do, however, deny that any of these conditions and events is fundamentally evil, the result of an evil force or an evil being of some sort. For the New Thought believer, there simply cannot be any reality besides God, the All Good. So, rather than admit to the appearance of limitation or distress, New Thoughters will seek to discover the true reality of God—to "know the Truth" about the situation, as the saying goes. Now, this may seem naive to some, but not to the New Thoughter. Quite the contrary, the New Thoughter will declare that such an exercise is the necessary process that needs to be undertaken in order to eliminate the condition, overcome the difficulty, or heal the injury.

The process itself is the basis for New Thought's most important religious rituals, all of which may be understood as healing rituals. They are used when confronted with specific healing needs or on a routine basis to cultivate greater awareness of Divine Mind and facilitate ongoing spiritual growth. The rituals themselves are often referred to as treatments, prayer treatments, or spiritual-mind treatments. They can also be referred to simply as prayer or knowing the Truth.

Healing rituals may be done individually, together with others (including professional religious practitioners and members of the clergy), and in larger community gatherings (such as classes and Sunday services). It is not uncommon in New Thought church services to have time devoted to healing rituals, usually just before, just after, or as part of the meditation ritual. No matter the context, the basic structure of these rituals is similar (and similar to healing practices in Christian Science), albeit there are technical variations between the various groups.

In all instances the ritual is an inner psycho-spiritual activity that occurs in the consciousness of the individual, which leads to her or his realization of the reality of God (Divine Mind), the omnipresent Good. This realization is the premise of all New Thought ritual practices. Once the realization is achieved, positive conditions will be established where they had not been present before. This may require persistence on the part of the believer, and treatments may need to be repeated.

When treatments are done to eliminate specific situations deemed undesirable, the situations themselves are referred to with terms and concepts that minimize negativity, such as "seeming challenges," "healing opportunities," "overcomings," and "seeming limitations." This is designed to get one's thoughts off the circumstances of the conditions and facilitate realization of the Truth. Thus, rather than claiming to be sick, a New Thoughter may say, "I have been given a healing opportunity." If someone has lost a job or is in financial distress, the New Thought treatment would be precipitated with the understanding that the person is faced with a "seeming limitation" and seeks a "demonstration of prosperity." The idea here is that it is not an actual limitation because Divine Mind has no limitations, and the All Good is the source of infinite supply.

In practice, the rituals usually involve specific mental operations, although experienced practitioners report often not needing to follow a specific process. Again, the key is always the realization of God. If that can occur without a systematic process, so be it—all the better. More often than not, specific practices are followed. Some of the more common ones are presented here.

What is typically the first step in all healing rituals has already been described. In one way or another, the undesired condition is minimized as a "seeming challenge." More explicitly, some forms of the ritual will involve a practice known as denial and affirmation, in which the undesired condition is not only minimized but entirely denied. The believer may declare, "There is no Truth in this appearance because Truth knows no limitation, and cannot be compromised in any way." The denial is then immediately followed by an affirmation of a reality of the All Good; for example, "I am one with Truth, and Truth is the All Good working in and through all things, and in my life now." In all instances, the statements may be offered silently or audibly, whichever technique is most effective for the individual. The ritual will be repeated whenever the "seeming limitation" comes to mind and until the believer is convinced of the reality of the Good. At that point, the negative situation will be eliminated.

Another approach is to move directly to the affirmation. This is called affirmative prayer, or affirmative mental treatment. This method gives no attention whatsoever to the "seeming limitation." Instead, the believer affirms what is known to be the Truth. In the case of a treatment for the elimination of fear, it might go like this: "There is one Love, that Love is God, that Love is Perfect, that Love is my Love now." Treatments for other positive conditions (e.g., peace, strength, health) follow the same pattern, with the ideal condition being used where "Love" was in the example. Again, the affirmation may be spoken or kept strictly in one's thoughts. Whenever the undesired condition comes to mind or is otherwise experienced, the individual will affirm this or some other appropriate statement about God and the reality of the All Good.

Silence may also be included in healing rituals. Following the statements, persons may become inwardly still, letting the truth of the statements settle into mind. If other thoughts intrude, the statements are made again, until silence is reached. Some New Thought groups even recognize an ideal spiritual state, which is called "The Silence."

Yet another technique is known as visualization. This method involves the use of mental imagery, with the believer creating a mental image of the desired condition. The image specifically excludes any conditions that may be undesirable. Visualization may be accompanied by denial and affirmation, affirmative prayer, or silence. In congregational settings, visualization is often included in guided meditations, described earlier.

As is evident, there are limitless variations for each of these ritual practices. What remains consistent is the realization of God and the reality of the All Good. When this occurs, the treatment concludes with a statement of completion and thanksgiving: "It is done, it is perfect, and all is well. Thank you, Infinite Lord."

Conclusion

At the outset of this chapter, we saw that participants in New Thought were not dropouts but seekers. As seekers, they seem to genuinely like religion or, better said, *religions*. Many have tried more than a few. For them, religion is serious business, but it is also something in which they find enjoyment and happiness. Enjoyment and happiness, after all, can be pursued quite seriously, and many Americans (not just those in New Thought) do exactly that.

The expression of enjoyment and a sense of happiness is something you may observe if you go to a New Thought religious service. You will probably notice that members of the congregation will appear positive, upbeat, and genuinely happy. They will laugh readily during the service, and there will be frequent applause. Happiness is important to these folks; in fact, it is part of their religion.

Over a century ago, the American philosopher William James described New Thought as "the religion of healthy-mindedness."[14] What struck James about the early New Thought movement (which he referred to as "Mind-Cure") was its sacralization of a positive worldview, which stressed optimism, joy, peace of mind, and happiness. A religion based on such a worldview was for him quintessentially American. This is, after all, the nation whose "Declaration of Independence" enshrines the belief that among the fundamental characteristics of the universe itself, as established by the "Creator" of the world, are "certain unalienable Rights" belonging to all people. The "Declaration" then cites three of these Rights: "Life, Liberty and the Pursuit of Happiness."[15]

New Thought followers treasure these rights, but it is the pursuit of happiness that they seem to have made a virtual tenet of their faith. The zealous pursuit of happiness by New Thought participants is what caught James's attention and is still a dominant feature of the movement. After all, for these seekers, the quest for happiness is not just a quintessentially American pursuit for the good life; it is a religious journey, a pilgrimage through the inner realms of consciousness to the new world of the All Good.

Notes

1. From Joseph L. Price, "An American Apotheosis: Sports as Popular Religion," in *Religion and Popular Culture in America*, ed. Bruce David Forbes and Jeffrey H. Mahan (Berkeley, CA: University of California Press, 2002), 212.

2. See Wade Clark Roof, *A Generation of Seekers: The Religion of the Baby Boom Generation* (San Francisco: HarperCollins, 1993).

3. For a helpful critique of Roof's "seeker" theory, see Andrew Greeley, "Review of *A Generation of Seekers: The Spiritual Journeys of the Baby Boom Generation* by Wade Clark Roof." *Political Science Quarterly* 109 (1, Spring 1994): 191–93.

4. William James, *The Varieties of Religious Experience* (New York: New American Library, Mentor, 1958), 88–89. First published in 1902.

5. Ibid., 76–111.

6. As quoted in J. Gordon Melton, "New Thought's Hidden History: Emma Curtis Hopkins, Forgotten Founder" *Journal of the Society for the Study of Metaphysical Religion* 1 (1, 1995): 18.

7. See James, *Varieties*, "Lectures IV and V: The Religion of Healthy-Mindedness," 76–108, esp. 87–108.

8. See the web site of National Presbyterian Church, http://www.natpresch.org/doxology.php (accessed March 8, 2008).

9. See hymnal, *Wings of Song* (Unity Village, Mo.: Unity Books, 1984), "Praise God That Good Is Everywhere," 1.

10. See chapter 14 on metaphysical communities for more on the allegorical method.

11. Some Gnostics believed that the world was made by an evil creator-god, that humans were spiritual beings trapped in physical bodies, that matter was evil, that salvation entailed freeing one's spiritual essence of its physical/material prison, and that Jesus brought the knowledge (*gnosis*) of how this escape could be made. This summary is derived from the *Oxford Concise Dictionary of the Christian Church*, ed. E.A. Livingstone (Oxford: Oxford University Press, 2000), s.v., "Gnosticism."

12. Charles Fillmore, *Christian Healing* (Unity Village, Mo.: Unity School of Christianity, 1959), 93. First published in 1909.

13. Ernest Holmes, with Maude Allison Lathem, *The Science of Mind* (New York: Dodd, Mead and Company, 1938), 119.

14. James, *Varieties*, 76–108, esp. 87–108.

15. "Declaration of Independence" as cited in *Religion and American Cultures*, vol. 2, ed. Gary Laderman and Luis León (Santa Barbara, Calif.: ABC CLIO, 2003), 723.

STUDY QUESTIONS

1. Compare and contrast New Thought and Scientology. Take into consideration similarities and differences between the founders of the groups, their relationship with other religions, and their basic worldview.

2. Isolate three key features of New Thought that make it a quintessentially American religion.

3. Explain the importance of idealism to the beliefs and practices of Christian Science and New Thought. What are the major similarities and major differences in these two forms of popular religious idealism?

4. Compare New Thought's view of Jesus with his role in traditional Christianity. In what ways do they differ?

5. Compared to Christian Science, Theosophy, and Scientology, New Thought has faced relatively little opposition from established forms of Christianity and the media. Give several explanations for why New Thought has faced less opposition than these similar groups.

6. What facts related to the ordination of ministers by Emma Curtis Hopkins are of importance to the early success of the New Thought movement? Give at least three and explain why they were important.

7. Why do you think New Thought has particular appeal to religious "seekers"?

8. On the basis of what you have learned in this chapter, comment on the spiritual responsibilities of individuals in New Thought. Are individuals given greater or less responsibility in New Thought than in other religions? Give examples to support your answer.

9. In what ways would a Catholic or a Protestant feel at home at a New Thought religious service? In what ways would she or he feel uncomfortable?

10. Explain why some might classify New Thought as Gnostic and why others would find such a classification inaccurate. See the short description of Gnosticism given in the notes to assist in organizing your response.

11. In light of their primary beliefs and teachings, why do New Thought communities have little involvement in politics and other forms of social activism?

12. If you were to use one word to capture the essence of New Thought, what word would you chose? Give the meaning of the word and tell why it best captures the essence of New Thought.

ESSAY TOPICS

The Life of Emma Curtis Hopkins: "Teacher of Teachers" and Founder of New Thought

Distinctions and Similarities between New Thought and the New Age Movement

The Schism between Christian Science and New Thought

The Appeal of New Thought to Religious "Seekers"

The Role of Women in New Thought

The Philosophical and Theological Roots of Religious Idealism

Same Tune, New Lyrics: New Thought and Protestant Christianity

WORD EXPLORATION

"Seekers"
Visualization
Brahman
The Christ Mind
Syncretism
Transcendentalism
"Doxology"
Prayer-Treatment
"Healing Opportunity"
"Love-Offerings"

Vedanta
Magus (magi)
Schism
Affirmative Prayer
Seminary
New Age
Guided Meditation
"Religion of Healthy-Mindedness"
Baby Boomers
Heresy

Idealism
Dogmatism
"The Instrumentalist Response"
Affirmation and Denial
Superconsciousness
All Good
Ordination
Gnosticism
Omnipresence
Universalism

FOR FURTHER READING

Albanese, Catherine L. *A Republic of Mind and Spirit: A Cultural History of American Metaphysical Religion*. New Haven, Conn: Yale University Press, 2007.

Braden, Charles S. *Spirits in Rebellion: The Rise and Development of New Thought*. Dallas: Southern Methodist University Press, 1963.

Cady, H. Emilie. *Lessons In Truth*. Unity Village, Mo.: Unity Books, [1894] 1988.

Cramer, Malinda E. *Divine Science and Healing*. Denver: Divine Science Federation International, [1902] 1988.

Harley, Gail M. *Emma Curtis Hopkins: Forgotten Founder of New Thought*. Syracuse: Syracuse University Press, 2002.

Holmes, Ernest, with Maude Allison Lathem. *The Science of Mind*. New York: Dodd, Mead & Co., 1957.

Hopkins, Emma Curtis. *High Mysticism*. Marina del Rey, Calif.: DeVorss, [1920], 1987.

James, William. *The Varieties of Religious Experience*. New York: New American Library, [1902], 1958.

Judah, J. Stillson. *The History and Philosophy of the Metaphysical Movements in America*. Philadelphia: Westminster Press, 1967.

Satter, Beryl. *Each Mind a Kingdom: American Women, Sexual Purity, and the New Thought Movement, 1875–1920*. Berkeley, Calif.: University of California Press, 1999.

WEB SITES

http://www.unity.org
   Association of Unity Churches

http://www.divinesciencefederation.org
   Divine Science Federation International Web site

http://emmacurtishopkins.wwwhubs.com
   Emma Curtis Hopkins home page

http://www.newthoughtalliance.org/
   International New Thought Alliance Web site

http://web.archive.org/web/20060907005952/http://etext.lib.virginia.edu/relmove/
   Religious Movements home page with links to numerous religious groups

http://www.rsintl.org/
   Religious Science, International Web site

http://www.religiousscience.org/
   United Church of Religious Science Web Site

http://www.uniteddivinescience.org
   United Divine Science Ministries, International Web Site

http://www.unityonline.org/
   Unity School of Christianity Web site

http://www.ufbl.org/
   Universal Foundation for Better Living

16

The Church of Scientology: A Very New American Religion

DELL DeCHANT AND DANNY L. JORGENSEN

1911	L. Ron Hubbard (LRH), founder of Scientology, born 13 March at Tilden, Nebraska
1920s	Hubbard family moves to Seattle, Washington
1930s	LRH becomes popular science fiction author
1940s	LRH serves in U.S. Navy during WWII
1950	First publication of LRH's *Dianetics: The Modern Science of Mental Health*; Hubbard Dianetic Research Foundation at Elizabeth, NJ, established
1954	Church of Scientology incorporated in California
1959	Saint Hill Manor near Sussex, England, serves as Hubbard's headquarters
1967	IRS removes Scientology's tax exempt status; establishment of Scientology's Sea Organization (Sea Org), a fleet of ships, with Hubbard as commodore
1970s	Headquarters of Scientology's Sea Org established in Clearwater, Florida. Scientology launches "Operation Snow White" to eliminate unfavorable public and private records; high-ranking Scientologists (but not LRH) convicted and imprisoned
1981	Scientology organizations unified under the Church of Scientology International
1982	Heber C. Jentzsch becomes president of the Church of Scientology International
1986	Death of L. Ron Hubbard on January 24
1987	David Miscavige (1960–) becomes Chairman of the Board of the Religious Technology Center and LRH's successor
1989	Scientology's Association for Better Living and Education (ABLE) established for the development of social service programs
1993	IRS recognizes church's tax-exempt status
2002	Sales of *Dianetics* pass the twenty million mark
2005	Scientology announces Golden Age of Knowledge involving the publication of all of LRH's books and over 5,000 other writings and lectures
2009	Scientologists operate in 159 countries and 66 languages worldwide

Super Bowl Sunday

The afternoon of January 28, 2001, was not a typical one at Scientology's Celebrity Center in Hollywood, California.[1] It was Super Bowl Sunday and, like Americans everywhere, about fifty Scientologists had gathered to watch the televised spectacle. Two large-screen televisions were set up in the hotel café so that the Scientology staff, students, and visitors to the Celebrity Center could enjoy the big game. They were rooting for one team or the other, cheering exceptional plays and debating contested ones, laughing at humorous commercials, and enjoying snack foods and beverages. The scene at the café was no different than you might find in thousands of other places around the United States on Super Bowl Sunday. In fact, most people probably would have found nothing at all unusual about that gathering of Super Bowl fans—until they learned that they were Scientologists.

For some Americans, unfortunately, that one fact—knowing that these fans were Scientologists—might have changed their view of the entire scene. It might have colored their perception of the people enjoying the game, and perhaps even their willingness to be a part of the gathering. New religions, as you have seen (or will see) from this and other chapters in this book, frequently are surrounded by controversy, much of it deriving from prejudice and misunderstandings. Scientology, over its very short, approximately sixty-year history, frequently has been dismissed as a "cult," and otherwise asked to defend itself as an authentic religion. It certainly is true that Scientology involves novel beliefs, practices, and organizational forms. It thereby is very different from many traditional American religions. No matter, the Church of Scientology, as you will see, is a religion of significance to scholars.[2]

Although Scientology is a very new American religion, it exhibits almost all of the ordinary features of the major world religions. It provides a sacred, supernatural myth of the origins and nature of humanity as well as an explanation of the human condition. The founder of Scientology, L. Ron Hubbard, resembles the prophet-like originators of many other religions, and some of his many writings form the sacred scriptures and define religious doctrines. Scientology contains religious practices and rituals, as well as moral principles and standards for ethical conduct, all aimed at the redemption and salvation of humanity. This new religion is supported by a community of believers, including a highly dedicated ordained clergy, and their activities are organized socially much like other, more traditional American religions. Scientology, like other religions, also is involved in a variety of social betterment programs in service to the larger, secular society.

A Sunday Morning Worship Service

Earlier that Super Bowl Sunday, many Scientologists around the country and the world did the same thing many other people did: they attended a church service. They arrived alone, as pairs or couples, and in family groups, sometimes with children. Some of them were dressed formally in dresses or suits and ties, while other people wore more casual clothing, like slacks and a shirt, as is common among many American religionists today. At the entrance to church, people frequently greeted one another, and they sometimes paused to enjoy friendly conversations. Visitors, newcomers, and nonmembers always are welcomed at these gatherings. The people entering the meeting room received a warm and positive reception from an ushering Scientologist, along with a printed program. The ushers busily greeted friends and newcomers, directed the congregants to available seats, and made sure that everyone had a copy of the program.

The program brochure was published by a central Scientology organization for its affiliated chapters (churches). It included the usual order of service, and it also contained an informative introduction to Scientology beliefs and principles. This "Introduction to Church Services" included, for instance, background information about Scientology and certain fundamental beliefs, a glossary of theological concepts, a foundational "Prayer for Total Freedom," and "The Creed of the Church of Scientology." Although the contents of these materials differ from more traditional American religions, just as these older religions differ to a greater or lesser extent among themselves, the preliminary activities at the meeting place were much the same as what transpires most everywhere in the United States on Sunday mornings.

The Sunday meeting places of Scientology often are buildings used for varied religious purposes, and their design is not particularly distinctive. You might or might not recognize them as a church building. In most ways, however, the interior of a Scientology meeting room or sanctuary resembles that of a typical Protestant church anywhere in America. It probably will be big enough for several hundred or more worshipers, and usually there are chairs or pews arranged in the customary, orderly manner. There also might be an elevated stage as well as a pulpit or lectern. Several features of this meeting space might strike you as unfamiliar. One of them is a bronzed, life-sized bust of the religion's founder, L. Ron Hubbard, elevated on a pedestal and situated in a prominent location. This representation of Hubbard is not surprising once you understand his central, almost prophetic role in the establishment of Scientology and his great veneration by contemporary practitioners. The other feature you probably would notice is a cross that appears different from the more familiar Christian one. You might wonder about the significance of the four diamond-shaped protrusions at the center of the Scientology cross. They, along with the four arms of the cross, represent what Scientology refers to as the eight "dynamics" of existence. These dynamics help define the theology of Scientology and some of its central beliefs.

The core principle of this Scientology theology is "survival," and revolving around it

are the eight dynamics. Survival thereby is one of this religion's basic goals and very much like the aim of "salvation" in older, biblical religions. The first dynamic is self, or survival of the individual's body and mind. The second dynamic is creativity, including the family and rearing of children. The third dynamic is group survival, for example, as a community, company, or nation. Survival as a species, all of humankind, is the fourth dynamic. The fifth dynamic is "life-forms," or the survival of other forms of life, such as plants, fish, birds, and animals. The physical universe is the sixth dynamic, and it is envisioned in terms of four components: matter, energy, space, and time. It, thereby, also is known by Scientologists as the "MEST" universe. Survival of all things spiritual is the seventh principle, and it is envisioned as the source of life. The eighth dynamic is "infinity," the "allness of all," or what may be called the supreme being, creator, or God. Each dynamic also may be represented by a circle, composing a series of concentric circles, beginning with the first principle at the center. This imagery has each person expanding his or her spirituality (spiritual awareness and ability) to survival across all of the dynamics. Survival, in all of these ways, therefore is a principal belief as well as one of the central salvation goals of Scientology.

Sunday worship services begin at 11:00 A.M., typically when the minister takes the lectern, welcomes the congregation, and recites "The Creed of the Church of Scientology." Congregants can follow along using the printed version of the creed in the church services brochure. The Creed affirms that the members of the church believe that all people "of whatever race, color or creed were created with equal rights." It specifies that all people have inalienable rights to their own "religious practices and their performance," "lives," "sanity," and "defense," as well as "inalienable rights to think freely, to talk freely, to write freely their own opinions and to counter or utter or write upon the opinions of others," and "to the creation of their own kind." The Creed holds that "the souls of men have the rights of men"; "[t]hat the study of the mind and the healing of mentally caused ills should not be alienated from religion or condoned in nonreligious fields; [a]nd that no agency less than God has the power to suspend or set aside these rights, overtly or covertly." It further maintains that the Church of Scientology believes that people are "basically good," they seek to "survive," and that survival depends on self and others as well as "brotherhood with the universe." God, according to the Scientology Creed, forbids people from destroying one another, the sanity of others, destroying or enslaving "another's soul," and destroying or reducing "the survival of one's companions or one's group." Finally, it asserts that "the spirit can be saved and that the spirit alone may save or heal the body."

Some of the specific language and beliefs of the Scientology Creed may seem unusual to you. Yet, you probably recognized the tone and content as fundamentally religious—rather than say, political or economic—in character. Some of you may find more than a few of these affirmations not only helpful and constructive but similar to your own beliefs. Perhaps you noticed that these affirmations are closely aligned with many of the sacred or almost sacred values of American culture. Regardless of how you reacted to the Scientology Creed, it reveals key elements of this religion. These ideals indicate that Scientology is a salvific religion (it aims to save, preserve from destruction, redeem, or deliver), and one that emphasizes human equality and freedom. You also may have noticed that Scientology beliefs stress the goodness of humanity and spiritual healing, which is viewed as profoundly religious. Surely you detected the belief in an ultimate, supernatural reality or God, and perhaps you recognized that Scientology, like many religions, envisions the ultimate reality as composed of "spirit" rather than "matter." These features of Scientology, along with other prominent

aspects of this religion, will be discussed in greater detail in this chapter.

The typical Scientology Sunday meeting also involves a sermon, much like other American religions. A minister reads Hubbard's statement on "Personal Integrity" and the text of a sermon taken from Hubbard's writings, many of which are considered doctrinal (or scriptural). On some Sundays, especially special occasions, an audio- or videotape recording of a lecture by Hubbard may be played rather than the minister delivering the message. As with Sunday services in most American churches, music is a part of the Scientology worship experience. This may include hymns, some of them written by Scientologists, sung by the congregation as well as inspirational musical performances by a solo entertainer and/or a choir. The mood of worship services, partly because of the music and other forms of audience participation, is very festive, stimulating, and upbeat.

"Group processing," a collective ritual activity, is another standard feature of Scientology services on Sunday morning. It is based on the elementary Scientology practice of "auditing" (as discussed below). The group-processing ritual also derives from a Hubbard text. A central function of this collective, religious ritual is meditative. In other words, it is a form of mental discipline or a focusing of the mind and body. These and related Scientology rituals very much resemble chanting or other meditation exercises as practiced in many Asian religions. They, however, are done in a playful, fun-loving, and celebratory manner, thereby contributing to the joyful mood of the occasion.

Following the group-processing ritual, the minister may make announcements, thereby providing relevant news and information to the congregation. There is no offertory ritual in Scientology services, as is customary among many American churches. Scientology instead (as discussed below) has a distinctive way of generating the financial resources necessary for sustaining any large, complex organization, religious or otherwise, in the world today. Sunday worship concludes with the reading of the "Prayer for Total Freedom," as printed in the church services brochure. It serves the usual purpose of providing a benediction to Scientology's Sunday worship service.

Scientology services on Sundays last for about an hour, as is customary among many American religious denominations. Afterward, parishioners may gather informally for continued fellowship before departing. In the afternoon Scientologists do many of the same things as other Americans. This might involve watching the Super Bowl in late January, going to a baseball game in July, taking their children to a playground, going to lunch or a movie, balancing the checkbook, or shopping for groceries. It also might entail additional religious study, ritual, and meditation or just putting their feet up at home and relaxing in preparation for the beginning of the workweek.

In short, then, the Sunday activities of Scientologists closely resemble those of many other Americans. The members of this very new American religion watch sporting events, have families, hold jobs, enjoy recreational activities, and otherwise actively participate in the larger society, as well as attend religious services once a week. Scientology worship services are not particularly different from those of other religions in their basic order and structure of activity. Scientology, like other religions, includes more and less devoutly active participants and members. It, like other faiths, affirms lofty spiritual beliefs about the origins and development of the universe as well as the nature and religious goals of humanity. It offers formal, ritual processes for humans to follow in achieving these goals, and it provides specific teachings on how to live a just and honorable life. Hence, Scientology contains the same elements of most other religions, including myths, scriptures, doctrines, worship, sacred practices and rituals, moral and ethical expectations, a community of believers, clergy, and ecclesiastic organizations.

L. RON HUBBARD AND THE ORIGINS OF SCIENTOLOGY

Scientology, like many religions, is a product of the activities of a founding figure, Lafayette Ronald Hubbard (1911–1986).[3] Hubbard ("Ron" or "LRH," as he sometimes is affectionately, respectfully, and reverently known to contemporary Scientologists) was colorful, complex, and enigmatic, very much like the founders of other religions. In some ways Hubbard's role in founding Scientology resembles that of biblical prophets, like Moses, Jesus, or Muhammad. In still other ways, Hubbard is more like the founders of Asian religions, such as the Buddha. Some of his voluminous writings form the scriptures of the movement, containing the spiritual teachings, mythology, theology, doctrines, practices, and rituals of Scientology. In addition, Hubbard's works supply the organizational structures and processes of this religion. From the Hubbard bust in Scientology buildings to the text of the Sunday sermon and the printed works that are ubiquitous in Scientology training centers, the founder's presence dominates the physical and spiritual environment of this very new American religion.

Lafayette Ronald Hubbard was born in 1911 at Tilden, Nebraska, but he grew up on a ranch near Helena, Montana. Partly since his father was a U.S. Naval officer, L. Ron Hubbard traveled widely throughout the world, especially Asia, before reaching twenty years of age. Over about the next ten years, he became a successful professional writer, particularly well known for numerous western, fantasy, and science fiction stories. During World War II, Hubbard served as an officer in the navy, and he spent part of 1945 recovering from war injuries in an Oakland, California, hospital. From these early life experiences Hubbard developed interests in Native American and

Asian religions as well as physical and mental healing. His studies resulted in the identification of certain therapeutic techniques, called "Dianetics," a part of which involved "auditing."

The subsequent publication of *Dianetics: The Modern Science of Mental Health* on May 9, 1950, is regarded by Scientology as "a seminal event of the century," and this date is designated as a religious holiday. *Dianetics* was an enormously popular success, resulting in Hubbard's establishment of "Hubbard Dianetics Research Foundations" in various parts of the United States. A primary activity of these centers was training people in the methods of auditing. The following year, Hubbard produced a second book on this subject, *The Science of Survival*, along with the "electropsychometer," or "e-meter" for short, a tool or instrument for auditing. During the early 1950s, Dianetics became a loosely organized movement with strong religious elements. The Hubbard Association of Scientologists and the *Journal of Scientology* were established out of the popular Dianetics movement in 1952, and the first church of Scientology was founded in Los Angeles in 1954. Very quickly, additional Scientology churches and centers were organized, first in the United States and then in other English-speaking countries. Scientologists today claim organizations in 159 countries worldwide.

Hubbard, as Scientology's executive director, supervised the development of the emergent religion from headquarters in Washington, D.C., beginning in 1955. Hubbard moved to Saint Hill Manor in Sussex, England, in 1959, where he continued producing and refining the basic teachings of this new religion. When Hubbard stepped down as executive director in 1966, Scientology was a fully functioning religion, although not yet complete. He officially received the title "Founder" and continued the elaboration of advanced Scientology principles. This portion of Hubbard's religious career, beginning in 1967, was conducted aboard the flagship Apollo, as part of a small flotilla called the "Sea Organization," or "Sea Org," for short. In 1975 the Sea Org moved to a land-based headquarters in Clearwater, Florida, as the "Flag Land Base." During the early 1980s Scientology was reorganized significantly, resulting in the Church of Scientology International, with responsibility for individual churches and worldwide expansion, and the Religious Technology Center, with ultimate authority for doctrine and, thereby in some sense, the entire religion. Hubbard moved to a residence in San Luis Obispo, California, at this time. Gradually, he also turned over authority for the religion he founded to a new generation of leaders, including David Miscavige, the current chairman of the Religious Technology Center. Even so, Mr. Hubbard continued writing—including the publication of new, popular science fiction works—up to his death on January 24, 1986.

PRIMARY SCIENTOLOGY TEACHINGS

Scientology, like most religions, is a syncretization (synthesis or blending) of existing ideas and a reflection of the particular cultural, social, and historical circumstances in which it was born and developed. Much like other religions born in the United States, such as the Latter-day Saint (or Mormon) religion, Scientology mirrors many essentially Western and American values, such as the almost sacred beliefs in democracy, individualism, and freedom. It, unlike other new religions discussed in this book, borrows very little from biblical religions, particularly Christianity. There are general similarities between Scientology and Asian religions, especially Hinduism and Buddhism, and strong indications that Hubbard viewed Buddhism, in particular, very favorably. Scientology seems to have incorporated portions of the diffuse Western esoteric tradition, and it thereby shares some features in common with Gnosticism, Theosophy, New Thought religions, and even the Latter-day Saint religion. It, very much like esotericism generally, mixes distinctively religious elements with more science-like ideas while simultaneously reflecting a religious critique of certain forms of science, especially psychiatry and psychology. This, of course, is hardly surprising during an advanced modern age in a sociocultural environment that has been massively affected by scientific ideologies. That this new religion is syncretic and a product of Western civilization at a particular historical moment does not diminishes its originality, uniqueness, or authentic religious character in the least. Scientology's success provides sound and independent sociological support for the conviction of adherents that it is a distinctly new path to religious salvation.

Mythology of Thetan

Scientology, like most religions, is anchored in a speculative concern for the origin and nature of everything or, more specifically, a mythology. Yet, contrary to the popular tendency to define *myth* as a fable or fictional story, scholars of religion take these sacred stories seriously as what members believe. Religious myths, in other words, are true (or True) for believers, although they usually are not historically accurate or verifiable by scientific methods. The mythology of Scientology develops around the unique notion of "thetan."

The thetan, according to Scientology, is an individualized expression of "theta" (derived from the Greek letter "θ")—the cosmic source and life force. The thetan is the true identity of all human beings, and it is intrinsically good, omniscient, immaterial, and unlimited in creativity. Humans, as thetans, are pure spirit and immortal or godlike. The thetan concept in Scientology therefore is somewhat analogous to the Western idea of soul with some notable exceptions, most importantly the belief that the true nature of all human beings is godlike. It, interestingly, resembles the Latter-day Saints' salvific belief in human progression toward a restored, godlike status in the celestial worlds.

The mythology of Scientology holds that in the primordial past (quite literally a time before "time"), thetans applied their creative abilities to form the MEST (physical) universe. In other words, the universe was created by theta in the form of individualized expressions, thetans, rather than solely by God, the supreme being and creator, as in biblical mythology. The exact nature of God is not defined by Scientology. While Scientologists do not hesitate to refer to "God" or use other like terminologies, this idea generally is presented in impersonal and highly abstract ways. This image of ultimate reality thereby is similar to the Hindu idea of Brahman. In the mythology of Scientology, human beings as thetans are godlike in their ability to expand across the seven dynamics to ultimate reality—the eighth.

With the creation of MEST, according to the Scientology myth, a spiritual crisis emerged when thetans came to identify with their creation rather than their original state of spiritual purity. Over time this identification with the MEST universe, and especially physical bodies, intensified. It finally reached a point where thetans became so enmeshed in MEST that they forgot their true identity as thetans and consequently lost their original spiritual, creative powers. In this way thetans became trapped in a MEST prison of their own creation. Consequently, most people do not realize that they are thetans, spiritually. Instead, they mistakenly believe that they are little more than physically embodied beings.

The thetan is immortal and it repeatedly returns to the MEST universe. For Scientology this transpires through a process called "assumption." This assumption occurs at each birth and it is somewhat analogous to reincarnation. The thetan, in other words, is repeatedly reborn. With each new birth and life, the effects of the MEST universe on the individual become stronger, unless there is special intervention (salvation). This happens because human experiences in MEST are stored in the "reactive mind," a concept that is very much like the Freudian notion of the "unconscious mind." The images of life after life MEST experiences contained in the reactive mind are called "engrams" by Scientology. With the accumulation of engrams, many of them painful and debilitating, people move further and further away from their true spiritual condition and identity as thetans. Salvation from this fate and restoration of the thetan is the fundamental goal of Scientology.

Scientology thereby is similar to Hinduism in recognizing a causal relationship between experiences of the present life and those of earlier incarnations. It is the thetan, like the *atman* of Hinduism, that is immortal, reincarnated, and functions as a person's true spiritual identity. Furthermore, it is the thetan that needs to be liberated and restored to its original spiritual state. The elemental problem of salvation, as it is envisioned by Scientology, is that thetans have become so entangled in MEST for so long that they virtually have forgotten their true spiritual nature. Overcoming this fundamental challenge further is envisioned by the Scientology beliefs in the "ARC Triangle," the previously discussed eight dynamics, and "The Bridge to Total Freedom."

The ARC Triangle

Scientology affirms that the goal of salvation, infinite survival, can be achieved in this life by acquiring the knowledge and understanding of the basic operation of the universe. Or, in other words, the ultimate salvific goal, survival, of immoral beings (thetans) requires a special knowledge and understanding of the universe. Scientology thereby resembles Western esotericism, particularly Gnosticism, in emphasizing the acquisition of special knowledge and related ritual practices as the means to salvation. In this way, it is also similar to Asian religions that stress the development of highly disciplined practices, such as yoga, as a method for religious enlightenment.

For Scientology, this special knowledge or understanding is summarily represented by the "ARC Triangle." It specifies three interdependent features of this unique "understanding," namely affinity, reality, and communication. *Affinity* is defined as the degree of affection or liking. More specifically, affinity is the emotional state, a feeling of love or liking, of the individual. *Reality* is envisioned as an agreement about what exists, such that what people take to be reality and agree exists is real. An interchange of ideas defines the Scientology concept of *communication*, and it is believed to be the most important element of the ARC triangle. According to Scientology, many human survival problems derive from ineffective communication, and at all levels of the movement great stress is put on clarity of communication. In this regard, standard unabridged dictionaries are commonly found at Scientology centers.

The Bridge to Total Freedom

"The Bridge to Total Freedom" provides the religious means whereby Scientologists increase their understanding, as defined by the ARC Triangle, and thereby their spiritual awareness. The Bridge itself is divided into two parts: Training and Processing. *Training* is essentially religious education in the principles and practices of Scientology, and *Processing* is personal spiritual development, which is based on the ritual known as auditing. Viewed as a step-by-step process, each increase in spiritual awareness is believed to result in a greater level of understanding of each of the ARC principles. As individuals acquire greater understanding, they in turn are believed to enhance their functioning across the eight dynamics. Or, in other words, the ability to survive as an individual, family, group, and species is improved greatly, along with the survival of other lifeforms and the physical universe. This further results in greater spiritual awareness and survival potential, ultimately leading to salvation, infinite survival, or infinity.

Therefore, the Bridge to Total Freedom generally is a metaphor for the Scientologists' overall spiritual life. But it also is an explicit and highly detailed outline of the process of personal spiritual development. This process is hierarchical, involving multiple degrees or levels, as charted in "The Bridge to Total Freedom: Scientology Classification Gradation and Awareness Chart of Levels and Certificates."[4] There are two basic stages or disciplines for increasing understanding, as defined by the Bridge, and within each of them a series of corresponding steps specified by particular ritual exercises. The primary objective of the first discipline is to free oneself from the limitations of the MEST universe, while the fundamental goal of the second discipline is to regain all creative powers as a thetan.

In the sacred language of Scientology, getting free of the debilitating consequences of repeated assumptions (lives) in MEST results in a status called "Clear." Until this level is reached, the person is "PreClear." Achieving the status of Clear specifically means that the reactive mind has been cleansed of engrams. These engrams might include painful past-life experiences, previous acts harmful to others, or anything that disguised the person's true creative powers as a thetan. When these engrams are stored in the reactive mind, the person's ability to think clearly, communicate effectively, and truly understand the nature of the universe and his or her true location in MEST is correspondingly diminished significantly. Or, in short, the person's ability to survive across the eight dynamics is reduced greatly.

These teachings involve a critical ethical component. Scientology believes that spiritual advancement goes hand in hand with moral development. Reaching the state of Clear, therefore, carries with it an expectation that PreClears necessarily will conduct themselves according to the highest moral standards. The ethical and moral standards of Scientology differ little from those of the major world religions, such as the biblical Ten Commandments. More specifically, the guiding prescript of Scientology's ethics is to seek the "optimum solution" for any problem based on the outcome that results in the "greatest good for the greatest number of dynamics."[5] Scientologists especially are prohibited from harming the mental and physical well-being of others, as well as damaging their own spiritual, moral, and physical well-being, for instance, by the use of drugs. PreClears, consequently, not only are expected to be spiritually responsible and mature, but also models of integrity and ethical behavior.

Upon becoming Clear, a person is ready to begin reacquiring his or her original creative abilities as a thetan. This more advanced discipline and set of related exercises makes use of the individual's "analytical mind" (rather than the reactive mind). It is known in Scientology as "Operating Thetan," or simply "OT." Free of the reactive mind's engrams, the OT has use of the more self-conscious, spiritually aware, reflective, analytical mind. The OT, by way of the analytical mind, gains spiritual mastery over MEST and the enhanced abilities necessary for promoting survival across all of the eight dynamics. Ultimately, the OT discipline is believed to result in "complete spiritual ability, freedom, independence and serenity, and freedom from the endless cycle of birth and death."[6] The final OT level, in other words, is the realization of the Scientology concept of salvation as infinite survival, or simply infinity.

The OT levels involve ritual practices aimed at increasing the ability of the individual to function across the eight dynamics, many of which increasingly carry with them greater and greater cosmic responsibility. The OT, as a more fully conscious thetan, now is in a position to effect not only his or her own creative powers and the lives of others—by way of service as an auditor, religious official, or public servant, for example—but also all of thetan-humanity and creation as a whole. Scientology specifically aims, ultimately, to "clear the planet" and restore everyone to their original thetan (spiritual) condition. Or, in other words, the OT's ethical and moral responsibilities and standards are envisioned by Scientology as genuinely cosmic in scope.

RELIGIOUS PRACTICES AND RITUALS

Scientology is not exclusivistic and it does not emphasize a singular religious doctrine, unlike most of the religions derived from biblical tradition. It is possible for Scientologists also to believe in Catholicism, Protestantism, or most other religions, and for them to participate in the activities of other religions, including the most sacred rites. Yet, very much like a similar situation with many Asian religions, Scientology does require orthodoxy in its practices (correct practice if not belief). In other words, religious practices, such as auditing, must be performed exactly in the manner prescribed by the Hubbard scriptures and texts. Any interpretation of the Scientology scriptures, furthermore, is unacceptable. The Sunday morning sermon, you may recall, was read by the minister from the scriptures without significant deviation so as to avoid any additional meanings. Put differently, the scriptures are held to be truth (or Truth) as written by Hubbard and canonized by the church. The membership, however, is permitted to believe in other teachings or subscribe to individualized belief in matters not treated by the scriptures, such as the precise nature of God (as noted above). Interestingly, while orthodox belief is not required by this new religion, orthodox practice and strict conformity to ritual standards does tend to result in more uniform, if not completely orthodox, belief in basic Scientology doctrines and teachings.

The most significant Scientology practices and rituals seek to process groups and individuals. All processing is related to the Bridge to Total Freedom and its aim to cross over from MEST bondage to the spiritual freedom of a thetan. The accomplishment of this salvation goal involves "training" in the beliefs and rituals, as well as performance of the "auditing" rituals. The auditing rituals are designed to permit the individual to progress from PreClear to Clear and then to Operating Thetan by way of a series of specific exercises in a step-by-step fashion. Scientology, like most religions, also provides sacred meaning to events like the birth of a child, the joining of a couple, and the death of members.

Auditing

Auditing involves an interactive relationship between a Scientology practitioner (trained auditor) and a parishioner, recruit, or almost anyone interested in participating in this religious practice. It aims to halt the decline of the individual's spiritual awareness, clear previous engrams believed to limit spiritual ability, enhance the person's spiritual understanding, increase survival across the eight dynamics, and eventually restore the individual to his or her original condition as a thetan. Auditing typically focuses on a particular problem or ability through certain exercises in a given session. It is a process, usually involving many sessions at each step as the individual progresses up the Bridge. In this way, auditing is a primary rite in this religion and perhaps the most important one.

Auditing, to a very limited extent, resembles pastoral counseling or confession. Yet, in other ways, it is more like the spiritual disciplines, such as meditation, of Asian religions. The auditor listens but, unlike the pastor or priest, he or she does not provide forgiveness or even advice. Instead, the role of the auditor is to assist the person in self-discovery and greater understanding of the ARC, more like the master teacher of Asian religions. In this way, auditing is designed to facilitate the individual's ability to learn and understand independently. Auditing sessions usually focus on uncovering and clearing particular engrams or previous experiences that limit the person's spiritual awareness, understanding, and creative ability. Increasing the person's ability to communicate effectively, as previously mentioned, is central to the auditing process. Scientologists strongly are encouraged to always look up the meaning of any word they do not understand, and interestingly, the dictionary therefore almost resembles a scriptural work.

Most auditing sessions are conducted with a ritual instrument or tool, the "E-meter." It resembles an electronic measuring device, with various knobs, settings, and displays. The person undergoing auditing holds two canisters loosely, one in each hand, that are connected by electrical cords to the main device. At the outset of an auditing session, the E-meter is calibrated to measure very low electrical voltages. According to Scientology beliefs, the engrams that are stored in the reactive mind as mental images carry minute electrical charges or currents. The purpose of the E-meter is to measure these electric charges or impulses and thereby assist the auditor in helping the parishioner identify spiritual problem areas. Once identified, the auditor repeatedly asks the person undergoing auditing specific questions about this problematic engram. Through questioning, the auditor helps the individual eliminate or clear particular engrams. The E-meter assists this process by measuring when the electrical energy changes and dissipates, thus indicating that the engram has been cleared. Auditing begins with the treatment of simple engrams, then more complex ones, and eventually the refinement of even more difficult spiritual abilities as the person makes his or her way up the Bridge to Total Freedom. At the more advanced OT levels of auditing, the individual acts as his or her own auditor. In other words, individuals conduct "solo" auditing sessions.

The Bridge to Total Freedom enables each person to advance spiritually, by way of auditing, at his or her own pace. It enables people to see precisely what level of spiritual awareness they have achieved and thereby where they stand in relationship to survival on the eight dynamics and salvation. It tells them exactly how far they have advanced and the explicit steps that are necessary to advance further. The Bridge consequently serves as a pilgrimage map that individual

Scientologists follow in conjunction with auditing in pursuit of infinite survival. Consequently, the Scientologists' pilgrimage, unlike that of other religions, is not an outer journey, but rather an inner quest.

Training

Scientology "training" involves serious, intensive religious study. Its primary aim is to educate persons in the theology and techniques of auditing. Much of this study is focused on Scientology scriptures and the various methods of auditing necessary for different levels of processing or grades of spiritual development. This training, much like the vocational education one might receive at a seminary, is divided into particular courses of study. In this way, once a student has completed a course of study, he or she is qualified to provide auditing up to a particular level. Each of the training courses is organized around a certain plan of study and a list of skills to be mastered. These courses are designed to be accomplished by an individual without a formal teacher. Instead, a supervisor of instruction helps students apply Scientology principles if necessary.

It should be emphasized that while Scientology's auditing and training rituals are inner directed, thereby resembling Asian religious disciplines, they are extraordinarily rational rather than mystical. Salvation in many Western, especially biblical, religions aims to perfect the individual by creating a revolutionary, utopian society. The salvific aims of many Asian religions are the religious transformation—by way of an inner-directed, mystical enlightenment—of the individual. Scientology aims to perfect the individual, by exceptionally rational means, who then is enabled to transform society, humanity, and all of the cosmos.

Other Rituals and Ceremonies

Scientology also provides religious practices, rituals, or ceremonies for special occasions. Friday services celebrate the completion of a person's services to the religion during the previous week. Weddings, child naming, and funerals are observed through other rituals. Any ordained Scientology minister may perform these rites. Scientology naming rituals are very much like christening ceremonies in other religions. This involves a welcome to the community, as well as introductions to parents and godparents, and the announcement of the child's name. The minister's other remarks on this occasion typically delineate basic Scientology principles, such as the eight dynamics. There are varied Scientology wedding ceremonies, all of them very much like those of more traditional religions. A minister officiates, the bride and groom exchange vows and rings. Yet, once again, the specific remarks revolve around basic Scientology principles. Likewise, Scientology funerals tend to resemble more traditional religious services in their basic design and structure. The main difference is that the contents derive from the Scientology belief that death is the beginning of a new life since by assumption the individual is reborn until he or she attains infinite survival. In addition to these ceremonies, Scientology celebrates a number of holidays. The two most important celebrations are the founder's birthday (March 13) and the date of the publication of *Dianetics* (May 9). On these days, Scientologists gather at churches, watch simultaneous live broadcasts from major centers of the religion, enjoy musical performances, and listen to speeches about Hubbard and the mission of the religion. Other Scientology holidays include Auditor's Day (the second Sunday in September) and the establishment of the International Association of Scientologists (on October 7).

ECCLESIASTIC ORGANIZATIONS AND COMMUNITY

Hubbard, as noted previously, defined specific guidelines for the organization of Scientology. His concern for the organization of this new religion is reminiscent of other religious visionaries, like the Buddha and Muhammad. They also communicated a revolutionary spiritual message and established a community to ensure the perpetuation and growth of the religions they founded. It must be emphasized that these two features—a message and a community—do not always go hand in hand. When they do, however, the consequences often are very dynamic. Clearly, this is the case with Scientology. Although many, perhaps most, new religions struggle to survive the founding generation, Scientology has moved into a second generation with tremendous vitality and energy.

The ecclesiastical structure of Scientology, like the Bridge to Total Freedom, is founded on two overarching principles: hierarchical design and uniform application. The structure of Scientology thus assures that all of its organizations operate with the same precise degree of order and certainty as does the Bridge. Each Scientology organization, from the smallest local mission to the Religious Technology Center, conforms to the same basic pattern and processes. The hierarchy of institutional roles, across all of Scientology and within each unit or organization, is based on the principles of merit and seniority. People with more education, training, demonstrated abilities, experience, commitment, and dedication to Scientology have authority over those people with lesser or fewer merits, and organizational advancement generally is based on these same merits.

Generally, Scientology and all of its inclusive units and organizations contain the same fundamental subdivisions. These subunits are designed to serve the basic functions, such as leadership, public relations, scripture and doctrine, ritual performances, financial management, and so on, of the particular organization. All Scientology organizations, for instance, have an "Ethics" section, which is responsible for ensuring the ethical conduct of all members of that organization. If an individual's actions are thought to be inappropriate, he or she is referred to Ethics for corrective measures. The primary aim of Ethics is to restore the individual to appropriate and competent functioning within the organization. The Ethics section of all Scientology organizations thereby operates on the related belief that people are basically good and that deviation essentially derives from a lack of knowledge or ability to act normatively. Scientology and all of its inclusive units consequently have a highly rational division of labor and hierarchy of authoritative roles designed for maximum efficiency. In many ways, this organizational structure resembles the bureaucracy of any well-ordered contemporary secular corporation. Indeed, some secular organizations have adopted the organizational designs of Scientology.

Religious Organizations

Two organizations, the Religious Technology Center (RTC) and the church of Scientology International (CSI), direct all of the activities of this new religion. The Religious Technology Center was formed in 1982 to safeguard Scientology's religious symbols, doctrines, and technical practices. Until then Hubbard held the legal rights to these matters. The RTC, as the legal owner of these religious symbols and materials, is responsible for sanctioning their use and otherwise maintaining religious orthodoxy. It seems likely that the RTC also controls the considerable funds derived from the sale of these materials. While the RTC therefore has tremendous power, it does not directly manage the routine activities of other Scientology organizations. Instead, most other Scientology organizations (such as the various churches, missions, and other units described below) are highly autonomous, self-sustaining units. They typically are independent corporations, governed by local boards and authorities, which are financially sustained by the contributions of members and, most substantially, fees collected for auditing.

While the RTC has ultimate responsibility for Church scriptures, doctrines, and rituals, the CSI supervises the religion's ecclesiastical operations. Recognized as the "Mother Church," the CSI manages and coordinates the worldwide activities of Scientology. The CSI, like the central leadership of any substantial religious organization, is responsible for such tasks as publication and distribution of religious literature, proselytizing, ministerial training, communication within the religion, and social outreach programs. Above all, the CSI oversees the correct and uniform delivery of Scientology's two primary religious services: auditing and religious training. Centers that offer these services are organized hierarchically on the basis of the ritual level they are permitted to offer.

The highest levels of training and auditing are provided exclusively at centers known as Advanced Organizations, two of which are based in Clearwater, Florida. They are the Flag Service Organization and the Flag Ship Service Organization, both of which derive their designations from Hubbard's flagship and the elite Sea Org. The Flag Ship Organization, operating from a 440-foot ship, offers the most advanced spiritual work, leading to the highest current Operating Thetan level, OT VIII. The land-based Flag Service Organization is the exclusive source of OT VI and VII training. At lower-level Advanced Organizations, practitioners begin the spiritual exercises necessary to reach OT and advance from OT I through OT V. These centers also provide advanced auditor training, for Class VI and above. The most famous of these training centers is the Saint Hill Church in England, where Hubbard systematized the higher levels of the Bridge. Today, three other Advanced Organizations bear the Saint Hill name, one each in Los Angeles, Copenhagen, and New South Wales (Australia).

Next in this hierarchy are Class V Churches, so designated because they offer training through Class V auditor status. They also provide the auditing needed to "go Clear," and have the authority to educate and ordain ministers. It is at the Class V Churches that the vast majority of Scientologists practice their religion. They hold regular

Sunday and Friday services, celebrate church holidays, and provide training and auditing as well as the naming, wedding, and funeral rituals. A few Class V Churches are designated as Celebrity Centers. While anyone may stay at a Celebrity Center and participate in the activities for which they qualify, these centers are designed specifically to minister to the abundance of famous Scientologists.

At the most elementary level of the religion's hierarchy are field auditors. At the next level up the hierarchy, there are Scientology Missions. It is at these smaller mission centers where many people first encounter Scientology, receive the introductory literature, attend a worship service, and undergo an auditing session. The field auditors and missions are on the vanguard of Scientology's worldwide expansion. Although the missions are found in all parts of the world, many of them are concentrated outside of the more industrialized Western nations. All told, Scientology operates more than 6,000 churches and centers throughout the world.

Social Service Programs

In the early 1970s, under Hubbard's guidance, Scientology turned its attention to pressing social issues and began developing social outreach programs to combat drug addiction, illiteracy, learning disabilities, and criminal behavior. Now operating under the independent heading of the Association for Better Living and Education (ABLE), these programs have grown in size and established themselves as remarkably successful. They are offered to schools, businesses, and community groups as purely secular techniques for social betterment, and although they are based on the works of Hubbard, participants are in no way required to join or even accept the religious teachings of Scientology. Among the more notable programs of this type are Narconon, Criminon, and Applied Scholastics. All three services are international in their outreach, and Criminon programs are found in more than two hundred correctional centers.

Clergy, Recruitment, and Membership

Scientology, like many religions, has a professional, ordained clergy. These people, of course, are among the most committed and dedicated members of the church. The clergy, like this religion generally, is exceptionally hierarchical, based on the level of training and auditing as well as the person's position within the organizational structure. The highest-ranking Scientologists therefore are functionaries of the RTC, the CSI, and the various Advanced Organizations. The most elite Scientology practitioners are members of the Sea Organization, an informal organization that traces its roots back to the original Sea Org established by Hubbard. Members of the Sea Org occupy the highest levels of the Scientology hierarchy, serving as the ministerial staff of all organizations above Class V Churches. They symbolically demonstrate their commitment and dedication by signing an eternal, "billion-year" covenant (which for that reason is not legally binding) with the church. In exchange for their full-time service to Scientology, these people are provided a small allowance for necessities, modest housing (typically a room or small apartment), and meals by the related church organization.

The majority of Scientologists are not ordained ministers. Instead, they are people otherwise employed who take auditing, attend worship services, and/or participate in other aspects of this new religion. In Scientology, unlike many American religions, there is no initiation ritual (like baptism) or other formal recognition of membership. Scientology does actively recruit members, although in a somewhat different way than other religions. Recruitment to Scientology occurs primarily through published literature and, especially, among people who enroll in the beginning auditing rituals. There are fees for ritual services, auditing, and training, and along with income from the sale of church-owned books, tape recordings, and other materials, they provide for the financial support of Scientology. Millions of peo-

Scientology and Psychiatry

Most Americans are familiar with Scientology's opposition to psychiatry and psychology, especially Tom Cruise's occasional and widely publicized outbursts on this subject, even if they know little more about this religion. Scientology's objections to secular beliefs about mental health and illness are religious, deriving from its conviction that people are perfectly divine beings who have been damaged by negative experiences over multiple earthly lifetimes. More specifically, Scientology holds that secular images of mental normalcy are not genuinely scientific, contrary to the claims of psychiatry and psychology. Scientologists teach that related theories are responsible for massive human tragedies, such as the Nazis' pursuit of the Second World War as well as other forms of evil and suffering. They also denounce therapies like lobotomy, electric shock, and drugs as atrocious and inhumane since they sometimes do more harm than good. Scientology, unlike some religions, is not opposed to secular medicine in general.

For most of human existence there was no divergence between sacred and secular images of reality because no culture made this distinction. In premodern cultures everything was understood religiously as a part of sacred reality. Clashes between the sacred and secular have arisen only recently, primarily in Western cultures, under the historical conditions of modernity whereby these socially defined images were distinguished and often times divorced from one another. Religion in the modern world has lost its monopoly on truthful definitions of reality and increasingly competes against multiple versions of itself in a complex, pluralistic religious environment—even as it also confronts upstart rivals like science.

Examples of this conflict between the sacred and secular, particularly religion and science, are legendary. Western Christianity objected strongly to the scientific contentions that the earth was round and revolved around the sun. Many contemporary Protestant fundamentalists reject biological evolution in favor of biblical images of human origins and development, and they object to teaching scientific theories of evolution, even in public schools. Many American Christians oppose medical birth control and/or abortion on religious grounds.

Religion and its adherents usually are passionate and zealous about their belief in sacred reality and its enactment; and science and its proponents commonly are equally fervent about secular reality and its appropriate enactment, sometimes to the point of looking like religion. Viewed in this way, Scientology's objections to psychiatry and psychology, including Tom Cruise's behavior, are hardly unique or unusual. This will not resolve the related disputes, any more than it settles contemporary debates about birth control, abortion, or evolution, but it makes such matters more understandable.

ple have taken auditing, leading the church to estimate the worldwide membership at around eight million to ten million. More conservative, scholarly estimates place the current size of this new religion at no more than a million members.

Unfortunately, there have been no formal scholarly studies of the clergy or membership of Scientology. What little is known about them therefore derives from simple observation. In general, Scientology seems to be composed of people from working- to middle-class social background. The membership appears to be predominantly of European decent, although there are people of color, especially middle-class blacks. The majority of Scientologists in the United States probably are Americans, although members, especially clergy, from other English-speaking and European countries are very common in all of the organizational centers. Consistent with these origins, the membership appears to be mostly people with an average education (at least high school and some college), as well as middle incomes and occupations. These people often are already competent in a middle-class American way, and they tend to be highly oriented to becoming more spiritually aware and, thereby, even more successful in life. With the exception of the children of the membership, few Scientologists seem to be under legal age, and members over sixty-five to seventy-five years of age appear rare. The majority of the membership therefore seems to range in age from their early twenties to late fifties, perhaps with the age distribution skewed toward younger people. Scientologists look to be about equally divided by gender, and women appear to be well represented in positions of authority, perhaps except for only the highest RTC level of the organization.

New Religions and Religious Pluralism

From a variety of backgrounds and for a host of reasons, Scientologists find in their unique religion a path to personal salvation. Following the Bridge, each is seeking realization and complete expression of the eight dynamics of existence and striving to live according to the high ethical ideals prescribed by the movement. For them life is a pilgrimage, a spiritual odyssey from the materialist snare of the reactive mind to the spiritual liberty of the Operating Thetan, from struggle and pain to survival and success, from MEST to Total Freedom and finally the reality of the eighth dynamic—Infinity. At every step along the way they have the strong clear assurance of the words of L. Ron Hubbard, the spiritual technology he discovered, and the Bridge itself that beckons them. For many, however, the spiritual pilgrimage brings them into contact with other, less encouraging elements—condemnation, malice, hatred, and rejection.

In light of its clearly religious character and its genuinely constructive spiritual features, why is it that Scientology has faced such intense opposition and generated such strong negative reactions? A general answer to this question may be offered in observing the simple (but unfortunate) fact that such reactions are typical in cases of new religions, especially successful ones. In this regard we must observe that the hostility Scientology faces today is strikingly reminiscent of the hostility that other young religions have faced in the past. Our chapters on the Latter-day Saints, apocalyptic communities, and metaphysical communities contain stories of how new religions of an earlier era faced the same type of hostility as Scientology faces today. In the case of Scientology, the attacks have been from the media, governments, the medical community (chiefly the psychiatric profession), and other, more established religions. These institutions are rather familiar critics of new religious movements, and their attacks on Scientology are not particularly unique in this context—aside, perhaps, from their intensity and persistence. Each of the secular institutions is a powerful force in our society, and their aggressive antagonism toward Scientology, especially when occurring in tandem with the other institutions, has created great challenges not only for the religion and its participants but also for people interested in learning more about it. Because of the rather complex relationship of Scientology to the institutions noted above, it is beyond the scope of this short study to elaborate in detail why Scientology has received such intense opposition. Nonetheless, three broad explanations seem worthy of brief consideration.

First, like other new religions, Scientology critiques certain social conventions and traditions, religious and secular, which in turn is a challenge to representative religious and secular organizations. Resistance to Scientology by established social institutions therefore is not surprising. Second, Scientology has been enormously successful, unlike many new religions, which seldom reach such a high level of visibility. Almost from the beginning, Scientology has been popular and extremely visible. Its initial challenge to the established social order thereby has been heightened. Consequently, the reactions of Scientology's antagonists have been all the more intense. Finally, Scientology has been extraordinarily vigilant in defending itself, especially against charges that it is not a religion. At one time these self-defense activities were excessive. For instance, they led to illegal activities, particularly by zealous members of a short-lived operation called the Guardian's Office.[7]

Scientology has otherwise conformed to American law and has been remarkably successful in resisting its attackers. In some instances its successful self-defense may have led to even more strident attacks and greater persistence on the part of its opponents. It is notable that, although Scientology immediately disbanded the Guardian's Office once its illegal actions came to light, most attacks on the church inappropriately cite its excesses as typical of Scientology as a whole.[8] Again, none of this is unusual for a new religion as it adjusts to the larger society and as traditional institutions adapt to the new religion. Many other new American religions have similar histories, and major world religions, like Christianity, also contain many instances of extreme tensions with their larger sociocultural environment, frequently resulting in violence and even warfare.

Scientology, then, has certain similarities with other religions, old and new. Like all religions, it faces the challenge of communicating its distinctive teachings and practices in a pluralistic culture, and elements in the larger society may resist its teachings and condemn its practices. With Scientology, like many young religions, the resistance and condemnation encountered has been especially severe. These similarities with other religions, however, do not minimize the distinctiveness of Scientology. It decidedly is a very new and unique religion in all meaningful senses, no matter how different it may be in particular ways from the more established world religions. Being different is what pluralism is all about. Yet, this challenges all of us to understand and, it is hoped, acquire respectful tolerance for others, especially when we hold different views and beliefs. We therefore hope you have gained a greater understanding for what Scientology truly is: one of America's youngest religions, a vital contribution to our healthy religious ecology, and a witness to the ideals of religious freedom that all of us cherish so dearly.

Notes

1. This and other portions of our account are based on field work conducted January 26–29, 2001, in Los Angeles, California, and other times, mostly in Clearwater, Florida, over the last ten years. The authors gratefully acknowledge the cooperation and assistance of the Church of Scientology with this scholarly research.
2. A Church of Scientology publication, *Scientology: Theology and Practice of a Contemporary Religion, A Reference Work* (Los Angeles: Bridge Publications, 1998), hereafter cited as *Scientology*, includes eight appendices by various distinguished religion scholars, all of whom consider and confirm that Scientology is a religion.
3. See Roy Wallis, *The Road to Total Freedom: A Sociological Analysis of Scientology* (New York: Columbia University Press, 1977); J. Gordon Melton, *The Church of Scientology* (Torino, Italy: Leumann, 2000, published in the United States by Signature Books, Salt Lake City, Utah); and "L. Ron Hubbard, Founder of Scientology," 87–93 in *Scientology*.
4. First published in 1965, the chart of the Bridge is reproduced in various Scientology publications, including *Scientology*, 56. It is easiest to read in poster form (L. Ron Hubbard Library, 1998).
5. *Scientology*, 27.
6. Quoted from "Operating Thetan, 27–28, in "An Introduction to Church Services."
7. See Melton, *The Church of Scientology*, 12–17, 19–21, and 53–60 for additional details.
8. Melton, *The Church of Scientology*, 16, 21.

STUDY QUESTIONS

1. Describe when and how the religion of Scientology emerged. How was the birth of this new religion influenced by American culture and society? And what did this involve?

2. List the key features that result in the conclusion that Scientology is a "religion" and indicate how, on this basis, it is alike or different from other American religions.

3. What are the major beliefs of Scientology? How are these beliefs related to and enacted through ritual?

4. Compare and contrast the central mythology of Scientology and the biblical genesis mythology. Does the "truth" of these myths depend on history or science? Why or why not?

5. How is Scientology socially organized? In what ways is the social organization of Scientology alike or different from other American religions? Why and how is it important for a religion to have a socially organized community of believers?

6. What is "auditing"? How is it alike and different from other religious rituals?

7. Why do new religions, like Scientology, often face prejudice on the part of the larger society and particular interest groups? Discuss this issue in terms of the basic ideals of religious freedom and pluralism in the United States.

8. Why is Scientology a "successful" new religion? What do you think Scientology will look like in another one hundred years? Why?

9. What is the central aim of the religion of Scientology? How is this alike or different from the primary objectives of other religions?

10. What is the principal appeal of the religion of Scientology? To what kinds of people does it appeal? Why?

ESSAY TOPICS

The Birth and Development of New Religions

Similarities and Differences between Old and New Religions

The Influence of Culture and Society on Religion

Social Responses to New Religions and the Responses of New Religions to Prejudice and Misunderstanding

The Uniqueness of New Religions

WORD EXPLORATION

The following words play significant roles in any discussion of Scientology in America and are worth careful reflection and discussion.

Dianetics	Assumption	Auditing
Processing	Syncretic	Thetan
Infinite Survival	Infinity	Eight Dynamics
MEST	Reactive Mind	Engrams
ARC Triangle	The Bridge	RTC

FOR FURTHER READING

Christensen, Darthe Refshund. "Inventing L. Ron Hubbard: On the Construction and Maintenance of the Hagiographic Mythology of Scientology's Founder," 227–258 in *Controversial New Religions,* ed. James R. Lewis and Jesper Aagaard Petersen. New York: Oxford University Press, 2004.

Kent, Stephen A. "Scientology's Relationships with Eastern Religious Traditions," *Journal of Contemporary Religion* 11, no.1 (1996), 97–126.

Kent, Stephen A. "The Creation of 'Religious' Scientology," *Religious Studies and Theology* 18, no. 2 (Dec. 1999):97–126.

Kent, Stephen A. "Brainwashing Programs in the Family/Children of God, and Scientology," 349–78 in *Misunderstanding Cults: Searching for Objectivity in a Controversial Field,* ed. Benjamin Zablocki and Thomas Robbins. Toronto: University of Toronto Press, 2001.

Melton, J. Gordon. *The Church of Scientology.* Studies in Contemporary Religion series. Salt Lake City: Signature Books, 2000.

DVD

ABC News 20/20: The Church of Scientology (DVD May 14, 2007, 40 minutes)

WEB SITES

www.scientology.org/
   The Church's official Web site, with FAQs, current statistics, and a brief history

www.rickross.com/groups/scientology.html/
   Information about Scientology's international presence and controversial issues

www.cesnur.org/testi/se_scientology.htm
   Center of Studies on New Religions, with scholarly and journalistic articles

17

Nature Religions: American Neopaganism and Witchcraft

DANNY L. JORGENSEN

1463	Latin translation of *Corpus Hermeticum* (foundational text for subsequent Western esotericism and occultism)
1700s	European revival of paganisms and occultisms and fascination with ancient religions
1875–1925	Syncretism of Western esotericism and occultism, especially by Hermetic Order of the Golden Dawn in Britain and Theosophy in the United States
1920s	Anthropologist Margaret Murray popularizes idea that witchcraft survived in Europe to the present as a secret underground religion
1950s	Gerald Gardner publishes book series announcing the revival of European witchcraft (Wicca) in Great Britain
1960s	Church of All Worlds, one of earliest American Neopagan organizations, founded by Oberon Zell-Ravenheart and others; the magazine *Green Egg* published; Raymond Buckland introduces Gardnerian witchcraft to the United States
1970s	U.S. Neopaganism and witchcraft become a visible religious movement with publication of Margot Adler's *Drawing Down the Moon* and Starhawk's (Miriam Simos) *The Spiral Dance*; increased feminist interest in ancient Goddess religions and emergence of Dianic witchcraft (Wicca)
1980s–1990s	Growth of American Neopaganism and witchcraft: increased visibility at public gatherings and festivals, diversification into eclectic and internet forms, and considerable scholarly attention
2001	Number of U. S. Wiccans estimated at over 400,000, though reliable numbers are hard to come by
2006	Don Larsen's application to become first Wiccan chaplain in the U.S. army denied

A WINTER SOLSTICE RITUAL

It was the eve of winter solstice (the short-est late December day of the year) in a state park in north central Florida, and by nearly midnight it was clear and almost cold.[1] Twenty-two of us from around the eastern United States, all connected by networks of friendship, had gathered here for a three-day weekend. There were single men and women, mostly between twenty-five and fifty years of age, single- and two-parent families with infants and/or older children, young adult couples without children, and middle-aged couples whose children were grown and inde-pendent. Most of those gathered to this state forest were college educated, and many of us were professionals with advanced degrees. By all appearances we were ordinary work-ing- to middle-class Americans enjoying a winter holiday in a state park.

We did come to this Florida park for the usual purposes of camping, hiking, and oth-erwise delighting in nature, making or renew-ing friendships, as well as sharing experiences and socializing. But we also planned on engaging in sacred activities and having reli-gious experiences. Our main religious event was to be a celebration of the winter solstice, marking the sun's return to North America as well as the end (death) of the darker half and the beginning (rebirth) of the lighter half of the solar year. We would find in this event and its religious commemoration an abun-dance of other sacred symbols and meanings, many of them involving the endless cycle of birth, death, and regeneration. Our winter solstice ceremony would remind us of our unity with nature and the cosmos. Indeed, it would prompt the recollection of the inter-connectedness of the heavens, earth, plants, animals, and all of us in a cosmic whole, succinctly captured by the hermetic (occult) expression "as above, so below."

We did not announce these religious intentions to state officials in making our camp reservations or checking into the park. They simply were told that we were a "family reunion" to avoid attracting any unwanted attention to our religious activi-ties. The practitioners of nature religions, especially witchcraft (or Wicca), feel that other Americans often misunderstand and sometimes oppose their religion.[2] Stories of religious prejudice and discrimination being directed toward Wicca and other nature religions are prevalent. Believers therefore sometimes conceal their religious identities and activities from outsiders.

Nature is sacred for these religions. Nat-ural cycles, such as the seasons of the solar year and the lunar months, provide occasions for celebration. The winter solstice—partic-ularly for nature religions borrowing from, reviving, and revitalizing the pre-Chris-tian religions of ancient Celtic Europe—is one of the "lesser sabbats," known as "Yule." The other lesser commemorations are "Litha" (summer solstice in late June), "Eostar" (spring equinox in late March), and "Mabon" (the autumn equinox in late September). The even more significant reli-gious holidays or "greater sabbats" on this ecological "wheel" of the seasonal solar year are: "Samhain" (November eve, the begin-ning of the new year), "Imbolc" (February eve), "Beltane" (May eve), and "Lugnasad" (August eve). The thirteen annual lunar events (full moons) also are celebrated by "esbats." The esbats typically are occasions for working magic and healing.

Ritual Preparations

On Saturday morning a small, volunteer committee was formed to plan our Yule sab-bat ritual. The rest of us spent much of the day exploring the forest and appreciating the natural environment. Many of us collected together for lunch and discussions of our nature (and sacred) experiences. Late that afternoon some of us built a campfire, an odd assortment of large and small drums were brought out, and a half dozen drummers beat out various rhythms. Other participants danced in a circle around the fire for several hours. Drumming and dancing often result in religious experiences, and these activities also help establish a mood and mentality for more formal religious rituals.

After cleaning up a communally prepared and consumed late-evening meal, the ritual participants began further preparations for the Yule sabbat. Most of them dressed in special ritual attire. The ritual costumes typically were long, loose, flowing robes in dark colors. Many of the robes were adorned with sacred symbols such as the sun, moon, stars, earth, water, fire, and air; or sundry deities like the Earth Mother or classical Greek or Roman goddesses. Some of the participants also painted these and other sacred symbols, like pentagrams or astrological signs, in bright colors on their faces or exposed skin of hands, arms, and legs. Several of the Yule participants wore headdresses of feather or horn. A few of us wore ordinary street clothes, typically dark jeans and a shirt, and most of us wore other warm clothing, including a jacket.

Worshiping in the nude or "skyclad" (clothed only by the sky) is common in many nature religions. Some of the people gathered for this solstice conduct rituals skyclad. This is done, most commonly, when they are engaged in "solitary" (alone and private) practices, or when they are participating in small, intimate, family-like groups (five–fifteen people) that regularly gather together for religious purposes, such as esbats. Our gathering was too large and diverse (including underaged children and people not previously well known to one another) for everyone to feel comfortable with a skyclad ritual. Besides, it was too cold for most of us to run around naked for several hours in the woods at midnight in late December, even in Florida.

All of the winter solstice participants helped collect the necessary ritual materials and implements (tools). The sacred items included candles, incense, water, salt, fire (matches or a lighter), as well as food (cookies and fruit juice), while a chalice (or cup), an athame (a dull-edged knife-like instrument), and a short wand or longer staff were the more usual tools. Another common rit-

ual tool is a sword, although none of these participants carried one. Once dressed, all of the ritualists began meditating or otherwise preparing mentally and emotionally for the Yule sabbat, either by themselves, in pairs, or in other small assemblies. Altogether, getting dressed and outfitted, collecting materials and tools, and reflecting on the sacred occasion is believed to be essential preparation for ritual. While the participants were very serious about ritual, they were not necessarily solemn. We often joked and played around, and these more jovial activities helped relieve the emotional excitement and tensions created by anticipation of the sacred Yule holiday.

Creating Sacred Space

Nature religions typically do not have permanent sacred buildings dedicated to religious purposes. These religions sometimes erect temporary structures for particular purposes, such as a sweat lodge. They also sometimes employ existing buildings, like a member's home, for religious activities. Yet, more prevalently, they create sacred space, physically and figuratively, out of the natural environment in a suburban backyard, a city park, the beach, a farm, or the wilderness. Our ritual committee formerly had selected a site for the Yule event. It was an opening in the forest, surrounded by tall pines, on a small rise about one-half mile from camp. This location was believed to be uniquely sacred and powerful, as determined by those who are regarded as gifted in discerning such matters. The ritual site, not insignificantly, also was out of immediate sight and sound of park officials and other campers.

At the selected ritual place the committee had constructed a small altar (about eighteen inches around) out of wood and stone found in the forest. It was erected at the northernmost point of an imagined circle large enough to hold all of the participants standing shoulder to shoulder around the perimeter. The other cardinal directions (west, south, east) of the circle were marked with rocks and candles on the ground. Just before the start of the ritual, the altar was equipped with candles, several statues of deities from classical mythology, burning incense, and bowls (or cups) of salt and water. With the creation of the circle, the committee also sanctified it "magically," by their related thoughts and deeds as well as by the use of incense (fire), sacred water, and salt. So prepared, the ritual circle thereby constituted a "portable temple," or sacred space appropriate for religious purposes.

About thirty minutes before midnight, several members of the ritual committee went ahead to the sacred circle in order to make further preparations. Shortly thereafter, the rest of us followed the other committee members through the forest. We filed along in pairs and bunches, sometimes whispering and even joking among ourselves. It was a beautiful night in spite of the upper-thirty-degree temperature. Away from the city, we could see the stars shining brightly in the winter sky. It was amazingly quiet, except for the sound of a few birds and the rustle of our feet as we walked through the woods. The pine added a wonderful aroma to the cold, clean air. The shadowy darkness provided a certain mystery as we moved toward the circle in anticipation of the impending ritual.

Just before reaching the ritual space we were instructed by committee members to line up in pairs, male and female, thereby preserving the natural balance of sexual energies, male to female, female to male. A committee member stood at the outer entrance to the circle. He "tested" each of us with the question: "Why have you come here tonight?" As each participant provided what apparently was a satisfactory response, we were permitted to move to the entrance of the circle. Here, each participant was welcomed into the circle by a committee member of the opposite gender. As a part of this welcome, each of us was anointed (blessed) with scented and previously sanctified oil touched to the forehead in the shape of a

pentagram. We also exchanged a hug and kiss on the cheek with the anointing person, before passing through a metaphorical portal cut for this purpose into the sacred space. Once inside the temple, we filed clockwise around the perimeter, carefully observing the female-male order and thereby defining the actual circle by our presence.

Opening Rites

One of the committee, performing the role of high priestess, declared the purpose of our gathering, namely to celebrate the end of the dark portion of the year, the return of the sun, and the beginning of the light half of the year. Another member, as high priest of the circle, reflected further on the symbolic significance of the mythic timelessness of life, death, and rebirth, and he generalized this natural cycle to various other polarities (gods and goddesses, good and evil, material and spiritual) forming the quintessential human quest for meaning. Following these remarks, both ritual leaders lighted candles on the altar, perhaps symbolizing the new sun and light.

Nature religions usually are very egalitarian collectivities with little formal social organization. Often all members are regarded as clergy (priestesses and priests), and any hierarchical (ranked) relationships are temporary and/or based on experience, age, and merit. Women as well as men perform leadership roles, and women—as priestesses or high priestesses—usually are the principal leaders of ritual events and groups. Many of the participants in our Yule sabbat perform leadership roles with the groups in which they ordinarily practice at home. Those designated as leaders for our ritual were such for this event only, not any subsequent activity, although they were selected (informally by general agreement) because of previous experience, skill, and knowledge.

Next, four members of the committee, alternately female and male, proceeded to "call the quarters," in sequence, beginning in the East, followed by the South, West, and North. This process sometimes is known as "charging the circle" since part of the intention is to draw magical or sacred energy to the ritual space. Each of the quarter callers began with a popular phrase, "Hail Guardians of the Watchtowers of the East" (or the appropriate, sequential direction). In each instance, this salute was followed by an invocation of the directional correspondences to the alchemical elements of air (East), fire (South), water (West), and earth (North), sometimes including additional remarks about each element. Then, the gods and goddesses were invited to join the ritual. In each instance, the callers of the quarters raised an actual or imaginary athame to the cardinal direction at the outset and the other ritual participants joined him or her in this action. This ended with most of the participants drawing an imaginary pentagram in the air and the collective verbal expression, "so mote it be" or, alternately, "hail and welcome," with the calling of each quarter. This opening portion of the ritual concluded with lighting the candle at each quarter in sequence.

Middle Rites

We then observed a few minutes of silence, during which some of the Yule participants took deep, heavy breaths, probably for the purpose of ritual cleansing and meditation. Following the silence, the high priestess and high priest moved to the north facing the altar. The priestess pointed an athame toward the sky, whispered a "spell" (a few words inviting the goddess to join with her), and visualized the goddess energy entering her, a practice known as "drawing down the moon." Then she picked up a chalice from the altar and turned to face the priest, who had turned facing her. He slowly lowered an athame into the chalice, symbolizing the union of male and female, an act also known as the "Great Rite." Together they blessed the cookies and fruit juice ("cakes and ale"), leaving offerings of each on

the altar to the deities. The food then was shared between them and passed around the circle to the other ritual participants. For about the next thirty minutes we talked and "feasted" together.

During the discussion some of the participants suggested that it would be appropriate to "raise a cone of power." All of us joined hands and drew very near, slowly raising our hands in the air, forming a tight bunch of people. Everyone then took about a dozen deep breaths, slowly releasing the air each time. Next, led by one of the participants, we started a chant, beginning with a deep, almost inaudible, vibrating sound and building to a loud, full chord. This was repeated several times as the ritual participants raised and lowered their hands, finally collapsing together in a heap on the ground.

Slowly recovered from the cone of power exercise, we once again joined hands and re-created the larger circle. As we began moving together in a clockwise direction, one of the participants began singing a folk song about the sun and light, appropriate to the Yule celebration. The rest of us gradually joined in song as we caught onto the music and lyrics. Singing and dancing around the circle continued for about ten minutes. The aim of this activity, in part, was to ease the participants from the altered, sacred consciousness of ritual time and space back to the ordinary world of daily life, sometimes called "grounding." Then, the high priestess signaled that it was time to dismiss the quarters, thank the deities, and close the circle.

Concluding Rites

The quarters were dismissed in reverse order along with raised athemas (actual or imaginary) and words thanking the guardians of the watchtower for joining and protecting our activities. This portion of the rite concluded with the expression "hail and farewell," or, alternately, "so mote it be." Skilled fingers extinguished each of the quarter candles in sequence. Then the priestess and priest thanked the deities and offered brief reflections on the return of the sun and light. Finally, the high priestess declared "the circle is open, but never broken; merry meet, merry part, and merry meet again." A joyous chorus of everyone else present joined her in this exclamation. The ritual, lasting almost two hours, was over. Most of us sat on the ground, quietly contemplating the religious experience, and the rest of them stood around talking softly about sacred experiences for a few minutes. These few moments also helped "ground" us further.

Before leaving the ritual site, the committee requested assistance with clearing up the area, restoring the altar to nature, and transporting all of the materials back to camp. Walking back to camp, the participants talked in still elated ways about the ritual and its magical, sacred power. Once back in camp, many of the participants began an all-night vigil aimed at welcoming the return of the morning sun. Some of them planned on conducting a brief ritual at dawn for honoring the sunlight.

NATURE RELIGIONS

The participants in this Yule holiday all are members of what may be described very loosely as "nature religions."[3] These religions take the natural environment, broadly construed to include almost everything in the universe not created by human beings (like material and nonmaterial culture), to be the sacred center of their beliefs and activities. Nature, moreover, generally is believed to be a dynamic, living entity, including such inanimate things as stars and planets. In this respect, these religions are similar to most of the primal religions of the world's indigenous peoples, such as Native Americans, although primal religions are different on many other accounts (and they are not a part of what is discussed here). Anthropologists sometimes use the term *animism* to describe the primal religious belief that all of nature—things like rocks and seemingly nonconscious life-forms such as trees—are

alive and possess a nonmaterial, "spirit" (soul) or spiritual quality. Animism also roughly describes the nature religions discussed here.

A closely related idea, characteristic of these nature religions, is that deities, or religious and spiritual qualities, are inherent in all of nature, literally or metaphorically. This notion sometimes is described as "pantheism." That spiritual qualities, deity, or deities are present in everything further indicates that they are "immanent." This concept—that deity is pervasive in everything—differs significantly from the image of a transcendental deity, external to and beyond the natural world, as in the case of the biblical God. For these religions then, nature is "sacred" or religious in character insofar as it is alive and animated by spirit qualities or entities that are present in everything in the universe not created by humans (immanent and pantheistic). Nature, in all of these senses, is at the center of these religions and, consequently, this is what is meant here by "nature religions." These religions believe that it is very important to respect and preserve the natural environment and, indeed, the entire planet earth.

Most of these religions, as previously illustrated, hold that everything in the universe is interrelated and interconnected in mysteriously and religiously complex ways. In other words, nature is alive, dynamic, enchanted, and fully interrelated in a cosmic totality. What connects all of this usually is envisioned as what is sacred, the life force, cosmic energy, and the like, or sometimes deity or deities. No belief in deity or deities is required, however, since the sacred, energizing life force may be envisioned as simply inherent in nature or its various manifestations, particularly human beings. This dynamic life force commonly is conceptualized as deriving from balanced polarities (opposites), such as light and dark, birth and death, female and male energies, and so on. Hence, for some of these religions everything in nature, humans included, are deity or deities.

When nature religions subscribe to deity or deities, they usually—but not always—are held to be plural and diverse. The belief in multiple deities commonly is known as "polytheism." Any belief in deities need not be actual or literal. Some of these religions and some adherents think literally in terms of embodied, personified deities. Other nature religions and some believers regard deities figuratively or metaphorically. Deities, in other words, may be envisioned as useful symbols but not literal descriptions of actual or spirit entities. Either way, most of these religions subscribe to and emphasize female deities, although not to the exclusion of male deities. The Great Goddess commonly is known by particular aspects, such as maiden, mother, or crone (referring to the human life cycle). She is usually symbolized by the moon. The Goddess also is known by a host of names, like Earth Mother, Aphrodite, Brigid, Isis, Venus, and so on. Male deity frequently is envisioned as the Horned God, the Great Mother Goddess's opposite and consort. He typically is symbolized by the sun or a bull. The God also may be known by many other names, such as Anubis, Apollo, Hermes, Jupiter, Odin, Osiris, Pan, or Zeus.

are substantially different from the original versions. In present-day form, these religions are composed of elements borrowed for pre-Christian Europe, for instance, as well as many other sources, including persisting folk traditions, and especially Western esotericism and occultism, synthesized and revitalized in new, contemporary forms.[4]

Indeed, American Neopaganism derives substantially from a synthesis of ancient religions, particularly of Egypt and Persia but including heterodox elements of biblical religions, assembled in the West during the first few centuries of the Common Era. During the Renaissance these ideas formed Christian Hermeticism, which incorporated a version of the mystical Jewish Cabala (often spelled Kabbala by the Hermeticists and their successors). Subsequently discredited culturally by what became orthodox Catholicism, the Hermetic-Kabbalistic tradition moved underground as Western occultism. It stimulated assorted European revivals, especially in Great Britain during the late nineteenth and early twentieth centuries.[5] Much of American Neopaganism derives from this source, particularly in the form of "ceremonial magic" and witchcraft or Wicca.[6]

Neopaganism

These nature religions are known by other labels. Many, perhaps a majority, of adherents think of them as a form of paganism. This term usually refers to the pre-Christian religions of ancient Celtic Europe or the specific religions of particular peoples, such as Italians, Norse folk, or Druids. However, it also may be used almost indiscriminately with reference to most any nonbiblical religion, such as those of indigenous world cultures, the religions of the ancient world (like Egypt), or even the world religions of Asia (such as Hinduism and Buddhism). "Neopaganism" is an increasingly popular description of most nature religions. Modifying the name paganism in this way explicitly acknowledges that the religions so described

Wicca

A majority of American Neopagans claim to be "eclectic."[7] What is meant by this is that they freely borrow from many sources of nature religion as well as many other contemporary religions and forms of knowledge. This includes primal religions, such as those of Native America and Africa, syncretic New World religions like Santeria and voodoo, the religions of Asia, and even biblical religions and modern sciences like astrophysics and psychology. Most of the participants in the Yule ritual described earlier are "eclectic" Neopagans. Many of them initially were trained in some variety of Wicca and/or ceremonial magic and later they began experimenting with and incorporating other elements of nature religions

The Pentagram

Religions are often represented by a distinctive symbol, such as the Star of David for Judaism or the cross for Christianity. The symbol most commonly but not universally used by Neopagans, especially Wicca, is the star pentagon, a five-pointed star formed with straight lines, best known as a *pentagram*. The star of the Neopagan pentagram conventionally is pointed up and enclosed in a circle.

In one form or another the five-pointed star symbol is probably at least six thousand years old. Many sacred meanings were associated with it in the ancient world, but like other Neopagan beliefs, it derives most substantially from a later era, namely Renaissance Hermeticism—especially as it was incorporated into subsequent occult revivals in Europe and related secretive societies, such as Freemasonry, the Rosicrucians, and the Golden Dawn. Western occult traditions commonly linked the five points of the star with the alchemical elements of earth, air, fire, and water, plus the unifying feature of Spirit. All are harmoniously united within the circle for Neopaganism. There are also other aspects of the pentagram's symbolism, such as its connection to Venus.

The usual pentagram symbol of Neopaganism should be distinguished from the inverted pentagram, with two points of the star directed upward, a symbol that is sometimes associated with evil and negative magic. Reflecting the American fascination with the occult and its perceived association with evil and the devil, the pentagram in its upright or inverted orientation is an ever-present feature of popular culture. It shows up in countless forms of mass entertainment, such as Hollywood movies and heavy metal music.

into their beliefs, practices, and collective activities. The Yule ritual is derived primarily from Wicca, but it also included other components.[8]

Witchcraft, Wicca, or simply the "Craft" is the largest single segment of American Neopaganism.[9] It largely is an "invented tradition," developed from the British witchcraft revival of the middle 1950s, especially as advanced by Gerald Gardner.[10] This Wicca was imported to the United States during the early 1960s.[11] Since the late 1970s, American Neopaganism generally, and Wicca in particular, were advanced further by a feminist disenchantment with patriarchal religions, a related fascination with ancient goddess worship—some of it derived from archeology—and the formation of women's spiritual alternatives.[12] Consequently, American Wiccans today are exceptionally diverse. Some focus on goddess worship (sometimes called *Dianic*

witchcraft); some follow the original or modified teachings of Gardner (Gardnerian) or another founding figure, Alexander Sanders (Alexanderian); some learned the Craft from family members (Hereditary, Family, or Kinship witches), as well as versions developed by particular people such as Raymond Buckland or Gavin and Yvonne Frost, among many others.[13] Contemporary American Wicca, it must be emphasized, has nothing to do with Satanism. Wiccans do not believe in the biblical Satan or devil, notwithstanding the popular tendency to equate witchcraft and Satanism.

A New Religion

Contemporary American nature religions therefore include Neopaganism and its largest single component, Wicca, along with a diverse assortment of women's spirituality groups, with focuses on goddess worship and feminist spirituality. While these religions borrow heavily from pre-Christian religions as well as Western esotericism and occultism, they mostly are recent religious innovations. Few contemporary nature religions are continuous socially with anything before 1900, and most of them derive from innovations of the middle 1950s. Furthermore, no sizeable nature religion movement existed in the United States before the late 1970s and early 1980s. Over about the last thirty to forty years, however, this new religious movement has grown very rapidly. It has produced a bewildering array of innovations, a proliferation of new literature, and a host of novel groups and associations. Solidified by extensive social networks, these nature religions now are supported by an elaborate "cultic milieu" (as discussed below).[14] Today, there are at least two hundred thousand American practitioners of nature religions. Estimates of twice that number are not implausible, and this does not include the "New Age" movement, which shares in common certain beliefs and practices but few social connections, networks, or collective activities.

NATURE RELIGIONISTS

Very little was known about the people involved with nature religions until recently.[15] Many of them are "solitary" practitioners for part or all of their religious careers, and many of them are secretive about their religious identities or selective, to a greater or lesser extent, about revealing this information to others. Most participants in nature religions were not born into them, and some of them maintain traditional religious affiliations as Catholics, Protestants, Jews, or something else, sometimes mixing and individualizing their old and new religious convictions and activities. It has become increasingly common for nature religion groups to incorporate or otherwise seek legal and public recognition. Yet the vast majority of these organizations—variously called churches, lodges, fellowships,

or covens, among other possible names—are small, informal, and usually independent of one another. Without permanent religious buildings or telephone listings (although some now have Internet addresses), nature religions consequently are mostly invisible to the larger American public.

The Participants

What is known about the nature religionists strongly suggests that they are rather ordinary Americans. A majority of them range in age from twenty-six to forty-one, not counting children, but younger and older people certainly participate in these religions. A slight majority of the participants are women, not unlike other American religions. Most of them are whites of European descent, living in or near urban centers. The participants in nature religions typically are working- to middle-class Americans. Substantial numbers of them are highly educated and employed in skilled occupations and professions.

Marriage, Family, and the Life Cycle

More impressionistically, the participants in nature religions seem to be about evenly distributed between singles and couples. They may be less likely to marry, formally, than other Americans. Most nature religions believe that human sexuality is normal, natural, and sacred. Consequently, they generally put few restraints on sexual expression between consenting adults, beyond the expectation that people conduct themselves with respect and responsibility for one another. There are, for instance, no general prohibitions against same-gender sexual relationships or premarital sexuality. The "Great Rite" (sexual union) or other symbolic expressions of sexuality are a part of many celebrations, especially Beltane (May eve—the second-most important holiday). The Beltane celebration frequently includes a sexually symbolic Maypole dance. With the notable exception of the Frosts' version of Wicca (which involves actual ritual sexuality), however, the physical act of intercourse almost never is performed publicly.

Because they are nature religions, the human life cycle is of special importance. The birth of a child usually is acknowledged in ritual, either in private, public, or both. There are few formal norms for these ceremonies, and the participants usually are creative in designing a specific ritual and/ or enacting one as part of another holiday. Puberty rituals perhaps are less prevalent, but girls and boys sometimes are welcomed to sexual maturity or adulthood in private and public ceremonies. When performed, these rituals tend to be highly individualized for the initiate. Many groups make provisions for the religious socialization of youthful members, and larger gatherings, such as festivals (as discussed below), typically have special activities for them. Children's activities may include games, music, and other arts as well as training in the gods and goddesses, magical practices, fire building, and so on.

Most nature religions have a wedding or coupling ceremony, although it too tends to be designed creatively and uniquely for the couple. Among Wiccans it usually is called "handfasting." Their view of handfasting differs from more conventional American marriages in that it may be contracted for a specific length of time, a year, five years, or whatever the couple desires, including until death. Wiccans may or may not exchange vows of sexual exclusivity as part of handfasting. Among nature religionists there is a lot of talk about alternative forms of sexuality and the inclusion of multiple parties, particularly threesomes, in relationships. The best available evidence, however, indicates that Neopagans are no less or more likely to be strictly monogamous than Americans in general.[16]

Nature religions, unlike American culture generally, value age—especially the experience and wisdom often accompanying it—very highly. Older members (commonly defined as over fifty or fifty-five years of age)

of these religious communities generally are assumed to have highly valuable experiences and knowledge to share with others. Mostly for this reason, they tend to be among the more prestigious and powerful people in a nature religion's community. This especially is true of women, among Wiccans and other goddess religions, who usually are acknowledged as "crones" by a special "croning" ritual. The crones often form a unique sorority and conduct rituals of purification and healing, for instance, exclusively among themselves. There is no specific male equivalent of the crone or the croning ritual. Men, however, may be "saged" and recognized as "sages," based on aging and, as importantly, individual merit deriving from accumulated experiences, skills, knowledge, and wisdom.

Many nature religions conduct remembrances of the dead and/or funeral rituals. Samhain (November eve and the beginning of the Wiccan New Year), the most important Neopagan holiday, is closely associated with decay, death, the deceased, and ancestors. Wicca and many other nature religions believe in some form of afterlife, sometimes called the "summerland" by Wiccans. Many of these religions also subscribe to a sort of reincarnation, or recycling of energy or spirit. Death, thereby, is viewed as a beginning of something else as well as the ending of this life, and, while it may be a sad occasion, it also contains the hopeful promises of a future. At Samhain, it commonly is believed, the "veil" (boundary) is very thin between the worlds of the living and the dead (as not inaccurately depicted in Hollywood horror films). Samhain celebrations usually have ways of remembering and honoring deceased friends and relatives. This often involves preparing special foods as an offering to the dead, and a subsequent feast among the living. It also may involve placing pictures of or articles belonging to the deceased on the altar, burning messages to them in the fire, or any number of other innovative ways of honoring the dead.

Funeral rituals sometimes are conducted, although there is no formal standard for these rites. Funeral rituals may be difficult to conduct when other family members are not nature religionists or especially when they are hostile to these religions.[17]

BECOMING A MEMBER

Since the nature religion movement in the United States is new, very few of the members were born into these religions. Only a slight majority of American Neopagans, for instance, report being involved with these religions for more than five years.[18] The best available evidence indicates that their previous religious backgrounds (including no religion) do not differ substantially from the religious affiliations of Americans generally. Neopagans, for instance, are a little less likely to be former Protestants, as likely to be former Catholics, and slightly more likely to be former Jews, or something else, than if their previous religious backgrounds mirrored the larger American population. How, then, did they become nature religionists?

Margot Adler, a journalist and witch, maintains that these are religions "without converts."[19] What she apparently means is that nature religions rarely proselytize in the same ways as many other religions and the process of becoming a member sometimes is selectively discriminate. Yet, insofar as a majority of nature religionists were not born into these religions, most members undergo some kind of "conversion," at least as this concept is understood and employed by scholars of religion.[20] The most recent evidence suggests that dissatisfaction with more traditional religions is the most important reason for Americans to become involved with a nature religion. Some of these people also indicate that interests in feminism, occultism, science fiction, and ecology were related to their attraction to a nature religion.

Most nature religions do not actively recruit, but members usually are willing and pleased to share their sacred experiences and beliefs with anyone who expresses more than casual interest. Conversion stories share the prevalent theme of the person's having discovered that the nature religion had been their true conviction and identity all along. Converting to some belief in a nature religion oftentimes is accomplished by reading related literatures, and it is entirely possible (perhaps even likely) that membership is acquired by a self-initiation. An untold number (probably many) of nature religionists, as previously noted, are "solitary" (individual/private) practitioners for part or all of their religious careers. Increasingly today, membership in a nature religion group may require little more than active involvement and participation. Yet membership in some groups still requires a period (typically a year and a day or thirteen months, for Wiccans) of learning and testing, followed by a formal initiation.

Nature religion groups typically are as small as three to five members; about a dozen members is considered ideal, and more than thirty to fifty members are unusual, not counting underage children. These groups usually think of themselves as extraordinarily intimate, family or kinship-like associations. Visitors or newcomers frequently are welcome at major celebrations, like the sabbats, but the regular monthly (more or less) meetings (such as esbats) may be inclusive of initiated members only. Part of the reason for this is that regular meetings frequently involve healing or magical rituals that are believed to require a small number of highly compatible participants. Since interpersonal conflict easily can disrupt or destroy magical practices and the solidarity of the group, membership typically is selective. Groups may have formal or informal standards for the composition of the membership, based, for instance, on gender, personality, experience, knowledge, and so on. It is not uncommon for groups to announce whether or not they are accepting new members.

Becoming a member therefore may be by invitation only, and if so, it usually involves training, testing, and—when this is successfully accomplished—initiation. There are several basic objectives to this process. It aims to ensure that newcomers become at least moderately knowledgeable about the religion. This means, for instance, that the person understands the significance of the major and minor celebrations. The pre-initiate is expected to learn the performance of basic rituals and some magical practices. Often there is some evaluation of whether the newcomer will be able to contribute to the group in ways that are compatible with collective goals (values) and ethics as well as the current membership. Conventionally, a teacher (or "adept") assists pre-initiates in this process, although more than one member may perform this mentoring role.

Formal initiation rituals are highly variable from group to group, and they frequently are individualized for the initiate. Among Wiccans, an initiation usually requires purification, and it is generally designed around the symbolism of death and rebirth, typically incorporating other central elements of this religion. Some groups, especially Wiccans, have two additional degrees of initiation, marked by rituals, that signify progressively advanced knowledge and skill. Some nature religion groups also perform initiations in recognition of other specialized roles, like healing, fire making, or other highly valued magical abilities.

EXPERIENCES, PRACTICES, ETHICS, AND BELIEFS

Correct belief (orthodoxy or dogma) is one of the more important features of traditional Western religions. This is not the case for most nature religions. These religions, as should be clear from the foregoing discussion, do more or less share certain beliefs or—perhaps more accurately—themes or an ethos in common: the sacredness of nature, for instance, alive and enchanted, energized by spiritual polarities and forces, all inter-connected, interrelated, and balanced in a cosmic whole. Yet, as the previous discussion also illustrated, exactly what is believed about the sacredness of nature is highly variable from group to group and individual to individual. No belief in deities is required, for example. Any such belief may be literal or symbolic, and goddesses and gods may be known in assorted aspects and by different names.

Even more significantly, the beliefs of nature religions are not defined or standardized by a scriptural text, equivalent to such documents, like the Bible, in other Western religions. There are many source texts and even theological or "thealogical" works, but none of them have canonical status.[21] The beliefs of these nature religions are highly pluralistic within and across particular groups, and there is no absolute or standard authority for truth or Truth. These beliefs tend to be exceptionally inclusive. Within the broad outlines discussed here, they may include almost anything, even beliefs borrowed from other religions, such as Buddhism, Hinduism, Judaism, and/or Christianity. Ultimately, the beliefs of the nature religion are very individualistic and, thereby, largely open to the interpretations and preferences of any particular believer.

Ethics

Although nature religionists may believe almost anything, their conduct usually is constrained by a central ethical principle. This ethic is that a person may do anything he or she wants, so long as it does not harm one's self or others. Exactly what this means and how it is to be applied, as with most ethics, is a matter of some interpretation. Yet "harm" usually is understood as doing physical, mental, or spiritual damage to self or others, including other animals and inanimate objects—since they too are alive and spiritual. This ethic, in other words, strongly encourages the members of these religions to behave respectfully and responsibly with regard to self, other people, the natural environment, the planet earth, and all of the cosmos. Furthermore, it is often reinforced by belief in a karmic principle. This principle (the threefold law) holds that whatever one does will return to that person threefold. The commission of a harmful or negative act toward someone or something else, in other words, will return three times worse to the individual who commits such an act. Good acts, similarly, are returned threefold.

Experiences and Practices

Most nature religions emphasize experiences of the sacred above everything else, especially beliefs. These religions, unlike traditional Western religions, do not subscribe to doctrines of sin or salvation. The aim instead is learning to act, live, and exist in harmony with other human beings, nature, and the cosmos. In this way, what members seek is an experience of the sacred, and a sacred existence. Religious belief, therefore, is less important than religious action, and religious actions, rituals, and practices are merely a means to the ultimate end of sacred experience, life, and existence. This, for example, was the intention of the Yule sabbat described at the beginning of this chapter. It aimed to bring the participants into harmony with the natural environment and to celebrate nature and our interrelationship with it. The Yule ritual celebrated nature, but not so much in the conventional sense of "worshiping" it. Instead, the participants were delighting in their experience of oneness with the sacred, natural world as accomplished through the Yule ritual.

The religious practices of most nature religion, aside from holiday celebrations and rituals (as discussed above), generally aim to employ the forces or energies of nature for the purposes of achieving religious experiences, transforming self or some state of affairs and, thereby, creating oneness with nature and the cosmos. These practices, typically called "magic," commonly are directed toward concrete results, such as changes in a person's consciousness and existence (life situation) or transformations of others, the humanly constructed world (culture and society), nature, or the cosmos. Magic (or "magick" to distinguish it from illusionism), in other words, is intended to produce results or changes in self and/or the natural world of our existence.

Almost anything that produces a result or change may be regarded as magical. If imagining one's self in terms of some aspect of the Goddess changes the person's self-conception, this act of imagination is a magical one. The list of magical practices therefore is almost endless, including such things as mediation, visualization, trance, chants, charms, divination, hexes, spells, healing, and so on. I once observed a witch "magically" break up a street fight and disperse the crowd by chanting the word "police." It worked: Very shortly thereafter the fighting stopped and the fighting parties, along with the crowd, left the scene. On another occasion this same witch gave me a bundle of the herb sage with instructions for using it to magically banish negative spirits or energies from my home. On still another occasion, she admitted "sending" a stray kitten to me so that I might "get in touch" with the mother goddess.

The practitioners of nature religions often meditate while burning a consecrated candle as a magical action directed toward attaining a job, money, love, or improved health. Many magical practices are directed toward physical, emotional, or mental healing of self, society, or nature. In all of these and many other ways, magical practices are a way of life for the members of many nature religions. Every situation they encounter and almost everything they do may be treated magically. Magic, it must be emphasized, is not something extraordinary. Nature religion practitioners see it as working with the forces and energies of nature to effect change or, specifically, to restore and harmoniously balance the natural order of the universe.

GROUPS, FESTIVALS, NETWORKS AND THE CULTIC MILIEU

Nature religion groups, as previously mentioned, tend to be small collectivities without authoritative (or strong) leaders, few hierarchies, and little formal organization. Typically they are composed of like-minded individuals of similar social characteristics (age, education, occupation) and backgrounds. Many groups seek to maintain an approximate balance between males and females, although there are exclusively male and female groups. Some groups formally recognize particular leaders (a high priestess and high priest among some Wiccans), while others rotate leadership or other specialized roles among the qualified members (based on knowledge, skills, and other achieved merits). Acknowledged differences among the membership usually are based on personal accomplishments, and otherwise, these groups tend to see themselves as associations of mostly equal people. Group decision making generally is democratic but informal, based mostly on consensus. Performing a ritual skyclad, for instance, generally requires that all the participants agree to being naked. If anyone objected, the rite usually would be conducted clothed.

Cults

Religious groups with these basic characteristics are "cults" as defined sociologically.[22] Obviously, this concept of a "cult" shares little in common with the popular imagery of autocratic leaders who coerce weak, sheeplike followers into conformity to demented visions. Indeed, nature religion cults are the opposite of the popular "cult" imagery. Very little holds them together except for whatever interests and experiences the membership share in common. Without authoritative leadership or orthodox beliefs, nature religion cults are exceptionally precarious and fragile organizations. They are highly susceptible to dissolution and disorganiza-tion as the interests and experiences of the members shift and change. Differences and especially conflicts among members regularly threaten the group's solidarity. Consequently, very few of nature religion cults survive for more than about ten years without undergoing substantial change in membership and reorganization.

Cult characteristics might seem to present serious challenges to the continued existence of the nature religions in America today. Interestingly, however, this is not the case. What initially appears to be a weakness, namely the lack of organizational stability, reflects an adaptation to contemporary social conditions, resulting in certain advantages. Nature religions, much like life generally in highly pluralistic societies, offer individuals an almost bewildering variety of choices. When people make these choices, their interests and actions change correspondingly. For group members, this means that they no longer share the same interests and, at least sometimes, find that their interests conflict. Americans today also are very mobile geographically. Hence, contemporary people constantly are finding and exploring new interests, changing our views, and moving from place to place. Altogether, these factors threaten the stability of most types of social organization, but especially tightly organized groups, such as traditional religious sects and denominations.

Cultic religious groups, however, are better prepared than many conventional sects and denominations to deal with these changes. The members of these groups expect change, understand that their association probably will not be permanent, and usually also know that sooner or later they will find another group. Put differently, while nature religion cults mostly are independent of one another, there are plenty of them around, and the members of different groups oftentimes get to know one another. The development of these social networks between individuals in different cults sometimes happens by chance meetings, but more often it transpires at "festivals" or other common meeting places, such as specialty book and supply stores.

The participants in the Yule celebration described above, for example, all were connected through a single Florida "lodge." Some of the lodge members moved away, many of them to go to graduate school in northeastern states. There, they joined new covens and other nature religion groups. When they returned to Florida, they often brought members of their new groups, as visitors, to the lodge. These social relationships and networks multiplied as members of the now linked groups joined still other groups, often as a result of individuals relocating to other states for jobs. The twenty-two participants in the Yule ritual consequently represented five or six independent cultic groups, all of them linked by overlapping friendships.

Festivals

Festivals, like the Yule celebration, gathered together newcomers, solitary practitioners, and the members of different nature religion groups for the purposes of fun, fellowship, and ritual. Larger festivals may attract several hundred or more religionists, while smaller events may involve only a few dozen participants, as with the Yule celebration described above. They commonly take place over a weekend (usually Friday evening to Sunday afternoon), but some festivals are weeklong events, especially during the summer. Several very large festivals, attracting nature religionists from across the country, have been held annually for ten or more years. Many smaller festivals, some of them now annual events, are held in most regions of the United States today.

At festivals, these nature religionists participate collectively in daily life by camping, eating, bathing, sleeping, playing, singing, dancing, and talking together. Nationally or locally recognized authors and other leaders frequently offer workshops on various beliefs and practices, and they may lead collective rituals. Merchants, some of whom circulate from event to event, offer artwork, ritual tools and supplies, as well as many other wares for sale. Consequently, festivals provide invaluable opportunities for the participants to recruit new members, make acquaintances and friends, and renew and strengthen previously established relationships. Or, in other words, nature religion festivals serve to create and sustain very extensive social networks of fellow religionists from different groups as well as solitary practitioners, locally, regionally, nationally, and even internationally.

The Cultic Milieu

The notion of the "cultic milieu" is a sociologically illuminating way of describing the collective organization of nature religions. The cultic milieu (or sociocultural environment) of nature religions consists of newcomers and potential recruits, solitary practitioners, authors and other experts, merchants and businesses, as well as a vast assortment of participants in various individual cults. Altogether they create and sustain a religious subculture of beliefs, values, ethics, practices, and the like, bound together by networks of social relationship and small cultic groups. This, then, is the social organizational basis for nature religions. It clearly is different from the sects and denominations, many of them with elaborate hierarchies as well as nationally and internationally centralizing organizations, that more typically support traditional American religions. Yet the cultic milieu is not a socially inadequate way of organizing religion. Particular cults may come and go, since they are rather precarious and fragile organizations, but new ones will emerge as individuals re-create them.

THE FUTURE OF NATURE RELIGIONS IN AMERICA

Historically, most new religions do not survive the death of the founders or maintain much organizational vitality for more than a couple of hundred years. This, perhaps, will be the fate of these nature religions. Yet, in spite of their newness and cultic type of organization, nature religions possess a number of features that strongly suggest far greater longevity.

These religions draw on very old religious themes centering on the sacredness of nature and unity of nature and humanity with the cosmos that still resonate in contemporary human experience. They also connect culturally with current religious issues, interests, and concerns. These include the conservation of the natural environment (ecology); human gender equality (feminism); less hierarchical and more democratic human organizations (freedom); spirituality or religion not bounded by rigid doctrines or authoritative organizations (individualized religion or spirituality); and more balanced, harmonious relationships among all persons and things, especially the world's people (peace).

Cultic nature religion groups are precarious, yet they provide at least a temporary basis for intimate, primary group relationships. Furthermore, cults are uniquely adapted to the more general conditions of contemporary social life. That they are easily formed on the basis of shared interests readily serves people who make choices among a wide variety of cultural and religious interests and alternatives, changing and re-creating themselves, and moving from place to place more or less frequently. Finally, the cultic milieu does provide a significant social basis for extensive networks of social relationships and a very resourceful religious subculture. That it seems to be a reflection and microcosm of contemporary American society generally suggests that these nature religions will be around for a very long time.

Notes

1. This account of a winter solstice holiday is based on participant observational investigation and field notes of this and many other similar events. The description offered here is not literal. Although it has been freely edited, it provides an accurate depiction of this and related types of circle rituals performed by contemporary American practitioners of some nature religions.
2. See Margot Adler, *Drawing Down the Moon: Witches, Druids, Goddess Worshippers, and Other Pagans in America Today* (New York: Penguin/Arkana, 1997, revised and expanded edition), 3–13.
3. See Catherine Albanese, *Nature Religion in America: From the Algonkian Indians to the New Age* (Chicago: University of Chicago Press, 1990); and Jo Pearson, "Wicca, Esotericism and Living Nature: Assessing Wicca as Nature Religion," *The Pomegranate: A New Journal of Neopagan Thought* 14 (November 2000): 4–15.
4. Antoine Faivre, *Access to Western Esotericism* (Albany: State University of New York Press, 1994).
5. Antoine Faivre, "What Is Occultism?" 3–9 in L. E. Sullivan (ed.), *Hidden Truths: Magic, Alchemy, and the Occult* (New York: Macmillan, 1989). These traditions, along with folk magics, also were imported to the Americas from the earliest colonialists through the more recent revivals. See, for instance, Jon Butler, "Magic, Astrology and the Early American Religious Heritage, 1600–1760," *American Historical Review* 84 (April 2, 1979): 317–46; H. Kerr and C. L. Crow (eds.), *The Occult in America: New Historical Perspectives* (Urbana: University of Illinois Press, 1986); and R. S. Ellwood and H. B. Partin, *Religious and Spiritual Groups in Modern America* (Englewood Cliffs, N.J.: Prentice Hall, 1988).
6. Aidan A. Kelley, *Crafting the Art of Magick, Book I: A History of Modern Witchcraft, 1939–1964* (St. Paul: Llewellyn Publications, 1991); and Francis King, *Ritual Magic in England, 1887 to the Present* (London: Neville Spearman, 1970).
7. Danny L. Jorgensen and Scott E. Russell, "American Neopaganism: The Participants' Social Identities," *Journal for the Scientific Study of Religion* 38 (3, 1999): 325–38.
8. For a description of another ritual, an initiation, I did with some of these people based on a mixture of Wicca and ceremo-

nial magic, see Danny L. Jorgensen, "Neo-paganism in America: How Witchcraft Matters Today," 60–83 in William Scott Green and Jacob Neusner (eds.), *The Religion Factor: An Introduction to How Religion Matters* (Louisville, Ky.: Westminster John Knox Press, 1996).

9. There are many debates about the origin and meaning of these terminologies. See, for instance, Margot Adler, *Drawing Down the Moon*, 9–13. The terms *Wicca* and *the Craft* oftentimes are used as less inflammatory ways of referring to contemporary witchcraft.

10. Gerald Gardner, *Witchcraft Today* (London: Rider, 1954).

11. James W. Baker, "White Witches: Historic Fact and Romantic Fantasy," 171–92 in James R. Lewis (ed.), *Magical Religion and Modern Witchcraft* (Albany: State University of New York Press, 1996).

12. Wendy Griffin (ed.), *Daughters of the Goddess: Studies of Healing, Identity, and Empowerment* (Walnut Creek, Calif.: Altamira, 2000).

13. Shelley TSivia Rabinovitch, "Spells of Transformation: Categorizing Modern Neo-Pagan Witches," 75–91 in Lewis, *Magical Religion and Modern Witchcraft*.

14. Collin Campbell, "The Cult, the Cultic Milieu and Secularization," 119–36 in M. Hill (ed.), *A Sociological Yearbook of Religion in Britain* 5 (London: SCM Press, 1972); and Danny L. Jorgensen, *The Esoteric Scene, Cultic Milieu, and Occult Tarot* (New York: Garland Publishing, 1992).

15. Jorgensen and Russell, "American Neo-paganism," 325–38.

16. Jimmy Moreland, "Neopagan Sexuality" (Master's thesis, University of South Florida, 2001).

17. Wendy Lozano and Tannice G. Foltz, "Into the Darkness: An Ethnographic Study of Feminist Witchcraft and Death," *Qualitative Sociology* 13 (3, Fall): 211–24.

18. Jorgensen and Russell, "American Neo-paganism," 332.

19. Adler, 14–23.

20. E. V. Gallagher, "A Religion without Converts? Becoming a Neo-Pagan," *Journal of the American Academy of Religion* 62 (3, Fall, 1994): 851–67.

21. Starhawk (Miriam Simos), *The Spiral Dance: A Rebirth of the Ancient Religion of the Great Goddess* (New York: Harper-Collins, 1979, 1989) is an exceptionally popular theological work, and there are many others pertinent to particular nature religions or aspects of these religions.

22. Steve Bruce, *Religion in the Modern World: From Cathedrals to Cults* (New York: Oxford University Press, 1996).

STUDY QUESTIONS

1. What are the distinguishing characteristics of "nature religions"? What components or religions are included?

2. How is nature envisioned by these religions? In what ways does this view of nature differ from traditional Western religions?

3. How is/are deity or deities conceptualized by nature religions? What are the features of deity or deities? What are they called?

4. Why are nature religions called "new religions"? What does this involve? Is a new religion less of a "religion" because it is new? Why or why not?

5. What kinds of people are involved with nature religions? How are these people alike or different from other Americans?

6. Why are people attracted to nature religions? How do they become members? In what ways is this like, or different from, how people become converts to other religions?

7. What kinds of rituals are involved in nature religions? What is the aim of these rituals? How are the rituals of nature religions like, or different from, those of other religions?

8. What are some of the basic sociological characteristics of "cults"? Why are cults fragile and precarious?

9. What are nature religion festivals? Why and how are festivals important for nature religions?

10. What is the "cultic milieu"? How is it related to nature religions? Why is the cultic milieu important for nature religions?

ESSAY TOPICS

The Significance of Sacred Space and Different Ways of Creating It

Differences among the Relative Importance of Religious Beliefs, Practices, and Experiences

New Religions vs. Old Religions

Sacred Images of Nature and the Cosmos

Religious Conversion

Religious Rituals and Practices

Images of Deity or Deities

Religion and the Human Life Cycle

WORD EXPLORATION

The following words play significant roles in any discussion of nature religions in America and are worth careful reflection and discussion.

Natural Cycles	Sabbats	Esbats	Skyclad
Animism	Pantheism	Polytheism	Neopaganism
Wicca	Eclectic belief	Handfasting	Conversion
Cult	Magic		

FOR FURTHER READING

Berger, Helen A. *A Community of Witches: Contemporary Neo-paganism and Witchcraft in the United States*. Columbia: University of South Carolina Press, 1999.

Berger, Helen A., ed. *Witchcraft and Magic: Contemporary North America*. Philadelphia: University of Pennsylvania Press, 2005.

Berger, Helen A., Evan A. Leach, and Leigh S. Shaffer. *Voices from the Pagan Census: A National Survey of Witches and Neo-pagans in the United States*. Columbia: University of South Carolina Press, 2003.

Clifton, Chas S. *Her Hidden Children: The Rise of Wicca and Paganism in America*. Lanham, Md.: AltaMira Press, 2006.

Davy, Barbara Jane. *Introduction to Pagan Studies*. Lanham, Md.: AltaMira Press, 2007.

Higginbotham, Joyce and River. *An Introduction to Earth-Centered Religions*. St. Paul, Minn.: Llewellyn Publications, 2002.

Hutton, Ronald. *The Triumph of the Moon: A History of Modern Pagan Witchcraft*. New York: Oxford University Press, 1999.

Lewis, James R., ed. *The Oxford Handbook of New Religious Movements*. New York: Oxford University Press, 2004.

WEB SITES

http://www.caw.org/
Official Web site of the neopagan Church of All Worlds

http://www.religioustolerance.org/neo_paga.htm
Neopagan traditions, history, and beliefs

http://www.sacred-texts.com/pag/index.htm
Internet Sacred Texts Archive

http://www.cog.org/
Home page of the Covenant of the Goddess

http://www.neopagan.net/
"Virtual stone circle" of practicing neopagans

18

The Latter-day Saint (Mormon) Religion in America and the World[1]

DANNY L. JORGENSEN

1805   Birth of Joseph Smith Jr., founding prophet for all Latter Day Saint churches
1830   Formal organization of a church in New York
1831   Church moves from New York to Ohio
1837   Church moves from Ohio to Missouri
1839   Saints expelled from Missouri and move to Nauvoo, Illinois
1844   Founding prophet, Joseph Smith, martyred at Carthage, Illinois
1847   Latter-day Saint religion established at Salt Lake City after long trek westward
1852   Utah Mormons acknowledge the practice of plural marriage
1860   Joseph Smith III accepts leadership of newly formed Reorganized Church of Jesus Christ of Latter Day Saints (RLDS)
1890   Practice of plural marriage officially discontinued by Church of Jesus Christ of Latter-day Saints
1896   Utah admitted as 45th state
1947   Worldwide LDS membership reaches one million
1960s   Latter-day Saint religion becomes significant outside of North America, approaching three million at decade's end
1978   The LDS prophet reveals that all worthy males may hold the priesthood, including men of color
1984   The RLDS open their priesthood to women
2001   RLDS renamed the Community of Christ
2007   Mitt Romney, a Latter-day Saint, vies for the Republican nomination for U.S. president
2008   LDS membership reaches 13.2 million worldwide
2090   Projections suggest as many as 250 million Latter-day Saints worldwide

Most Americans today know a little something about the Latter-day Saints and their religion. You most likely are familiar with this religion and its people by the popular but unofficial nickname of "Mormon." Perhaps you have encountered a pair of the many clean-cut, youthful Latter-day Saint missionaries, neatly dressed in dark slacks and white shirts with ties and nametags, canvassing neighborhoods throughout the United States, possibly on bicycles. They, no doubt, were eager to teach you the basic principles of the Latter-day Saint gospel. These young men may have told you something about modern-day prophecy and the restoration of the priesthood, the Book of Mormon scripture, or about their religiously required abstinence from coffee, tea, tobacco, alcohol, illegal drugs, and premarital sexual relationships. Or, perhaps you have listened to or watched the spectacular Mormon Tabernacle Choir on radio or television, probably around the Christmas or Easter holidays, jubilantly singing familiar hymns of praise.

Many of you probably learned in an American history class about the Latter-day Saints' epic, mid-nineteenth-century trek from the Mississippi River to the Rocky Mountains. Surely you heard about how the seagulls ate the swarm of crickets threatening the Saints' first wheat crop in Utah. You also may have learned about some of the other hardships these religiously inspired American pioneers endured in making the desert valley of the Great Salt Lake "blossom as the rose."[2] Perhaps you have visited the world headquarters of the Saints' in Salt Lake City, Utah. If so, surely you toured the centrally located Temple Square and observed the many markers and monuments to the early Latter-day Saint pioneers. These and related features of this otherwise all-American city may have seemed somehow different. Did you wonder, for example, why so many banks in Utah carry the name "Zion"?

Wherever you live in the United States, there probably is a Latter-day Saint meeting house (chapel) or even a temple located not too far away. Perhaps you have wondered about these different buildings and what transpires in them. You may be familiar with the Saints' passion for genealogical research and family history, or perhaps their custom of maintaining a year's supply of food at home. Do you understand why these matters are important for the Latter-day Saints? All of this, and much, much more, is part of the story of the Latter-day Saints and their unique religion in the United States today.

A New American Religion

Most of the American religions you will learn about in this text originated centuries ago in other, distant cultures and societies. They were imported here, adapting to and influencing the development of American culture and society. The Latter-day Saint religion, however, is very new, and its origin is eminently American.[3] It was formally organized on April 6, 1830, in upstate New York by an American prophet, Joseph Smith Jr. (1805–1844), and a few followers. From this very modest beginning until about the middle of the twentieth century, the Latter-day Saint religion steadily and gradually attracted converts; and it was influential, but mostly in the western United States. Today, less than two hundred years later, there are about six million Saints spread across North America and approximately another seven million Latter-day Saints located elsewhere around the world.[4] This, you should appreciate, truly is extraordinary!

There is, of course, nothing particularly unusual in and of itself about the appearance of new religions. They are commonplace enough: Hundreds, perhaps even thousands, of would-be new religions arise annually.[5] Most of them, however, fail and disappear in less than ten years. Very few of them survive their founders. Only under the most unusual circumstances does a new religion persist, attract significant followings, or develop a viable culture and community. The odds against a new religion becoming successful are immense. In order to survive, a new religion must offer people a perceivably meaningful alternative to the existing religions. The new faith must do this, moreover, without seeming to be so unusual that its basic tenets, practices, or adherents are defined socially as unattractive or even deviant. Novel themes and appeals therefore must be balanced and coordinated with social and cultural traditions. To prosper, a new religion also must be able to generate needed resources, such as members and money, and mobilize them in the form of a unified, goal-directed organization. The Latter-day Saint religion is indisputably and genuinely exceptional on all of these accounts.

Founded on the basis of a novel mixture of biblical and folk traditions, the Latter-day Saints redefined Christianity in distinctively American ways.[6] This new religion revealed that the Americas were the site of the biblical Eden and the location of a theretofore unknown Christian nation of native American peoples (this is the Book of Mormon story as discussed below). The "history" of the New World thereby is understood as a part of the biblical story. The United States, in particular, is envisioned as a divinely inspired nation. It is the Promised Land prepared by the biblical God especially for His Chosen People, namely European Americans generally and, in particular, the Latter-day Saints. America is the place of a New Dispensation (biblical age or epoch) where divine Authority for the Holy Priesthood and Christ's original church has been restored. All of this, moreover, now is being directed by the divine revelations of the Latter-day Saint prophets of God.

The United States, according to the Latter-day Saint religion, also is one of the eventual locations of the Advent or second coming of Jesus Christ and the site of the millennial kingdom of God (also called "Zion") on earth. The Saints see themselves as descendants of the ancient House of Israel and God's Chosen People, whose divine mission is to build up the theocratic kingdom of God on earth. While some of this may sound odd to you, every single one of these ideas is a part of

what many Americans (not just the Latter-day Saints), past and present, believe about the United States and what it means to be an American. The Latter-day Saint religion is unique mostly in terms of how these themes are arranged and placed into practice.

Even, or especially, when it initially is successful, internal conflicts over basic goals and beliefs, leadership, and organizational forms commonly threaten the very existence of a new religious movement. These internal conflicts frequently result in schisms (organizational splinters) that severely weaken the new movement, resulting in a loss of basic resources and significant decline. The Latter-day Saint religion has produced more than a hundred different organizations in its brief history.[7] All but two of them are very small and relatively insignificant in the overall picture of American religion. The Community of Christ (formerly called the Reorganized Church of Jesus Christ of Latter Day Saints, or RLDS), with headquarters at Independence, Missouri, is the much smaller of the two largest organizations.[8] Partly for this reason, the more moderate, Protestant-like Community of Christ faith is not described except indirectly here. This chapter focuses primarily on the largest and more distinctive form of this religion, The Church of Jesus Christ of Latter-day Saints (LDS), headquartered in Salt Lake City, Utah.

Besides founding a new, distinctively American religion, the Latter-day Saints created a unique subculture (comprehensive way of life) and social (ethnic) identity for themselves.[9] Their religious beliefs and practices differentiated the Saints from other Americans and their religions, serving as a way for the Latter-day Saints to identify themselves as socially different. These differences, in turn, provided the Saints with the grounds for developing very cohesive, self-sufficient communities. Throughout the late nineteenth and early twentieth centuries, conflicts with other Americans over their distinctive religion and way of life reinforced the Latter-day Saints' sense of being "peculiar" and chosen by God for a special mission.[10]

The Saints responded by re-creating American social institutions (marriage and family, economies, polities, education, and the like) in their own characteristic ways. This was especially true in Utah, where the Saints were away from the direct control and influence of the larger secular culture and society. It is true that, over the last fifty years or so, the Latter-day Saint subculture increasingly has been Americanized (accommodated to the main currents of American culture). Their subculture, nevertheless, still remains distinctive, supporting somewhat unique forms of social identity and community, particularly in Utah. This religion, along with the subculture and people which was created by and now supports the Latter-day Saint faith, today is the largest, most successful, and fastest growing new faith to emerge entirely from the culture and society fashioned by European immigrants in North America.

THE AMERICAN SAINTS TODAY

The Latter-day Saints are a significant religious minority in the United States today.[11] They comprise about 2 percent of the American population (or about the same proportion as Jewish Americans). They form one of the country's five largest religious denominations. The LDS religion is the first or second largest in nine western American states. An impressive number of American Saints have served or do serve as leaders at every governmental level, including federal cabinet secretaries, presidential advisors, legislators, ambassadors, national party officials, federal agents, military officers, and mayors. Mitt Romney, the former governor of Massachusetts who tried to win the Republican presidential nomination in 2008, is a Mormon, as is Harry Reid, who as a Democratic Senator is on the other end of the political

Prominent Latter-day Saint Americans

Latter-day Saints increasingly became involved in American society during the second half of the twentieth century. They have served with distinction in the military, sometimes as high-ranking officers. Brent Scowcroft, three-star general and former national security advisor, is a Mormon, as is Paul A. Yost Jr., four-star admiral. Latter-day Saints have held positions in other federal agencies, most notably the FBI and CIA. Significantly, Mormons repeatedly have been selected by Democrats and Republicans for high-level federal service, including U.S. presidential cabinets (Ezra Taft Benson, Agriculture; Stewart Udall, Interior; David M. Kennedy, Treasury; Terrel Bell, Education; and Mike Leavitt, Health and Human Services). Republican businessman George Romney was a candidate for the U.S. presidency in 1968, and his son Mitt Romney was perhaps an even more vital contender in 2008. Democrat Harry Reid currently serves as the majority leader of the U.S. Senate; and at least fifteen additional Mormons, mostly Republicans, serve in the U.S. Congress from a variety of states.

Latter-day Saints are eminent and sometimes famous for their contributions to American business, including the Romney and Marriott families, gun designer John Browning, Alan Ashton of WordPerfect, Kevin Rollins of Dell, and consultant-author-entrepreneur Stephen Covey. Mormons have their share of writers, journalists, and scholars, including novelists Orson Scott Card, Anne Perry, and Stephenie Meyer; Harvard historian Laurel Thatcher Ulrich; and political cartoonist Steve Benson. Conservative television talk show host Glenn Beck is LDS, as are entertainers Gladys Knight, Julianne Hough, David Archuleta, and the Osmonds. Mormons are also well represented in professional sports, including football players and coaches Todd Christensen, Ty Detmer, Andy Reid, and Steve Young; basketball players and coaches Danny Ainge, Shawn Bradley, and Mark Madsen; and baseball players Jeff Kent, Harmon Killebrew, Vern Law, and Dale Murphy.

spectrum. The Saints excel in business and agriculture, and they contribute significantly in the arts, literature, entertainment, and professional sports. They also founded and sometimes still operate educational facilities, hospitals, and a wide variety of social welfare and humanitarian services throughout the nation. LDS historic sites and visitors' centers dot the American landscape; temples are found in many states; and chapels are located in most cities in every region of the country.

MARRIAGE AND FAMILY LIFE

For the Latter-day Saints, daily life and religion are not separate domains of human existence. They are, instead, highly interrelated, interdependent, and coordinated in a total way of life. Their religion defines what it means to be a Latter-day Saint and, in turn, their subculture and communities support and reinforce the religious faith. Being a Latter-day Saint requires a tremendous commitment of a person's time, energy, and other resources, ordinarily on a daily or weekly basis. Marriage and family life provide the social foundation for the Saints' exceptionally cohesive, orderly subculture and communities. Life within Latter-day Saint families is defined and ordered on the basis of age and gender roles as well as related activities. Age and gender, in other words, socially define who you are and what is expected of you as a member of a Latter-day Saint family and community.

Marriage for the Saints is much more than simply a civil contract between consenting adults. Rather, it is an extremely sacred, loving relationship whereby a man and a woman coordinate their different interests and roles in support of one another, the family, and the community. Marriage is defined strictly as a monogamous relationship between heterosexual couples.[12] Any form of pre- or extramarital sexuality is prohibited by their religion as is any expression of homosexuality. The marriage partnership provides the foundation for the family, and the family is the basic social, economic, and religious institution of the Latter-day Saint way of life.

A slightly higher proportion of Latter-day Saints marry and at a younger age than other Americans.[13] They, like other Americans, contract marriages that are intended to last for this lifetime, typically by way of a religious ceremony performed by an LDS "bishop" (local leader). Some of them also are married ("sealed" together) for all eternity in a very special, sacred ceremony that can only be performed in a Latter-day Saint temple. The Saints are more likely than most other Americans to marry within their religion. Divorce is permitted but discouraged by the Latter-day Saints' religion. Overall the Saints' divorce rate is about the same as that of the larger American population; however, marriages solemnized in a temple are much less likely to end in divorce.

Latter-day Saint couples are expected to have children. Many of them anticipate having as many children as they are able to nurture and support. Latter-day Saint families therefore tend to be somewhat larger than the American average. Their religion prohibits abortion (except in instances of rape or serious danger to the mother's health) and it discourages, but permits, birth control for family-planning purposes. The Saints are as likely as other Americans to use birth control, although it typically is employed for the spacing of children rather than for limiting family size. The LDS religion also strongly encourages men and women to perform traditional American gender roles. Men are expected to sustain, economically and otherwise, the family's well-being and direct family life; women are expected to manage the children and home life. Many of the Saints, however, find it economically necessary for wives and mothers to work outside of the home; and many LDS women have occupational or professional careers. Hence, while the Latter-day Saints subscribe to traditional images of gender, their actual enactment of these roles does not differ significantly from other working- and middle-class Americans.

Children are expected to obey their parents and otherwise exhibit respect for authority, conform with social and religious standards, develop their talents, and contribute to the life of the family and community. They ordinarily attend American public schools, and regularly are assigned responsibilities for helping their parents with the routine tasks (laundry, cooking, cleaning, home maintenance, and the like) that sustain daily life at home. Many Latter-day Saint high school students also attend special seminary classes devoted to religious instruction before, during, or after the public school day.

Almost everything the Latter-day Saints do revolves around family life. Families live, work, play, and worship together. They, for instance, typically gather together for a brief period of scripture reading and prayer before retiring each night. One evening a week, called "family home evening," is set aside exclusively for family activities. Sundays are reserved for worship, religious study, and family activities. Besides religious worship and study, Latter-day Saint communities commonly sponsor an extensive, weekly calendar of family and youth-oriented events. These include music, art, dances, plays, picnics, sports, scouting, and many other similar activities.

Latter-day Saint children receive a religious blessing shortly after birth. It welcomes them into the LDS community and seeks God's protection and direction in their lives. Children born to parents whose marriages have been solemnized in the temple are already considered "sealed" (or joined) to them eternally, and children otherwise may be sealed to their parents eternally in a sacred temple ordinance. At eight years of age children become eligible for baptism, always by immersion in water, for the remission of sin. Baptism is followed by a "confirmation" (a blessing prayer and laying on of hands) whereby the new member receives the gift of the Holy Ghost.[14] Until this time children are not deemed to be responsible and accountable for their own decisions and lives. The Latter-day Saints, in other words, do not subscribe to the doctrine of "original sin," and they do not practice infant baptism.[15] The Saints, furthermore, believe that all people after the age of eight have, by their God given nature, free will or agency. They, in other words, have the right and responsibility to make their own decisions, whether for right (good) or wrong (evil). Children are encouraged to develop their own personal "testimonies" concerning the basic gospel and regularly share them with others. Most Latter-day Saint children choose baptism at the age of eight or shortly thereafter. Besides attending regular family worship services, children also receive formal religious instruction by age groups at Sunday meetings and weeknight activities.

By the time they are teenagers, the Saints begin assuming adult responsibilities and gender roles. All worthy males are eligible for "ordination" to the almost entirely lay (nonprofessional) priesthood.[16] At about twelve years of age, young men who are obedient to religious and community standards usually are "ordained" to the office of "deacon" (the first rank of the lesser or "Aaronic Priesthood"). Continued conformity usually results in subsequent ordinations to the successive offices of "teacher" and "priest" in the Aaronic Priesthood at approximately two-year intervals. At about age eighteen (or high school graduation), worthy young men usually are ordained to the office of "elder" in the (high) "Melchizedek Priesthood." Older adult males who have demonstrated religious commitment may be ordained to the last regular office of "High Priest."

Each Latter-day Saint priesthood office is defined by certain religious responsibilities. These religious roles also encompass many of the more ordinary, mundane affairs of daily life, especially including service to other members of the LDS community. Some of the responsibilities of deacons, for example, include caring for meeting houses and cemeteries, ushering, distributing information, helping widows and the poor, collecting offerings, and assisting the other priesthoods. Elders perform all of the functions

Americanization, Polygamy, and Mormon Groups

During the formative period, 1830–1844, Mormonism ambitiously advanced itself not merely as a new faith but as an alternative to American culture and society. Mormons favored theocratic government, modifying capitalism with collective economics, and a form of Old Testament plural marriage (polygamy or specifically polygyny, whereby a man may marry more than one wife). These challenges to American values and institutions resulted in conflicts, some of them violent, between the Saints and other Americans—including local, state, and federal governments—through the nineteenth century.

In spite of the Latter-day Saints' isolation in the intermountain West, the confrontation intensified following the Civil War. The LDS agreed to compromise on polygamy and other issues in 1890 when the U.S. government poised to take control of church assets. The church relinquished control of some business interests and submitted to conventional American capitalism. The Mormon political party was dissolved in favor of the two principal parties and American democracy. It was agreed that no additional plural marriages would be sanctioned in the United States. In exchange, Utah was promised and granted statehood in 1896. During the first half of the twentieth century members of the LDS Church moved increasingly toward the center of American culture and society while still retaining their religious distinctiveness.

A few Latter-day Saints resisted theological and social changes, resulting in schisms. Former members of the LDS Church continued practicing plural marriage after 1890, resulting in a small subculture. Efforts to enforce antipolygamy laws have been selective and not successful except in a few isolated cases of individuals. A 1953 raid, for instance, on the Fundamentalist Church of Jesus Christ of Latter Day Saints (FLDS) community at Short Creek, on the Utah-Arizona line, resulted in stalemate. Prosecution of plural marriage is difficult, and other Americans found the breakup of families, especially the separation of mothers and children, extremely distasteful. A similar result, involving important legal questions, is the most likely outcome of efforts to prosecute members of the FLDS community in Texas today.

The reconciliation of Mormonism and American culture, a process of Americanization, has been genuinely amazing. The overwhelming majority of Latter-day Saints today are as American as anyone else, notwithstanding the persistence of the fundamentalist plural marriage subculture and the media's preoccupation with it. Today the LDS Church is a staunch opponent of plural marriage and promotes itself as a champion of American democracy, capitalism, and family values.

of the lesser priesthood offices, such as visiting the membership, teaching, expounding the gospel, as well as blessing the sacrament. They also have the priesthood authority for administering to the sick and elderly (by a ritual laying on of hands for healing) and performing ordinances (like marriage). High Priests manage congregational activities and perform other leadership roles. Following high school graduation many, but not all, elders perform an unpaid, two-year mission for the church at home or abroad.

LDS women are not ordained to the priesthood. They instead have primary responsibility for the care, socialization, and teaching of young children (in Sunday school and otherwise), much of the work associated with the church's extensive social calendar, many aspects of the operation of the Saints' far-reaching welfare programs (such as canning and preparing food as well as providing clothing), assisting and supporting the priesthood (as with teaching and sharing the gospel), and many other activities traditionally associated with the roles of wife and mother. LDS women begin assuming some of these responsibilities and roles as teenagers. At age twenty-one, women may serve on a mission at home or abroad, and thousands of young LDS women have availed themselves of this opportunity.

Education and Work

The Latter-day Saints subscribe to a biblical sense of "stewardship," which is envisioned as much more than being economically efficient and contributing financially to the church. "Wherefore, seek not the things of this world but seek ye first to build up the kingdom of God, and to establish his righteousness, and all these things shall be added unto you."[17] All of the Saints are expected to develop and maintain their bodies and minds in conformity with the basic principles of the gospel and in service to the fundamental goal of building the kingdom of God on earth. "Thou art called to labor in my vineyard, and to build up my church, and to bring forth Zion, that it may rejoice upon the hills and flourish."[18] Education, viewed broadly to include more than formal schooling (as noted earlier), therefore is highly valued by the Saints. An LDS scripture, for example, proclaims that "The glory of God is intelligence, or, in other words, light and truth."[19] They are more likely than other Americans to graduate from high school, and a higher proportion of the Saints also have some college education.[20]

In spite of the emphasis on traditional gender roles, Latter-day Saint women now are encouraged to become formally educated and some of them are completing college as well as pursuing graduate and professional educations.[21] While they perhaps are most likely to undertake careers in fields like nursing and teaching, Latter-day Saint women also have been successful in medicine, law, and other professions traditionally dominated by American men. The Saints founded numerous educational institutions and colleges, especially in the American West (many of which have been donated to the states). Brigham Young University in Provo, Utah, is the largest religiously sponsored institution of higher education in the United States.

The Saints expect to cultivate their individual talents. Men, especially, are expected to work hard and become economically productive, independent, and self-sufficient. Women are encouraged to adopt traditional family roles and devote their lives to the welfare of their husband and children. Even today, some families raise small gardens and preserve foods; the men may be skilled in building trades as well as in operating and fixing mechanical equipment; and the women may have special expertise in sewing and related homemaking enterprises. The principal goal of work and economic productivity is collectively building the kingdom of God. Obedient Saints contribute 10 percent of their income as tithing to the church. (Some Latter-day Saints contribute 10 percent of gross income, and some 10 percent of after-tax income; this is decided by the individual or family.) They commonly make additional financial contributions for the poor and special projects. Youthful missionaries, for instance, depend on their families for financial support. The Saints sometimes contribute money or labor to building, repairing, decorating, landscaping, and maintaining meeting houses, visitors' centers, historic sites, and other facilities. Most of the activities of LDS congregations, religious and social, are dependent on unpaid, donated labor. For many adults, this sometimes involves extensive, almost full-time religious and community responsibilities in addition to regular, secular employment in and away from the home.

Subcultural Uniformity and Diversity

Latter-day Saint communities constitute a comprehensive way of life for many of these people, even in the modern, secular world. In many regions of the United States, especially where there are large LDS communities, these people not only worship together but they also socialize and engage in many otherwise secular activities as a community of brothers and sisters. In Utah, for instance, a Latter-day Saint family may have purchased a home built by a LDS contractor and tradespeople from materials and land supplied by Saints with money borrowed from an LDS-owned bank. The family automobile may have been financed by the same bank, purchased from a dealership owned by a Latter-day Saint, and it perhaps is operated and maintained by supplies, parts, and labor from other Saints. Latter-day Saints possibly own the companies that insure the car, house, and lives of this family. The father (and perhaps the mother too) may work with other Saints, possibly in an LDS-owned business or organization. The family most likely reads, watches, and listens to media (newspapers, books, TV, radio) owned and operated by the Saints. The entire family, but especially the children, probably participate in scouting and sporting activities sponsored by the Saints at the local meeting house. Furthermore, some of the family's basic needs and desires, from the clothes purchased at the Deseret Industries thrift store, lawnmower and fertilizer, furniture, electricity, and phone service to medical and legal services, groceries, entertainment, fine arts, transportation, motels, and burial in the family plot at the local cemetery, may involve the substantial participation of many other Latter-day Saints.[22]

The Saints' commitments to strong family values, work in the interest of God's kingdom, and serving one another greatly contribute to an orderly, uniform subculture wherever these communities are located in or out of the United States. While every Saint is strongly encouraged to cultivate his/her individual talents and abilities, individualism is restrained by collective, community goals. This discourages individual excess and deviance in all aspects of everyday life. The Saints are admonished to be financially responsible and avoid unnecessary debt, waste, conspicuous consumption, and excessive fashion. They, furthermore, generally are encouraged to sustain healthy, productive, moderate lifestyles and lives. They tend to dress in modest, practical attire, and generally maintain a clean-cut appearance in conformity with conservative, middle-class, American standards. Young men, for instance, are discouraged from wearing excessive jewelry (including earrings), growing facial hair, and sporting hairstyles worn below the ear; while young women are discouraged from using excessive makeup or wearing immoderate hairstyles; and both genders are discouraged from dressing or conducting themselves in a sexually provocative manner.

The LDS religion generally encourages moderation in all things.[23] The basis for this is scriptural: "A Word of Wisdom . . . showing forth the order and will of God in the temporal salvation of all saints in the last days."[24] This "word of wisdom" is understood to prohibit the use of illegal drugs, tobacco, any form of alcohol, and strong (or hot) drinks, defined especially as coffee and tea (and, for some LDS, any other caffeinated beverage). Long before it became popular among other Americans, the Saints' dietary customs discouraged eating meat, except in moderation, and encouraged eating plenty of whole grains, fresh fruit, and vegetables. "And all saints who remember to keep and do these sayings, walking in obedience to the commandments, shall receive health in their navel and marrow in their bones."[25]

Some of the Saints, as previously noted, grow and raise some of their own food. All of the Saints are expected to maintain a one-year supply of foodstuffs at home in the event of an emergency or shortage. "And I, the Lord, give unto them a promise, that the destroying angel shall pass by them, as the children of Israel, and not slay them. Amen."[26]

The tendency for the LDS religion to direct the activities and lives of the membership results in tremendous individual conformity as well as a very orderly and uniform subculture. Yet, it would be a serious mistake to conclude that the Saints are absolute conformists, all of whom think, feel, act, and look alike. The American Saints are moderately diverse, and with worldwide expansion they have become increasingly so, as well as more tolerant of other cultures and people.

Many of the early Latter-day Saints, the people who pioneered Utah and the inter-mountain West, were former New Englanders. They were reinforced by British converts, followed by immigrant converts from Scandinavia and, to a lesser extent, from France, Italy, and Germany. As Latter-day Saints, all of these European Americans viewed themselves as part of the biblical tribes of Israel in contrast with non-members, who traditionally were described as "gentiles." The aboriginal peoples of the Americas, called "Lamanites" in the Book of Mormon story (as discussed later), also are viewed as a part of the biblical tribes of Israel. The Saints therefore have a special, scriptural obligation for the Christian redemption of Native Americans. LDS missions to Native Americans, particularly in the American southwest, have been moderately successful in attracting new members.[27] Additionally, Pacific Islanders, and smaller numbers of converts from around the world, gathered to the Utah region before immigration slowed and officially was discouraged in the 1920s.

In 1978 the LDS prophet received a revelation opening the priesthood to all worthy men without regard for color or race.[28] Since this time growing numbers of African American converts have contributed further to the diversity of the North American Saints. There now are many predominately African American congregations.[29] Increasingly, distinctive ethnic groups have been encouraged to value their heritage and unique cultural traditions, while sustaining the fundamental values of the LDS subculture. When there are a sufficient number of non-English-speaking American members, it has become commonplace for them to organize in congregations based on the native language, such as Spanish. In many areas, unmarried Saints also form separate singles branches (congregations).

The American Saints predominately are working-to-middle-class people. A few of them have been extraordinarily successful in business (motels, computer software, management), entertainment, professional sports, and governmental service.[30] The LDS tend to be politically conservative to moderate, and they are represented in the Republican Party, especially, and to a lesser extent in the Democratic Party. Their communities are organized around marriage, family, kinship, and religion. This subculture provides the Saints with a way of life that in many respects has been and still is remarkably independent of the larger society. While they are devoutly religious, the Saints also are a highly energetic people who greatly enjoy working and playing together. Ultimately, however, what ties them together is a common religious faith and its principal objective of building the kingdom of God.

The Latter-day Saints' Religion

The Latter-day Saints tend to be somewhat more religious (as indicated by various measures of belief, practice, and commitment) than Americans in general.[31] They believe in a living prophet (not unlike the Catholic Pope) who communicates the will of God to the people. Joseph Smith and all of his successors as president of the LDS church down to the present are regarded as modern-day prophets of God. The first Latter-day Saints, like other early European immigrants to North America, were convinced that the original church of Jesus Christ had become irretrievably corrupted over the centuries. They aimed to restore Christianity, as directed by a modern-day prophet of the biblical God, to the purity of the primitive, early New Testament church.

> We believe all that God has revealed, all that He does now reveal, and we believe that He will yet reveal many great and important things pertaining to the Kingdom of God.[32]

Scripture

The Saints accept the Bible (King James Version) as the word of God insofar as it had been translated correctly.[33] The Pearl of Great Price, another canonical work, includes Joseph Smith's corrections to the King James Bible and his divinely inspired translation of other documents.[34] The Latter-day Saints, mostly unlike other Americans committed to the restoration of primitive, New Testament Christianity, also emphasize the Old Testament. They, much like the early American Puritans, envision themselves as God's Chosen People, part of the House of Israel, and continuous with the Old Testament story. By way of a patriarchal blessing, most Latter-day Saints receive a divinely inspired message identifying their Old Testament lineage and directing their lives. As God's Chosen People in a new land (the Americas) selected especially for them, the primary mission of the LDS restoration is to build the kingdom of God on earth (Zion) in preparation for the second coming of Jesus Christ and his millennial (thousand) year reign on earth before God's Final Judgment on humanity.

> We believe in the literal gathering of Israel and in the restoration of the Ten Tribes; that Zion (the New Jerusalem) will be built upon the American continent; that Christ will reign personally upon the earth; and, that the earth will be renewed and receive its paradisiacal glory.[35]

Two additional scriptures, along with the previously mentioned Pearl of Great Price, are entirely unique to this new American religion. The Book of Mormon, from which the Latter-day Saints received their popular (but officially disavowed) nickname, is Joseph Smith's prophetic translation of an abridged ancient record of the Americas.[36] It tells the sacred story of pre-Christian migrations of biblical peoples from the old world to the Americas and, most important, Jesus Christ's establishment of his church in the Americas. Nephi, an ancient American prophet, recorded that:

> And I saw the heavens open, and the Lamb of God [Christ] descending out of heaven; and he came down and showed himself unto them. And I also saw and bear record that the Holy Ghost fell upon twelve others; and they were ordained of God, and chosen. And the angel spake unto me, saying: Behold the twelve disciples of the Lamb, who are chosen to minister unto thy seed.[37]

The Book of Mormon follows the story of these ancient Christian Americans, in a King James style, concluding with their extermination by wicked kinfolk who rejected Christianity and survived as the "Lamanite" ancestors of the contemporary native Americans. For the LDS, the Book of Mormon solves the much debated mystery of the Native Americans' origins; it provides the Americas with a Christian history continuous with biblical tradition; and, most important, it supports the Christian Bible as a second testament to the divine mission of Jesus Christ.

The third LDS scripture, called the Doctrine and Covenants, contains the prophecies of Joseph Smith and his successors up to the present day. It includes instructions for the restoration of the priesthood as well as the basic structure and organization of the Church; other directions, rules, and patterns pertinent to building Zion; as well as words of wisdom and advice about the Saints' daily lives. The Saints believe, as previously discussed, that God continues to reveal Himself to the people, providing new revelations to guide them in building the kingdom.

Beliefs about God

The Latter-day Saints "believe in God, the Eternal Father, and in His Son, Jesus Christ, and in the Holy Ghost."[38] Yet, their image of God and salvation also is unique. The biblical God is believed to be a material being, and likewise, Jesus Christ is envisioned as a corporeal person of flesh and bones. The

Holy Ghost, however, is seen as a personage of spirit. The Saints' God doctrine also includes a female deity, a Heavenly Mother. In the words of a favorite LDS hymn:

> I had learned to call thee Father,
> Thru thy Spirit from on high,
> But, until the key of knowledge was
>   restored,
> I knew not why.
> In the heav'ns are parents single?
> No, the thought makes reason stare!
> Truth is reason; truth eternal
> Tells me I've a mother there.[39]

The Father God is the husband of this female deity, and She is the mother of all the "pre-mortal spirits" who become humanly embodied as earthly children. The Eternal Father God is supreme in organizing and ruling over a council of gods in the eternal world. Heaven is hierarchically arranged in three degrees of glory: celestial, terrestrial, and telestial (in order from the highest to lowest). Human beings, based on their spiritual progress on earth, attain lower or higher degrees of heavenly glory. It therefore is possible for human beings, depending on their spiritual development (knowledge of God, conformity to His laws, and performance of related ritual ordinances) to attain exalted, god-like status in the celestial world.

LDS Temples

There are several sacred LDS salvation rituals that can only be performed in a special "temple" building (based on Old Testament imagery).[40] These sacred rituals include: "washings" and "annointings" for purification and sanctification; an "endowment" whereby individuals gain a knowledge of and enter into a covenant (mutually binding promises) with God pertinent to salvation; baptism (by a proxy, usually a family member) for the deceased (for the salvation of those who lived without the opportunity to embrace the LDS gospel); the eternal "sealing" of marriage partners and other family members (so that families are united and joined together eternally in the celestial world); and a very rare "second anointing" through which a highly ranked church authority and his wife make and receive promises pertinent to their embodied existence with God in the celestial world. The Saints, as part of their endowment, receive a sacred undergarment (reminding them of their covenant and providing God's protection) which always is to be worn whenever possible and practical. For all temple ordinances, furthermore, the Latter-day Saints dress in special ritual attire: a white dress for women, and a white shirt and slacks for men.

LDS temples are devoted to the performance of these special sacred rituals. They also are used by the leadership for special purposes, like prophetically seeking the will of God; but temples are not used for ordinary worship, regular sacrament services, or regular blessings of children, baptisms, ordinary priesthood ordinations, or marriages for time. Temples are designed to serve the functions of the sacred salvation ordinances, with baptismal fonts, gender-segregated locker rooms for bathing and dressing, rooms for the endowment and sealings, and so on. Before a temple is dedicated (or rededicated after remodeling), it usually is open for public visitation. Thereafter admittance to a Latter-day Saint temple is closed to everyone, members included, unless they have a special "recommend." To hold a "temple recommend" a Saint must submit to two worthiness interviews with local church leaders and be strictly obedient to the laws of God.

Priesthood and Administration

The Latter-day Saint religion is formally organized in terms of the hierarchical priesthood.[41] This priesthood is authorized exclusively by God for the responsibility of building His kingdom on earth and all that it entails. The Prophet-President, assisted by two counselors forming a First Presidency, heads the LDS priesthood and church organization. The First Presidency presides over a special Quorum of Twelve Apostles. The twelve apostles, ranked by seniority in this special quorum, have primary responsibility for the gospel (witnessing for Christ), the church, and the entire kingdom of God wherever it is located in the world. The First Presidency and the Twelve are appointed for life as full-time, salaried ministers/administrators.

Other special priesthood offices with general, administrative authority for particular aspects of the kingdom include: a three-man Presiding Bishopric, with many regional area directors, primarily responsible for the temporal (economic and other mundane) affairs of the church; and the Quorums of Seventy, with responsibility for assisting the ranking administrators, usually in particular geographic areas. These "general authorities" are appointed to various terms as full-time, salaried ministers/administrators. The general authorities are supported by an extensive staff of several thousand employees composing an elaborate bureaucratic organization which oversees the worldwide management of the LDS religion.[42]

The LDS Kingdom of God is administratively divided into specific geographic areas, such as the United States, Latin America, and western Europe. The definition of an area depends substantially on the number of members; and the specification of these jurisdictions therefore changes, sometimes rapidly, based on membership growth. Each area includes several "regions" and "missions." A region consists of several "stakes," including several "wards." A mission is composed of several "districts," each of which includes several "branches." Each of these divisions is managed by special officers (Area Authorities, Mission Presidents, and so on). With the exception of area-level administrators, none of the other administrative offices are paid positions. The basic congregational unit is a ward (or, if smaller, branch). There ordinarily are about two to four hundred members of a ward. All ward activities are directed by a local "bishop,"

with the assistance of two counselors, forming the ward bishopric. The ward bishopric, for instance, is responsible for duties of the lesser and greater priesthood quorums, the various "auxiliaries"—such as the women's "Relief Society"—and Sunday schools, the local welfare and missionary programs, and all of the other religious and social activities of the local LDS community.

The ward chapel or meeting house is the center of the Saints' daily lives and activities outside of the home. Most resemble ordinary American houses of worship (churches). Many of them look alike since ward meeting houses and chapels (as well as all other buildings) are constructed on the basis of a few designs approved at LDS headquarters. Ward meeting places, much like other American church buildings, contain a sanctuary, complete with a pulpit and pews, large enough to accommodate several hundred worshipers; as well as separate rooms designed for classes and smaller meetings of the priesthood and auxiliaries. Most of them also include a large kitchen for preparing food for ward social events and welfare programs, and typically a large, multipurpose room (frequently designed in the form of a basketball court) for worship overflow, as well as social and recreational activities. Because of rapid membership growth, two (or more) congregations sometimes share a single ward meeting facility, necessitating staggered sessions of activities.

The Saints are expected to attend and participate fully in the ward serving the geographic division in which they reside. On Sundays they typically gather for an hour-long family worship and sacrament service. The ward bishop and his two counselors preside over this service, although men, women, and children all may participate by offering brief talks, prayers, testimonies, music, and the like. This service includes the sacrament, or a serving of bread and water for the remembrance of Christ's atoning sacrifice. While entirely serious, LDS worship services tend to be somewhat informal, casual, family-oriented events. Outsiders (non-members) sometimes are surprised at the informality of Latter-day Saint worship services, the lay priesthood leadership, the joyful fellowship of family, kinfolk, and friends, and, especially, the playful activities of vibrant young children.

After the sacrament meeting, members attend other sessions involving meetings of the priesthood quorums for men, the Relief Society for adult women or other auxiliaries for younger women, and Primary (Sunday school) for children. Other activities such as baptisms, the blessing of children, priesthood ordinations, and so on also transpire on Sundays in the ward meeting house. For many of the Saints, the remainder of Sunday very likely will be devoted to family meals—which regularly are extended- and multi-family affairs—and social activities ranging from musical and dramatic performances to games or simply talking and interacting with one another. The ward meeting house, as previously mentioned, may be used for other religious and social activities throughout the week.

Several or more LDS wards form a "stake." It ordinarily is housed in a building that also is used as a ward meeting house. The stake building usually contains a large meeting hall for conferences (business meetings) and worship; offices for the stake administrators; class-sized meeting rooms; a media center for receiving telecommunication programs from LDS headquarters; and commonly a library and special facilities for conducting genealogical research. Researching family genealogy is extremely important for identifying deceased relatives who lived before the Latter-day Saint restoration. It serves as the basis for the performances of temple ordinances for these people, including proxy baptisms and the sealings of family members eternally. Although the LDS priesthood forms a theocracy, a democratic principle also operates at all levels from the local ward and stake to the Council of the Twelve Apostles and First Presidency. All priesthood officers, from the top to the bottom of the organiza-

tion, and some collective decisions require a sustaining vote from the entire membership at regular "conferences" of the ward, stake, and entire church. While it rarely if ever happens, the membership in principle could reject candidates for the ward bishopric or even the First Presidency.

A WORLD RELIGION

The Saints believe strongly that they have a prophetic mission to take the gospel to "every nation, and kindred, and tongue, and people."[43] From the very beginning of this new religion, LDS missionaries were sent out with "no purse nor script" fulfilling the revelation to: "Arise and shine forth, that thy light may be a standard for the nations."[44] As of 2008, there are more than fifty-two thousand LDS missionaries in the field, about 30 percent of whom serve outside of the United States.[45] While most of them are young men, several thousand married couples (typically retired people) and a good number of young women also are serving on missions. To replenish this missionary force, about twenty-five thousand new recruits are enlisted annually. They usually receive intensive preparation for teaching the gospel and foreign languages, as necessary, at the LDS Missionary Training Center in Provo, Utah, and similar training centers located in several other countries.

Since the 1960s, the LDS religion has become an increasingly important international movement outside of Canada and the United States.[46] There are more than three hundred thousand Saints in Great Britain, Scandinavia, and elsewhere in western Europe. In Australia and the South Pacific there are about 420,000 members. However, the real growth of the LDS Church is happening in Latin America and Africa. LDS growth in Mexico (more than 1.1 million members), the Caribbean (over 153,0000 members), as well as Central and South America (with more than 3.7 million members combined) has been tremendous. Africa now has more than a quarter of a million

Latter-day Saints, with most of that growth happening in the last decade. While less remarkable, LDS growth in Asia (with close to a million members) also is significant. Although some scholars point out that not all of the people "on the books" as baptized Mormons regularly attend church, especially in the developing world, the growth is still remarkable.

In the developing countries of the world, the Latter-day Saint religion is especially attractive to people who identify with American cultural values and are intent on improving their social and economic status. To aid them in this effort, the LDS Church established the Perpetual Education Fund in 2001 to help young Saints in developing nations obtain an education. Increasingly, the LDS religion has encouraged people from other cultures to preserve and value their own heritage. Even so, this North American religion and the subculture supporting it (as described earlier) exhibits an amazingly high degree of uniformity wherever it is transplanted around the world. Except for the people, their native language, and a few other, relatively minor adaptations to other cultures and societies, the LDS religion and subculture mostly is the same wherever it is found in the world today. Family life and ward meetings, for instance, fundamentally are the same, even in the vastly different social and cultural contexts of South America, Asia, and Africa.

CONCLUSION

This, then, is the Latter-day Saint religion, subculture, and people in the world today. It is different from almost all of the other religions you will study here, and a truly remarkable story: a new faith, born in American and forged out of the experience of European immigrants in the new world. It is the most successful new religion born in America, and now, through international exportation, this American original is an emergent world religion. At its current rate of growth, there will be more than 250 million Latter-day Saints worldwide, a majority of whom will be Third-World converts, before the close of the twenty-first century.[47]

Notes

1. The author gratefully acknowledges the helpful readings and comments of Marie Cornwall, Maureen Ursenbach Beecher, Larry Dahl, Jessie L. Embry, and David L. Paulsen on various drafts of this chapter.

2. "The wilderness and the solitary place shall be glad for them; and the desert shall rejoice, and blossom as the rose" (Isa. 35:1).

3. Jan Shipps, *Mormonism: The Story of a New Religious Tradition* (Urbana: University of Illinois Press, 1985); and Richard L. Bushman, *Joseph Smith and the Beginnings of Mormonism* (Urbana: University of Illinois Press, 1984).

4. *Church Almanac* (Salt Lake City, Utah: Deseret News, 1998).

5. Robert S. Ellwood and Harry B. Partin, *Religious and Spiritual Groups in Modern America* (Englewood Cliffs, N.J.: Prentice Hall, 1988); Timothy Miller, 2d ed., *America's Alternative Religions* (Albany: State University of New York Press, 1995); and J. Gordon Melton, *Encyclopedic Handbook of Cults in America* revised and updated (New York: Garland Publishing, 1992).

6. Leonard J. Arrington and Davis Bitton, *The Mormon Experience: A History of the Latter-day Saints* rev. (Urbana: University of Illinois Press, 1992).

7. Steven L. Shields, *The Latter Day Saint Churches: An Annotated Bibliography* (New York: Garland Publishing, 1987).

8. Richard P. Howard, *The Church through the Years*, vol. 1, *RLDS Beginnings, to 1860*, vol. 2, *The Reorganization Comes of Age, 1860–1992* (Independence, Mo.: Herald Publishing House, 1992–3). Today there are approximately 250,000 members of the Community of Christ (formerly RLDS Church) worldwide, most of whom reside in North America.

The RLDS movement initially attracted dissidents from the Nauvoo, Illinois, Church, many of whom remained scattered throughout the American Midwest following Joseph Smith's murder in 1844. This schismatic movement, headed by the founding prophet's oldest son, Joseph Smith III (after 1860), rejected many of the more innovative features of Latter-day Saints' Nauvoo theology (principally the temple salvation doctrines). Instead, the RLDS emphasized a more Protestant-like, biblical Christianity. Beginning in 1984, the RLDS also began ordaining women to the previously all-male priesthood.

9. James B. Allen and Glen M. Leonard, *The Story of the Latter-day Saints*, 2d ed. (Salt Lake City, Utah: Deseret, 1992); Thomas F. O'Dea, *The Mormons* (Chicago: University of Chicago Press, 1957); and Klaus J. Hansen, *Mormonism and the American Experience* (Chicago: University of Chicago Press, 1981).

10. R. Laurence Moore, *Religious Outsiders and the Making of Americans* (New York: Oxford University Press, 1986); Kenneth H. Winn, *Exiles in a Land of Liberty: Mormons in America, 1830–1846* (Chapel Hill: University of North Carolina Press, 1989); and Marvin S. Hill, *Quest for Refuge: The Mormon Flight from American Pluralism* (Salt Lake City, Utah: Signature Books, 1989).

11. Barry A. Kosmin and Seymour P. Lachman, *One Nation Under God: Religion in Contemporary American Society* (New York: Harmony Books, 1993); and D. Michael Quinn, *The Mormon Hierarchy: Origins of Power, Extensions of Power*, 2 vols. (Salt Lake City, Utah: Signature Books, 1994, 1997).

12. Between about 1843 and 1890 the Latter-day Saint religion permitted the marriage of one man to more than one wife (called plural marriage, polygamy or, technically, polygyny), although a substantial majority of the Saints never engaged in this practice and were monogamous. Richard S. Van Wagoner, *Mormon Polygamy: A History*, 2d ed. (Salt Lake City, Utah: Signature Books, 1989); Carmon B. Hardy, *Solemn Covenant: The Mormon Polygamous Passage* (Urbana: University of Illinois Press, 1992); and Jessie L. Embry, *Mormon Polygamous Families: Life in the Principle* (Salt Lake City, Utah: University of Utah Press, 1987).

13. Kosmin and Lachman, *One Nation Under God*; and Tim B. Heaton, Kristen L. Goodman, and Thomas B. Holman, "In Search of a Peculiar People: Are Mormon Families Really Different?" 87–117 in Marie Cornwall, Tim B. Heaton, and Lawrence A. Young, *Contemporary Mormonism: Social Science Perspectives* (Urbana: University of Illinois Press, 1994).

14. The LDS "Articles of Faith," number four, states: "We believe that the first principles and ordinances of the Gospel are: first, Faith in the Lord Jesus Christ; second, Repentance; third, Baptism by immersion for the remission of sins; fourth, Laying on of hands for the gift of the Holy Ghost." B. H. Roberts, *A Comprehensive History of The Church of Jesus Christ of Latter-day Saints*, 6 vols. (Salt Lake City, Utah: The Church of Jesus Christ of Latter-day Saints, 1930), 4:535–41. Hereafter cited as *History of the Church*.

15. The LDS "Articles of Faith," number two, states: "We believe that men will be punished for their own sins, and not for Adam's transgression" (*History of the Church*, 4:535–41).

16. The LDS "Articles of Faith," number five, states: "We believe that a man must be called of God, by prophecy, and by the laying on of hands by those who are in authority, to preach the Gospel and administer in the ordinances thereof." The "Articles of Faith," number six, further indicates with respect to the priesthood that: "We believe in the same organization that existed in the Primitive Church, namely, apostles, prophets, pastors, teachers, evangelists, and so forth" (*History of the Church*, 4: 535–41).

17. The Pearl of Great Price: A Selection from the Revelations, Translations, and Narrations of Joseph Smith (Salt Lake City, Utah: The Church of Jesus Christ of Latter-day Saints, 1986), Matthew 6:38. Hereafter cited as Pearl of Great Price.

18. *The Doctrines and Covenants of the Church of Jesus Christ of Latter-day Saints* (Salt Lake City, Utah: The Church of Jesus Christ of Latter-day Saints, 1986), 39:13. Hereafter cited as *D&C*.

19. *D&C* 93:36.

20. Armand L. Mauss, *The Angel and the Beehive: The Mormon Struggle with Assimilation* (Urbana: University of Illinois Press, 1994).

21. Maureen Ursenbach Beecher and Lavina Fielding Anderson, eds., *Sisters in Spirit: Mormon Women in Historical and Cultural Perspective* (Urbana: University of Illinois Press, 1987); and Maxine Hanks, ed., *Women and Authority: Re-emerging Mormon Feminism* (Salt Lake City, Utah: Signature Books, 1992).

22. See Quinn, *Extensions of Power*, 214–17, for an even more specific example.

23. Lester E. Bush Jr., *Health and Medicine among the Latter-day Saints: Science, Sense, and Scripture* (New York: Crossroad, 1993).

24. *D&C*, 89.

25. *D&C* 89:18.

26. *D&C* 89:21.

27. Bruce A. Chadwick and Stan L. Albrecht, "Mormons and Indians: Beliefs, Policies, Programs, and Practices," 287–309 in Cornwall, Heaton, and Young, *Contemporary Mormonism*.

28. *DC*, Official Declaration 2. From about 1844 until 1978, men of black African ancestry were prohibited by custom from ordination to the LDS priesthood. See Newell G. Bringhurst, *Saints, Slaves, and Blacks: The Changing Place of Black People within Mormonism* (Westport, Conn.: Greenwood Press, 1981); and Mary Lou McNamara, "Secularization or Sacralization: The Change in LDS Church Policy on Blacks," 310–25 in Cornwall, Heaton, and Young, *Contemporary Mormonism*.

29. Cardell K. Jacobson, Tim B. Heaton, E. Dale LeBaron, and Trina Louise Hope, "Black Mormon Converts in the United States and Africa: Social Characteristics and Perceived Acceptance," 326–48 in Cornwall, Heaton, and Young, *Contemporary Mormonism*.

30. Kosmin and Lachman, *One Nation Under God*; Mauss, *The Angel and the Beehive*.

31. Mauss, *The Angel and the Beehive*, 141–56.

32. "Articles of Faith," number nine (*History of the Church*, 4: 535–41).

33. "Articles of Faith," number eight (*History of the Church*, 4:535–41). Also see Philip L. Barlow, *Mormons and the Bible: The Place of the Latter-day Saints in American Religion* (New York: Oxford University Press, 1991).

34. Pearl of Great Price.

35. "Articles of Faith," number ten (*History of the Church*, 4: 535–4).

36. Joseph Smith Jr., trans., The Book of Mormon (Salt Lake City, Utah: The Church of Jesus Christ of Latter-day Saints, 1981).

37. Book of Mormon, Nephi 12:6–8.

38. "Articles of Faith," number one (*History of the Church*, 4:535–41).

39. Eliza R. Snow, "My Father," *Hymns of the Church of Jesus Christ of Latter-day Saints* (Salt Lake City, Utah: The Church of Jesus Christ of Latter-day Saints, 1985), 292–93.

40. James E. Talmage, *The House of the Lord: A Study of Holy Sanctuaries, Ancient and Modern* (1912; reprint, Salt Lake City: Deseret, 1976); and David John Buerger, *The Mysteries of Godliness: A History of Mormon Temple Worship* (San Francisco: Smith Research Associates, 1994).

41. Quinn, *The Mormon Hierarchy*.

42. Quinn, *Extensions of Power*, 161.

43. Bible (KJV), Revelation 14:6.

44. *D&C* 24:18 and 115:5.

45. Gordon Shepherd and Gary Shepherd, "Sustaining a Lay Religion in Modern Society: The Mormon Missionary Experience," 161–81 in Cornwall, Heaton, and Young, *Contemporary Mormonism*.

46. Rodney Stark, "The Rise of a New World Faith," *Review of Religious Research* 26 (1, 1984), 118–27; and Allen and Leonard, *The Story of the Latter-day Saints*, 652–53.

47. Rodney Stark, "Modernization and Mormon Growth: The Secularization Thesis Revisited," 13–23 in Cornwall, Heaton, and Young, *Contemporary Mormonism*.

STUDY QUESTIONS

1. Discuss some of the similarities and differences between American culture and the Latter-day Saint subculture. Did the information discussed in this chapter change your views of the Latter-day Saints? Why or why not?

2. How are new religions different from more traditional religions? Discuss how the Latter-day Saint religion is similar to or different from other new religions.

3. What are the main beliefs and practices of the Latter-day Saint religion? Discuss how the Latter-day Saint religion is alike and/or different from other forms of Christianity. What, specifically, do you learn about religion in general by comparing and contrasting new religions with traditional religions?

4. Describe the ways in which the Latter-day Saint religion is a distinctive product of American culture. Is the Latter-day Saint religion unique in this regard? Why or why not?

5. Describe how the Latter-day Saint religion influences the daily lives of its members, especially in terms of marriage and family, education and work, as well as their relationships with the larger society. In what ways is this similar to or different from other religions in America?

6. What is the Book of Mormon? What role does it play in the Latter-day Saint religion? Why did many Americans find this story attractive? How is it alike or different from other religious scriptures?

7. What is the meaning and significance of a "temple" for the Latter-day Saint religion? How does it differ from other Latter-day Saint facilities? Describe and discuss the role of the temple in the lives of the faithful.

8. Describe the development of the Latter-day Saint religion outside of the United States. What accounts for the success of the Latter-day Saint religion elsewhere in the world?

ESSAY TOPICS

The Role and Significance of New Religions and the Conditions under which They Are or Are Not Likely to Be Successful

The Theocratic Kingdom of God and Its Role in the Latter-day Saint and Other American Religions

The Americanization of Religion or Specific Forms of Religion

The Influence of Religion on Daily Life in a Pluralistic Society

The Emergence and Development of New Religions as World Religions

WORD EXPLORATION

The following ideas play a significant role in the Latter-day Saint religion and therefore merit deliberate consideration and discussion.

Bible	Book of Mormon	Doctrine and Covenants
Priesthood	Temple	Word of Wisdom
Mission	Prophecy	Stewardship
Zion	Conformity/Obedience	Heavenly Mother
Ward/Stake	Theocracy	Chosen People

FOR FURTHER READING

Bringhurst, Newell G. and Lavina Fielding Anderson, eds. *Excavating Mormon Pasts: The New Historiography of the Last Half Century*. Salt Lake City: Greg Kofford Books, 2004.

Bushman, Claudia L. *Contemporary Mormonism: Latter-day Saints in Modern America*. New York: Praeger Publishers, 2006.

Bushman, Richard Lyman. *Joseph Smith: Rough Stone Rolling, A Cultural Biography of Mormonism's Founder*. New York: Random House, 2005.

Davies, Douglas J. *An Introduction to Mormonism*. New York: Cambridge University Press, 2003.

Ludlow, Daniel H., ed. *Encyclopedia of Mormonism: The History, Scripture, Doctrine, and Procedures of the Church of Jesus Christ of Latter-day Saints*. 4 vols. New York: Macmillan, 1992.

WEB SITES

http://www.mormon.org
    Basic beliefs and practices of the Latter-day Saints

http://www.familysearch.org
    The LDS Church's global genealogy Web site

http://newsroom.lds.org/ldsnewsroom/eng/
    Official news and statistics of the LDS Church

http://earlylds.com/
    Mormon Trail Pioneer Database

19

The Unification Church

GEORGE D. CHRYSSIDES

1920	Sun Myung Moon born
1935	Moon claims vision of Jesus on Korean mountainside
1946	Moon returns to Pyongyang; imprisoned by authorities
1948	Prison sentence in Ton Nee Special Labor Concentration Camp, Hungnam
1951	Moon's first church constructed near Seoul
1954	Holy Spirit Association for the Unification of World Christianity founded
1956	Pastor Joshua McCabe visits Moon's church; helps translate *The Principle* into English
1959	Young Oon Kim starts evangelizing in United States
1960	Marriage of Sun Myung Moon and Hak Ja Han
1965	Sun Myung Moon's first visit to U.S. First Blessing Ceremony outside Korea
1972	U.S. government allows Moon residential status
1973	Publication of *Divine Principle*
1974	Moon's 32 City Tour. During Watergate scandal, Moon supports U.S. President Richard Nixon
1981	Moon convicted of U.S. tax evasion
1983	Death of Heung Jin
1984–1985	Moon serves prison sentence in Danbury, Connecticut
1987	Black Zimbabwean Cleopus Kundiona claims to be Heung Jin's "returning resurrection"
1989	Death of Hak Ja Han's mother Soon Ae Hong
1996	New name "Family Federation for World Peace and Unification" (FFWPU) adopted
1997	Death of Dr Sang Hun Lee, from whom members claim spirit messages; beginning of Hoon Dok Hae period
2001	Lee purportedly presides over ceremony in spirit world, with political and religious leaders acknowledging Moon's messiahship
2004	"Coronation" at Capitol Hill
2008	Death of Moon's eldest son Hyo Jin; Moon hands over presidency of FFWPU to Hyung Jin

Of all the new religions that emerged in the West in the 1960s and 1970s, the Unification Church—popularly known as "the Moonies"—is probably the most controversial. Critics have accused it of "brainwashing" its members, splitting up families, and forcing its members to work for long hours in mobile fund-raising teams (MFTs). Critics allege that its authoritarian leader enjoys a sumptuous lifestyle while rank-and-file members lived modestly in dormitory-style accommodation in various communes, remote from the outside world. Evangelical Christians, particularly in the Protestant tradition, have accused the Unification Church (UC) of heresy, since its definitive writing *Divine Principle* appeared to be a new scripture, and its teachings about Jesus and about Moon as a new Messiah on earth were at variance with mainstream Christianity's understanding of the Bible. The UC gained further notoriety when the Rev. Moon was convicted of tax evasion in 1982 and sentenced to eighteen months' imprisonment.

Sun Myung Moon has repeatedly said that he never intended to found a new religion. It is therefore ironic that members of Moon's Unification Church are popularly known as "the Moonies." Unificationists are adamant that they are a Christian organization, and, as the name "Unification" suggests, that they seek to unite, not divide, Christianity and the world's religious traditions.

ORIGINS

Unificationists insist that Sun Myung Moon's teachings cannot be properly understood without knowing his life. It is sometimes hard to distinguish between hagiographical tales and genuine history, but it seems certain that he was born as Young Myung Moon in the P'yeongan Pukta province of North Korea on January 6, 1920. (Moon changed his name to Sun Myung in 1953. "Young Myung Moon" means "shining dragon," which he felt was inappropriate for a religious leader, since the dragon has Satanic associations.) His parents converted

to Presbyterianism when he was nine years old, having previously espoused a Korean blend of Confucianism, Buddhism, and folk shamanism.

He frequently went to the mountainside to pray, and in 1935, around Easter time, the teenage boy claimed to have received a vision of Jesus, who instructed Moon to complete the mission that he was unable to accomplish fully in first-century Palestine. Moon claims to have continued to receive supernatural revelations, not only from Jesus but also from God, Confucius, Lao Tzu, the Buddha, and Satan, among others. Moon did not commit his teachings to writing for a further fifteen years, but preached them orally. His principal innovations were that Jesus' crucifixion was not part of God's original redemptive plan, and that Jesus' premature and unnatural death prevented him from marrying and fathering sinless children. Additionally, Moon claims to have discovered the true origin of sin, which was due to illicit sexual relationships between Lucifer, Eve, and Adam, rather than to Adam and Eve's being tempted to eat fruit from a forbidden tree in the Garden of Eden. Unificationism is not fundamentalist in its interpretation of scripture, holding that not all of the Bible is to be understood literally. Much of Christianity's scriptures are to be understood symbolically, and are to be supplemented by the additional revelations afforded to its founder-leader, Sun Myung Moon.

At the age of eighteen, Moon went to Seoul to study electrical engineering, after which he went to Waseda University in Japan, where he became involved with the Korean Independence Movement. He returned to Korea in 1945, when he began his public ministry. Moon appears to have sought out a number of religious groups, both in Japan and Korea, that he thought would be sympathetic to his ideas. In particular, he had hoped that the Israel Jesus Church, headed by Kim Baek-Moon, and which he joined in 1945, would acclaim him as the Second Adam. (The Israel Jesus Church is perhaps more familiar by the name of the Israel Monastery, among other names.[1])

Disappointed by his of lack of recognition, Moon returned to Pyongyang in North Korea in 1946. However, he fared no better in the north, and was arrested and imprisoned for allegedly heretical teaching and espionage little more than a month after his arrival. In 1948, Moon received a further prison sentence, to five years' hard labor in the Tong Nee Special Labor Concentration Camp in Hungnam, but was liberated when UN forces arrived in 1950. He became reunited with a small number of supporters, and returned to Seoul, where he began to commit the Principle to writing. In 1954, Moon's own organization, The Holy Spirit Association for the Unification of World Christianity, was founded; its premises consisted of a small shack, constructed by Moon himself in 1951 from old cardboard and wood. It was there that Moon would give intensive teachings to his early group of disciples, often far into the night.

UNIFICATIONIST TEACHINGS

The generic collective name for the Rev. Moon's key teachings is "the Principle." It has been set out in writing in various texts over the years. Originally the teachings were written as a set of notes, dictated by Moon to a close disciple who is said to have transcribed them in pencil. In 1956 an English translation was made, largely with the assistance of a pastor from the Apostolic Church, Pastor Joshua McCabe. Apparently twelve copies of this translation were made and circulated, but none appears to have survived. Two later translations were made, bearing the name *The Divine Principle*, one by Dr. Young Oon Kim and another by Colonel Bo Hi Pak, both of whom evangelized in the United States in the early 1960s. In 1973, a more substantial version was completed by Hyo Won Eu, which served as the principal text until 1996, when it was replaced by *Exposition of the Divine Principle*, a retranslation.

In addition to these writings, *Outline of the Principle Level 4* covers the main teachings of *Divine Principle*, but in a more concise and reader-friendly way. The reference to "levels" in this title alludes to a number of forms in which the Principle is disseminated at Unificationist seminars. The most basic and condensed version is Level 1, and instructors used to recommend inquirers to progress through these various "levels" of the Principle: each successive one had greater length and detail. In addition to *Exposition of Divine Principle*, Moon's various speeches to his followers have been collected and translated into English. Some of these form complete short books, while others are short sermons.

The Principle is arranged into three main divisions:

1. The Principle of Creation
2. The Fall
3. Principles of Restoration

As to its teachings on creation, Unification theology is an interpretation of the Jewish-Christian Bible, but with additional elements that members believe to derive from subsequent revelations afforded to Sun Myung Moon. According to Unification teaching, God created the universe for the purpose of its attaining perfection. Perfection does not occur instantly, but as a result of a three-stage process: formation, growth, and completion. The first man and woman—Adam and Eve—were expected to attain perfection by undergoing marriage and giving birth to sinless children, who would subject themselves to God's dominion. However, at the age of sixteen, having attained the highest level of the "growth" stage, Eve was seduced by Satan in the Garden of Eden, and subsequently entered into a sexual relationship with Adam. Thus there were two types of fall: a spiritual fall (the illicit relationship with Satan, a spiritual being), and a physical fall (the illicit premature sexual relationship with Adam). By so doing, Adam and Eve entered into a new relationship, subjecting themselves to Satan's dominion rather than God's.

The original relationship between humankind and God therefore needed to be restored, and in order to accomplish this, it was necessary for God to send a messiah. This could not be done instantly; according to Unificationism, humanity must pay "indemnity" before the messiah can appear. Indemnity is a key concept in Unification thought, although its meaning differs from that of common parlance: it is more akin to compensation than to a guarantee. There are two requirements for indemnity, known as the foundation of faith and the foundation of substance, reflecting the two types of fall that Adam and Eve experienced. For the foundation of faith to be accomplished, humanity must unite around a central figure who pays appropriate indemnity and establishes a correct "vertical" relationship (that is, a relationship between humanity and God). The foundation of substance involves humanity establishing appropriate interhuman relationships under God's dominion. Only then have the foundations been set for the messiah to come.

Various key individuals in the Bible came as central figures: Abel, Noah, Abraham, Jacob, and Moses. *Divine Principle* gives quite a detailed and complex explanation of why these individuals assumed the role at the time they did, and why they all failed to accomplish their mission. The next central figure after Moses was John the Baptist, who heralded Jesus as the coming Messiah. At first, John was loyal and witnessed to Jesus, but subsequently began to doubt Jesus' messianic status and became more concerned with his own popularity, which was diminishing as Jesus' ministry progressed. As a result of John's failure, the majority of Jews were unable to accept Jesus' messiahship, and consequently Jesus was crucified rather than heralded as the world's redeemer.

Although it is sometimes said that Unificationism teaches that Jesus' mission was a failure, Unificationists are emphatic this was not the case, for two reasons. First, it was not Jesus who failed, but rather humanity in general for not accepting his messianic status, and John the Baptist in particular for failing to witness consistently on his behalf. Second, Jesus' mission did accomplish something: on the cross, Jesus told one of the dying thieves that he would be with Jesus that day in paradise (Luke 23:43). Unification theology distinguishes between paradise and the kingdom of heaven: earthly existence is the foundation stage; paradise, the growth stage; and the kingdom of heaven, the completion stage.

Although Jesus' death secured the opening of paradise, Jesus died without marrying and fathering children who, being the Messiah's offspring, would have been free from original sin. A new messiah is therefore needed to accomplish the mission that Jesus was unable to complete, and again *Divine Principle* goes into considerable detail to determine where and when this new messiah would be born. By recognizing parallel events in the Old Testament and New Testament, it concludes that a new era—the Completed Testament era—must begin somewhere between 1917 and 1930, and that the country chosen by God to accomplish the new mission is Korea. There are several reasons for God's choice of Korea: the Book of Revelation speaks of an angel arising from the east (Rev. 7:2–4), and several Korean prophecies allude to the country's role in receiving the messiah. Also of key importance is the fact that Korea is perceived as the battleground between communism and democracy, being split into North and South, with competing ideologies. Unificationism is vehemently opposed to communism, seeing it as oppositional to God and inspired by Satan.

Divine Principle does not explicitly identify Moon by name as the new messiah, although the introduction makes this claim:

With the fullness of time, God has sent His messenger to resolve the fundamental questions of life and the universe. His name is Sun Myung Moon.

For many decades, he wandered in a vast spiritual world in search of the ultimate truth. On this path, he endured suffering unimagined by anyone in human history. God alone will remember it. Knowing that no one can find the ultimate truth to save mankind without going through the bitterest of trials, he fought alone against myriads of Satanic forces, both in the spiritual and physical worlds, and finally triumphed over them all. In this way, he came into contact with many saints in Paradise and with Jesus, and thus brought into light all the heavenly secrets through his communion with God. *(Divine Principle, 1973, 16)*

To remove any doubt, he explicitly declared in 1992 that he and his wife Hak Ja Han Moon were jointly the messiahs of the Completed Testament Age:

In early July, I spoke in five cities around Korea at rallies held by the Women's Federation for World Peace. There, I declared that my wife, WFWP President Hak Ja Han Moon, and I are the True Parents of all humanity. I declared that we are the Savior, the Lord of the Second Advent, the Messiah. *(Moon, 1992, 5)*

Moon names both himself and his wife as joint messiahs: this is because humanity's restoration can only be effected through the messiah's marriage and procreation of blessed children, who are sinless under God's dominion. This marriage took place on March 16, 1960, and is referred to as "the marriage of the lamb," being the messianic marriage that Jesus was unable to accomplish. Since one of the principal functions of the messiahs is to establish a new lineage, giving birth to "true children under God," Sun Myung Moon and Hak Ja Han Moon are known as the True Parents. Hak Ja Han Moon has given birth to fourteen children in all, although only ten have survived. Members frequently refer to Moon as

Father; however, by so doing they are not conferring divine status on him—the Principle teaches that the messiah is human, not divine. When members pray, they address God, not Moon, although it is common to end a prayer with the words, "in the name of True Parents."

By enabling humanity to enter into a new lineage, the messiah offers entry into the kingdom of heaven. Like everything else in the universe, life in the spirit world has three stages: a formation stage, a growth stage (Paradise), and a completion stage (the kingdom of heaven). This final stage can only be opened by the messiah and, as previously noted, it can only be entered by married couples. Unificationism is universalist in its views on salvation: it is expected that, in time, the whole of humanity will gain entry into this kingdom, not just a predetermined elect group, as in Calvinist Protestantism. Even Satan himself will be saved, although he and his bride will probably be the last to enter heaven's gates.

BEGINNINGS IN THE UNITED STATES

Entrusted with the salvation of the entire world, the Unification Church desired to spread its message beyond Korea's boundaries, and the year 1959 saw the beginnings of attempts to bring Unificationism to the United States. Early members sought out promising opportunities. Colonel Bo Hi Pak (b.1930), one of Moon's earliest disciples, had been appointed to the Korean Embassy in Washington as assistant military attaché, and became one of the first Unificationist missionaries in the United States. Success in attracting Western seekers, however, was largely due to Miss Young Oon Kim (1915–1990), who had a keen interest in the spirit world and was particularly influenced by the teachings of Emmanuel Swedenborg. She had taught at a women's Bible college in Pyongyang before meeting Moon and coming to accept his teachings. She brought out an English version of the Principle, typewritten and mimeographed, titled *The Divine Principles*: it covered the same ground as the later, professionally produced *Divine Principle* (1973), but in less detail. Two principal factors were influencing mainstream Christianity at that time: the charismatic movement, which stressed healing and ecstatic experiences, and the ecumenical movement, which sought to unite diverse religious groups. The Unification Church endeavored to tap into both of these, combining the enthusiasm and spontaneity of the charismatics with the professed desire to unite Christendom of the other. The UC's initial attempts therefore involved promoting itself as a brand of charismatic and ecumenical Christianity, with a view to being seen as part of the mainstream Christian tradition.

Kim managed to attract a small band of around half a dozen Western converts, who lived with her in rented accommodation. Her strategy was to send them out leafleting the public and visiting members of the local Christian clergy, attempting to sell them copies of *The Divine Principles*. These attempts were largely unsuccessful. What really saved them from extinction was the coming of its founder-leader to the United States, which did much to unify the rival groups that were then working in the Bay Area, and to encourage renewed vigor amongst the early UC missionaries. Moon paid three visits in all in the early years: in 1965, 1969, and 1972. Perhaps surprisingly, Moon did not engage in any public preaching or lecturing whatsoever during these first two visits, or attempt to win over Christian clergy. In fact, Moon's activities seemed almost guaranteed to demonstrate that his movement was outside the mainstream Christian tradition.

The main purpose of Moon's first visit was to establish "holy grounds." Although this practice of establishing, using, and maintaining holy grounds is not widely known, such sacred places are regarded as highly important to Unification members. Their locations may be unmarked, and hence unnoticed by the public, but Unification members know where they are and use them for private prayer, vigils, and the Pledge service (a weekly ceremony in which members reaffirm their commitment). Their creation involves a form of geomancy: careful instructions are given on where holy ground sites should be located, and exact ritual instructions are prescribed about how such grounds should be set up.[2]

Apart from being an aid to devotion, holy grounds bear a theological significance. The ritual is believed to reinstate God's ownership of the land, which has previously belonged to Satan. The holy ground is thus a "representative area," providing hope that the entire country will be released from Satan's hold and returned to God. The ability to create such sacred space is attributed to Moon's "holy marriage" in 1960, when Sun Myung Moon and Hak Ja Han achieved what Jesus was unable to accomplish: holy matrimony. Thus, it is taught that Jesus himself could not have created holy grounds, since he was only able to work in the spirit world. Moon's second U.S. visit lasted thirty-nine days in February and March of 1969 and focused on the Blessing ceremony (the "mass weddings," as the media labeled them). At these ceremonies, the Rev. and Mrs. Moon presided over the marriage of multiple couples—sometimes thousands—simultaneously. During the 1969 visit, thirteen American couples received the Blessing, the first such event to be conducted outside Korea. It formed part of the landmark "43 Couples Blessing": on departure from the United States, Moon presided over further ceremonies in Germany and Japan, where a further eight and twenty-two couples respectively were blessed.

It was Moon's third visit to the United States that gave decisive impetus to the movement. He arrived in Washington, D.C., on December 18, 1971, initially as part of a further world tour, but was granted permission to reside in the country the following year. Moon's arrival was significant in a number of ways. His presence not only ensured that the movement was stable and truly unified: this time Moon emerged as a public speaker, being the focus of numerous rallies in U.S. cities. Perhaps surprisingly, Moon had never spoken to the public before; previously he had only taught his own followers. In 1973 his International One World Crusade toured twenty-one U.S. cities, but his supporters cite his Day of Hope Crusade as the beginning of his real success, when on September 18, 1974, an estimated audience of 25,000 heard him speak at Madison Square Garden. The following month (Oct. 8, 1974) Moon spoke before Congress on the topic "America in God's Providence." The year 1976 marked the bicentennial of American independence, and on June 1 Moon spoke at Yankee Stadium, his theme being "God's Hope for America." This event was somewhat marred by high winds, which blew down many of the signs and decorations. Much more successful was the "God Bless America Festival" on September 18 at the Washington Monument, where Moon declared that America would only retain its status as an advanced country if it became united with God. According to the Unification Church, there were some 300,000 attendees, but critics believe that this claim is somewhat exaggerated.

Moon has typically sought audiences with leading politicians in various parts of the world. In 1965 he had gained an audience with former U.S. President Dwight Eisenhower. When the Watergate scandal erupted in 1974, Moon took the unpopular step of supporting Nixon. Although Moon did not condone Nixon's actions, his "Forgive, love, unite" speech brought him to the fore in the media once again, and Moon appeared publicly in the President's company. Moon's relationships with mainstream churches have been less successful, however. In 1974, the Unification Church in Korea applied unsuccessfully to join the Korean National Council of Churches. In 1976 the New York City Council of Churches received an application, which it promptly rejected. This application prompted a study of Unificationist teachings by the Commission on Faith and Order of the National Council of Churches, which firmly

concluded that "the Unification Church is not a Christian Church."[3] The grounds for rejection were several, and all theological: their doctrine of the Trinity, the person of Christ, grace and salvation, the Unificationist interpretation of scripture, Moon's own revelations, and—most especially—his claim to offer a "new, ultimate, final truth."[4] A subsequent attempt in the United Kingdom to the (then) British Council of Churches also failed in 1978.

A further endeavor to spread the Unification movement's ideals lay in a number of related organizations that Moon created. The Collegiate Association for the Research of Principles (CARP), founded in Korea in 1955, established a presence in the West, aiming principally at university and college students. As well as encouraging the study of the Principle, it campaigned against social ills, such as drugs and pornography. Other developments included the setting up of the International Conference of the Unity of the Sciences (ICUS) in 1972, the International Cultural Foundation in 1976, and the International Religious Foundation in the early 1980s. These conferences sought to bring together academics from various disciplines and members of the clergy. Although essentially nonproselytizing, they afforded an opportunity to disseminate information about the Unification Church and to create sympathetic understanding of its major goals.

FURTHER DEVELOPMENT IN THE WEST

After his rallies in the United States in the early 1970s, Moon began to attract a group of Western followers, both in America and in Europe. Small communities were set up, where seekers could come for seminars on the Principle. Members of the public were invited initially to a two-day seminar (sometimes called a "workshop"), at which a leader would expound the Principle sequentially, beginning with the Principles of creation and the fall of man, and ending with the Lord of the Second Coming. The program was interspersed with prayers and the singing of holy songs; some seminars had a "rest and relaxation" period, which consisted of organized sports or homespun entertainments. Since living accommodation was communal, there was little opportunity for solitude or personal reflection. The intensity of these seminars led to the now-familiar accusations of "brainwashing," which are associated particularly with the Unification Church.

Converts also engaged in street preaching in major cities and in the distribution of their *One World* magazine. The church's Go-World Brass Band attracted attention as it toured major cities worldwide. Financing the movement was important, and Moon's followers were organized into mobile fundraising teams (MFTs), who would go out in vans into cities, and sell candles and flowers, often working long hours to help finance their newly found faith. It has been estimated that around fifteen percent of the movement's income at the time came from the MFTs. The rest came from Moon's own financial ventures: his investment portfolio is vast as well as diverse, and his financial interests include seafoods, catering, ginseng, and various sectors of the media, including *The Washington Times*. At the time of writing, his assets were estimated at $990 million.[5] Members seldom expressed disapproval of the striking contrast between Moon's own living conditions and those of rank-and-file members and seekers, who lived in dormitory-style accommodations in Camp K and Boonville, and who worked long hours with the MFTs. Members believed that their leader was entitled to the honor due to humanity's new messiah, pointing out that he had endured much hardship to bring himself to his present situation, and that he also worked long hours, taking little sleep.

Rites and festivals

Although the Unification Church has made claims to be authentically Christian, its worship, rites of passage, and celebration of festivals differ substantially from those of mainstream Christian denominations. The weekly Sunday service is somewhat in the style of Protestant Presbyterian worship, involving the singing of holy songs (some of which are mainstream Christian hymns), readings from the Bible, *extempore* prayer, and a sermon. *Divine Principle* is not normally used liturgically. It is here that close similarities end, although it should be noted that many Unificationists attend the Sunday services of mainstream Christian denominations. It is expected that, in addition to Sunday congregation worship, members will attend the weekly pledge ceremony, usually held very early in the morning. Members don holy robes and assemble in a shrine room, where a picture of the Rev. and Mrs. Moon is prominent. There they pledge their allegiance to God's will and promise to follow the way of the True Parents and to help to achieve an ideal restored world under God's dominion.

Additionally, there are five major festivals: True God's Day, True Parents' Day, the Day of All True Things, True Children's Day, and True Parents' Birthday. The first Parents' Day was established on October 1, 1960, shortly after the marriage of Sun Myung Moon and Hak Ja Han, and celebrates the reestablishment of the original matrimonial state that God intended. True Children's Day reminds members that God and the True Parents now have their own "true children," and that the rest of humanity can be engrafted into this true family. The Day of All True Things is a reminder that the entire cosmos can now be brought under God's dominion. Adam and Eve would have achieved this if they had progressed towards perfection, and would have received God's blessing. God's Day is celebrated on New Year's Day and highlights the belief that, through the work of the True Parents and True Children, perfection is once more a realistic hope. True Parents' birthday is celebrated on the anniversary of the birth of Sun Myung and Hak Ja Han Moon, according to the lunar calendar. (They share a common birthday.) These festivals are celebrated, first within the individual family at home and then with an elaborate ceremony, over which the True Parents preside. At Unification Church Centers, festivals begin with the pledge, and continue with prayers and holy songs. With modern technology, it is often possible to have a video link with the True Parents, so that rank-and-file members can watch them live as they lead the celebrations.

As well as these five major festivals, there are several minor ones. Particular significance is attached to the Day of the Victory of Love (early January), which Moon established when his son Heung Jin was dying in the hospital, believing that the sorrow would be transformed into great accomplishment in the spirit world. The anniversary of the establishing of the HSA-UWC is celebrated on May 1. The Day of the Love of God (mid-May) reaffirms Heung Jin's work, emphasizing the relationship between the True Parents on earth and those who remain in the spirit world: God, Jesus, and Heung Jin. Foundation Day (Sept. 18) commemorates important U.S. public rallies held in 1974 and 1976. The Day of the Victory of Heaven (Oct. 4) celebrates Moon's release from prison in North Korea on October 14, 1950, and in South Korea on October 4, 1955. In addition, the birthdays and Blessing anniversaries of Moon's children receive recognition within the church.

Unification Church members have their own distinctive ways of celebrating rites of passage. When a baby is born, a birth ceremony is held to which family and friends are invited. Seven ceremonially prepared "birth candles" are lit by designated attendees, and prayers are offered. On the eighth day after the child's birth, parents put on holy robes and conduct a further early-morning ceremony—the Eight Day Dedication Ceremony—with invited friends looking on. Gifts are discouraged: the ceremony is for God, not for the child. Birthdays are marked in a religious context as well as a more celebratory one, reminding parents and children of the importance of the gift of life.

Death rites mark the passing ("ascension") of the Unification member from the physical world to the spiritual world. These involve several separate stages, one at home for the deceased's immediate family (the *Gwi Hwan* ceremony); the second (*Seung Hwa*) for members, in front of an altar; and the third (*Seung Hwa*) resembling a more mainstream Christian funeral, consisting of holy songs, prayers, and a tribute. A constant vigil is kept for either three, five, or seven days, until the coffin is finally removed for burial (cremation is disallowed). The burial rites (*Won Jeun*) consist of a holy song, prayers, and a sermon. Food is offered at the cemetery, and subsequently at the home altar. (It is customary in the East to make food offerings to departed spirits.) Finally, the graveyard is visited three days after the funeral, when the final "ceremony of ascension" (*Sam Oje*) is performed: this involves offering incense, flowers, fruit, and other foods. These ceremonies, as described, are for members who have undergone the Blessing; a simplified set of ceremonies is used for single members.

THE BLESSING

Most important of all the Unificationist ceremonies is, of course, the Blessing. Because the messiah's mission is to marry and to beget sinless children, Unificationism has attached great importance to marriage and the family. Eve's sin was sexual misconduct, and Moon teaches the importance of confining sexual relationships to the bonds of marriage. Moon teaches that the kingdom of heaven can only be entered by married couples, not by individuals. Consequently, great importance is attached to members undergoing the Blessing ceremonies, popularly called "mass marriages" by the media. Moon has attracted considerable publicity for marrying record numbers of couples at the same ceremony. In 1982, Moon married 5,837 couples from 83 different countries simultaneously in the

Chamsil Gymnasium in Seoul, gaining him recognition in the 1986 *Guinness Book of Records* for presiding over the largest multiple wedding at that time.

The number of couples whom Moon marries can vary. Sometimes the declared numbers are misleading and do not always indicate the number of participants at a single event. For example, the so-called "36 Couples" Blessing of 1961 encompassed three ceremonies that took place in that year and the previous one. Moon blessed an inner coterie of three founder-disciples (Hyo Won Eu, Young Whi Kim, and Won Pil Kim) in 1960, followed by a further nine in the same year, and another twenty-four in 1961. The numbers who are blessed were initially given numerological significance: thus, in the first Blessing, the three were said to correspond to Jesus' inner core of close disciples—Peter, James, and John—with the subsequent nine making up the apostolic number of twelve. The number 777—the number of couples married at a ceremony in 1970—was said to represent three times the number seven, which signifies perfection; hence, 777 meant the completion of the three stages of formation, growth, and completion. The declared numbers are not always exact: for example, the so-called "777 Couples" ceremony actually involved 791. Such discrepancies are explained by the fact that the declared numbers are targets set by Moon; because human beings bear an important measure of responsibility for advancing the messiah's work, they may either fail to meet these targets or else exceed them.

From the Unification Church's inception until the 1990s, the procedure for undergoing the Blessing was that one had first to have belonged to the Unification Church for at least three years, to have three "spiritual children" (in other words, attract three new members), and to pay the Blessing fee (which can vary according to the ceremony and to one's country). In the wake of the AIDS epidemic, one must now also be HIV-negative. Having satisfied these conditions, the pro-spective marriage partner would send an application and photograph to the Blessing Committee. The next stage was a "matching ceremony," at which Moon presided over a gathering of eligible applicants, where he would pair off couples, many of whom had not met previously. On account of the Unification Church's international character and its desire to bring together different cultures and nationalities, in a significant number of cases the matched couples have not shared a common language. The matched partners would then leave the room, being allowed several minutes in which to decide whether or not they would accept Moon's matching. A few have been known to reject the matching, but most were more than willing to place their trust in the messiah's decision, acknowledging that he was being guided by God and that their partnership had an important role in his mission.

If a couple were already married before joining the UC, then they would not be rematched, although they would be required to fulfill all the other requirements for the Blessing, and undergo the same ancillary ceremonies. Their Blessing in effect would be a rededication of their existing marriage. It is sometimes asked whether the Blessing ceremony constitutes a legal marriage. This depends on the country and its prevailing legislation: Unificationists wish to ensure that members' marriages have legal as well as religious status, and members are asked to ensure that they participate in an appropriate civil ceremony.

The high-profile "mass wedding" is merely the visible part of Unificationist marriage. The couple must participate in three other associated ceremonies for the marriage to be complete. First, the Chastening Ceremony (previously called the Indemnity Ceremony, or Indemnity Stick Ceremony) is carried out in private by the couple. It involves beating each other with a large stick, symbolically signifying the driving out of Satan and obtaining God's forgiveness for past sin. The driving out of Satan paves the way for the new lineage into which the couple will become engrafted. (Members affirm that this is a genuine beating—somewhat painful, but not causing permanent injury.) Second, there is the Holy Wine Ceremony, at which an officiant offers the bride a glass of wine (grape juice may be substituted). She bows, drinks half, and offers the remaining half to the bridegroom, who bows to her, empties the glass, and gives it back to the officiant. In the early years Moon himself was the officiant, but a senior member now typically represents him at the ceremony. The meaning of the ceremony is that, by consuming the wine, the bride acts as an antitypical Eve—she reenacts Eve's original submission to Satan, in which she entered into a Satanic lineage, but this time she does so in a "principled" way. The woman then symbolically restores this lineage to her husband, who assumes the role of the antitypical Adam. At the close of the Holy Wine Ceremony, a few drops of wine are put onto a new white handkerchief, which is given to each couple. It is referred to as the "holy handkerchief"; its recipients must let it dry before putting it away for further use at the subsequent Three Day Ceremony—the third private ceremony, which takes place after the public wedding.

The major public celebration is the Holy Blessing Ceremony. The exact pattern of the ceremony varies, but it invariably involves the couples processing before the Rev. and Mrs. Moon, who sprinkle them with holy water. Unificationists sometimes compare this part of the liturgy to Christian baptism: the water symbolizes their cleansing from sin, and—in common with baptism—it initiates them into the organization that claims to offer the means of attaining the kingdom of heaven.

Another essential component of the Holy Blessing Ceremony is the recitation of the Unification Church's marriage vows. The couples vow to keep God's unchanging law, to create ideal families, to raise children who will become obedient and loyal to God's will, and to act as a nucleus by which they and their progeny will establish the creation of a family, a society, a nation, and a world of goodness. The couples pledge to do this by responding, "Ye!" Finally, rings are exchanged: these are special "Blessing rings," designed by the Unification Church, and should be worn by each partner on the third or middle finger of the right hand. There is a concluding prayer, and the couples are pronounced husband and wife.

The Holy Blessing is not consummated immediately. Couples are required to observe a forty-day separation period, involving sexual abstinence. The number forty is significant, being the number of days Jesus fasted in the desert, finally gaining victory over Satan, who tempted him during that period. Members are taught that abstinence during this period highlights the belief that sexual relationships are not merely a means of sense-gratification, and that the period of abstinence highlights the nature of true love between marriage partners.

When the marriages are finally consummated, it is done in a prescribed manner known as the Three Day Ceremony. Couples are instructed to begin each day by praying together in private. Before engaging in sexual activity they shower; the holy handkerchief is then placed in wine and dipped into cold water, and smeared over their bodies. The couple then put on their holy robes. During the first two nights, the couple must adopt the female-superior position, then the male-superior position on the third night. This symbolizes a sanctification process, in which the wife first adopts the position of the "restored Eve." She symbolically "restores" the two sexual acts that occasioned the spiritual and the physical fall of humanity, while the husband successively adopts the positions of Satan and Adam. On the third night "principled" sexual activity can take place: the couple are now restored and can fulfill the second original blessing that God entrusted to humanity's original parents: to be fruitful and multiply.

The Case of Archbishop Milingo

Emmanuel Milingo (b. 1930) was ordained as Roman Catholic Archbishop of Lusaka, Zambia, in 1969. In the 1970s he made himself controversial by claiming to perform miraculous healings and conducting exorcisms. He also introduced indigenous African elements into masses that he conducted, which some people associated with witchcraft. He was officially investigated at the time, and Pope John Paul II permitted him to remain in office, since the Roman Catholic Church has no inherent objections to present-day miracles, exorcism, or indigenization. Milingo became more controversial, however, when he started to criticize the tradition of the priesthood's celibacy. It has been claimed that some 150,000 priests who have been ordained by the Roman Catholic Church have subsequently married, and are therefore unable to perform their priestly functions. Milingo also criticized the Catholic Church hierarchy, describing them as followers of Satan and making particular criticism of their tolerance of homosexuality.

Milingo became acquainted with the Unification Church, and in 1999 he attended the first seminar of the International Federation for World Peace—a UC-sponsored organization—where he studied Moon's *Divine Principle* and some of the Hoon Dok Hae texts (official texts authorized by Moon after 1997). He was invited to participate in one of the UC's Blessing Ceremonies, and accepted. Then seventy-one years old, he was matched with Maria Sung, a forty-three-year-old Korean acupuncturist, and they participated in a sixty-couple Blessing on May 27, 2001. Unsurprisingly, this action proved unacceptable to the Roman Catholic hierarchy, and Pope John Paul II, together with Cardinal Tarcisio Bertone—the Vatican secretary of state—met with Milingo, persuading him to leave his newfound wife, Maria. Milingo initially complied and was reconciled to the Church. The Vatican authorities confined him to a Capuchin monastery, but his wife began a hunger strike as a protest against Rome's verdict.

In July 2006, Milingo reconsidered his situation and went back to his wife. He held a press conference in which he stated that he was embarking on an independent charismatic ministry, endeavoring to bring the Unification Church and Sun Myung Moon closer to the Vatican. Further, in order to promote the cause of married clergy, he founded a group called Married Priests Now! He also conducted a ceremony on September 24, 2006, in which he ordained four married clergy as Roman Catholic bishops. This action made him subject to *latae sententiae* excommunication—automatic expulsion, which does not require the sentence of an ecclesiastical court. Milingo then decided to take more interest in Unification teachings. In February 2007 he departed for Seoul, Korea, for further study of Unificationist theology.

CHANGES IN THE 1990S

Although the Unification Church attracted publicity in the 1970s and 1980s for its zealous evangelizing, the Blessing is the means of securing full salvation, not mere membership. The question therefore arose about the possibility of undergoing UC-style marriage without necessarily subscribing to all the church's doctrines. The qualifications for undergoing the Blessing were exacting: might there be a less demanding way of attracting nonmembers into UC matrimony? Moon claimed that members had now paid sufficient indemnity for the traditional Blessing ceremony not to be needed for those outside the organization.

In 1996 the Unification Church changed its name to the Family Federation for World Peace and Unification (FFWPU). This reflected the fact that the Unification movement wanted to move away from encouraging couples formally to undergo the Blessing in its traditional form. One method was for members to set up a stand in a public place, displaying literature extolling the virtues of traditional married life, marital fidelity, and abstinence from sexual relationships outside the confines of marriage. Couples drawn from members of the public were invited to renew their marriage vows and to sign a declaration subscribing to such values, whereupon both partners were asked to consume a small glass of wine as a token of their action.

The wine was important, since it contained a small portion of Unificationist holy wine, which Moon had blessed—although this was not explained to most participating couples. The consumption of the wine meant that the couples had undergone one important requirement of Unification marriage: they were exempted from the other ceremonies that Unification members had been expected to undergo. There were other means of persuading nonmembers to consume the holy wine: a Unificationist family might invite outsiders to a dinner party and add a drop or two of holy wine as a cooking ingredient. There are stories of members putting small drops of wine into candy bars and distributing them. One member is alleged to have put some holy wine into a reservoir, thus ensuring that a whole community received the Blessing!

RECENT DEVELOPMENTS

The widening of the Blessing was only one of a number of recent changes in the Unification movement. Having its origins in Korean shamanic culture, interest in the spirit world has always remained a major preoccupation. The present-day interest in spiritism can be traced back to Moon's second eldest son, Heung Jin, who died following an automobile crash in December 1983. Shortly after his death, some members began receiving messages that purported to come from the deceased Heung Jin, who reassured them that he was faring well in the spirit world and continuing his work for the Unification Church. In 1987 a further phenomenon was reported: a black African member in Zimbabwe was claiming not merely to have received communications from Heung

Jin but to be his "returning resurrection." ("Returning resurrection" is a Unificationist term, approximately equivalent to possession, in which a spirit takes control of a human body.) The Zimbabwean's name was not disclosed to members, although it is now known to be Cleopus Kundiona. At the time they referred to him as "the black Zimbabwean" or straightforwardly as "Heung Jin Nim" or "HJN." The Zimbabwean took members to task for allowing their behavior and spiritual practice to decline, and exhorted members to improve their lives.

The phenomenon was reported to Moon, who sent one of his principal aides, Chung Hwan Kwak, to investigate. Kwak vouched for the Zimbabwean's authenticity, and Moon accepted his judgment. Moon did not meet the Zimbabwean until November of that year, when the Zimbabwean was brought to the States and received as Moon's own son. However, the Zimbabwean's zeal proved too much for the majority of Unification Church members, particularly when he reprimanded the senior Korean leader Bo Hi Pak and beat him with a stick. Bo Hi Pak was hospitalized for a week as a result. After this incident, Moon disowned the Zimbabwean, sending him back to Africa, where he seceded with a small group of supporters to found his own schismatic group. He claimed that he, not Moon, was the Lord of the Second Advent, and that Moon was merely his herald. Some members believed that Heung Jin had returned to heaven, and there appeared to be no further messages after Kundiona's withdrawal.

The Zimbabwean affair did not mark the end of interaction with the spirit world, however. Life in the spirit world is not static, and Unificationists believe that important events continue to occur there. Moon continues to use his own personal shaman,[6] and the movement's spiritism seems to be given even greater emphasis. Sun Myung Moon's late mother-in-law (known to members as Dae Mo Nim, or "revered mother"), who died in 1989, has now become a cult figure and the focus of a sacred shrine at Cheong

Pyung, Korea. There, a medium named Mrs. Hyo Nam Kim claims to be spiritually linked with her, and members have recently been asked to undergo substantial periods of spiritual training.[7] However, the happenings in Cheong Pyung are not merely for the benefit of members who are alive on earth. Members of the spirit world need help to progress in order to reach their final goal of the kingdom of heaven. Unificationism teaches that everything that happens in the spirit world needs a physical base, and living members' activities on earth are necessary in order to afford assistance to the dead.

Additionally, members of the spirit world need the Blessing, which only the True Parents can offer. Even if they are already married, they must undergo the Unificationist Blessing, and not merely a civil marriage, if they are to be allowed to enter the kingdom of heaven. Moon, therefore, does not merely offer spiritual guidance to the departed, but offers them the Blessing and has performed ceremonies to bond spirit partners in matrimony. Deceased Unificationist leaders now offer seminars in the spirit world, facilitating the spirits' progress. (Details of precisely how these ceremonies are conducted have not been disclosed.) It is claimed that these have been attended by a host of religious and political leaders, including Confucius, the Buddha, Jesus, Muhammad, and St. Augustine, as well as Marx, Engels, Lenin, Stalin, Trotsky, and Mao Zedung, to name but a few.[8]

Dr. Sang Hun Lee, a senior member of the Unification Church who died in 1997, is believed to have journeyed in the spirit world and to have communicated to a medium—Mrs. Young Soon Kim—messages concerning his encounters with religious and political leaders, ranging from Jesus of Nazareth to Adolf Hitler. These have been transcribed, and a number are published in a slim paperback titled *Life in the Spirit World and on Earth*. Lee's text is recognized as one of a number of writings, now known as Hoon Dok Hae texts: these are writings, authorized by Moon since 1997,

which stand beside *Divine Principle* as authoritative texts, appropriate for study. On December 25, 2001 Lee is said to have presided over a ceremony in the spirit world, in which the historical leaders of Buddhism, Christianity, Confucianism, Islam, Hinduism, and Communism proclaimed a written resolution: "We resolve and proclaim that Reverend Sun Myung Moon is the Savior, Messiah, Second Coming and True Parent of all humanity." While Moon has professed the goal of the unification of world religions, such claims only serve to demonstrate that such unification is not to be understood merely as interfaith harmony, but rather to bring about a recognition from all the world's religious communities that he is the messiah.

THE SECOND GENERATION

Eileen Barker, who has studied the Unification movement extensively, has pointed out that one important contrast between new religious movements and traditional religions is that the former inevitably consist of converts rather than those who have been brought up in their faith by parents. This factor explains their enthusiasm and evangelistic zeal. As Unificationism has become more established, however, it is no longer an organization composed only of first-generation converts; those original members have undergone Moon's Blessing and have been encouraged to have children. (Moon does not absolutely forbid contraception, but members are advised not to limit their families unnaturally.) The phenomenon of second-generation (and now third-generation) members has raised a new set of issues. How could members ensure that their children remained in the faith? What arrangements should be made for their marriages? How was the new generation to be understood theologically? For example, were children of rank-and-file blessed couples reckoned to be sinless in the same sense as the Rev. Moon's own family? How can they be sinless, when they continue to perform apparently sinful acts? In what sense can Moon's own children be regarded as sinless, since their behavior has given rise to serious concern?

With the expansion of the Blessing to non-members of the Unification Church, attracting new followers is now less important. The once-familiar sight of Unificationists street-preaching and selling copies of *One World* now belongs to the past. Seminar workshops for interested seekers are largely discontinued, as emphasis is now given to organizing similar events for children who belong to the second and third generations, to enable them to understand their parents' faith. Regarding marriage, it is expected that Unificationist children will marry within the movement, and, in accordance with Eastern practice, responsibility lies with their parents to arrange suitable partners for them. This is now largely done through the Internet, where parents can come in contact with members worldwide who wish to match their offspring. Once a pairing has been agreed, a form is completed online and photographs are sent to the organization. Second-generation members must comply with Moon's decision on such matters, agreeing that they are "[r]esolved to accept True Parents' matching with absolute faith."[9]

Not all of the second generation is happy to acquiesce with such arrangements. Some have left the movement, either because they are concerned about having to marry a partner whom they may not know, or who does not share their language, or because they have simply experienced a loss of faith. Even some of the Moons' own second-generation family have provided cause for concern, inspiring some members to reflect on what it means to be a blessed child, free from original sin. In 1994 Moon himself was reported as stating that there were "unresolved relationships in my family," making particular mention of his eldest son and eldest daughter. His eldest son, Hyo Jin, attracted much adverse publicity for his addiction to drugs and alcohol. On a number of occasions he had used the services of prostitutes, and he physically abused his wife, Nansook Hong,

who recounted her experiences in a book titled *In the Shadow of the Moons*. According to Nansook, the Moons did little to discipline their son, although he was barred from succeeding his father. Hyo Jin finally died prematurely from a heart attack in March 2008. Ye Jin, the eldest daughter, apparently condemned her father for showing insufficient concern for the welfare of his members. Another daughter, Sun Jin, left her husband only a few weeks after undergoing the Blessing.

There have also been allegations regarding Moon's personal life, suggesting that he has had sexual relationships outside marriage, resulting in the birth of children. Such events have caused disquiet among some members, causing a few to leave. Most, however, implicitly believe that, if such allegations are true, they must serve some providential purpose that their leader knows better than they do. One long-standing member argues that restoration is not something that is instantly accomplished, but rather takes up to three generations to establish.[10]

THE ISSUE OF SUCCESSION

Problems in Moon's family have inevitably raised questions about the leadership succession. At the time of this writing, the Rev. Moon is in his late eighties, and for some time he has given thought to the question of who will succeed him. His oldest surviving child is a woman—Ye Jin (b. 1960)—but Moon has always minded that his successor would be male. Heung Jin, his second eldest son, died in 1983, and the second youngest son, Young Jin, died mysteriously in 1999, having fallen from a hotel balcony. His eldest son Hyo Jin (1962–2008) was once the obvious candidate, although members believe that Hak Ja Han Moon might continue to lead the movement during the remaining years of her lifetime, since she is jointly the messiah, together with her husband.

In these circumstances, it was commonly expected that Moon would nominate Hyun Jin (b. 1969), the oldest surviving son, as his successor. However, in April 2008, in a ceremony held near Seoul, his youngest son, Hyung Jin (b. 1979) was anointed as the new chairman of the Family Federation for World Peace and Unification. Hyung Jin obtained an M.B.A. degree from Harvard University, during which time he became a practitioner of Zen Buddhism, shaving his head and donning the robes of a Zen priest. Although this may seem a surprising background for the new leader of a movement that claims a Christian heritage, Hyung Jin believes that he brings a wider understanding of the world's religions to the organization.

OTHER INNOVATIONS

Recent developments in the movement include various "coronation" ceremonies involving Sun Myung Moon and his wife, which have gained media publicity. On March 23, 2004, an event occurred on Capitol Hill, Washington, that attracted worldwide publicity. Initially publicized as an awards banquet, it was hosted by Moon and his supporters and involved a pageant in which Moon donned a ceremonial costume and received a crown, which U.S. senator Danny Davis (D-Illinois) carried ceremonially and placed on his head. This event was one of a number of coronations of the Rev. Moon, and their significance may initially seem puzzling. Unificationists interpret it as signifying that Moon is now king of the "second and third Israels"—the United States being construed as the second Israel, being the most powerful Christian nation. Korea is the "third Israel," being the country from which the Lord of the Second Advent comes.

The symbol of the crown is important to Moon for a further reason: he believes it is a preferable symbol than the cross. To Unificationism the cross signifies failure: as we have seen, Jesus' death on the cross prevented him from fully accomplishing his mission. The cross is also a symbol that is inimical to Jews and Muslims, since historically the Jews have been blamed for Jesus' death, and some interpret the Qur'an as denying that

Jesus was crucified. Accordingly, Moon has attempted to persuade church leaders to take down the crosses in their churches and to replace them with crowns. Although the Christian church has been largely unaffected by Moon's request, a few pastors, particularly in the Black Pentecostal tradition, have complied. (Pentecostalism, being more spontaneously open to new promptings by the Holy Spirit, has tended to be slightly more sympathetic to the Unificationist movement than other denominations, which have largely remained hostile.) In 2003 Moon gave the instruction, "Bury the cross in Golgotha where Jesus was crucified." On May 18 that year, at an event organized by the American Clergy Leadership Conference (ACLC—a Unificationist-sponsored organization), a number of representatives of Christianity and Judaism set out to do this. Finding that it was not possible to bury a cross in the Church of the Holy Sepulchre—the traditional site of Golgotha—they set out for the Potter's Field, the ground that Judas Iscariot is believed to have purchased with the silver he obtained for betraying Jesus. Here they deposited a cross into a six-feet-deep hole. Afterwards, one rabbi apologized for the Jews' treatment of Jesus, while one Christian participant deplored past Christian anti-Semitism. Such incidents highlight the fact that, while the Unification movement seeks to unify, the outcomes of its methods can prove to be highly divisive.

CONCLUSION

It is always tempting to end by speculating about the future. New religions tend to be volatile, however, and scholars are not clairvoyants. Moon is particularly prone to implementing new ideas and projects, causing the academic community constantly to revise its material. Without doubt, Moon's days on earth are limited, but while he remains alive it is unlikely that the new leadership will take the movement in any markedly different direction. As with Heung Jin and Hun Sang Lee, members will no doubt claim to receive his messages from the spirit world, together with claims of his accomplishments there. Meanwhile, back on earth, religious believers are less inclined to acknowledge his messianic status. The UC's numerical strength lies between one and three million members worldwide (estimates vary considerably), including somewhere between 30,000 and 50,000 in the United States, between 600 and 700 practicing members in Britain, 210,000 in Japan and 300,000 in Korea. If Moon's aim is to be acknowledged as the true messiah and king of the world, he is still far from accomplishing such a goal.

Notes

1. For a further discussion of these names and of the possible relationship between Moon's teachings and Kim-Baek Moon's, see George D. Chryssides, "Heavenly Deception? Sun Myung Moon and *Divine Principle*," in *The Invention of Sacred Tradition*, ed. James R. Lewis and Olav Hammer (Cambridge: Cambridge University Press, 2007), 118–40.

2. Holy Spirit Association for the Unification of World Christianity, *The Tradition* (New York: Rose of Sharon Press, 1985), 59–71.

3. Quoted in Kelley, D. A. Affidavit on behalf of Defendants in the High Court of Justice, Chancery Division, between Her Majesty's Attorney General and Alexander Frederick Herzer, et al. 1984-A-6263 and 1984-A-6264. November 4, 1987, 3.

4. This is a direct quotation from *Divine Principle*, 15.

5. "Son of Moonies' Founder Takes Over as Church Leader." *The Guardian* (April 25, 2008). http:www.blnz.com/news/2008/05/10/Moonies_founder_takes_over_church_9/_1.html. Accessed January 9, 2009.

6. Nansook Hong, *In the Shadow of the Moons: My Life in the Reverend Sun Myung Moon's Family* (Boston: Little, Brown & Co., 1998), 70–71.

7. Sang Hun Lee, *Life in the Spirit World and on Earth: Messages from the Spirit World* (New York: Family Federation for World Peace and Unification, 1998).

8. Family Federation for World Peace and Unification (2002). "A Cloud of Witnesses: The Saints' Testimonies to True Parents." http://www.ffwpu.org.uk Accessed November 10, 2002.

9. BC Blessing Department, "Guideline for the Blessing." http://bcblessing.familyfed.org/index.php?option=com_content&task=view&id=4&Itemid=7. Accessed May 15, 2008.

10. Peter Nordquist, "Sammy Moon? The Pure in Heart Will See God." http://groups.google.com/group/alt.religion.unification/msg/7abc5ffdca859735. Accessed May 15, 2008.

STUDY QUESTIONS

1. Examine the claims that converts to the Unification Church are "brainwashed." What gives the brainwashing theory momentum? How plausible is it?

2. How useful is it to claim that new religious movements commence as a result of a charismatic leader? How appropriate is it to describe Sun Myung Moon as "charismatic"?

3. Can Unificationists legitimately claim a Christian identity? Consider arguments for and against.

4. Unification theology claims that Jesus did not fully accomplish his mission. How plausible is such a claim, and should mainstream Christians discount it?

5. How effective is Unificationism likely to be at unifying the world's religions or the world's nations?

6. Several Christian writers and organizations have produced literature aimed at refuting the Unification Church's beliefs and practices. How effective is such literature, and what motives do its authors have?

7. Are non-Unificationists abandoning their faith by participating in the Blessing? To what extent is it appropriate for Unificationists to persuade those who do not share their beliefs to participate?

8. What problems has the Unification Church encountered in accommodating a second generation of followers? Critically examine how effectively they have been dealt with.

ESSAY TOPICS

Evangelization Strategies among Unificationists

The Role of the Spirit World in Unificaton Thought

The Significance of the Blessing Ceremony in the Unification Church / Family Federation

Public Reaction to the Unification Church / Family Federation

Charismatic Leadership and Sun Myung Moon

Divine Principle as a New Interpretation of the Bible

The Unification Church and How New Religions Develop

WORD EXPLORATION

Blessing (Holy Blessing)	Central figure	Completed Testament Age
Divine Principle	*Exposition of Divine*	Fall (of Man)
Family Federation for	*Principle*	Holy Wine
World Peace and	Hyung Jin	Indemnity
Unification	Kingdom of Heaven	Lord of the Second Advent
Matching Ceremony	Messiah	(Lord of the Second
Paradise	Pledge	Coming)
Returning resurrection	True Parents	

FOR FURTHER READING

Breen, Michael. *Sun Myung Moon: The Early Years, 1920–1953*. Hurstpierpoint, West Sussex: Refuge Books, 1997.

Chryssides, George D. *The Advent of Sun Myung Moon: The Origins, Beliefs and Practices of the Unification Church*. London: Macmillan, 1991.

Gorenfield, John. *Bad Moon Rising: How Reverend Moon Created* The Washington Times, *Seduced the Religious Right, and Built an American Kingdom*. Sausalito, Calif.: PoliPoint Press, 2008.

Holy Spirit Association for the Unification of World Christianity. *Exposition of Divine Principle*. New York: HSA-UWC, 1996.

Hong, Nansook. *In the Shadow of the Moons: My Life in the Reverend Sun Myung Moon's Family*. Boston: Little, Brown & Co., 1998.

HSA-UWC. *Divine Principle*. New York: Holy Spirit Association for the Unification of World Christianity, 1973.

Introvigne, Massimo. *The Unification Church*. Salt Lake City: Signature Books, 2000.

Kwak, Chung Hwan, Kwang Yol Yoo, and Joong-Hyun Choe, eds. *Footprints of the Unification Movement*. 2 vols. Seoul: HSA-UWC, 1996.

Lofland, John. *Doomsday Cult: A Study of Conversion, Proselytization, and Maintenance of Faith*. Englewood Cliffs: Prentice-Hall, 1966.

Sontag, Frederick. *Sun Myung Moon and the Unification Church*. Nashville: Abingdon, 1977.

WEB SITES

http://www.reverendsunmyungmoon.org/
   Official Web site of the Universal Peace Federation

http://www.familyfed.org/
   Official Web site of the Family Federation for World Peace and Unification

http://science.gcc.edu/reli/kemeny/new_page_238.htm
   Lengthy bibliography on the UC

PART SIX

Issues in American Religion

20

Religion and Women in America

ELEANOR J. STEBNER

1631	Margaret Winthrop arrives in Massachusetts Bay colony
1638	Anne Hutchinson and family banished from Massachusetts
1642	Mary Kittamaquund baptized as a Christian in Maryland
1660	Mary Dyer hanged in Boston for spreading Quakerism
1692	Rebecca Nurse executed for witchcraft in Salem, Massachusetts
1727	Ursuline Sisters establish school in New Orleans
1766	Barbara Heck brings Methodism to New York City
1767	Massachusetts slave Phillis Wheatley publishes her first poem
1774	Ann Lee, founder of Shakerism, arrives in the colonies
1790	First Carmelite monastery founded in Maryland
1800	Boston Female Society for Missionary Purposes established
1819	Female Hebrew Benevolent Society established
1825	Fanny Wright creates Nashoba community near present-day Memphis
1827	Cynthia Farrar is first single, female missionary to India
1833	Lydia Maria Child publishes antislavery book
1836	Evangelist Jarena Lee publishes autobiography
1837	Mary Lyon opens Mount Holyoke Female Seminary in Massachusetts
1841	Catherine Beecher publishes *A Treatise On Domestic Economy*
1844	Ellen Gould White's religious vision leads to founding of Seventh-day Adventist Church
1848	Women's rights convention held in Seneca Falls, New York
1849	Fox sisters begin to speak in public; become famous for Spiritualist seances
1851	Sojourner Truth speaks at women's convention in Akron, Ohio
1853	Antoinette Brown (Blackwell) ordained as first woman Congregationalist minister
1858	Young Women's Christian Association set up in the United States
1861	Ex-slave Harriet A. Jacobs publishes autobiography
1863	Olympia Brown ordained the first woman Universalist minister
1874	Woman's Christian Temperance Union established
1879	Mary Baker Eddy founds Christian Science
1883	Sarah Winnemucca Hopkins publishes autobiography; first Native American woman to secure copyright for English-language book
1888	Women's Missionary Union established

1893	Women's Congress of Representative Women meets in Chicago; Jewish Women's Congress meets in Chicago; National Council of Jewish Women founded
1895/98	Publication of *The Woman's Bible*
1896	National Association of Colored Women established
1902	Esther Ruskay publishes *Hearth and Home Essays* First Ladies Philoptochos established in Greek Orthodox Church
1906	Lizzie Robinson experiences "baptism of the Holy Ghost"
1912	Hadassah established
1913	National Federation of Temple Sisterhoods established
1914	Fujinkai women's groups formed in Japanese Buddhist communities
1915	Women's Peace Party organized
1920	Nineteenth Amendment passed
1924	Aimee Semple McPherson begins her radio sermons
1933	Dorothy Day cofounds Catholic Worker Movement
1935	National Council of Negro Women established
1941	Church Women United established
1943	Kateri Tekakwitha beatified by Roman Catholic Church
1955	Rosa Parks initiates Montgomery, Alabama, bus boycott
1964/65	Sister Mary Luke Tobin attends sessions at Second Vatican Council
1970	Elizabeth Platz ordained as first woman minister in the Lutheran Church in America
1971	Las Hermanas organized
1972	Sally Priesand ordained as first woman Reform rabbi
1974	Eleven women ordained in "irregular" service in the Episcopal Church
1975	Elizabeth Seton named as Roman Catholic saint
1980	Four American Catholic women murdered in El Salvador
1983	Publication of *An Inclusive Language Lectionary: Readings for Year A*
1984	Southern Baptist Convention votes to prohibit the ordination of women
1992	North American Council for Muslim Women organized
1993	Re-imagining Conference held in Minneapolis, Minnesota
2002	Religion and the Feminist Movement Conference held at Harvard Divinity School
2006	Katharine Jefferts Schori elected as presiding bishop of Episcopal Church; Ingrid Mattson chosen as first woman president of Islamic Society of North America
2009	Rev. Sharon Watkins, president of the Disciples of Christ, becomes first woman to give sermon at National Prayer Service after a presidential inauguration

A recent report released by the Pew Forum on Religion and Public Life indicates that women are significantly associated with every religious tradition in the United States. Women comprise the majority of people who claim to be Christian, whether they identify as Protestant, Catholic, or Orthodox, and they outnumber men in Mormon and Jehovah's Witness traditions. Men outnumber women slightly within Jewish, Muslim, and Buddhist religious traditions; only within Hinduism do men substantially outnumber women. The report indicates as well that women are much less likely than men to claim that they have no religious ties or that they are agnostic.[1] The study also analyzed connections between religious identification and variables such as race, levels of education and income, age, and geographical regionalism. Yet the gender findings are significant in confirming what many people may sense intuitively or know from firsthand observations: women are religious. While women differ greatly in how they participate within their various religious traditions and in how they understand the place of religion within their own lives and the role of religion within the broader society, the presence of women within religious groups cannot be ignored if one wants to better understand religion in America.

The irony is that scholars who have studied religion have usually ignored the presence and contributions of women in religion. This is true within the broad discipline of history itself. Clara Barton, the founder of the American Red Cross, wrote almost one hundred years ago in a letter to her friend, Mary S. Logan, "From the storm-lashed decks of the Mayflower . . . to the present hour, woman has stood like a rock for the welfare and the glory of the history of the country, and one might well add . . . unwritten, unrewarded and almost unrecognized."[2] American historian Mary R. Beard published a book in 1946 called *Woman as a Force in History*, where she argued that it is of utmost necessity to place women in the history of humankind and to understand that women were not simply passive participants in history but were also shapers of it. At the time of its publication, Beard's study had little impact on influencing the discipline of history to be more inclusive of women. Yet almost twenty years later Gerda Lerner, who was then in her forties and applying to do graduate study at Columbia University, told her admissions committee that in her intended studies she wanted to "put women into history." Then she corrected herself: "No . . . not put them into history, because they are already in it." Rather, she said, she wanted to "complete the work begun by Mary Beard."[3] Gerda Lerner later became a founding leader in the development of women's studies and a respected scholar in the blossoming field of women's history.

RECLAIMING WOMEN'S HISTORY

Thanks to women such as Beard and Lerner, and the dozens of other scholars who came after them, studies of women in history greatly multiplied during the last decades of the twentieth century. This has made women—at least some women—less hidden. Great strides have been made in identifying women within religious histories, especially women who are considered unique in some way. Therefore women who were "firsts" are often named, such as Antoinette Brown (Blackwell), the first white woman ordained in a Christian church; or Sally Priesand, the first Jewish rabbi; or Mother Elizabeth Seton, the first woman born in the United States to be canonized as a saint by the Roman Catholic Church. Other women who are deemed prophetic or inspirational are uplifted, such as Sojourner Truth, who spoke so eloquently for black women's experiences at an 1851 women's conference. Women rendered as troublemakers are remembered (sometimes very fondly in some circles), such as Anne Hutchinson, the Puritan dissenter. We remember those who founded new religious movements or institutions, such as Theosophist leader Helena Blavatsky, or the founder of Christian Science, Mary Baker Eddy. (Both of those two women are discussed at length in this book's chapter on metaphysical religious movements.)

The inclusion of such women as named above is necessary for the writing of a more inclusive history of religion in America. Yet many lesser-known women have also contributed to their religious traditions. Women have often worked through organizations and movements and have made their impact not so much as individuals but as collectives of women pursuing what they considered to be religious ends. From the numerous congregations of Roman Catholic sisters (or nuns) to organizations such as the Woman's Christian Temperance Union, Hadassah, and the National Council of Negro Women, women have organized themselves, often on the basis of their religious identities, to pursue goals that they considered religious. Such religious goals were also social and political, and they were influential in shaping the nation.

Although the singular term *woman* was used as a collective label for women into the early decades of the twentieth century (as seen in the quote from Clara Barton and the name of the WCTU), it is a misnomer. Women have always represented a gamut of religious, social, and political commitments. Despite the various differences that exist between women, however, two commonalities seem to emerge across distinctions of race, class, and regionalism: First, women have often found themselves occupied with major familial—or caring—responsibilities in their roles as daughters, wives, mothers, and grandmothers. Even today in the early twenty-first century, studies show that most women hold primary responsibility for household duties and childrearing. Second, women have also, with the exception of the most privileged of women, hardly been excluded from labor and from making economic contributions. In the history of the United States, they have done this through indentured servitude, enslavement, and both paid and unpaid work; they have labored on farms and sweated in tenement hovels. Caring for immediate family members and eking out a living, while challenging in many ways, has not prevented women from religious pursuits.

Even though women have been excluded until recently from official positions of leadership in most religious traditions or confined to the realm of the home (there are some exceptions, such as the Quakers and Shakers), women have also broken out of social and religious norms and expectations, and they have found within their religious cultures sources of meaning that have enabled them to understand their world. Women have therefore played huge roles in transmitting the teachings of their particular religions to the next generations through participating in household rituals, hosting community dinners, mentoring, and establishing schools and colleges. They have regularly taken care of the sick, prepared the dead for burial, and been instrumental in the establishment of hospitals. While these actions have often been taken for granted, it is hard to imagine how any religious group could have survived the centuries without the participation of women. From the colonial period through the various wars, from racial segregation and civil rights through feminism, women have claimed their religious identities and experiences and have contributed to their communities in a multitude of ways. They have not only accepted and embodied the basic tenets of their religion but have also modified and critiqued them, and in doing so, women have contributed to the mosaic of religious life in America.

COLONIZATION AND CHRISTIANIZATION

Women were not among the first Europeans to arrive in what was to become the United States. Spain, France, England, the Netherlands, and Sweden all staked claims in what for them was a new world; these male explorers, *conquistadores*, and priests did not have settlement as their primary purpose but rather the acquisition of wealth for their homelands. They, like the settlers who followed, did not see the indigenous peoples of the continent as practicing religious traditions or holding worldviews of merit; the indigenous peoples were not like them, they thought, and were indeed "other" to sixteenth-century Europeans imbued by the Catholic or Protestant cultures of their homelands.

European women arrived with the establishment of permanent settlements, which was a slow but steady process during the seventeenth century. No women were part of the initial establishment of Jamestown in 1607, for example; the first two women—a Mrs. Forrest and her servant—arrived a year later. African women were brought to Jamestown in 1619 aboard a Dutch ship, the first of many ships that were to participate in the Atlantic slave trade. Only a quarter of the settlers (or Pilgrims) aboard the *Mayflower* in 1620 were women, and most of them did not live through their first winter. The first Jewish women, along with their men and children, arrived in New Amsterdam in 1654 as refugees from Brazil.

While the roots of what became America were therefore religiously diverse from the earliest years of colonization, American history has often been told from the perspective of the early Puritans. In part this is because of written records and the national mythos that developed from them. Margaret Winthrop, for example, the third wife of John Winthrop (his first two wives died in England), arrived in the Massachusetts Bay colony in 1631, one year after her husband. From letters exchanged between them, historians know of how she raised their eight children and helped her husband in his duties as governor of the colony. In many ways Margaret Winthrop embodied what was understood to be a good Puritan wife: she was a helpmate to her husband, and she knew her place in the order created by God. Order and obedience were central tenets to Puritan theology, and women especially were to be godly mortals who did their duties in supporting their husbands and fulfilling their familial obligations. The well-ordered Puritan family—while allowing for love and affection between husband and wife—was understood to be the building block of a stable and pure society. Puritans believed that women were to be pious, virtuous, and genteel. Cotton Mather wrote in 1691 that there were "far more Godly women in the world" than "Godly men." Indeed, by the early eighteenth century more women than men held church membership. Whether this is because women were more religious than men or because church involvement provided them with an acceptable social outlet is debatable.

Exemplifying high morals was one way that women could protect themselves against the Puritan idea that women embodied Eve, the temptress, and were more responsible for original sin than were men. It was this fear of women that accounts in part for the violence directed toward them during the Salem witch trials of 1692 and 1693. While some men were also accused of and executed for witchcraft, women were more often targeted than men: fourteen women and five men were eventually hanged for the felony of witchcraft in these years. One of the saddest examples relates to the arrest and execution of Rebecca Nurse, a seventy-one-year-old blind woman with grandchildren and great-grandchildren. She was a longtime church member. Some twenty years after she was hanged, Salem leaders cleared her name by revoking her conviction and making monetary restitution to her family.

While the Salem witch trials are an extreme example of Puritan culture gone awry, the trial and banishment of Anne Hutchinson is an example of how important it was for Puritan women not to claim too much religious authority. Hutchinson, who along with her family became followers of Puritan minister John Cotton while they still lived in England, began to teach a weekly class in her home that became very popular. She was soon accused of antinomianism, a theological heresy for Puritans because it was understood to place too much emphasis on grace and not enough emphasis on law and order. Hutchinson and her family were banished in 1638. Banishment was a dangerous punishment during these years of intermittent European and American Indian wars and raids; within six years Hutchinson and her family were dead from an Indian raid on the shores of Long Island Sound.

The colonial period included more than Puritan women in the English colonies, however. The majority of colonists, especially along the southern Atlantic, were Anglicans (or members of the Church of England).

Little is known about Anglican women in the early colonial period, but evidence suggests that they were active in their churches even though they could not hold official church roles. Records from colonial Virginia, for example, indicate that more men than women were cited for not attending church services. By the eighteenth century, some Anglican women served as sextons in their parishes, which allowed them to clean and care for the physical maintenance of ritual objects, buildings, and cemeteries. Anglican women held major responsibilities for the education of the young and supervised the preparations necessary for weddings and funerals, since these activities were usually held in households during this time period.

English Catholics were also present, especially in Maryland and in eastern Pennsylvania. Margaret Brent arrived in St. Mary's (which is now Maryland) in 1638 with her sister and brothers, for example, where they were granted land. Brent is sometimes called America's "first feminist" because she requested the right to vote; even though she was a landowner and represented Lord Baltimore, the Maryland Assembly declined her request. The continental lands claimed by Spain and France were predominantly Roman Catholic, of course. The Ursuline Sisters became the first women's congregation established in Quebec, New France, in 1638, and by 1727 they had established a school for girls in New Orleans. Given the antagonism between Catholics and Protestants and Anglicans in Europe and England, it is not surprising that anti-Catholicism raged in the colonies.

Dissident groups, such as the Quakers and Shakers, came early to the colonies and met with great resistance from those in authority. Quakers Mary Fisher and Ann Austin arrived in Boston in 1656, only to be deported, and in 1660 Mary Dyer was hanged for spreading Quakerism in the colonies. Quakers emphasized the spirit of God moving in all people as a form of inner light and recognized the public leadership of women; Puritans saw them as dangerous heretics. Ann Lee, a former Quaker who began her own religious movement of "Shaking Quakers" (Shakers), arrived in New York City in 1774, just before the outbreak of the Revolutionary War. Based on the visions received by Mother Ann, as she was called, Shakers believed in gender equality. Although Lee was accused of witchcraft and her converts met with some mob violence in the colonies, by the time of her death almost a dozen celibate Shaker communities had been established. In addition to practicing their beliefs through communal singing, dancing, and working, Shaker communities often took in and educated orphaned children.

Some sectarian groups (i.e., not part of the established Catholic or Protestant hierarchies) also came to the colonies. For example, Moravians, a Protestant group tracing its origins to John Hus in the fifteenth century, arrived in the colonies of Georgia, Carolina, and Pennsylvania in the early eighteenth century. The early Moravians utilized a communal living arrangement (called "choirs") where groups of people lived together on the basis of their age, gender, and marital status. Single women lived together, as did widowed women, for example. As a result of this arrangement Moravian women were responsible for the physical and spiritual care and education of other women and had a remarkable degree of autonomy for the time period.

Africans brought to the colonies as slave laborers also had their own traditions. Many of their beliefs and practices were based on African indigenous customs, but some Africans enslaved in the colonies had Muslim roots. Given the divisive and violent structure of the slave society in the colonies, it was difficult for Africans to maintain the practices of their homelands, although the roots of these traditions did not completely disappear. Most slaveholding colonists were not initially concerned about converting enslaved Africans to Christianity, and some debated among themselves as to whether baptized Africans would need to be seen as equal in social and spiritual terms and therefore freed. In the seventeenth and eighteenth centuries more enslaved African women than men converted to Christianity, perhaps in part because of their proximity to Christian women who taught their households (which included African women) about their religious faith. Phillis Wheatley, for example, who was bought as a young girl by a merchant family in Massachusetts, was educated by the white mistress of the family and began to write poetry that was evangelically religious in content. Wheatley's poem "On Being Brought from Africa to America," considered controversial in our day, shows her eighteenth-century Christian faith:

Twas mercy brought me from my
    Pagan land
Taught my benighted soul to
    understand
That there's a God, that there's
    a Saviour too
. . . .
Remember, Christians, Negros,
    black as Cain,
May be refin'd and join th'
    angelic train.[4]

American Indians continued to practice their religious traditions. Some Europeans endeavored to civilize them through enforced settlements in mission outposts and in so-called "praying towns"; here Native American men and women were taught how to dress, work, and live according to European standards. A few Puritan and Jesuit missionaries translated biblical texts into Native languages. Some Native women married Europeans and were significant as mediators between their peoples and the invading Europeans. Mary Kitomaquund, for example, was the daughter of a Piscataway chief brought by a Jesuit priest to St. Mary's as part of an alliance between her people and the English. She married the brother of Margaret Brent and was baptized a Christian in 1642. While her liaison with an English man was not atypical for the time period, most American Indian women did their best

to uphold their own people in the midst of disease, war, famine, and looming annihilation. Some American Indians did convert to Christianity. Perhaps the best known is Kateri Tekakwitha, a Mohawk woman who came under the influence of Jesuit missionaries and was baptized in 1676. Revered for her devotion and humility, in 1943 she became the first Native American woman to be beatified—named "blessed"—by the Roman Catholic Church.

A series of revivals broke out in the English colonies between the 1720s and 1740s, prompted by the preaching of Englishman George Whitefield and Puritan minister Jonathan Edwards. These religious experiences, referred to as the First Great Awakening, changed the tenor of American Christianity by sustaining the creation of hundreds of local study and prayer groups, which were often organized and led by women. Some women, such as Sarah Edwards (wife of Jonathan), wrote of their mystical experiences and the place of affection (or emotion) in their religious experiences. A kind of democratization of colonial religious institutions occurred through these revivals. African Americans converted to Christianity in large numbers. Many of the converts were women who could speak with religious authority because of their conversion experiences. Their speaking was not considered preaching, however, because male church leaders did not equate their testimonies or assertions with the authorized teachings of the churches. Nevertheless, women's varied contributions to religion became more public throughout the colonial period.

The revivals themselves led to an emerging identity among the thirteen British colonies and contributed to their ability to join together in revolting against their British overlords. Some colonial women opposed the independence of the colonies, and some were in favor of it. Barbara Heck, for example, considered one of the founders of Methodism in America, was a Loyalist who fled north with her family into what is now Canada; Nancy Ward of the Cherokee Nation, aided the revolutionaries; Quaker Charity Cook preached pacifism for both sides.

The religious history of women during the colonial period was varied, although a concept of what was called Republican Womanhood emerged in the 1770s. This ideology attempted to define the proper qualities of white middle- and upper-middle-class women. Women were to focus on the home and on motherhood and thereby influence the emerging nation through their moral example and persuasion of their husbands, sons, and brothers; and they were to teach their daughters to do the same. It was a social and religious ideology that advanced the idea of separate spheres for women and men. One perhaps unforeseen result of it, however, was a new emphasis on the need to educate women so that they could fulfill what was considered to be a high calling for them in the new republic. As numerous scholars have suggested, access to education has been key to women's religious and social emancipation.

THE NINETEENTH CENTURY: A FLOWERING OF NEW RELIGIOUS MOVEMENTS

Between the end of the Revolutionary War and the Civil War the former colonists, supplemented by new arrivals from Europe and England, pushed inland. The United States expanded geographically, from the Louisiana Purchase of 1803 through the annexation of Texas in 1845 and the acquisition of the Pacific southwest in 1848, and it successfully removed Native Americans from their traditional lands.

With all of this geographic expansion and a population spike caused by immigration, religious diversity flourished in the nineteenth century. Many new religious movements emerged, such as the Church of Jesus Christ of Latter-day Saints (LDS), the Adventists, and the Spiritualists. Women were attracted to these new movements as well as more traditional religions, partly because the new movements answered many of the concerns of the age. For example, some of the new religions rejected Calvinism and embraced instead a belief in the power of the individual to decide her own religious fate. Mormonism (LDS), begun by Joseph Smith and Brigham Young, was notorious for its controversial introduction of plural marriage (polygamy), but it was also known for its doctrines of eternal progression of the soul and the unique role of the United States in salvation history. LDS women were highly respected in their roles as wives and mothers, and were also spiritual leaders in their time. Although they were not ordained to the priesthood, many nineteenth-century LDS women were empowered to give sacred blessings to women and children—a privilege that was gradually taken away from them in the mid-twentieth century.

Women's leadership was also an attractive element of Seventh-day Adventism, which emerged in 1844 after Jesus failed to appear despite some very scientific-seeming calculations pointing to that date. A young woman named Ellen Gould White experienced a vision and enabled her generation to reinterpret that apparent failure as an actual fulfillment of prophecy: Jesus *had* returned in 1844, White taught, but he had returned first to the heavenly realm where earthly followers could not yet see him. White's teachings galvanized the faithful and resulted in the creation of the Seventh-day Adventist Church, which emphasized a healthful life and observance of the Sabbath on Saturday.

In addition to beliefs in progress and women's leadership, a third attractive feature of some new religious movements was their emphasis on communication with the dead. Many women were active in Spiritualism, a movement that enabled the living to communicate with the dead. The young Fox sisters, for example, were very popular in the late 1840s, as was the young Cora Richmond in the 1850s; such Spiritualists drew thousands of listeners to their lectures, both in the United States and abroad. The popularity of Spiritualism increased after the Civil War, as thousands of women sought to communicate with beloved soldiers lost in the conflict: fathers, sons, husbands, brothers. The nineteenth-century fascination with heaven and the afterlife also sparked one of the age's great best sellers, Elizabeth Stuart Phelps's novel *The Gates Ajar*, which took readers on a tour of a recognizably domestic heaven.

Overall, despite the concern over death, the age was one of great optimism, and many religions were affected by the desire for both social and spiritual change. Some women were members of utopian communities, often short-lived ones, such as the Owenite community at New Harmony, Indiana, and the Oneida community in New York. Free Thought societies attracted women who were critical of traditional religion and advocated for more rational thought. Fanny Wright, for example, who founded the utopian community of Nashoba, Tennessee, in 1825, also advocated for political and sexual liberty for women; she often encountered mob violence at her lectures but refused to give up her right to think freely.

THE NINETEENTH CENTURY: PROTESTANT REVIVALS AND THE MISSIONARY MOVEMENT

While the United States was therefore home to numerous religious movements and varying religious ideas, various forms of Protestant Christianity remained its principle religious expression. Another series of religious revivals occurred between the 1790s and 1830s. These revivals were especially significant along the frontiers where camp meetings were social and religious events. Referred to as the Second Great Awakening, these revivals were popular among African Americans and women, but some Protestant church leaders were highly critical of them. Evangelist Charles Finney, one of the most important revivalists of this period, was criticized, for example, because he allowed women to pray with men in public; women speaking in so-called "promiscuous" (or mixed) assemblies were controversial

because they were seen as threatening the proper order between women and men. Yet the revivals empowered women to speak as evangelists in their own right. Jarena Lee, for example, converted to Christianity when she was in her early twenties. Although not approved as a Methodist preacher, she spent decades traveling as an evangelist. Her autobiography, *The Life and Religious Experience of Jarena Lee, A Colored Lady*, was the first autobiography published in the United States by an African American woman, and in it she speaks powerfully of her "call" to preach the gospel.

The Protestant Christian revivals of the late eighteenth and early nineteenth centuries not only empowered a few women to speak as evangelists and teachers but also prompted women to form organizations in order to engage in missionary work. A Baptist woman, Mary Webb, founded what may have been the first such organization in 1800, namely, the Boston Female Society for Missionary Purposes. Literally dozens of such organizations followed throughout the nineteenth century. Through them Protestant women raised money, sewed clothes for the poor, and sometimes sent workers to live among those deemed in need of evangelization, both at home (i.e., within the United States or its territories) or abroad. The first missionary women were sent with their husbands: Moravian Anna Gambold, for example, became a missionary with her husband among the Cherokees in 1805, and Baptist Anne Judson sailed with her husband to India in 1812 and ended up living (and dying) in Burma. Congregationalist Cynthia Farrar became the first single woman to be sent abroad by the American Board of Commissioners for Foreign Mission when, in 1827, she arrived in India to organize schools for girls.

Women engaged in benevolent work, as it was called, through networks they established within their local congregations and in newly formed educational institutions for women. For example, Sarah Allen, the wife of Richard Allen who founded the African Methodist Episcopal Church, was not only active in the Underground Railroad but also raised money for the formation of her denomination's missionary society. Mary Lyon, who founded Mount Holyoke Female Seminary in 1837, believed that one of the purposes of educating women was to train them not only for their future roles as wives and mothers but also for their future contributions in benevolent and missionary work.

Roman Catholic women also formed benevolent associations and sodalities, where lay and married women could support "works of mercy." New women's religious congregations were also established. All women's congregations embraced a specific calling or purpose, such as providing education for children or caring for the needy. While some sisters lived in cloisters, many actively engaged in their society. The Sisters of Charity, founded in Maryland in 1809, ran schools and orphanages. Its founder, Elizabeth Seton, was not only an able administrator but also a mystic who wrote numerous texts on her spiritual insights. Seton became the first woman born in the United States to be named a saint, in 1975. Ann Teresa Mathews founded the first Carmelite monastery in Maryland in 1790, and the Religious of the Sacred Heart founded their first mission in Missouri in 1818 and dedicated themselves to educating women. While most of these religious congregations involved only white women, not all of them did. The Sisters of the Holy Family, founded in 1842 in New Orleans, included African American and Creole women, for example.

Historians have suggested that the dominant ideology regarding the nature and role of women moved from that of Republican Motherhood to that of the Cult of True Womanhood in the decades before the Civil War. First articulated by historian Barbara Welter in a 1966 article, Welter said that with the expansion and consolidation of the United States women were to exhibit qualities of "piety, purity, submissiveness, and domesticity."[5] Congregationalist Catherine Beecher published her book, *A Treatise On Domestic Economy*, in 1841. Although she

herself was single and not a mother, her manual educated women on how they could fulfill their wifely and motherly duties, and contained instructions on everything from how to dress and garden to how to keep a clean household and ensure the health of family members. Beecher aspired to educate women so that they could instill in their children everything that was necessary to live Christian lives and therefore contribute to the nation.

Directed toward urban middle-class women, the ideology of domesticity was not applicable to most Native American and African American women, women of Mexican and Chinese descent, and pioneer women. Yet it provided a basis for the involvement of women within the broader society by suggesting that women had a special role in educating and influencing not only the members of their immediate households but also all children. It fed, for example, the growth of the Sunday school movement among Protestant, Catholic, and Jewish women during the 1830s and 1840s. The Female Hebrew Benevolent Society, for example, was the first of many Jewish women's organizations in the nineteenth century. Founded in 1819 under the leadership of Rebecca Gratz, it sponsored the Hebrew Sunday School in Philadelphia in 1838. For both Jewish and Christian women, education became a way not only to instill religious identity but also to reform society. Christian women addressed what they considered to be moral concerns, such as temperance, upholding Sunday as a day of worship and rest (i.e., Sabbatarianism), and the elimination of prostitution. Some women began to advocate for women's suffrage, and women's conventions were organized throughout the various states. These conventions provided forums for women to network and to engage in public speaking and leadership opportunities. Some white women feared that allowing black women to speak at these conventions would confound the causes of women's rights and black abolition. This was the case when Sojourner Truth, a frequent speaker at antislavery rallies, got up to speak at an 1851 women's convention in Akron, Ohio. "Ain't I a woman?" she asked, addressing some of the ministers who had stated their belief that men were superior to women not only in their intellect, but also because Jesus had been a man and Eve had brought the first sin into the world. Sojourner Truth refuted the notion of white racial and male gender superiority in her speech.

THE NINETEENTH CENTURY: WOMEN AND SLAVERY

Among the many moral reform movements of the nineteenth century, the abolition of slavery was an ultimate concern for some women. Christian women in the northern states formed antislavery and abolitionist groups. Lydia Maria Child was one of the first women to write against slavery in her 1833 book, *An Appeal in Favor of That Class of Americans Called Africans*. In the preface she begged readers to read her book: "I am fully aware of the unpopularity of the task I have undertaken," she wrote, "but though I *expect* ridicule and censure, I cannot *fear* them."[6] Other women embraced the abolitionist cause, including Angelina and Sarah Grimké, sisters who appealed to southern Christian women and clergy and argued that Christianity and slavery were incompatible. After the passage of the Fugitive Slave Act in 1850, Harriet Beecher Stowe (sister of Catherine Beecher) began to write a series of stories later published as *Uncle Tom's Cabin*; her book became a best seller that exposed the cruelty of slavery and argued that it was antithetical to Christian morals.

Ironically, of course, southern slaveholding white women and enslaved African women both drew on the biblical tradition, but they interpreted it differently: Southern slaveholders believed that slaves were to obey their masters, while slaves upheld the exodus to freedom. Some slave women saw their white owners as hypocrites. Harriet A. Jacobs, who became a fugitive in the 1830s

and published an autobiography in 1861, uncovered the "great difference between Christianity and religion [in] the south":

> If a man goes to the communion table, and pays money into the treasury of the church, not matter if it be the price of blood, he is called religious. If a pastor has offspring by a woman not his wife, the church [would] dismiss him, if she is a white woman; but if she is colored, it does not hinder his continuing to be their good shepherd.[7]

While the antislavery movement united some women and men in a shared cause, it also divided families and religious institutions and communities. When the Civil War broke out, women on both sides of the conflict ended up doing what women often did, namely, taking care of the wounded. Even Harriet Tubman, the fearless leader of the Underground Railroad, worked as a nurse during the Civil War, as did Episcopal deaconess Adeline Tyler, reformer Dorothea Dix, and Sister of Charity Mary O'Connell. The Civil War was horrifying in the number of dead it left in its wake. Although it resulted in amendments to the United States Constitution regarding the abolition of slavery and "involuntary servitude" and the extension of voting rights to men regardless of "race, color, or previous condition of servitude," the war did not eliminate racism or other looming social and political problems.

AFTER THE CIVIL WAR: SUFFRAGE AND REFORM

Women gained confidence and respect through their efforts during the Civil War, which led to their increased religious, social, and political activities after the war. Waves of new immigrants arrived, many of them Roman Catholic and Jewish. With the expanding nation came the challenges of poverty, inadequate housing, and illiteracy, which all burgeoned in both urban and rural areas. Women formed organizations to direct their efforts on a whole spectrum of concerns. Ideals regarding the True Woman were challenged with calls for a New Woman; such women would be well-educated and articulate, active in public realms, attired in clothes that did not restrict their physical movements, and assertive of their own political and religious independence.

Often referred to as the first wave of feminism in America, such ideas and actions eventually resulted in the 1920 passage of the Nineteenth Amendment, which granted the vote to all citizens of the United States regardless of their sex. (Native Americans were not automatically considered citizens until 1924 and, even then, some—depending on what state they lived in—were not allowed to vote until 1948.) While Elizabeth Cady Stanton and Lucretia Mott had organized the first convention for women's rights in Seneca Falls, New York, in 1848, the Civil War had diverted attention and energy from suffrage. After the war, however, some women continued their advocacy for women's political and social rights, and for some it was a matter of religious principle. Susan B. Anthony, unrelenting in her push for women's suffrage, was a born Quaker who later in life embraced Unitarianism; suffrage was to her an ultimately religious matter regarding women's basic equality. But other women were staunchly opposed to women's suffrage on their religious principles. Helen Kendrick Johnson was one such opponent. Johnson believed that separate gender roles needed to exist within America, and that women (and men) who supported voting rights for women were spurning the teachings of the Bible and the essential directive for women to obey their husbands.[8]

Women such as Johnson were adamantly opposed to the publication of *The Woman's Bible* (1895/98), in which Elizabeth Cady Stanton and the women scholars on her revising committee argued that the authority granted certain biblical texts resulted in women's secondary status in religious organizations and in society itself. *The Woman's Bible* met with much opposition in its day from both men and women. Most

women did not equate religious teachings with women's subordination, but rather found within them a source of meaning and empowerment in their lives.

Women's organizations and movements became significant agencies of social change in this time period. Women continued to organize and support missionary societies and address the needs of the poor. The Women's Missionary Union (WMU), an auxiliary of the Southern Baptist Convention, was founded in 1888, for example; Martha McIntosh, a daughter of former slaveholders in South Carolina, became its first president but resigned her position upon her marriage. The WMU grew into one of the largest Protestant missionary unions for women in the world. In Greek Orthodox communities women's clubs were formed by the end of the nineteenth century in urban centers where immigrants from Greece, Asia Minor, and Constantinople had settled. By 1902 the first women's Philoptochos group was established in New York City as a way to engage women in charitable activities specifically directed toward the poor in their own communities; by 1931 the Philoptochos Society was incorporated as a national auxiliary organization.

Within Roman Catholic circles religious women took on major tasks, and within Protestant circles deaconesses became vital church workers. Religious Roman Catholic women established more schools and hospitals in attempts to address growing needs, especially among Catholic immigrants. The Little Sisters of the Poor founded their first American congregation in 1868 to work among elderly poor urban people, for example, while the Sisters of the Blessed Sacrament for Indians and Colored People, established in 1891 by Katherine Drexel, worked with Native and African Americans. Other sisters founded and staffed colleges for Catholic women. Susan McGroarty, for example, a Sister of Notre Dame de Namur, founded Trinity College in Washington, D.C., in 1897. Anti-Catholic sentiment was rampant in parts of the United States, and sisters often met with antagonism from their Protestant neighbors who accused them of being anti-American (in their allegiance to the Roman papal office) and engaging in "superstitious" actions.

The Protestant deaconess movement, although established in the United States in the mid-nineteenth century, became significant after the Civil War. Deaconesses were single women who were "set apart" for church-related work; that is, they were officially recognized as workers in the churches but were not ordained. (They were sometimes simply considered Protestant nuns.) The Chicago Training School for City, Home, and Foreign Missions, opened by Methodist Lucy Rider Meyer and her husband in 1885 became one of the best-known training centers in the world, but Anglican, Lutheran, Methodist, and Presbyterian denominations had all opened schools for the training of deaconesses by the end of the century. Deaconesses worked as educators, nurses, and missionaries. Episcopal deaconess Adeline Tyler, for example, first established an infirmary in Baltimore; then during the Civil War she took care of wounded northern and southern men, after which she established a children's hospital in Boston.

Most women in America, of course, were not Catholic religious sisters or Protestant deaconesses. Married, single, and divorced women were active in various organizations, often as an extension of their religious commitments. Some of them were active in the settlement house movement, for example. While some settlement houses attempted to be free of religious or sectarian persuasions, such as Hull House, established by Jane Addams and Ellen Gates Starr in 1889, other houses were more like missions and were officially sponsored by religious groups. Wesley houses, for example, were established by Methodist churches to work among urban and rural European immigrants as well as in Hispanic and Mexican communities; Roman Catholics and Jews and an array of Protestant denominations also organized such neighborhood centers. The first generation of college-educated women was key to the success of this movement, even though men were involved in it. Some women spent the bulk of their lives in such settings. Donaldina Cameron, for example, lived in a Presbyterian mission house in San Francisco's Chinatown for over thirty years, where she sought to empower and educate Chinese young women; she came to be fondly called "Lo Mo," old mother, by the neighborhood women.

Scores of the alliances formed by women were organizations that mustered support from across religious identities and institutions, however. The Young Women's Christian Association (YWCA) was started in the United States in 1858 and was especially important in providing support to working women in terms of employment, housing, and social activities. The YWCA included women of various religions, races, and ethnicities. Eva Bowles became the executive secretary of the Harlem branch in New York City in 1905, for example, and worked for decades on expanding services offered among African American women and on interracial integration, and a Chinese YWCA began to operate in San Francisco in 1916. Although the YWCA was initially Christian in its theology, its leaders very early on attempted to build consensus around less sectarian social goals for women. The YWCA provided a model for other organizations as well, such as for the Young Women's Hebrew Association, which was founded in 1902.

The Woman's Christian Temperance Union (WCTU), emerging out of earlier women's crusades against alcohol, united mostly white Christian Protestant women in the goal of prohibiting alcohol. Temperance and prohibition were needed, WCTU members argued, to prevent violence toward women and the impoverishment that resulted when drinking husbands and fathers neglected their dependents. Under the leadership of its second president, Frances Willard, the goals of the WCTU expanded to include not only temperance but also women's suffrage and wider issues of women's independence. The ideology of the WCTU was based on the foundational idea that women needed certain rights in order to protect their households. The WCTU became the largest women's organization in the United States by the first decade of the twentieth century and did not lose its influence until prohibition was repealed in 1933. While the WCTU was mostly viewed as an organization for respectable women, not all women who advocated temperance engaged in respectable protest activities. Carry Nation, for example, a member of the WCTU, went around smashing saloons in Missouri and Kansas; she held a Bible in one hand and a hatchet in the other, and believed that she was doing what God required of her in destroying what she considered the greatest evil in America.

Jewish women's organizations engaged in a variety of reform efforts during these decades. Hannah Solomon and Sadie American founded the National Council of Jewish Women (NCJW) in 1893, the first Jewish women's organization in America. Hannah Solomon was especially concerned with educating women regarding their domestic duties and in helping newly arrived immigrant women. Esther Ruskay was the first speaker at the formation of the New York NCJW in 1894, where she defended Judaism against those who argued that it was obsolete in modern America. Even though Ruskay was the first woman to speak from the Reform Temple Emanu-El in 1894, her concern was with promoting and defending Jewish family traditions. In 1902 Ruskay published her *Hearth and Home Essays* in which she strove to encourage Jewish women to maintain their identity in the overwhelming Christian ethos of America. Some women, such as Carrie Simon, believed that the NCJW was too focused on social reform, so in 1913 she formed the National Federation of Temple Sisterhoods, which worked with the women's groups within Reform synagogues on specifically religious matters, such as holiday celebrations and religious instruction. Hadassah, another significant women's organization, was founded in 1912 under the leadership of Henrietta Szold. As part of the American Zionist movement, Hadassah supported education and provided medical care for the women and children of Palestine; its work relied on the grassroots commitment of countless local chapters or groups of women.

African American women, excluded from most white women's associations, organized among themselves. The formation of the National Association of Colored Women (NACW) in 1896—a merger of the National League of Colored Women and the National Federation of Afro-American women—under the initial leadership of elected president Mary Church Terrell was important in giving voice to middle- and upper-middle-class black women. Like with members of the WCTU, members of the NACW advocated temperance, women's suffrage, and "good morals." Its motto, "Lift as we climb," became central to its commitment to education for racial justice and social equality. Educator Mary McLeod Bethune, who was to organize the National Council of Negro Women in 1935, was shaped by her experience with the NACW, even though she believed that it was not committed enough to empowering working poor black women.

By the end of the nineteenth century, many Native American young people were being sent to boarding schools. Operated by Christian missionaries with the encouragement of the government, it was a practice that was to last well into the 1970s. The aim was to Americanize and Christianize them. Despite the devastation of their traditional way of life, a Native woman such as Sarah Winnemucca Hopkins of the Paiute (Nevada) people lectured through the eastern United States and even before Congress to make non-Native Americans aware of the wrongs inflicted on her people. Her book, *Life Among the Piutes* (1883), was probably the first autobiography written by an American Indian woman.

NEW RELIGIOUS CHOICES
AT THE TURN OF THE CENTURY

Women were also drawn to newer religious movements in this time period, such as the Stone-Campbell, Holiness, and Pentecostal movements. Participants in the Stone-Campbell movement, with roots into the pre-Civil War period, believed that the churches needed to be restored to their earlier unity and expression. Selina Campbell, wife of one of its founders, became a significant leader after the 1866 death of her husband. Also, Clara Babcock, a lecturer for the WCTU, became active in the movement during the 1870s and was its first ordained woman pastor in 1888. Within the Holiness movement, which aimed to turn Methodism away from overintellectualization toward an emphasis on the experience of God, women such as Phoebe Palmer and Amanda Berry Smith were important preachers who called their listeners—both black and white, male and female—to repentance and a new life of holiness. The emergence of Pentecostalism in the early part of the twentieth century relied on the religious experiences and leadership of women such as Lizzie Robinson, who became a significant leader in the Church of God in Christ after she experienced "baptism of the Holy Ghost" in 1906. Mary Tate even started her own Pentecostal denomination, the Church of the Living God, after her 1908 experience of healing and speaking in tongues.

Other women were active in Christian Science, founded by Mary Baker Eddy in 1892, or Theosophy, promoted by women such as the charismatic Helena Blavatsky and Alice Bailey. Few women in this time period were active in Eastern religions. Marie Canavarro was probably the first European American to convert to Buddhism, and her lectures throughout the United States in the early twentieth century received substantial media attention. Asian Buddhists, of course, had practiced their beliefs in their homes for decades. By 1914 Japanese Ameri-

can women had formed their own society, Fujinkai, which was key in fund-raising and providing social support for Buddhist Japanese women. Numerous Chinese benevolent societies were also established in the late nineteenth century and provided tremendous support for Chinese women and families.

The World's Parliament of Religions held in Chicago in 1893 was significant in introducing Buddhism, Hinduism, Islam, and other religions to Americans. Protestant Christian men dominated it, but a few women were invited as speakers. Unitarian minister Julia Ward Howe, for example, spoke on "What is Religion?" "Any religion which sacrifices women to the brutality of men is no religion," she stated, for religion was to exist for the "sake of humanity."[9] The parliament also provided the opportunity for a west coast woman, Mrs. Alexander Russell, to become acquainted with the Japanese Zen teacher Soyen Shaku. Mrs. Russell and her husband were to become significant patrons of Buddhism in America.

More important to women than the World's Parliament of Religions were the Women's Congress of Representative Women and the Jewish Women's Congress, both held in conjunction with the Columbian Exposition of 1893. Although the women's congress was dominated by white middle-class women and chaired by the wealthy socialite, Bertha Palmer, it nevertheless featured women from around the world who spoke on a variety of topics, many of them religious. The Jewish Women's Congress was the first of its kind in the United States. Organized by Hannah Soloman, it provided the opportunity for twenty-five women to speak on their understanding of Judaism and resulted in the formation of the National Council of Jewish Women.

WARS AND ECONOMIC DEPRESSION

American women have always been divided on the question of war, and World War I was no exception. Most women (and their religious communities) supported the entrance of the United States into the war. Some American women, however, advocated various pacifist positions. Settlement house leader and social reformer Jane Addams, for example, was one of the most respected women in the United States until she began to advocate for pacifism. Addams and the other women who formed the Women's Peace Party in 1915 viewed their opposition to military solutions to national disputes as merely extending their "motherly" concerns onto the world stage, but they were blasted as silly, hysterical, and naïve women by the media, politicians, and religious leaders. Quaker women, of course, continued their pacifist stance, and some, like Emily Greene Balch, devoted their entire lives to peace. (Addams was awarded the Nobel Peace Prize in 1931, and Balch received it in 1946.) The end of the war resulted in great jubilation and ushered in a period of economic boom for the United States in the 1920s, but was soon followed by economic depression.

The Great Depression was a crisis for religious groups. Protestant Christians, divided into so-called liberal and fundamentalist camps, and Roman Catholics, growing in numbers but not yet in the American mainstream, struggled with how to maintain their institutions while addressing huge economic and social needs. Two very different women became well-known religious leaders in these years, Aimee Semple McPherson and Dorothy Day. Aimee Semple McPherson emerged as one of the most popular evangelists in the interwar years, and her International Church of the Foursquare Gospel provided thousands of people with a sense of community during the Great Depression. In addition to holding tent meetings and services at her Angelus Temple in Los Angeles, McPherson utilized the new medium of radio to enlarge her audience. Considered controversial by many religious people (she was twice divorced), McPherson drew huge crowds that were diverse in race, class, status, and political opinions. Employing highly theatrical methods in her church services, she

was perhaps the first modern-day celebrity preacher in America. A preacher, healer, and performer, she also sponsored soup kitchens and medical clinics for the hungry and ill.

Dorothy Day, who had been influenced by socialism and communism in her younger years and had made her living as a writer, converted to Catholicism in 1927. The tradition of Catholicism fed her spirit and also spurred her to care for the poor. In 1933 she and Peter Maurin, an itinerant teacher and laborer, founded the Catholic Worker Movement; they not only printed a newspaper but also established houses of hospitality for anyone in need. Day, as an intellectual and a single mother, was often criticized as immoral and not obedient enough to church authorities, but she insisted on seeing God even in the most downtrodden of human beings and on not separating her faith from her actions for social justice.

The entrance of the United States into World War II brought the nation out of its economic slump, but it also raised huge questions about political systems such as fascism and communism, the place of conscientious objection, and the use of nuclear weapons. The plight of European Jews did not concern most non-Jewish Americans prior to or during the war, nor did the near-devastation of the Japanese-American communities trouble most non-Japanese Americans. After the war, however, some American women helped displaced European peoples and addressed the horrors of the Jewish Holocaust (or Shoah). Jane Evans, for example, as director of the National Federation of Temple Sisterhoods, chaired a commission on displaced persons for the American Jewish Conference, and Irma Jung, along with her rabbi husband, raised funds for students at the Yeshiva University and for Holocaust survivors. Other women, such as Lutheran Cordelia Cox, oversaw the resettlement of thousands of post-World War II Europeans and directed services for immigrants to the United States.

The post-World War II ethos saw anti-communist campaigns, the emergence of a Cold War, and an emphasis on middle-class consumerism. Women were expected to focus on their primary role as homemakers and mothers, and provide stable "behind the scenes" support to their religious communities. Although not stated in the ideology of the good Puritan wife or the Republican mother, gender expectations for women existed both within religious communities and in larger public arenas. Although the United States saw a baby boom and the growth of suburbs, uncertainty existed. As anthropologist Margaret Mead—herself a faithful Episcopalian who became active in the World Council of Churches (f.1948)—noted in 1946,

"Women—and men—are confused, uncertain and discontented with the present definition of women's place in America."[10]

CIVIL RIGHTS, ORDINATION, AND WOMEN'S GROUPS

The civil rights and the women's movements of the mid-twentieth century held revolutionary consequences for American society. Many women were active in civil rights. Mary Church Terrell, for example, lectured and protested against segregation in the 1940s and 1950s, and Rosa Parks, as a

---

Religion, Feminism, and Social Change

Are religions and various forms of feminism diametrically opposed? Some religious people, for instance, may not support ideas regarding the basic equality of men and women, or they may support ideas regarding the complementary nature of gender relations that uphold distinct social and religious roles for men and women. On the other hand, some feminist critics of religion may totally trounce religious traditions as oppressive and harmful to women, or they may judge women who are religious as not really feminist. As Nancy K. Frankenberry has observed, "Feminist scholarship in general has had a hard time with religion."[1] Yet many women profess both identities.

Religion and the Feminist Movement was the topic of a 2002 conference organized by the Women's Studies Program at the Harvard Divinity School.[2] Twenty-five women spoke, some of them academics, others activists, and yet others church, community, and spiritual leaders; they represented a variety of religious traditions. All speakers addressed how feminism and religion were connected in their own lives and work. Some saw themselves as contributing to the transformation of religion through their embrace of both feminism and religion, and indeed, the three hundred conference attendees seemed to applaud the speakers' significance as "women who changed American religion." Time will only tell, however, whether the efforts of such women will be a blip on the historical screen or result in enduring changes to religious institutions and traditions.

If the feminist movement may result in changing religions in America, one must also ask about the role of religions in social change itself. To what extent do religions play a role in promoting social change? Scholars note that religions have never been static entities and their very human proponents have always adapted to emerging circumstances and cultures. It may also be well to remember that women have a long history of addressing societal concerns as part and parcel of their religious commitments and engaging in social actions through their assorted religious networks. In light of looming twenty-first century issues, this may be a comforting thought.

1. Nancy K. Frankenberry, "Feminist Philosophy of Religion," *Stanford Encyclopedia of Philosophy*, ed. Edward N. Salta (March 2005). See http://plato.stanford.edu/entries/feminist-religion.

2. Refer to Ann Braude, ed., *Transforming the Faiths of Our Fathers: Women who Changed American Religion* (New York: Palgrave Macmillan, 2004) for a selection of the addresses given.

member of the National Association for the Advancement of Colored People (NAACP), set off the 1955 Montgomery, Alabama, bus boycott by refusing to yield her bus seat to a white passenger. While men held the official leadership positions in civil rights organizations, such as Martin Luther King Jr. in the Southern Christian Leadership Convention (SCLC), women were key to the movement, as were the churches in which they were actively involved. Ella Baker, for example, unrelentingly labored for civil rights alongside men such as W. E. B. DuBois and King in the NAACP and the SCLC, and in her later years associated with the Women's International League for Peace and Freedom. Baker's stubborn determination to work for freedom and liberty for black people—and all oppressed peoples—was celebrated in "Ella's Song," written and performed by Bernice Johnson, founder of the a cappella group Sweet Honey in the Rock.

While the civil rights movement was highly divisive within the United States, so too was the women's movement. Not all women agreed with feminist goals, such as economic equality, women's reproductive and sexual rights, and the proposed Equal Rights Amendment (ERA). Catholic laywoman Phyllis Schlafly and evangelical Beverly LaHaye, for example, became well-known in their opposition to the ERA, while the Women's League for Conservative Judaism and the Evangelical and Ecumenical Women's Caucus advocated for its passage. Mormon Sonia Johnson supported the ERA, while her church opposed it. Opponents of the ERA did not view women as second-class citizens, as has sometimes been assumed, but many believed that it would take away traditional privileges of wives and children.

Questions regarding sexual orientation also became controversial among women. Singer and entertainer Anita Bryant, for example, campaigned against gay rights in the late 1970s on the basis of her Christian beliefs. The Evangelical Women's Caucus was split in 1986 over the question of including homosexual rights among their goals; some members feared that they would weaken their broad support for women's rights by including lesbian rights in their agenda. Sexual orientation, as well as gay covenants and marriages, became controversial in religious denominations and traditions and continues to be debated by religious bodies and in political arenas.

The broad feminist movement resulted in a major change within religious institutions, namely, the ordination of women by some Protestant Christian and Jewish bodies. A few women had been ordained as Protestant ministers prior to the mid-twentieth century: Congregationalist Antoinette Brown (Blackwell), ordained in 1853, is upheld as the first woman ordained by a local congregation in America, and Universalist Olympia Brown, ordained in 1863, is considered the first woman ordained by a wider denominational structure. Women, of course, preached and taught and worked as religious sisters and deaconesses throughout the history of the United States. Women had also been ordained in some of the smaller denominations, such as the Church of God (Cleveland, Tenn.) in 1909 and in the Mennonite Church in 1911, and had worked as officers within the Salvation Army since its founding. Some of the Methodist and Presbyterian denominations approved the ordination of women in the late 1940s to mid-1950s, but it was not until the Lutheran Church in America ordained its first woman, Elizabeth Platz, in 1970, and Reform Judaism ordained its first woman rabbi, Sally Priesand, in 1972, that women's ordination became a matter that could not be ignored by religious institutions. It did take time and struggle, however. Within the Episcopal Church, for example, eleven women were ordained in a so-called "irregular" ordination in 1974; the church took two years of further debate to authorize (i.e., approve) women's ordination.

Not all religious traditions moved toward accepting women's ordination, however. Even though a Southern Baptist congregation ordained its first woman pastor, Addie

Davis, in 1964 and other individual congregations followed suit, the Southern Baptist Convention voted in 1984 to prohibit women's ordinations; and in 2000 the convention affirmed that the office of pastor was limited to qualified men. In the Roman Catholic Church, despite unrelenting advocacy from groups such as the Women's Ordination Conference and the National Coalition of American Nuns, and in the Orthodox Christian churches, women remain excluded from the priesthood. Orthodox Judaism also does not allow women into the rabbinate.

The first generation of ordained women did not always find their paths easy. Many experienced a professional glass ceiling (sometimes called the "stained glass ceiling") that made it difficult for them to move beyond entry-level positions or even into full-time appointments. Women's caucuses were formed in some denominations to address such concerns. The United Methodist Church elected its first woman bishop, Marjorie Matthews, in 1980, and the Episcopal Church elected its first woman bishop, Barbara Harris, in 1988. In 2005, the Disciples of Christ became the first mainline Protestant denomination to elect a woman, Sharon Watkins, to head a major denomination. The Episcopal Church made history the following year by electing Katharine Jefferts Schori to be the Presiding Bishop over all Episcopalians in the United States; she was the first woman to ever be elected as a primate in the entire worldwide Anglican Communion.

RELIGIOUS CHANGES AND REALIGNMENTS INTO THE TWENTY-FIRST CENTURY

The entrance of women into ordained ministry has been made possible by the growing number of women receiving theological education and by a resultant increase in theological scholarship done by women. Increasing numbers of women have completed professional degree programs (such as the Master of Divinity), which provide them with the credentials they need to be approved as official religious leaders. As more women have pursued postgraduate studies, they have become better equipped to engage with their religious roots and offer critical interpretations of texts and traditions. Such scholarship has resulted in a surge of publications in theology, history, and ethics that examine the place of women within religious traditions. Some resources have aimed to make religious traditions more inclusive of women. In 1983, for example, *An Inclusive Language Lectionary* was published under the auspices of the National Council of the Churches of Christ. A product of twelve scholars (men and women) who had worked on a committee for over three years, the project garnered mixed reactions ranging from "great joy to bitter hostility."[11] At the same time, a few women such as former Catholic scholar, Mary Daly, became convinced that religion—in her case, Christianity—was ultimately irredeemable from its patriarchal clutches and came to advocate a "post-Christian" theology from the 1970s onward.

The variety of scholarship generated has not only affected the academic study of religious disciplines but also fostered prolific study among grassroots women's groups. The Grail and Church Women United were significant groups in the post–World War II era. The Grail was started by a Dutch Jesuit priest in 1921 and established in the United States in 1944. Through retreats and a collective of women living on a farm in Ohio, it initially attracted Catholic laywomen who sought a spiritual and liturgical renewal in their church. It became a locus for Catholic feminist theology in the 1970s and networked with other women's groups. By 1969 it admitted women of any Christian tradition and in 1975 welcomed the participation of Jewish women. The Women-Church movement that emerged in the 1980s was in part based on the grassroots foundation established by groups such as the Grail. In a similar trajectory of increasing openness, Church Women United, founded in 1941, has come to include Protestant, Roman Catholic, and Orthodox women. It has sought to be theologically inclusive and to work for racial and social justice. It has coordinated the annual World Day of Prayer (an event with roots into the nineteenth century), a program that brings together American women, both Protestant and Catholic, with women throughout the world in educational and worship activities.

Roman Catholic American women have been greatly affected by the Second Vatican Council. Sister of Loretto Mary Luke Tobin was the only American woman invited to attend two sessions of the council, where she advocated for greater inclusion of women in the church. While American women's religious communities lost thousands of members after Vatican II and were divided on issues of dress and liturgy, many also experienced renewed commitments to their ministries. Although women's religious communities differ widely (just as in the past), many sisters are leaders in movements supportive of women's ordination, social justice, and peace. Las Hermanas, founded in 1971 as an organization by Hispanic religious women, for example, works to support the social and economic struggles of Latina people and thereby gives voice to a frequently overlooked segment of the American populace. The rape and murder of four Catholic women—Ita Ford and Maura Clark (Maryknoll sisters), Jean Donovan (a laywoman), and Dorothy Kazel (an Ursuline sister)—by members of El Salvadoran military in 1980 brought to the attention of Americans the idea of "solidarity with the poor" that many Catholic women had adopted.

Some of the recent innovations or changes wrought by feminists have been controversial. The 1993 Re-imagining Conference in Minneapolis, for example, was one of the more contentious gatherings in the last decade of the twentieth century. Organized by Christian ecumenical leaders in response to the call from the World Council of Churches for an Ecumenical Decade of Churches in Solidarity with Women (1988–1998), over two thousand people (mostly women) gathered to worship and celebrate, share their stories, and pray for what they called the "transformation of the church." Women theologians and church leaders uplifted Sophia (an understanding of God as wisdom) and critiqued traditional theology, which many participants said was too patriarchal. When word leaked out about the conference, some church leaders called it heretical and even pagan. Presbyterian church executive Mary Ann Lundy, one of the organizers of the conference, was forced to resign her position in the face of heavy protest. Nevertheless, the Re-imagining community has continued to network and hold periodic conferences. Such conferences raised basic questions as to whether or not most religions are patriarchal and therefore need transformation if women are to be inherently valued within them.

Women's groups have not only involved Christian or Jewish participants, however. Native Americans, although mostly Christianized, began to claim their own traditional teachings in the 1970s, and some women emerged as key leaders. Essie Parrish, for example, became a spiritual and political leader among the Pomos people. While some religious groups acknowledge in public gatherings or meetings that "they sit on native lands" and some Christian denominations have issued apologies for their treatment of Native American peoples, Native women remain among the most impoverished and underrepresented groups in America.

Since the passage of the 1965 Immigration Act, the United States has become more religiously diverse. Large numbers of Muslims and Hindus have immigrated to the United States and have built mosques and temples. Muslim women, at first largely invisible to mainstream society, began to organize by the 1990s. American-born Sharifa Alkhateeb, for example, founded the North American Council for Muslim Women in 1992 and was key in teaching non-Muslim Americans about Islam. She also chaired the Muslim caucus at the Beijing (1995) United Nations World Conference on Women. In addition to growth through immigration, Islam has also gained tens of thousands of African American converts, who comprise approximately one-third of the religion's adherents in the United States. The vast majority of these are Sunni Muslims, with a small group following the teachings of the controversial Nation of Islam sect. The NOI's growth in urban centers especially has been supported by the work of women members who teach children in a network of schools scattered through the country, a practice started by Clara Muhammad, the wife of founder Elijah Muhammad.

Since the 1970s some women began to involve themselves in Wiccan practices and goddess traditions. Women such as Starhawk and Yvonne Frost became leaders in the nascent Wiccan movement, and women such as Carol Christ and Selena Fox, in opposition to traditional Christian and Jewish understandings of a male deity, began to claim a goddess tradition. More American women also became associated with various branches of Buddhism. Some, like Pema Chödrön and Tsultrim Allione, became nuns who were based in retreat centers or monasteries, while others, such as Maxine Hong Kingston and Joanna Macy, became popular writers. Such women advocated not only their particular religious perspectives but also built broad alliances based on what they consider ultimately "spiritual" issues, such as environmentalism and antinuclear proliferation. Concerns for the earth and for the welfare of future generations as expressed in various forms of environmentalism—from ecofeminism to deep ecology—may unite women in the twenty-first century across their various religious, social, and political identities.

Women in America have generally been and will probably continue to be religious. Reflecting a mosaic of practices and beliefs, many women have faithfully participated in their religious communities, and accepted and passed on their religious traditions and teachings. However, women have also been innovators. Sometimes, at various points in the history of American religion, they have been accused of heresy, but mostly, they have been able to shape their religious traditions—and their society—through collective actions and sheer presence.

Notes

1. "U.S. Religious Landscape Survey," The Pew Forum on Religion and Public Life (Washington, D.C.), 2008, 62–64.
2. Clara Barton to Mary S. Logan, June 16, 1911, Container 73, Clara Barton Papers, Manuscript Division, Library of Congress.
3. Gerda Lerner, "A Life of Learning," Charles Homer Haskins Lecture for 2005, American Council of Learned Societies. ACLS occasional paper, no. 60, 9.
4. Phillis Wheatley, "On Being Brought from Africa to America" (1773). Numerous copies are online, e.g., Archiving Early America, http://www.earlyamerica.com/review/winter96/wheatley.html.
5. Barbara Welter, "The Cult of True Womanhood: 1820–1860," *American Quarterly* 18 (Summer 1966):151–74. http://www.pinzler.com/ushistory/cultwo.html.
6. Lydia Maria Child, *An Appeal in Favor of That Class of Americans Called Africans* (Boston: Allen & Ticknor, 1833). Available online: Stephen Railton, "*Uncle Tom's Cabin* and American Culture," http://www.iath.virginia.edu/utc/abolitn/childhp.html.
7. Harriet A. Jacobs, *Incidents in the Life of a Slave Girl, Written by Herself* (Cambridge: Harvard University Press, 1987), 74.
8. Helen Kendrick Johnson, *Woman and the Republic* (New York: D. Appleton & Co., 1897).
9. Julia Ward Howe, "What is Religion?" http://womenshistory.about.com/library/etext/bl_1893_pwr_howe.htm.
10. Quoted by S.J. Kleinberg in *Women in the United States, 1830–1945* (London: Macmillan Press, 1999), 309.
11. Bernice Johnson Reagon, "Ella's Song" (Songtalk Publishing Co. 1981). http://www.bernicejohnsonreagon.com/ella.shtml.
12. Burton H. Throckmorton, Jr., "Why the Inclusive Language Lectionary?" *Christian Century* (August 1–8, 1984); 742. http://www.religion-online.org/showarticle.asp?title=1414.

STUDY QUESTIONS

1. How did the "feminization" of religion take place during the eighteenth and nineteenth centuries in America? What was women's role in organized religion at that time? How much change do you think has taken place since then?

2. What role did women play in the American Great Awakening?

3. What issues in the North were most affected by women's religious convictions? How did Northern women's religious experiences differ from those of women in the South? What role does slavery play in understanding women in the South and their understanding of religion?

4. What were women's views toward slavery? Do you see a difference between the views of women in the North and women in the South? Do you see any relation between the plight of slaves and the lives of white women during the nineteenth century?

5. What was the "Cult of True Womanhood"? Do you believe that such an image exists today?

6. How did the role of women in American religion change during the post–Civil War period? What do you see as the most significant change? Do you believe that there is no difference between men's and women's relations to religion in America?

ESSAY TOPICS

Religion, Women, and Slavery during the Civil War

Women, Their Religion, and the American Temperance Movement

Harrier Beecher Stowe's *Uncle Tom's Cabin:* An Antislavery Novel

Women and Ordained Clergy in America

Men and Women in American Religion: Still No Equality

WORD EXPLORATION

The following terms play significant roles in any discussion of religion and women in America and are worth careful reflection and discussion.

Abolitionist
Ordination
Settlement Houses
Young Women's
    Christian Association

Cult of True Womanhood
Republican Motherhood
Suffrage

Deaconess Movement
Salem Witch Trials
Woman's Christian
    Temperance Union

FOR FURTHER READING

Braude, Ann. *Women and American Religion*. New York: Oxford University Press, 2000.

Brekus, Catherine A., ed. *The Religious History of American Women: Reimagining the Past*. Chapel Hill: University of North Carolina Press, 2007.

Keller, Rosemary Skinner and Rosemary Radford Ruether, eds. *Encyclopedia of Women and Religion in North America*. Bloomington: Indiana University Press, 2006.

Lindley, Susan Hill. *"You Have Stept Out of Your Place": A History of Women and Religion in America*. Louisville, Ky.: Westminster John Knox Press, 1996.

Lindley, Susan Hill and Eleanor J. Stebner, eds. *Handbook to Women in American Religious History*. Louisville, Ky.: Westminster John Knox Press, 2008.

WEB SITES

http://womhist.alexanderstreet.com
  Dublin, Thomas and Katherine Kish Sklar, "Women and Social Movements, 1600–2000"

http://hirr.hartsem.edu/research/women_religion.html
  Hartford Institute for Religion Research, "Women and Religion"

http://womenshistory.about.com/od/essentials/a/etext_index.htm
  Lewis, Jone Johnson. "Index to Women's History Etexts." About.com: Women's History

http://www.mtsu.edu/~kmiddlet/history/women/wh-rel.html
  Middleton, Ken. "American Women's History: A Research Guide—Religion." Middle Tennessee State University Library

21

Religion and Politics in America

ANDREW M. GREELEY AND FRED FROHOCK
WITH ESBEN GERHAUGE

1619   Anglican Church becomes legally established religion in Virginia

1630   Puritan experiment in Massachusetts Bay Colony

1636   Roger Williams founds Rhode Island, America's first colony to separate church and state

1786   Virginia enacts Statute of Religious Freedom, ensuring freedom of religion throughout the state

1791   Bill of Rights ratified, stipulating free exercise of religion and prohibiting government sponsorship of religion

1833   Congregational Church disestablished in Massachusetts

1854   "Know Nothing" political party organized to keep immigrant Catholics out of public office

1865   Congress authorizes use of "In God We Trust" on some U.S. coins

1925   Scopes trial in Tennessee raises issue of the teaching of evolution in public schools

1933   Prohibition repealed

1960s   Religion a major factor in the civil rights movement

1973   Supreme Court hands down *Roe v. Wade* decision, angering many religious groups that opposed abortion

1993   Congress passes the Religious Freedom Restoration Act, which the Supreme Court declares unconstitutional in 1997

2008   Conservative religious groups help to ban same-sex marriage in California

Religion and politics don't mix in America, it is often said. Church and state are separated by a wall. Religion is a matter of private life; politics pertains to public life. In your heart and in your church on Sunday (or whatever day of the week) you can be religious if you want to, but the political life of the country ought to be purely secular. Many Americans would agree with those clichés, though fewer would agree with the logical conclusions that can be drawn from them, such as the prohibition of prayer in public schools and of Christmas decorations in public parks.

The Constitution forbids the establishment of a state religion, as well as interference in the free exercise of religion. Historically, however, these two clauses have not created an impenetrable wall between church and state. Judicial interpretations that take the metaphor of the "wall" literally are heavily influenced by secularist theory, which often seems to others to want its "anti-religion" established as the only permissible approach to religion. Religious behavior should be banned, it would seem, from every area of life where its presence might be an embarrassment to those who are not religious. Some of these controversies will be addressed later in this chapter. It should be noted, however, that balancing the "establishment" clause with the "free exercise" clause has always required a neat tightrope act by the courts.

In fact, as a description of American history and American life, the metaphor of the "wall" between religion and public life could not be more inaccurate. The Pilgrims and Puritans came to New England for religious reasons. Religion has shaped decisive turning points in American history: the abolition of slavery in the nineteenth century; the prohibition of alcohol sales and consumption in the early years of the twentieth century (remnants of which still persist in state alcohol laws); and, more recently, the black civil rights movement. Religion is also part of the personal identity of most Americans; their denominational affiliation is an essential component of the way they think about themselves. Those who think religion has

no place in the public life of America only deceive themselves. Indeed, what they often mean is that *other* people's religions have no place in the public life of the country.

There are three aspects of the relationship between religion and public life: (1) religion and personal identity; (2) religion and party affiliation and voting; and (3) religion and public controversy.

RELIGION AND WHO YOU ARE

In most American communities, when a new family moves in people want to know "what they are." This includes a number of questions: What kind of occupation are they engaged in? Where do they come from? What is their religion? "He's Catholic and she's Jewish." "They're Protestants, Methodist I think." "They're Irish Catholics. Can't you tell by the name?" "Italian Catholics—she's devout, he doesn't go to church much." "Staunch Christians." "They're Missouri Synod Lutherans." "They're some kind of Asian religion."

None of these comments is meant to put down the new family. Rather, they locate the newcomers on a map of religious differences that most Americans carry around in the back of their heads. These maps are a kind of quick and easy way of figuring out where other Americans come from and who they really are. If the new neighbors are a certain kind of Protestant, you hardly will bring them a bottle of wine as a welcoming present or invite them to a card party or a dance. If they are Jewish you would want to be sure that bacon will not cause them a problem at brunch. If you're active in Democratic politics, you'd have reason to suspect that they might be on your side should they be Catholic.

If you know someone's religion, you have some preliminary hints about what kind of a person he or she might be. You may revise or confirm these preliminary notions as you get to know the person better, but they are tools that enable you to begin your relationship with the other in something more than total ignorance.

Moreover, when you tell someone what your religion is you're laying down for that person some preliminary notions of who you are and where you stand: "I'm Jewish, so don't tell anti-Semitic jokes in my presence," for example. Religion defines some of the boundaries that make us different from other people—not totally different, perhaps, but different enough to be important. Even if we tell others that we have no religion, or if we think the question is irrelevant and offensive and say so, we nonetheless place ourselves on the religious map and tell them something important about who we are and how we want to be treated. Even those who think religion is a purely private matter still have a pretty good idea of the religious identification of their friends and neighbors.

Religious affiliations, then, are part of the map that enables us to navigate through the uncharted waters of human relationships. Instead of encountering a mass of people about whom we know nothing and who seem totally like one another, we sort them out on several different criteria, one of which is religion. Think of the people you know reasonably well, your friends, neighbors, and family. How many are there whose religious affiliation you don't know? Chances are you can locate them in the three-part paradigm that embraces most Americans: Protestant, Catholic, Jew.

The more heterogeneous the place you live or go to school, the more likely religious identification is to be important to you and to others. If you live in a neighborhood where four out of five people are Italian Catholics, then the only codes that make much difference are "Italian" and "other." But if your neighborhood is a mix of many different kinds of people, then you are more sensitively tuned to these differences, not as a matter of principle but as a matter of practical necessity. This is an important point: Consciousness about religious identity does not result from an explicit conviction that you *should* know the religion of other people. Rather, it is an implicit and unself-conscious diagram that you need to have to find your way among others.

If you give a group of American young people a list of last names and ask them to provide the religion and ethnic background of each name, some of them will be right more than 90 percent of the time; none of them will be right less than 70 percent of the time. How do they know? They just know, that's all. "I mean, Kelly is Irish Catholic, isn't it?" Usually it is, though not always. (Indeed there are more Irish Protestants in the United States than Irish Catholics. The former tend to live in the South and in rural areas and to be descended from immigrants who came before 1820.)

"Gargiulo, that's Italian Catholic for sure."

You got it.

"Lewis . . . that's hard, but maybe it's Welsh and probably Methodist."

"Washington? If she's black I bet she's Baptist."

"Greenblum? Most likely Jewish."

Then ask them what kind of behavior they would expect at a party organized by these various people.

If the name is Kelly there would be, you'll be told, a lot of drinking. If the name is Gargiulo, there'll be a lot of hand waving. If Washington is a good Methodist or Baptist, there's not likely to be much drinking. If it's a Greenblum party, there'll only be a beer or two and a lot of heavy conversation.

These predictions are not necessarily accurate, nor does anyone believe that they are a hundred percent true. They are rather presuppositions with which we operate, models to be tested against further experience. They are benign stereotypes until one holds them despite contrary evidence.

Kelly may in fact be a Lutheran. Or she may be one of those rare Irish Catholics who don't drink at all. (I never had a drop to drink, save wine at the Eucharist, till I was thirty-six years old. Then I went to Italy and fell in love with wine but two glasses at the most.) If this happens we are mildly surprised but quickly correct our assumptions. Then we ask if Ms. Kelly's father is a lawyer and active in politics and learn that he is. Well, some of our predictions were accurate.

Religion (sometimes combined with ethnicity) provides us with a set of questions to ask (discreetly of course) about other people—and also a set of questions we expect to be asked about ourselves. No one is particularly surprised or offended by these sets of questions. They are considered "natural" questions to ask in our society.

In a country like Italy, where almost everyone has the same religion, or a country like England, where most people are vaguely identified with the same church, the religious question seems much less "natural" and other questions are necessary to shape our first and tentative impressions of strangers.

Why is it different in America? Mainly because we are a "nation of immigrants" (as President Kennedy said) from many different places and backgrounds (including the first Asian tribe that migrated across the Bering land bridge and settled in North America, though of course it didn't become North America for many thousands of years). In Italy the Italian style of intense family relationships is taken for granted by almost everyone. In the United States, the first time you meet a person you don't know how that person relates to his or her parents and brothers and sisters, and how tight a control the family is likely to exercise on his or her behavior. Religious (and ethnic) background gives you a hint of what to expect. The diversity of our origins makes religious affiliation so important (and so useful) in our country. It is a way to tell others who we are and to learn from others who they are.

These differences do not go away over time. Research shows that there is very little difference between the family patterns of those who identify as Irish in the United States today and the Irish in Ireland (a lot of conversation in both countries). And there is no difference at all on a wide variety of measures between Italians and Italian Americans (both groups are more likely than anyone else to turn to family members when they need help).

We usually are not conscious of the subtle but important role that religion plays in tentatively defining people and relationships and indeed are inclined simply to deny that role when someone begins to talk about it. It is therefore necessary to think about it for a while and to understand that in a religiously heterogeneous society, especially one with a long history of intense religious devotion, religious affiliation is a terribly important map through our society. This fact of religious pluralism and identification is the basis for the intricate and at times difficult relationship between religion and politics in America.

PARTY IDENTIFICATION AND VOTING

American electoral politics has been shaped through the years roughly by four major events:

1) The emergence of urban-rural differences at the time of the country's formation (Federalists tended to be urban, Republicans rural)

2) The Civil War (the North tended to be Republican, the South Democratic)

3) Industrialization (workers tended to be Democratic, businesspeople Republican)

4) Immigration, especially the massive immigration around the turn of the century (immigrants tended to be Democratic, native-born Americans Republican). Perhaps the most significant change in this pattern occurred in the 1930s when blacks, who had been Republicans because that party was responsible for the end of slavery, turned to the Democrats, who were on their side economically.

Obviously, the components of this four-part model overlap, which is why the great political coalitions that constitute the American political parties are so fractious. Moreover, a tendency is not an absolute prediction. Some immigrants and their children vote Republican. Some businesspeople are Democrats. Many people vote one way in presidential elections and another way in congressional elections—before 2008, most notably Democratic in congressional elections and Republican in presidential elections. Party identification is not as strong an influence in voting as it used to be.

Most Americans do tend to identify, however weakly, with one political party, usually the same party as their parents. Moreover, the choice of a party identification takes place at about the same time (early adulthood) as does the choice of religious identification—and as part of the same process: for example, Catholics who identify strongly with their church also tend to identify strongly with their political party. Both party and religious choice are components in forging your identity as you mature. Not everyone, of course, has both forms of identity, but most people do.

All that need concern us in this chapter is the generalization that Catholics and Jews tend to be Democrats, while Protestants, especially white Protestants who do not live in the South, tend to be Republicans. (And white Protestants in the South are shifting to Republican identification, particularly in presidential elections.) There are many reasons for these tendencies. When Catholics and Jews came to this country in large numbers, they were poor urban workers. The Republican Party represented—or was perceived to represent—the native born, who did not like the immigrants, and the well-to-do, who exploited them. The Democratic Party, on the other hand, already the party of white urban workers, quickly organized the immigrants and persuaded them that the party supported their causes. To look at the same process from a different perspective, the urban Democratic "machines" wanted the immigrants in their party and the affluent and native-born Republicans did not. The Democrats offered immigrants political power and jobs; the Republicans were much less likely to do so.

The Democrats also supported or came to support reforms that would benefit the immigrants and were congruent with their more communal social policies, while the Republicans remained the party of "rugged individualism." Thus social security, regulation of business and banks, unemployment insurance, legalization of unions, occupa-

tional health, and, in the case of Jews, support for Israel, became standard planks of the Democratic platform in the years between 1930 and 1950. These kinds of legislative programs confirmed the allegiance of Catholics and Jews to the Democratic Party despite subsequent developments.

Party positions on critical issues, however, were no more important than the matter of jobs in the big cities. The "machines" (which had been Protestant in many cities before immigration) were Catholic and Jewish, and they effectively traded influence, money, favors, and jobs for votes in the cities for many years. Republican Protestants often thought this exchange was corrupt and supported "reform" movements to "clean up" the cities and end political "corruption." However, when they gained political power it was usually their allies who got the jobs and the contracts.

The old "machines" are less powerful than they used to be because the children of the immigrants are no longer poor and Democratic Party organizations have less to offer the more recent immigrants (though they tend to be Democrats, too). The Irish Catholics, the first of the large immigrant groups and those with the most political skill, are reputed to have been the masters of "machine politics" and the dominant force in urban politics. There remain many big-city Irish mayors (think of Boston, San Diego, and especially Chicago in the early 1990s), and Irish Catholics still disproportionately choose political careers, in part it would seem because of their love for the political game.

It is often said that as Catholics became more affluent and moved to the suburbs they left the Democratic Party and joined the Republican Party because that's where their self-interest would be best served. In fact, most Catholics still identify as Democrats and almost two-thirds of them still vote for Democratic congressional candidates, as do four-fifths of Jews.

Is there a "Jewish vote" and a "Catholic vote"? If you mean, *Can the leaders of either*

Hispanic Voting Patterns: A Case Study of Immigrant Groups

The conventional wisdom has long been that Democrats hold sway with recent immigrants while subsequent generations may swing more toward the Republican Party after the immigrant group becomes more established, affluent, and educated. One contemporary immigrant group on which to test this theory is the growing Hispanic voting population. From the 1990s through 2004, this group voted for Republicans in growing numbers. Republican Bob Dole took home only 21 percent of the Hispanic vote in 1996, but in 2004 George W. Bush took home 40 percent of the group's vote, nearly doubling Republican inroads in less than a decade.

Moreover, by that 2004 election the Hispanic voting group had grown significantly in terms of size and influence, constituting nearly eight million actual election voters (which would become ten million by 2008). Also a hopeful sign for Republicans was that Hispanics had changed somewhat in their religious preference. Once almost wholly Roman Catholic, this immigrant group had begun diversifying religiously, sometimes embracing religions that were more likely to be conservative politically, such as evangelical Protestantism and Mormonism. Some pundits predicted that the growing Hispanic identification with the Republican Party might help swing the 2008 election for Republican candidate John McCain, especially in key battleground states like Florida, which has a sizeable Hispanic population.

However, this was not to be. Democratic candidate Barack Obama took the Hispanic vote in something approaching a landslide, with 67 percent, according to the Pew Research Center. This was especially impressive given that most Hispanic voters had supported Hillary Clinton, not Barack Obama, in the primary season, and some analysts had predicted that it would be difficult for them to transfer their loyalties to Obama in the general election.

What are the lessons to be learned here? First, of course, that elections boil down to each individual candidate as much as they do to broad general trends. Barack Obama was a tremendously popular, even historic, presidential candidate. Second, we learn that immigrant groups, like other communities, tend to vote their pocketbooks along with everyone else, perhaps even more so. In a year when an ailing economy became voters' paramount concern, Hispanics were no different from many other groups in voting Democratic. And finally, immigrant groups, no matter how well established in America, often vote for the candidate who is perceived as immigration-friendly. Although John McCain's personal positions on immigration were not substantively different from Barack Obama's, McCain's association with the Republican Party—some of whose spokespersons had taken a strong stand for strict border controls and English-only schools—may have hurt him with Hispanic voters.

---

religion "deliver" the votes of their people the way a skilled precinct captain could in the old days of the urban machines? then the answer is certainly no. Catholic bishops, for example, have been notoriously ineffective in persuading their laity to vote against "pro-choice" candidates—and most major Catholic political leaders believe that in a pluralistic society the woman herself must make the choice about abortion, despite what bishops might say. Jewish voters are deeply concerned about government policy toward Israel, but they do not need the guidance of Jewish leaders to demonstrate that support by voting for pro-Israel candidates (just as the Irish did not need their clergy to tell them to vote for congressional candidates who supported Irish Independence in 1920). Voters of both religions think for themselves. Their leaders do not dictate to them and indeed are often unsuccessful when they try to do so. In that sense there is no "Jewish vote" or "Catholic vote."

How, then, does it happen that Jews and Catholics still tend to be Democrats even when their purely economic interests might put them in the other party? Why do affluent Jews and Catholics still vote Democratic? Why are Jewish and Catholic Democrats more likely to vote for Democratic "pro-choice" presidential candidates, even when they don't like the candidate and think, as they have more often than not for the last twenty years, that the candidate is a "loser"? There are two reasons, one rational, the other non-rational (but not irrational).

The rational reason is that the religious imaginations of Jews and Catholics tend to be "communal." They picture society as organized into families, local groups, and communities, and they picture humankind as relating to God as members of such clusters of people. Therefore, they have a strong inclination to identify with a party that historically has supported human and community well-being over against rugged individualism. Neither religious tradition sees government intervention as inherently wrong or dangerous. Thus, they do not abhor an activist government and are more at ease with a party heritage that favors such government.

The "non-rational" reason is that Catholics and Jews still tend to think of Democrats as "us" and Republicans as "them." "They" didn't like "us" when "we" first came here and "they" still don't like "us" all that much. Only those who think that the history of one's religious community is unimportant will have trouble understanding this argument.

Another way of viewing the same phenomenon is to observe, as we have said, that party identification (at least a weak link to one party tradition or the other) is part of the personal identity of most Americans. Most, though not all, Americans end up choosing to identify with the party of their parents in young adulthood. Thus, party affiliation is to some extent a matter of inheritance, of choosing for "us" against "them."

By itself the inheritance of party affiliation would not be so strong if it were completely "non-rational" (as support for the Cubs or the White Sox is in Chicago, a very powerful if utterly "non-rational" choice—

particularly if you have the bad taste, as this writer thinks, to identify with the White Sox). However, when it is combined with different pictures of what a "good society" is and how humans relate to God, party inheritance on religious lines remains an important factor in American political life, regardless of how the mass media (whose commentators tend to be alienated from all traditions) try to minimize it.

There is no single "Catholic" issue like the State of Israel is a "Jewish" issue, which perhaps makes Catholic affiliation with the Democratic Party somewhat weaker. It also makes it more difficult for Democratic candidates on the national level to activate their potential Catholic supporters—not that any of the presidential candidates in recent decades have tried to do so. Thus, to appeal to the Catholics in their coalition, Democrats would have to stress issues of family, neighborhood, and local community that have special appeal to Catholics, though they appeal to many other Americans too.

It also should be said in passing that there is a certain kind of political style, an impression of somber self-righteousness, that may appeal to many Protestants but turns off many Catholics. (Some historians say that Catholics were virtually driven into the Democratic Party by the prohibition of alcohol during the 1920s.) Unfortunately for the Democrats, the style of their candidates from the 1960s to 2008 tended to rub Catholics the wrong way. The Catholic political "style" tends to emphasize loyalty and compromise, whereas one kind of Protestant political style tends to emphasize high political principle and integrity. Neither style is necessarily better than the other, but they are different and there's no point, particularly for the politician, in pretending that the difference does not exist.

Is there a Catholic vote or a Jewish vote or a Protestant vote? A directly and explicitly religious vote based on doctrine? No. An indirect vote, a correlation based on history, image, and style? Yes. And there is no sign of it going away.

How Does Religious Diversity Affect Political Behavior?

There is no doubt that religious identification is vital in shaping beliefs, values, and public life, and that it is instrumental in providing incentives for political action. The religion story, after all, is archetypal, tracking back to antiquity, and always vital in ordering the relations we have with one another in a political society. But, like all stories, the religion narrative is changing in the American political landscape. It is important that we monitor and understand these changes in order to understand politics in America.

Here are some recent findings: Various surveys show that the relative size of Christianity as a religious group is diminishing, and that many of the numerically small religious denominations, Christian and non-Christian, are on the rise. Also, and of most significance, the group that considers itself religiously unaffiliated has increased dramatically in the past few decades. Such findings do not present a tight and coherent pattern, or an irreversible trend, but they do suggest an historical shift towards greater religious diversity and volatility. These findings also indicate that the three-part paradigm traditionally used to depict religious identification now only extends to 80 percent of all Americans.

Two interesting and contrary observations can be drawn from these transitions: First, greater overall diversity, in part attributable to the strengthening of small religious groups, intensifies the need for religion as a *plural*, not a singular, marker of social and political orientations. If people are religious in many more ways than in the past, a thick *and* varied set of religious identifications is eminently useful in negotiating the political scene. Second, we need more information on the increasing number of Americans who report no religious affiliation (a group that presumably can range from diehard atheists, conventional secular believers, and people who just provide benign report that religion means very little to them). This unaffiliated group is not traditionally considered part of the religious history of the United States. But it must be considered now given its increasing size. Also, the religious origins of the group are relevant. One sector consists of people who have disaffiliated themselves from previous religious memberships. This is an important fact. A disaffected religious believer—an ex-Catholic, for example—is obviously different from a nonbeliever with no history of religious affiliation.

What do these changes suggest in practical terms? The creation of independent value systems? A heightened complexity in religious beliefs? A new sense of social identification? Then what are the empirical implications? The notorious burlesque line is apt: Predictions are unreliable, especially when they refer to the future. Changing patterns of religious affiliation *may* affect party identification and voting behavior. The spectacle of a growing segment of the American population declaring that they have no affiliation with a religion is the main puzzle, a practical spectacle that demands explanation. It is a simple fact that any group consisting of 14 percent of the population—in this case the group professing no religious affiliation—constitutes an important segment of the electorate. But, like many groups, the religious-unaffiliated group is not really a group in the political sense. It is not monolithic. Its constituency is distributed unevenly across both the Democratic and Republican Parties. Some of its members are politically independent. Little in the way of political demands is associated with the group. Perhaps a contrarian conclusion can be drawn: the growing numbers of people professing no religious affiliation might be yet one more correlate of the decline in party identification acknowledged in American politics today.

At one time religion was an excellent indicator of political convictions and actions. But now the landscape is different. Religion in America is undergoing change, both across religions and from the religious to the unaffiliated. But the meaning and causal effects of these changes are unclear. Religious diversity and the growth in nonreligious affiliation may be decisive in carving out social and political norms, or they may not be. What we are bearing witness to may itself be a transient phase on its way to a past configuration. The one verity in this set of mutable conditions is that religion, as the expression of some of our deepest and unassailable beliefs, remains a critical though more complicated entry in the vast panorama of American politics.

RELIGION AND PUBLIC CONTROVERSY

Religion, it is often said, ought not to be involved in public controversy over political issues. That often means, however, that it's all right for religious leaders to take a stand in favor of my side, but it's wrong when they oppose my side. If I support a war and religious leaders support it, they're nothing but patriotic Americans. If I support the same war and they oppose it, they are traitors. If I oppose a war and they oppose it, they are courageous leaders. If I oppose a war and they support it, they have failed to teach religious truth. One must beware, therefore, of those who tell you that religion should not become involved in politics. What they usually mean is that religion ought not to be on the other side.

A certain Catholic bishop in a western state condemned a Catholic candidate who was running on a ticket of racial hatred, and the bishop was praised by many good "liberals" for this outstanding exercise of religious leadership. Subsequently, he denounced a "pro-choice" Catholic candidate and was roundly condemned for interfering in a political campaign by many of the same people. When I pointed out the inconsistency to a pro-choice supporter who was appalled at the bishop's action, I was told, "But racial hatred is sinful!"

Many conclusions about the relationship between politics and religion in America can be drawn from that little story, not least of which is the old dictum that it depends on whose ox is being gored. If my ox is being gored, then I want the clergy on my side. If your ox is being gored, the clergy have no right to intervene.

A second conclusion is that the typical American (indeed the typical human) tends to think that morality is on his or her side and immorality on the other side. Religion should back morality and condemn immorality. Hence, it should always be on my side.

A third conclusion is that Americans are not very good at listening to the "story" that lies behind the position that the other side is taking. Nor are they very good at admitting that those who disagree with them can do so in goodwill and good faith.

The abortion issue currently is a classic case. Pro-choice and pro-life activists do not listen to each other and do not concede to each other even the beginnings of good faith and goodwill. It is not the first time in American history that such conflict has occurred and presumably it will not be the last.

In fact, there is little difference between typical Catholics and typical Protestants in their attitudes toward the *legality* of abortion. More than nine out of ten approve of the legality of abortion when there is a threat to the mother's life or health. More than six out of ten disapprove of it when the mother simply does not want another child. (Black Protestants are more likely to disapprove of legal abortion than white Protestants, indeed more likely to disapprove of it than white Catholics.) However, such "balanced" or "inconsistent" opinions (depending on your perspective) are anathema to the activists on both sides of the debate, and the activists set the tone and terms of the public debate. Jews are more likely to support "abortion on demand" than are Christians, though not by any means all Jews, especially the Orthodox. The "secularists" (those with no religion at all) are the most likely to approve of abortion.

Both sides of the controversy are in favor of life in the sense that they think their position is the most supportive of human life. Very few people think that it would be permissible to kill a newborn baby if the mother did not want it. Almost everyone would agree that the baby is a human person. Most people would also say that a fetus that can survive outside its mother's womb is a human person. The pro-choice side (generally) denies that a human person is present until viability is achieved and hence argues that the termination of a pregnancy is not murder. The pro-life side says that the human person exists from the first moment of conception and hence abortion is murder.

Moreover, most of those on both sides are convinced that their position is self-evidently true and that the other side is not only in error but in bad faith.

"Life begins at the moment of conception," a Catholic pro-life advocate will tell you. "We've always known that is true because God has revealed it to us."

One might want to argue that many Catholic theologians in ages past disagreed, believing that life did not begin for several months (though they had different biological models than we do today). However, the point is that the Catholic tendency is to think of life beginning early. (The fundamentalist pro-life advocate would probably say the same thing as the Catholic in this dialogue.)

"We don't consider a fetus to be a person," a Jewish pro-choice advocate might reply, "until it exists outside the womb."

"You're wrong," says the Catholic, "and you know you're wrong."

"No," says the Jew. "You're wrong and you're trying to impose your religious ideas on me."

"Abortion is mass murder just like the holocaust," says the Catholic.

"Don't talk to me about holocaust," says the Jew.

If a secularist were present at this shouting match, he or she might contend that both are wrong to worry about when human life begins. The issue is really the welfare of the mother. No one may tell a woman what to do with her body. She and she alone has the right to choose what is best for her own happiness. It is certainly true that society has always found it difficult to force a woman to bring a baby to term when she does not want to. However, many pro-choice advocates see no problem with accusing the mother of a baby born addicted to cocaine, or with a law that imposes punishment on a woman who ingests too much alcohol into her body and then drives a car. In fact, this response would not bother the secularist, who in all probability does not believe in God or life

after death, does not accept the need for a consistent moral system, and thinks that human happiness is necessarily the basis for all moral choice.

Each of these positions is profoundly religious in the sense that it is based on a religious "story" that tells of the meaning and purpose of human life and of the way humans should live if they are to be fully human. Each story comes from a tradition that is ancient and usually unexamined. In most people the traditional story is so strong and so unself-conscious as to seem self-evident and unarguable. Therefore, the other side is wrong and proper religion has no choice but to denounce it.

The conflict, then, is less about abortion than about why humans exist at all (a profoundly religious question). Each side assumes that anyone with half an ounce of sense and a modicum of integrity *knows* that its story is correct.

A related issue, of course, is whether in a pluralistic society like the United States, in which many different stories are told, one has the right to try to impose by law on others the conclusions drawn from one's own religious story. However that question may be answered, one might still make a case that religious leadership ought to ask its members to at least listen to the story on the other side.

On issues that involve major moral questions (issues about how humans should behave, and hence what human existence means) religion will inevitably be drawn into public conflict. Northern religious leaders were among the leading advocates of the abolition of slavery. A certain kind of Protestant religious leadership, convinced that the consumption of alcohol is wrong, imposed the Prohibition amendment on the rest of the country (and still imposes laws regulating the sale and consumption of alcohol). The leaders of the civil rights movement were and are for the most part black clergy. The Constitutional right of freedom of speech guarantees the right of religious leaders to take public stands on what they take to be critical moral issues. Such public intervention in the political order can be prohibited only by denying freedom of speech to religious leaders. (Whether such intervention is always wise, prudent, appropriate, or even likely to be effective is another matter.)

The suggestion of some secularists that churches ought to lose their tax-exempt status if they take such moral stands on public issues is in effect an attempt to deprive religion of freedom of speech by taking away from it a privilege that it has long enjoyed. Despite the secularist complaint, the tradition of religious involvement (based on religious stories) in major political issues that are also moral issues is too old and too powerful in America ever to be abolished. We must understand that this involvement becomes exceedingly controversial when the issues are based on conflicts between underlying stories about human nature and the meaning of human existence.

For example, a strong component in the traditional Protestant story is a conviction that human nature is "fallen" and is therefore fundamentally perverse. Left to its own amusements, human nature will engage in all kinds of "wicked," "unseemly," or "Godless" behavior. Therefore, to preserve social order and to protect men and women from their own wickedness, the government should intervene to forbid such evil as drinking, gambling, dancing, and smoking, especially on the Sabbath. Dancing you can pretty much get away with these days. Smoking has become a public health rather than a religious issue. What President Hoover called the "noble experiment" of Prohibition ended more than seventy-five years ago. But you still can't buy liquor on Sunday in many states. And many states forbid gambling or regulate it closely.

The Catholic story of human nature is more benign. The human personality may be "flawed" but it is not fallen. Legal efforts to constrain humans to virtuous lives are not likely to work. There is nothing wrong with a drink, a game of cards, or a dance (though the old-fashioned Irish clergy would have disagreed on the last). They are harmless human amusements that, within proper limits, can legitimately be enjoyed.

To the strict Protestant this story sounds like a pact with the devil. To the Catholic the Protestant response sounds like Puritanism (which may be a bad word for Catholics but is not so bad for their Protestant counterparts).

Hence, when a law was being proposed in my state that would permit charitable organizations to run bingo games, a Protestant cleric said to me, "But gambling is wrong!" To him that conclusion was so self-evident that only the irredeemably corrupt or hypocritical could possibly deny it. So gambling continues to be illegal in one form or another in many states, although the laws are routinely broken in taverns, country clubs, athletic stadiums, and family card parties. Similarly, teenage drinking laws are on the books in every state, laws which are no more effective in preventing consumption of alcohol by young people than gambling laws are effective in preventing football pools.

Americans are often astonished to learn that other countries, especially Catholic countries, are much more lenient on the subject of young people's drinking than our country is. Currently, arguments about the effect of teenage drunken driving are used to support these laws, but logically such arguments would lead again to total Prohibition. A twenty-two-year-old is no less likely to be drunk at the wheel of a car than a twenty-year-old. It would be more appropriate to use mechanisms in cars such as combination locks on the ignition that would prevent someone who was drunk, at whatever age, from starting a car. Moreover, young people might drink less if it were not forbidden.

Another current controversial issue is the matter of religion in public places. Secularists, along with many other Americans

(Protestant, Catholic, and Jewish), believe that there should be no religious instruction or prayer in the public schools, no displays of religious symbols (nativity scenes, menorahs, etc.) in or near public places, no prayer at high school or state college graduations, and no prayer before athletic contests in public stadia or when the contestants are from public schools.

The courts currently are wrestling with these issues. It should be clear, however, that the legal arguments are masks for underlying "stories" about the meaning of human life. One story believes that human life will be better if religion is banned in every possible place, or at least that the "purity" of religion is contaminated if it is used at every possible secular occasion. The other story believes that religion is an essential part of human life and ought not to be excluded.

National survey data show that, despite court rulings, Americans overwhelmingly support some kind of prayer in public schools. However, that issue, like the others mentioned above, is not sufficiently important for enough people to generate massive voting blocs. Hence the conflict is waged between elite pressure groups (and their lawyers) on both sides.

The "story" still matters and matters greatly in American political life.

CONCLUSION

Most Americans are repelled by noisy religious controversy. The self-righteousness and dogmatism that often accompany such controversy somehow offend the American propensity to permit the other person the right to his or her own opinion. Many American religious leaders are also cautious about becoming too involved in political debate because they sense such involvement may be more harmful than helpful to religion. Yet, because of the different stories that underpin the different religious traditions (and the different versions of the stories within each tradition), major political disagreements over moral issues will certainly call forth some religious participation—always welcome when the leaders happen to be on your side!

Such exercise of the rights of freedom of expression and freedom of assembly are part of the American way. They seem messy and troubling only when the alternative is not seriously considered. Nonetheless, it does not seem contrary to the American tradition to hope that those who mix religion and politics will remember that it is also part of the American way to respect the opinions, integrity, and goodwill of others and at least to listen sensitively when they try to present the "stories" that support their political positions.

STUDY QUESTIONS

1. What does "separation of church and state" mean to you? Give examples of how you see such separation reflected in American society. Give examples of how church and state appear not to be separated.

2. How does your religion reflect who you are? Why do we often want to know what religious community people belong to when we first meet them? What does the author mean when he says that religious affiliation is a "map" for guiding us through human relations?

3. How does religious affiliation affect the way Americans vote? Give specific examples. Do you believe these examples are merely stereotypes? Can there really be a "Jewish vote" or a "Catholic vote"? Why? Why not?

4. Why do people believe that it is powerful to have religion on their side in arguments about public policy? Does religion always stand on the side of morality?

5. Why is it important to place positions on public policy within the context of religious story? In this context, what gives "story" its power?

6. What is the secularist position concerning religion and public policy in America? Why do secularists argue that religion should not interfere in public policy?

ESSAY TOPICS

The Separation of Church and State in America: Why It Does Not Exist

The Separation of Church and State in America: Why It Is Important

Images of Church and State in Government and Religion

Religion, State, and Abortion (feel free to choose any other issue)

Being American and Jewish (or Christian, Muslim, Buddhist, etc.)

The Seculariziation of America

WORD EXPLORATION

The following words play significant roles in any discussion of religion and politics in America and are worth careful reflection and discussion.

Secular	Nationalism	Patriotism
Public Policy	Secularist	Religion

FOR FURTHER READING

Bishop, Bill. *The Big Sort: Why the Clustering of Like-Minded America Is Tearing Us Apart.* Boston/New York: Houghton Mifflin Company, 2008.

Campbell, David E., ed. *A Matter of Faith: Religion in the 2004 Presidential Election.* Washington, D.C.: Brookings Institution Press, 2007.

Gutterman, David S. and Andrew R. Murphy, eds. *Religion, Politics, and American Identity: New Directions, New Controversies.* Lanham, Md.: Lexington Books, 2006.

Hargreaves, Alec G., John Kelsay, Sumner B. Twiss, eds. *Politics and Religion in France and the United States.* Lanham, Md.: Lexington Books, 2007.

Hulsether, Mark. *Religion, Culture and Politics in the Twentieth-Century United States.* New York: Columbia University Press, 2007.

WEB SITES

http://www.rna.org/library.php
  Online resources and links on religion

http://pewforum.org/
  The Pew Forum On Religion and Public Life

http://www.thearda.com/
  The Association of Religion Data Archives

22

Religion and Society in America

WILLIAM SCOTT GREEN

1670	William Penn publishes his *Great Case of Liberty of Conscience*
1776–1783	Revolutionary War
1818	Congregational Church is disestablished as the official religion of Connecticut
1868	The Fourteenth Amendment requires states to provide equal rights to all their residents
1879	Supreme Court determines that religious duty is not a sufficient defense for criminal activity
1947	Supreme Court applies religious establishment clause of the First Amendment to the states
1962–1963	Supreme Court finds it unconstitutional for schools to impose mandatory prayer for students
1972	Supreme Court grants Amish students an exemption from secondary school requirements on the grounds of free exercise of religion
1994	Supreme Court nullifies a school district that had been drawn to accommodate a Hasidic sect

When it comes to religion, America is different. The uniquely American value of the separation of church and state makes the role of religion in American society, politics, and culture distinctive and complex. Religions from the ends of the earth converge and flourish in America. What does the presence of the world's religions in America tell us about the country's character? Conversely, how does the American experiment with religion affect religion? This chapter considers these questions.

THE CHRISTMAS CHALLENGE

Religion matters because it affects people's daily lives, so a good way to begin thinking about religion in America is to focus on a typical, real-life event. Consider the following story:

It is a cold December morning in a small rural northeastern city, and Joey's father is going to school. Joey is the only Jew in the second grade of the municipal grammar school, and his father is going there to tell his son's class about the Jewish holiday of Hanukkah.

Explaining Jewish holidays to his son's schoolmates is not something Joey's father normally does. He did not go to his son's school in the fall to explain the Jewish New Year (*Rosh Hashanah*), the Day of Atonement (*Yom Kippur*), and the Festival of Booths (*Sukkot*), and he is not planning to go again in the spring to tell them the stories of Purim and Passover (*Pesah*). Although all those holidays are more important than Hanukkah in the Jewish religious calendar, they usually do not attract much general interest. But Hanukkah falls in the winter, usually in December, and its proximity to Christmas gives it a visibility in American culture and a consequence in American Jewish life that are far out of proportion to its minor significance in Jewish religion. Many Americans, Jews and non-Jews alike, regard Hanukkah as a Jewish counterpoint to Christmas. And, in fact, it is precisely the impact of Christmas on the life of Joey's

school that prompted his father to ask permission to make his visit.

Joey goes to a public school, but the Christmas holiday has been the center of the school's activities since before Thanksgiving. Christmas decorations are everywhere. Trees and ornaments blanket the corridor walls, Santas are stenciled in classroom windows, Christmas cookies are served in the cafeteria, the third and fourth grades are writing in-class letters to Santa Claus, and the fifth grade plans a Christmas pageant for the whole school.

Most of the people in this small city either are Christians or have a Christian heritage. For them the sights and sounds of Christmas are natural, uncontroversial, culturally affirming, and inviting. But for non-Christian Americans—whether Muslims, Jews, Buddhists, Hindus, secularists, or others—those same sights and sounds can be, and often are, vivid indicators of separation, exclusion, and minority status. Indeed, recent court cases about the permissibility of displaying a nativity scene on public property suggest that the symbols of Christmas may now exemplify the challenge of living with differences that religious pluralism presents to American society.

The presentation about Hanukkah begins well. The students are intrigued by the special Hanukkah candelabra (*menorah*) and the prospect of lighting candles. They delight in the Hanukkah top (*dreydl*) children play with during the holiday. Most of all, they love the idea of eight nights of gifts. In the midst of this easy cheer, one student turns to Joey with a question, "Do you celebrate Christmas too?" Before the father can answer, another boy blurts out, "Oh no! Jews can't have Christmas because they think Jesus hasn't come yet." This remark makes some students uncomfortable. They look at Joey. "You don't believe in Jesus? Why not?" Joey stiffens, uncertain how to answer. His father, feeling awkward, begins to reply, but the teacher quickly intervenes. "There are many different religions and peoples in the world," she says, "and we should respect them all. But the important thing is that people are really the same underneath." The tension eases, and the lesson ends.

Almost every day across America—in schools, clubs, and homes; on dates; at weddings, funerals, and family reunions; in living rooms and even bedrooms—some version of this story takes place. Americans of varied religious traditions and convictions encounter one another and try to deal with their differences. That encounter frequently—perhaps usually—creates tension and confusion. Typically, the tension and confusion are resolved, as in our story, through an easy affirmation of pluralism ("There are many different religions and peoples in the world . . .") but a denial of the significance and consequences of difference (". . . people are really the same underneath"). In a down-to-earth way, our story illustrates a central feature—some might say a dilemma—of religion in America. At the level of political principle, America has a national commitment to religious liberty. But at the practical level of everyday living, religious difference is a sensitive and awkward topic in American life. The story and the problem it illustrates prompt a question: What is unique about the American context for religion? Is there something special about religion in America?

DISESTABLISHMENT: THE SEPARATION OF CHURCH AND STATE

The political principles that preserve religious liberty in America illustrate the core American values of freedom of religion and the separation of church and state, as expressed in the First Amendment to the Constitution of the United States. These values have shaped the way Americans perceive, understand, and practice religion. Let us briefly review the main features of the First Amendment and then ask about its consequences for religion in America. The First Amendment states: "Congress shall make no law respecting an establishment of religion, or prohibiting the free exercise thereof; or abridging the freedom of speech, or of the press; or the right of the people peaceably to assemble, and to petition the Government for a redress of grievances." The First Amendment declares freedom of religion to be a fundamental civil right of all Americans. Significantly, it lists religious liberty together with other freedoms, particularly freedom of speech and freedom of the press. This is an important and revealing association that Americans often overlook. Just as free speech and a free press shape, ground, and define American politics, society, and culture, so too does freedom of religion. Religious liberty is a basic freedom that gives American life its distinct character.

It is well to note that the language of the First Amendment applies only to the federal government, not to state governments. However, in two important modern cases, *Cantwell v. Connecticut* (1940) and *Everson v. Board of Education* (1947), the Supreme Court of the United States included the First Amendment within the Fourteenth Amendment, which was ratified in 1868. The Fourteenth Amendment reads, in part, "No State shall make or enforce any law which shall abridge the privileges or immunities of citizens of the United States; nor shall any State deprive any person of life, liberty or property, without due process of law." By asserting that the Fourteenth Amendment applies to and includes the First Amendment, the Supreme Court holds all states to the standards of the First Amendment.[1]

American freedom of religion is based on an idea called "disestablishment," which denies to the government the power to endorse or support ("establish") religion. The disestablishment of religion—more popularly known as the separation of church and state—aims, in the words of Justice Wiley B. Rutledge, to "create a complete and permanent separation of the spheres of religious activity and civil authority."[2] The United States was the first nation in history to apply the separation of church and state as a practical political principle, the first nation to make disestablishment of religion a foundation of its national life. It is important to note that the disestablishment of religion was advocated by and largely achieved through the efforts of religious minorities—from Baptists to Quakers—in several of the original states. They did not want the denominations that constituted the majority in their states to control their religious life.

The First Amendment is composed of two clauses: the so-called Establishment Clause and the Free Exercise Clause. The meaning of the Establishment Clause ("Congress shall make no law respecting an establishment of religion") is explained in a classic statement by Justice Hugo L. Black:

> The "establishment of religion" clause of the First Amendment means at least this: Neither a state nor the Federal Government can set up a church. Neither can pass laws which aid one religion, aid all religions, or prefer one religion over another. Neither can force nor influence a person to go to or remain away from church against his will or force him to profess a belief or disbelief in any religion. No person can be punished for entertaining or professing religious beliefs or disbeliefs, for church attendance or nonattendance. No tax in any amount, large or small, can be levied to support any religious activities or institutions, whatever they may be called, or whatever form they may adopt to teach or practice religion. Neither a state nor the Federal Government can, openly or secretly, participate in the affairs of any religious organizations or groups and vice versa. In the words of [Thomas] Jefferson, the clause against establishment of religion by laws was intended to erect "a wall of separation between Church and State."[3]

The Free Exercise Clause of the First Amendment (". . . or prohibiting the free exercise thereof") inhibits the government—except in certain kinds of cases, such as child welfare—from restricting or controlling people's religious beliefs or behavior.

How are these two clauses applied in practice? For our purposes two brief examples will suffice. In interpreting and applying the Establishment Clause, the Supreme Court has ruled that a school district may not display the Ten Commandments in classrooms because that would be government advocacy of religion.[4] To protect free exercise, the Court has ruled that the state may not require the children of the Old Order Amish to attend public secondary school because the group regards such schooling as a sin.[5] The government would be forcing people to transgress their own teachings and would thereby violate their right to the free exercise of their religion.

It is useful to observe—particularly for readers of this book—that most of the legal battles over the Establishment Clause have been fought in the arena of education. The combination of a system of compulsory education and the separation of church and state has made the expression of religion in public schools—from prayers in classrooms or at assemblies or graduations, to Bible study on school property, to the content of textbooks—a thorny and difficult legal issue.

In fact, American education divides over the issue of religion. On the one hand, although studying religion—as opposed to instruction in religion or in how to be religious—has been affirmed by the Supreme Court as legitimate, concern about violating the Establishment Clause or offending local constituencies keeps religion out of the curricula of most American public school systems. On the other hand, more than 90 percent of private schools in America are religious or of religious origin. One important reason that religious difference is a delicate topic in American conversation is that, historically, too few Americans have had the opportunity to study it and learn how to think about it.

Let us now explore how the First Amendment shapes the way religion is understood and practiced in American life, and how it

The Religious Origin of Freedom of Religion

In the United States, the freedom of and from religion depends on what we call the separation of church and state, on the idea that religion and government do not and should not coincide. The separation of religion and government depends on the conception that religion and government are distinct entities, and that they serve different purposes.

People often think that the separation of religion from government is a secular idea. However, the separation of church and state could not work as a guiding social, legal, and political principle if it were plausible only to secular thought. To be effective and actually shape a society, the idea has to make sense to the society's religion as well. The biblical heritage of the West helps explain why both Judaism and Christianity are traditionally comfortable with the religious pluralism guaranteed by the First Amendment.

Judaism and Christianity are both ancient Mediterranean religions that developed under foreign domination. They were not religions of free people. When they began, neither religion could constitute a government or run a state. The Pentateuch (the first five books of the Bible), which is basic to both religions, was edited under the domination of the Persian state. Judaism persisted in the ancient Mediterranean in large measure because of Roman indulgence. Julius Caesar granted privileges to the Jewish religion that lasted for three centuries and made Judaism both politically legitimate and politically dependent. As a breakaway version of Judaism, early Christianity was seen by Rome as illegitimate and had no possibility to govern. Until the conversion of Constantine in the fourth century, it operated under Roman domination but largely outside of Rome's political structures.

We can see this context in the biblical texts both religions produced. The Pentateuch, for example, barely mentions a king for Israel, and the king plays no role in Israel's worship. The Hebrew Bible as a whole supposes that while God can be king, the Israelite king cannot be a god. It thus draws a clear distinction between religion and government. In the New Testament, Jesus' famous admonition to render unto Caesar what is Caesar's and unto God what is God's assumes that Caesar is *not* God, and thus presupposes this biblical distinction.

The heritage of the Hebrew Bible created a legacy of a religion without politics, of a religion that did not need to govern in order to succeed. There is no mandate to govern in either Judaism's or Christianity's earliest texts and conceptions of politics. This is why the separation of church and state can make sense in religious as well as secular terms. If Judaism and Christianity had regarded the separation of church and state as blasphemy, heresy, or irredeemable nonsense, freedom of religion might not have taken root in American life as it has.

reveals and expresses a distinct American attitude toward religion.

RELIGION AS A NATIVE CATEGORY

The very language of the First Amendment assumes a domain of behavior and thought, a realm of experience, called "religion," that is a normal and familiar aspect of American life. By naming religion and setting it apart for special consideration, the Constitution embeds the notion of religion in American culture so that it seems a natural part of the way things are. Because of the First Amendment, American culture easily assumes that there is an aspect of life called religion that can be distinguished from other aspects, such as politics, law, psychology, or economics.

This does not mean that the First Amendment assumes or requires that all Americans are or must be religious. On the contrary, in America freedom *of* religion implies freedom *from* religion, both from religion in general and from someone else's religion in particular.

Religion is so unquestioned and uncontroversial a part of American life that it can be called a native category. A native category is a fundamental concept, a basic classification, that people use to identify and explain to themselves what is happening to them. A classification is a native category if it is so elemental in a society that it carries cultural weight and so familiar that people use it constantly and intuitively; they know what it means without needing to define it.

Native categories usually don't travel well from one culture to another. They have connotations, nuances, and shades of meaning that are understood in one society but not in another. Sports terms are a kind of native category. Terms like "strike out" and "home run" have meaning for most Americans beyond the baseball field. But these terms, so familiar to us as categories of value ("I hit a home run on my math test," "I struck out with Laura last night"), are meaningless to Europeans, and explaining them to people from other cultures is not easy. The idea of "stress" is one of modern America's newest native categories. People use it constantly to explain their feelings or account for their actions. They know that "stress" can make you ill, or worse. They know what stress is, acknowledge its importance, but would have difficulty giving a precise definition of it.

Because of the First Amendment, religion is a native category of American culture. The Constitution assumes religion as a given. Americans use religion prominently both to distinguish our culture from others (as when elected officials once described Communist states as "godless") and to differentiate individuals within our culture. A consequence of the First Amendment is that Americans take religion for granted as a meaningful and conventional trait of being human. But because religion is a native category, we grasp it intuitively rather than spell it out. We think better *with* religion than we do *about* it.

RELIGION AS PLURALISM

By restricting government control over religion, the First Amendment guarantees that America will have more than one religion. It affirms that religion is a legitimate, legally protected form of difference in American society. Americans are supposed to differ from one another religiously. The First Amendment means that America is multireligious by design and not because of an accident of history or immigration. As we have seen, America is the first nation of history to declare itself religiously pluralistic. Religious difference was built into America from the start, and it is a hallmark of national life.

The guarantee of multiple religions undermines any claim that America has a particular or even a fundamentally national religious character. Some people commonly assert that "America is a religious nation" or "a Christian nation." Even if, in a general way, such claims reflect major preferences of Americans at certain times in the nation's history, they misrepresent the character of America. Freedom of religion is a basic civil right that allows multiple religions to flourish in America.

Let us see how the First Amendment works to ensure religious pluralism in America. We often suppose that the First Amendment limits only how the government may act, but that view is somewhat misleading. Because it protects the "free exercise" of religious behavior, the First Amendment forbids any religion to use the legal system to restrict another religion. No religion in America can plausibly claim that it is the only one here or that it alone has a mandate to shape, govern, or monitor people's values and behaviors. The legal scholar Stephen L. Carter notes that the "fundamental message of the Establishment Clause . . . is one of religious *equality* . . ."[6] As its earliest advocates intended, the First Amendment protects and preserves the perspective of religious minorities. It thereby makes religion into an effective vehicle for the expression of dissent.

The First Amendment limits the way religion can manifest power in American life. Although religions may seek to affect the government, they cannot control it. In America, religions can attempt to influence the government by persuading individual voters or elected officials—as they have done on a host of important issues, including slavery, prohibition, civil rights, the war in Vietnam, and abortion—but religions cannot become the government or advance or enforce their doctrines through it. American culture regards religion and government as distinct categories, and the two in principle are not to be confused with each other.

Because they cannot have the backing, confirmation, and power of governmental resources and agencies, religions in America are by necessity voluntary. Many observers think that religions retain their strength among Americans—as they decline in importance in other nations—because, with the separation of church and state, they have to earn their keep. To persist, religions in America must know how to appeal to, and engage the interest of, a broad public audience. Moreover, they must perpetually contend with one another as well as with non-religion and even anti-religion. As they compete to keep their members and attract new ones, religions in America watch one another and adapt as in the case of Hanukkah and Christmas.

But the adaptation of America's diverse religions to a context of freedom and competition—and the constant option of non-religion—can only go so far. By their nature, religions tend not to compromise on their core beliefs, teachings, and rituals but to affirm that they are right and that they work. As readers of this book doubtless have already learned, different religions really are different, and their values, practices, and worldviews often are irreconcilable. In a word, for all their capacity to adapt to different political and social settings, at a fundamental level religious teachings are non-negotiable. That is another reason religious difference makes people uncomfortable. Often there is no way to overcome the difference. When it comes to religion, people are not "the same underneath," as Joey's teacher claimed.

The American doctrine of religious liberty, as expressed in the First Amendment, holds out the promise that American society can maintain the delicate and exquisite balance of the absoluteness of religious teaching and the relativism of religious pluralism, that it can allow religions to be true to themselves and to the American vision of a diverse society. It can make this promise, and make good on it, because the separation of church and state frees American society from needing to decide among religions, to prefer one over all, or all over none. The world's religions can thrive in the American setting because, although each may judge the others misguided, in error, or just plain wrong, America as a nation cannot, and need not, pass such a judgment on any of them.

To see what is at stake in America's religious pluralism, let us conclude with an instructive historical example. In 1863 a group known as the National Reform Association, composed of eleven Protestant denominations, sought to amend the Constitution of the United States to say that America was a Christian nation. In place of the Constitution's preamble, which reads:

> We the People of the United States, in order to form a more perfect Union, establish Justice, insure domestic Tranquility, provide for the common defense, promote the general Welfare, and secure the Blessings of Liberty for ourselves and our Posterity . . .

they advocated the following words:

> We the people of the United States, humbly acknowledging Almighty God as the source of all authority and power in civil government, and the Lord Jesus Christ as the Ruler among the nations, His revealed will as the supreme law of the land, in order to constitute a Christian government . . . [7]

In light of the First Amendment, the differences between these two texts are stark and require no comment. Needless to say, the proposed amendment was defeated. Two years later, in 1865, in his Second Inaugural Address, Abraham Lincoln reflected on how both sides in the Civil War had invoked religion in behalf of their cause:

> Both read the same Bible, and pray to the same God; and each invokes his aid against the other. It may seem strange that men should dare ask a just God's assistance in wringing their bread from the sweat of other men's faces; but let us judge not that we not be judged. The prayers of both could not be answered—that of neither has been answered fully.

The American concept of religious liberty holds out the possibility that different religions—despite their often irreconcilable worldviews, value systems, and patterns of behavior—can coexist freely in a single country, and that, in Lincoln's terms, though the prayers of all will be offered, none will be answered fully. Religion is at the core of America's pluralism, and the First Amendment to the Constitution has made the recognition of religious difference in American life both a promise and a reality.

Notes

1. Leonard W. Levy, *The Establishment Clause: Religion and the First Amendment* (New York: Macmillan, 1986), 123.
2. Ibid., 124.
3. Ibid., 123–24.
4. *Stone v. Graham* (1980).
5. *Wisconsin v. Yoder* (1972).
6. Stephen L. Carter, *The Culture of Disbelief* (New York: Basic Books, 1993), 93.
7. Cited in James E. Woods Jr. and Derek Davis, eds., *The Role of Religion on the Making of Public Policy* (Waco, Tex.: J. M. Dawson Institute of Church-State Studies, 1991), 8–9.

STUDY QUESTIONS

1. Why, when it comes to religion, does the author believe that America is different? How do the ideas of Christmas and Hanukkah reflect the author's claim? Do you agree that America has a national commitment to religious liberty? Why?

2. Is the First Amendment to the Constitution a religious statement, a political statement, or both? What do you think the First Amendment says about the separation of church and state? Be specific.

3. What are the Establishment Clause and the Free Exercise Clause of the First Amendment? How is each important for religious liberty in America?

4. Why does the author believe that religion is a "natural part" of the way things are in America? Do you agree? What are the implications of such a statement for our understandings of religion? Does it help to explain the world's, as well as America's religious diversity?

5. What is the meaning of religious pluralism? Is America religiously pluralistic?

ESSAY TOPICS

David Koresh and the Branch Davidians: An Abuse of Religious Freedom?

Is America a Religious Nation?

The Christmas Holiday: Is It about Religion?

Prayer in School: Both Sides of the Issue

WORD EXPLORATION

The following words play significant roles in any discussion of religion and society in America and are worth careful reflection and discussion.

Liberty	First Amendment	Pluralism
Disestablishment	Religious Liberty	Civil Rights

FOR FURTHER READING

Feldman, Noah. *Divided by God: America's Church-State Problem and What We Should Do About It.* New York: Farrar, Straus, & Giroux, 2005.

Greenawalt, Kent A. *Religion and the Constitution.* Vol. 1: *Free Exercise and Fairness.* Princeton, N.J.: Princeton University Press, 2006.

———. *Religion and the Constitution.* Vol. 2: *Establishment and Fairness.* Princeton, N.J.: Princeton University Press, 2008.

Hamilton, Marci. *God vs. The Gavel: Religion and the Rule of Law.* Cambridge: Cambridge University Press, 2005.

Nussbaum, Martha C. *Liberty of Conscience: In Defense of America's Tradition of Religious Equality.* New York: Basic Books, 2008.

Sullivan, Winnifred. *The Impossibility of Religious Freedom.* Princeton, N.J.: Princeton University Press, 2005.

Witte, John Jr. *Religion and the American Constitutional Experiment.* 2nd ed. Boulder, Colo.: Westview Press, 2005.

WEB SITES

http://www.baylor.edu/church_state/splash.php
Web site of the J.M. Dawson Institute of Church-State Studies

http://www.firstamendmentcenter.org
Comprehensive coverage of First Amendment topics, including freedom of religion

GLOSSARY

A glossary is an important tool for study and reflection. Yet a glossary should never be read as the final or complete definition of the words contained within it. Words should be explored within the context they are written and with the studious awareness of the cultures out of which they come. Please keep in mind that the following words were taken from the preceding chapters and that the glossary serves only to point you back to your readings and reflections. These are not "the most important words" of each chapter; rather, they represent a beginning place for the study of all the words within each chapter.

abolitionists. People who were against slavery. Certain women played prominent roles in the abolitionist movement.

acculturation. The encounter of two or more cultures in which each adopts, subsumes, and/or embraces traditions, practices, and beliefs from the other culture(s).

Adventism. A religious tradition made up of many groups, of which the Seventh-day Adventists is the largest. Seventh-day Adventists believe in the imminent return of Jesus and the observance of the seventh day of the week (Saturday) as the Sabbath.

Adventists. People associated with the Seventh-day Adventist religious group, which stresses the second coming of Christ, or *parousia*, as a literal and imminent event.

African spirituality. The religious traditions and influences brought from Africa, often practiced in secrecy, that maintained African identity and influenced the American Christian tradition.

Allah. The Muslim name for God, who is the Creator, Sustainer, and Judge of the universe.

allegorical interpretation. Understanding the Bible as a symbolic or metaphorical document.

alternative religions. Religious communities that advocate religious doctrines and customs that are decidedly different from those in the cultures in which they emerge.

Anne Hutchinson. A powerful leader and representative of female piety in America during the 1630s, who claimed equal religious authority to her male counterparts.

apocalyptic groups. Groups that affirm that the second coming of Jesus will occur in the very near future.

apocalypticism. A collective term referring to religious views that focus on the revelation of divine mysteries relating to the end time, when God will appear to bring history to a closure. Most notable writings are the book of Daniel in the Hebrew Bible and the book of Revelation in the New Testament, though Islamic messianic themes also speculate about the final days.

ARC Triangle. In Scientology, the basic operatives of the universe: Affinity (emotional states), Reality (consensus on existence), and Communication (interchange of ideas).

astrology. The belief that the natural universe, the stars and planets, have an influence on life. Through the use of divination, signs, horoscopes, and other techniques, astrology has frequently encountered opposition from major religious groups because of its tendencies toward supplementing beliefs in the divine with dependence on the mysteries of the universe.

atman. The Hindu concept of the eternal spiritual essence of all persons, which is united with the universal principle of being—Brahman. Analogous to the "soul."

auditing. In Scientology, a formal process of spiritual treatment that occurs between a trained auditor and a parishioner. It functions to restore awareness of one's spiritual nature and facilitate spiritual growth, freedom, and progress toward salvation.

Báb. ("the Gate" in Arabic) Formerly known as Siyyid 'Alí-Muhammad (1819–1850), he is known as Báb to fellow Bahá'ís, one of the founders of the Bahá'í religion. He claimed to be the bearer of a new religion that succeeded the religion of Islam. The name also applies to the Bahá'í shrine in Haifa, Israel.

Babism. An early Iranian religion centered on the teachings of the founder Siyyid 'Ali-Muhammad. As a forerunner to Bahá'í, the movement challenged established Muslim teachings and suffered great persecution.

Bahá'í. A faith found in Iran in the mid-nineteenth century; the main tenets are the unity of all religions and the unity of all humankind.

Bahá'u'lláh. ("The Glory of God" in Arabic) The prophet and founder of the Bahá'í Faith. Formerly known as Mírzá Husayn-'Alí (1817–1892), he was a follower of the Báb, who taught that he fulfilled the many messianic hopes of religions around the world.

bar mitzvah. The advent of puberty for the male, a sacred ceremony in which family and friends celebrate a young boy's becoming responsible to his religious duties.

bat mitzvah. The advent of puberty for the female, a sacred ceremony in which family and friends celebrate a young girl's becoming responsible to her religious duties.

Bhagavad Gita. The most important religious text of classical Hinduism. The translation is, "Song of the Lord."

Bible. The sacred book of Christianity, including both the Old Testament (Hebrew Scripture) and the New Testament.

Blessing Ceremony. In the Unification Church, a mass wedding conducted by Rev. and Mrs. Moon.

blue laws. Laws aimed at regulating commercial and other activities on Sunday.

bodhisattva. The ideal Buddhist in Mahayana Buddhism and the path one must follow in order to become a Buddha.

Book of Mormon. For Latter-day Saints (Mormons), a second testament (after the Christian Bible) to the divine mission of Jesus Christ.

book of Revelation. The final book in Christian Scripture.

Brahma. In Hinduism, the creator God and one of three basic forms of the ultimate or absolute.

Brahman. The universal principle of being in Hinduism. The Absolute that exists in and beyond all things.

Brahmin. The priestly class of the Hindu religion; it is the highest caste of four castes in India and considered to be the most pure and educated of the peoples of India.

canon law. The rules and regulations that govern a church.

chosen people. Those who believe they have been selected by God for a special mission on earth.

The Christian Science Monitor. The daily newspaper of the Church of Christ, Scientist. *The Monitor* is published along with *The Herald of Christian Science*, *The Christian Science Sentinel*, and *The Christian Science Journal*.

Christotokos. The divine place of Mary in the Orthodox tradition. The word *Christotokos* means "the bearer of Christ."

Church of Scientology International. As one of the central organizations in Scientology, this group is responsible for managing the basic operations of the religion, such as ministerial training, publications, and the missions programs.

civil rights. The suggestion that in a democratic society all people are guaranteed the right to live freely within the nation's laws without discrimination because of race, gender, or national origin.

concealed church. The slave community's private practice of Christianity, which emphasized the Bible's treatment of such issues as freedom, exodus, and relief from suffering.

Confucianism. The practice, begun in China, that teaches that the family is the essence of social order and that filial piety is the origin of virtue. Particular ethical teachings are at the heart of its teachings. Its founder is Confucius, 551–479 B.C.E.

Constantinople. This city in Turkey, now known as Istanbul, represents to the Orthodox community what Rome represents to the Catholic community: the spiritual and geographical center of the church.

creeds. Formal statements of faith which reflect and embody the basic beliefs of a particular religious community.

cultic milieu. The collective term for the various nature religions in America, their organizations, members, beliefs, and practices.

Dao de jing. Written by Laozi, it is the basis of the tradition known as Daoism.

Daoism. A Chinese-based religious tradition that encourages its believers to follow the Way or Path in which the universe is unfolding. Human life must be at one with the natural order of all things.

denominationalism. The variety of churches within the Protestant tradition: Baptist, Methodist, Holiness, Presbyterian, Episcopalian, etc.

Dharma. Symbolized by a wheel, which has become the symbol of Buddhism, Dharma is the Buddha's teaching and embodies all that is the Buddha's life. As morality and righteousness, Dharma in Buddhism is universal, and social class is not relevant to it. In Hinduism, Dharma means virtue. Specifically it refers to the duties of a person's caste and the belief that those duties should be fulfilled willingly and well.

Dianetics. (Full title: *Dianetics: The Modern Science of Mental Health*) The best-selling book by L. Ron Hubbard, the founder of the religion of Scientology. The book focuses on individual self-enhancement through the experiences that are pure and clean in the present life.

disestablishment. Also known as the separation of church and state, this notion denies a government the right to encourage, endorse, or support a particular religion.

Divine Mind. A commonly used synonym for God among some Christian groups, including The Church of Christ, Scientist.

Divine Principle. The definitive writing for Rev. Sun Myung Moon and the Unificationist Church, dealing with the creation, fall, and restoration.

Doctrine and Covenants. For Latter-day Saints (Mormons), this is the third scripture (after the Christian Bible and the Book of Mormon). It contains the prophecies of Joseph Smith and his successors up to the present day.

El Cid. A great warrior considered a Christian hero in Spain following Spain's defeat at the hands of the Moors. "Cid" is an Arabic word meaning Lord.

encomiendas. A group of natives entrusted to Spanish settlers who, in turn, were responsible for their Christian education.

evangelical. The emphasis in Western Christianity on the proclamation of the Gospel that centers on conversion to the Christian faith as a way of salvation through faith in Jesus Christ.

feminist. A person who believes that women have equal rights, legally and economically, to men.

First Amendment. States that "Congress shall make no law respecting an establishment of religion, or prohibiting the free exercise thereof; or abridging the freedom of speech, or of the press; or the right of the people peaceably to assemble, and to petition the Government for a redress of grievances."

free will. The belief that individuals have complete control over their moral choices and their relationship with their God.

Gabriel. The Messenger Angel of Allah, who spoke the divine revelations of the Quran to Muhammad, the founder of Islam.

Great Awakening. A period before the American Revolution in Protestant America's religious development, which saw intense religious fervor and conversion to Protestant Christianity.

Hagia Sophia. The sixth-century church of Emperor Justinian, located in Constantinople. Hagia Sophia means "holy wisdom."

Hajj. The pilgrimage to the holy city Mecca required of all Muslims who have the health and the financial ability to make such a journey.

Heavenly Mother. According to Latter-day Saints (Mormons), a female deity who is the mother of all the "pre-mortal spirits" who become humanly embodied as earthly children.

Holocaust (Shoah). The murder of nearly six million Jews by Germany and its allies during the years between 1933 and 1945.

holy wine. In Unificationism, this is drunk at a marriage (Blessing Ceremony) and then sprinkled onto a white handkerchief, which is later used by the couple during the Three Day Ceremony (consummation).

iconography. Images of sacred value, often representing the lives of the saints of the church, which are honored with worship and adoration.

idealism. A philosophic and theological position that claims the highest reality, and foundation of existence, is mental.

imam. The prayer leader during Muslim worship. There is no priesthood in the Islamic tradition.

Islamic Fundamentalism. Also called *Islamic revivalism*, a movement that expresses the desire to restore Islam as a complete way of life in a Muslim society and state.

jihad. The Islamic notion of holy war in the more specific sense, or the defense of Islam against any opposition. The concept also applies to the general struggles in life for each Muslim who follows the will of Allah.

Joseph Smith. The founder of the Latter-day Saint (Mormon) religion lived from 1805 to 1844.

Kaba. The "House of God," or sacred cubical positioned in the center of the open-air mosque in Mecca. The most holy site in Islam, the Kaba is the point of focus for all Muslim *salat*, or prayers.

kami. In Japan, the gods, without human form, who make the divine presence known through image and symbol.

karma. In Buddhism, the belief that a person's life is governed by his/her actions.

Kingdom Hall. The congregational centers for Jehovah's Witnesses.

Kitáb-i-Aqdas. "The Most Holy Book" of the Bahá'í Faith, written by Bahá'u'lláh.

Laozi. The author of the *Dao de jing*, the primary text of Daoism.

limited atonement. The Christian belief that the death of Jesus on the cross effected the salvation for only those who have been predestined by God to become believers.

Madonna. Mary, the Mother of Jesus, is the most distinctive symbol of Catholicism. She represents the "mother-love" of God and a saintly intercessor for all believing persons.

Mahabharata. One of the great epic stories of India includes within its writings the *Bhagavad Gita*.

Mahayana. A movement within Buddhism, four centuries following the Buddha's death, which emphasized the life of the bodhisattva as the ideal life for the Buddhist to follow in order to be like the Buddha.

manifest destiny. The belief, beginning in the early 1800s, that the United States had the moral right to gain, hold, and develop all land from "sea to sea."

mass. A service of liturgy, song, and sacred text in celebration of the Eucharist, during which the body and blood of Christ become present in the elements of bread and wine.

Mecca. The holy city of Muhammad's birth and the city to which all Muslims must make a pilgrimage during their lifetime.

Medina. (Arab: *Yithrib*) The city located three hundred miles north of Mecca where the Islamic community was founded by Muhammad in 622 C.E. following his Hijra, or migration from Mecca. Muhammad is buried in Medina.

mental healing. The belief, held by members of the Church of Christ, Scientist, and other metaphysical communities, that the conscious (mental) realization of reality can eliminate all adverse physical conditions.

metaphysical. Literally: "beyond the physical." As an identifying term for religious communities, it refers to a general belief that the physical world is secondary to a higher spiritual realm and that the true identity of humans is found in the spiritual realm.

middle passage. The long, inhumane, and deadly ship journey between Africa and America, when slave traders brought Africans to the Americas.

millenarianism. The belief that Jesus' return will be followed by a thousand-year period (the millennium) when his followers will live with him in heaven.

Moors. Muslims who were conquerors of Spain in 711 C.E.

mosque. The sacred place of worship for Muslims.

Muhammad. Born in Mecca, lived 570–632 C.E., is the revealer of God's message to all Muslims and the supreme prophet of the Islamic tradition.

Muslim. One who submits to the teachings of Islam, believed to be God's will for human life, and belongs to the worldwide community of individuals (*ummah*) who embrace Islam.

Nation of Islam. A form of Islam (in the West), associated primarily with African Americans, which stresses separatism for the superior African American from a deceptive, white-dominated society.

nationalism. Devotion to one's nation, its policies, and actions.

nature religions. Systems of religious beliefs that view the natural universe to be a sacred, living entity. Pantheistic qualities of the divine are pervasively interrelated throughout the natural world.

New Age. An international socio-religious movement that originated in the West in the late 1960s and became prominent in the 1980s. It is syncretistic, strongly influenced by the Western esoteric tradition, and promotes personal and planetary spiritual transformation.

new dispensation. A biblical age or epoch.

nirvana. The end to the cycle of reincarnation and the ultimate moment of true peace with self and the world.

occultism. In the West, a system of beliefs in a supernatural realm that is accessible to trained initiates who, through practice, can learn its secrets and gain spiritual knowledge, wisdom, and power.

Omoto. Meaning "great source," a Japanese-inspired movement that began in 1892 with revelations given to a peasant woman, Deguchi Nao. The Omoto Movement emphasized healing, the importance of religious art, and the power of the mind.

oral tradition. Stories told orally by one person to others in order to pass a community's tradition from one generation to another, especially in Native American tribes.

orthodoxy. The right method of worship, theological practice, and belief. In the "Orthodox" tradition, orthodoxy is considered the right way to give "glory" to God.

pacifism. Opposition to violence and/or military service.

patriotism. The feeling of love, devotion, and support for one's country.

pillars of Islam. The heart of the Muslim faith contained in five elements: Shahadah (confession of faith), Salat (daily prayer or worship), Zakat (charity for the poor), Sawm (practice of fasting), and Hajj (pilgrimage to Mecca).

pluralism. The recognition and affirmation that there are many different peoples and many different religions in the world.

polytheism. The belief in the manifestation of the divine in diverse ways.

pope. The head of the worldwide Catholic Church; in traditional Catholic theology believed to be a direct, authorial descendent of the apostle Peter.

posadas. An ancient Hispanic American tradition, which begins on the evening of December 16 and continues until Christmas Eve. People enact the journey of Mary and Joseph seeking "lodging" for the birth of the Christ Child and celebrate the event that lodging is found. Posadas means "lodgings."

priest. An ordained minister authorized to perform the sacred rites of a religion. In Catholicism, a celibate male who leads the local parish in liturgy, ritual, and sacrament.

prophecy. The inspired utterance of a prophet, believed to be inspired by divine will.

Protestant Individualism. The belief that each person is responsible for his or her belief without dependence on outside authority.

Protestant work ethic. The belief that a person receives material as well as spiritual gain in relation to the depth of his/her faith and hard work.

public policy. The generally accepted attitudes and beliefs of a particular government.

Puritanism. A form of Protestant Christianity that places equal, if not greater, importance on the belief of the heart to the "religion of the mind." The Puritans sought a "pure" form of religious practice in America.

Quran. The holy scripture of the Muslim people is the recorded revelations of Muhammad as received from Allah.

Ramadan. The month of fasting, which all Muslims are required to observe, if physically able. It is a special time for devotion and reflection. The fast is each day of Ramadan from dawn to dusk, during which Muslims abstain from eating and drinking.

reincarnation. The belief that the human existence embodies various lives throughout the history of the world. It is at the heart of the Indian tradition of samsara, a word that literally means "wandering" from one life to the next.

religion. The belief in some pivotal value; the seeking and the responding to what a person and/or community believes to be holy.

religious liberty. The belief that all people are free to worship and to practice their religion as they please.

religious order. A community of men or women who carry out the specialized work of the church: missions, education, medicine, etc. Examples are the Benedictines, the Jesuits, the Franciscans, the Dominicans, and the Carmelites.

Requerimiento. A document read to native peoples by Spanish explorers that claimed that Christ was the ruler of the known world and required that the native peoples were to give their lands to Christian Spain.

rite of passage. A formal practice, procedure, or event that initiates a person or community into a new understanding of self.

ritual. A sacred performance, often celebratory, the goal of which is to bring about change in the status quo through an encounter with the sacred or holy.

Rosh Hashanah. The Jewish New Year, which represents a time for penitence and personal reflection.

Sabbath. In the Jewish religious calendar, the seventh day (Saturday), set aside for worship and the observance of various Judaic traditions. Christians maintain Sunday as a form of Sabbath, while Muslims observe Friday as a day of prayer and worship.

sacrament. A solemn ceremony or religious ritual which embodies the mystical presence of God. The Catholic Church recognizes seven sacraments: baptism, confirmation, matrimony, Communion, ordination, anointing of the sick, and penance.

sacred. Persons, events, places, and time that are set apart from ordinary existence and deemed appropriate for a community's religious acts and their gods.

samsara. In Buddhism, the cycle of rebirth that parallels the endless and cyclic unfolding of time. The life into which one is reborn is governed by the person's karma.

Sanskrit. The sacred language of India and the language of texts previous to and including the Vedas.

Satan. Also called the devil, the chief adversary or enemy of God and God's will for creation.

Satanism. The belief in and the worship of the source or origin of evil, also known for its challenge to the traditional dependence on God as the source of truth and power for living.

schism. A division in the unity of the church, a separation in which a community of believers leaves an existing church to form a different community of faith.

Science and Health. Full name: *Science and Health with Key to the Scriptures*, premier writing by Mary Baker Eddy, founder of the Christian Science movement.

Scientological Creed. The statement of faith in Scientology that upholds freedom of the self and the individual worth and goodness of humanity.

second coming. Also called the Second Advent of Christ, or *parousia*. Related to Christian beliefs in the future return of Christ. Elements in the theme include the establishment of the kingdom of God, the final day of judgment, and the thousand-year reign of Christ (see *millenarianism*).

secularist. A person who is not religious or connected to any religious institution.

secularization. Acts or events considered separate from all things religious and sacred.

shaman. A Native American community's holy person who uses "ecstatic techniques" such as trance, visions, and dreams to bring sacred knowledge and healing powers to the community.

Shariah. "Path," or Islamic law, believed to be divine revelation sufficient for doctrine and practice in Islam. The law includes two major divisions: the Quran and the Sunnah.

Shavuot. A sacred event held fifty days after Passover to commemorate the revelation of the Torah to Moses at Mount Sinai fifty days after the exodus from Egypt.

Shinto. The ancient Japanese religion which dates back to prehistoric times and reflects a belief in many local gods and shrines.

Shiva. In Hinduism, the destroying God and one of three basic forms of the ultimate or absolute.

Shoghi Effendi. The great-grandson of 'Abdu'l-Bahá, son of Bahá'u'lláh, leader of the Bahá'í Faith from 1921 to 1957. He was perhaps the most influential person for the Bahá'í religion in America.

shrine. Within the Japanese tradition, a container holding sacred relics that reflect the presence of the kami.

Siddhartha Gautama. Born of a princely family, he lived around 500 B.C.E. His spiritual development led him to become a Buddha, someone who is enlightened. Gautama is the "first" Buddha and the founder of Buddhism.

soul-sleep. A condition that Seventh-day Adventists and Jehovah's Witnesses enter into at death. At the time of the second coming of Jesus, those in "soul-sleep" will awaken to be judged, with the righteous receiving eternal life and those who are evil being annihilated.

spirituals. Among slavery's most lasting legacies to America. Spirituals represented the story of the slave's suffering, endurance, and hope told in song.

stake. A geographic region in the Latter-day Saint (Mormon) Kingdom of God. Each stake includes several "wards."

Sunnah. The collected traditions about the prophet Muhammad that constitute the second part of Islamic Shariah, or law; the Quran is the first and foremost in authority.

syncretistic. The merging of religious beliefs and practices, thus accommodating the influences of various cultures and religions upon one another. An example would be the development of Hellenistic Judaism during the Greek/Roman periods or Gnosticism during the early period of Christianity.

temple (synagogue). A sacred space, building, used as a gathering place for prayer and worship, for the study of the Torah, and the fellowship of the Jewish community.

testimonials. A special feature of the Church of Christ, Scientist, services, in which believers report successes in life due to Christian Science principles.

theocracy. Government by religious leaders or officials claiming divine authority.

Theosophy. Translated as "divine wisdom," a modern movement, closely associated with Christian Science, that stresses the personal experience of God is the only way to know the divine.

thetan. In Scientology, a term referring to the spiritual essence of an individual, which is believed to be entrapped by its own previous experiences of life, from which liberation can come through the teachings of Scientology. It is similar to the Western notion of "soul" and the Hindu concept of "atman."

Torah. The revelation of God's will and word to humanity. The first five books of the Hebrew Bible, which include the Ten Commandments given by God to God's people.

tribe. A gathering of people who form a community that claims a common ancestry and tradition.

Trinity. The Christian belief that the eternal God is revealed in three ways; as Father, as Son, and as Holy Spirit.

True Parents. For Unificationists, this phrase refers to Rev. Sun Myung Moon and his wife, Hak Ja Han Moon, who are regarded as joint messiahs.

ulama. The "learned" clergy or scholar within Muslim leadership whose responsibility includes teaching Islamic law and directing the affairs of the Muslim faith and its traditions.

Universal House of Justice. The supreme governing body for the Bahá'í religion. The body was first chosen in 1963 and has nine members, who are elected every five years by the members of the National Spiritual Assembly.

Upanishads. A collection of writings from the ninth and eighth century B.C.E., which reflects much of the philosophical underpinnings of Hinduism.

vedas. An extensive body of sacred utterances of hymns, chants, and religious instruction learned by Hinduism's priestly class in order to perform ritual sacrifice.

Virgin of Guadalupe. A sacred image to the poor and disenfranchised of Mexico. Shortly after Spain conquered Mexico, the Virgin Mary appeared in Guadalupe to a young, poor Indian and promised hope for the downtrodden natives of his country.

Vishnu. The preserving God in Hinduism and one of three basic forms of the ultimate or absolute.

Wicca. A religious group within the category of Neopaganism in America, associated with witchcraft and natural religion.

Witnesses. A term that refers to Jehovah's Witnesses, a sect that originated within the Seventh-day Adventist religion.

Woman's Christian Temperance Union. A group of women in the late nineteenth and early twentieth century devoted to issues that were pro-family, working in particular with the young and the elderly. They also opposed the legalization of alcohol.

Word of Wisdom. For Latter-day Saints (Mormons), a scripturally based prescription for proper behavior and dietary practices. It prohibits the use of illegal drugs, tobacco, alcohol, coffee, and tea.

yarmulke. A small skull cap that is worn as a sign of humility and respect in Jewish worship.

Yin and Yang. They make up the power of the Dao and are composed of male (yang) and female (yin) energies and the five elements of our world: earth, water, wood, fire, and metal.

yoga. The practice of disciplined meditation, the aim of which is total focus on a personal god.

Yom Kippur. "The Sabbath of Sabbaths" for the Jewish community, a day of atonement that is marked by prayer and fasting.

Young Women's Christian Association. The YWCA became a strong organization during the last quarter of the nineteenth century. The organization paid special attention to single women and their responsibilities as Christians.

Yule ritual. Also called the "lesser sabbat," the practice in nature religions of celebrating the oneness with the sacred natural world during the winter solstice.

zen. The doctrine of emptiness best exemplified in Japanese Buddhism. Zen practice involves intense meditation and study and leads to spiritual awakening.

Zion. The site of the millennial kingdom of God on earth.

INDEX